ARMORED BEARS, VOLUME ONE

ARMORED BEARS, VOLUME ONE

THE GERMAN 3RD PANZER DIVISION IN WORLD WAR II

VETERANS OF THE 3RD PANZER DIVISION

STACKPOLE
BOOKS

Published by
STACKPOLE BOOKS
5067 Ritter Road
Mechanicsburg, PA 17055
www.stackpolebooks.com

Printed in the United States of America

10   9   8   7   6   5   4   3   2   1

Library of Congress Cataloging-in-Publication Data

Geschichte der 3. Panzer-Division, Berlin-Brandenburg, 1935–1945. English
    Armored Bears : the German 3rd Panzer Division in World War II. Vol. 1 / Veterans of the 3rd Panzer Division.
            p. cm.
    Originally published: Geschichte der 3. Panzer-Division, Berlin-Brandenburg, 1935–1945. 1967.
    ISBN 978-0-8117-1170-8
    1. Germany. Heer. Panzer-Division, 3.   2. World War, 1939–1945—Tank warfare.   3. World War, 1939–1945—Campaigns—Eastern Front.   4. World War, 1939–1945—Regimental histories—Germany.   I. Traditionsverband der Ehemaligen Dritten Panzer-Division.   II. Title. III. Title: German 3rd Panzer Division in World War II.
    D757.563rd.G47 2012
    940.54'1343—dc23
                                                                        2012033432

CONTENTS

FOREWORD

The veteran's association of the former *3. Panzer-Division* presents its history of the division.

This is the result of an analysis of daily logs, diaries, individual letters from the time, firsthand accounts, maps, and a gratifying number of images from Werner Haupt of the Bibliothek für Zeitgeschichte in Stuttgart. Official daily logs were not available to any great extent. New items of information made numerous revisions necessary. The many collaborators—from *General* on down to *Obergefreiter*—need to be thanked one more time here. Thanks are also extended to our comrade, Günther Richter, for his time-consuming preparations for printing and distributing the book.

If some formations are mentioned with differing degrees of emphasis—some achievements and noteworthy events are not even mentioned at all—it results from the incompleteness of the source material.

Despite that, the book will evoke many memories among those still living, since it names so many persons and locations. It will also provide those left behind of the fallen with a picture of the experiences and the suffering of their loved ones.

Continuously renewed trust and proven comradeship have molded our community together and enable it to do what it has done. The victims discussed in this book are a reminder to those responsible to do everything in their power to spare us the horrors of a new war.

Franz Westhoven[1]
Generalleutnant a.D.[2]
Honorary Chairman of the Veterans
Organization of the former *3. Panzer-Division*

---

1. In addition to commanding the *3. Panzer-Division* (1 October 1942 to 15 October 1943), he also commanded the *2. Panzer-Division* in May 1944. He was awarded the Knight's Cross on 25 October 1943 for his command of the *3. Panzer-Division*. Westhoven survived the war and passed away on 9 October 1983. (All notes are by the translator.)
2. *a.D. = außer Dienst* = Retired.

CHAPTER 1

From Training to Baptism of Fire: The *3. Panzer-Division* in Peacetime

The Activation of the Division

The German government issued the "Law Concerning the Build-Up of the Armed Forces" on 16 March 1935. That signaled the start of the new German armored force, which would steer the conduct of warfare into new avenues a few years later. The already existing motorized elements of the army conducted their training and exercises more intensively in order to perfect their organization and weaponry. Assorted formations were consolidated into an exercise division in May 1935 at Döberitz. The training exercises took place under the direction of *Generalmajor* Hoth. The *I./Kraftfahr-Lehrkommando*[1] of *Oberstleutnant* Harpe and other motorized forces under the command of *Major* Breith were issued the first German fighting vehicle, the *Panzer I.*

The 15th of October 1935 was the birth date of the German armored force. It was established on that date as its own combat arm within the framework of the army and not just as an accompanying weapon of the infantry or a part of the cavalry. The *3. Kavallerie-Division* in Weimar, the two motorized instructional commands, all of the motorized battalions, a few artillery regiments, and, later on, the cavalry divisions in Frankfurt and Breslau all reassigned complete units as cadre for the first three armored divisions.

---

1. Motorized Instructional Command. This was the genesis of the future *Panzer-Regiment 5.*

The *1. Panzer-Division* was activated in Weimar.[2] *Generalleutnant Freiherr*[3] von Weichs was its commander. *Oberst* Guderian assumed acting command of the *2. Panzer-Division* in Würzburg. The *3. Panzer-Division* under *Generalleutnant* Fessmann was established in Berlin.

The *3. Panzer-Division* had been in the process of being formed since the summer of 1935; by 15 October 1935, it had completed its initial activation. A division had been created within the Germany Army that was intended to continue the long-standing traditions of the best regiments. The division headquarters was located in Berlin, with the staff and support agency offices located at the high rise at the corner of Kurfürstenstraße and Burggrafenstraße. *Generalleutnant* Fessmann was fifty-four years old and a longtime cavalryman, hailing from the *2. Bayerisches Chevaulegers-Regiment*. He had already been the commander of the first armored brigade established in Germany.

The division staff consisted of the following officers and civilian officials in 1935:

Operations (Ia): *Hauptmann i.G. Graf* von Sponeck[4]

Logistics (Ib): *Hauptmann* Keppel
Adjutant for Officer Personnel (IIa): *Rittmeister* von Necker[5]
Judge Advocate General (III): *Kriegsgerichtsrat* Dr. Schweinsberger[6]
Administration (IVa): *Intendanturrat* Zur Neiden[7]
Division Surgeon (IVb): *Oberstarzt* Dr. Muntsch[8]

One armored and one rifle brigade were assigned to the division. *Oberst* Kühn[9] was assigned as the commander of *Panzer-Brigade 3*, while *Oberst* Bernard assumed command of *Schützen-Brigade 3*.[10] *Hauptmann* Thomas served as Kühn's adjutant, while *Hauptmann* Schulte-Mönting served in the same capacity for Bernard.

The most important and most powerful formations assigned to the division and serving under the command and control of *Panzer-Brigade 3* were *Panzer-Regiment 5* and *Panzer-Regiment 6*. Both regiments combined old German cavalry tradition with the modern capabilities of a motorized force.

Panzer-Regiment 5: The regiment was formed by the reassignment of elements from *Kraftfahr-Lehrkommando Zossen* and *Reiter-Regiment 4*

---

2. The cities listed are the garrisons for the division headquarters. The division troops and the major subordinate support and combat commands were usually in other garrison cities. There was no garrison in Germany large enough to house an entire division.

3. *Freiherr* = Count.

4. *i.G. = im Generalstab* = General Staff (the traditional suffix applied to rank to denote membership in the General Staff). Theodor *Graf* von Sponeck rose to the rank of *Generalleutnant* during the war. He also commanded a division in North Africa (*90. leichte Afrika-Division*), where he received the Knight's Cross (12 September 1941). He was taken prisoner by the British upon capitulation of the German forces in North Africa in May 1943. He survived the war and died on 13 June 1982.

5. Hans-Horst von Necker became a General Staff officer following his assignment to the *3. Panzer-Division*. He served in a variety of armored and mechanized divisions during the early war years, primarily as an operations officer, and he eventually served as the operations officer of a field army (*16. Armee*). He was transferred to the *Luftwaffe* in 1944, being assigned to *Fallschirm-Panzer-Division "Hermann Göring,"* which he eventually commanded (October 1944–February 1945). He received the Knight's Cross on 24 June 1944, while serving as the commander of *Fallschirm-Panzer-Grenadier-Regiment 2 "Hermann Göring."* He survived the war and passed away on 27 February 1979.

6. A *Kriegsgerichtsrat* was the senior judicial officer on a division staff, with a rank roughly equivalent to that of *Major*. To receive the life-long appointment, the individual had to be qualified to be a judge under German law. This was a uniformed civilian position.

7. An *Intendanturrat* was a senior armed forces civilian official whose rank corresponded roughly to that of a *Major*.

8. Medical rank equivalent to *Oberst*.

9. Following his assignment to the *3. Panzer-Division* (October 1940), Friedrich Kühn assumed divisional command three times (*33. Infanterie-Division*, *15. Panzer-Division*, and *14. Panzer-Division*). Toward the end of the war, he was placed in charge of the army's motorization department, but was killed in an air raid on Berlin in February 1944. He reached the rank of *General der Panzertruppen* and also received the Knight's Cross (3 July 1940).

10. *Schützen* generally equals rifle in translation; however, its use within the German Army of this period is for motorized formations, as opposed to *Infanterie* (infantry), *Jäger* (light infantry), *Gebirgsjäger* (mountain or alpine infantry), or *Kradschützen* (motorcycle infantry).

1

(Potsdam). The latter regiment had already transitioned from being horse-mounted to motorized in the spring of 1935. *Panzer-Regiment 5*, which, out of fairness, should have received the numerical designation of *Panzer-Regiment 1*,[11] since its tank companies were the very first ones in the *Reichswehr*, carried on the traditions of the Guard Cuirassiers in its 1st Battalion and the 2nd Guards Ulan Regiment in its 2nd Battalion. *Oberst* Zuckertort, who had previously commanded the *Kraftfahr-Lehrkommando*, became its first commander.[12] *Major* Breith and *Major* Streich were the battalion commanders. The regimental adjutant was *Oberleutnant* Kühlein. The signals officer was *Oberleutnant* Voss. Company commanders were *Hauptmann* Thomale, *Hauptmann* Volckheim, *Hauptmann* Schenk, *Hauptmann* Wagner, *Oberleutnant* von Heinemann, and *Oberleutnant* Mildebrath.[13]

Panzer-Regiment 6: The regiment also received cadre elements from *Kraftfahr-Lehrkommando Zossen* and *Reiter-Regiment 4*. In addition, it also received a company from *Panzerabwehr-Abteilung 6* (Hannover) and its sister regiment, *Panzer-Regiment 5*. *Reiter-Regiment 4* transferred most of its 1st Squadron, with the 1st, 2nd, and 4th Troops. The 1st Battalion of the regiment carried on the traditions of the *Garde du Corps*. *Oberst* Meyer, the former commander

of the motorized forces in East Prussia, was named as the first commander. *Major* Lendle[14] and *Major* Linnarz were the respective battalion commanders. The company commanders were *Hauptmann* von Lewinski, *Hauptmann* von Heimendahl, *Hauptmann* von Heydebreck, *Hauptmann* Ilgen, *Hauptmann* Munzel, *Hauptmann* von Gersdorff, *Hauptmann* Ziegler, and *Hauptmann* Crohn. The regimental adjutant was *Oberleutnant* Nedtwig.

The combat forces of the division serving under the command and control of Schützen-Brigade 3 were as follows:

Schützen-Regiment 3: The regiment was activated in Altengrabow. The advance parties for the formation of the regiment arrived on 15 September 1935, including *Oberst* Stumpff,[15] the first regimental commander. The cadre of the regiment was received from personnel from *Reiter-Regiment 7*[16] and *Reiter-Regiment 11* (*Reiter-Regiment Gera*). The latter regiment had transitioned from being horse-mounted to motorized prior to being deactivated on 15 October 1935. Most of its personnel went to form the 1st Battalion. Additional cadre came from *Infanterie-Regiment Meiningen* of the *3. Kavallerie-Division* in Weimar. These personnel helped form the 2nd Battalion. The 1st Battalion was commanded by *Major* von Felbert,[17] who had

11. The actual *Panzer-Regiment 1* was assigned to the *1. Panzer-Division*.

12. Karl Zuckertort went on to assume a variety of staff positions, primarily in weapons design and procurement, after giving up command of the regiment on 1 October 1937. He left the military for unknown reasons on 31 July 1941. He survived the war, passing away in 1982.

13. *Panzer-Regiment 5* was later reassigned from the division to help form the *5. leichte Division* for service in North Africa. The regiment's history is covered in depth in the two volumes of Bernd Hartmann, *Panzers in the Sand* (Mechanicsburg, PA: Stackpole Books, 2010, 2011).

14. Hubert Lendle went on to regiment and division command after his assignment as battalion commander ended in January 1938, but this was to be his last assignment within the *Panzertruppe*. He advanced to *Generalleutnant* by war's end and passed away in Stuttgart in 1970.

15. Horst Stumpff left the division in late 1940, assuming command of the *20. Panzer-Division*. While in command, he was awarded the Knight's Cross. He gave up command in the fall of 1941 and assumed staff positions for the remainder of the war, culminating in his appointment as the Inspector General of Armored Forces for the Replacement Army in July 1944. He passed away in Hamburg in 1958. His younger brother, Hans-Jürgen, was a *Generaloberst* in the *Luftwaffe* and one of the signatories of the unconditional surrender in Berlin in May 1945.

16. *Reiter* is generally translated as "rider"; however, in German Army usage of this period, it means a horse-mounted element (cavalry).

17. Paul von Felbert rose to *Generalmajor* by war's end. He transferred to command of *Kavallerie-Schützen-Regiment 9* of the *3. leichte Division* in November 1938 and again served with the *8. Panzer-Division* as the commander of its *Schützen-Regiment 8*. He was captured by the British in late 1944 while serving as a local area commander in occupied France. He passed away in Wiesbaden in 1973.

already been the commander of the *II./Reiter-Regiment 11*. *Major* von Unger commanded the 2nd Battalion. The 2nd Battalion had the following company commanders when it was raised: *Hauptmann* Riederer *Freiherr* von Paar, *Oberleutnant* Wellmann, *Hauptmann* Zimmermann, *Oberleutnant* Reckleben, and *Hauptmann* Hildebrandt. The regiment maintained the traditions of two famous German formations. The 1st Battalion was responsible for *Infanterie-Regiment "Generalfeldmarschall Prinz Friedrich Karl von Preußen" (8. Brandenburgisches) Nr. 64* and the 2nd Battalion for the *"Armin-Dragoner" (Dragoner-Regiment 12) Gnesen*.

Kradschützen-Bataillon 3 (3rd Motorcycle Infantry Battalion): This formation received personnel assets from *Reiter-Regiment 16* (Erfurt), from the Rural Police Academy (Köslin), and from units of the Silesian Rural Police. The battalion maintained the traditions of the *1. Brandenburgisches Dragoner-Regiment Nr. 2 ("Schwedter Dragoner")*. Correspondingly, the motorcycle infantry of the battalion wore the gilded eagle and king's crown with the motto "With God for the King and the Fatherland" on their caps. The battalion's headquarters and 2nd and 4th Companies were assigned wooden barracks in Bad Freienwalde, while the 1st, 3rd, and 5th Companies of the battalion were quartered in the garrisons at Wriezen. Those same garrisons had housed elements of the Schwedt Dragoons in the eighteenth and nineteenth centuries. The commander of the battalion was *Major* von Manteuffel.[18] His adjutant was *Leutnant* Pape. The company commanders were: *Hauptmann* Hänisch, *Major* von der Schulenburg, *Haupt-*

mann Ottens, *Hauptmann* Schlieckmann, and *Hauptmann* Gorn.

Aufklärungs-Abteilung 3 (3rd Reconnaissance Battalion): The battalion was formed from the oldest motorized formation of the *Reichswehr*, the *3. Preußische Kraftfahrabteilung Berlin-Lankwitz*, which had once been commanded by *Major* Guderian. On 1 April 1934, it had become the *Kraftfahr-Abteilung Wünsdorf* of *Oberstleutnant* Paulus.[19] That battalion was redesignated as *Aufklärungs-Abteilung 3* and was moved to Berlin-Stahnsdorf. *Major* Schroetter then assumed command. His troop commanders were *Hauptmann* von Wietersheim,[20] *Hauptmann* von Prittwitz und Gaffron, *Hauptmann Freiherr* von Lüttwitz, and *Oberleutnant* von Uslar-Gleichen. The reconnaissance soldiers of the battalion maintained the traditions of the *1. Garde-Ulanen-Regiment*.

Artillerie-Regiment 75: The divisional artillery regiment was formed from cadre from the *I. motorisierte Artillerie-Abteilung Ohrdruf*. That battalion had been formed from the *11./Artillerie-Regiment 3* (Potsdam) in 1934 and transferred to Thuringia. The battery was expanded to a battalion there and motorized. When the armor divisions were formed, the 1st Motorized Battalion provided the nucleus for the *I./Artillerie-Regiment 73* (*1. Panzer-Division*), the *1./Artillerie-Regiment 74* (*2. Panzer-Division*), and the division's own 1st Battalion.

Effective in the fall of 1935, the *I./Artillerie-Regiment* was assigned to the division. The first personnel came from Ohrdruf with the 1st Battery of *Hauptmann* Kiersch. Two additional batteries were provided from *Artillerie-Regiment 2*

---

18. This is Günther von Manteuffel, not the more famous Hasso von Manteuffel, to whom he was related. He left the division in January 1942 as an *Oberst*. He went on to brigade command (ski forces) and short-term acting command of the *16. Panzergrenadier-Division* (January to April 1944). He then led various defense districts in northern Germany and Denmark until the end of the war. He passed away in 1962.

19. The same Paulus of Stalingrad fame. Following his assignment as commander, Paulus was transferred to the position of chief of staff of the Armored Forces as Guderian's successor.

20. Wend von Wietersheim left the division in March 1940 to assume command of *Kradschützen-Bataillon 1* (*1. Panzer-Division*). He later successfully led *Schützen-Regiment 113* (*1. Panzer-Division*). By August 1943, he had assumed acting command of the *11. Panzer-Division* and was designated commander of the division in November 1943, after promotion to *Generalmajor*. He held that position until May 1945, when his division surrendered to U.S. forces, but he was not taken prisoner. He ultimately received the Swords to the Oak Leaves to the Knight's Cross of the Iron Cross. He passed away in 1975.

and *Artillerie-Regiment 4*. All of the batteries were equipped with the 10.5-centimeter light field howitzer, the *leichte Feldhaubitze 18 (lFH 18)*. Since the initial allotment of guns was designed to be moved by horse—wood-spoked wheels—and the battalion received prime movers, the guns had to be placed on castors in order to transport them until newer versions of the guns with better suspension and rubber tires could arrive. The battalion was moved to Neuruppin, where it was garrisoned in the See-Kaserne and the Friedrich-Franz-Kaserne. That meant that the old garrison town of Neuruppin had artillerymen within its walls for the first time; up to then, there had only been infantry. The formerly garrisoned formation, elements of the *I./Infanterie-Regiment 5*, had to be moved to Neustrelitz. The commander of the battalion was *Oberstleutnant* Weidling, who came from *Artillerie-Regiment 1*. He was later to become the defender of Berlin.[21] The battery commanders were *Hauptmann* Kiersch, *Hauptmann* Schwarz, and *Major* von Colbe. The battalion adjutant was *Oberleutnant* Dous, and the signal officer was *Oberleutnant* Oll. The 1st Battalion assumed the responsibility for maintaining the traditions of the *3. Garde-Feldartillerie-Regiment* from its predecessor unit, the Potsdam-based *11./Artillerie-Regiment 3*.[22]

Nachrichten-Abteilung 39 (39th Signals Battalion): This battalion was also formed from troop elements located in Thuringia, including *Nachrichten-Abteilung (mot.) Weimar*, which had itself been formed the previous year from the *6./Reiter-Regiment 16* (Langensalza), *Nachrichten-Abteilung 3* (Potsdam), and *Nachrichten-Abteilung 13* (Magdeburg). The new battalion maintained the traditions of *Luftschiffer-Bataillon Nr. 1* (1st Dirigible Battalion). The battalion was temporarily housed in the garrisons of *Korps-Nachrichten-Abteilung 43* and *Artillerie-Regiment*

23 in Potsdam. When formed, the battalion consisted of a headquarters and two companies. The senior duty positions of the battalion were filled as follows:

Headquarters: *Hauptmann* Kempf (commander); *Oberleutnant* Henrici (adjutant); *Hauptmann* Lackner (staff captain)
1st Company: *Oberleutnant* Heintke (commander); *Leutnant* Ültzen (platoon leader)
2nd Company: *Hauptmann Baron* von Behr (commander); *Leutnant* Wilff (platoon leader)

Panzer-Abwehr-Abteilung 39: The battalion was formed from *Kampfwagen-Abwehr-Abteilung 3*, which had previously been designated as *Kraftfahrabteilung Döberitz*. The antitank forces were initially assigned to the infantry divisions, since the experience of the Great War had shown that special weapons and personnel trained in that special mission needed to be on hand for the destruction of motorized and armored vehicles. To that end, the German engineers had designed a light, easily moved, and low-silhouette cannon with a caliber of 3.7 centimeters. This gun was initially referred to as a *TaK (Tankabwehrkanone)* but later became universally known as a *PaK (Panzerabwehrkanone)*. Later on, in soldier jargon, this truly good and practical gun became known as the *Panzeranklopfkanone*, or "tank-knocker cannon" (i.e., a door knocker), since the fighting vehicles of the opponents that were faced were so heavily armored that the small 3.7-centimeter round was no longer able to penetrate.

The battalion was housed in the area around Wünsdorf. The commander was *Major* von Tippelskirch. In 1937, the battalion was designated to maintain the traditions of the *1. Garde-Dragoner-Regiment* and the *2. Garde-Dragoner-Regiment* (inherited from *Reiter-Regiment 9*).

---

21. Helmuth Weidling is mentioned in a variety of sources with regard to his final assignment as the Local Area Commander for Berlin.
22. The regiment's 2nd Battalion was not formed until nearly a year later, in September 1936, and will be covered at that point in the narrative.

Pionier-Bataillon 39: This battalion was the last element that was assigned to the division. Its history was different from the rest of the formations of the Berlin-Brandenburg regiments and battalions. The battalion was formed in 1935 from personnel from *Pionier-Bataillon 9* and *Pionier-Bataillon 44*. Their cadres, in turn, had come from *Pionier-Bataillon 4* (Magdeburg) and *Pionier-Bataillon 5* (Ulm). The battalion was initially housed in the garrisons at Wittenberg (Elbe). *Oberstleutnant* Müller was the commander.

In October 1937, the battalion in Wittenberg was redesignated as *Pionier-Bataillon 37*. The original 1st Company from that battalion (*Hauptmann* Beigel) and another company formed from personnel from all of the remaining companies (*Oberleutnant* Groeneveld) formed the nucleus of the new *Pionier-Bataillon 39*. It was only at that point that the two companies officially became part of the *3. Panzer-Division*. The new battalion was commanded by *Oberstleutnant* Müller, who also initially continued to command the newly redesignated *Pionier-Bataillon 37*.[23]

The Years of Peace

The officers, civilian officials, noncommissioned officers, enlisted personnel, and civilian employees of the division had little time to get acquainted before the division was faced with its first major mission. Armed forces draftees were being called up in November to perform their service obligations. That meant that young men started pouring into the garrisons and provisional housing of the division and had to integrate themselves into the cohort of men who had already volunteered to perform armed service.

The swearing-in of the recruits took place in ceremonial form at the various garrisons of the division on 7 November 1935. The new *Reich* war flag fluttered from the mast and over the assembled columns and curious public in attendance. All of the troop elements in Potsdam assembled their new soldiers, including those of *Nachrichten-Abteilung 39*. They swore their oath to the flag in the presence of the *Reichswehr* Minister, *Generaloberst* von Blomberg. The recruits from *Kradschützen-Bataillon 3* were sworn in in the middle of the assembled battalions at the parade ground at Wriezen. Following the ceremonies, the daily training and duties started in the garrisons, on the parade grounds, in the maintenance facilities, at the firing ranges, and at the training areas. Ceaseless work and tenacious willpower allowed the division to grow into a formation of single-minded purpose.

The division was alerted at the end of February and beginning of March 1936 and left its garrisons in the Berlin area. The rail transports headed west. The General Command of the *Panzertruppe* had assembled its motorized formations at Camp Staumühle at the Senne Training Area for an exercise. For days and nights on end, exercises, combat drills, armored reconnaissance, and gunnery (including from a moving vehicle) were conducted. It was not until the national radio service announced that German forces had entered the demilitarized Rhineland on 7 March that the soldiers of the division knew that their exercises at the Senne Training Area had served an important military purpose. Like all of the other motorized formations assembled at Senne, the division had been earmarked to defend against any potential attack by the western powers, which might have felt threatened by the occupation of the Rhineland. Fortunately, an "emergency situation" did not arise. Despite that, the exercises were continued and did not end until 7 April.

---

23. *Lexikon der Wehrmacht* gives a somewhat different history for these two battalions. *Pionier-Bataillon 39* is listed as having been activated on 6 October 1939 and stationed in Rathenow in Military District III. It was formed using cadre from *Pionier-Bataillon 9* (*9. Infanterie-Division*) and *Pionier-Bataillon 44* (corps asset). *Pionier-Bataillon 37* is listed as having been activated on 12 October 1937 and garrisoned in Wittenberg. According to *Lexikon*, the battalion received cadre from *Pionier-Bataillon 39* in its formation. *Pionier-Bataillon 37* became the divisional engineers for the *1. Panzer-Division*. *Lexikon* lists no *Oberstleutnant* Müller. (www.lexikon-der-wehrmacht.de/Gliederungen/PionierBat/PiBat39-R.htm and www.lexikon-der-wehrmacht.de/Gliederungen/PionierBat/PiBat37.htm).

Some of the divisional elements did not receive their permanent peacetime quarters until the weeks and months that followed. For instance, *Panzer-Regiment 6* left Zossen on 14 June 1936. It moved as a regiment through Altruppin to Neuruppin. During a rest, the German crown prince arrived to demonstrate his solidarity with the forces that were carrying on the traditions of the Guards. That afternoon, the regiment marched into Neuruppin, accompanied by a military band. The local populace greeted its "black" soldiers[24] with heartfelt joy and enthusiasm.

Kradschützen-Bataillon 3 also received new quarters; they moved into the modern garrison in Bad Freienwalde. On 30 June, *Nachrichten-Abteilung 39* moved from Potsdam-Nedlitz to Stahnsdorf. As the battalion marched into Stahnsdorf, it passed in review past *Oberst* Kühn, the commander of *Panzer-Brigade 3*; *Oberst* Löweneck, the corps signal officer for Military District XIII; and *Oberstleutnant* Gimmler, a staff officer from the Signals Directorate at the Army High Command.

For the summer of 1936, the main effort in training was directed toward familiarity with the new weapons and the vehicles. Neither of the two armored regiments had sufficient quantities of vehicles and had to make do with "dummy" vehicles. On 29 July, *Panzer-Regiment 5* went to Putlos for the first time for tank gunnery for five weeks. On 25 August, both of the armored regiments were rail loaded to Döberitz, where they conducted two weeks of gunnery and driving exercises. At the same time, the *I./Artillerie-Regiment 75* and the rifle brigade conducted long marches with all of its assigned and attached elements.

In addition to its engineer battalion, the division received an additional reinforcement in the fall of 1936. Using its own personnel, the *I./Artillerie-Regiment 75* formed the 4th and 5th Batteries of its newly formed 2nd Battalion. The 6th Battery came intact from Ulm, which meant that the divisional artillery was complete with regard to men and materiel in accordance with its tables of organization. The new battalion moved into its garrison in Eberswalde, accompanied by a big turnout from the local populace.

In 1936, *Panzer-Regiment 6* was directed to provide officers and good specialists for a German armor contingent being sent to Nationalist Forces in Spain. In September 1936, the German Army High Command directed the establishment of a directorate to manage army elements that had been earmarked for sending to Spain to support the training of Nationalist Forces in their fight against Spanish Reds[25] being supported by the Soviet Union. In addition to *Panzer-Regiment 6*, *Panzer-Regiment 4* (2. *Panzer-Division*) was directed to provide training personnel and vehicles for the mission. That meant that officer and noncommissioned officer volunteers from the two battalions would be the first ones to lead the new weapons into combat and test them out. *Hauptmann* Ziegler (7th Company) and *Oberleutnant* Wolf (4th Company) left the regiment with an additional 160 noncommissioned officers and enlisted personnel to provide the cadre for the tank battalion that was being formed by the army. They were discharged from active duty so that they could serve in a foreign army.

As early as 1936, the first three armored divisions had to transfer personnel and materiel for new activations. For the establishment of *Panzer-Regiment 8*, *Panzer-Regiment 5* had to give up its 6th Company. *Panzer-Regiment 6* had to give up two companies: the 3rd Company of *Hauptmann* von Heydebreck and the 6th Com-

---

24. German tankers were often referred to as being "black" because of the special-purpose black tanker uniforms they wore. Modeled on ski fashions of the time, the color black was used in order to minimize the appearance of stains from petroleum products and working on tracked vehicles.

25. Republican forces, generally left-wing and anti-monarchist in political orientation, but democratic rather than Communist.

pany of *Hauptmann* von Gersdorff. *Panzer-Regiment 6* rebuilt those companies from out of its own ranks. *Hauptmann* Schmidt-Ott assumed command of the newly formed 3rd Company and *Hauptmann* von Winterfeld took over the 6th Company. The commander of the armored regiment's 2nd Battalion, *Major* Linnarz, was transferred to the General Command of the *Panzertruppe* as its adjutant. *Major* Rothenburg, a *Pour le mérite* recipient from the Great War, replaced him; Rothenburg was reassigned to the regiment from *Panzer-Regiment 1*.

The troop elements of the army that were stationed in the Berlin area formed up on Wilhelmsplatz on the evening of 19 April 1937 to receive their standards. These included elements from the *3. Panzer-Division*. The commanders of the regiments, battalions, and detachments accepted their new colors in a ceremonial fashion. *Unteroffizier* Schmidt (4th Company) and *Unteroffizier* Teichmann (5th Company) carried the colors for *Panzer-Regiment 6*. The escort officers for the colors were *Oberleutnant* Bernewitz, *Leutnant* von Kiekebusch, *Leutnant* Markowski, and *Leutnant* Voigts.

On 28 June, the division moved out for its summer exercises in the western portion of the Brandenburg Province, after special exercises for the signal elements had taken place in May and the beginning of June around Rathenow and the tanks had conducted gunnery at Putlos. The exercises were intended to improve the coordination between and among the differing combat arms, effect a unified command, and continue to familiarize the men with their weapons and vehicles. The exercises took place in a wide area bounded by Braunschweig, Jüterbog, and Halle.

An unfortunate event happened during the exercises. The division commander's vehicle had an accident while traveling to inspect divisional elements. *Generalleutnant* Fessmann and his operations officer, *Hauptmann i.G. Graf* von Sponeck, were badly injured. The division logistics officer, *Hauptmann* Keppel,

later died of his injuries. The division leadership was effectively eliminated. *Oberst* Kühn was given acting command of the division, while his adjutant, *Hauptmann* Thomas, was made the provisional operations officer. The exercise and training continued. Combined exercises were conducted in Jüterbog in July with the newly formed *4. Panzer-Division*. One month later, the division moved in its entirety to the Bergen Training Area in the Luneburg Heath.

From 14 to 29 September, the division participated in the so-called "Mussolini Maneuvers" in Mecklenburg. On 1 October 1937, *Generalleutnant Freiherr* Geyr von Schweppenburg was named as the division commander. He immediately worked up a new training plan for the division. It was emphasized that the forces were not to be found on the parade grounds but in the field! According to Schweppenburg, a future war would not be decided on the ground by infantry alone. Instead, it would involve all dimensions and weapons systems.

Following the annual army maneuvers in October, a number of reorganizations, transfers, and reassignments took place, since it was necessary to activate new armored and motorized formations. Among other force structure changes, the divisional signals battalion had to give up its 2nd Company to help form *Korps-Nachrichten-Abteilung 62*. In addition, noncommissioned officers and men from the 1st Company were also assigned to the newly forming battalion. The battalion's 2nd Company had already lost its company commander the previous April. *Hauptmann Baron* von Behr was transferred to the Army Sports Academy in Wünsdorf. His successor from the time, *Oberleutnant* Schulz, was transferred to the corps battalion. *Oberleutnant* Weiz remained behind to rebuild the 2nd Company. Even deeper cuts were made to the two armored regiments. *Panzer-Regiment 5* transferred its 6th Company to help form *Panzer-Regiment 15*; half of the 8th Company was transferred to the Gunnery School at Putlos.

Oberst Nehring, who was one of Guderian's closest associates, assumed command of the regiment.[26] *Panzer-Regiment 6* was also tasked with reassigning some of its elements. With the activation of the *I./Panzer-Regiment 10*, 9 officers and 355 enlisted personnel were sent to distant East Prussia from Neuruppin. Just a few weeks after that, the regiment had to give up its 5th Company to help in the formation of *Panzer-Regiment 31* in Jägerdorf (Silesia).

In November 1937, new recruits again arrived at all of the garrisons of the division. The following year, 1938, also saw a number of changes in duty positions, commands, and transfers. The face of the officer corps changed once again. The arrival of *Oberst* Nehring in November 1937 had marked the arrival of the first new regimental commander in the division. *Oberst* Meyer, who commanded *Panzer-Regiment 6*, was transferred to Mainz on 1 February 1938 to become its local military commander. His position was taken by *Oberst* Crüwell.[27] The two brigades also had changes of command at the same time. *Oberst* Stumpff assumed command of the *3. Panzer-Brigade*. He had previously been the commander of *Schützen-Regiment 3* and followed *Oberst* Bernard into command of the *3. Schützen-Brigade*. *Oberst* Gawantka assumed command of the *3. Schützen-Brigade*.[28] *Oberstleutnant* Kleemann assumed command of *Schützen-Regiment 3* and *Major* von Bernuth took over the antitank battalion, *Panzerabwehr-Abteilung 39*.

In the spring of 1938, the division finally received its engineer battalion. *Major* von Mertens's *Pionier-Bataillon 39* held its last formation in Wittenberg on 31 March 1938, whereupon it moved to Rathenow. It made its move into its new garrison on 2 April. The division commander received the report of the battalion commander on Kaiser-Wilhelm-Platz in the town.

The summer months were marked by even more intensive training and a complete immersion into a knowledge of weapons, equipment, and terrain. The armored brigade spent some time at the Baumholder Training Area, followed by more training at Bergen. During those exercise periods, the division commander's plan of seeing his forces work together with the *Luftwaffe* and other elements of the army came to fruition.

Oberst Nehring's *Panzer-Regiment 5*, with its two battalions (under *Major* Schäfer and *Major* von Wilcke), was a centerpiece of the large-scale exercises. Infantry from *Infanterie-Regiment 17* (*31. Infanterie-Division*) participated, as did the division artillery of *Oberst* Weidling. *Panzer-Regiment 5*, along with its attached elements, conducted a long road march that developed into an enveloping attack and ended with a breakthrough of the "enemy" front. During the exercises, which lasted several days, a gunnery competition (moving vehicles) was held, which was won by *Hauptmann* Wendenburg's 4th Company.

After the fields had been cleared and the harvest brought in during the fall, large-scale marches and exercises commenced, just as they did every year in armies throughout the world. The division left its garrisons. Its marches took

26. Walter K. Nehring would command the regiment for nearly one and a half years before being transferred to Guderian's *XIX. Armee-Korps (mot.)*. He went on to division command (*18. Panzer-Division*), several corps commands (including the *Deutsches Afrika-Korps*), and field army command (*1. Panzer-Armee*). He was a recipient of the Swords to the Oak Leaves to the Knight's Cross of the Iron Cross. He survived the war, became a prolific writer on military subjects, and died in Düsseldorf in April 1983.

27. Ludwig Crüwell would command for slightly more than a year before being reassigned. He went on to division (*11. Panzer-Division*), corps (*Deutsches Afrika-Korps*), and field army (*Panzerarmee Afrika*) command. While conducting aerial reconnaissance in North Africa in May 1942, his aircraft was shot down. He survived but was captured by the British. He was a recipient of the Oak Leaves to the Knight's Cross (1 September 1941). He was released from captivity in 1947 and passed away in September 1958.

28. Georg Gawantka had previously commanded *Schützen-Regiment 2* (*2. Panzer-Division*) before assuming this command. It was relatively short-lived (February to August 1938). Upon promotion to *Generalmajor*, Gawantka was transferred to the *2. Schützen-Brigade* to assume command. After commanding it in Vienna for around six months, he was given command of the *10. Panzer-Division* on 1 May. He died of natural causes in Prague in the middle of July of the same year.

it south. The division troops and formations assembled at the Königsbrück Training Area, only to move farther south and into Silesia.

German armed forces occupied the Sudeten-land in accordance with a schedule that had been approved by four European powers (Germany, France, Great Britain, and Italy). Zone 5 was the last to be occupied. It encompassed the areas bounded by Ratibor (present-day Racibórz in southern Poland) and Olmütz (present-day Olo-mouc in the Czech Republic), including the Hultschiner and Kuhländchen regions (the pres-ent-day Hlučín and Kravařsko regions in the Czech Republic). The division was placed on the extreme left wing of the army forces prepared to march into the area. Its lead elements arrived on 24 September. The formations were quartered in the area west of Ratibor. A rather carefree bivouac and rear-area atmosphere prevailed until orders were received to continue toward the designated border. The division moved adminis-tratively (as opposed to assuming tactically based march formations and serials). The reservists were not called up, with the exception of the two maintenance companies, which were established between 9 and 11 September in Niemegk and used to supplement the rear-area services.

On 8 October, the division crossed the border near Cosel right at noon with *Panzer-Regiment 6* in the lead. *Oberstleutnant* Rothenburg was in command since *Oberst* Crüwell had assumed acting command of the armored brigade for *Oberst* Stumpff, who had taken ill. The regimen-tal musicians, under the direction of *Stabsmusik-meister* Quader,[29] set up at the border marker and played marches. The division's formations rattled into the pretty countryside. They were heartily greeted by the German-speaking popu-lation and presented with wine and flowers. The first quarters for the armored regiment were in Kuchelna, where a close relationship was estab-lished with the local populace. The remaining formations and elements of the divisions also

reached their objectives in accordance with the time schedule. As a result, the *Wehrmacht* High Command announced on the radio at 1900 hours: "German forces have reached their day's objectives for 8 October."

The march continued the next morning. They were joined by the other formations of *Gener-aloberst* von Rundstedt—the *3. Panzer-Division* was attached to his command—and moved south from a line defined by Grulich–Moravian Schönberg–Braunseifen–south of Tropau. The areas and localities were occupied without any resistance on that day as well. The tenth of Octo-ber marked the last day of the movement, which came to a close around 1900 hours. *Pionier-Bataillon 39* had had a great deal to do during the three days. The engineers had to remove the road obstacles that had been erected by the Czechs, as well as the mines emplaced along the former frontier. The battalion's 1st Company was employed around Tropau and the 2nd Com-pany around Odrau.

The division was located in the Neutitschein–Stramberg–Wagstadt areas. In some instances, the detachments and battalions were quartered in open barracks-like arrangements. The soldiers were well taken care of wherever they went. It was only in the places where there was a purely Czech element, such as around Vresina-Pist, that the relations were cool. Small acts of sabotage were quickly identified and the damages fixed.

The bivouac life was not of long duration. The division started moving back by 20 October. The division transferred its sector to Silesian ele-ments of the *VIII. Armee-Korps*. The way back home lead through Tropau and Breslau and then along the Autobahn to Berlin. The troop ele-ments and formations returned to their garrisons between 23 and 27 October and were greeted enthusiastically.

The division then had to give up more experi-enced commanders and officers and received in their place hitherto unknown men, who were nonetheless able to rapidly integrate themselves

---

29. *Stabsmusikmeister* is the musician's equivalent of *Hauptmann*.

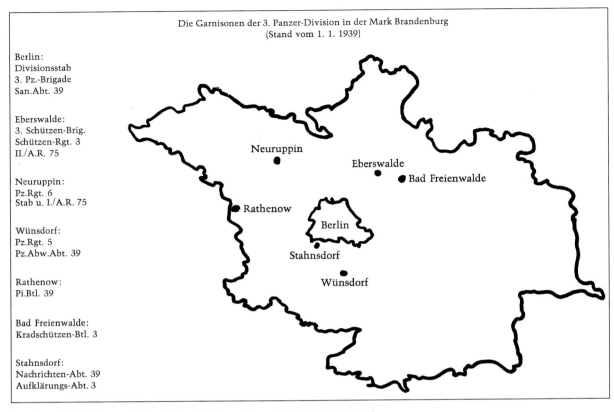

Die Garnisonen der 3. Panzer-Division in der Mark Brandenburg
(Stand vom 1. 1. 1939)

Berlin:
Divisionsstab
3. Pz.-Brigade
San.Abt. 39

Eberswalde:
3. Schützen-Brig.
Schützen-Rgt. 3
II./A.R. 75

Neuruppin:
Pz.Rgt. 6
Stab u. I./A.R. 75

Wünsdorf:
Pz.Rgt. 5
Pz.Abw.Abt. 39

Rathenow:
Pi.Btl. 39

Bad Freienwalde:
Kradschützen-Btl. 3

Stahnsdorf:
Nachrichten-Abt. 39
Aufklärungs-Abt. 3

Garrisons of the *3. Panzer-Division* in the Mark Brandenburg (as of 1 January 1939).

into the structure of the division. In the division headquarters, *Major i.G. Graf* von Sponeck was replaced by *Major i.G.* von dem Borne as operations officer. In addition to his many duty requirements, *Graf* von Sponeck had also designed the special-purpose over-garment that was worn by military motorcyclists. *Hauptmann i.G.* Krasà,[30] an officer originally hailing from Austria, became the division logistics officer, a position in which he gained the complete trust of the division in the coming years. *Major* Materne, the division intelligence officer, was replaced by *Hauptmann* Barth. *Rittmeister* von Wietersheim became the division adjutant. *Oberst* von Angern assumed command of the *3. Schützen-Brigade*.[31] *Oberst* Forster, who had transferred to the army from being a police officer three years previously, assumed command of the divisional artillery. *Oberst* Weidling, who had commanded the divisional artillery since its formation, left the division to assume command of *Artillerie-Regiment 56*, the divisional artillery

30. Krasà apparently went on to become at least an *Oberstleutnant i.G.* and recipient of the relatively rare German Cross in Silver (for support achievements) while serving as the quartermaster for the *XXIV. Panzer-Korps*. The date of the award is listed as 23 October 1942.

31. Günther von Angern is perhaps more famous for subsequent assignments and his ultimate fate. After successfully commanding the *3. Schützen-Brigade* during the campaign in Poland, he was reassigned to command the *11. Schützen-Brigade*, a separate motorized infantry brigade that later became known in the campaign in France as the "Ghost Division" for its exploits. It formed the nucleus of the *11. Panzer-Division*. Angern assumed acting command of the division in Russia, only to be badly wounded. His recovery lasted until September 1942, when he was sent back to the Eastern Front as the commander of the *16. Panzer-Division*. He committed suicide rather than being taken captive by the Soviets. He received the Knight's Cross on 5 August 1940.

of the *20. Infanterie-Division (mot.)*. Battalion command also changed within the artillery regiment's two battalions, with *Major* Lorenz and *Major* Wimmer assuming command. Within the rifle battalions of *Schützen-Regiment 3*, *Major* Meese (1st Battalion) and *Oberstleutnant* Dr. Ehlermann (2nd Battalion) assumed command. *Major Freiherr* von Wechmar replaced *Oberstleutnant* Schroetter in command of *Aufklärungs-Abteilung 3*. *Oberstleutnant* Negendanck assumed command of the division's signals battalion.

No major changes occurred among the personnel during the first few months of 1939. Of course, there were transfers, temporary duty assignments, and reassignments within the division, but routine was the daily norm.

It was therefore quite by surprise that the division was alerted on 12 March. Elements of the division were immediately loaded by rail and dispatched to the Königsbrück Training Area. Not all of the division was sent. For instance, one battalion from each of the armored regiments remained in garrison. The divisional artillery only rail loaded four batteries. Reservists were not called up for that "exercise." Nonetheless, the powerful *Kampfgruppe* (battle group) of the *3. Panzer-Division* that left the training area in stormy weather was sent to the area around Zittau. The tanks that were loaded in Neuruppin had the destination of Zittau as well.

The divisional elements headed toward the Czech border during the night of 14–15 March. It was a difficult march. Biting cold, a stormy eastern wind, and wild snow squalls made a rapid advance by the motorized elements along the ice-covered roads impossible. Engineers and construction battalions first had to clear the meter-high snow. As a result, the march of the armored brigade was delayed for several hours.

The riflemen, reconnaissance elements, engineers, signalers, motorcycle infantry, and cannoneers had already crossed the border at first light; it was not reached by the tanks until 1405 hours. The march continued through heavy snow and black ice through Jung-Bunzlau, Neu-

Benatek, Alt-Bunzlau, and Brandeis. It was there that the commander of the Czech Armor School reported to *Generalleutnant* von Schweppenburg. Initially, the Czech military and civilian populace acted in a very reserved manner. But for the time being, there were no major sources of friction, acts of sabotage, or even resistance.

Exerting a special effort, the lead platoon of *Aufklärungs-Abteilung 3* reached the high ground outside the Czech capital by 0820 hours. The commanding general of the *XVI. Armee-Korps (mot.)*, *Generaloberst* Hoepner, arrived a few minutes later and assumed command over all German forces in the greater area of Prague. The *I./Schützen-Regiment 3* and *Panzerabwehr-Abteilung 39* followed close behind and immediately occupied the Prague Castle, whose first military administrator became *Major* Meese. *Generalleutnant* von Schweppenburg was able to establish his command post there at 0930 hours. The combat formations of the division slowly entered Prague. *Oberstleutnant* Rothenburg reported at the castle at 1700 hours that his armor regiment had arrived, entering Prague demonstrating exemplary march discipline. Elements of the *24. Infanterie-Division*, a Silesian formation, and the *4. leichte Division*, coming from Austria, reached the "Golden City" at 1900 hours. Together with the *3. Panzer-Division*, they secured the area. For the time being, the division remained in the city.

The division passed in review in front of the division commander on the Wenceslas Square on 17 March. It then left the city and occupied localities to the north in the area around Alt-Bunzlau–Brandeis–Podebrady. The division command post was located in the latter town. *Schützen-Regiment 3* was billeted in the Czech training area at Milowice, where it disarmed the Czech military stationed there. Only the tank battalions remained in Prague. On 18 March, they took part in the final parade held in front of *Generaloberst* Blaskowitz, the commander in chief of the German forces involved with the occupation.

Oberst Crüwell left the division after its return to its garrisons. He was transferred into the Army High Command to become a department head. *Oberstleutnant* Rothenburg assumed command of *Panzer-Regiment 6*, while *Major* von Boltenstern assumed command of the 1st Battalion. In the summer of 1939, the *Panzerwaffe* was further increased in size by the activation of the *10. Panzer-Division* in Prague. The *3. Panzer-Division* was again tasked to provide personnel and materiel to assist in the activation

process. Among other officers, *Oberleutnant* Poretschkin left the signals battalion, from which *Hauptmann* Brinkmann had also been transferred only a short time previously.

The next senior command over the division remained with the *XVI. Armee-Korps (mot.)* of *Generalleutnant* Hoepner. *Oberst i.G.* Paulus was the corps chief of staff; *Oberstleutnant i.G.* Heim was the corps operations officer. Those three men would indelibly leave their mark on the *Panzertruppe* in the course of the next few years.

Neuruppin. Nach dem Kupferstich von Merian. 1650.

The two oldest garrisons in the division area. Neuruppin was the home of *Panzer-Regiment 6* and the *I./Artillerie-Regiment 5*. (Copperplate engraving from 1650 by Merian.)

Rathenow was home to *Pionier-Bataillon 39*. (Copperplate engraving from 1650 by Merian.)

Generalleutnant Fessmann, the first commander of the division (1935–37).

Generalleutnant Freiherr Geyr von Schweppenburg, the division commander from 1937 to 1940. Schweppenburg went on to command the *XXIV. Armee-Korps (mot.)*, to which the division had a long-time association.

General Ludwig Crüwell served as the regimental commander of *Panzer-Regiment 6* from 1 February 1938 to 15 March 1939. Crüwell went on to command the *11. Panzer-Division* and then the *Deutsches Afrika-Korps*. He became the commander in chief of *Panzer-Armee Afrika* but was shot down in a Fieseler *Storch* over British lines and captured in May 1942.

General Walther K. Nehring served as the regimental commander of *Panzer-Regiment 5* from 1 October 1937 until 30 June 1939. He went on to serve with distinction, eventually assuming field army command by the end of the war.

Oberst Fritz Kühn served as the commander of the
3. Panzer-Brigade in 1940. He went on to serve as
a division commander three times (*33. Infanterie-
Division*, *15. Panzer-Division*, and *14. Panzer-
Division*). He was killed in a bombing raid in
February 1944 while serving in Berlin.

General der Artillerie Weidling served as the
commander of *Artillerie-Regiment 75* from its
activation until November 1938. He went on to
corps command, but is most famous as the last
commander of the Berlin military district,
surrendering to the Soviets and remaining
imprisoned by them until 1955, when he died in
KGB custody.

Oberst Rothenburg served as the commander of *Panzer-
Regiment 6* for one year, from March 1939 until March
1940. He later commanded *Panzer-Regiment 25*
(*7. Panzer-Division*) and was killed in action shortly after
the start of Operation "Barbarossa" on 28 June 1941.

Panzer-Regiment 6 enters Neuruppin in 1936.

Entrance to the garrison of *Kradschützen-Bataillon 3* in Bad Freienwalde, with a view toward the 5th Company.

The commander of *Kradschützen-Bataillon 3* and his adjutant: *Oberstleutnant* von Manteuffel and *Oberleutnant* Pape.

The officers and civilian officials of *Nachrichten-Abteilung 39* in 1937–38. From left to right:
Inspekteur Sylvester, *Zahlmeister* Bauck, *Oberzahlmeister* Kahle, *Leutnant* Polack, *Hauptmann* Brinkmann, *Leutnant* von Borries, *Regierungs-Baurat* Weil, *Major* Kempf, *Leutnant* Porestchkin, *Hauptmann* Lackner, *Waffenmeister* Rohwerder, *Oberleutnant* Weiz, *Leutnant der Reserve* Lohrmann, *Leutnant* von Arnim, and *Leutnant* Mangelsdorf.

Employed with the *Legion Condor. Leutnant* Buchterkirch (viewer's left), who later became the first Oak Leaves to the Knight's Cross recipient of the division, and *Unteroffizier* Blaich (second from the right), another future Knight's Cross recipient.

Training personnel from *Panzer-Regiment 6* in Spain.

A *Panzer I* at the location of the German maintenance facilities at Kubas (Spain).

The barracks of *Schützen-Regiment 3* at the Groß-Born Training Area in August 1939.

Panzer I's of the division during the so-called "Mussolini Maneuvers" in 1937.

SIZE, FUNCTION, MOBILITY

General Headquarters	Armed Forces Governor	Army Group Headquarters	Army Headquarters	Group Headquarters	Corps Headquarters	Division Headquarters	Brigade Headquarters	Regiment Headquarters	Battalion Headquarters	Company Headquarters	
Infantry	Motor Transport	Panzer Troops	Cavalry	Reconnaissance	Signal	Combat Engineer	Bridge Engineer	Railroad Engineer	Supply	Medical	Veterinary
Infantry	Mountain	Bicycle	Machine Gun	Mixed Mobility	Motorized	Motorcycle	Tank	Anti-Tank	Construction	Military Police	Traffic Control
Artillery	Mountain Artillery	Artillery Observation	Rocket Artillery	Infantry Antiaircraft	Army Antiaircraft	Luftwaffe Antiaircraft	Assault Artillery	Recoilless Artillery	Fortress	Field Replacement	Sich Security
Foot / Horse-Drawn	Mountain	Pack Animal	Bicycle	Mixed Motorized	Motorized	Motorcycle	Halftrack-Towed	Motor-Towed	Self-Propelled	Halftracked	Train

WEAPON SYMBOLS

Light Machine Gun	Heavy Machine Gun	Anti-Tank Rifle	28mm Anti-Tank Rifle	20mm Anti-Tank Gun	37mm Anti-Tank Gun	47mm Anti-Tank Gun	50mm Anti-Tank Gun	75mm Anti-Tank Gun	88mm Anti-Tank Gun	
50mm Light Mortar	81mm Heavy Mortar	75mm Light Infantry Gun	150mm Heavy Infantry Gun	Flame Thrower	20mm Antiaircraft Gun	20mm Quad Antiaircraft Gun	37mm Antiaircraft Gun	88mm Antiaircraft Gun	Antiaircraft Searchlight	

INFANTRY UNITS AND MOUNTAIN UNITS

Infantry Platoon	Infantry Company	Infantry Heavy Company	Infantry Bicycle Platoon	Infantry Pioneer Platoon	Infantry Signal Platoon	Infantry Anti-Tank Platoon	Infantry Gun Company	Light Antiaircraft Co. (mot)	Medium Antiaircraft Co. (mot)	Infantry Mounted Recon. Plt.	Infantry Light Column
Mountain Platoon	Mountain Company	Mountain Heavy Company	Mountain Bicycle Platoon	Mountain Pioneer Platoon	Mountain Signal Platoon	Mountain Anti-Tank Co. (mot)	Hvy Infantry Gun Company (self-propelled)	Light Antiaircraft Co. (self-propelled)	Medium Antiaircraft Co. (self-propelled)	Machine Gun Company (motorized)	Mountain Transport Column
Infantry Platoon (motorized)	Infantry Company (motorized)	Heavy Company (motorized)	Motorcycle Infantry Platoon	Infantry Pioneer Plt. (mot)	Infantry Signal Plt. (mot)	Lt. Inf. Gun Platoon (motorized)	Infantry Gun Company (motorized)	Lt. Inf. Gun Platoon (motorized)	Infantry Gun Company (motorized)	Lt. Mtn. Anti-Aircraft Co. (mot)	Infantry Light Column (motorized)

REAR ECHELON UNITS

Horse-Drawn Transport Column (15 t)	Horse-Drawn Transport Column (30 t)	Horse-Drawn Transport Column (60 t)	Motor Transport Column (30 t)	Motor Transport Column (60 t)	Supply Company (motorized)	Motor Fuel Transport Col (25 cbm)	Motor Fuel Transport Col (50 cbm)	Motor Water Transport Col (25 cbm)	Maintenance Platoon (motorized)	Maintenance Company (motorized)	Park
Bakery Company (motorized)	Butchery Company (motorized)	Commissary Office	Medical Company (motorized)	Motor Ambulance Platoon	Casualty Transport Company	Decontamination Company	Field Hospital	Light Casualty Hospital	Military Hospital	Hospital Train	Medical Park
Veterinary Company	Veterinary Hospital	Horse Transport Column (mot)	Veterinary Examination Section	Veterinary Park	Remount Park	Survey Printing Det (mot)	Survey Detachment (motorized)	Survey Company (motorized)	Map Detachment (motorized)	Printing Platoon (motorized)	Construction Company
Carrier Pigeon Dovecot	Motorcycle Messenger Platoon	Field Post Office (motorized)	Band	Military Police Platoon (motorized)	Military Police Company (motorized)	Traffic Control Company (motorized)	Secret Field Police Detachment	Tire Supply Detachment (motorized)	Tire Repair Detachment (motorized)	Fuel Examination Det (mot)	Gasoline Leading Det (mot)

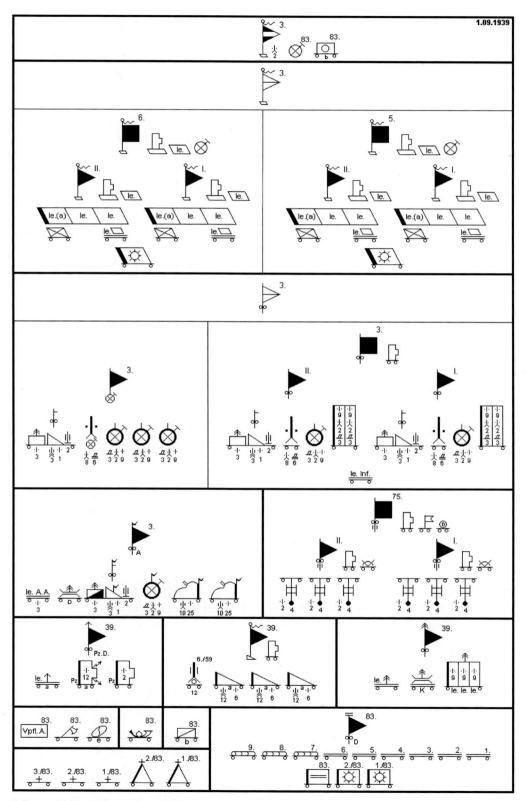

3. Panzer-Division, 1 September 1939.

CHAPTER 2

From the Spree to the Bug: The Campaign in Poland, 1939

August 1939 approached. The weather was warm and sunny. There was a lot of activity in the fields and pastures; the harvest needed to be brought in. Who knew when the next bad weather would come? But the sun still smiled down from the clear blue skies.

The headquarters and staff sections were filled with secretive and fast-paced work. The adjutants and liaison officers ran around with serious faces, and even the clerks and staff noncommissioned officers became unapproachable. The first batch of reserve officers arrived in the garrisons at the beginning of August. The soldiers, who had been called up for eight weeks, had given up hope of being released. It was the same picture every year. The annual maneuvers were around the corner. But this time, there was no real anticipation; the reports coming in from east of the *Reich* frontier were too serious.

In July, at the Bergen-Belsen Training Area, the division had activated the logistical units that belonged to it in accordance with its mobilization plans. They received the designation *Divisions-Nachschubtruppen 83* (Division Support Element 83). By the beginning of August, ten truck columns[1] had been established. That was followed by the division rations section

---

1. *Kolonne* is literally translated as "column," but organizationally, it was roughly equivalent to a company. Generally, *Kolonnen* were organized by lift capacity, with a *kleine Kolonne* capable of transporting thirty tons and a *große Kolonne* capable of sixty tons.

under the direction of *Stabszahlmeister* Flitner.[2] The division bakery company was under the command of *Hauptmann* Nagel. There was also the division's meat-processing platoon, the field post office (*Feldpostinspektor* Mollweide), and the two maintenance companies.

On 17 August, the whistles of the noncommissioned officers in charge pierced through the hallways of the barracks and the living areas: "Load up!" Later on, the company commanders revealed the march objective of the movement that had been ordered: the training area at Groß-Born. The elements of the division gradually moved out of their various garrisons. The advance parties of the rifle regiment left Eberswalde the next day, with elements of the motorcycle battalion following on 19 August and the armored regiments the day after that. That was followed by the artillery. Everyone thought to himself: Were we really just going to Groß-Born? Only a few actually knew that the Army High Command had already taken the preliminary measures for a mobilization. That meant that the formations capable of "moving out expeditiously" were to be prepared to move. That included all motorized divisions.

As the forces marched out, the family members of the soldiers gathered to bid farewell, as did the civilian employees of the mess halls, the canteens, and the administrative elements.

Many career officers and noncommissioned officers had to depart from the divisional elements during that period. They were transferred to new commands, activating formations and schools. It was not easy taking leave of their units. Now that the time had come to prove themselves, their common experiences and common efforts had to be given up. Reserve officers and noncommissioned officers took their places. Some of them were from the times of previous exercises and the march into the Sudetenland, thus allowing them to find a bridge to foster trust and understanding.

The commanders of the 4th and 5th Batteries changed within the 2nd Battalion of the division artillery. *Major* Wöhlermann and *Hauptmann* Hellmers gave up their commands to *Hauptmann* Haselbach and *Oberleutnant* Nebel (promoted to *Hauptmann* on 27 August). *Major* Burmeister assumed command of the 2nd Battalion of *Panzer-Regiment 6*.

The march route of the individual elements of the division took them past Stettin, across the Oder, and through Pomeranian Switzerland (*pommersche Schweiz*, the hill country of lower Pomerania, now Poland). On 22 August, a rumor spread through the march serials of a non-aggression pact between Germany and Russia. That evening, the rumor was confirmed. By then, all elements of the division were at the training area. The next few days were spent with the daily duty routine and passed quickly. Weapons and equipment were maintained; classroom instruction alternated with drill. Engineers instructed other formations with regard to electrically detonated obstacles and disarming them. No one thought that a military confrontation was possible.

Suddenly, on 25 August, marching orders arrived. The code word was "Tannenberg." At 1800 hours, the formations assembled in the camps for a final formation. The commanders discovered from the division that the surreptitious mobilization was to take place, with D-Day being 26 August. The die had been cast.

The march east started. The border was to be reached that same evening. The motorcycle battalion took the lead as far as Barkenbrügge. The armored brigade was to pass through at that point. The lead elements reached the border east of and to both sides of Preußisch Friedland around 2300 hours. The motorcycle battalion staged in the forests along the border. Its 1st Company screened along the railway line to Königsberg.

At 2345 hours, orders to halt arrived.

The lead elements were promptly pulled back ten kilometers; the artillery set up in the thick

---

2. A uniformed civilian official with a rank equivalent to *Hauptmann*.

woods forty kilometers west of the border. No one knew exactly what was going on. The rumor started to circulate slowly that the attack had been called off. It was said that the government had made new proposals to Poland with regard to regulating the Danzig and corridor problems and that it was waiting for the Polish response.

In an order that must be considered a masterpiece of planning, the German Army in the East—around half a million strong at this point—had to be halted at and over the border. The division set up a bivouac site in the Friedland area. The days spent in the camp were certainly a test of nerves for the forces, but they also represented a bit of a breather after the feverish preparations. Hardly any traces of normal duty activities could be seen. The only thing was pulling guard. On 27 August, an order prohibiting the sending of mail was imposed for the next few days. Portions of the companies were detailed to assist in the harvest in the surrounding farmlands. Some colorful evening celebrations took place, with the one hosted by the 2nd Battalion of the divisional artillery on the evening of 28 August in Peterswalde counting among the most impressive. The highlight of the evening was a singing competition, which the choir from the 5th Battery won. *Gefreiter* Salchow was an entertaining master of ceremonies who was not afraid to inject some political humor. The 2nd Battalion of *Panzer-Regiment 6* also held a singing competition, with the 6th Company taking the prize.

On the evening of 26 August, the motorcycle battalion returned to the border area again to secure the staging area of the division. The 3rd Company of *Oberleutnant* Adler advanced as far as a line running from the Grünkirch customs building to Grunau. Within the company, the platoon of *Leutnant* Arent,[3] who was the *Reichsbühnenbildner* in civilian life, was positioned on the right. *Leutnant* Stadie's platoon was in the middle and *Leutnant* Schmidt's platoon on the left. Across from them were the Polish village of Wilkowo and Hill 162, which featured a tall wooden watchtower.

Contrary to expectations, everything remained quiet on the Polish side, even though some movement could be identified. One antitank gun and one machine-gun position could be identified. There was little to be seen of civilians. On the German side, all traffic was forbidden between 2200 and 0500 hours. During that time, the patrols and engineers were active, cutting tank lanes through the barbed wire.

All of a sudden, around 0100 hours on 29 August, advance parties from the *III./Infanterie-Regiment 25* of the *2. Infanterie-Division (mot.)* showed up. It was part of a deception, whereby the armored division was being pulled back from the front. The motorcycle battalion moved to the forestry office at Linde. The next day passed quietly. It rained. There was no change in activity on 31 August, either. In the midst of all the quiet, orders arrived around 1600 hours: "Be prepared to move!"

As it started to turn dark on that rainy day, the columns began to move forward again. The tanks moved into the area on both sides of Grunau, followed by the rifle regiment. Just after midnight, an attack order arrived. The war was on!

To that end, the *4. Armee* had moved up to the border in Eastern Pomerania. The commander in chief was *General der Artillerie* von Kluge. It was directed for the field army to force a crossing over the Braha, rapidly reach the west bank of the Vistula in the Kulm–Graudenz area, and eliminate the Polish forces in the corridor. The main effort of that aspect of the operation was the *XIX. Armee-Korps (mot.)*. The commanding general, *General der Panzertruppen* Guderian, was the creator of the German armored force. *Oberst i.G.* Nehring, a longtime assistant to

---

3. Benno von Arent was a prominent member of the National Socialist Party. In addition to his title as the Reich Stage Designer, he was also designated as the Reich Agent for Fashion. He had close ties to Himmler and eventually joined the Waffen-SS in 1944 and was given the rank of *SS-Oberführer*.

Guderian in the creation of the *Panzertruppe* and prewar commander of *Panzer-Regiment 5*, was his chief of staff.

The corps consisted of the *2. Infanterie-Division (mot.)* of *Generalleutnant* Bader and the *20. Infanterie-Division (mot.)* of *Generalleutnant* Wiktorin, in addition to the *3. Panzer-Division* of *Generalleutnant Freiherr* Geyr von Schweppenburg. Also attached to the corps was the *23. Infanterie-Division* of *Generalmajor Graf* von Brockdorff-Ahlefeldt, which was its operational reserve.

As the formation with the most combat power of the corps, it was to be employed as its main effort. That aspect had already been determined at a conference at the headquarters of the *4. Armee* in Kolberg. According to the decision made there, the division would advance up to and into the Tuchel Heath, with its armored brigade in the lead. It was intended for the reinforced reconnaissance battalion of the division to advance as far as the Vistula after the bridge over the Braha had been taken. The long, open flanks were to be screened by the motorized rifle divisions. The first mission given to the division: "Reach the Braha east of Prust in the vicinity of Hammermühle and continue the advance to the Vistula in the vicinity of Schwetz!"

To execute that mission, the division received the following assets in attachment: *Panzer-Lehr-Abteilung* (*Major* von Lewinski),[4] *Flak-Regiment 101*,[5] and a flight of army utility aircraft. At the start of hostilities, the armored brigade had 324 *Panzer I*'s and *Panzer II*'s at its disposal. By contrast, the *Panzer-Lehr-Abteilung* was already fielding some of the first *Panzer III*'s and *Panzer IV*'s.

What did things look like from the Polish side? It goes without saying that the Polish government was prepared for the German attack and had already initiated mobilization of its own forces for some time. Starting in the spring of 1939, it had started to systematically "ripen up" its military and populace for the possible confrontation with Germany. The Pomeranian Army of General Bortnowski had completed its movement into the corridor by the end of August. The field army was organized into western and eastern groups. The Eastern Group of General Boltuc had the mission of protecting the western flank of the Modlin Army with its 4th and 16th Infantry Divisions. In addition, it was directed to defend along a line running Straßburg–Graudenz in the event of a German offensive. The Western Group of General Skotnicki was directed to hold the corridor, including the flanking position of Bromberg–Nakel, with its 9th and 15th Infantry Divisions, as well as the Pomeranian Cavalry Brigade. The 27th Infantry Division was the field army's operational reserve. Its orders were to eventually march on Danzig with the 13th Infantry Division, which would be brought in from Thorn.

The morning of 1 September 1939 dawned . . .

An early-morning fog appeared eerily in the woods; it was already perceptibly cold. There was an unearthly disquiet everywhere. The rattle of engines that quickly died off . . . the almost silent marching of columns . . . whispering and cursing, the light clinking of weapons . . . the division was ready. The officers continuously looked at their watches. The hands seemed to move imperceptibly slowly. Then: 0445 hours! There was a wailing from somewhere, but our artillery was still silent.

---

4. The Armored Instructional Battalion was composed of cadre from the armor school. The intent was to make sure that school personnel had valid wartime experience in order to teach in the military schooling system. Throughout the war, various elements from the school would be sent to the front to familiarize cadre personnel with the trends developing in armored tactics and fighting. By the end of the war, an entire division would be formed from school personnel. Rather than return to the "schoolhouse," it remained committed in fighting in the West until the end of the war. It was usually equipped with the latest equipment in order to keep it on the "cutting edge" of armor doctrine.

5. This was a *Luftwaffe* formation, primarily a command-and-control headquarters, with differing *Flak* formations attached to it.

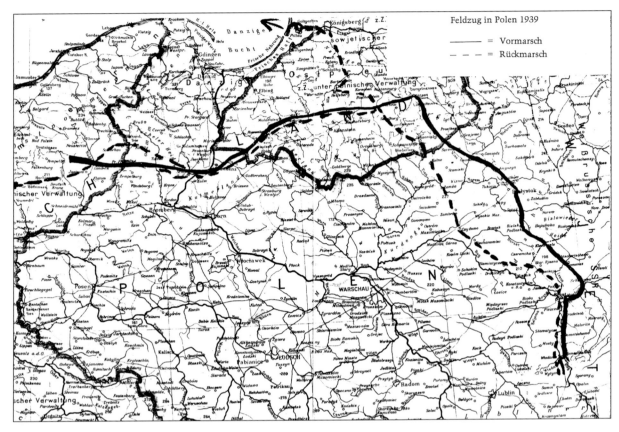

Campaign in Poland, 1939.

All of a sudden, the tank engines howled, tracked rattled, motorcycles roared. It was as if all unrest and all doubts had been lifted all at once and wiped away. The *3. Panzer-Division* of Berlin and Brandenburg was marching into war as the lead division of the *4. Armee.*

The small tanks were the first ones to make their way through the lanes created in the wire obstacles by the engineers. It was the light platoon of the *I./Panzer-Regiment 6* of *Oberleutnant* Buchterkirch. The mission: "Conduct reconnaissance in the attack zone of the regi-ment and press through across the Prust to secure the railway crossing!"

Tank after tank followed, with the *Panzer-Lehr-Abteilung* in the lead. Following close behind, dispersed across a wide frontage, was the rest of the armored brigade. Interspersed were a few squads of riflemen, mounted in the few *SPW*'s[6] that were available. The rifle brigade followed closely behind the armored elements in two groups. *Oberst* Angern, the brigade commander, led one group, while *Oberst* Kleemann was in charge of the second one. The riflemen crossed the border

---

6. *Schützenpanzerwagen* = armored personnel carrier. These were undoubtedly the *Sonderkraftfahrzeug (Sd.Kfz.) 251*, which was the standard German half-track of World War II. The original German refers to these as *Mannschaftstransportwagen* (personnel carriers), but it is obvious in context that the *Sd.Kfz. 251* is meant here. These vehicles were always in short supply, and for much of the war, only one company within a motorized/mechanized infantry regiment was so equipped. The light half-track was the *Sd.Kfz. 250*, but it was primarily used as a special-purpose vehicle and for reconnaissance duties. It was likewise in short supply for the entire war.

on foot. The motorcycle battalion started moving through the barbed wire at 0500 hours and was committed behind the armored regiments.

Panzer-Regiment 5 rolled forward on the righthand side of the attack zone, followed closely by the motorcycles of the *2./Krad-schützen-Bataillon 3*. The battalion's 3rd Company followed it, leading a *Flak* battery, the 1st Company of the motorcycle battalion, and the 4th and 5th Batteries of the divisional artillery into sector. *Panzer-Regiment 6* was employed on the left-hand side of the attack zone; its 1st Company was on the right, the 2nd Company on the left, and the 4th Company following. The remaining motorcycle elements, the 2nd and 3rd Companies of the divisional engineers, and a light *Flak* battery followed the tanks. Guderian rode at the front in an *SPW* among the regiment's tanks.

Fog cascaded over the terrain. Despite that, the tanks rolled forward across the potato and stubble fields. There wasn't a Polish soldier to be seen anywhere. Only the civilian populace could be seen in individual farmsteads along the way, some raising their arms in greeting, others glancing fearfully out from behind windows.

Oberleutnant Buchterkirch's tanks had already advanced fifteen kilometers when a column of horse-drawn carts suddenly appeared in front of the entrance to Zahn. It was guarded by a few horse-mounted soldiers. The first Poles! The *Oberleutnant* immediately opened fire. The tanks that were following close behind did likewise. There was confusion among the ranks of the enemy, with a few horses bolting and tossing their riders. Trains vehicles flipped over. After a few minutes, the enemy column scattered. The tanks rolled on. Behind them were the first Polish dead.

The morning fog slowly grew denser. Hardly anything could be seen. But that also meant the enemy could not see the tanks. *Oberleutnant* Buchterkirch had his tanks form up in column.

The tank engines howled and the march continued at maximum speed. Klein Klonia was passed and the Prut reached without encountering any trace of Polish resistance. At 0915 hours, the tanks were positioned along the railway line east of Prust. All of a sudden, a few vehicles appeared in the fog. They were the lead vehicles of the divisional reconnaissance battalion. Nothing had as yet been seen of the enemy. A single motorcycle approached along the roadway. Machine guns bellowed; the motorcycle stopped, with two men jumping off and raising their hands, flabbergasted. They were Polish officers, the first prisoners.

Farther to the rear, *Panzer-Regiment 6* had also encountered enemy forces. Around 0600 hours, its tanks were outside of Zahn. Visibility was poor, even though the sun was starting to peek through. A creek was crossed, followed by a large tract of marshland, which caused the first losses. A heavy tank got bogged down and churned itself ever deeper into the marshland with its running gear. A few minutes later, the same fate befell two other vehicles. The other tanks passed them, unconcerned. The maintenance contact teams were summoned forward by radio. The artillery liaison officer, *Oberleutnant* Weymann, also had bad luck. When he moved onto the Zahn–Großlossburg with his armored vehicle, the rear track came off the running gear. The disabled vehicle was discovered by a Polish bicycle patrol, which approached the vehicle's crew, which had dismounted and was working on the track. But before the Poles could become dangerous, German tanks appeared and shot the patrol to pieces.

The clocks showed 1000 hours, when the fog lifted all at once. The 7th Company of *Panzer-Regiment 6* (*Hauptmann* Friedrichs), moving on the left, suddenly encountered strong defensive fires coming a patch of woods jutting out near Gross Klonia.[7] The Poles had dug in and

---

7. In German, this was Groß Klonia, the equivalent of Large Klonia. Since "large" seems awkward in English, the Groß was retained but Anglicized into Gross. The same will be done for villages prefaced with *klein* (small). The reader should bear in mind that these extended villages were often broken into sections, usually separated by a natural obstacle, resulting in differentiation on maps into "large" and "small" sections.

become invisible in the woods and were firing antitank guns at pointblank range at the tanks. Two vehicles were hit and immobilized immediately, while the others went into cover behind in the rolling terrain. The company attempted to bypass the patch of woods, but was forced to halt again by the enemy's fires. The riflemen bringing up the rear also ran into Polish infantry fire, with the result that it was impossible to advance in that sector.

The regiment ordered a general halt in order to wait for the other formations to close up. The 2nd Battalion of the division, which was following the armored regiment, was ordered forward. Likewise, the 1st Company of the motorcycle battalion, under the command of *Oberleutnant* von Cochenhausen, which had heretofore not had any enemy contact, was ordered to attack.

Things were getting urgent. The 7th Company had already lost a number of vehicles. The first soldiers of the division killed in the war were lost during that engagement: *Leutnant* Nienaber, *Gefreiter* Fromm, *Gefreiter* Hopp, and four *Panzerschützen* (Meyer, Litmann, Godenschweig, and Kirschke). The 5th Battery of *Artillerie-Regiment 75* (*Hauptmann* Haselbach) went into position in a potato field and took the patch of woods under fire from 800 meters. The shells exploded in the crowns of the trees, and soon there were smoke and flames above the wood line. Some of the Poles fled their positions, others approached the Germans with raised hands. After the artillery observers saw that two enemy antitank guns had been destroyed, they ordered a stop to the artillery fires.

The 2nd Battalion of *Panzer-Regiment 6* made only slow progress. Every Polish pocket of resistance had to be eliminated individually. *Feldwebel* Wolschina of the 6th Company distinguished himself in that round of fighting by his aggressive advances. As a result, he became the first soldier of the regiment to receive the Iron Cross, Second Class.

By then, the motorcycle infantry had arrived. *Oberleutnant* von Cochenhausen had his company deploy and enter the thick woods. It was difficult to advance. The underbrush was thick and large trees and branches, knocked over or off by gunfire or felled, blocked the way. There were still Polish riflemen everywhere putting up a defense. While clearing the woods, the company suffered its first soldier killed in action; *Leutnant* Hiltmann and a junior noncommissioned officer were wounded.

At that point, the armored regiment was able to continue its march in the direction of the Brahe. All of the motorcycle battalion had closed up around Willkowo in the meantime. A motorcycle patrol under *Unteroffizier* Petreins from the 3rd Company was dispatched in the direction of Gross Klonia. A solo rider, *Kradschütze* Löwenstein, brought the news that the route was clear of the enemy. At that point, the battalion headed out in the direction of Bagnitz.

Panzer-Regiment 5 made faster progress. Moving through Prust, *Hauptmann Edler*[8] von der Planitz's tank company reached the Brahe shortly after 1100 hours. By then, Buchterkirch's platoon had advanced along the railway line, where it was promptly taken under fire from the elevated embankment by numerically superior Polish forces. The regiment's tanks arrived in time to assist. *Leutnant* Rommel's platoon was directed by Buchterkirch in an attack on the embankment and the enemy antitank guns. The tanks overran everything that got in their way, but they were finally stopped by a field position protected by wire. They were wedged between the creek and the marshland, and they had to take up fire from exposed positions. All ammunition was expended after ten minutes. Fortunately, the regiment's 1st Company (*Hauptmann* Nedtwig), which had been called forward, arrived by then. The other tanks were able to pull back under its covering fires.

---

8. A title of nobility, which is normally translated as "noble." *Edler* was below a knight (*Ritter*), but above untitled nobility in rank.

Schützen-Regiment 3 had moved out in the morning with the tanks, but its main body remained behind the advancing fighting vehicles. In searing heat, the riflemen marched and rode across the broad, flat terrain. In the villages that were predisposed to the Germans, the soldiers were greeted heartily. The greetings were especially heartfelt in Lossberg. Men, women, and children stood on the streets, waving flags. Who knew how long and where they might have hidden them?

The two armored regiments, which had worked their way forward to the Brahe, halted along its western banks. The vehicles and men were somewhat the worse for wear and waited for the rest of the divisional elements to close up. By that afternoon, they were thirty kilometers deep in enemy territory, along with the elements of the reconnaissance battalion that had been attached. They had driven a wedge into the Polish Army.

But to the right and the left of that wedge, there were powerful elements of the Polish 9th Infantry Division that were threatening the flanks. An actual threat materialized from the north from the Tuchel Heath. A Polish cavalry brigade attacked the left wing of the division.

The troops charged with drawn sabers. It was a scene straight out of the opening days of World War I. Unfortunately, the Polish cavalryman did not want to believe or were not allowed to believe that the German tanks were made out of steel and not wood and cardboard. The machine-gun fire from the tanks wreaked havoc among the ranks of the enemy riders. But they did not give up. The rode back, reorganized, and attacked again.

In the meantime, friendly artillery had gone into position in the open fields between Bagnitz and Prust. Its fires completely destroyed the Polish cavalry charge. Elements of the rifle regiment were also there. The heavy machine-gun section of the regiment's 1st Company was able to thin the enemy's ranks with well-aimed fire. *Hauptmann* von Bosse's 1st Battalion assumed a flank guard mission north of Gross Klonia.

By early afternoon, the division had reached its day's objective. The commander went to the corps headquarters to make his report. Everything seemed to be going according to plan.

The commanding general was not satisfied. Guderian ordered the crossing of the Braha that very afternoon. He wanted to remain on the enemy's heels—just as he had always preached.

It was directed that the motorcycle battalion move first across the Brahe with all of its available companies. The 2nd Company, together with support from the engineers, succeeded in crossing the river on rubber boats and floats about three kilometers south of the railway line. The 3rd Company followed shortly thereafter. That same night, the 1st Company established a bridgehead on the east bank of the Kamionka. The bridgehead was held until the arrival of the rifle platoons.

The reconnaissance battalion forced the river in a surprise attack directly outside of Hammermühle. The bridge was taken. The tanks that followed took a Polish bicycle company that was hastily arriving to defend the bridge prisoner.

By then, it had turned midnight. Hammermühle and the farmsteads all around it were blazing like torches. To both sides and the rear, pyrotechnic flares were being shot skyward, a sure sign that the division was well ahead of the remaining forces of the corps. *Oberleutnant* von Manteuffel did not allow his motorcycle infantry any rest. His men were able to reach Swiekatowo. That was as far as they got; the battalion set up an all-round defense in the woods. That same night, there was a wild firefight. A large Mercedes suddenly showed up with headlights on, driving right into the encampment of the 1st Company. The German guards were just as surprised as the two Polish officers in the car. The Poles entered captivity with glowering faces. A few minutes later, they received company in the form of a mounted patrol that also rode into the bivouac site without a clue.

Major Freiherr von Wechmar's reconnaissance battalion received orders during the night to continue advancing east, along with the attached 2nd Battery of the artillery regiment and some tanks from the *Panzer-Lehr-Abteilung*. The next objective for the newly formed advance guard was the Vistula.

As it started to dawn on the second day of the war, the reconnaissance and motorcycle battalions continued their advance east. They knew that the armored brigade and the rifle regiment would close up behind them. The division had created a strong second wave in the form of a *Kampfgruppe* under *Generalmajor* Stumpff. It consisted of the *II./Panzer-Regiment 5*, the *II./Panzer-Regiment 6*, the *II./Artillerie-Regiment 75*, and the remaining elements of *Kradschützen-Bataillon 3*. The elements of the rifle regiment that remained behind in Kamionka moved out and into the Tuchel Heath around 0800 hours. The gigantic expanses of woods had an eerie quality to them. No one knew what could be hiding in them.

The Poles then upset the apple cart a bit with regard to the German plans. Strong elements from the Polish 9th and 27th Infantry Divisions, as well as the Pomeranian Cavalry Brigade, conducted a surprise attack on the German bridgehead at Hammermühle early in the morning and established themselves along the road to Swiekatowo. That meant that the advanced elements of the division were threatened with being cut off. Even worse, a loss of the bridgehead would have negative effects on the continued attack of the entire corps.

That morning, only *Hauptmann* Beigel's 1st Company of the engineer battalion was arrayed along the Hammermühle. The division commander, unaware of what was happening, continued toward the front in order to receive the reports from the formation commanders. All of a sudden, heavy machine-gun fire flared up from the nearby woods. The enemy fires increased in intensity by the minute. *Generalleutnant* von Schweppenburg; his adjutant, *Major* von Wietersheim; and an assistant operations officer, *Oberleutnant* von Levetzow, had to take cover immediately. The headquarters of the division and of the divisional artillery,

which arrived a short while later, also got caught in the fire. The division's command-and-control ability was lost for a short while on that day. The two headquarters and the accompanying radio operators from the divisional signals battalion suffered their first casualties. The officers had no choice but to bound back across the 100 meters of open meadowland to get to a steep downward slope to the rear. They were received there by the combat outposts of the rifle regiment.

That did not accomplish much, since Polish fires started to impact there as well and stymied every attempt to pull back and occupy better positions. Although the engineers attempted an immediate counterattack into the thick woods, they were unable to dislodge the well-entrenched enemy.

The division commander had the *Kampfgruppe* of *Oberst* Kleemann, which was still relatively far back, brought forward to relieve the beleaguered force. Unfortunately, that battle group had changed its direction of march just a few minutes previously and had not turned its radios back on to receive. As a result, hours passed. The division commander had no idea at that point where his individual battalions and regiments were.

Finally, German soldiers appeared from the west. They were not formations from the *3. Panzer-Division*, however. Instead, it was the reconnaissance troop of *Rittmeister* von Götz from the divisional reconnaissance battalion of the *23. Infanterie-Division*, which was in the second wave.

The Polish attack not only cut off the command-and-control elements of the division that morning, it also hit the elements of the division that had already ranged well to the east. During the night, the 2nd Battalion of *Panzer-Regiment 6* had assumed the mission of screening the bottleneck between the lakes at Swiekatowo. The enemy thrust early that morning slammed right into that area with full force. The 5th and 6th Companies were able to turn back the first attack effort until 0900 hours. Two platoons from the

6th Company particularly distinguished themselves in the engagement. They were the platoons of *Leutnant Graf* von Kageneck and *Leutnant* von Diest-Koerber. Also worthy of note were the achievements of *Unteroffizier* Wehrmeister and *Gefreiter* Deuter, who were in the thick of things with their fighting vehicles. Nonetheless, that company suffered its first five dead in that fighting: *Feldwebel* Fiedler, *Unteroffizier* Fleher, *Gefreiter* Schreiber, *Oberschütze* Feldhahn, and *Panzerschütze* Bischoff.

By noon, the enemy had pulled back to his original line of departure. Due to a lack of fuel, the friendly vehicles were not able to attack him. When the commander of *Panzer-Regiment 6* brought up reinforcements in the afternoon, the 2nd Battalion attacked to the north and was able to drive the enemy back. At the same time, the 5th and 8th Companies screened the flank to the east. The 6th Company attacked identified enemy antitank-gun positions and put the guns out of commission. The 5th Company was also able to eliminate some antitank guns—three in all. In the process, it rescued a platoon from the 4th Company, which had advanced the farthest north but had also shot off all of its ammunition. By late afternoon, all threats had been eliminated and the battalion moved out to continue east after rearming.

The 1st Company of the motorcycle battalion was immediately ordered back to Hammermühle, as was the 1st Company of the rifle regiment. The 2nd Battery of the divisional artillery turned its guns around 180 degrees and fired with everything it was capable of.

Hauptmann Boehm's riflemen moved as quickly as they could to Hammermühle. Along the way were ammunition vehicles and baggage trains that had been overrun by the tanks, as well as the corpses of horses and of Poles killed in action. General Guderian appeared and encouraged the soldiers, waving them on. After moving four kilometers through woods, a halt was ordered. Polish artillery held up any further movement and was raking the road with heavy fire. The company's vehicles were brought forward, and the march continued through Johannisberg and Stansilawa to Koritowo.

All of a sudden, *General* von Schweppenburg was standing in front of the men. He personally directed the 3rd Platoon of *Feldwebel* Hillinger against the enemy battery.

Panzer-Regiment 5 then moved out to attack Gross Lonk. On the far side of Koritow, the fighting vehicles ran into the artillery positions of the enemy. Disregarding the intense fires and brave resistance, the tanks plunged into the Polish lines and individually took out the guns. That did not occur without perceptible losses, however.

The 1st Company of *Kradschützen-Bataillon 3* assumed the mission of protecting the division command post with one of its platoons. The remaining two platoons advanced into the woods north of Hammermühle. Two Polish infantry companies were wiped out in tough fighting. The two platoons lost two dead and four wounded in that engagement and only had thirty men altogether by the end of the evening. The batteries that were brought forward fired over open sights. The 3rd Battery lost *Hauptwachtmeister*[9] Hippe in the process, the first *Spieß*[10] of the division to be killed, an indicator of the toughness of the fighting and also the bravery of the enemy. By evening, the division had mastered the dangerous situation with its own forces. It was then able to rapidly move its elements to the east across the Brahe.

In the meantime, the motorcycle battalion had taken Klonowo with its remaining two companies and a few tanks from the *Panzer-Lehr-Abteilung*. Unconcerned about the sounds of fighting to their rear, the motorcycle infantry and reconnaissance troopers continued their advance

---

9. *Hauptfeldwebel* was specific to artillery and cavalry units and indicated a unit's first sergeant. This was a duty position, not a rank, as the position could be filled by an *Oberfeldwebel* or a *Feldwebel*.

10. *Spieß* = pike. This was the common soldier jargon for the first sergeant of a unit.

east. The sun blazed mercilessly that day, with rain following in the afternoon. The tanks and riflemen moved, marched, and advanced. The roads were poor and frequently only had a single lane. All of the traffic had to work its way around that. The roads became clogged and there were unpleasant stops. The reconnaissance battalion was far ahead of the division and moved right through the middle of enemy detachments, which were equally shocked and surprised and incapable of offering a defense. *Major* von Wechmar intended to reach the Vistula before the onset of darkness. But intertwined enemy columns or vehicles and trees that had fallen victim to *Stukas* blocked the way. The enemy was not falling back uniformly. Resistance around Rozana was especially hard.

The reconnaissance battalion was unable to advance any farther. The armored car crews, supported by the 1st Battery of the artillery regiment (*Leutnant* Hoffmann), had a hard fight on their hands at the Poledno Estate, which was being defended by Polish cavalry. The advance guard suffered its first officer casualties. The commander of the *2./Aufklärungs-Abteilung 3*, *Rittmeister* von Prittwitz und Gaffron, the former adjutant to *Generaloberst* von Fritsch,[11] was wounded in the stomach. The brave officer refused to be operated on at the main clearing station, insisting that the surgeons operate on the more severely wounded first. *Leutnant* Adam died on the battlefield at the head of his reconnaissance platoon. Once stopped, the battalion "circled the wagons" with its vehicles, the village of Rozana, set alight by air attacks and artillery, forming a backdrop.

The motorcycle battalion pivoted from its movement east to head south in order to help the reconnaissance battalion. But the motorcycle infantry were not able to get beyond the line reached by the armored cars. In contrast, the divisional engineers had more success in the effort to take Rozana. They had been directed there by the division commander. *Major* von Mertens led his engineers in the assault on the shot-up and burning town and took possession of it that night.

The 2nd Battalion of *Panzer-Regiment 6* also moved out in the evening (around 2000 hours). *Hauptmann* Bernewitz's 8th Company advanced as far as Polskie-Lakie. At that point, the tanks encountered a surprisingly strong antitank defense. Three friendly tanks were knocked out. The battalion then pulled back 1,000 meters, set the village alight, and then set up an all-round defense for the night.

The division could be satisfied with its achievements that day. Its formations had not only stymied the efforts of the Poles to break through, but they had also broken into the front of the Corridor Army. The corps brought the *23. Infanterie-Division* across the Brahe and employed it to the left of the division.

The 1st Battalion of the rifle regiment assumed the flank guard mission for the division during the night. The plucky riflemen succeeded in orienting themselves in the dark woods and fields and taking up good positions. They throttled all attempts by the Poles to find a gap in the German lines. The division discovered with certainty that its tanks had advanced so far into the corridor that elements of the Polish forces had been bypassed.

The night was very cool. That was especially noticeable after a humid summer's day, as the past one had been. Something else had a negative impact on the soldiers as well: hunger and thirst. The supply elements were still far to the rear as a result of the rapid advance and the poor road network. They had barely gotten beyond Hammermühle. Some of the men found the courage to sneak across the fields in an effort to milk some cows that had gone astray. Among artillery circles within the division, that night was always referred to as "the hour of the *Ortsbäuernführer*."[12]

11. This, of course, was the famous Werner von Fritsch of the Blomberg-Fritsch Affair and prewar intrigue.

12. The *Ortsbauernführer* (Village Farmer Leader) was the lowest-ranking organization leader for food production of a village as part of the *Reichsnährstand* (usually not translated, but sometimes rendered as Reich Food Corporation).

The advance started all over again at 0400 hours across the entire frontage of the division. The march route ran parallel to the Vistula along the Poledno–Drozdowo road. The reconnaissance and motorcycle battalions were the first to move out, followed by the armored brigade (at least those elements that had been refueled). The 2nd Company of the motorcycle battalion, which was in the lead, received heavy fire from Drozdowo shortly after moving out and bogged down. The battalion commander quickly brought his 3rd Company forward and employed it north of the road, along with the 1st Company, which was still exhausted from the previous day. The 1st Company approached the railway embankment behind Belno. *Oberleutnant* von Cochenhausen intended to let his men rest after that. It remained an

intent. A transport train steamed in. The motorcycle infantry forced it to halt; 4 officers and 128 enlisted personnel were taken prisoner.

All of the remaining elements of the division also advanced against numerically superior Polish forces. The enemy field army command had recognized the situation it was in—the rapidly growing threat of encirclement—and was doing everything in its power to pull its division across the Vistula on the road leading to Kulm.

The armored brigade attacked at first light from Swiekatowo in the direction of Heinrichsdorf and Biechowoko toward the northwest in an effort to interdict the retreat routes. Both of the division's armored regiments and the attached *Panzer-Lehr-Abteilung* moved at "full speed ahead." But it was soon discovered that the Poles had placed very strong antitank defenses

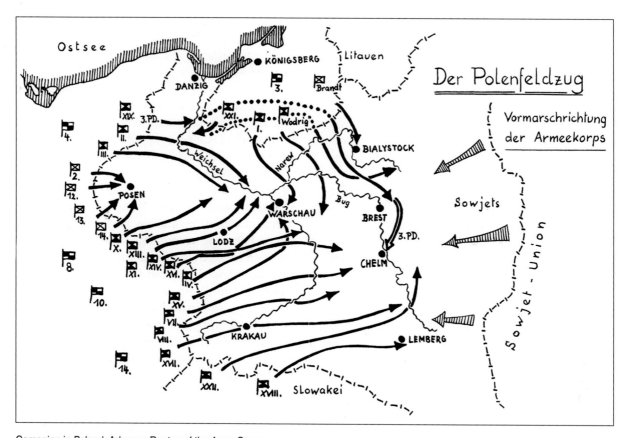

Campaign in Poland: Advance Routes of the Army Corps.

at the entrance to every village. As a result, there was hard fighting that was not without casualties.

Panzer-Regiment 6, moving on the right, crossed the Terespol–Tuchel road, with *Hauptmann* Schneider-Kostalski's 2nd Company eliminating three Polish machine-gun tanks in the process. Defiles then held up further advance. The regiment pivoted to the left and ran into elements of the advancing *Panzer-Regiment 5*. Enemy infantry continued defending everywhere after being bypassed by the tanks and made life difficult for the riflemen following.

The tanks reached the Terespol–Oslowo area and then pressed on to the east, but the following formations ran into strong enemy forces. Only the 4th Battery of the artillery regiment was able to successfully stay on the heels of the enemy. The remaining battery received considerable fire from the village of Heinrichsdorf. *Hauptmann* Haselbach assumed command of the forces in the area and had the 5th and 6th Batteries unlimber in a depression. Patrols were sent out in all directions. Sections under *Wachtmeister* Rademacher and *Unteroffizier* Himmel searched the nearby farmsteads, while *Leutnant* Grotewald occupied the industrial area of Heinrichsdorf with the ammunition section of the 4th Battery, which had been left behind.

The Poles tried to open the road to Terespol with all the means at their disposal. But it was already too late at noon on that hot summer day to accomplish that, even though elements of the Polish 9th Infantry Division—especially elements of the 16th Cavalry Regiment, as well as the 25th and 35th Infantry Regiments—fought bravely. By then, the rifle regiment was able to join the developing fray by moving via Poledno and Drozdowo.

At 1240 hours, the artillery took the Poles attempting to break out under heavy fire. The effect along the road was horrific. Horses bolted, soldiers ran head over heels into the fields, and limbers and trains vehicles flipped over. They were followed by fires from *Hauptmann* Hasel-

bach's 5th Battery and *Leutnant* Jaschke's 6th Battery (Jaschke was acting battery commander). *Hauptwachtmeister* Reinig of the 6th Battery identified a Polish battery going into position along the northern edge of Heinrichsdorf. He brought up the spotting gun of the battery. The gunner, Wenzel, had the target in range with his second shell. A few minutes later, the enemy battery was silenced. For his efforts, *Hauptwachtmeister* Reinig later became the first soldier of the artillery regiment to receive the Iron Cross, Second Class.

The rifle regiment attacked at just the right time to interdict the hard-fighting enemy. Heavy fighting ensued; it was conducted by the Poles with the courage of desperation. The 1st and 3rd Rifle Companies assaulted along the road in the direction of Polskie. *Hauptmann* von Lany, the commander of the 3rd Company, and *Leutnant* von Heydebreck, his platoon leader, were killed. The 1st Company lost its first man with *Schütze* Krämer.

By then, the Poles had had enough. There was no way to get out. In addition to twenty artillery pieces and six antitank guns being destroyed, there were vehicles, ammunition wagons, machine guns, horses, and articles of equipment scattered everywhere. The rifle regiment took 36 officers and 800 men prisoner that afternoon; fifteen artillery pieces were among the spoils of war.

The division did not allow itself to be distracted from its objective by the fighting to encircle the enemy forces. The reconnaissance battalion received orders to take Schwetz, while the motorcycle battalion was sent in the direction of Liepo–Biala–Taszarko. Fortunately, the advance of *Infanterie-Regiment 96* of the *32. Infanterie-Division* on the right side of the division was starting to make its presence felt. Despite that, Polish cavalry sections continued to surface across the front and created temporary disruptions here and there. There no longer appeared to be unified command among the Poles; operations seemed to be left up to the individual unit and formation commanders.

Around 1000 hours, the *II./Panzer-Regiment 6* crossed the Czerna-Woda at F.W. Dedienke. The lead tanks identified the rapid movement of trains, one after the other, four kilometers away. *Oberstleutnant* Rothenburg, who was up front with his tanks, ordered *Hauptmann* Schneider-Kostalski to block the reported rail traffic along the stretch between Derispol–Oslowo. The tanks moved along the sandy road as far as the rail line without encountering any resistance. The railway crossing guard shack was locked up and the gate crossing lowered. Schneider-Kostalski was undeterred. He ordered: *"Panzer marsch!"* The gate flew in the air with a crash. A cloud of smoke could be seen to the south. Schneider-Kostalski had his company take up firing positions on the far side of the line. The train's engineer must have noticed the movement, however, since the train slowed and finally stopped. The company commander opened fire at 250 meters. With the first round, the locomotive's boiler exploded with a monstrous cloud of smoke. The doors to the passenger cars opened everywhere. Polish soldiers jumped out and attempted to flee into the nearby woods. The tanks of the 4th and 7th Companies showed up at that moment and joined in the engagement. Sixty Polish soldiers were sent back as prisoners. They were the last men of a battalion that had boarded the train.

The three tank companies immediately took up the advance on Lakowicz. At Krapjewitce, they were able to scatter horse-drawn trains elements. Once past Polskie-Lakie, they encountered Polish cavalry and antitank elements. The 2nd Company encountered its first enemy tank on the Rozana–Bledno road at 1100 hours; it was knocked out at 300 meters with two rounds.

The armored brigade reached the training area at Schwetz in the afternoon and continued its advance north. Toward 1800 hours, the tanks took Oslowo. The forces reorganized for the attack on the Grupa Training Area. The rear areas also had to be secured, since there were still strong Polish forces in the area around Terespol. Those forces did not remain quiet; they continued to fight to break free. *Leutnant* Lange, the adjutant of the artillery's 2nd Battalion, was captured by the enemy during a patrol. He was stabbed, but he lived to tell the tale.

Major von Wechmar's reconnaissance battalion pressed past Schwetz at the onset of darkness without regard for the scattered enemy groups. He immediately pressed along the Vistula to the north with all of his troops. To help keep the movement fluid, the division sent the engineer companies of *Major* von Mertens, which had just become available, and *Hauptmann* Reinke's 3rd Battery, after the reconnaissance battalion. The engineers and the artillery made it into Schwetz, but the Poles then started a stubborn defense there. There was a danger that the engineer battalion might be encircled. The engineers had to defend from all directions and lost contact with the remaining elements of the division. Despite that, it was able to prevail. In the end, the battalion occupied and held Schwetz. The 3rd Battery captured a war chest in the city hall.

The Polish command knew what was at stake. Energetic officers rallied their men again and again to bravely defend. As a result, the German rifle companies did not advance any farther that night. As a result, *Generalleutnant* von Schweppenburg ordered the 1st Battalion of the rifle regiment pulled back to Poledno. The division operations officer, *Major* von der Borne, expressed a contrary opinion. He believed the riflemen should remain where they were. But the division commander wanted to lead his forces in a traditional cavalry style: pull the forces back tonight so that they could be used to conduct a "fencer's leap" the following morning. As a result, he ordered the battalion back and directed it to hold Poledno "to the last bullet," as the pivot point of the entire division.

Only *Panzer-Regiment 5* was able to score a success that evening. It did not remain in Oslowo; instead, it pushed its companies along sandy routes through the dark woods as far as Dubielno, which was reached around 0200 hours.

That meant that the encirclement of the enemy forces fighting in the corridor was just around the corner. The division could see the blazing fires and hear the sounds of fighting in the nearby fortress of Graudenz, which had fallen to the East Prussian *21. Infanterie-Division* that day. The *XIX. Armee-Korps (mot.)* was only a few kilometers from the borders of East Prussia.

The Polish Pomeranian Army had been split in two in three days of fighting. The field army headquarters was located in Thorn at that point and was attempting to establish contact with the Modlin or Posen Armies with its remaining regiments.

General Guderian went to the division headquarters during the night and ordered the advance to continue, irrespective of the condition of the beleaguered men and vehicles. The Poles could not be given any time to cross the Vistula west of Graudenz. Correspondingly, orders were sent to all elements of the division to move out at first light again.

The reconnaissance battalion started its movement along the Vistula in the direction of Graudenz at 0400 hours. The armored cars and motorcycles moved without regard for the scattered enemy elements, which were still offering a defense from out of individual farmsteads and barns. The men of the division had only one objective: to establish contact with their East Prussian comrades as soon as possible. Whoever fell back had to fend for himself. The disabled vehicles had to be repaired with only the means available. Fortunately, the Poles were no longer in a position to offer energetic resistance. Most of them automatically raised their hands in the air as the vehicles raced past them. Only a burst of machine-gun fire was necessary to fish them out of their hiding places—trenches, haystacks, houses, and gardens—where they had spent the cold night in order to try to find a place that morning to get over the river somewhere and head south.

The movements of the reconnaissance battalion took place on the right wing of the division;

the main effort of the day's efforts was to be in the center, however. The armored brigade, reinforced by the motorcycle battalion and the 2nd and 4th Batteries of the divisional artillery while it staged during the night, received orders to cross the Matave quickly and attack the Grupa Training Area from the west along a broad front. The enemy was to be driven east to the Vistula, where *Oberst* Angern, with elements of the rifle brigade and the reconnaissance battalion, had been directed to interdict him. *Oberst* Rothenberg was entrusted with the screening of the division north of Schwetz. In addition to *Panzer-Regiment 6*, he had the *I./Schützen-Regiment 3*, the *1./Pionier-Bataillon 39*, the *I./Artillerie-Regiment 75*, and the *6./MG-Bataillon 59* at his disposal. Of those forces, the 2nd Battalion of the armored regiment (*Major* Burmeister) would face a few dangerous situations over the course of the next few hours.

The elements of the division that were still hanging back were collected into a *Kampfgruppe* under the command of *Oberst* Kleemann. It was directed for Kleemann's elements to move as expeditiously as possible to follow the armored brigade, ferreting out the Polish forces still hiding in the woods and fields in the process. Since the movement of the entire force was delayed, *Hauptmann* Beez decided to race forward with a hastily assembled advance party. That small element, to which *Leutnant* Behrend, *Leutnant* Franzke, and *Inspektor* Tries were also a party, collected almost 300 prisoners in a short period. *Leutnant* Behrend ensured the prisoners were properly transported to the rear, while the rest continued moving toward the increasingly loud sounds of fighting coming from Grupa.

The armored brigade moved out around 0400 hours and portions crossed the creek in their first attempt. The Poles did not open fire until the following elements arrived. The brigade suffered considerable casualties, particularly in the streets of Grupa proper, where the enemy had barricaded himself in houses and set up strong anti-tank-gun positions. *Oberstleutnant* Wimmer assumed command of the motorcycle, antitank, and artillery elements left behind. Despite the more unified command of those forces, the Poles still thwarted every attempt to cross the creek by means of well-placed artillery fire. It was not until four light tanks of the armored brigade turned around and rolled up the Polish positions from the rear that it was possible to cross the water obstacle.

Hauptmann Hinniger's 2nd Battery was the first unit that could be guided through. It was high time, since the tanks and riflemen that were attacking Grupa had run into a bind. The Polish forces—later, it was discovered that there were nearly 20,000 men there—were attacking with the courage of desperation in order to break out of the encirclement.

Oberst Angern led the forces of the division that were arrayed around Grupa. The tank attack on the training area was not making any progress due to heavy and well-aimed antitank-gun fire. The friendly companies needed to be pulled back. The 1st Company of the motorcycle battalion also bogged down in the Polish fires. The company commander, *Oberleutnant* von Cochenhausen, was badly wounded.

The 3rd Company of the motorcycle battalion (*Oberleutnant* Adler) pulled back from the crossroads east of Grupa and worked its way back in the woods to the south as far as Hill 87. The company was subjected to an intense infantry attack. The numerically superior enemy approached the company, which was fixed in place, by leaps and bounds. If the position were broken through there, then the enemy would create a gap from which to escape.

Oberst Angern gave responsibility for the southern portion of the sector to *Oberstleutnant* Wimmer, who arrived in Grupa-Dola at 0745 hours. At the time, the 3rd Company of the rifle regiment, the 3rd Company of the motorcycle battalion and elements of two tank and one machine-gun company were positioned there. Wimmer brought the heaviest firepower with him—his 2nd Battery. To the right of the road leading from Grupa to the training area, the battle group had contact with the 2nd Battalion of

the rifle regiment (*Oberstleutnant* Dr. Ehlermann). That battalion's 7th Company was widely dispersed in the vicinity of the observation posts of the 2nd Battery and was exchanging fire with Polish snipers.

The 2nd Battery then opened well-aimed fire on identified Polish positions. That enabled *Oberleutnant* Adler and his men to disengage from the enemy. His company left behind three dead (*Unteroffizier* Bruns, *Unteroffizier* Fiss, and *Unteroffizier* Petreins), as well as four men missing (two *Gefreite* and two *Schützen*). Wimmer employed the freed-up motorcycle infantry on the right, where the Poles also attacked.

The battery fired off all but twenty of its rounds. In the broken terrain, the machine gunners had no fields of fire and had to allow the enemy to approach to pointblank range. Fortunately, elements of the two tank companies arrived at that point. But they also had little ammunition left. The enemy recognized his advantage and pressed ever more energetically by the minute against the German positions. Both of the brigade commanders, *Generalmajor* Stumpff and *Oberst* Angern, had to employ their messengers in the defense of Grupa. The time moved inexorably forward . . . if a miracle did not happen soon.

And miracles do happen.

The 4th Battery of the artillery regiment arrived from the Matave just in time and unlimbered at the edge of the woods. Its fires forced the enemy to call off his attacks for the time being. Fortunately, the ammunition section of *Inspektor* Tries also arrived. The guns once more had ammunition and started to fire with everything they had. *Hauptmann* Lorenz, the commander of the 1st Battalion, then arrived with the 1st Battery.

At that point, the Poles gave up on their intent of breaking out in the direction of Graudenz. The Poles only conducted limited attacks, but they were all turned back, since large portions of the rifle regiment had also arrived and started to get committed to the fighting. On that afternoon of 4 September, the division had also passed its

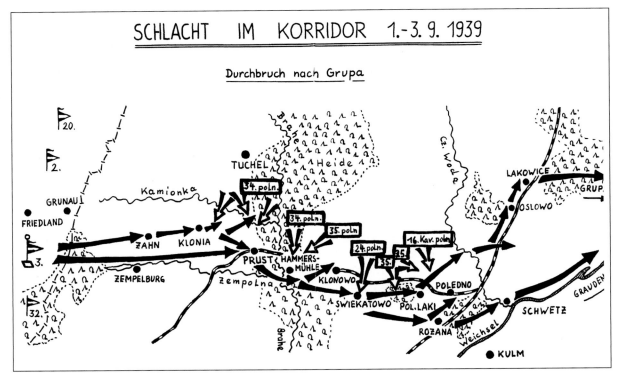

Fighting in the corridor, 1–3 September 1939: Breaththrough to Grupa.

baptism of fire in the defense. *Generalmajor* Stumpff was able to report that to the commanding general, who arrived late in the afternoon. Because Stumpff became ill, however, he had to give up command of the armored brigade temporarily. *Oberst* Rothenburg assumed acting command, with Major von Lewinski taking over *Panzer-Regiment 6*. The commander of the latter regiment's 1st Battalion, Major von Boltenstern, also took ill and had to be relieved by *Major* Schmidt-Ott.

The motorized elements were gradually withdrawn from the encirclement over the next few hours and replaced by infantry, since the other divisions of the corps had closed up to the division by then and established contact. They assumed responsibility for finishing the encirclement of the Polish Corridor Army.

The ethnic German villages between Graudenz and Schwetz served as the quartering area for the division. The cannoneers and riflemen were especially warmly welcomed in Wiag. The rear-area services, supply elements, and maintenance companies were brought forward through Swiekatowo to Stanislawie. The tanks, trucks, and motorcycles were in desperate need of maintenance, but it could only be conducted hastily, since the fighting in the corridor was not yet over.

The majority of the division did not see action on 5 September. The neighboring infantry divisions did not allow the Poles to break through and forced them to give up the fight that day. The first battle of encirclement of World War II was over.

Despite the "peaceful" hours of that day, the division was not idle. The artillery occupied positions to assist in fending off any potential enemy attacks. The maintenance companies were brought up closer to the motorized elements and quartered in the former Polish military facilities in Schwetz. The engineer battalion, which was never employed as a complete entity up to that point—it had been parceled out to all of the battle groups of the division—built a bridge over the Vistula at Weisshof. The motorcycle battalion combed the bottomlands of the river for scattered Polish elements. Its 3rd Company screened along the embankment, while a reinforced platoon under *Leutnant* Schmidt became the first element of the division to cross the Vistula to Graudenz.

On 6 September, the first German formations were moved to the eastern portions of East Prussia. They were to conduct a new assault from there. The *XXI. Armee-Korps* took Graudenz. In the next two days, the *XIX. Armee-Korps (mot.)* was to follow, crossing the bridges at Käsemark (north of Dirschau), at Mewe, and at Topolno.

The corps situation on the evening of 6 September was as follows. The *20. Infanterie-Division (mot.)* was already marching across the bridge at Käsemark in the direction of Elbing and had already reached Bartenstein with its lead elements. The *2. Infanterie-Division (mot.)* was preparing to cross at Mewe, while the *3. Panzer-Division* remained west of Graudenz behind the latter motorized infantry division.

The division moved out on 7 September with its lead elements. The columns once again experienced the "beauty" of the Polish road system under their wheels. It seemed to the soldiers that ever since that area had come under Polish control, not a single spade had been turned to maintain the roads. The deep sand and the broad craters made the march difficult. Many vehicles became disabled, because the gas lines or the suspension springs broke. The men of the maintenance companies were not idle.

The movement led north. In the shadow of the *Ordensburg*[13] at Mewe, all of the divisional elements crossed on a pontoon bridge constructed by the engineers over the broad, calm waters of the Vistula. At Kurzebrack, to the west of Marienwerder, most of them saw for the first time in their lives the four-meter-wide access to the Vistula provided to the Germans.[14] At that point, the men of the division were in East Prussia, a beautiful province with large tracts of woods, broad hills, vast fields, and quiet lakes.

The movement took place under magnificent sunshine through the resplendent cities of Marienwerder, Rosenberg, Auerswald, Deutsch-Eylau, Osterode, the Tannenberg Memorial, Allenstein, Guttstadt, Lötzen, and Arys. The long route of 380 kilometers was covered in three days. But no one felt the hardships. The weather put on a sunny face. The reception in the individual localities was indescribable. All people, especially the youth, could not contain themselves in decorating the vehicles with flowers and cheering the soldiers.

Guderian requested that his corps be directly allocated to the field army group. He intended to range far to the east on the left wing of the *3. Armee*, reach the Bug at Brest, and encircle the Polish field armies in Eastern Poland. *Generaloberst* von Bock picked up on the idea; in the end, the Army High Command approved the operation.

When the Polish front in front of the *3. Armee* started to waver, the *XIX. Armee-Korps (mot.)* was employed on the left wing to conduct a bounding pursuit. Guderian gave his divisions the following intermediate objectives:

- *20. Infanterie-Division (mot.)*—through Zambrow to the Bug crossing at Nur
- *10. Panzer-Division*—to Bielsk via Bransk
- *3. Panzer-Division*—to the area north of Bielsk
- *2. Infanterie-Division (mot.)*—to be brought forward into the area around Zambrow–Bielsk

The long-range objective for all of the formations remained the fortress of Brest-Litowsk.

---

13. The *Ordensburgen* were fortresses constructed in the Middle Ages by military orders such as the Teutonic Knights to defend Christian Germanic lands from pagans.

14. As part of the Versailles Treaty, Germany was guaranteed access to the Vistula, but only through this small channel. It was a bone of contention for Germans of that era, and the authors obviously felt there was no further need for explanation.

Sunday, 10 September, was a day of rest for the division at the large training area at Arys. The sun smiled warmly on the soldiers. As it started to disappear behind the hills and woods, marching orders arrived. The individual formations left the training area one after the other until about midnight and headed to the southeast to the border. That same night, Polish territory was entered for the second time by the forward elements of the division. The main body of the division crossed the border at Szczuczyn. *Panzer-Regiment 6* followed the next day. It had moved out with the following vehicles: 55 *Panzer I's*, 55 *Panzer II's*, 3 *Panzer III's*, 6 *Panzer IV's*, 132 trucks, 60 staff cars, and 114 motorcycles.[15]

That meant that the time for cursing had started all over again for the drivers of the tanks, staff cars, trucks, prime movers, and especially the motorcycle riders. "Roads" was not the right word, and the entities that were so marked on the maps would not even have qualified as routes of the worst order back in the homeland. But there was to be no rest. There was only one objective and one mission: Forward!

Wasosz and Przytuly were a few of the places on the route before the columns reached the broad bottomlands of the Narew. The terrain came across as monotonous and bleak; there was something of the unearthly quality of the steppes of the Far East about it. The whitewashed wooden houses of the villages came across as simple structures and the people there as poor and raggedy. For the first time, the soldiers saw faces that expressed neither joy nor sorrow, just a resignation to fate.

The engineers had already constructed a pontoon bridge over the Narew at Wizna, since the large bridge there had been blown up, and its remnants were lying in the water. The crossing went very slowly, since the heavy prime movers had to be guided individually. The planks were only as wide as the heavy vehicles, and it cost a lot of sweat on the part of those drivers to make it across in one piece.

The lead elements—the reconnaissance battalion and the motorcycle battalion—crossed the river in the course of the day, while the artillery crossed during the night. The supply elements were still far to the rear. Moving from Schwetz, they did not follow up until 13 September, when the fighting elements were already deep in Poland. They quickly closed up with the fighting elements, however.

The division did not remain in the Wizna area; it ordered the immediate continuation of the march in the direction of Jedzewo, the large transportation hub south of the river. There was nothing to be seen of the enemy yet. Only the destroyed bunkers, the wire entanglements, the foxholes, and the artillery and bomb craters gave witness to the fact that the *10. Panzer-Division*, moving ahead of the *3. Panzer-Division*, had to take this area in a fight.

Once again, the reconnaissance battalion and the motorcycle battalion, reinforced by engineers and artillery, had taken the point. The objective for both battalions was Sokoly. But soon after it had moved out, the motorcycle battalion was pivoted sharply to the west.

"Polish forces are attacking the corps headquarters in the vicinity of Wysokie-Masowieki!"

The motorcycle infantry did their utmost to come to the aid of Guderian. When they reached Zambrow late in the afternoon, their efforts had been overcome by events. The commanding general was unharmed and was happy to see the enthusiasm of his soldiers.

Despite that, the battalion did not get any rest, even though the night brought rain with it. The battalion was employed by Guderian against Wysokie, where it was to throw down the gauntlet and cut off the enemy fleeing from the direction of Lomscha. When *Oberstleutnant* von Manteuffel and his men entered the completely destroyed village of Wysokie, they were too late.

---

15. It is obvious from this list how few of the heavier *Panzers* were available at that time. The *Panzer I*—intended only as a training, not a combat, tank—was pressed into service because of a shortage of armored vehicles.

The battalion then returned to the command and control of the division.

The *20. Infanterie-Division (mot.)* had thrown back the enemy south of Zambrow and pushed him right into the arms of the *21. Infanterie-Division* and the *206. Infanterie-Division*, which were advancing from the west on Andrzejewo. The Polish 18th Infantry Division met its end there.

The general situation for the *XIX. Armee-Korps (mot.)* on the evening of 11 September was as follows: the *20. Infanterie-Division (mot.)* was south of Zambrow and fighting; the *10. Panzer-Division* was advancing from Bransk in the direction of Bielsk; the *3. Panzer-Division* was still right to the north of it; and the *2. Infanterie-Division (mot.)* was rolling in the direction of Bielsk from the north.

In order to protect its open flank, the division formed a *Kampfgruppe* composed of engineers and the platoon of *Wachtmeister* Rademacher of the 5th Battery of the artillery regiment and employed it at Jedzewo. The terrain was completely open and flat. The remaining elements assaulted in generally southerly direction. The reconnaissance battalion, supported by the 6th Battery, advanced as far as the area southeast of Sokoly. The advancing armored cars were suddenly attacked from some woods by Polish cavalry and had to halt. The battery went into position in some vegetated terrain in the nick of time and shot the attacking Poles to pieces at 2,500 meters. When snipers appears during the continued advances in some woods, fire was opened for the second time under the direction of *Oberleutnant* Kersten and *Leutnant* Krause, allowing the battalion to continue its march. During its move through Sokoly, the rifle regiment was fired upon by civilians in ambush positions. The riflemen immediately searched the poverty-stricken houses.

Bielsk was reached on 12 September and taken in the face of weak resistance on the part of the Polish 35th Infantry Division. The tanks moved to the Brest–Bialystock rail line and blocked all traffic. Elements of other formations took up the mission of guarding the east flank of the division, which was growing ever longer. The primeval forests of Bialowieza spread out on the far side of the rail line. The czar located his hunting lodge there once, and the last bison of Europe lived in its thickets.

The motorcycle battalion sent two patrols into that area. *Unteroffizier* Voutta moved into the thick woods with his men, and *Gefreiter* Steffen was sent to Hainowka. Steffen's group was lured into an ambush, but it was able to fight its way out and establish contact with the 1st Company of the rifle regiment, which was screening the road east of Bielsk. *Hauptmann* von Bosse, the commander of the rifle regiment's 1st Battalion, immediately initiated a reprisal operation against Hainowka. The 4th Battery of the artillery regiment went into position against Hainowka with one of its platoons, under the direction of the battery commander, *Hauptmann* Nebel. It returned to Halody toward noon.

The advance over the next few days headed toward Brest-Litowsk. The motorcycle battalion was once again in the lead, with its 3rd Company the tip of the spear. The motorcycle infantry rattled carefree into the village of Zabinka, only to find themselves confronted by an armored train at the rail station. Before *Leutnant* Schmidt could issue orders, the armored trains started spewing fire. At the same moment, things turned lively in the town. Machine guns and carbines started hammering away from the houses. The motorcycle infantry had no other choice but to turn and pull back as quickly as possible. The accompanying artillery forward observer, *Leutnant* Jaschke, and his men were also fired upon. Vehicles exploded, wounded moaned, and the radio equipment ripped apart. It was a devilish situation. The situation went from bad to worse when four Polish tanks appeared out of nowhere and enemy antitank guns also started firing.

The 6th Battery then raced in and took the town under fire. *Leutnant* Jaschke, *Unteroffizier* Killat, and *Gefreiter* Mieritz directed the fires of the battery by means of a radio set that had been brought quickly forward. The armored trains steamed away. When the first shells destroyed the enemy's pockets of resistance, he gave up. The motorcycle infantry were able to take Zabinka by 1400 hours. Once again, the town appeared to be dead. Only the four disabled tanks and the burning houses indicated the severity of the fighting. The 7th Company of *Panzer-Regiment 6* arrived in time to fend off an immediate counterattack by Polish cavalry. The entire 2nd Battalion then cleared the battle area.

The motorcycle battalion assumed the mission of securing the town and formed a bridgehead over the Muchawiec. The forward observers from the artillery, *Leutnant* Meyer and *Oberwachtmeister* Berlin, appeared there. They directed the fires of the friendly batteries against a Polish battery at Zamoszany, which was protecting the rail line.

The division did not allow itself to be distracted from its objective, the fortress of Brest. By the afternoon of 14 September, *Panzer-Regiment 5*, the reconnaissance battalion, and the 3rd Battery of the artillery regiment were east of the city, in an effort to cut it off from that side. (Fate would have it that the division would once again move out from the same spot on 22 June 1941.)

Guderian's intent was to attack Brest with his division on 15 September. He led his four major formations up to the fortress in a night march, leaving only the *2. Infanterie-Division (mot.)* to protect the broad flank of the corps in the direction of the Bialowies Forest. The lead elements of both the *10. Panzer-Division* and the *20. Infanterie-Division (mot.)* made it to the fortress on 14 September.

The division moved out to attack from the east. To that end, it formed a *Kampfgruppe* consisting of elements of *Panzer-Regiment 6*, the motorcycle battalion, the engineer battalion, the 6th Battery of the artillery (*Oberleutnant* Kersten), and a platoon from the 4th Battery (*Leutnant* Stiller).

The battle group moved out around 0345 hours in its attack on Brest. Its mission was to take Fort III. The city was reached without a shot being fired. The Poles did not defend Fort III, either. The 2nd Company of the motorcycle battalion (*Hauptmann* Pape) rested in the fort. The forces continued unscathed as far as the central train station and occupied the high rail overpass.

From the overpass, the enemy was nowhere to be seen in the immediate area; however, the guns at the citadel were firing with everything they had and there was a lively exchange of fire at the rail yards. The motorcycle infantry screened the southern part of the city, where they were also under constant fire from the citadel.

Contact was established with the *20. Infanterie-Division (mot.)*, which was attacking from the north. The *III./Infanterie-Regiment 86* of that division maintained the contact. The batteries of the *3. Panzer-Division* were attached to *Oberst* Weidling—former commander of *Artillerie-Regiment 75* and current commander of the divisional artillery of the motorized infantry division—in an effort to provide unity of command for fire support.

The first attack of the *20. Infanterie-Division (mot.)* around 1430 hours against the citadel did not succeed. A bit later, the *III./Infanterie-Regiment 86* and *Pionier-Bataillon 39* attempted an attack with a limited objective against the eastern edge of the fortress. The Polish defensive fires also forced the German attackers to ground there as well. Small groups from *Schützen-Regiment 3*—for example, the 2nd Platoon of the 1st Company—attempted to conduct reconnaissance-in-force efforts against the southern part of the fortress, but they were also turned back. The 2nd Battalion of *Panzer-Regiment 6* attacked the citadel, which was being placed under heavy German artillery fire, from the east. The 2nd Company (*Hauptmann* Schneider-Kostalski) and the 4th Company (*Hauptmann* Weiß) approached the fortress from the southeast. Around 2200 hours, the armored regiment received orders to call off the attack. Both battalions disengaged from the enemy during the night.

The motorcycle battalion remained in the city that night to screen its southern sector. The 1st Platoon of the 3rd Company (*Leutnant* von Brauchitsch) screened the prison, where civilian and military prisoners taken the previous day were being housed. The battalion was pulled out of Brest on the morning of 16 September and quickly returned to direct divisional control. The division proper was moving in the direction of Wlodawa. As a result, only two batteries of the divisional artillery remained behind. They continued to support the attack of the motorized infantry division on the citadel. Their fires were directed by *Leutnant* Meyer, assisted by his radio operators, *Unteroffizier* Göhler and *Kanonier* Elsholz. The fires were so effective that all three men later received the Iron Cross, Second Class.

The *3. Panzer-Division* no longer took part in the fighting for the fortress. Instead, it went around the city with the majority of its forces to then thrust south. Its new objective was Wlodawa. This time, the reconnaissance battalion, *Panzer-Regiment 5*, and the 3rd Battery were in the advance guard. The terrain appeared monotonous and gray to the men of the advance guard. The rain of the last few days had softened up the roads and the pastures. There was hardly a tree to be seen; only sandy soil and more sandy soil, with small, dirty localities here and there. There were few people to be seen, and those that were encountered were shy and uncommunicative. They were quite different from the White Russians, who had been encountered at Bialystok and Hainowka.

The division moved in *Kampfgruppen* on Tomaszowka. The armored cars encountered an energetic defense when they arrived there towards noon on 16 September. The tanks were called up by radio. The commander of the *I./Panzer-Regiment 5, Major* Wendenburg, ordered the 2nd Company forward. The nineteen tanks caught up with the lead elements at the Przaborowo rail station. The commander of the lead element reported that it was impossible to advance any farther, because the terrain, with

many woods and lakes, was full of Poles. Prisoner statements indicated that the organizational staff directing the retrograde movements of the entire Polish Army was located there.

Hauptmann Schmidt, the tank company commander, assumed command of the available motorcycle infantry and turned to the east on the path leading from behind the rail station. *Leutnant* Nitschke took over the lead with his tanks. To his right was Lake Sielachy. Then Perczspa came into view. The small village was ablaze. The riflemen discovered enemy soldiers and smoked them out. The *Leutnant* left a few men with their motorcycles back at the entrance to the village and gave them orders to reconnoiter the southwest in the direction of the railway embankment. The tanks raced through the village and reached the woods to its south. By then, it was already fairly dark, so the *Leutnant* and his men had to wait until the rest of the company closed up.

Just outside of the crossroads at Tomaszowka, movement was identified. Nitschke sent a short burst in that direction, which immediately caused the activities to cease. The *2./Panzer-Regiment 5* turned onto the road leading to Tomaszowka. There was no break in the action. The battery, following to the rear, was unable to maintain contact in the darkness and went into position along the railway embankment. The engineers mounted up on the tanks, which then moved into the woods.

When an enemy armored car turned up on a trail by surprise, it was shot to bits in short order. But there were more and more movements along the road by the minute. *Hauptmann* Schmidt had his vehicle pivot sharply right and take anything that blocked the route under fire. Trucks, horse-drawn wagons, pontoon equipment, and many other major items of equipment and materiel went up in flames. The Polish drivers fled into the protection of the woods on both sides of the road as quickly as they could. The speedometers on the tanks registered forty-five kilometers an hour, and the pace picked up from there. The Wlodawa–Kowel telegraph line was disrupted by knocking over the poles; horse-drawn columns were scattered and vehicles destroyed.

Just as the darkness of the night made further progress impossible, the company reached Tomaszowka. A single antitank gun, which was positioned not far from the rail station and took the German tanks under fire, was put out of commission. The tankers had only been able to identify the gun by its muzzle flashes. Some batteries were firing from somewhere into the burning village, but the tanks had moved through it by 1945 hours.

Hauptmann Schmidt and *Leutnant* Nitschke fired white signal flares. The signals were made out by *Wachtmeister* Gaebler, the forward observer from the 3rd Battery, and understood: Shift the fires forward! On that day, the battery fired some 350 rounds.

Hauptmann Schmidt's 2nd Company was not satisfied with what it had achieved. There was still fuel in the tanks, so it continued south. The route turned increasingly worse by the minute. The motorcycle infantry were no longer able to keep pace and fell back. The tanks rattled on by themselves. It was difficult to stay oriented in the darkness. The movement grew slower, since woods and marshland became the next obstacles.

During the night, *Major* Wendenburg assembled his tanks as best he could. The 4th Company took over the lead. The officers moving out front had to illuminate their way with flashlights. At some places, Polish trains vehicles were passed. As it started to turn first light around 0300 hours, the battalion was outside of Opalin. The village was swarming with Polish soldiers. Since the battalion was almost out of fuel—the 2nd Company was already stranded—*Major* Wendenburg had his forces turn eight kilometers to the west. He had his battalion set up an all-round defense on a small rise. Patrols were sent out in all directions to maintain security.

The motorcycle battalion left *Kampfgruppe Wendenburg* and turned west toward the Bug. The Poles expected an attack there, however, and had blown up the bridge over the Bug in

time. That meant that the men of the division had to remain on the east bank of the river in order to wait for the engineers coming forward.

The next day was one of decision. The motorcycle infantry crossed the river on inflatable craft and floats and entered the city of Wlodawa from the northeast. The 2nd Battalion of the divisional artillery had already been firing on the northern portion of the city since the morning, concentrating on the military facilities. The enemy resistance had been weakened by the well-placed fires, with the result that it did not prove too difficult for the motorcycle battalion and elements of the rifle regiment, which had been brought forward, to take the city in its entirety that morning. *Major* Burmeister's 2nd Battalion of *Panzer-Regiment 6*, which also closed upon the city, was not needed to enter the fray. Two platoons from the 6th Company of the armor regiment, those of *Leutnant Graf* von Kageneck and *Leutnant* von Diest-Koerber, were sent west to reconnoiter around 1500 hours. After both platoons had forded the broad but shallow riverbed and moved out of Wlodawa after moving through it, they were immediately engaged by heavy enemy artillery fire and had to pull back to behind the forward combat outposts of the riflemen.

It was not until the afternoon of 17 September that the Poles had reorganized their forces. They attacked from the wooded terrain west of the city to retake it. A storm that broke out at the same time prevented the German defenders from offering a proper defense. The artillery was unable to join directly into the fray. Instead, it was limited to firing on targets that had been previously identified by the forward observers. The companies of the rifle regiment finally gathered themselves, and their rifle and machine-gun fire tore big gaps in the ranks of the Poles. The 3rd Company of the motorcycle battalion was committed to a flanking effort outside of the city, and the 6th Company of *Panzer-Regiment 6* (*Hauptmann* von Winterfeld), which was quickly called forward, was finally able to bring the enemy attack to a complete standstill.

According to prisoner statements, nine companies had been involved in the enemy's effort.

The enemy then gave up on Wlodawa and pulled back into the thick woods south of the city.

After Tomaszokwa was occupied, the 1st Company of the rifle regiment advanced farther along the railway line. The final meters leading up to the Bug were a race against death. It was certain that the Poles had prepared the large bridge for demolition. The riflemen and engineers took long strides across the railway ties, and the risky venture succeeded. They got across the bridge, reached the railway guardhouse on the south bank of the river, and formed a small bridgehead. It was 0030 hours.

The engineers immediately set about searching for charges. Despite the darkness, they found some and started the laborious task of removing them.

At first light, the 3rd Platoon of the 1st Company attacked Orchowek, which was burning. *Obergefreiter* Janik was killed. Because the village had completely burned down, the riflemen dug bunkers and dugouts next to the rail line. Although the Poles attempted to reduce the small bridgehead a few times during the day with infantry and cavalry, their attacks were always turned back.

From the area where it had encamped, the 1st Battalion of *Panzer-Regiment 5* had observed enemy groups attempting to flee since early morning, by swimming across the Bug. The tanks were unable to prevent those attempts, however, since they were stranded due to a lack of fuel.

Major Wendenburg had sent out two patrols during the night that had been directed to blow up the bridges over the Bug. The numerically strongest patrol made good progress. *Feldwebel* Hass took the lead with his medium tank. Following behind him was the commander's tank of the 4th Company. *Leutnant* Brandt and an engineer *Unteroffizier* had also mounted it. *Leutnant* Zorn brought up the rear with the two remaining light tanks and the rest of the engineer squad.

The movement of the patrol took it through Huszcza and Rowno in the direction of Wilzcy–Przewo. Along the route, a few vehicle columns were shot up. The crews of the two light tanks watched over the prisoners. After a few minutes, however, they simply let the Poles flee, after their weapons had been taken away. The prisoners would only have been a burden for the patrol. The enemy received the patrol in Przewo with heavy small-arms fires. But *Leutnant* Zorn, *Leutnant* Brandt, and the engineers fought their way through the middle of the enemy to the wooden bridge, which they set on fire. The two light tanks held down the Poles on the far side with well-aimed fires.

The tankers even managed to capture a Polish 7.5-centimeter field piece from 1917. *Leutnant* Zorn limbered the piece to his tank and started to bring it back. Unfortunately, his fighting vehicle became immobilized after a few minutes with running gear problems.

The heavy commander's tank with the engineer officer went forward as far as the rail line. Just as *Leutnant* Brand was starting to place a demolition charge on the tracks, a transport train started to approach. Fortunately, its locomotive was knocked out by the tank, thus blocking the line. As a result, this mission was also accomplished.

Leutnant Wisniewski, who led the second patrol, returned around 1000 hours and reported that the railway bridge had been successfully blown up. As a result, the immobilized tank battalions had at least cut off the retreat route over the Bug to the Poles.

It was not until 1600 hours that the regimental logistics officer, *Hauptmann* Hackermann, arrived and reported that fuel was on its way. It took another hour before the fuel arrived. *Major* Wendenburg immediately had his battalion form up.

It approached the village of Przewo as it started to turn dark. The tanks did not allow themselves to be held up by either the hastily emplaced road obstacles or by the heavy flanking fires coming from the woods. The 1st

Company thrust through the burning village, while the 2nd Company took down the Polish resistance in the woods. The sole heavy tank of the battalion overran everything and reached the rail line. It encountered an enemy battery there, which forced the tank to pull back. The tankers saw that the train that had been engaged that morning by the patrol was still there, making all traffic impossible.

Major Wendenburg had his companies assemble between Przewo and Rowno. In the process, the tank companies encountered the lead company of the rifle regiment. It was the 8th Company, along with *Major* Zimmermann. The riflemen were immediately employed screening in the direction of Przewo. The tank battalion set up an all-round defense.

On 17 September, the reconnaissance battalion received the mission to blown up the Kowel–Chelm rail line at Luboml. The 2nd Battery of the artillery regiment and some engineers were attached in support. The movement of those elements took place on sandy, softened and seemingly endless roads to the southeast. There were still individual occurrences of enemy resistance, but they were quickly eliminated by a few bursts of fire from the machine guns on the armored cars. There wasn't a true engagement until it started to turn dark, when the battalion approached Scack. The Poles had dug in there in the houses and gardens.

Major Freiherr von Wechmar had his companies halt and wait until the battery had closed up. The guns unlimbered in an open field and took the locality and individual pockets of resistance under direct fire. After a few minutes, the enemy was silenced, and the companies were able to take the locality in an envelopment. The battalion set up defenses for the night, putting out security in all directions.

The *Kampfgruppe* was ordered to break camp at first light on 18 September. The march continued relentlessly, and Luboml was reached that same morning. The reconnaissance battalion encountered a large grouping of enemy forces. The armored cars moved into position behind hills and ditches. The riflemen took up the infantry fight and the artillery battery fired. But the enemy no longer had any desire to become engaged in protracted and casualty-intensive fighting. First individually and then in ever-larger groups, the enemy surrendered. In the end, the 400 men of *Kampfgruppe Wechmar* counted almost 3,000 Polish prisoners. The reconnaissance battalion had accomplished its mission, transitioning to a screening mission.

The tanks of the division continued their own advance about 0700 hours that morning. But the enemy had pulled his forces across the Bug during the night and only put up minimal resistance. Przewo, the railway embankment, and the railway bridge were taken practically without a fight. The tanks advanced across the river and established a small bridgehead. The 6th Battery of artillery arrived and assumed the direct-support mission. Three *Unteroffiziere*—Killat, Grothe, and Schröder—discovered the gun that had been captured the previous day and included it in the firefight.

At 1357 hours, the division ordered the bridge to be blown up. At that point, the battalion moved back across the river without any enemy interference. At that point, the enemy started to get continual reinforcements. Starting at 1530 hours, strong artillery fire started to fall on the friendly positions. The division was concerned about its *Kampfgruppe*, which had ranged far forward, and sent out the following radio message in the afternoon: "If the tactical situation requires it, pull back to *Aufklärungs-Abteilung 3* in Luboml, since larger regular-army formations are moving from west to east. Report your decision." *Major* Wendenburg reported back shortly: "Position will be held!"

Far ahead of the other major formations, the *3. Panzer-Division* was the southernmost division of the field army group at that point. Correspondingly, it had covered more ground than any other German division during the campaign. The division was closer to the elements of the *10. Armee* approaching from the south than it was to its sister divisions within the corps. The division commander ordered the 2nd Battalion of the rifle regiment (*Oberstleutnant* Dr. Ehlermann) to break through to *Heeresgruppe Süd*. Attached to Ehlermann's battalion were the *6./Panzer-Regiment 6*, the *1./Artillerie-Regiment 75*, and the *1./Panzerabwehr-Abteilung 39*. The lead elements of the southern field army group were trying to take Chelm from three sides with the *4. Infanterie-Division*, the *4. leichte Division*, and the *2. Panzer-Division*.

The reinforced rifle battalion moved out right on time. Forward movement was made difficult by the clogged roads, blown-up bridges, and recurring resistance form Polish formations that were led by especially brave officers. They had established themselves skillfully along wood lines and the outskirts of villages. The fights for Osowa and Malinowka were especially hard for the rifle companies. Leading the way in an exemplary fashion, *Hauptmann* Wellmann stormed the last village with his 6th Company. The battalion worked its way forward slowly and had to bring down new enemy strongpoints in sacrificial fighting. During that fighting, the 2nd Battalion suffered the heaviest losses of the entire division for the campaign. Since night had fallen in the meantime, the idea of a continued advance was discarded.

A motorcycle infantry patrol under the command of *Unteroffizier* Panzlaff was sent farther south, however, reaching the area just outside of Chelm. The expected forces of the *10. Armee* attacking from the south were not there. The Wehrmacht High Command reported a linkup between the two field army groups, but none ever took place in the campaign.

The division instructed the Ehlermann's battalion not to continue its operation and to pull back slowly on the direction of Wlodawa. The division pulled back the rest of its battle groups to Wlodawa as well. They were widely dispersed over a large area. It wanted to protect the force and not cause unnecessary casualties, since the Polish Army was already in a state of dissolution. Ehlermann evacuated the positions his reinforced battalion had taken near Chelm and pulled back under sharp pressure from individual Polish formations. *Hauptmann* von Winterfeld's tank company provided the *Kampfgruppe* with the requisite covering fires. Four German fighting vehicles were lost that day. Around 1000 hours, *Major* Wendenburg received similar orders: He was to pull back to Luboml and link up with the reconnaissance battalion. Around 1600 hours, the two advance guards of the division linked up.

All forces of the division that were east of the Bug left their forward positions and pulled back across the river, as ordered. There had been no encounters with the Red Army anywhere, but the senior commanders took precautionary measures to ensure that the encounters took place without any friction.[16]

In order to mark the German lines for Russian aircraft, the division ordered recognition panels set out.

The fighting slowly abated. That meant that there was some movement between and within the fronts. The Polish soldiers no longer knew what they should do. Unarmed, they gave up by the hundreds, so as not to fall into the hands of the Red Army. For example, *Hauptmann* Eikmann's maintenance company took in some 1,500 prisoners in the Puchaczewo area from 19 to 21 September. *Leutnant* Müller of *Panzer-Regiment 6*, who went deer hunting in some woods, wound up bringing in 165 prisoners. The civilian populace was also on the run.

The elements of the division assembled in Wlodawa. For many of the soldiers, the village became a place to recover. They saw an actual city for the first time, which stood out considerably in its appearance from the dirty villages that had been crossed through and fought for up to

---

16. In accordance with the Treaty of Non-Aggression between Germany and the Soviet Union (23 August 1939), Poland had been divided into two spheres of influence between Germany and the Soviet Union. On 17 September, Soviet forces entered Poland from the east, thus hastening the end to the short war.

that point. Its two churches, the Baroque Roman Catholic one and the Orthodox one with its characteristic onion dome, dominated the landscape of the city. Its populace was composed of Poles, White Russians, and a large number of Jews.

After the forces had rested a bit and the men could wash off the dirt and grime from the many days of dust and rain, they had a pleasant surprise. The first field mail arrived.

The return march for the division was set for 21 September. The individuals left their quartering areas around Wlodawa at first light and moved along the road back to Brest. The large city had already been decorated with red flags with the hammer and sickle and black-white-red flags. The first Russian soldiers had arrived; they were assigned to a tank brigade.

The march then continued twenty-five kilometers to the demarcation line, moving through Widomla–Giechanowiec–Zambrow and on to Lomscha, where the divisional formations arrived on 22 September. For the fourth time in a month, the German border was crossed just south of Johannisburg. The men forgot about the hardships of the campaign that was behind them. The friendly and tidy East Prussian villages, the nice people, and the thoughts of reuniting with loved ones back home put wind in the sails of all the soldiers.

The division quartered in the area around Bartenstein. The individual companies and detachments were quartered privately in the surrounding localities. Everyone felt as though they were on maneuvers. The *XIX. Armee-Korps (mot.)* was disbanded on 26 September,[17] and the last general order from the field army group was issued a few days later. That signaled the end of the campaign in Poland.

---

17. The corps was not truly disbanded. In actuality, the command-and-control relationship of the corps over the division was rescinded and the division reverted to its peacetime command-and-control structure. Until 1944, there were no fixed major subordinate commands (divisions and brigades) assigned to corps; they were only attached.

1 September 1939. The first Polish prisoners in a path in the woods between Prucsz and Zepolna.

General Guderian is briefed by the commander of *Panzer-Brigade 3*, *Generalmajor* Stumpff, outside of Grupa.

A field mess from the division support command distributes food to Polish civilians.

The *1./Kradschützen-Bataillon 3* in Brest-Litowsk.

Motorcycles from *Kradschützen-Bataillon 3* in front of the police headquarters in Brest-Litowsk. The crews were inside, searching the building.

A Polish light tank, a licensed version of the French Renault, knocked out by forces of the division at Zabrinka, east of Brest-Litowsk, on 15 September.

Motorcycles crossing a light-duty pontoon bridge over the Bug at Wlodawa.

Polish prisoners being led back across the same footbridge seen in the previous image.

The tanks are loaded on ship at Pilau for transport back to their home garrison.

Return march of *Kradschützen-Bataillon 3* on an engineer bridge over the Vistula at Neuenburg.

CHAPTER 3

From East Prussia to Westphalia: Between the Campaigns, 1939–40

The division left its quarters in East Prussia on 1 October 1939. Many of the officers and enlisted personnel received the awards they had earned just before departure and were proud to be wearing the Iron Cross. At the same time as the first wartime awards were presented, many members of the division also received the medal commemorating the march into the Sudetenland.[1] That had happened a year previously and had been forgotten in the face of the most recent events.

The long columns of the division started their trek westward. The local populace waved a final farewell to them in all the villages and towns. The march route went through Heilsberg, Osterode, and Deutsch-Eylau. The soldiers then reached the Vistula. The tanks and other tracked vehicles were loaded on ships at Pillau. They were sent home that way to avoid wear and tear on the equipment.

The wheeled elements of the division crossed the Vistula on the same bridges as it had arrived. The movement continued through Tuchel, and the borders of the Reich were crossed at Konitz, some twenty kilometers north of where it had originally crossed. The first signs pointing to Berlin could be seen.

---

1. The Sudetenland Commemorative Medal (*Medaille zur Erinnerung an den 1. Oktober 1938*) was presented to all who participated in the actual march into the ethnic German region of Czechoslovakia on 1 October 1938. Since it was a medal, it was generally represented as a ribbon on a ribbon bar after the first day of presentation.

The vehicles were washed, the uniforms cleaned up, and the weapons gleamed like new. The faces of the soldiers were beaming with joy: they were home. The closer they got to their home garrisons, the more excited they became. In every locality they passed through, the people stood on the streets and waved. Just before entering the garrisons, there was a short halt. A final formation was held . . . and then they were really there. The people lining the way were familiar to them. The local citizenry formed a cordon and tossed flowers. The command rung out: "Eyes . . . right!"

The commander was standing there with his staff and received the pass-in-review by the returning victors. It was the same picture in all of the garrison cities of the division on that 5 October. That's the way it was in Wünsdorf with the tankers, in Eberswalde with the riflemen, in Neuruppin with the cannoneers and the tankers, in Bad Freienwalde with the motorcycle infantry, and everywhere else that the soldiers of the division called home.

The division commander, *Generalleutnant* von Schweppenburg, who had taken ill prior to the start of the campaign and who had undergone all of the hardships, had to relinquish command of the division he had formed due to health reasons. *Generalmajor* Stumpff, the commander of the armored brigade, was entrusted with acting command of the division until further notice.

The coming months saw other changes in various command positions. *Oberst* Angern left the rifle brigade at the end of the year, with *Oberst* Kleemann assuming command. *Oberstleutnant* von Manteuffel became the new commander of the rifle regiment. *Oberstleutnant* Tröger[2] assumed command of the motorcycle battalion from him on 1 December. Tröger had arrived at the division from the staff of the senior cavalry officer at the Army High Command. *Oberstleutnant* Conze, who had assumed acting command of *Panzer-Regiment 5* during the campaign in Poland, relinquished that command on 15 October to *Oberst Freiherr* von Funck, who had previously served as the military attaché to Lisbon.[3] *Oberstleutnant* Negendank, who had commanded the signals battalion before the war and in the campaign in Poland, turned over command to *Major Baron* von Behr on 20 April 1940. *Oberstleutnant* Dr. Ehlermann turned over his *II./Schützen-Regiment 3* to *Major* von Olszewski. By the following March, the command again changed hands, with *Major* Zimmermann coming on board. *Oberstleutnant* Wimmer, the commander of the 2nd Battalion of the divisional artillery, returned from the campaign desperately ill, dying of the hardships he had endured there on 12 December 1939. He was followed in command by *Major* Wöhlermann.

The division underwent a decisive change during that period, as did many other large formations of the armed forces, which affected its organization. The campaign in Poland had brought with it many lessons learned, with one being the fact that the motorized divisions with their three rifle regiments were too unwieldy for the command and control of rapid movements. Consequently, each motorized infantry division had to give up one regiment, which were then reassigned to the armored divisions by battalion.

As a result, the *I./Infanterie-Regiment 69* was assigned to the division in the middle of

2. Hans Tröger had a distinguished career as a cavalry officer before joining the *3. Panzer-Division*. Following his assignment to the division in June 1941, he went on to command in the *14. Panzer-Division* (*Kradschützen-Bataillon 64*). He went on to regimental command within that division and after an administrative assignment was given acting command of the *27. Panzer-Division*. He commanded three more armored divisions by war's end (25th, 17th, and 13th). He ended the war as a *Generalleutnant* and was also awarded the Knight's Cross to the Iron Cross. He was held by the Soviets until 1955 and passed away in Schwangau in 1982.
3. Hans Emil Richard Freiherr von Funck had held various positions of responsibility in Spain during the Civil War. Following his assignment to the *3. Panzer-Division*, he went on to command the *7. Panzer-Division* and the *XXXXVII. Panzer-Korps*. He ended the war as a *General der Panzertruppen* and recipient of the Oak Leaves to the Knight's Cross. He died in Versen in 1979, after remaining a prisoner of the Soviets until 1955.

October. The battalion had formerly belonged to the *20. Infanterie-Division (mot.)*, which the division had shared some common fighting experience with at Brest. The new officers, non-commissioned officers, and enlisted personnel came primarily from the North German area, mostly Hamburg. They soon grew accustomed to the Berlin dialect and accent, and after a few weeks, no one noticed the differences anymore. The commander of the battalion, *Oberstleutnant* Hoernlein, was transferred out a short while later. He would later work with the division again as the commander of *Infanterie-Regiment (mot.) "Großdeutschland"* (Tula) and, later, as the commander of the mechanized infantry division with the same honorific (Kursk). *Major* Kratzenberg assumed command of the battalion, which was redesignated as the 3rd Battalion of *Schützen-Regiment 3*.

On 29 November 1939, movement orders arrived. The divisional troops and the formations left the garrisons that afternoon. This time, the division was headed to the West. Everyone, whether enlisted man or officer, breathed a sigh of relief. The perpetual waiting for something to happen, which was always being postponed, got on one's nerves over time.

The division split up among various villages in the Teutoburg Woods. The quartering area for the division extended across an area bounded by Osnabrück–Glandorf–Warendorf. The units were put up in farmsteads, where they also took their vehicles. Tanks, trucks, and motorcycles were camouflaged in barns and courtyards. But when a few of the vehicles were discovered being used for private "joy rides," orders were issued to park the vehicles in barns or outbuildings by platoon and to guard them.

Duty during that period was easy and simple, and good contacts were soon made with the locals. Not a few marriages resulted from the friendly relationships. Life was therefore not so bad, even if guards had to be posted here and there. Since the time of year was not exactly pleasant and brought ice, snow, and rain with it, pulling guard was not always a pleasure. Christmas approached.

Married personnel were allowed home on leave; single personnel remained and waited.

Then, one day, more movement orders arrived, at a time when no one thought the situation would ever change. The division's elements left the hospitable area among the heartfelt good wishes of the local population—a few tears were to be seen—and armed with decently sized "food packages." Through night and fog, snow and ice, the route led farther west through Münster and Hamm as far as the vicinity of Dortmund and Soest. February 1940 brought with it snowstorms and gruesome cold. The division was on the move. Its formations crossed the Rhine at Duisberg, thus reaching the operational zone of the Western Front. The new quartering area for the division was around Krefeld and Viersen.

Generalleutnant Schweppenburg was given command of the *XXIV. Armee-Korps (mot.)* on 15 February. He took his leave of the officer corps of the division where it was located in the field. He said goodbye to the men of his headquarters with a firm handshake. For the first two years of the war in the Soviet Union, the general officer would have the division under his corps command. Starting in July 1944, he would become the last Inspector General of the *Panzertruppe*.

Effective that same 15 February, *Generalmajor* Stumpff was designated as the division commander. *Oberst* Kühn, the former commander of the armor school who was known to his friends as "Brother Cellarer," assumed command of the *3. Panzer-Brigade*. The commander of *Panzer-Regiment 6*, *Oberstleutnant* Rothenburg, also left the division at the end of the month, with *Oberstleutnant* von Lewinski taking his place. Two other officers left the division, who later went on to be noted armor commanders. *Major* von Wietersheim assumed command of *Kradschützen-Bataillon 1 (1. Panzer-Division)* on 1 March 1940; as the division commander of the *11. Panzer-Division*, he would receive the Swords to the Oak Leaves to the Knight's Cross in March 1944. The armored brigade's adjutant, the tall-as-a-tree *Hauptmann* Ziegler, was transferred to the General Staff. He later fell in the final fighting in

Berlin as a *Generalmajor der Waffen-SS* and the division commander of the *11. SS-Freiwilligen-Panzer-Grenadier-Division "Nordland."*[4]

At the beginning of March, orders arrived detaching the 3rd and 6th Companies from *Panzer-Regiment 6* for a special operation. The officers and men took leave of their regimental commander in Viersen in a parade; they then occupied new quarters in Dabendorf, near Berlin. Those companies later took part in the occupation of Norway.[5]

Krefeld! That was a city no one would forget who spent time there until the start of new operations. Although the troops received instructions on dealing with the local civilian population . . . a hit from the time is perhaps telling: *"Die Nacht ist nicht allein zum Schlafen da!"*[6] Quite a few tippling tankers and riflemen followed that advice and not only in the various restaurants and pubs with names like Seidenfaden, Bosi, Parkstübchen, Dortmunder Hof, and Nachtlokal Barth, but they also did it at private quarters as well. One wonders how many returned to Krefeld after the war in order to live there permanently.

And so many hoped that spring might finally arrive. . . . But then the news arrived about the occupation of Norway and Denmark.[7] Over the next few nights, columns from nondivisional formations moved through the city and the soldiers began to get the feeling that it would soon be time for them to start marching again as well.

By the end of April 1940, the division had received its first *Panzer III's* (thirteen) and *Panzer IV's* (twenty), which were distributed to the two regiments.

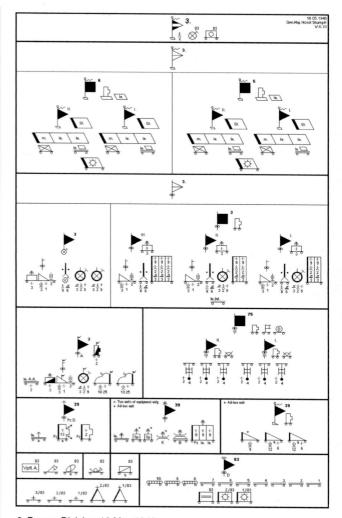

3. *Panzer-Division*, 10 May 1940.

---

4. Joachim Ziegler served with the German contingent in the Spanish Civil War, where he received the Spanish Cross. He served with distinction as a General Staff officer after his transfer out of the division. On the staff of the *XXXXII. Armee-Korps*, he was awarded the German Cross in Gold. He was detailed to the *Waffen-SS* in June 1943, serving as the chief of staff of the *III. (germanisches) SS-Panzer-Korps*. He eventually assumed command of the *"Nordland"* division. As mentioned in the text, he died in the final fighting around Berlin, but it was after he had been relieved of command for disputed and unclear reasons. He was mortally wounded while attempting to break out of the encirclement and died on 2 May 1945.

5. *Lexikon der Wehrmacht* makes no mention of the detachment of the 1st Company for this purpose. The 6th Company, however, was definitely used to form cadre for the formation of *Panzer-Abteilung z.b.V. 40*, which was used during the operations in Norway and, later, Finland. z.b.V. = *zur besonderen Verwendung* = special purpose. An extensive discussion of the battalion can be found at www.lexikon-der-wehrmacht.de/Gliederungen/Panzerregimenter/PR6.htm.

6. "The Night's Not Just There for Sleeping!"

7. *Unternehmen Weserübung* commenced on 9 April 1940.

CHAPTER 4

From the Rhine to the Somme

The German Army was ready for the campaign in the West. It tossed aside the old and traditional strategic concepts and introduced a new epoch in the art of war. After Germany's enemies had later copied those methods, it was defeated by its own invention. The Army High Command decided to rip open the enemy front by having a single point of main effort. The plan originated with *Generalleutnant* von Manstein, who had sought Guderian's advice as an armor expert. As a result, most of the armored divisions were concentrated in the middle of the front. They were to advance through Luxembourg, move through and near Sedan, and advance on St. Quentin and Amiens as far as the mouth of the Somme. By doing so, they would hit the main Allied forces in their deep flank or even in their rear.

Ever since the start of the war, the enemy had assumed there would be a repeat of positional warfare and expanded the Maginot Line as far as the English Channel by the construction of bunker networks. It was intended that the main front would be protected by the two Dutch and two Belgian lines of fortifications. It was also assumed that the Germans would reuse the old Schlieffen Plan and descend on Belgium with a strong wing. That German thrust was to be interdicted by the Allied field armies in the Dyle Line (Meuse–Wavre–Löwen). The motorized forces stationed in northern France were to move into Belgium immediately and hold up the German attack on the Dyle Line.

The German field armies went into battle well armed. They not only had a full complement of personnel, weapons, vehicles, and equipment, but they had also trained theoretically and learned on a practical basis for to conduct this fight.

The divisions were given tactical insignia to place on their vehicles to differentiate the formations, identifying them quickly on the battlefield or in congested movements on roads. The symbol for the division was similar to a sideways E.[1]

The *3. Panzer-Division* was attached for operations to the *XVI. Armee-Korps (mot.)* of *General der Kavallerie* Erich Hoepner. Hoepner's chief of staff was *Oberstleutnant i.G.* Chales de Beaulieu. The corps' mission was to advance rapidly to the Albert Canal and blaze a path to Brussels for the *6. Armee* of *Generaloberst* von Reichenau. Von Reichenau's chief of staff was *Generalmajor* Paulus, who had once held command of *Aufklärungs-Abteilung 3*.

At the start of the campaign, the division received welcome reinforcements: *MG-Bataillon 7*[2] (with a headquarters, signals platoon, motorcycle infantry platoon, three machine-gun companies, and an antitank company); the *II./Flak-Lehr-Regiment*; and the *II./Artillerie-Regiment 49*.[3]

At this point, the formations of the division were resting and in quarters around the Krefeld area. Many of the officers and married enlisted personnel were on leave for Pentecost. The remainder spent their days with the usual Prussian duty routine and the evenings seeking entertainment.

At 2103 hours on 9 May 1940, the code word "Danzig" arrived at the division headquarters.

Tactical insignia of the division. The first was used in Poland and France in 1939 and 1940 and the second in Russia in 1941. The third is a later variant also used in Russia.

The code word meant: "Immediately start preparations for movement and be prepared to move out no later than 0700 hours on 10 May 1940!"

That same hour, the telephones rang, the Morse code keys tapped, the motorcycle messengers roared off and the duty personnel blew their whistles: "Alert!" The messengers raced through the streets of Krefeld and the surrounding localities to alert the officers and personnel that had been put up in private quarters. Telegrams cancelled leaves. A hasty farewell was said everywhere. Some thought it was just a practice alert. It turned out to be a big surprise when everyone discovered they were really moving out.

The night was short and when the soldiers stepped out of their quarters at first light, they already heard a rushing sound high in the heavens. Squadron after squadron of bombers and fighters were headed west. At that point, there was no longer any doubt that the hour of attack was close at hand. The division started departing Krefeld around 1000 hours.

The division moved in two large march serials to the south. Initially, everyone thought they were headed straight towards Holland. When the march turned along the major road to Neuß, even the "know-it-alls" had second thoughts.

---

1. The author is not entirely correct. The tactical insignia were introduced for the Polish campaign and retained in usage through the campaign in the West. They were modified several times again during the course of the war. The insignia were painted on the hull front, rear, and sides in a subdued yellow.

2. The battalion was raised in Saxony in 1935 as a separate formation. It served as a reserve for the *10. Armee* during the campaign in Poland. In August 1940, it became the nucleus of *Kradschützen-Bataillon 64* of the *14. Panzer-Division*.

3. The regiment was intended as a separate formation with a command-and-control headquarters and two battalions. The 2nd Battalion was outfitted with heavy field howitzers (15 centimeters). After the campaign in France, it became the 3rd Battalion of the divisional artillery of the *3. Panzer-Division*.

That was because that route led towards Aachen and, by extension, to Belgium.

The righthand march serial under *Oberst* Kühn marched in the following order: *Panzer-jäger-Abteilung 39*; division headquarters; *Nachrichten-Abteilung 39*; headquarters, *3. Panzer-Brigade*; the two tank regiments; the *3./Pionier-Bataillon 39*; one battery from the *II./Flak-Lehr-Regiment*; and one and a half fuel sections. The lefthand march serial was under the command of *Oberst* Kleemann. Its order of march was as follows: *Aufklärungs-Abteilung 3*; one battery from the *II./Flak-Lehr-Regiment*; headquarters, *Schützen-Brigade*; *Kradschützen-Bataillon 3*; headquarters and *I./Artillerie-Regiment 75*; headquarters, *Schützen-Regiment 3*; *Schützen-Regiment 3*; the *II./Artillerie-Regiment 75*; and one fuel section.

The division headquarters established its command post in Linnich. The division's elements had moved past Neuß through Titz and as far as the area around Jülich. The armored brigade had moved via Mönchen-Gladbach and occupied that afternoon in the villages along the Erkelenz–Linnich road. The rifle regiment bivouacked with all of its elements around Jülich, with its headquarters initially taking quarters in Jackerath, followed by Pattern. The 3rd Battalion of the rifle regiment had its headquarters and 12th and 15th Companies in Koslar, its 11th and 14th Companies in Freialdenhoven, and its 13th Company in Engelsdorf. The motorcycle battalion also took up quarters in Jülich, while the reconnaissance battalion provided security in Linnich. The antitank battalion remained in Gereonsweiler. The divisional artillery bivouacked in the area between Titz und Ameln, with its 6th Battery, for instance, spending the night in the Mündt Farmstead. The divisional troops were spread all over the assembly area. The elements of the division support command were quartered all across the area in assorted villages.

This time, as opposed to the campaign in Poland, the division was not in the first attack wave. Instead, it was in the second wave, following the *4. Panzer-Division*. The latter division was directed to reach the Albert Canal in the vicinity of Maastricht in its first thrust, where it was to relieve the airborne and special forces protecting the bridges.

Hauptmann Barth, the division's intelligence officer, visited the *4. Panzer-Division* on the morning of 10 May. Its headquarters was already in Maastricht. He made his way back with some difficulty in the face of the advancing columns. That evening, he reported back to *Generalmajor* Stumpff. Barth reported on the capture of Maastricht, the demolition of the bridges by the Dutch, the capture of Eben-Emael, and the taking of the bridges over the Albert and Juliana Canals. *Leutnant* Oelrich of the Headquarters Company of the 1st Battalion of *Panzer-Regiment 6*, served as the route reconnaissance officer for the armored brigade and also went forward.

The soldiers of the division were up early on the morning of 11 May. Many of them were entering combat for the first time and correspondingly nervous. Those who slept out in the open were awakened by the cold. The morale was good everywhere and the soldiers were confident of victory. They heard about the initial fighting along the border from the radios they had brought along, messengers passing through and the local populace.

The division started its movement toward the border with its lead elements, including the headquarters and the reconnaissance battalion, around 1000 hours. The movement was hindered by the congestion on the roads. The congestion was caused by the demolition of the bridges over the Meuse. Despite supreme efforts, it was not possible to guide the jammed-up formations over the provisional bridges quickly. The *XVI. Armee-Korps (mot.)* was delayed in its advance by exactly twenty-four hours.

The leading formations of the division, which started rolling forward at noon, reached the Dutch border around 1500 hours. The countryside was pretty and tidy; the soldiers had their first glimpse into Holland from the small, squat hills. The fruit trees were in bloom; it would

Einsatz West der 3. Panzer-Division

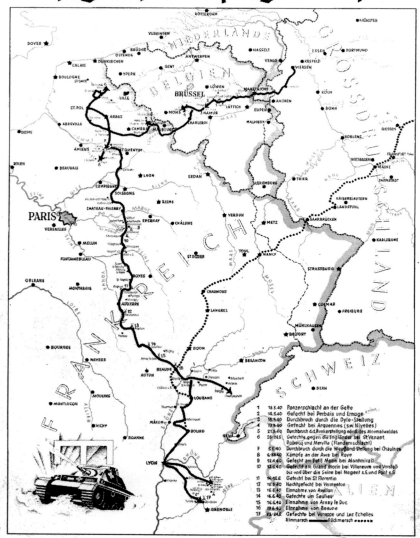

Operations of the *3. Panzer-Division* in the West:

1	13 May 1940	Armored engagement along the Gette
2	14 May 1940	Fighting in the vicinity of Perbais and Ernage
3	15 May 1940	Breakthrough at the Dyle Position
4	17 May 1940	Fighting at Arquennes (southwest of Nivelles)
5	21 May 1940	Breaking through the bunker positions north of the Mormal Woods
6	26–29 May 1940	Fighting against the English at St. Venant, Robecq, and Merville (Battle of Flanders)
7	5 June 1940	Breaking through the Weygand Position at Chaulnes
8	6–7 June 1940	Fighting along the Avre near Roye
9	12 June 1940	Fighting at the Petit Morin at Montmirail
10	13 June 1940	Fighting at the Grand Morin at Villeneuve and Advance to and across the Seine at Nogent and Pont
11	14–15 June 1940	Fighting at St. Florentin
12	15 June 1940	Night fighting at Vermenton
13	15 June 1940	Taking of Avallon
14	16 June 1940	Fighting around Saulieu
15	16 June 1940	Taking of Arnay le Duc
16	17 June 1940	Taking of Beaune
17	23–24 June 1940	Fighting at Vareppe and Les Echelies

have been a peacetime picture had it not been for the clouds of smoke that darkened the skies to the north and west.

The motorcycle infantry, reconnaissance elements, and first tanks crossed the border at Locht. The move continued in fits and spurts via Simpelveld–Schin-op-Geul–Valkenburg. The motorcycle battalion was then outside the gates of Maastricht. It was shortly after 1500 hours. Long columns—tanks, engineers, *Flak*, medical vehicles—closed up on the broad, attractive streets of the city and waited for a crossing over the newly erected pontoon bridge. All of a sudden, *Flak* on both sides of the street went into position. Before the motorcycle infantry grasped what was going on, the first rounds were being fired. Twelve British Blenheims raced in and dropped their loads on the bridges.[4] The fireworks were soon over, however, and the motorcycle battalion was able to cross the bridge. *Leutnant* Schmidt and his platoon from the 3rd Company were the first to reach the far side.

By then, the division headquarters had moved forward. The corps chief of staff held a situation briefing at 1640 hours. He announced that the *4. Panzer-Division* had already taken Tongern and had been directed to reach Grandeville. The *3. Panzer-Division* received orders to move quickly in the direction of Bilsen–Tongern after crossing the Meuse and advance north of the *4. Panzer-Division*. It was also to conduct reconnaissance through Tongern in the direction of St. Trond.

Correspondingly, the motorcycle and reconnaissance battalions received missions around 1800 hours to cross the Belgian border at Veldvezelt and screen the area for the divisions that were following. By 2200 hours, the reconnaissance battalion was engaged with Belgian *franctireurs* and scattered Belgian elements in Bilsen, while the motorcycle battalion reached the border at the same time.

Most of the division was still east of the Meuse and on German soil during the night of 11–12 May. The rifle regiment had continued its march with march serials D and E at noon, but there were delays again, since it proved impossible for the individual columns to infiltrate the march routes at the designated times. The regimental headquarters had the individual companies pass it at Ahlsdorf. The border was crossed around 0200 hours at Simpelveld. The commander, *Oberstleutnant* von Manteuffel, went ahead to Maastricht in his staff car. He reported in to the bridge commander, *Oberst* Kleemann, to receive additional orders. At 0415 hours, the regimental headquarters and the 2nd Battalion were the first elements of the regiment over the engineer bridge.

The elements of the division support command did not leave their original quarters until around evening of 11 May. They not only brought the supplies the division needed forward, but also the men returning from leave who did not arrive until that day. Starting in Ahlsdorf, the supply routes of the division were marked by signs, which showed the division's tactical insignia, an arrow and the letter N (for *Nachschub*). The marking of the supply route was done by a messenger section on motorcycles that was under the direction of *Leutnant* Seibt. The system proved itself, and many vehicles were able to find the division without knowing the location of the assembly area ahead of time.

The leading elements of the division reached the Albert Canal during the evening and rapidly got across. The bridges had been taken intact the previous day by airborne and air-landed forces. The lead elements of the corps had encountered tough resistance in the first Belgian villages entered. That could be seen by the soldiers of the *3. Panzer-Division* in the destroyed and burned farmsteads, the scattered materiel of war, and the many dead horses.

Elements of the reconnaissance battalion and the 1st Battalion of the divisional artillery went into position during the night north of Tongern, where they screened and waited for the rest of the division, which was slowly closing up. No

---

4. Probably from 15 Squadron RAF. Six Blenheims were shot down and three heavily damaged.

enemy could be determined. Since he was expected at any time, however, security was established in all directions. It was completely dark, and the eyes of the soldiers on outpost duty strained as they gazed into the darkness. The 3rd Battery oriented its guns north, while the 1st and 2nd Batteries aimed west.

The enemy had been prepared for the German attack across the Meuse. All of his plans hinged on preventing a repetition of the envelopment attempt of the German field armies as had happened in World War I. The French field armies moved into Belgium immediately after the start of the offensive in order to position themselves along the Dyle Line. To the north of Gembloux, there was still a gap in the fortified positions, which the French intended to close. To that end, the French High Command pushed a cavalry corps forward, which included the 2nd and 3rd Mechanized Divisions.

Since the *XVI. Armee-Korps (mot.)* ordered the *4. Panzer-Division* to also advance on Gembloux, the two enemy corps were approaching one another on the evening of 11 May. In terms of personnel, equipment, mobility, and firepower, they were equals.

Around 0150 hours, orders arrived at the division command post from the corps that stated that the enemy had been forced back to the west by the *4. Panzer-Division*. The corps intended to continue its advance to the southwest on 12 May and directed the *3. Panzer-Division* to advance next to the *4. Panzer-Division* on the right. The objective: the area on both sides of Hannut.

On that twelfth of May, Pentecost Sunday, the division attempted to move its elements that were still in Reich territory forward as quickly as possible. Despite that, there was no rapid move forward, since British aircraft were constantly bombing the engineer bridges across the Meuse, expanding their attacks as far as Linnich. The divisions suffered no casualties, but the 1st Company of the rifle regiment had to dive into position "head over heels" while it was crossing

the river and a truck from the bakery company received minor damage.

The *II./Flak-Lehr-Regiment*, attached to the division, reported its first "kills." For example, the 8th Battery shot down four bombers and three fighters (Spitfires) on 12 May alone.[5]

Oberstleutnant von Manteuffel was put in charge of traffic control along the Meuse to facilitate the smooth crossing of the different formations. *Oberleutnant* Stein, the commander of the 5th Company of the rifle regiment, was made temporary bridge-site commander. The rifle regiment had all of its elements on Dutch soil and crossed the engineer bridge at 1620 hours with its 1st Battalion. The 3rd Battalion followed at 1845 hours. The artillery regiment was in Belgium, as was the antitank battalion. The later formation suffered its first three wounded after an attack by British Wellington bombers. The antitank elements continued forward and moved through Mopertingen, which had been completely destroyed by *Stukas*. Elements of the division support command crossed the Meuse around 2100 hours. By doing so, the division found itself completely in enemy territory . . .

What was the situation at the front?

The *4. Panzer-Division* had moved out from its staging area around Grandville at 0600 hours on 12 May. One and a half hours later, its *5. Panzer-Brigade* reached Hannut after crossing rolling countryside that was populated with numerous villages. At 0950 hours, the division submitted the following report to the corps: "*5. Panzer-Brigade* has broken the resistance between Lens–St. Remy!" Then, all of a sudden, French tanks approaching from the northwest moved against the Germans. A tough tank engagement developed that did not turn in favor of the *5. Panzer-Brigade* until noon. The German fighting vehicles were unable to pursue the withdrawing enemy forces, since they were running out of fuel. *Ju-52* transporter aircraft flew in the fuel in the early afternoon and enabled the tanks to continue the attack. The brigade's forces

---

5. There were no RAF Spitfires operational in France or Belgium; these aircraft were probably Hawker Hurricanes.

bogged down at Thisnes in the face of strong defensive fires. The French employed their heavy Somua[6] tanks, against which the main guns of the German fighting vehicles were powerless.

The commander in chief of the *6. Armee, Generaloberst* von Reichenau, arrived at the division command post at 1215 hours, along with his chief of staff, *Generalmajor* Paulus. A few minutes later, the commander in chief of the field army group, *Generaloberst* von Bock, also arrived. The two senior commanders were adamant in insisting that the *3. Panzer-Division* enter the fray as soon as possible with all of its combat elements.

The forwardmost elements—such as the motorcycle and reconnaissance battalion, as well as the two armored regiments, which were rapidly closing up, and the 1st Battalion of the divisional artillery—had already established contact with the enemy. The first prisoners, mostly from the Belgian 4th Infantry Division, had been brought in. The cannoneers of the 1st Battalion had even succeeded in capturing the 9th Battery of the Ardennes Light Infantry Regiment. The motorcycle battalion arrived at the battlefield around Hannut late in the afternoon, soon joined by the reconnaissance battalion. The antitank battalion, which had assembled in the Mopertingen area in the meantime, was also sent forward as soon as possible. Its 1st and 3rd Companies were attached to the armored brigade, its 2nd Company to the reconnaissance battalion. *Panzer-Regiment 6* followed the reconnaissance battalion through Heers and reached Hannut with its first battalion around 1800 hours.

The division received orders during the night: "Advance on Gembloux!" The division commander thereupon ordered an attack with the armored brigade in front with the main effort on the right. The attack was to cross the line Houtain–l'Eveque–Avernes–le Baudoin with the objective of taking the crossroads southwest of Jodoigne. *Major* von Wechmar's reconnaissance battalion was given the guard mission on the open right flank during the advance. It made its first enemy contact against reconnaissance elements at Hemitienne around 1000 hours. The rifle battalions formed up behind the armored regiments, with the 3rd Battalion held in reserve.

In the meantime, the tactical reconnaissance established contact with the enemy. Around 0800 hours, it brought in its first prisoners around Hannut. They were two officers and three dragoons of the Dragoon Regiment (motorcycle infantry regiment); four prisoners were taken at Racourt from the 12th Cuirassier Regiment (motorized rifle regiment). That allowed identification of the enemy. The French 33rd Mechanized Division from Paris was facing the *3. Panzer-Division* from Berlin.

The division prepared itself for its baptism of fire in the campaign in the West. This action would also prove to be the first major tank engagement of World War II.

The division completed its preparations by 1230 hours. The two armored regiments were in front. *Panzer-Regiment 5* was at Trognée, with the 1st Battalion of the rifle regiment behind it. *Panzer-Regiment 6* was at Montenaeken, with the 2nd Battalion of the rifle regiment behind it. The artillery, reinforced by the *II./Artillerie-Regiment 49*, was arrayed across the entire front. The 1st Company of the antitank battalion was supporting Panzer-*Regiment 6*, while the 3rd Company of the battalion was supporting the other armored regiment. The division command post was located one kilometer south of Montenaeken.

Right at 1230 hours, *Stukas* raced through the air and dove on identified enemy positions. Fountains of smoke and fire as high as a house rose skyward and moved slowly through the pretty countryside, from which so many church towers were jutting. The engines of the tanks starting up didn't allow for a peaceful mood, however. The steel-gray monsters with the white crosses rolled along a wide front through the depressions and across the green hills, which were being bathed in the hot midday sun streaming down. The division was attacking.

---

6. The Somua S-35 mounted a 4.7-cm main gun and had relatively heavy frontal turret armor of 55 millimeters.

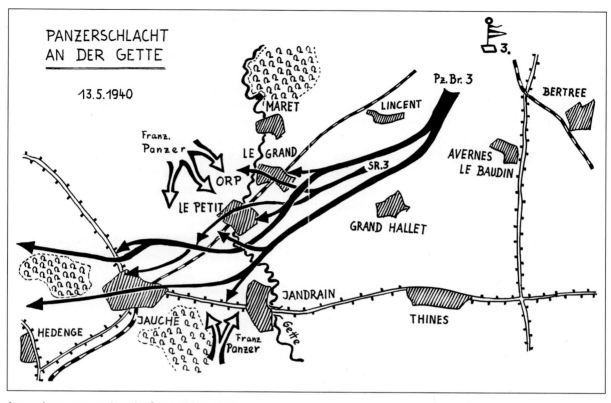

Armored engagement along the Gette, 13 May 1940.

By 1300 hours, the armored brigade had already reached the high ground along the Gette. From there, the hills descended sharply to the creek, which snaked its way through woods, vegetation and villages, one following the next. The tank drivers had no time to take in the idyllic picture. All of a sudden, there was a rumbling sound approaching and the earth pitched skyward between the fighting vehicles. The enemy artillery had identified the German position. The tanks halted briefly and sought out the enemy. They took aim and fired. Then there was a crackling sound in the headphones: "*Panzer marsch!*"

Oberstleutnant von Lewinski's *Panzer-Regiment 6* advanced on Orp-le-Grand with its 1st Battalion and Genville with its 2nd. The terrain was rolling and open and well suited for an attack, since the riflemen were still able to follow the tanks without problems. *Hauptmann* Schneider-

Kostalski's 2nd Company entered Orp-le-Grand first. It was supported by two heavy tanks from the 4th Company (*Leutnant* Schewe and *Unterfeldwebel* Krajewski) and the regimental light platoon of Oberleutnant Buchterkirch. The enemy had set up obstacles along streets, so that it was not possible to advance quickly. Despite that, the advance continued and then moved on to Orp-le-Petit. *Major* Schmidt-Ott's 1st Battalion attacked with all of its resources. Once again, it was Schneider-Kostalski's and Buchterkirch's men, who blazed a path. The tanks of the 1st Company followed a short while later. An artillery direct hit killed one soldier and wounded seven more, including *Leutnant* von Kriegsheim, who was badly wounded. It proved further unfortunate that the company commander, *Hauptmann* von Zedlitz und Leipe, became ill and had to turn over his command to *Leutnant* Fechner. By then, the 4th Company of

Hauptmann Weiß had advanced. It destroyed two antitank guns in its first assault and then advanced into the village, where there was intense house-to-house fighting. The French defended stubbornly and fired from the houses after the tanks had rolled past. The crews of the fighting vehicles had to dismount more than once and resort to pistols and carbines to clear a path. *Leutnant* Schewe suddenly discovered a small emergency bridge over the Gette. What would have been considered impossible in peacetime happened there: The heavy tracked vehicles rolled over the wooden beams and made it to the far side.

Oberst Freiherr von Funck's *Panzer-Regiment 5* also had to fight its way through tough enemy resistance. The 4.7-centimeter antitank guns turned out to be dangerous. They had to be out-maneuvered and engaged individually. Despite that, the regiment was able to locate a crossing point towards 1430 hours. The engineers from the 1st Company of the engineer battalion erected a provisional bridge through their aggressive actions while under French machine-gun fire. The tanks then rolled across it.

Around 1515 hours, *Panzer-Regiment 6* crossed the Gette with its tanks and continued its attack. The tanks advanced on Jandrain. Belts of antitank guns held up the tanks there. Fortunately, the fires of *Hauptmann* Hinninger's 2nd Battery were placed so well that two guns were knocked out almost immediately. At that point, the companies rolled forward. *Leutnant* Schewe encountered two more antitank guns at the western outskirts of the village, which he was able to eliminate. All of a sudden, a French tank appeared, but it was also knocked out. While moving on, Schewe's fighting vehicle received a hit at Hill 110, but it was still able to move. The young officer was wounded in the left arm. *Unterfeldwebel* Krajewski, following behind in his *Panzer III*, was killed in the enemy fire. *Leutnant* von Krause was able to mount the tank in the middle of the engagement and bring it back in one piece.

Additional French tanks appeared from the south and slammed into the wide-open flank of *Panzer-Regiment 6*. Even before the antitank elements were summoned forward by radio, that battalion was closing in. *Major* von Bernuth immediately employed his 1st Company under *Oberleutnant* Polentz. The antitank crews started unlimbering their guns while still moving and took up the fight at 800 meters. Twenty-five Somua and Hotchkiss tanks were approaching. They did not turn away until three of their number had gone up in flames. The lefthand platoon of the *1./Panzerjäger-Abteilung 39* (*Leutnant* Rehberg) contributed significantly to that success. *Oberleutnant* Schacht's *4./Panzerjäger-Abteilung 39* had also closed up in the meantime. It was called away, however, to assist *Panzer-Regiment 5*.

The enemy had not used up his offensive combat power by a long shot. Indeed, he committed additional fighting vehicles into the fight. The armored brigade's commander, *Oberst* Kühn, correspondingly ordered the 1st Battalion of *Panzer-Regiment 5* to support its sister armored regiment. The 2nd Battalion of *Panzer-Regiment 6* was having an especially hard time of it. After it was determined that the light tanks with their machine guns and light automatic cannon could not accomplish anything against the heavily armored enemy fighting vehicles, the *Panzer I's* and *Panzer II's* were called back to a rear-slope position and given a flank-guard mission. The *Panzer III's* and *Panzer IV's*, on the other hand, fired with everything they had.

The enemy counterattack was taking place with forty fighting vehicles from the area around Jauche–Genville. The *I./Panzer-Regiment 6* had to exert itself to deflect that dangerous thrust to the flanks. The regimental light platoon was directed to reconnoiter in the direction of Genville. *Oberleutnant* Levin led the way in his tank. While he was searching the terrain with his binoculars, he was fired upon by a French sniper. The young officer became the first officer of the regiment to be killed in the campaign.

The 2nd Company of *Panzer-Regiment 6* had moved up and encountered enemy tanks around Jauche. By 1700 hours, the company was able to knock out another Hotchkiss, eliminate two anti-tank guns, and take 3 officers and 120 enlisted personnel prisoner. Shortly after that, *Hauptmann* Schneider-Kostalski's tank was knocked out. The fighting continued. *Oberleutnant Graf* zu Dohna and his gunner, *Unteroffizier* Eisel, were able to take out another three antitank guns and bring in 150 French prisoners. *Unteroffizier* Sandberg and his crew set a tank alight, before he and his driver, *Gefreiter* Diesener, were killed by enemy fires. *Feldwebel* Wolf and his platoon destroyed an enemy tank at Jandrain and captured five machine guns and ten motorcycles in a surprise attack. The 2nd Battalion of the regiment, under the command of *Oberstleutnant* Burmeister, did not remain idle either. In his heavy tank, *Oberleutnant Baron* von Nolte and his crew knocked out five enemy fighting vehicles all by themselves.

The 2nd Battalion of *Oberst Freiherr* von Funck's *Panzer-Regiment 5* was attacked from the northwest by enemy tanks at Orp-le-Grand. They were holding the high ground to the north of Jauche. The fight was taken up and soon all the vehicles were firing and curving around one another. The German tanks slowly started to gain the advantage, since their cohesiveness and coordination were vastly superior to those of the enemy. Our tanks remained intact as platoons or even companies, while the French moved individually or in very small groups. Correspondingly, they dissipated their effectiveness. Since the rate of fire for the Germans was also considerably higher, the enemy soon pulled back.

The rifle regiment had been following the tanks since noon. The riflemen ran along between the fighting vehicles so as to eliminate infantry threats in a timely manner. *Major* Zimmermann's 2nd Battalion reached Orp-le-Grand shortly after *Panzer-Regiment 6* did. At 1530 hours, it forced a crossing over the creek. The battalion remained on the heels of the tanks and provided effective protection to the flanks.

Major von Bosse's 1st Battalion moved forward with equal élan. *Hauptmann* von Plato's 1st Company eliminated a hard-fighting machine-gun position, before the battalion made it to Orp-le-Petit. The riflemen wound up in a tank attack there, and had to temporarily move back to the Gette to set up defensive positions there, along with the antitank battalion. *Panzer-Regiment 5* succeeded in driving the enemy back to the southwest by itself, however. The rifle battalion joined in the pursuit, with its 5th Company particularly distinguishing itself. The battalion took in more than 400 prisoners. *Major* von Bosse, leading from the front, was badly wounded, however. *Hauptmann* Haspel assumed temporary command of the battalion. When the 1st Battalion of *Panzer-Regiment 5* arrived around 1600 hours, the engagement was finally decided in favor of the German forces.

The 1st Battalion of *Panzer-Regiment 5* and *Panzer-Regiment 6* did not halt; instead, they continued advancing farther west. In the process, both formations encountered immediate counterattacks by the French, but they were unable to stop the German advance. *Leutnant* Rentsch's platoon from the 1st Company of the antitank battalion was employed in a screening mission oriented toward Jauche. The antitank gunners shot a French baggage train to pieces and took two officers and eighty-five men prisoner in Jauche after sending an assault detachment in. The 4th Company of the battalion screened in the direction of Enien. Since the platoon leader of the lead platoon, *Leutnant* Schenk, was reconnoitering new positions when enemy tanks started rolling forward again, *Stabsfeldwebel* Gericke assumed command. Only the middle gun of *Unteroffizier* Westricht (the gunner was *Obergefreiter* Günther) was able to take the tanks under direct fire, since the lefthand gun of *Unteroffizier* Behring was firing at identified machine-gun nests and the righthand gun of *Unteroffizier* Großkreutz was prevented from opening fire by grazing cows. Despite those difficulties, the platoon was able to knock out two enemy tanks, causing the enemy to give up his attack.

The well-placed fires of the divisional artillery and the attached *II./Artillerie-Regiment 49* played no small role in the success of the aforementioned operations. The fires from the German batteries enabled the tanks to continue advancing west. *Panzer-Regiment 6* moved past Jauche to the north—in the lead were the platoons of *Oberleutnant* Buchterkirch and *Oberleutnant Baron* von Nolde—and bypassed a small patch of woods, all the while still continuing to engage individual enemy tanks. The 1st Battalion of *Panzer-Regiment 5* screened in the direction of the Jandrain–Jauche road, while the regiment's 2nd Battalion oriented along the Jauche–Orp rail line. The latter regiment reached the rail line at 2020 hours and moved its fighting vehicles forward through Jauche. Around 2100 hours, as a result of the onset of darkness, the advance came to a close for the day along a line running Jauche–Marilles–Jodoigne rail line–Geest Gerompont–two kilometers south of Huppays. The rifle regiment followed closely behind the tanks, with its 1st Battalion reaching the Jodoigne–Hedenge rail line at 2230 hours. In the course of its movements, it had brought in 200 prisoners and knocked out five tanks and thirty-four trucks. At the onset of darkness, the reconnaissance battalion was in Libertange, where it had established contact with the neighboring *18. Infanterie-Division*. The division command post was moved forward to Grand-Hallet. The rifle regiment and its headquarters moved to Orp-le-Petit.

The French 3rd Mechanized Division pulled farther back to the west. On that day, it had lost thirty Somuas and almost seventy Hotchkiss. The personnel losses were likewise grave, with the three battalions of the dragoon regiment forced to consolidate into one battalion.

For 14 May, the *6. Armee* intended "to continue the attack along the entire front, maintaining the main effort in the general direction of Nivelles." For its part, the *XVI. Armee-Korps (mot.)* issued the following order: "eject the mechanized enemy force to the front and advance via Perwez in the general direction of Gembloux." The division moved out at 0900 with its armored brigade in the lead. *Panzer-Regiment 5* moved on the left, once again followed by the 1st Battalion of the rifle regiment. Following *Panzer-Regiment 6* on the right was the 2nd Battalion of the rifle regiment. As before, the reconnaissance battalion remained on the right wing, advancing via Pomel and the bridge at Walhain-St. Pol as far as Thorembais-les-Beguines. The 2nd Battalion of *Panzer-Regiment 6* took the point in its sector and advanced inexorably forward. The enemy started pulling back as soon as the tanks approached. The delaying actions of the French appeared to no longer have any decisiveness. The division's advance proceeded rapidly. The Löwen–Eghezée road was crossed and, a short while later, the Wawre–Perwez road. A recently installed steel-beam fence south of Roux–Miroire was intended to hold up the German tanks, but they were able to simply overrun it.

Panzer-Regiment 6 reached Walhain–St. Pol in a single bound. *Oberleutnant Baron* von Nolde's 8th Company shot to pieces the first Somuas that appeared. Together with his platoon, he was able to knock out seven more fighting vehicles in the ensuing engagement. That cleared the path for the companies that were following. The action was mentioned in the Armed Forces Daily Report on 20 May, where it was stated that "During the tank engagements of the last few days in Belgium, Nolde, an *Oberleutnant* in an armored regiment, distinguished himself through his cold-blooded actions."

The enemy resistance then became noticeably stronger. The lead elements of the division were approaching the Dyle Position, which was heavily fortified. The defensive effort increased considerably in the Ernage area, with the result that the armor brigade had to pull back about 600 meters from the locality around 1830 hours in order to find better cover. Five vehicles were lost to enemy antitank and artillery fires. The rifle regiment, which had received orders to attack the Dyle Position, dug in along the limits of its advance at 2130 hours, after its 1st Battalion had taken about fifty prisoners right outside of the village.

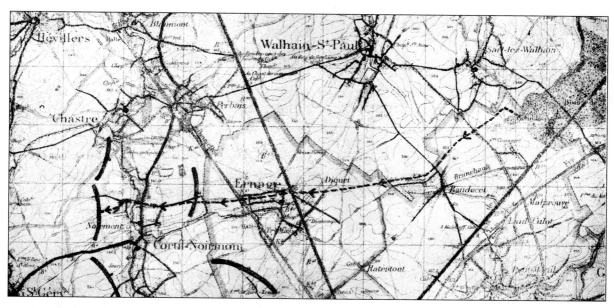

Breaking through the Dyle Position.

At that point, the corps formed the main effort of the offensive within the field army group. It intended to break through the enemy front. Around 1400 hours on 14 May, *Generalobersten* von Bock and von Reichenau visited the division command post in Mont-St. André. Both of them emphasized the importance of a relentlessly moving advance. The field army commander in chief placed special emphasis on bounding leaps forward so as to always have the requisite amount of artillery available.

By the evening of 14 May, the field army group, the field army, and the corps all came to the conclusion that the fighting morale of the enemy, which had already sunk considerably, and the previously demonstrated offensive momentum allowed a thrust against the Dyle Position on 15 May. Hoepner issued his orders: "*XVI. Armee-Korps (mot.)* attacks at 0900 hours on 15 May, with the *3. Panzer-Division* and the *4. Panzer-Division* in front and supported by all available artillery, to break through the Dyle Position on both sides of Ernage."

The following enemy forces had been identified as facing the division: elements of the French 3rd Mechanized Division; the French 1st Infantry Division; and elements of the Belgian 2nd and 7th Infantry Divisions. By employing those active-duty forces, the enemy demonstrated his intent to hold the Dyle Position under all circumstances.

The engines of the *Stukas* howled through the air shortly before 0900 hours on 15 May. They were headed to both sides of Ernage to drop their bomb loads on the enemy positions. Unfortunately, the bombs did not land exactly in the designated target areas. Instead, they exploded right in front of the German lines. The fires from the German artillery also did little damage to the enemy, since they were firing from the map. The forward observers had not been able to make it up front. It was intended for the division's attack to start at 0900 hours with the rifle brigade, but the whole operation seemed to be under a bad sign that day. Unnoticed by the enemy, the 2nd Battalion of the rifle regiment had advanced during the night and occupied Hills 161 and 165. By doing so, the battalion was unintentionally farther forward on the right than planned. As a result of the enemy's continuous and well-aimed rolling artillery barrages, it was impossible to reorganize at daylight. The neighboring 1st Battalion was able to be pulled back and redirected, however, when the German artillery fires started.

As a result of the reorganization, the attack of both battalions was delayed half an hour. On his own initiative, *Major* Zimmermann had his 2nd Battalion move out, even though he knew his companies were well ahead of the rest of the division. To protect the completely open right flank, Zimmermann employed the machine-gun platoon of his 9th Company there. *Leutnant Graf* von Arnim, the platoon leader, was killed shortly after the battalion moved out. The companies in the middle—*Oberleutnant* Müller-Röhlich's 7th, *Oberleutnant* von Kayser's 8th, and *Hauptmann* Zabel's 10th—descended the front slope more quickly and were thus spared receiving fires from the German artillery, which was landing much too short on that day of all days. Fortunately, a forward observer, who showed up in time, was able to stop the fires and shift them forward. The enemy had turned lively and mercilessly hammered the battalion. A total of eleven batteries had been identified. As the riflemen slowly approached the Perbais–Ernage road, French machine guns began rattling away on all sides. The defensive fires were terribly effective and forced the 2nd Battalion to give up its advance about 200 meters west of the road, just south of Perbais, around 1030 hours. The company commander of the 9th, *Oberleutnant* Seidler, was badly wounded with a round to the heart. In the 8th Company, *Unteroffizier* Zimmer, one of the "old hands" of the rifle regiment, was killed, among others. It was clear that the 2nd Battalion was not going to get any farther. The men had reached a long and wide depression. They were unable to get out of it as a result of the horrific flanking fires to make the final 100 meters to the railway embankment.

Hauptmann Haspel's 1st Battalion also did not enjoy any success that morning. It moved out along both sides of the Walhain–St. Pol–Perbais road, minus its 2nd Company, which was screening toward Ernage. The 1st Company of *MG-Bataillon 7* was attached to the battalion and enabled *Hauptmann* von Plato's 1st Company to make good progress as a result of its well-placed fires. The riflemen were taking considerable casualties. All of the officer candidates of the battalion were killed that day. Despite all their efforts, *Hauptmann* Haspel's men were unable to get across the Perbais–Ernage road.

The two battalion commanders conferred on how to continue the advance. By then, however, the regiment had ordered *Major* Kratzenberg's 3rd Battalion forward, to help get the bogged-down attack flowing again. Kratzenberg was briefed at the command post of the 2nd Battalion, before he continued on to the brigade command post. He received the mission there to close the gap between the division and the *4. Panzer-Division*, staging on Hill 169 west of Baudeset. It was intended for the battalion to attack Ernage from there and then swing left after crossing the railway line.

The other elements of the regiment did not remain idle. The 7th and 8th Companies reached the Wavre–Gembloux railway line just south of Perbais. *Major* Zimmermann then employed *Oberleutnant* Engelen's 6th Company, which had been held in reserve up to that point, to take the village.

By then, *Major* Wöhlermann's 2nd Battalion of artillery had ranged on the road and was supporting the continued advance of the riflemen. The forward observer from the 6th Battery, *Leutnant* Leese, moved forward to the location of the 3rd Company of the rifle regiment on the road with his two radio operators, *Gefreiter* Mieritz and *Gefreiter* Szagunn. From there, he directed the guns of *Leutnant* Kersten's battery on the field positions of the Moroccan forces arrayed along the outskirts of Perbais.

The 1st Battalion of the rifle regiment then moved out. The companies, exploiting the artillery fire and a *Stuka* attack farther to the front, succeeded in getting to and then into the village. *Hauptmann* von Plato's 1st Company was able to clear the rest of the village through aggressive employment of his platoons, whereby the 1st

Platoon of *Leutnant* Zitzewitz was able to take fifty prisoners all by itself. The company secured the village but continued to receive casualties from enemy artillery fire. By contrast, squads from *MG-Bataillon 7* were able to proceed beyond Perbais and take Hill 154.

Major Lorenz's 1st Battalion of artillery, as well as the *II./Flak-Lehr-Regiment*, joined the fray and supported the advance of the riflemen. The battalion's forward observers were all up front with the attacking riflemen. *Leutnant* Guthke, forward observer of the 2nd Battery, was killed, the first officer lost by the artillery regiment in the war.

By then, elements of the 2nd Company of the rifle regiment and the *2./MG-Bataillon 7* had entered Ernage. The companies became embroiled in heavy street fighting, made all the more difficult by the fact that friendly artillery was also causing casualties. It took some time for radio contact to be established with the batteries. The riflemen disengaged from the enemy and did not take up the attack again until the German guns fell silent. The enemy's defensive effort started increasing in the afternoon. The well-placed enemy artillery fires tore large gaps in the ranks of the attackers.

Around 1400 hours, the rifle brigade ordered the 3rd Battalion of the rifle regiment to attack left of the 2nd Battalion to close the gap between the two divisions that still existed. The battalion marched by foot as far as the Baudeset Farm. The staging was completed by 1600 hours. The attack was scheduled for 1630 hours. The forces were arrayed as follows: on the right, the 11th Company, reinforced by one heavy machine-gun platoon, one heavy mortar section, one infantry gun, one antitank gun, and one platoon from the divisional engineers; and on the left, the 12th Company, reinforced by one heavy machine-gun platoon, one heavy mortar section, one infantry gun, one antitank gun, and two sections from the divisional engineers. The 13th Company was held in reserve. With the battalion headquarters was a fire-support coordination officer from the 1st Battalion of artillery, but his radio equipment was not functioning properly. It was only possible to communicate with the brigade via landline. Just before the attack started, the 1st Company of *Panzer-Regiment 6* arrived.

The 3rd Battalion moved out punctually and, despite heavy enemy fire, reached its intermediate objective, the road east of Ernage, by 1715 hours. The enemy's fires increased by the minute, and the engineers were continuously clearing mines in order to make the attack on the village easier for the riflemen. Machine-gun rounds pelted against the attackers from all of the houses, but the men were eventually able to run through the village. The 11th Company was the first one to reach the railway embankment behind the village and, after hard fighting, took the high ground 900 meters west of Ernage. The attack of the 12th Company, on the other hand, stalled at the embankment, since friendly artillery fire once again made it impossible to move forward. The radio set of the forward observer had been shot to pieces, and the green signal flares were not seen in the rear. That meant that messengers had to be sent back. They reached *Leutnant* Jaeger from the 12th Company, who had become separated. He immediately rallied his platoon. Moving through friendly artillery fire, it assaulted the Moroccan positions.

Since the rifle battalion was fighting with an open flank, the two platoons from the 1st Company of *Panzer-Regiment 6* were employed there. *Oberfeldwebel* Meyrhofer's platoon, moving on the right, encountered six enemy antitank guns at the embankment. All of them were shot to pieces by the fighting vehicles and then overrun. *Feldwebel* Burusiak's platoon supported the advance of the 12th Company through fires from his vehicles. The riflemen were finally able to cross the railway embankment. *Oberleutnant* von Werthern's 11th Company followed the tanks and reached the road leading to Noirmont around 1900 hours. Once there, the company received heavy fire from antitank guns. Two fighting vehicles bringing up the rear, a *Panzer I* and a *Panzer II*, were lost to antitank-gun hits. *Gefreiter* Maylach, who was wounded, dismounted. On his way back to the clearing station, he took in some thirty French as prisoners. In the meantime, *Oberfeldwebel* Mayrhofer had moved on the antitank guns with his vehicles. Two were knocked out in the space of a few minutes. *Leutnant* Fechner set a third gun alight at the edge of the village. The enemy finally weakened and approached the German lines with raised hands. All of a sudden, however, machine guns and antitank guns rang out to the rear. The Moroccans threw themselves on the ground and then continued fighting. The enemy's resistance became especially tough on the right flank, where the enemy had barricaded himself in the village of Chastre. A few individual French tanks also appeared. They were engaged by the German fighting vehicles. *Leutnant* Fechner reorganized his tank company and employed his 3rd Platoon, as well as the battalion's light platoon, which was attached, to protect the open flank.

Since the 12th Company was still hanging back, *Major* Kratzenberg pushed the engineer platoon into the gap on a hill east of Cortil–Noirmont. An enemy immediate counterattack, comprised of 300 soldiers and supported by tanks, hit the flanks and rear of the battalion a few minutes later. Receiving a shock, the engineers pulled back in the face of the superior numbers.

But the fighting vehicles arrived in the nick of time. *Oberleutnant* Buchterkirch had received orders at 1930 hours to support the *1./Panzer-Regiment 6* up front. When he was at the western outskirts of Ernage with his light tanks, he saw eight enemy tanks approach. He immediately had his vehicles deploy into firing order and started the fight. Buchterkirch's platoon knocked out five enemy tanks and forced the accompanying infantry to turn back 200 meters from the positions of the *6./MG-Bataillon 7*. The German tanks then resumed advancing, bringing the machine-gun company with them. *Oberleutnant* Buchterkirch and his men then eliminated

an antitank-gun position with three guns. He wanted to report his actions to the company commander of the machine-gun company and dismounted his vehicle. At that point, enemy fires started howling in from the other side. His tank flew into the air, and two other fighting vehicles also went up in flames. Under the leadership of *Unteroffizier* Reinicke, the remaining tanks continued the attack, knocking out an additional three antitank guns. Then Reinicke's tank received a direct hit. Reinicke lost an arm; the remaining two members of his crew were killed. The *Unteroffizier* changed tanks in the middle of the fight and brought the remaining tank safely back.

Hauptmann Dr. Sturm's 13th Company had also moved out again with support from *Leutnant* Arnold's platoon from the *1./Panzer-Regiment 6*. The riflemen and tankers were able to eliminate two machine-gun carriers and capture a lot of equipment and weapons in their attack. The Moroccan soldiers evacuated the battlefield and pulled back.

Hauptmann Weiss's *4./Panzer-Regiment 6* was then directed to advance. The company crossed a minefield northwest of Ernage, with *Unteroffizier* Korbella distinguishing himself through a combination of circumspection and temerity. The company then rattled through Noirmont and positioned itself on the right wing of the *1./Panzer-Regiment 6*. The tanks moved forward and approached Villeroix. A *Panzer I* was lost during the advance. *Feldwebel* Krause shot up a machine-gun position with his tank, which had been causing the riflemen a lot of problems up to then. *Leutnant* Andersen's platoon from the 4th Company drove an enemy baggage train to flight.

By then, the rifle companies had closed up to the front. *Oberleutnant Freiherr* von Werthern's 11th Company started attacking Cortil-Noirmont. *Hauptmann* Orts's 12th Company attacked into the village at the same time and occupied the high ground to its east. At 2045 hours, regimental orders arrived: "Stop the attack; hold the lines reached!"

The enemy was placing well-aimed fires into the positions of the 3rd Battalion of the rifle regiment. When orders came to pull back *MG-Bataillon 7*, *Major* Kratzenberg decided to pull back the left wing of his battalion to eliminate the threat to his wide flank. *Oberleutnant* von Brodowski and *Feldwebel* Thévoz arrived there with their heavy vehicles from the *4./Panzer-Regiment 6* and were able to effectively support the pulling back of the 12th Company with their fires. Since the tanks had radio equipment, it was possible to establish radio contact with the brigade for the first time. Up to then, only *Leutnant* Schnitzler, a liaison officer from the brigade, had maintained any contact.

In the meantime, the situation in the sector of the 2nd Battalion of the rifle regiment had changed so much that the commander of the 8th Company, *Oberleutnant* von Kayser, brought himself to the decision to support the advance of the neighboring battalion. He placed the 7th Company under his command as well. With the two companies, he then reached the first attack objective of the division: Hills 152 and 155, west of Noirmont. The companies broke through the weak resistance and crossed the creek outside of Noirmont at 2130 hours. *Oberleutnant* von Kayser established contact with the 11th Company, which was in position there, and reported to *Major* Kratzenberg.

A retrograde order from the brigade forced those brave men to slowly move back behind the creek. The regiment set up for defense. The 1st Battalion was on the right, the 2nd in the middle, and the 3rd on the left in a general line running: railway crossing at Perbais–Hills 164 and 165–1,000 meters west of the railway crossing at Ernage. To support the regiment, the division brought a company of *MG-Bataillon 7* forward, as well as elements of the divisional engineers and the antitank battalion. The *II./Flak-Lehr-Regiment* also dispatched a platoon with 8.8-centimeter *Flak*.

It was clear that the rifle regiment had forced a breakthrough through the Dyle Position, thus opening up the path for the continued advance of the division to Belgium. Friendly losses were not inconsiderable, however. In addition to forty noncommissioned officers and enlisted personnel killed, the rifle regiment had also lost *Leutnant* Lemke, *Leutnant* Amede, *Leutnant* Koch, *Leutnant* Strauß, *Leutnant* Hessler, and *Leutnant* Graf von Arnim. The wounded included 144 noncommissioned officers and enlisted personnel, as well as 9 officers (*Hauptmann* Peschke, *Oberleutnant* von den Heyden-Rynsch, *Oberleutnant* Seidel, *Oberleutnant Freiherr* von Werthern, *Leutnant* Busch, *Leutnant* Büschen, *Leutnant* Busack, *Leutnant* Jenoquel, and *Leutnant* Rosemeyer).

The *35. Infanterie-Division*, which had been marching behind the *3. Panzer-Division* on 15 May, moved its lead elements forward during the night and relieved the 1st and 2nd Battalions of the rifle regiment, which had not eaten in thirty-six hours. *MG-Bataillon 7* was inserted into the line next to the 3rd Battalion of the rifle regiment, both of which were to remain in the front lines for the time being.

As special recognition for the difficult fighting in Belgium, two officers of the *3. Panzer-Division* would later receive the Knight's Cross to the Iron Cross for the actions just described. One was *Oberleutnant* Buchterkirch, the platoon leader of the Light Platoon of the 1st Battalion of *Panzer-Regiment 6*. He had already been a recipient of the Spanish Cross in Gold.[7] The recommendation for the award stated that "through his brave and decisive actions had favorably influenced the conduct of the attack in his sector. His fighting vehicle, which later burned out as the result of a direct hit, was responsible for putting six enemy tanks out of battle and his platoon destroyed a total of eighteen enemy fighting vehicles."

The commander of the 3rd Battalion of the rifle regiment, *Major* Kratzenberg, also received

---

7. The Spanish Cross in Gold was presented to members of the *Legion Condor* who had proven themselves well in combat in Spain. Some 1,126 of these were awarded.

the high-level award for the actions of his capable formation in breaking through the Dyle Position.[8]

The sixteenth of May passed with reorganizing the forces, improving the positions that had been won and even some rest. The reconnaissance battalion and the *II./Panzer-Regiment 6* reconnoitered far to the front. Late in the afternoon, the area around Tilly was reached, and the town was crossed by the troops of the reconnaissance battalion around 2200 hours. The battalion, which had been reinforced with riflemen and tanks, took Marbais around 2300 hours, where it screened for the night.

The corps issued orders to the division at midnight that the pursuit was to continue with all available forces at daybreak and that the crossings over the Brussels Canal were to be taken. The division formed an advance guard consisting of rifle, armored, and antitank elements. It was already moving by 0100 hours. The route led through Tilly and Marbais, to the south of Nivelles, and on to the canal. The lead troops of the reconnaissance battalion were already outside of Arquennes at 0535 hours, where they were engaged by tanks that appeared there. Elements of the 2nd Battalion of *Panzer-Regiment 6* assisted the reconnaissance elements in that engagement and rolled on as far as Arquennes. The 8th Company of the tank regiment encountered the French fighting vehicles outside of Grenfaux. *Oberleutnant Baron* von Nolde knocked out five enemy tanks in the first exchange of fire.

At 0850 hours, the corps directed that a bridgehead be established over the canal. That mission could not be executed. The village was occupied with strong forces and the bridges had been blown up. The bridge at Chaumont, two kilometers north of Ronquieres, was also in the water, where enemy elements were also identified along the banks of the canal. The Light Platoon of *Panzer-Regiment 6*, under the leadership of *Leutnant* von Diest-Koerber, knocked out two fighting vehicles during his reconnaissance-in-force. The 7th Company of the armored regiment was directed to take the bridges in Arquennes. The lead platoon of the company entered the village, but it was forced to halt due to intense enemy antitank fire. The platoon leader's vehicle was set alight, with *Oberleutnant* Schoen and his crew all being killed. It was impossible to get closer to the bridges. The 5th Company, which had been following, also bogged down in the face of the enemy's antitank gun belt. Since artillery fire then started to hamper the approach of the remaining companies, the regiment decided to protect the flanks of the advance guard to both sides of Arquennes for the time being.

While the lead elements were still fighting it out with the enemy, the main body was still far to the rear and moving in three march serials. The majority of the forces were under *Oberst* Kühn and consisted of major elements of the armored brigade, including *Panzer-Regiment 5*, and the headquarters of the rifle regiment and its 3rd Battalion. The second march serial, under the control of *Major* von Bernuth, had the 1st Battalion of the rifle regiment and the antitank battalion as its combat elements. The third serial, under *Oberstleutnant* Fuhrmann, consisted of the rest of the division. The artillery was split among all of the serials.

The corps headquarters issued orders at 1400 hours. The division was to advance in the general direction of Soignes and Ath, while the rifle brigade crossed the canal with elements and established a bridgehead. The 12th Company of the rifle regiment and platoons from the divisional engineer battalion were directed to cross

8. Ernst-Georg Buchterkirch received his award on 29 June 1940, although Veit Scherzer, *Die Ritterkreuzträger*, 1st ed. (Ranis/Jena: Scherzers Militaire-Verlag, 2005), 226, lists Buchterkirch as having been assigned to the *2./Panzer-Regiment 6* at the time of his award. Buchterkirch later went on to become the forty-fourth recipient of the Oak Leaves to the Knight's Cross on 21 December 1941, while serving as the commander of the same company. He ended the war as an *Oberstleutnant i.G.* and passed away on 17 July 1969. Kratzenberg received his award on 15 August, ending the war as an *Oberst* and passing away on 24 January 1976.

the canal in Arquennes, while the 3rd Company of the motorcycle battalion was to look for a crossing point at Renissart. The remaining companies of the motorcycle battalion and the 3rd Battalion of the rifle regiment were given Château de la Rocq as their crossing point.

The rifle brigade then ordered that the formation of the bridgeheads was to be delayed. While the motorcycle battalion and the 3rd Battalion of the rifle regiment could be stopped in time, *Hauptmann* Orts 12th Company entered Arquennes. The riflemen were all by themselves. Nonetheless, they crossed the canal. It turned out that the enemy had pulled back during the evening and had evacuated the village. The attached engineers did not cross over with the riflemen. They had already been called back. Thus, Orts's company remained on the west side of the canal the entire night. It was only after express orders were received from the brigade the next morning that it pulled back from the bridgehead it had won.

The 3rd Company of the motorcycle battalion was finally given the green light to attempt a crossing at Renissart. While approaching, *Oberleutnant* Beck's company received heavy enemy machine-gun fire. The motorcycle infantry halted. *Unteroffizier* Lowa was sent forward to reconnoiter. His squad entered the village and called the neighboring squad of *Unteroffizier* Liebich forward. But both squads were unable to counter the fire from the Moroccans, who were able to take every movement in the village and in the open under fire from improved positions. Fortunately, light tanks arrived along with the rest of *Feldwebel* Hauff's platoon. The fighting vehicles were called back a few minutes later, after one tank flew into the air. That meant that the motorcycle infantry also had to pull back. Five dead men were left behind in the village (*Unteroffizier* Steinmetz, *Gefreiter* Müller, *Gefreiter* Maciejewskie, *Kradschütze* Feige, and *Kradschütze* Wauer). The company set up to defend outside of Renissart. It did not advance again until that night. By then, *Hauptmann* Pape's 2nd Company had also arrived. Both

companies succeeded in making it through the completely destroyed village and crossing the canal.

The visible conclusion to the first phase of the campaign in the West was the orders received from the corps on 18 May which stated that all further attacks were to be put on hold for the time being. The divisions were to disengage from the enemy. The corps was relieved in sector by the *XXVII. Armee-Korps*, with the division being relieved by the *35. Infanterie-Division* of *Generalleutnant* Reinhard.

The Army High Command directed a reorganization of the motorized forces that day. Two strong armored groups were formed. It was intended to cut off the enemy forces withdrawing to the Channel with them. One group was formed under *General der Infanterie* Hoth, comprised of the *3., 4., 5.,* and *7. Panzer-Divisionen,* the *20. Infanterie-Division (mot.),* the *SS-Totenkopf-Division,* and the *11. Schützen-Brigade.* Hoth's forces were to reinforce the *4. Armee,* pivoting north, along with the infantry divisions, in the direction of Flanders and Artois. *General der Kavallerie* von Kleist commanded the second group of forces, consisting of the *1., 2., 6., 8.,* and *10. Panzer-Divisionen* and the *2., 13.,* and *20. Infanterie-Divisionen (mot.),* which was to advance directly for the Channel. Two days later, the *2. Panzer-Division* of *Generalleutnant* Veiel and the *8. Panzer-Division* of *Generalleutnant* Kuntzen reached the coast at Abbéville and Montreuil-sur-Mer. That started the encirclement of the main body of French, Belgian, and British forces.

The *3. Panzer-Division* rested the next two days, if that's what one wanted to call it. Weapons were cleaned, formations held. The first replacements arrived and were assigned. The move was scheduled to begin at 0800 hours on 20 May. The division command staff crossed the French border at Cousolre, east of Maubeuge, around 0800 hours. The division followed in two large march serials. The rifle brigade moved to the left of the armored brigade on two roads to the border, which was not reached until 2200 hours in the area between Grandrieu and Hestrud. The march serial of the rifle brigade was structured as follows: Group A (*Major* Kratzenberg), consisting of the *III./Schützen-Regiment 3*, the *6. and 10./Flak-Regiment 26*, and *Panzerjäger-Abteilung 39*; and Group B (*Major* Zimmermann), consisting of the *II./Schützen-Regiment 3*, the *7./Flak-Regiment 26*, the light engineer section, and a medical company. The large march serial on the right consisted of the two armored regiments, the motorcycle infantry battalion, and the divisional artillery.

The advance guard of the division was under the command of *Major* Meese, the commander of the 1st Battalion of the rifle regiment. In addition to his battalion, the reconnaissance battalion, elements of the motorcycle battalion, and batteries from the divisional artillery were also attached. The advance guard encountered enemy fighting vehicles at 1140 hours at the northeast portion of the Mormal Woods. The corps ordered the broad expanse of woodland to be cleared. The rifle battalion and the motorcycle infantry elements were employed to that end, but were soon called back when aerial reconnaissance revealed that the woods were still full of enemy forces.

The division bypassed the woods to the north and moved in the direction of Denain, while the *4. Panzer-Division* went around the woods to the south. The motorcycle infantry battalion established a bridgehead over the Sambre at Boussières at 1300 hours. Around 2100 hours, the corps ordered *Generalleutnant* Koch-Erpach's *8. Infanterie-Division* to comb the Mormal Woods from the north, while corps forces cut off the woods from the east, south, and west. For that operation, the *3. Panzer-Division* was directed to guard the northern flank of the corps in the direction of Valenciennes and to advance on Denain.

The advance guard was pivoted in the direction of the Sambre to screen. To that end, the 1st Battalion of the rifle regiment established positions in the bend of the Sambre from Hargnies to Pont-sur-Sambre. The engineer battalion was attached to the riflemen in support. The motorcycle infantry battalion remained behind to screen in the direction of the woods, along with the artillery and antitank elements. Soldiers took thirty prisoners from the French 101st and 143rd Infantry Divisions there. The antitank elements shot up five trucks in a convoy, which was attempting to escape from the woods.

The division, whose command post was located in St. Remy-du-Nord, formed a strong *Kampfgruppe* at 0100 hours and gave it the mission of breaking through the line of enemy bunkers north and west of Amfroipret on the northwest tip of the Mormal Woods and throw back the enemy forces west and southwest of Bavai. *Oberst Freiherr* von Funck assumed command of the battle group, which consisted of *Panzer-Regiment 5*, *Kradschützen-Bataillon 3*, the *III./Schützen-Regiment 3*, the *I./Artillerie-Regiment 75*, the *8./Flak-Lehr-Regiment*, the *3.Pionier-Bataillon 39*, and the *1./Panzerjäger-Abteilung 39*.

The armored regiment moved out at 0630 hours and made enemy contact starting at 0744 hours at the western outskirts of Mecquignies. The enemy was ejected there. Two hours later, the line of bunkers at Amfroipret was reached. The armor was then unable to proceed any further. The armored brigade commander, *Oberst* Kühn, directed *Panzer-Regiment 6* forward, which was able to take out two bunkers in its first effort. The 2nd Battalion of that regiment bore the brunt of the fighting, in which *Oberleutnant* Rohrbeck and *Feldwebel* Zipplies distinguished themselves. At 1800 hours, the same battalion stormed the village of Wargnies-le-Grand. After the tanks had passed through the village, the trains vehicles that were following received heavy fire. *Leutnant* Hildebrand raced back to support the trains elements, but his fighting vehicle was knocked out. The *I./Panzer-Regiment 6* then arrived on the battlefield. Together with *Leutnant* Oelrich and his assault detachment, *Hauptmann* Schneider-Kostalski and *Feldwebel* Thiele from the 2nd Company eliminated four enemy bunkers east of Jenlain.

The armored brigade concluded that the elimination of individual bunkers along the line of fortifications was not enough. It was directed that riflemen, antitank elements and *Flak* cannoneers clear the line. The two armored regiments were pulled back. After minor skirmishes, *Panzer-Regiment 5* made it to Preux-au-Sart. The antitank battalion took Orsinval, where the reconnaissance battalion was engaged. The armored brigade was located just southwest of Jenlain that evening and continuing to advance west. In the process, Valenciennes and the heavily fortified Fort Curgies on the right were left alone.

The 12th Company of the rifle regiment, reinforced by engineer elements, was then employed to engage the bunker complex. After a surprise attack failed, a struggle commenced that lasted for hours. By 1800 hours, one platoon of riflemen and two sections of assault engineers were still attempting to put one of the concrete blocks out of commission. The defenders were putting up a tough fight and inflicted heavy losses on the attackers. German medics were constantly on the go. Two medics, *Obergefreiter* Corssen and *Oberschütze* Meyer, were cut down in the performance of their duties. When a platoon from the 11th Company arrived to assist its sister company, the bunkers were finally taken down.

During the fighting, the 3rd Battalion of the rifle regiment was ordered to follow right behind *Panzer-Regiment 6*, which was spreading out into battle formation. The rifle brigade reached the area around Villers-Pol toward 2200 hours with its formations, securing the area, along with the armored brigade, which was also there. The 3rd Battalion of the rifle regiment was employed against the high ground at Mareches, while the regiment's 2nd Battalion screened to the west and *MG-Bataillon 7* to the north. The *6.* and *9./Flak-Regiment 26* were entrusted with protecting the flanks. Behind those formations, the 1st Battalion of the artillery regiment oriented to the right, while the 2nd Battalion trained its guns to the left. The front lines of the rifle brigade were reinforced with *Leutnant* Fechner's *1./Panzer-Regiment 6* and *Hauptmann* von

Versen's *3./Panzerjäger-Abteilung 39*. The badly battered 12th Company remained in reserve. The armored brigade had established a blocking position in front of the division along the creek north of Artes. *Oberstleutnant* Burmeister, the commander of the *II./Panzer-Regiment 6* was in charge of the forces arrayed there, which consisted of the *13./Schützen-Regiment 3*, the *7./Panzer-Regiment 6*, and one platoon each from the *8./Panzer-Regiment 6* and *Panzerjäger-Abteilung 39*.

The mission for the next day had the corps breaking the enemy's resistance in and around the Mormal Woods and then continuing to advance on the de l'Ecaut Canal. The *3. Panzer-Division* had to take the canal running along the line Marly–Denain. To that end, the division formed an advance guard at 0920 hours under the command of *Oberst Freiherr* von Funck, to whom the *II./Schützen-Regiment 3* was still attached.

But by 1145 hours, the corps sent out a directive that all of it was to start marching to the southwest. The *Leibstandarte SS "Adolf Hitler" (mot.)* was directed to assume the division's sector. *SS-Obergruppenführer* Dietrich, the reinforced regiment's commander, arrived at the division command post a few minutes after receipt of the order in order to be briefed.

The division staged its formations for the new operation. Most of the armored brigade, along with the 3rd Battalion of the rifle regiment, the motorcycle infantry battalion, and elements of the divisional artillery screened the reorganization and assembly in the Préseau–Guérenaing–Sommaing area. The advance guard continued to remain in contact with the enemy. Toward noon, the reconnaissance battalion took the enemy's bunkers and positions in the woods east of Préseau. Around 1600 hours, *Leutnant* von Viebahn of the 2nd Troop of the reconnaissance battalion advanced as far as the center of the city of Valenciennes with a dismounted patrol, bringing back valuable information. By then, *Panzer-Regiment 5* had made it to the canal and was able to take the bridge at Thiant intact after hard fighting. In that round of fighting, the 2nd Battalion of the rifle regiment lost four dead and thirteen wounded, including *Oberleutnant* von Kayser and *Leutnant* Dittmer.

At 1630 hours, *Oberstleutnant i.G.* von dem Borne brought the corps movement order. The division was directed to advance to the area around Cambrai. To that end, two march serials were formed, which were to move independently of one another. They were to be prepared to move no later than 1830 hours. The division deliberated whether the bridge that had just been captured at Thiant should be blown up. That measure proved unnecessary, as the *Leibstandarte* elements showed up in time and assumed control of the bridgehead.

Oberstleutnant von Manteuffel led March Group I. The order of march: *Kradschützen-Bataillon 3*; headquarters, *Schützen-Regiment 3*; *1./Pionier-Bataillon 39*; *8./Flak-Lehr-Regiment*; *II./Artillerie-Regiment 75* (minus its 4th Battery); *II./Flak-Regiment 26* (minus its 8th and 9th Batteries); *III./Schützen-Regiment 3*; *I./Artillerie-Regiment 75* (minus its 1st Battery); *Panzerjäger-Abteilung 39*; and *Panzer-Regiment 5*. The route of the march group: Ruesnes–Beaudignies–Neuville–Vendegies–Ovillers and on as far as Beugny, east of Bapaume. The sixty-kilometer route was covered without regard to the enemy. Contact was frequently lost between the units and formations; there were too many destroyed bridges and other obstacles. Since the route led through the battlefields of World War I, individual military cemeteries could occasionally be seen along the sides of the road. The tank companies had an especially tough time of it during the night march, which placed a terrific strain on both personnel and materiel. *Panzer-Regiment 6* suffered the mechanical loss of the following vehicles that night: four *Panzer I's*, two *Panzer II's*, one command tank, three motorcycles, and three trucks.

The field army headquarters issued the following order telephonically at 2100 hours: "*Gruppe Hoth* advances to the right of the line Hesdin–Lillers–Merville. It is sufficient if the line Arras–Vimy Hills–Aire–St. Omer–Gravelines is reached."

On that day, *General der Infanterie* Hoth commanded two armored corps: the *XXXIX Armee-Korps (mot.)*, with the *5.* and *7. Panzer-Divisionen*, the *SS-Totenkopf-Division*, and the *11. Schützen-Brigade*; and the *XVI. Armee-Korps (mot.)*, with the *3.* and *4. Panzer-Divisionen* and the *20. Infanterie-Division (mot.)*.

The division intelligence officer, *Hauptmann* Barth, went forward the next day around 1700 hours to establish contact with the *SS-Totenkopf-Division*. The division also started marching again with its two march groups. Shortly after moving out, reports came in about the appearance of enemy armored forces that were approaching on both sides of the Arras–Bapaume road. The antitank battalion, the *8./Flak-Lehr-Regiment*, and the 1st Company of engineers were immediately employed around Ervilles in defensive positions. The enemy tank attack did not run into the *3. Panzer-Division*, however, and the march continued unimpeded. The men of the divisions saw their first captured British soldiers. Around midnight, the division was in its new rest area.

The twenty-fourth of May was another day of intense activity. From within the sector of *Gruppe Hoth*, the *12. Infanterie-Division* was already at Arras. The *11. Schützen-Brigade* and the *5. Panzer-Division* were fighting. The *4. Panzer-Division* was sent forward through Béthune, while the *SS-Verfügungs-Division*[9] established a bridgehead along the d'Aire–La Bassée Canal and was advancing on St. Vènant. At 0900 hours, the corps ordered the *3. Panzer-Division* to have a reinforced motorized *Kampfgruppe* standing by. Two hours later, it was given orders to take the bridges at Robecq and Busnes.

9. The *SS-Verfügungs-Division*, the first division of what was to later become known as the *Waffen-SS*, was itself later redesignated numerous times, ending the war more famously as the *2. SS-Panzer-Division "Das Reich."*

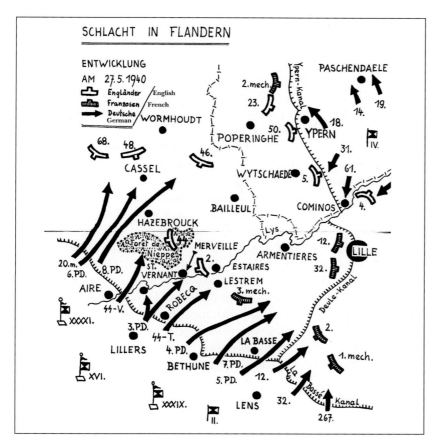

The Battle of Flanders: Development of the Situation on 27 May 1940.

The division gave the mission to the rifle brigade at 1415 hours to take those bridges and then force a crossing over the Lys canal at Merville. The rifle regiment attacked in the direction of the canal with its 1st and 2nd Battalions, reinforced by the antitank battalion and the 1st Battalion of the divisional artillery. The forward observer from the 6th Battery enjoyed great observation over the entire attack sector from the church tower in Busnes. The battalions reached the canal north of Busnes, after stubborn fighting against formations of the British 2nd Infantry Division. The engineers immediately started erecting a bridge, soon allowing the riflemen and antitank elements to cross and advance as far as the northern outskirts of Robecq. English snipers caused a great deal of disruption.

Generalmajor Stumpff then summoned all of his senior commanders to Busnes to explain to them as best he could—he really did not know the reason, as did none of the other major commanders—why Hitler had halted his armored divisions, allowing the English and French field armies time to withdraw their forces and to evacuate Dunkirk. It was assumed by all of the officers of the division—at least that was what was recorded in the daily logs of the intelligence officer—that the enemy would attempt to break out to the south. The La Bassée Canal provided the best natural line of defense for interdicting that attempt. Furthermore, it was assumed that the broken-up terrain of Flanders posed an obstacle to tanks, thus preventing the full mobility and firepower of an armor division from being brought to bear. But even considering that, given the enemy situation, only a rapid pursuit of the enemy could led to victory over the enemy—that much was also recorded in the daily logs.

At 1825 hours, the rifle brigade was surprised to receive the order that the mission to take Merville had been rescinded. The brigade was directed to immediately cease work on the engineer bridge and pull back the elements that had already crossed the canal. Shaking their heads, the officers and enlisted personnel followed those directives. The engineers were allowed to mine the terrain on the far side, however. Once they were done, they also crossed back under covering fire from an antitank platoon.

Under the command of *Oberst* Kleemann, the 1st and 2nd Battalions of the rifle regiment, along with *MG-Bataillon 7*, occupied a deep defensive zone along the canal. All formations were brought back across; only a few combat outposts were left on the far side along a line running Carvin–Les Amusoises. Their mission was to turn back enemy reconnaissance elements but to pull back in the face of superior enemy forces. The divisional engineers prepared all other bridges over the canal for demolition in case of the enemy's approach, after it had taken down its sixteen-ton bridge at Robecq. All boats and watercraft along the canal were destroyed. The engineer platoons of the two rifle battalions built footbridges for the combat outposts. A forward observer from the artillery continued to be posted in the Robecq church tower. The imposing tower was also prepared for demolition. The artillery regiment went into position. All of the vehicles of the division were sent back to the Rieux–Lillers–Cauchy area. The motorcycle infantry battalion, the *8./Flak-Lehr-Regiment* and the 3rd Battalion of the rifle regiment were quartered in the Floringhem–Pernes area and held as a reserve.

The *XVI. Armee-Korps (mot.)* remained on line with its three divisions in the area between Béthune and Lillers. The *SS-Totenkopf-Division* was inserted in the front between the two armored divisions, thus become the right-hand of the *3. Panzer-Division*. The lefthand neighbor was the *SS-Verfügungs-Division*, which was part of the *XXXXI. Armee-Korps (mot.)* of *Panzergruppe Kleist*. Elements of the British 2nd Infantry Division were reported in front of the division's sector.

In general, 26 May was quiet. The division had only a strong battle group from the rifle brigade in position. The weather was poor, with rainy storms sweeping over the fields of Flanders. Fortunately, the first mail arrived from home that day and allowed the soldiers to forget the wind and the rain.

Major Meese's 1st Battalion of the rifle regiment crossed the canal the previous night and encircled Robecq from the east and north. The brigade provided the battalion with additional elements of the 1st Battalion of the artillery regiment, the antitank battalion and the engineer battalion. At 0900 hours, the *Kampfgruppe* attacked the village straight on. The British defended doggedly. A fight developed for every intersection and every house. The enemy machine guns fired from basement windows, roof access doors and every hole in a wall. The riflemen had no other choice but to smoke out each house individually. The 5th Company of the rifle regiment, the engineers and two heavy tanks, which had been brought forward, reported the most success. It was not until 1600 hours, whoever, that Robecq was firmly in German hands.

Two officers and thirty-six enlisted started their journey to Germany as prisoners. They had been assigned to the following formations: The Durham Light Infantry Regiment, the Royal Berkshire Regiment and the Royal Welsh Fusilier regiment (all from the 6th Infantry Brigade). With the exception of the officers, all of the prisoners thought they were going to be summarily executed. That was the reason why they had fought so stubbornly. In addition, the spoils of war for the day included two antitank guns and two mortars. The difficulty in taking Robecq could be measured in the high number of friendly casualties. The 1st Battalion of the rifle regiment had suffered one officer (*Leutnant* Kayser) and sixteen noncommissioned officers and enlisted dead. *Hauptmann* Haspel, *Oberleutnant* Wüst, *Leutnant* Schmittchen, *Leutnant* Dziewas, and twenty-five enlisted personnel were wounded.

The battalion improved its positions within the newly won bridgehead and held it against the immediate counterattacks launched by the British. Some ten heavy tanks, approaching from Estaires, were identified by the riflemen. One of the fighting vehicles was immobilized by mines in front of the positions and was finally put out of commission by well-placed artillery fire.

The division was attached to *Generalleutnant* Reinhart's *XXXXI. Armee-Korps (mot.)*. Reinhart's chief of staff was *Oberstleutnant i.G.* Röttiger. A commander's conference was held at the division command post around 2200 hours. It was directed for the division to move out from the vicinity of its combat outposts in the direction of Merville–Bailleul at 0800 hours on 27 May. To help accomplish that mission, *SS-Infanterie-Regiment (mot.) "Deutschland"*[10] was attached, as was a light artillery battalion, an engineer company, a company from *Heeres-Panzerjäger-Abteilung 521* (with nine 4.7-centimeter self-propelled antitank guns), and a heavy *Flak* battery from *Flak-Regiment 101*.

The division formed two strong attack groups. The *Kampfgruppe* on the right was commanded by *Oberstleutnant* von Manteuffel and consisted of the *III./Schützen-Regiment 3*, the *I./Panzer-Regiment 6*, the *I./Artillerie-Regiment 75*, and *Panzerjäger-Abteilung 39* (minus the 3rd Company). *Kampfgruppe Kleemann* on the left consisted of *MG-Bataillon 7*, the *II./Schützen-Regiment 3*, the *II./Artillerie-Regiment 75*, and the *I./Panzer-Regiment 5*. *Oberst* Kühn's armor brigade was positioned in the southern portions of Lillers and Mensecq to break through once the rifle attack succeeded. The 1st Battalion of the rifle regiment was held at the division's disposal in Robecq.

The rifle battalions that formed the main effort of the attack were staged during the night and early in the morning. *Major* Kratzenberg's 3rd Battalion had his 11th Company on the right, his 13th Company on the left, and the 12th Company and an engineer platoon in reserve. *Hauptmann* Schneider-Kostalski's 2nd Company of *Panzer-Regiment 6* was attached to the

rifle battalion. *Oberleutnant* von Brodowski's and *Feldwebel* Höhe's platoons provided direct support to the 11th Company, while *Oberleutnant Graf* zu Dohna's platoon assisted the 13th Company. *Leutnant* Schneider, *Leutnant* Falkenthal, and *Wachtmeister* Fritz, all from the 1st Battalion of artillery, arrived as fire-support officers. *Leutnant* Kramm of the 2nd Company of the engineer battalion reported in as the leader of an engineer reconnaissance party, whose mission it was to find the best place to erect a sixteen-ton bridge at Merville.

Major Zimmermann's 2nd Battalion, which had been directed to take St. Vénant, positioned its 7th Company on the right and the 8th Company on the left. The 9th Company was inserted into the middle, while the 10th Company was held back. The 2nd Company of *Panzer-Regiment 5* (*Major* Schmidt's 1st Battalion) was attached in support and provided each rifle company with a platoon of tanks.

The division command post moved to the high ground 1.5 kilometers southeast of Burbure at 0730 hours. The *Stuka* attack, which had been requested to start at 0745 hours against the woods at Amont and Moyen, as well as Merville proper, was called off due to the heavy ground fog. A few bombers flew over the friendly lines, but their targets were unknown.

After a short artillery preparation, which provided *Oberst* Kleemann's *Kampfgruppe* with the brunt of its fires, the division's attack started promptly at 0800 hours. The rifle companies, which moved out immediately, made only slow progress in the completely flat terrain. The sparse vegetation provided little concealment and made it easier for the enemy snipers to take aim. The British soldiers stubbornly defended the outskirts of St. Vénant. The 8th Company was being led by *Oberleutnant* von Wallenberg, who had only taken command of the orphaned company two hours previously. Despite the enemy's defensive fires, his riflemen entered the village and fought their way forward along

10. The regiment came from the *SS-Verfügungs-Division*.

the main street between the individual farm-steads in the direction of the railway embankment. The British continued to hold out among the ruins, however, and took every movement under fire. Von Wallenberg was cut down by a burst of machine-gun fire. *Oberleutnant* Müller-Röhrbach's 7th Company had moved out from Busnes in the direction of the water tower in the meantime, but it was only able to gain ground slowly as a result of the enemy's defensive fires. *Leutnant* von Bismarck was badly wounded in that advance and died a short while later of his wounds.

The 8th Company, which was then being led by Leutnant Englisch, did not succeed in reaching the bridge over the canal until around noon. Its elements were joined by elements from the neighboring *SS-Verfügungs-Division*. *Major* Zimmermann immediately employed his 6th Company and advanced through the village with it in order to form a bridgehead. The British elements fighting in the houses along the road leading to Haverskerque were overcome and three officers were taken prisoner. By then, the tanks of *Major* Schmidt and the antitank elements of the 10th Company (*Hauptmann* Zabel) had come forward. Enemy armored cars and fighting vehicles attempted again and again to reduce the bridgehead, which had been reinforced by the 7th Company. It was not until *Unteroffizier* von der Horst and *Gefreiter* Stöcker and their small antitank guns knocked out four tanks and two armored cars that the British gave up their offensive efforts. The battalion had an easier time holding on to its positions after the batteries of the 2nd Battalion of the divisional artillery moved forward to the southern approaches to St. Vénant in the afternoon.

The righthand *Kampfgruppe* of *Oberstleutnant* von Manteuffel was committed directly against Merville, where it not only encountered deep water ditches but also strong resistance. Despite that, the riflemen were in Calonne forty-five minutes after the attack had started. The many drainage ditches that crisscrossed the countryside were difficult to cross. For the crews of the heavy machine guns, the infantry guns,

and the mortars, the heavy clay soil presented a significant obstacle.

The fighting vehicles of the *I./Panzer-Regiment 6* arrived in Calonne starting at 0900 hours. They attempted to get as far as Merville in a *coup de main*. *Hauptmann* Schneider-Kostalski, the commander of the 2nd Company, had a few men from the 11th Company of the rifle regiment mount his tanks. They then thrust into the village. Approaching from the southwest were the medium tanks of *Oberleutnant* von Brodowski and *Oberleutnant Graf* zu Dohna's platoon. One platoon, under the command of *Feldwebel* Biesicke, approached the British airstrip. Acting quickly, it set three machines alight, as well as several trucks and two antitank guns. *Feldwebel* Wolf's platoon eliminated two antitank guns and a fighting vehicle. At that point, the lead elements of the company reached the railway crossing, where it started receiving murderous defensive fires. *Leutnant* von Winterfeld's tank received a direct hit. The tank's turret flew high into the air and landed on the road with a crash. None of the crew survived. There were road obstacles everywhere in Merville that made forward movement impossible. In addition, English machine guns were hammering away from all directions: from the roofs, cellar windows, and house windows. Interspersed were the sounds of British field howitzers that had camouflaged themselves well after going into position off the side of the road and in front of the large memorial. The *2./Panzer-Regiment 6* had a total loss of one more tank in addition to the platoon leader's vehicle. Two other tanks received battle damage. Nonetheless, the company was able to silence six guns. Friendly losses were not inconsiderable. *Oberarzt* Dr. Koch, the battalion surgeon, who had come forward, had his hands full in recovering the wounded. Since the fighting continued to increase in intensity, *Hauptmann* Schneider-Kostalski decided to pull back. The maneuver was successfully supported by fires from the 1st Company, which had reached the Merville battlefield in the meantime.

It had turned noon by then. The sun burned down from the skies in between rain showers. The 1st Battalion of the divisional artillery took Merville under concentric fire, after the tank companies had returned to the outskirts of the town. The 3rd Battalion of the rifle regiment then attacked. The lead company—*Oberleutnant Freiherr* von Werthern's 11th—crossed the railway embankment south of the locality at 1130 hours and entered the town for the second time. The enemy, who could barely be made out, fired on the riflemen like he had before. Once again, there were dead and wounded. The tireless surgeons and medics had no rest that day.

The regiment ordered the bridge to be taken immediately. It had been identified by aerial reconnaissance as being intact. But the British resistance grew from street corner to street corner and from house to house. Although the brave men of the 11th Company made it as far as the northern canal, the drawbridge had been raised there and was apparently rigged with demolitions. The company had to take cover. Likewise, the 13th Company was unable to make any further progress. The company commander, *Hauptmann der Reserve* Dr. Sturm, was badly wounded and died a short while later. Even *Oberleutnant Graf* zu Dohna's tanks were unable to help in any significant fashion. Contact was lost between the two forward companies. The 12th Company, which was sent forward, was finally able to establish a cohesive front after some time. *Oberstleutnant* von Manteuffel decided to call off the attack until such time as the neighboring *SS-Totenkopf-Division* and *Kradschützen-Bataillon 3* had gone around Merville and encircled it.

MG-Bataillon 7 had been able to establish a small bridgehead north of St. Floris at noon. The reconnaissance battalion reached Korbis and advanced with patrols into the d'Amont and Moyen Woods. The attack by the *SS-Verfügungs-Division* was starting to have a positive effect in the sector of the *3. Panzer-Division* around 1500 hours. The *III./SS-Infanterie-Regiment (mot.) "Deutschland"* was in Meurilon and pressing on

La Brianna. The rest of the battalions of that regiment were screening in the direction of Estaires.

The division issued orders to erect a sixteen-ton bridge across the Lys canal south of Le Sart. The 1st Company of the rifle regiment (*Hauptmann* von Plato) succeeded in establishing a bridgehead after a sharp skirmish in the village and then holding it against all attacks. During the operation, the company took forty prisoners and captured or destroyed five trucks, three Cardon-Lloyd tankettes, three infantry guns, and one armored car.

The armored brigade moved across the bridge in order to break the remaining resistance in Merville. *Oberst* von Funck and *Oberstleutnant* von Manteuffel brought their regiments forward to attack. The *II./Panzer-Regiment 6* was attached to *Panzer-Regiment 5* for the attack. *Oberstleutnant* Tröger's motorcycle infantry battalion reinforced the armored regiments. *Leutnant* Panzlaff and his lead platoon from the 3rd Company of the motorcycle infantry established contact with the 3rd Battalion of the rifle regiment around 1845 hours and reached the railway embankment. But the advance of the motorcycle infantry and the tanks then bogged down. The medium tanks were pulled out of the firing line so as to take the village under fire with their 7.5-centimeter main guns. The senselessness of continuing the attack in that pitch-black and rainy night became increasingly clear. Correspondingly, the division ordered its forces to pull back from Merville around 2240 hours.

The division pulled its forces out of the town and established a combat-outpost line along the railway embankment south of Merville–Calonne bridgehead–eastern outskirts of Cornet-Male. It remained in contact with the forces of *SS-Infanterie-Regiment "Deutschland"* along that line. Occupying the forward positions were the *3./Schützen-Regiment 3*, *Kradschützen-Bataillon 3*, the *1./Schützen-Regiment 3*, the *3./Panzer-jäger-Abteilung 39*, and *Heeres-Panzerjäger-Kompanie 527*. The total number of prisoners taken that day amounted to 310 British and 20

French soldiers. The British belonged to active-duty formations, including guards regiments, of the I Corps. Losses within the rifle regiment in dead amounted to 3 officers and 15 enlisted personnel; in wounded, the numbers totaled 5 officers and 66 enlisted personnel.

The corps issued orders that night to repeat the attack the next day. The division's objective was the area around Bailleul. By 0430 hours, the division had established its objective as the high ground southwest of Bailleul. It was to leave Merville alone.

The division moved out at 1000 hours in stormy and rainy weather. Patrols from the 3rd Battalion of the rifle regiment could no longer find any enemy forces in Merville, with the exception of the area around the church, where a few prisoners were taken. Correspondingly, the battalion moved immediately into the town, supported by the 4th Company of *Panzer-Regiment 6* (*Hauptmann* Weiß). It moved through the town and then established contact with *MG-Bataillon 7* and *SS-Infanterie-Regiment "Deutschland"* just east and north of Merville. *Panzer-Regiment 6* then screened from the northern portion of the town with its 1st Battalion and the western portion with its 2nd Battalion. The reconnaissance and motorcycle infantry battalions marched forward on foot due to the intractable mud and the continuously misting rains. The motorcycle infantry were able to establish a bridgehead at St. Tournant at 1200 hours, while the reconnaissance elements made it to the northern edge of the Hamont Woods.

At 1330 hours, the corps ordered the division to transition to the defense, since it was feared the British were going to launch an immediate counterattack. That did not materialize, and three hours later, a new attack was ordered for 1800 hours. The enemy was still holding out in the Lestrem–Estaires area and was making life difficult for the *SS-Verfügungs-Division*. That also did not materialize, since the division was reattached to the *XVI. Armee-Korps (mot.)* at 1900 hours, after the attack had been postponed for an hour. A commanders' conference was held two hours later at the *Generalmajor* Stumpff's command post. The division commander announced the plans for the next day. After the 1st Company of the division engineers built a sixteen-ton bridge at Merville, the division would attack with all of its forces.

The British were very active with their artillery that night. The harassment fires caused unwelcome unrest among the companies that were screening and also caused a few casualties. A direct hit slammed into the positions of the 5th Battery of artillery. The British fires were intended to cover the retrograde movements of their own forces. When patrols entered Neuf-Berquin the next morning, they found it to be clear of the enemy.

The division then started its advance at 1100 hours. *General* Hoepner had visited the command post just prior to that and indicated for the first time that the corps might be pulled out of the attack frontage. The reinforced rifle brigade bore the brunt of the attack that day, while most of the armor brigade was held in the previously reached area awaiting the opportunity to follow up once the riflemen had gained sufficient ground. The objective of *Kampfgruppe Kleemann* was the line La Doulieu–La Couranne; that of the armored regiments was the high ground south of Meteren.

The rifle brigade employed the 3rd Battalion of the rifle regiment on the right and *MG-Bataillon 7* on the left. The 2nd Battalion of the rifle regiment was positioned behind the machine-gun battalion, with the motorcycle infantry battalion echeloned to the left rear. Both of the lead battalions received a company of light tanks from *Panzer-Regiment 6* and a company of antitank elements. The 1st Battalion of the divisional artillery was directed to support the advance of the first assault group. *Leutnant* Fechner's 1st Company of the armored regiment was attached to the righthand group, with *Leutnant* Hilpert, *Leutnant* Falkenthal, *Leutnant* Buhrmann, *Leutnant* von Stosch, *Wachtmeister* Schwarz, and *Wachtmeister* Tschechamowski functioning as forward observers for the artillery.

The 3rd Battalion advanced through Neuf-Berquin without encountering the enemy and moved as far as north and east of Le Doulieu. The machine-gun battalion crossed the railway embankment to the north of Vieux-Berquin, and the reconnaissance battalion moved beyond that as far as Bailleul. The sectors of the companies employed kept getting narrower. The continuing reduction of the pocket around the English and French forces was unmistakably noticeable.

At 1645 hours, the corps headquarters issued orders not to cross the Bailleul–Meteren road any longer. The lead elements of the *6. Armee* had already advanced past the lead elements of the *XVI. Armee-Korps (mot.)*, advancing from the south. Correspondingly, the rifle brigade set up a screening line along a line running two kilometers outside of Bailleul–Outersteene–Meteren. The machine-gun battalion remained on the left wing, followed by the 2nd and 3rd Battalions of the rifle regiment and then the reconnaissance battalion. The 1st Battalion of the rifle regiment was positioned behind the reconnaissance battalion as a backstop, and it was also sent to the area around Pacaut, south of Merville, to conduct clearing operations. The rear-area services of the division were allowed to close up at that point. *Hauptmann Graf* Plauen's 2nd Maintenance Company set up shop in Lillers and, along with other elements of the division support command, confiscated a shoe factory with 3,000 pairs of shoes, a sugar factory with 100 tons of ready-to-consume sugar and a large fuel depot at the rail station.

On the evening of 29 May, the division had its forward combat outposts six kilometers from the French-Belgian border and fifteen kilometers outside of Ypern. That was the hotly contested battlefield of World War I, dominated in the distance by Kemmel Mountain.

Another phase of the campaign was over for the division. It then moved south from the positions it had taken and occupied rest areas in the vicinity of Aire–Pernes–Busnes. Most of the brigades remained in quarters, but the motorcy-cle infantry battalion, the reconnaissance battalion, and the 1st Battalion of the rifle regiment were employed clearing the area of the enemy between the Lys, Aire, and La Bassée Canals. The division command was moved from the mill in Calonne to Isbergues.

The next few days passed without any serious incidents, although the maintenance and repair companies and facilities could not complain about a lack of work. The riflemen, cannoneers, engineers, and radio operators got their uniforms cleaned up. The two division chaplains, Heidland and Laub, held field services and set up memorials for the fallen. The division's musical elements performed at village squares and helped raise the spirits of the many refugees who had taken up provisional quarters in barns and outbuildings.

Generalmajor Stumpff held a commanders' conference on 2 June, in which the movement of the division to the south and along the Somme was discussed. The orders for that movement had arrived from the corps the previous day. The division intelligence officer, *Hauptmann* Barth, went with *Leutnant* von dem Knesebeck and *Sonderführer* (translator) Winkin to the headquarters of *Panzergruppe Kleist*. From there, they went on to the *33. Infanterie-Division* of *Generalmajor* Sintzenich, in whose sector the future operations of the division were to take place. The infantry division was positioned in a bridgehead at Péronne, facing the French 19th Infantry Division. The French division was holding the localities south of the Somme with strong forces.

Starting at 2100 hours, the division moved south from its previous quartering area along to march routes. The movement led through St. Pol, Arras, and Bapaume and the broad and open terrain with its young stands of woods, ripening wheat fields, and many military cemeteries from World War I in the area north of the Somme. The division headquarters set up in Le Transloy and the armored and rifle brigades in the area around Péronne. The leader of the division support command, *Major* Haker—promoted to that rank on 2

June—brought up his sections behind the combat formations as soon as possible. All of the ammunition for the light howitzers was unloaded at Maurepas. *Oberfeuerwerker*[11] Kaulfers looked for ammunition distribution points, while the supply columns under *Leutnant Graf* Asseburg continued on to St. Quentin to pick up more ammunition. *Panzer-Regiment 6* sent a detail to Mons to pick up the following new vehicles for the regiment: thirteen *Panzer I's*, seven *Panzer III's*, and one *Panzer IV*. The maintenance and repair companies worked ceaselessly to maintain weapons and equipment in a combat-ready status.

11. An ordnance specialist equivalent in rank to *Feldwebel*.

An engineer bridge over the Meuse at Maastricht. The *3. Panzer-Division* used it in its march west.

The first captured Belgians are led back.

Attack on the Gette on 13 May 1940.

Orp le Grand has been taken.

Shot-up French fighting vehicles on the streets of Jauche after the fighting.

Forming up for the attack on the Dyle Position on 14 May 1940.

Along the edge of the woods in front of the Dyle Position.

The advance continues—the men of the *5./Schützen-Regiment 3* are proud of their achievements.

Discussing the situation on 27 May 1940. From left to right: *Major* Kratzenberg, *Oberstleutnant* von Manteuffel, and *Assistenzarzt* Dr. Türk.

The final minutes before the attack. From left to right: *Hauptmann* Orts, *Major* Schmidt-Ott, *Major* Kratzenberg, and *Oberleutnant Freiherr* von Werthern.

Attack on Merville: *Major* Kratzenberg leads his *III./Schützen-Regiment 3*. Next to him is *Leutnant* Lange. In the black *Panzer* uniform is *Hauptmann* Schneider-Kostalski of *Panzer-Regiment 6*.

Entering Merville across the blown-up bridge.

Antitank elements in Robecq.

Captured British soldiers in Merville.

The armored brigade stages around Péronne.

CHAPTER 5

From the Somme to the South of France

The second part of the campaign in the West started for the *3. Panzer-Division* on 4 June 1940. On that day, the division reached its staging area west and northwest of Péronne with all of its elements. Once again, it was attached to the *XVI. Armee-Korps (mot.)*, along with the *4. Panzer-Division*. In contrast to the attack on 10 May, however, it would be employed in the first wave this time, while the sister division would remain behind to the northeast of Péronne.

The division commander, *Generalmajor* Stumpff, and his operations officer, *Major i.G.* von dem Borne, were busy preparing their operations order for the next day. The logistics situation was discussed by the division logistics officer, *Hauptmann i.G.* Krasá; the division support commander, *Major* Haker; the division armaments officer, *Hauptmann* Hein; and *Oberleutnant* Gesenger. The commanders of the two brigades and the divisional troops established contact on 4 June with the elements already at the front, in order to be briefed on the situation and terrain.

At 1700 hours, the division issued orders for the occupation of the assembly area, which would be conducted the next night. According to the order, the main body of the division would move across the Somme into the bridgehead, while weak elements and the majority of the vehicles would remain north of the river. The division inserted itself into a narrow area between the *33. Infanterie-Division* on the left and the *44. Infanterie-Division* on the right. Previously occupying the new divisional sector was *Oberst* Fuchs's *Infanterie-Regiment 104* of the former infantry division. Its sector ran a line running Dompierre–Assevillers–north of Belloy.

The following formations were attached to the division in support for the new offensive: the *II./Flak-Lehr-Regiment*, the *9.(H)/Lehrgeschwader 2*,[1] *schwere Panzerjäger-Abteilung 605*,[2] *Nebel-Abteilung 1*,[3] *MG-Bataillon 7*, and an additional heavy *Flak* battalion.

The division started organizing for the operation at 1900 hours and established two *Kampfgruppen*. The righthand group, in the Dompierre–Becquincourt area, consisted of *Infanterie-Regiment 104* (with two battalions), the *1./Pionier-Bataillon 39*, and the heavy *Flak* battalion. The second group, in the Asseviliers area, was comprised of the *III./Schützen-Regiment 3*, *MG-Bataillon 7*, *Panzerjäger-Abteilung 605*, the *II./Infanterie-Regiment 104*, and reconnaissance parties from the *2. Pionier-Bataillon 39*. The divisional artillery sent all of its batteries across the Somme. The armored brigade was also represented there with *Panzer-Regiment 5* on the right and *Panzer-Regiment 6* on the left. The division's antitank battalion was brought forward to the vicinity of the village of Herbécourt, as was the 1st Battalion of the rifle regiment. The *II./Flak-Lehr-Regiment* and elements of the signals battalion crossed the river, while all of the remaining elements of the division remained north of the river. The division command post was moved forward across the river to Buscourt by 0400 hours.

The operations plan of the German Army High Command for the second part of the campaign envisioned *Heeresgruppe B* moving out for the offensive from its positions on the lower course of the Somme on 5 June, with the objective of occupying northern and northwest France. It was intended for *Heeresgruppe A* to advance to the southeast in the direction of the Swiss Alps on 9 June, with the objective of encircling the French field armies in the Vosges Mountains and along the Maginot Line. Depending on how the situation developed, *Heeresgruppe C* was to break through the Maginot Line frontally at an appropriate time.

The armored divisions were once again to be employed as the main effort of the offensive. *General* von Kleist's armored group was to support the attack of *Heeresgruppe B*, with the 5. and 7. *Panzer-Divisionen* west of Amiens, the 9. and 10. *Panzer-Divisionen* to both sides of Amiens, and the 3. and 4. *Panzer-Divisionen* in the area around Péronne. *General* Guderian's armored group, consisting of the *1., 2., 6.,* and *8. Panzer-Divisionen*, was to initially stand by on the Aisne as part of *Heeresgruppe A*.

The night of 4–5 June passed relatively quickly. As the new day started to dawn, it promised to be sunny and warm. Around 0300 hours, the French suddenly fired several artillery missions on Asseviliers. The lead combat outposts had fired green signal flares on orders of the division in an effort to draw out enemy fire. That was intended to give the forward observers opportunity to identify the enemy batteries. The hands of the clock moved slowly forward . . .

Right at 0500 hours, 384 guns of all calibers sent their fiery greetings across to the French positions, villages and road network from along a frontage of ten kilometers. At the same time, the squadrons and groups of bombers and *Stukas* rushed through the air to drop their deadly loads on Estrées-Deniecourt, Ablaincourt, and Chaulnes. The battle had started.

When the artillery fires started, the riflemen, infantry, engineers, and tanks moved out to exploit those fires and get as close as possible to the enemy lines. The fighting vehicles of the two armored regiments soon passed the riflemen and

---

1. This was a *Luftwaffe* short-range reconnaissance squadron: 9th Squadron (Army) of the 2nd Instructional Wing.

2. This was a separate heavy antitank battalion. At the time of the campaign, it had three batteries of four 8.8-centimeter antitank guns each.

3. *Lexikon* lists the battalion's designation as *Nebelwerfer-Abteilung 1* by this time. It was initially equipped with the *Nebelwerfer 35*, a 10-centimeter mortar, designed primarily to deliver smoke and chemical munitions, but also capable of firing high-explosive rounds. It was in the latter capacity that the weapon system was used most often. Later on, the German Army had multiple-barrel rocket launcher systems developed, which were used to the end of the war to good effect.

moved without stopping in and over the initial enemy trenches.

The lead elements of the armored brigade had already crossed the Villers–Estrées road west of Villers at 0540 hours. They went around the village of Estrées and, twenty minutes later, were rolling along the "Roman road" at Estrées-Deniecourt. The 4th Company of *Panzer-Regiment 6*, leading the columns, received heavy artillery fire, causing it to stop for the first time and also causing some losses. The French batteries were identified as being on the northern edge of the woods at Chaulnes and at the southwest outskirts of Ablaincourt. It appeared that the friendly fires that had been fired there earlier had had no visible effect.

The crews of the fighting vehicles were imbued with the "spirit of the attack" and continued to roll on, disregarding the enemy's fires. Just before 0630 hours, *Panzer-Regiment 6* reached Démécourt. It was greeted there by heavy artillery fire, which caused the companies to scatter. The enemy's batteries were firing at the tanks from unidentified positions at Berny-en-Santerre. Both of the armored regiments continued their advance through the French lines. By 0850 hours, *Panzer-Regiment 5* had crossed the Chilly–Hallu road, soon reaching the high ground south of Hallu and north of Fransart.

The enemy batteries recognized the danger they were in and started placing well-aimed interdiction fires on the tanks. The attack of the armored brigade increasingly dissolved into individual engagements by the companies. The 2nd Company of *Panzer-Regiment 6* turned on the first enemy battery northwest of Berny and silenced the 7.5-centimeter guns. *Feldwebel* Kannenberg's 3rd Platoon was especially successful, knocking out three guns on its own.

Oberstleutnant Freiherr von Funck's *Panzer-Regiment 5* was able to break through all of the enemy positions and advance directly towards Chaulnes through the woods. *Oberstleutnant* von Lewinski's *Panzer-Regiment 6*, moving on the left, advanced past Ablaincourt with its 2nd Battalion in the lead. Another three enemy bat-

teries were eliminated. The heaviest resistance was encountered north of Pressoir. The enemy artillery fire forced *Panzer-Regiment 6* to split up and sidestep to the south. In the 4th Company of the regiment, *Gefreiter* Moritz's light tank was knocked out. The crew was able to dismount and make its way back to a defile, where wounded from differing companies had assembled. They set up an all-round defense and held out there the entire day.

The *4./Panzer-Regiment 6* approached Chaulnes. The 1st Company of the regiment cleared the wooded terrain and eliminated two enemy antitank guns. The two companies then attacked west of the locality. The 4th Company overran an enemy battery with its heavy tanks. In the course of the fighting there, four friendly fighting vehicles were lost, with ten tankers being wounded. *Oberleutnant Graf* zu Dohna was among them; one of his arms was shot off. Two hours after the start of the attack, the tanks were far to the enemy's rear and between his artillery positions. But where were the riflemen?

Initially, those two battle groups had been able to follow the tanks rapidly. But when they got to the first built-up areas, they started receiving murderous defensive fires, which caused the attack to bog down. The Weygand Line did have its strengths. The French forces had established positions south of the Somme that placed their main efforts on the villages and towns. They were well fortified and interconnected with the other villages by means of trenches, thus creating a small system of fortifications. The defense was organized along a narrow frontage and in depth. Its mission was to allow the German tanks to pass and take on the following infantry.

Major Kratzenberg's 3rd Battalion of the rifle regiment received antitank and machine-gun fires from Estrées. The attackers had to go to ground. Only *Leutnant* Alter and his 13th Company were able to swing out to the east and enter the first few houses of the village. But then Alter's men also got bogged down in the ruins and could barely lift their heads. The French were firing at the slightest movement. *Haupt-*

mann Orts's 12th Company got bogged down on the western outskirts of the village and was unable to move a single meter farther. The battalion was being hit by intense fires from the flanks and rear that were coming from Fay and the woods to its south. The battalion's frontage was more than 1,800 meters at that point. The two companies lost all contact with one another. Finally, the 11th Company of *Oberleutnant Freiherr* von Werthern was able to plug the gap between the two in a provisional way. By then, the riflemen had run out of steam. Neither of the two engineer platoons of *Leutnant* Ziegenbalg and *Leutnant* Weigel was able to provide relief. The only perceptible relief came from the fires of the 4th Battery of the divisional artillery, which were directed by the two forward observers, *Leutnant* Graf and *Leutnant* Braun, and caused some damage to the enemy. The *II./Infanterie-Regiment 104* was able to close to within 600 meters of the outskirts of Estrées, but it was also forced to ground.

The attack of the other battalions of the rifle brigade also got held up by the strong enemy resistance. For instance, *Hauptmann* Hansen's brave *MG-Bataillon 7* was employed against Belloy. Although the companies reached the initial houses, they soon became decisively engaged in casualty-intensive street fighting.

Infanterie-Regiment 104, which was advancing on the right, worked its way with some difficulty to Fay and entered the village shortly after 0700 hours with its lead elements. The French also defended there with doggedness and determination and an unflappable will to fight. Hard-fought close combat developed, which eventually ejected the German infantry from the village. The antitank elements that were following were likewise unable to accomplish much of anything. Although the two assault groups of *Leutnant* Prause and *Feldwebel* Wiemer brought some relief, they also suffered heavy casualties. All of Wiemer's men were cut down by machine-gun fire.

The armored regiments reached their attack objectives by 1100 hours and continued to advance. The 1st Battalion of *Panzer-Regiment 6* turned to the southwest and moved on Hattencourt, receiving heavy fire from there. It had to take up a defensive posture, oriented to the south. When information arrived that a few scattered fighting vehicles and wounded were holding out east of Chaulnes, the regiment ordered their relief. The regimental liaison officer, *Oberleutnant* Suhr, moved there with the last two tanks of the light platoon, but his vehicle was knocked out. Despite that, the stranded crew was able to assault a French machine-gun position along the eastern outskirts of Chaulnes and then use the captured weapon to stop a French truck. The resourceful *Oberleutnant* then used the truck to get to the encircled comrades. *Oberleutnant* Schaary's tank, which was also headed there, was likewise knocked out. *Oberleutnant* von Kiekebusch suffered the same fate an hour later. Despite the fact that the tankers were surrounded by superior enemy numbers, they did not give up. Instead, they conducted energetic immediate counterattacks and were even able to take 120 French prisoners, before they finally boxed their way through to the neighboring *4. Panzer-Division*.

By noon on that first day of the offensive, the armored brigade was far ahead of the division and in the midst of the enemy. Contact had long since been lost with the riflemen. Fuel and ammunition were running out. *Oberst* Kühn ordered his forces to set up security on both sides of Hallu. Although a few rifle and motorized elements attempted to force their way forward to the tanks, they were always turned back by the French fires from the fortified villages. Only the adjutant of *Panzer-Regiment 6*, *Oberleutnant* Markowski, succeeded in reaching his regiment after several attempts through enemy fire coming from Chaulnes and Omiécourt.

The commander of the *I./Panzer-Regiment 6*, *Major* Schmidt-Ott, attempted to rejoin his companies in Hattencourt. In the process, his tank come off the roadway and landed in a tank ditch. But the tank did not land on earth and stones; instead, it slammed against steel walls. There was another German fighting vehicle in the ditch, which was anywhere from three to four meters deep. Unfortunately for Schmidt-Ott, the tank commander of the other tank was his own adjutant, *Leutnant* von Twardowski. *Feldwebel* Thévoz, who had been following behind, recognized the unfortunate situation his commander had gotten into. He moved forward in his heavy tank to assist the two officers. The enemy artillery also seemed to have identified the unfortunate situation. Just as the *Feldwebel* was starting to recover his commander, the rounds landed. Thévoz was wounded. In the end, however, all the efforts were crowned with success. A second heavy tank was able to recover the two tanks of the officers and their crews.

As it started to turn evening that fifth of June, the armored brigade from Berlin had turned open the French front and broken through. The victory cost dearly. Eleven noncommissioned officers and enlisted personnel of *Panzer-Regiment 6* were killed; another three officers and twenty-seven enlisted personnel were wounded. Tank losses totaled eleven *Panzer I's*, thirteen *Panzer II's*, five *Panzer III's*, one *Panzer IV*, and one small command tank.

The commander of the armored brigade, *Oberst* Kühn—promoted to *Generalmajor* after the campaign in the West—later received the Knight's Cross to the Iron Cross for the actions of his two regiments that day. Part of the award recommendation read: "on 5 June, the brigade penetrated the stubbornly defended Weygand Line southwest of Péronne to a depth of fifteen kilometers and destroyed fourteen French batteries, including three heavy ones, thus eliminating their fires. That brought about decisive relief for the further attack and breakthrough."

The commanding general of the *XVI. Armee-Korps (mot.)*, *General* Hoepner, arrived at the division command post two hours after the start of the attack on 5 June, wanting to be briefed on the status of the advance. The commanding general ordered that the division was to reconnoiter as far as the area around Roye that same day. So that the division would not have to bear the brunt of the fighting, Hoepner declared he intended to bring up the *4. Panzer-Division* ahead of time and insert it into the fighting to the left of the *3. Panzer-Division*.

The employment of the *5. Panzer-Brigade* of the *4. Panzer-Division* on the high ground northwest of Etalon began to be felt in the division's sector starting at 1100 hours. The regiments of the *4. Panzer-Division* were employed south of Flauciourt and east of Ablaincourt against the high ground around Chaulnes in an effort to exploit the success of the *3. Panzer-Brigade* and to rally forward the *33.* and *44. Infanterie-Divisionen*, whose offensive efforts had stalemated.

What was the division's rifle brigade doing at noon?

The sun was burning hot from the almost cloudless skies and made things even more difficult for the riflemen hunched over in the cornfields, meadowland depressions and blown-up walls of houses. The enemy resistance had not slackened in the least and had brought the attack between the villages to a standstill. A few officers and noncommissioned officers attempted to lead the forces forward, but the French fires kept pinning the assaulting forces. The brave commander of the 13th Company of the rifle regiment, *Leutnant* Alter, was killed while undertaking just such an effort. *Leutnants* Wördemann and Wietbrock of the regiment were likewise killed that day. The 3rd Company of the divisional engineers also suffered heavy casualties.

The battalion surgeons and medics had no shortage of work. The division surgeon, *Oberstarzt* Dr. Böhm, established his main clearing station with one of his medical companies at the western outskirts of Buscourt. The two ambulance platoons of the division were constantly on the go to pick up wounded from the forward clearing stations. The battalion surgeon of the 3rd Battalion of the rifle regiment, *Stabsarzt* Dr. Marr, had already dressed 100 wounded from his battalion by noon. *Oberstabsarzt* Dr. Grünewald and his medical company also worked ceaselessly.

Early in the afternoon, *MG-Bataillon 7* achieved the sole visible success of the rifle brigade that day. *Hauptmann* Hansen and his small band of soldiers were hard pressed for some time and, indeed, some of his elements were encircled, but the Saxons were finally able to rally and occupy Belloy around 1430 along with a few attached light tanks from *Panzer-Regiment 5*. The prisoners taken from the French 117th Infantry Regiment numbered 450.

The artillery was called to help the hard-pressed rifle formations. *Oberst* Forster used all available batteries to support the rifle brigade. *Leutnant* Hoffmann's 1st Battery and *Oberleutnant* Kersten's 6th Battery were pushed forward as close as possible to Estrées-Deniecourt and fired over open sights into the twin villages, setting them alight. *Leutnant* Leese, the forward observer, was wounded; he was immediately replaced by *Leutnant* Schröder to ensure there was no lull in the firing.

Toward 1600 hours, the batteries all placed concentrated fires on Estrées. *Major* Kratzenberg's 3rd Battalion stormed into the village while the rounds were still impacting. It was finally taken in close combat. *Major* Meese's 1st Battalion, which had been brought forward after noon, supported its sister battalion in its efforts. The 2nd Company attacked Estrées from the front, while *Leutnant* Hilliger's 3rd Company screened in the direction of Fay. Kratzenberg and his tireless men continued their assault and occupied the high ground south of the village. Only the 12th Company remained behind in the destroyed village, eliminating the final enemy resistance by the onset of darkness. In that round of fighting, 700 prisoners were taken.

Major Zimmermann's 2nd Battalion was then inserted into the line to the left of the 3rd Battalion so as to reinforce the position that had been taken. *Infanterie-Regiment 104* also fought its way slowly forward in the face of heavy enemy fire in the direction of Fay. *Oberst* Fuchs, who was a shining example to his men, would be killed in combat two weeks later.

Around 1830 hours, the division ordered that contact be established with the armored brigade far to the front, which was defending against strong enemy forces. The battalions that had previously been held in reserve—the reconnaissance battalion, the motorcycle infantry battalion, and *Panzerjäger-Abteilung 605*—were brought forward to surge past Pressoir and Chaulnes. The armored brigade was ordered to pull back to Chaulnes, since the *44. Infanterie-Division* to the right had had to pull back from terrain it had taken in the face of enemy forces that had proven to be too strong. As a result, a gap had developed between the two divisions.

Since the situation was growing increasingly critical, the division reinforced the *Kampfgruppe* that was being sent forward with the 1st Battalion of the rifle regiment and the 2nd Battalion of the divisional artillery (*Major* Wöhlermann). All of the formations were then placed under the command of *Oberstleutnant* von Manteuffel. The reinforced *Kampfgruppe* moved out at 2100 hours. Shortly after moving out, the lead elements, composed of the reconnaissance battalion and the 1st Battalion of the rifle regiment, encountered heavy infantry and artillery fire coming from Ablaincourt. Elements of the 1st Battalion fought their way into the village under extremely difficult circumstances by 2230 hours. But the enemy resistance was too great, and *Oberstleutnant* von Manteuffel decided to pull his entire force back to Hill 105 and screen from there for the rest of the night.

The armored brigade found itself alone in the area it had taken around Hallu, where it set up an all-round defense. Since the fuel had run out and the ammunition had been practically shot up, the men of the two armored regiments had to rely on their small arms and hold their positions until the rifle brigade could close up the next day.

The troops of *Major Freiherr* von Wechmar's reconnaissance battalion started moving out against at 0500 hours. *Oberstleutnant* von Manteuffel followed a short while later with the rest of the *Kampfgruppe*. The riflemen encountered the French positions at Ablaincourt and Pressoir. The 1st Battalion of the rifle regiment succeeded in taking both villages by 0615 hours. In the process, it took 295 prisoners and captured two antitank guns and a few trucks. The advance then continued relentlessly.

The armored brigade was aware of the rapid advance and put together all of its vehicles that could still move and entered the fray. The fight was especially hard around Chaulnes, which had been reduced to rubble by artillery and *Stuka* attacks. The armored brigade was able to take several hundred prisoners on its own, before *Kampfgruppe Manteuffel* arrived there. *Leutnant* von Quast and his reconnaissance platoon from the 2nd Battalion of *Panzer-Regiment 6* was the first one through to the encircled tankers. When the young officer later tried to bring up the combat trains, he was killed at Omiécourt.

The eastern part of Chaulnes was still being stubbornly defended by the enemy. The riflemen did not give up; they started attacking the French strong-points at 0900 hours. The fierce fighting in the village lasted three hours, before the enemy was finally cleared out of it. The enemy lost 5 officers and 150 men as prisoners. Four antitank guns, four 7.5-centimeter guns, eight machine guns, twenty trucks, and twelve staff cars were the spoils of war. All by themselves, *Leutnant* Doerner, *Unteroffizier* Ulrich, and *Gefreiter* Borgmann—all from the headquarters of the rifle regiment—were able to take an enemy battalion staff with four officers and forty enlisted prisoners at the southern outskirts of Chaulnes.

The streets of the village were littered with military equipment of all types. Among the many guns were shot-up vehicles, crates and boxes with uniforms, equipment, radio sets and ammunition and dead horses and soldiers. Worthy of note were the many defensive measures. In the second floor of a house, there was a heavy machine gun on the side that was on the main street and faced the attacker's direction. It had excellent fields of fire between the two houses across the street and into the open ground outside of Chaulnes. There was an antitank gun at

an intersection. It was well protected by sandbags and wooden beams. It had been emplaced in a slightly raised gateway and had good fields of fire to all sides. In the vicinity of the destroyed rail station and in the many gardens, there were dugouts for the riflemen. It was not only the actions of the enemy, but also the defensive system that he had established that showed that the French wanted to stem the Germans at the Weygand Line.

The reconnaissance battalion did not allow itself to be held up in its advance by the fighting in Chaulnes. Around 0930 hours, it reached the lead elements of the armored brigade. *Major Freiherr* von Wechmar reported to the commander of the 2nd Battalion of *Panzer-Regiment 5*. Physical contact had been reestablished with the armored brigade for the first time in twenty-four hours.

While the armored regiments refueled and rearmed, *Kampfgruppe Manteuffel* kept advancing. The reconnaissance battalion was sent in the direction of Hattencourt. The remaining elements of the battle group were south of a line running Chilly–Hallu early in the afternoon of 6 June. *Oberstleutnant* Tröger's motorcycle infantry battalion screened to the south and southwest outside of Hattencourt, while the *II./Infanterie-Regiment 104* screened west from the western outskirts of Chaulnes. Both battalions of the divisional artillery were pushed forward and employed in the area around Chaulnes.

The field army inserted the *SS-Verfügungs-Division* next to the *3. Panzer-Division*, since the *44. Infanterie-Division* was hanging back and the division's right flank was "hanging in the air." Up to that point, that area had been screened against the strong enemy strongpoints by *Infanterie-Regiment 104* and the 3rd Battalion of the rifle regiment.

The division could not give the battered enemy any chance to recover if it wanted to exploit the breakthrough it had achieved. Correspondingly, all combat-capable elements of the division moved out in blazing heat that afternoon to initiate the pursuit in the direction of

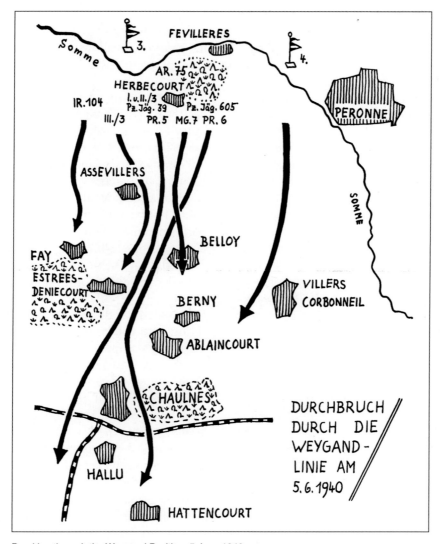

Breaking through the Weygand Position, 5 June 1940.

Avre. The armored brigade was in the lead again, with *Panzer-Regiment 5* on the right and *Panzer-Regiment 6* on the left. Following it was *Kampfgruppe Manteuffel* with the motorcycle infantry battalion on the right and both the 1st Battalion of the rifle regiment and *Panzerjäger-Abteilung 605* on the left. The artillery regiment covered the advance from new positions around Chaulnes. On the left wing, the 1st Company of the rifle regiment took Fransart from the east. The regiment's 2nd Company, supported by attached antitank-gun platoons, attacked at the same time from the north. The fighting for the heavily defended village was not decided, however, until the 3rd Company entered the fray. Two hundred thirty-five French soldiers were captured.

Panzer-Regiment 5 moved through Fransart around 1800 hours and continued advancing south. It reached Fresnoy and a line running Roye–Goyencourt. *Oberleutnant* Buchterkirch from *Panzer-Regiment 6* conducted combat reconnaissance as far as Avregrund, near St. Mard. The reconnaissance battalion, racing ahead, was able to reach the banks of the Avre with most of its troops just after 2000 hours and take the undamaged bridge at St. Aurin.

The enemy had recognized the danger posed by the breakthrough and employed his air force to prevent the armored brigade from crossing the river. Some painful casualties were taken. The 2nd and 5th Companies of the rifle regiment lost three dead and fifteen wounded. But it was no longer possible for the enemy aircraft to hold up the attack.

At 2020 hours, *Panzer-Regiment 5* crossed the Avre at Villers-les-Roys; *Panzer-Regiment 6* crossed at St. Mard. The motorcycle infantry battalion was sent forward as rapidly as possible to support the armored regiments. *Oberleutnant* Beck's 3rd Company, along with the heavy-machine-gun platoon of the 4th Company, was able to cross the river at L'Echelle. *Major* Meese's 1st Battalion of the rifle regiment reached the high ground south of St. Mard and started screening south. *Panzer-Regiment 5*, *Kradschützen-Bataillon 3*, and *Aufklärungs-Abteilung 3 (mot.)* rapidly formed a bridgehead in a line running L'Echelle–St. Aurin. The rifle regiment, which closed up later, assumed the screening mission in that area, with the riflemen continuing to improve the positions until midnight.

The motorcycle infantry battalion was positioned in the righthand portion of the sector; the 1st Battalion of the rifle regiment was on the left. The 2nd Battalion of the rifle regiment was pushed forward during the first few hours of darkness from Parvillers to Villers-les-Roys, where it was employed to the right of the 1st Battalion. All of the battalions sent out patrols to the nearby villages of Marquivillers, Dancourt and Lancourt. It was determined that all were occupied by the enemy.

The daily report of the division contained the following: "*3. Panzer-Division* took Chaulnes, Hattencourt, and Fresnoy on 6 June, crossing the Avre and then screening with its lead elements in the direction of the line formed by the villages of Marquivillers, Dancourt and Lancourt. The localities are occupied by the enemy

and most likely improved to strong-points like the previous localities in the Weygand Line. It is anticipated that additional enemy artillery will appear . . ."

The spoils of war for that day, captured or destroyed, numbered eight to nine batteries, four thirty-two-ton tanks, and five aircraft. The number of prisoners was in the neighborhood of 3,000 men from the French 19th and 29th Infantry Divisions.

That success would never have been possible had it not been for the logistics personnel, who performed their duties in a quiet and modest but conscientious fashion. Their story is rarely told. The daily logs of the division support command recorded the events of 6 June as follows:

Based on a discussion with the division logistics officer, the headquarters and the supply company will be moved to Ham-Monacu. Movement orders were issued to the units. Departure at 1000 hours. As a consequence of the rapid advance, it is anticipated the 1st Maintenance Company may move. The 1st Maintenance Company reported it would need thirty-six hours to clear its workload. At 1130 hours, message traffic arrived, according to which two sections of ammunition needed to be sent to Chaulnes immediately. To that end, the 2nd and 3rd Truck Sections (Light) were dispatched. . . . At 1200 hours, radioed orders arrived for two fuel sections to be pushed forward to Ablaincourt immediately. The 8th and 9th Truck Sections (Heavy), as well as the 7th Truck Section (Light), continued their march. The units reached their march objectives in a seamless movement, with only the 2nd Truck Section (Light) winding up in heavy ensnarled traffic. The 10th Truck Section (Heavy), which had distributed its fuel in Feuilléres, was sent to Henencourt, to the west of St. Albert, to refuel. . . . The 2nd Maintenance Company was pushed forward to Herbecourt. . . . Some elements of the 7th Truck Section

(Light) and the 8th and 9th Truck Sections (Heavy) in Ablaincourt came under artillery fire and air attack. . . . From the ammunition sections, the 4th and 6th Sections are to be sent forward to Hallu. The 1st Truck Section (Light) is to go to Ablaincourt. . . . Radio message: "Bring forward infantry ammunition and the 6th Truck section (Light) with a platoon from the supply company. Ammunition to be dropped off at Maurepas. The section will be sent to St. Quentin to pick up light howitzer ammunition."

Nowhere along the frontage of the division was it quiet during the night of 6–7 June. Patrols were sent out everywhere and machine-gun fire hissed through the air. Both friend and foe fired harassing fires. For instance, the 6th Battery fired on Marquivillers shortly after midnight. During that time, the division formed two new *Kampfgruppen* for the continued attack.

The righthand group, under *Oberstleutnant Freiherr* von Funck, consisted of *Panzer-Regiment 5*, *Kradschützen-Bataillon 3*, the *II./Schützen-Regiment 3*, the Headquarters of *Schützen-Regiment 3*, and the *I./Artillerie-Regiment 75*. On the left, under *Oberstleutnant* von Lewinski, were *Panzer-Regiment 6*, the *I./Schützen-Regiment 3*, and the *II./Artillerie-Regiment 75*. The initiation of operations was originally scheduled for the division at 1230 hours, but it was postponed to 1430 hours. In the meantime, the reconnaissance battalion reconnoitered to the front and reported enemy antitank positions at La Boissière and artillery batteries at Guerbigny and south of Popincourt. Those were the combat outposts of the French 47th Infantry Division, which had been brought in from the Alsace region.

Oberstleutnant von Lewinski ordered the 1st Battalion of the rifle regiment to take Dancourt the morning of 7 June in order to open up terrain for the later attack by the tanks. Mortars, infantry guns, and heavy tanks opened the operation with a short artillery preparation. *Leutnant* Hilliger's 3rd Company assaulted from its posi-

tion in a defile with the German battle cry of "Hurrah!" Hilliger reached the edge of the village without taking any casualties with the squads of *Unteroffiziere* Röske, Gertner, and Schöning. Four machine guns were captured and fifty French taken prisoner, but heavy and devastating flanking fire started in from Popincourt. Using the infantry guns of his 5th Company, *Oberleutnant* Stein covered the enemy positions in such a way that the 3rd Company was able to continue its assault. But the enemy appeared to come alive everywhere at the same time. There was a racket from all directions—from basements and rooftops, from behind hedges and trees. *Gefreiter* Sust and *Unteroffizier* Schröder were killed; a short while later, the company headquarters section leader, *Feldwebel* Kügler, was also killed. *Major* Meese and *Oberleutnant* Wüst were also forward with the men, who were smoking out the houses in hand-grenade duels. *Oberleutnant* Buchterkirch moved forward with five light tanks of the 1st Battalion of *Panzer-Regiment 6*. The tanks directed their fires on identified machine-gun nests; they destroyed an antitank gun and were able to take sixty prisoners. That only reduced the intensity of the fighting a little bit. The company commander of the 4th, *Oberleutnant* Wüst, was killed by a round to the head. His father had been killed in Lothringen in 1914 as an officer. The riflemen continued to attack. They were finally able to make it all the way through Dancourt. *Feldwebel* Ruhland's platoon was able to make it as far as Popincourt. In all, seventy-seven prisoners were taken, and the spoils of war numbered one antitank gun, four heavy machine guns, and eleven light machine guns.

The main attack of the division was initiated by the assault against Armancourt. It had been identified the previous night as being a heavily fortified strongpoint. *Hauptmann* Pape's 2nd Company of motorcycle infantry attacked the locality after an artillery preparation. The enemy defended stubbornly and inflicted heavy casualties on the motorcycle infantry before he suddenly fled the village at 1400 hours. The company lost seven men dead during that operation, as well as many wounded. Among the wounded was the dashing *Leutnant* Erdmann.

Around that time, *Generalmajor* Stumpff arrived at the command post of the armored brigade. He halted the tanks, which had been in the process of moving out. Orders had been received from higher headquarters that the attack was not to be continued until 8 June. The division started screening. The armored brigade left only weak forces south of the Avre and moved into the area around Hallu–Fransart–Hattencourt along with all of the non-essential vehicles of the rifle brigade. Remaining up front under the command of *Oberstleutnant* von Manteuffel were the 1st Battalion of the rifle regiment, along with elements of *Panzer-Regiment 6* and *Panzerjäger-Abteilung 605*, on the left wing and the 2nd Battalion of the rifle regiment, along with elements of *Panzer-Regiment 5*, on the right wing. On the left, contact was maintained with the *4. Panzer-Division*, while it was with the *SS-Verfügungs-Division* on the right. The motorcycle infantry battalion occupied positions in the defile south of Hill 99 and from Armancourt as far as the St. Aurin–Dancourt road.

The rifle regiment ordered its forward battalions to reconnoiter to the west and southwest in their sectors during the night. In doing so, the 6th Company conducted a reconnaissance-in-force against Marquivillers. The enemy was initially driven from the northern and western edges of the village, but the company had to pull back in the face of growing resistance, which increased by the minute. Another patrol determined there were a large number of enemy forces in Crivillers.

At 0500 hours on 8 June, the division ordered the attack continued at 1100 hours. To that end, the division was reinforced by the *Leibstandarte SS "Adolf Hitler."* The SS regiment was committed up front with the 2nd Battalion of the rifle regiment. Echeloned behind those forces were the 1st Battalion of the rifle regiment, *Panzerjäger-Abteilung 605* and *MG-Bataillon 7*. The armored brigade received orders to follow

immediately as soon as the *Leibstandarte SS "Adolf Hitler"* had overcome the first enemy position.

Then, by surprise, orders arrived from the 6. *Armee* at 0900 hours that the attack was to be postponed indefinitely.

Starting at 1200 hours, the division set up for the defense south of the Avre. The 2nd Battalion of the rifle regiment remained at Laucourt on the right wing, with the 1st Battalion to its left. The SS regiment was held back east of St. Aurin as reserve. One heavy platoon each from *Panzerjäger-Abteilung 605* was attached to the forward battalions. From the ranks of the armored brigade, only the 1st Battalion of *Panzer-Regiment 5* was forward, being positioned south of the river line. All of the remaining elements of the division pulled back across the Avre to the north.

Generaloberst von Reichenau arrived for a short visit to the division command post at 1300 hours. At the same time, the commanding general of the *I. Flak-Korps, General der Flakartillerie* Weise, also appeared. The division operations officer, *Major i.G.* von dem Borne, went to the corps command post and brought back the information that the *3. Panzer-Division* was to be pulled out of the line. It was directed for the *33. Infanterie-Division* to assume the division's sector and continue the attack.

The combat outposts continued to patrol to clarify the enemy situation and keep the withdrawing division from being unpleasantly surprised. At the onset of darkness, the *Leibstandarte SS "Adolf Hitler"* was pulled out of its positions, being relieved by *MG-Bataillon 7*. The *33. Infanterie-Division* moved into the former positions of the division. *Infanterie-Regiment 104* took over the positions of the 2nd Battalion of the rifle regiment, while *Infanterie-Regiment 115* assumed those of the 1st Battalion. The rifle battalions then pulled back from their trenches.

Generalmajor Sintzenich, the commander of the relieving infantry division, arrived with his headquarters staff at Fresnoy during the morning of 9 June and formally assumed the sector of the

3. Panzer-Division. The division command post moved back to Péronne via Liancourt and Omié-court. Both of the brigades and the divisional troops were taken back across the Somme on 9 and 10 June, where they were quartered between Péronne and Ham. The formations rested, cleaned weapons and vehicles, and took care of personal hygiene, all the while also enduring formations. A fuel dump for the division was established at the railway fuel stop at Roisel, to the east of Péronne. Replacements arrived. For instance, the rifle regiment received 200 new officers, noncommissioned officers and enlisted personnel from the replacement battalion in Eberswalde, where *Hauptmann* Wellmann had been conducting courses for officer candidates. The division's supply elements received forty-six men, of which twenty-seven had been trained as drivers.

Oberstleutnant i.G. von dem Borne and *Hauptmann* Barth reported to the command post of the *XVI. Armee-Korps (mot.)* in Gauchy at 1100 hours on 10 June to be briefed on the future operations of the division. The corps was assembling in the St. Quentin–Soisson area and was staged behind the right wing of the *9. Armee*, whose commander in chief was *General der Infanterie* Strauß and whose chief of staff was *Generalleutnant* Hollidt. The corps' mission was short and to the point: "*Panzergruppe Kleist*, with the *XVI. Armee-Korps (mot.)* on the right wing of the *9. Armee*, is directed to cross the bridgehead established by the *XVIII. Armee-Korps* east of Château-Thierry and advance in the direction of Montmirail as soon as possible."

The *XVI. Armee-Korps (mot.)* was inserted between the *XVIII. Armee-Korps* of *Generalleutnant Ritter* von Speck[4] and the *XXXXIV. Armee-Korps* of *Generalleutnant* Koch. The two divisions of the *XVIII. Armee-Korps*—the *81. Infanterie-Division* on the right and the *25. Infanterie-Division* on the left—had established a small bridgehead over the Marne. During the

course of the day on 11 June, it was expanded enough so that *Pionier-Bataillon 72*[5] was able to erect the first sixteen-ton bridge over the river on 12 June.

Starting on 10 June, the division set up its quartering areas in the area around Villers–Cotterets. It moved there on two march routes: Roupy–Flavy–Houvron–Coevre and St. Sulpice–Berlancourt–Coevre. The division headquarters established itself in Château La Poterie. The operations officer, returning from a corps meeting, returned with orders directing the division to cross the Marne on 12 June. The intermediate objective of its attack was the line running Viffort–Mont Levon; the day's objective was Montmirail. The enemy in front of the division belonged to the French 6th Army and consisted of the 27th Infantry Division, as well as elements of the 7th and 8th Infantry Divisions. Up to that point, those enemy forces had offered the *XVIII. Armee-Korps* stubborn resistance.

Hauptmann Barth, the division intelligence officer, went forward on the morning of 12 June to reconnoiter a location for erecting a bridge. Since the approach route to the crossing point was blocked by the ruins of shot-up houses, Barth commandeered some nearby prisoners and had them clear the route. Advance parties from both of the brigades found the routes in order by noon and had the division come forward. When the engineer bridge was finished at 1345 hours, the division's elements prepared to move across.

Oberst Kühn's armored brigade was in the lead with both of its armored regiments, the motorcycle infantry battalion, and the reconnaissance battalion. The first elements crossed the river at 1415 hours. The rain misted from the heavens and placed a thin veil over the beautiful Marne Valley, which featured hills filled with deciduous trees on both sides. The reconnaissance and motorcycle infantry battalions passed through the positions of the *81. Infanterie-Division*—the Silesian division was commanded

---

4. Speck became the first commanding general of the German Army to fall in combat. He was killed in action on 15 June.
5. That engineer battalion was assigned to the *72. Infanterie-Division*.

by *Generalmajor* von Loeper—and advanced into the enemy forces, which had been pulling back since noon as the result of heavy artillery fire.

The 3rd Company of the motorcycle infantry sent a large patrol in the direction of Hill 222. The patrol, under the command of *Feldwebel* O.A. von Plessen,[6] moved rapidly as far as the Railler Woods northeast of Soudan. There it encountered surprisingly strong resistance and did not have time to turn around. The motorcycle infantry set up a desperate defense. But when the rest of the company arrived a few minutes later, it only found dead. *Feldwebel* von Lessen, *Unteroffizier* Schörnborn, *Obergefreiter* Kurz, *Gefreiter* Müller, and *Gefreiter* Zimmermann were the first dead of the division in its new sector.

At the same time, the troops of the reconnaissance battalion were positioned in the woods south of Fontanelle. The village proper was full of enemy forces. The battalion had to hold up until the tanks had closed up. With their support, the village was taken in difficult house-to-house fighting by 2000 hours. Elements of the armored brigade had gone around the village by then and set up in the high ground to the south.

Oberst Freiherr von Funck's *Panzer-Regiment 5* was in the lead. Neither the onset of night or the enemy machine guns and antitank guns prevented the battalions from continuing their advance. At 2130 hours, the fighting vehicles approached Marchais. In a bold move, the regiment succeeded in taking the two bridges south and west of the city over the next hour. Kühn then ordered his regiment to continue advancing to open up the crossings at Montmirail from the south.

Generalmajor Stever's *4. Panzer-Division*, employed to the left of the *3. Panzer-Division*, crossed the high ground west of Mont Levon, encountering little French resistance. On the division's right, the *1. Gebirgs-Division*[7] of *Gen-*

eralleutnant Kübler was still hanging far back in the vicinity of Essières. By the end of the first day of the attack, the corps had pressed a deep wedge into the enemy's front. Correspondingly, during the night, the corps directed a ceaseless pursuit.

As it turned dark, the rifle brigade reached the Marne and crossed the river in two series, starting with the 2nd Battalion of the rifle regiment at 2100 hours. All of the remaining battalions were immediately brought across. The movement was not so simple, since the roads were ensnarled with traffic and the misting rain had softened them as well. The brigade bivouacked for the night in the Fontanelle–Marchais area.

The armored brigade had established itself in the vicinity of La Saulsette–Courtoux–Villegeruis–St. Martin–Foucheries during the night, with security being posted in all directions. It started its advance again the next morning at 0800 hours. The motorcycle infantry battalion took the lead and got involved in engagements in the small woods and individual farmsteads two kilometers northwest of Marchais. They were able to break all resistance, however, and had reached La Haute Epíné an hour after they had moved out.

The armored regiments moved in two groups to the south. The enemy was by no means defeated. The fighting vehicles frequently had to halt and let their main guns do the talking. *Panzer-Regiment 5* was able to force Le Vezier, which was full of enemy forces, after a sharp fight. The regiment immediately moved on the Grand Morin, after the *4. Panzer-Division* succeeded in taking Montmirail.

The division ordered *Oberst* Kleemann and his rifle brigade to exploit the situation and establish a bridgehead over the Grand Morin. In the meantime, the armored brigade had encountered heavy resistance outside of Villeneuve, and the enemy demonstrated he knew how to employ artillery. *Panzer-Regiment 5* was able to

---

6. *O.A.* = *Offizier-Anwärter* = officer-candidate.
7. 1st Mountain Division.

cross the road south of Reveillon, and it took the bridge at La Fossé at 1400 hours, while *Panzer-Regiment 6* overran the enemy positions in and around Tréfols.

The division ordered the continuation of the pursuit of the battered enemy at 1400 hours. Two battle groups were formed under the respective brigade commanders. Both received orders to establish bridgeheads over the Seine.

Kampfgruppe Kühn was employed in the direction of Nogent. The reconnaissance battalion took the lead, followed closely by *Panzer-Regiment 5*. The 2nd Battalion of the rifle regiment was attached to the tankers. Following behind was the headquarters of the rifle regiment and its 3rd Battalion and the motorcycle infantry battalion. The 3rd Battalion was initially designated as the division reserve. *Kampfgruppe Kleemann* consisted of *Panzer-Regiment 6*, the 1st Battalion of the rifle regiment, and the 2nd Battalion of artillery. Engineers, signalers, and antitank elements were split out among the two battle groups. Kleemann also formed an advance guard for his battle group. It consisted of the *II./Panzer-Regiment 6*, elements of *Panzerjäger-Abteilung 605*, the *II./Artillerie-Regiment 75*, and the *10./Flak-Lehr-Regiment*. In addition to the separate companies and detachments, the remaining formations—the *I./Panzer-Regiment 6*, the main body of *Panzerjäger-Abteilung 605*, and *MG-Bataillon 7*—constituted the main body of Kleemann's forces. *Oberleutnant* Buchterkirch once again took the lead with his light tanks. By then, the bold officer had reinforced his platoon with five captured French fighting vehicles, enemy personnel carriers and English ammunition carriers. *Oberleutnant* von Brodowski was attached to the advance guard with his two *Panzer IV's* and a platoon of motorcycle infantry.

Kleemann's advance guard reached the high ground south of Rieux shortly after 1000 hours and advanced on strong enemy forces at Tréfols an hour later. The batteries of the 2nd Battalion had to go into position for the first time there. At 1250 hours, the lead tank elements entered the village and had it firmly under German control by 1320 hours. The advance guard took 350 men prisoner and captured one 15-centimeter gun and one antitank gun. The march continued.

When the lead elements of the division reached the three-road intersection at Neuvy at 1545 hours, a halt was ordered, with security posted in all directions, even though there was no serious enemy resistance far and wide. The commanding general arrived a few minutes later and ordered *Oberstleutnant* von Lewinski to continue the pursuit immediately.

The tanks and reconnaissance elements encountered a few French strong-points, but the resistance was quickly broken. It was only outside of Villeneuve that enemy artillery fires became particularly noticeable. One armored car and one tank received direct hits before the enemy battery could be identified. The fighting vehicles then rolled forward and eliminated one gun after the other. The stockpiled artillery rounds caught fire and went up in the air with a loud bang. In the process of that engagement, *Panzer-Regiment 6* took 600 French from differing formations prisoner.

The advance guard of *Oberst* Kühn's battle group was outside of Reveillon around 1900 hours, after crossing rough terrain and practically impenetrable woods. It entered St. Genest. The lead elements of *Oberst* Kleemann's *Kampfgruppe* right neared the Seine as it turned dark. Once again, they had to contend with heavy artillery and antitank-gun fire. Infantry fire from the woods also hampered friendly movements. Despite the uncertain situation, *Oberleutnant* Buchterkirch ordered an immediate attack on the bridges over the Seine.

Buchterkirch's men moved out immediately with two heavy and two light tanks. They raced through the enemy fire towards the first bridge. *Leutnant* Busse and his platoon of engineers sprung towards the obstacle there and made a lane for the fighting vehicles. Buchterkirch was the first one to move across the bridge, ripping out the demolition charges on the far side. The same "game" was played at the second bridge, although the engineers had to remove three obstacles there. In front of the third bridge, *Feldwebel* Thiele shot up a 7.5-centimeter field piece and two antitank guns. The third bridge was then taken. Then it was the turn of the riflemen of the 1st Battalion. *Leutnant* Weiss stormed ahead with his men. Under the covering fires provided by the tanks, they crossed the fourth bridge. By 2040 hours, the fighting vehicles, riflemen, motorcycle infantry and engineers had established the first bridgehead over the Seine at Pont-sur-Seine.

Oberst Kühn's *Kampfgruppe* had not been idle, either. His advance guard was at the high ground around Courtnoux by the evening of 13 June. A sunny day, filled with success, was behind the tankers and riflemen. The spoils of war in terms of artillery, vehicles of all types, small arms, and equipment could neither be counted nor used. Frequently, it was not even reported—the pursuit had moved so fast. On that day, the division took some 3,000 prisoners from the French 20th, 53rd, and 59th Infantry Divisions and the 27th Mountain Division. By then, the silver ribbon of the Seine presented itself to the soldiers of *Oberst Freiherr* von Funck and *Major* Zimmermann. It snaked and curved its way through the countryside.

Kühn ordered his commanders together around 2200 hours. He issued orders to *Major Edler Ritter* von Peter to take the bridge over the seine at Nogent-sur-Seine in a *coup de main* with his tank battalion, the 6th Company of the rifle regiment and a platoon of divisional engineers. The riflemen sent out a patrol under *Unteroffizier* Heinrich, which already started encountering enemy forces six kilometers from the bridge. That meant that surprise was out of the question. Making a snap decision, Peter had his tanks close up, followed closely by the riflemen and the engineers. Unfortunately, the lead fighting vehicles encountered an obstacle in front of an eight-meter-wide creek. The main guns set the beams alight. Leading the riflemen, *Major* Zimmermann and his adjutant, *Oberleutnant* Siegelmann, had already climbed over the

beams and reached the far side. There were twenty abandoned buses to either side of the road; they had probably been transporting French forces just a few hours earlier.

Oberleutnant Engelien's 6th Company moved forward silently. To the left was a railway embankment; on the right, a large gas works. A machine-gun section was posted at the road leading to Paris. The riflemen then sprang across the railway bridge in long strides. The silence of the night was broken by machine-gun and anti-tank-gun fire. That was coming from the bridge's guard detail. The engineers with the company tossed hand grenades. *Unteroffizier* Schrank brought the first machine gun into position, *Unteroffizier* Reschke and *Unteroffizier* Klemusch their mortars. Reschke was able to eliminate the antitank gun. Then the words came: "Get up! Move! Move!"

The bridge over the Seine had been taken. In the course of clearing the demolitions, the engineers suffered two dead and four wounded. The riflemen kept moving forward. *Leutnant* Tank and his platoon assaulted and were able to take a second bridge over a tributary. The French had already abandoned their positions there. The first German fighting vehicles started to arrive. It was 0330 hours. By 0400 hours, Engelien's 6th Company had assembled in Nogent. The squads of *Unteroffizier* Heinrich and *Unteroffizier* Franz, which had been left behind, were able to bring twelve officer and thirty enlisted prisoners with them when they came forward. The town proper was not defended by the enemy. Large numbers of refugees were dwelling in the streets. *Feldwebel* Gabler combed the town and brought back a few more prisoners, as did *Unteroffizier* Schmidt, who took in 4 officers and 140 enlisted while screening in the direction of Ferreux.

The bridgehead was expanded until noon and combat outposts sent out to Sorigny–Avant le Marcilly–Ferreux. The neighboring division on the left, the *4. Panzer-Division*, had also established a bridgehead at Marcilly with its *Panzer-Regiment 35*. The *1. Gebirgs-Division* on the

FROM THE SOMME TO THE SOUTH OF FRANCE 105

right continued to hang back in the vicinity of Petit Morin. The forces of the corps were arrayed far to the rear of the French front. The orders for the next day: "Pursue to the utmost and prevent any enemy breakthroughs from the east!"

The division started moving out again with two *Kampfgruppen* around 1400 hours. *Kampfgruppe Kühn—Panzer-Regiment 5, Kradschützen-Bataillon 3*, the *II./Schützen-Regiment 3*, the *I./Artillerie-Regiment 75*, the *1./Pionier-Bataillon 39*, and the *II./Flak-Lehr-Regiment*—moved out from Nogent. The route led it past seemingly endless columns of refugees through Marcilly, where weak enemy resistance was eliminated. The pursuit continued via Planty–Vulaines–Rigny–Bérulles–Boeurs.

One episode from the pursuit may shed some light on the conduct of the fighting as the French field armies started to disintegrate, which was more evident with each passing day. *Unteroffizier* Ulrich of the headquarters of the rifle regiment took a wrong turn on his motorcycle and found himself on a secondary road. He was surprised to encounter a motorized column. Making a snap decision, he raised his carbine, which had only three rounds loaded, and had the eight vehicles halt. He took three officers and forty men prisoner.

Kampfgruppe Kleemann—Panzer-Regiment 6, the *I./Schützen-Regiment 3*, the *II./Artillerie-Regiment 75*, and division troops—pursued the enemy through le Peje–Palis–Villemaur. *Hauptmann* von Plato's 1st Company of the rifle regiment was able to push back enemy forces that unexpectedly appeared and continued the advance at the head of the column. Elements of the armored regiment stopped a French transport train at the Villemaur rail station and forced the personnel on board to surrender.

The division intelligence officer made the following notation in the daily logs that evening:

Enemy pulling back in complete dissolution. Formations above regimental level no longer identifiable as entities. The appear-

ance of numerous medical personnel make it apparent that the breakthrough is far in the rear-area services area. While moving the division command post forward to St. Mard, there were long columns of prisoners without German guards on and next to the avenue of advance to the north. The number of prisoners for the day is estimated at 10,000.

Panzer-Regiment 5 and the *II./Schützen-Regiment 3* were only fifteen kilometers north of St. Florentin when it turned dark. *Major* Zimmermann received orders: "take the crossings over the Armance, the de Bourgogne Canal and the Armançon and enter the city of St. Florentin!" *Major* Hohmann's tank battalion was to support him in that effort.

That started the memorable operation of Zimmermann's men, supported by *Leutnant* Bonacker's tank platoon and *Leutnant* Weigel's engineers. The two machine-gun tanks and the light cannon tank rattled on ahead, followed by the engineers and then the 6th and 10th Companies of riflemen. The raiding party passed long columns of refugees and a French bicycle company. *Unteroffizier* Landgräber, a patrol leader from the 6th Company, returned with his men and reported that St. Florentin was full of the enemy but that the bridges were still intact.

Major Zimmermann ordered the tank platoon to head for the city. Without regard for the dispositions and resistance of the enemy, the 6th Company and the engineers were to follow right behind. They were to take the bridges and establish a bridgehead. The first houses of the city soon appeared. The streets were full of refugees, mixed in among them were innumerable French army trucks. Up to that point, not a single shot had been fired. The French probably thought the German forces were their English Allies until someone, somewhere, shouted out: "*Les Allemands!*"

But by then, the main guns and machine guns were doing the talking. The riflemen charged the nonplussed enemy with cold steel. None of them thought about defending. In the blink of an eye, 30 . . . 50 . . . 100 men were captured. The tanks reached the first bridge, but were unable to proceed in the entanglement of vehicles and horse-drawn conveyances. *Major* Zimmermann and *Oberleutnant* Engelien charged forward with their men. They got on to and then across the bridge. The battalion commander was badly wounded by a round to the chest. *Unteroffiziere* Moder and Böhm, along with *Stabsgefreiter* Jordan, took their commander back to *Stabsarzt* Dr. Schreck. Despite the setback, the attack did not falter. *Oberleutnant* Siegelmann, the battalion adjutant, made a snap decision and assumed command of all German forces in St. Florentin.

Feldwebel Schieblon charged on with his platoon, with *Unteroffizier* Moder in the lead. The riflemen cleared a path by means of close combat and soon broke all resistance. Despite the Gordian knot of vehicles, the men continued advancing. Sleeping Frenchmen were pulled from their vehicles and simply sent back through the city without guards. *Unteroffizier* Klemusch and *Gefreiter* Borsdorff were killed in the fighting. *Unteroffizier* Moder was the first to reach the railway bridge. He was able to cut off the retreat route of a vehicle column, and he forced two fighting vehicles to stop.

By then, *Leutnant* Bonacker was able to blaze a trail with his tanks and occupy the bridge. He arrived at just the right time; a long transport train wanted to depart. The few German fighting vehicles immediately attacked the armored train and stopped it. Hundreds of French left the freight cars with raised hands.

It was slowly turning light. There were enemy truck columns, guns and tanks everywhere in the streets; among them was an immense crowd of prisoners. The 6th Company had taken five bridges and set up to secure the bridgehead. *Feldwebel* Franke's platoon from the 8th Company of the rifle regiment, which was rushed forward, was able to turn back the first and only French immediate counterattack to relieve St. Florentin.

Oberleutnant Siegelmann arranged the companies in such a fashion that they could turn back any attempted enemy attacks. *Hauptmann* Riedl brought up his 9th Company and assumed acting command of the battalion from Siegelmann. *Oberleutnant* Müller-Röhlich's 7th Company was positioned along the northern outskirts of the city. Later on, the 9th and 10th Companies reinforced those positions. The 6th Company screened in front of the railway facilities to the south of the city, and the 8th Company cleared the city and engagement areas of the enemy.

In the process of clearing, *Unteroffizier* Knoll was able to round up 20 officers and 105 enlisted and secure them in a building. *Unteroffizier* Dickfeld, *Gefreiter* Tamm, and *Gefreiter* Leuendorf captured an additional 250 French. *Oberfeldwebel* Arndt and a platoon form the 9th Company forced three columns of trucks with 400 soldiers back into the city, while *Schütze* Wegener of the 6th Company personally held 50 French captive. All of the prisoners were placed in a collection point in the city square that had been set up by *Hauptmann* Zabel's 10th Company.

Two French companies attacked the outposts of the 7th Company from the north. After a short firefight, they were forced to surrender. Six hundred French, including many coloreds, put down their arms. *Gefreiter* Noack, armed only with his pistol in his had, succeeded in bringing in 25 prisoners. When *Major* Hohmann arrived in St. Florentin around noon, the fighting was over. The 2nd Battalion reported an overwhelming success that day:

Prisoners: 112 officers and 2,360 noncommissioned officers and enlisted personnel
Spoils of war: More than 500 vehicles of all types; 4 tanks; 4 armored cars; 4 antitank guns; 6 antiaircraft guns; 11 artillery pieces; 17 ambulances; and a fuel depot with 6 million liters of fuel

The German losses consisted of three dead and three wounded. The victory was reported in the Armed Forces Daily Report of 18 June as follows: "As a result of his decisive personal actions, the commander of a rifle battalion,

Major Zimmermann . . . prevented the demolition of important bridges by the enemy at the last minute."

Later, Zimmermann received the Knight's Cross for this operation. The same award was presented to Willy Moder, who was also promoted to *Feldwebel*. His award recommendation read, in part: ". . . entered St. Florentin with his motorcycle infantry squad, moving through French columns during the night of 14–15 June. In two hours of close combat, he eliminated numerous French soldiers with cold steel and blocked the retreat route for an enemy column, forcing it to surrender."

At that point, the French Army no longer offered a cohesive defensive front. Nonetheless, individual strong points and troop elements offered stubborn resistance, and the enemy conducted immediate counterattacks here and there. For instance, the antitank elements had to turn back a French cavalry attack from out of the woods east of Villemoiron. Another cavalry thrust struck the rest area of the 6th Battery of the division artillery at Aix-en-Othe. *Unteroffizier* Arndt, in an outpost with a machine gun on the right side of the perimeter, was able to see the horsemen fleeing, however. The enemy lost ten soldiers.

The division continued its pursuit starting at 1400 hours on 15 June. The day's objective was Auxerre/Yonne. The corps had issued its orders in that regard at 1120 hours. Once again, the armored brigade took the lead. A reinforced advance guard under the command of *Oberstleutnant* von Manteuffel followed. It consisted of the *III./Schützen-Regiment 3*, the *3./Panzerjäger-Abteilung 39*, the *3./Pionier-Bataillon 39*, the *8./Flak-Lehr-Regiment*, the *5./Artillerie-Regiment 60*, and the *II./Artillerie-Regiment 75*. Manteuffel's men marched via St. Florentin–Brienon–Moneteau without enemy contact. During the movements that day, the 1st and 2nd Companies of *Panzer-Regiment 6* set a transport train loaded with high-explosive ammunition alight. The reconnaissance battalion was ahead of all the other battalions and encountered the enemy at the eastern outskirts of Auxerre around 2000 hours. The battalion immediately moved on the enemy and was able to take an airfield with fifteen operational aircraft.

The division continued its movements without pausing and advanced via Cravant–Vermenton–Arcy to Avallon with both of its battle groups. The latter locality was reached during the night of 15–16 June around 0200 hours. The reconnaissance battalion was only able to enter and move through the village with the help of the 11th Company of the rifle regiment, which was quickly brought forward. In the process, several hundred prisoners were again taken.

The French were surprised by the sudden appearance of the German tanks. Situations developed that bordered on the farcical. For example, the lead armored cars of the reconnaissance battalion approached the La Côte de Chaux Mountain, south of Arcy. The tunnel through the mountain was completely illuminated. The French guards posted there greeted the waving armored reconnaissance soldiers in a friendly manner and seemed happy to encounter their British Allies. They were mightily disappointed when they looked down the barrel of a pistol after the tunnel was firmly in the hands of the few reconnaissance troopers.

The 1st Company of the rifle regiment, part of *Oberst* Kleemann's march group, was able to book another success that night. *Oberleutnant* Buchterkirch's light platoon had the riflemen mount up and then conduct a reconnaissance in force in the direction of Chabois. The nighttime march was successful and brought good reconnaissance information for the command. But with the great distances that were being covered during the day, there were also a few difficulties that had not been anticipated. For example, the forces did not have any good military maps for southern France. Commercial roadmaps with a scale of 1:300,000 or travel guides had to be used. The number of prisoners was another issue that had not been taken into account in the operations plans. The mass of prisoners grew by the day. The division could barely spare any more men to guard them. *Generalmajor* Stumpff requested the corps send forward a guard regiment that would accept responsibility for the French.

The fuel situation presented the greatest problem. The supply sections were barely able to keep up with the pace of the advance, since there were no supply dumps. Even when some were reported, as was the case on 14 June in Crisolles, they either did not exist or their existing stocks had already been distributed. It was a daily worry for the division logistics officer and the division support commander: How was the division going to get fuel? The division had not received a single cubic meter of fuel for two days. When a report arrived on 15 June that *Ju-52's*[8] were landing at the airfield at Bethon with fuel, *Major* Haker immediately stopped the movements of all of his sections and ordered them there to pick up fuel. But when *Oberleutnant* Gesenger and *Leutnant* Bömcke arrived in Bethon, there was nothing there. The officers from the other divisions that had shown up for the same purpose also had to leave with unfinished business. *Oberleutnant* Gesenger flew in a Fieseler *Storch*[9] to four neighboring airstrips, including one that was still under French artillery fire, but he was unable to find fuel anywhere. In the meantime, *Panzergruppe Kleist* announced that fuel would be coming to Crisolles "sometime." *Oberleutnant* Günther's 10th Truck Section (Heavy) was ordered there immediately; but that effort was also in vain. Only *Leutnant Graf* Douglas's 8th Truck Section (Heavy) had success; it brought fifty cubic meters of fuel from Roisel to Nogent. The *3. Panzer-Division* thus became the only division of all of *Panzergruppe Kleist* that received any fuel that day. It was not until the large dump in St. Florentin was discovered that all worries

were temporarily gone. *Hauptmann i.G.* Krasá confiscated all of the stockpiles there for the division.

Despite that, the fuel situation continued to remain strained. *Panzer-Regiment 5* sent a report back with *Leutnant* Müller-Hauff on 16 June that it was stranded without fuel. Guided by *Leutnant* Bömcke and *Leutnant* Haug, corps assets were then sent forward as soon as possible with twenty-five cubic meters (6,600 gallons) of fuel. A few hours later, the armored brigade adjutant, *Hauptmann* Friedrichs, arrived at the division support command and reported that the brigade was out of fuel. The 7th and 9th Truck Sections were sent forward with *Leutnant Graf* Asseburg with another twenty-five cubic meters of gasoline and three cubic meters (790 gallons) of diesel. Since the brigade's fuel situation was really a cause for concern, the division ordered more fuel to be brought forward to the Quarré–les Tombes area immediately. Fortunately, *Leutnant* Thorhauer of the 9th Truck Section (Heavy) had been able to locate some fuel in Paris[10] and bring it forward to the division on 17 June.

During the night of 15–16 June, the division reorganized its forces in such a manner that the two battle groups under the brigade commanders marched behind the reinforced advance guard, which had already reached Avallon around 0230 hours without encountering any enemy resistance. Outside of that town, however, were French forces. They were completely surprised by the arrival of the Germans. After the 3rd Battalion of the rifle regiment had closed up, the attack started. *Oberleutnant Freiherr* von Werthern's 11th Company made it through the town in its first attempt in an effort to cut off the roads leading to the north, northeast and east. The French were quickly overrun. Some 52 officers

---

8. The Junkers *Ju-52*, a trimotor aircraft, was the standard transporter of the *Luftwaffe* for the entire war. It was a sturdy and reliable aircraft, but there were never enough on hand to address supply issues such as the one under discussion.

9. The Fiesler *Storch* ("Stork") was a light utility aircraft used in a wide variety of roles. It had a single engine and was noted for its ability to take off and land at unimproved airfields.

10. Paris was declared on "open city" on 13 June and occupied by German forces on 15 June.

and 2,500 enlisted personnel, including many men from the Alsace region and Negroes, surrendered, resigned to their fate. Among other things, the reconnaissance battalion captured the war chest of the garrison, which held 14,000 Francs. It also destroyed the telephone lines by means of a special detail.

The corps radioed orders at 0800 hours: "The main body of the division moves on Arnay-le-Duc; the advance guard to Beaune!"

The armored brigade was already approaching Saulieu and was four kilometers northwest of the city around 1700 hours. The 2nd Battalion of *Panzer-Regiment 6*, using tried and true methods, went around the city to gain some open ground. All of a sudden, Hotchkiss tanks rolled against the battalion's left flank from some woods. They belonged to formations that had previously been positioned in the Maginot Line and were pulling back in the face of the frontal attack by the *1. Armee* to the west. The surprise was equally great on both sides. The enemy was first to fire, however, and unfortunately knocked out the command tank of the regimental commander. The regimental liaison officer, *Oberleutnant* Rohrbeck, was badly wounded. One of the crew was killed. Fearlessly, *Obergefreiter* Jahr moved forward to the road in his *Panzer II* and blocked it. The brave soldier paid for the bold move with his life. Nonetheless, he held up the enemy temporarily. *Oberstleutnant* von Lewinski sent motorcycle messengers forward to the tanks that were already far ahead. A short while later, the first ones returned. It was *Oberleutnant Baron* von Nolde and his platoon from the 8th Company. A sharp tank engagement ensued. After the smoke had cleared, there were twelve knocked-out enemy tanks littering the landscape between the woods and the road. At the same moment, the regiment's 1st Battalion rolled up, which immediately started pursuing the French. Their fighting vehicles were able to knock out another tank and destroyed another eighty vehicles of all types and descriptions.

Oberstleutnant von Lewinski assembled his regiment. One battle group attacked the woods in an enveloping maneuver, while a second one turned directly on Saulieu. The tanks that advanced against the woods only found infantry forces. For the most part, they were Moroccans, who put up a defense. They allowed themselves to be overrun, only to fire on the following riflemen or the dismounted tankers. Finally, the last resistance in the woods was overcome, and 780 men started their march into captivity. *Major* von Bernuth's antitank battalion also arrived. The fires from the small 3.7-centimeter antitank guns were just able to reach the fleeing enemy fighting vehicles. Five enemy tanks were set alight by the antitank elements. A short while later, the motorcycle infantry battalion also appeared; its companies brought about the decisive turning point in the fight for Saulieu. After the last infantry resistance in the woods had been eliminated, the motorcycle infantry attacked the city frontally. The motorcycle infantry, supported by the 1st Company of *Panzer-Regiment 6*, were able to push through the city rapidly and take 450 prisoners.

With that action, the division found itself to the rear of the French 2nd and 4th Armies. The troop elements that put up a fight belonged to formations from a large number of divisions. There was no more unified command among the enemy forces, and every officer fought with his element at the spot he found himself in when the German tanks appeared.

To the soldiers of the division, it seemed they only moved in their vehicles and marched. The countryside grew prettier by the day. The division found itself in the fruitful and rich Burgundy region. Small rivers snaked through the hilly countryside, which reminded the men of the wheat fields and blooming meadows of the Rhineland. The vineyards stretched for kilometers on the slopes of the wooded hills. The roads were good and straight as an arrow.

The reconnaissance battalion made it to the outskirts of Arnay. Nothing to be seen of the enemy far and wide. But, all of a sudden, there was a crack! The lead armored car was hit. There were two French tanks in front of it. An antitank gun from the battalion was immediately brought forward and was able to knock out one of the two fighting vehicles. The other vehicle cleared the route. *Major Freiherr* von Wechmar sent a motorcycle infantry platoon in pursuit. It was unable to enter the village, because it was halted outside by machine gun and antitank fire. The battalion stopped its movements and waited for the rest of the advance guard to catch up. *Oberstleutnant* von Manteuffel ordered the 3rd Battalion of the rifle regiment to attack around 1600 hours. Valuable time was lost, since the battalion dismounted to early and tried to envelop too far to the west. The 1st Battalion of artillery supported the attack with its 1st and 3rd Batteries, as well as the attached *5./Artillerie-Regiment 49*. *Leutnant* Graf directed the short artillery preparation as a forward observer. At 1915 hours, the rifle battalion finally launched its attack. The 12th Company was on the right and the 13th Company on the left. Both of the companies had been reinforced with infantry guns, antitank guns and heavy mortars. The 11th and 14th Companies were employed against the high ground north of the road.

Initially, the battalion made good progress. But five enemy tanks appeared right outside of Arnay, which caused the momentum of the attack to peter out. It was not until the friendly antitank guns fired that the French fighting vehicles pulled back. *Hauptmann* Orts's 12th Company then entered the city. The 13th Company followed, somewhat more slowly. House-to-house fighting ensued that lasted two hours and caused many casualties. It was made all the more difficult by the appearance again and again of French tanks. The fighting was especially intense around the cemetery, which changed hands several times. It was not until 2100 hours that Arnay was firmly under German control.

The advance guard moved to the high ground west of the city to screen, leaving behind the 11th Company of the rifle regiment, which was reinforced by the *4./Panzer-Regiment 6*, two platoons from the antitank battalion and the engineer platoon of the regiment's 15th Company.

The night was fitful, since groups of enemy riflemen tried to take back Arnay in immediate counterattacks. While defending against one such attack, the 3rd Battery of artillery set eight enemy trucks alight. The personnel on board surrendered.

The entire division went over to a screening posture. The 1st Battalion of the rifle regiment was assigned to guard the armored brigade, which had assembled at Saulieu. The rifle battalion commander, *Major* Meese, was wounded during an enemy reconnaissance-in-force. In addition, three other officers from the regiment were wounded that day: *Hauptmann* Haspel and *Leutnant* Deckert and *Leutnant* von Pfuhlstein. The French were hiding out in the woods around Saulieu and attempting to break through the German lines to reestablish contact with their own forces. A large fuel column under *Hauptmann* Schütte was engaged several times by one such group.

The constant rain hindered the conduct of combat operations. It didn't bother the riflemen, who were resting in the vineyards on the high ground around Arnay, at all.

Without warning, a French first lieutenant arrived at the German positions with a white flag. *Major* Kratzenberg and *Major Freiherr* von Wechmar were amazed when the emissary offered them the surrender of the Dijon Fortress! The French officer was taken back to the division command post. Instead of the *3. Panzer-Division*, however, the corps directed the *4. Panzer-Division* to initiate the capitulation of the fortress. Dijon was in the latter division's attack sector. Starting at 1700 hours on 17 June, the Reich war flag was waving from the fortress walls.

Oberstleutnant von Manteuffel reorganized his advance guard. Instead of placing the reconnaissance battalion in front, he inserted a tank company, which would enable him to break any potentially significant enemy resistance faster. The battalion moved out right at noon. *Hauptmann* Weiss led with his battle-tested 4th Company of *Panzer-Regiment 6*. The 12th Company of the rifle regiment and one platoon from the

3rd Company of the antitank battalion were attached to him in support. The main body of the advance, under the command of *Oberstleutnant* von Lewinski, followed behind in this order: Headquarters, *III./Schützen-Regiment 3*; Headquarters, *Schützen-Regiment 3*; Headquarters, *Panzer-Regiment 6*; Headquarters, *I./Artillerie-Regiment 75*; *1./Artillerie-Regiment 75*; *III./Schützen-Regiment 3*; *3./Pionier-Bataillon 39*; and one platoon from the *3./Panzerjäger-Abteilung 39*. The rest of the division followed in two battle groups.

The lead elements of the advance guard received rifle fire from both the left and right outside of Bligny. The tank company was able to break the resistance rapidly, however, with the result that the advance could be continued unimpeded at 1330 hours. The first batch of prisoners for the day numbered forty. The reconnaissance battalion was sent in the direction of the rail line that turned off to Dijon. In the course of its reconnaissance, it destroyed five locomotives and a transport train.

When the lead armored elements reached the high ground northwest of Beaune, they encountered defending enemy motorized columns. They had been directed to cover the withdrawal of the garrison to the west. *Oberstleutnant* von Manteuffel immediately brought the 14th Company of the rifle regiment forward, as well as the 1st and 3rd Batteries of artillery. They took the valley and the railway station under fire. Unfortunately, they did not succeed in stopping the trains that were just pulling out. Later on, however, *Leutnant* Hiltmann of the motorcycle infantry battalion was later able to capture them. By then, *Major* Schmidt-Ott's 1st Battalion of *Panzer-Regiment 6* had closed up. He advanced down on Beaune with his battalion and entered the city. In the process, the lead tanks were able to knock out a French tank and then work the enemy over with machine guns and main guns. There was a great number of Indochinese among them. Mounted up, the 11th Company of the rifle battalion followed behind the *1./Panzer-Regiment 6*. The riflemen were able to overcome the frequently tough resistance in the houses and then establish a defensive position along the creek northeast of the city. After clearing the city, the 12th and 13th Companies of the rifle regiment were sent east of the city to reinforce. The 12th Company blocked the railway line to Chagny.

The advance guard was then allowed to rest. The Headquarters and *I./Panzer-Regiment 6* stayed in Beaune; the *II./Panzer-Regiment 6*, along with the *12./Schützen-Regiment 3*, the *3./Pionier-Bataillon 39*, and a platoon from the 3./Panzerjäger-Abteilung 39 in Alexe-Corton; the *III./Schützen-Regiment 3* and the rest of the *3./Panzerjäger-Abteilung 39* around Serrigny; and the *I./Artillerie-Regiment 75* and the *II./Flak-Lehr-Regiment* in Vignolles. Screening elements were sent out in all directions and combat outposts established.

Rumors started circulating from mouth to mouth that were confirmed a short while later by those who could listen to a radio: Marshal Pétain was asking for a ceasefire. It goes without saying that the troops were overjoyed that evening and night.

The patrols that had been sent forward reported by the morning of 18 June that the bridge at Seurre had had a span of fifteen meters blown out of it on its west side. The enemy was nowhere to be seen along the river. The division moved out immediately with its forward elements around 0700 hours. The leaders of the battle groups had been issued orders beforehand: "Reach Verdun sur le Doubs immediately and establish a bridgehead over the Saone, screening to the south!" That was to be followed by a later crossing over the Doubs at Chaussin, with an attendant advance on Mouchard and the Swiss border.

The division had reorganized that day as well. The two strong battle groups of *Oberst* Kühn and *Oberst* Kleemann took over the lead, while the former advance guard was sent to the right-hand march group. *Kampfgruppe Kühn* placed the reconnaissance battalion in the lead; it was able to take the bridge in Verdun sur le Doubs at 0732 hours after a short engagement. The troops moved out again immediately, and the bridge north of Pagny la Ville, eight kilometers north of Seurre, fell to them a short while later. That bridge was negotiable for all vehicles.

At that point, *Kampfgruppe von Manteuffel* moved out with the mission to guard the advance of the two battle groups to the east and north. His forces consisted of the Headquarters, *Schützen-Regiment 3*; the *III./Schützen-Regiment 3*; the *I./Artillerie-Regiment 75*; the *3./Panzer-jäger-Abteilung 39*; and the *I./Flak-Regiment 51*. The aviators from the attached *Luftwaffe* short-range reconnaissance squadron had been in the air ever since the morning in an effort to monitor the entire divisional sector.

Kampfgruppe Kühn reached the Saone around noon with most of his forces, crossing the river. The reconnaissance battalion continued to advance and turned in the direction of Mont Vaudery. *Oberst* Kleemann was with his forces at the same time outside of Aumont, while *Kampfgruppe von Manteuffel* formed a bridgehead at Allery.

The enemy was generally falling back everywhere. In cases where a defense was being offered, there were strong officers in charge. There were frequent instances where machine gun and carbine fire suddenly broke out far behind the lead elements. In one case, *Krad-schützen* Pohl, Gerbsch, and Kiebitz of the 3rd Company of the motorcycle infantry battalion noticed that the village of Chagny was still full of French soldiers. Under the direction of *Leutnant* Hiltmann, who was bringing up the rear because he was wounded, the three motorcycle infantrymen convinced the garrison there to surrender. Eight officers and three hundred fifty men surrendered. In addition, they also captured three intact freight trains and one hospital train.

Major Freiherr von Wechmar's reconnaissance battalion was turned in the direction of Champagnole. His troops did not encounter any serious resistance anywhere. The reconnaissance elements did run into columns of refugees again and again, however. Some soldiers tried to hide themselves among them, who were hoping to escape undetected. There was no fighting at all

on 19 June along the entire Western Front. *Oberst* Kleemann and his battle group reached the area around Mouchard–Arbei without practically any enemy contact. *Oberst* Kühn and his forces advanced into the area around Chaussin, after the brigade had crossed the Doubs at 1715 hours.

Over the last few days, *Major* Beigel's engineer battalion had seen constant employment. The engineers practically needed to be everywhere at the same time in an area that was dotted with rivers in order to scout bridges or erect them. For example, the battalion determined at noon on 18 June that the bridge at Pt. Noir was too weak for tanks. Correspondingly, it prepared the bridge at Lays for tank crossing. The destroyed bridge at Peseux was likewise repaired around 1800 hours and, within the same hour, the bridge at Orrain, west of Chaussin, was checked for its load-bearing capacity. The 3rd Company of engineers completely repaired the large bridge in Seurre by midnight.

Like the rest of the forces of the division, *Kampfgruppe von Manteuffel* started its nighttime rest around 2000 hours that day. The quartering area spread across Allery, Bragny, Chauvort, St. Pussey, La Parre, Verdun, and St. Jean. Elements of the 3rd Battalion of the rifle regiment and the 3rd Company of the antitank battalion guarded the bridge over the Saone at Chauvort, as well as the most important roads and bridge of the entire sector. The 13th Company of the rifle regiment established a large prisoner collection point at Verdun. By midnight, some 600 prisoners from the following regiments had been counted: 34, 49, 134, 168, 305, and 402. There were also soldiers assigned to territorial training, replacement and work detachments. That evening, the 12th Company of the regiment found a burning fuel depot at the Gergy rail station. A platoon from the supply company that was sent there by the division support command was undeterred and put out the fire. *Feldwebel* Röhl's men were able to save one million liters of gasoline for the division.

The nineteenth of June was a day of rest for the division. It remained in the positions it had previously reached. The troops found the necessary time to bring weapons, uniforms and vehicles back into order and enjoy the well-deserved rest. More replacements arrived from the homeland. Only the reconnaissance battalion enjoyed no rest. It attacked Champagnole and occupied the village without encountering major resistance. By doing so, the lead elements of the division were only fifteen kilometers from the Swiss border that evening.

That day had been blessed with great weather. The sun shone from clear skies, inviting the soldiers to bathe in the Saone or simply take it easy in the soft green meadowlands along the river and in the pretty villages of Burgundy. Vineyards on ridgelines stretched all the way around. Old palaces and ruins greeted the soldiers from the peaks of the hills and mountains. Rich villas and tidy houses invited the soldiers to spend some time in the small towns with their gardens and parks. The roads were smooth and well maintained and wound in serpentines down into the river valley.

Unfortunately, there was hardly any rest time for the officers of the headquarters. After Marshal Pétain had exhorted his army to fulfill its duties to the last man, we knew that the war was not quite over yet. *Oberstleutnant i.G.* von dem Borne went to the corps headquarters and brought back new directives for the division. According to them, the corps was to fall in behind the *XIV. Armee-Korps (mot.)* and advance in the direction of Marseille or the Spanish border. The new direction of march was caused by the fact that *Panzergruppe Guderian* had reached the Swiss border, encircling the French field armies in the Alsace region. *Panzergruppe Kleist* was to move down the Rhone. The armor group consisted of the *XIV. Armee-Korps (mot.)*, with the *9.* and *10. Panzer-Divisionen, Infanterie-Regiment (mot.) "Großdeutschland,"* the *Leibstandarte SS "Adolf Hitler,"* and the *SS-Totenkopf-Division*, and the *XVI. Armee-Korps (mot.)*, with the *3.* and *4. Panzer-Divisionen*, the *13. Infanterie-Division (mot.)*, and the *SS-Verfügungs-Division*. In a supplement to its

directive of 14 June, the Army High Command had designated the long-range objectives of German operations to be a line running from the area south of Lyon in the east and the area around Bordeaux in the west.

The *XVI. Armee-Korps (mot.)* followed the *XIV. Armee-Korps (mot.)* in the direction of Lyon on 20 June. On that day, the *10. Panzer-Division* and *Infanterie-Regiment (mot.) "Großdeutschland"* took that major city. The corps was directed to advance into the area southeast of Lyon, whereby the *3. Panzer-Division* had a flank guard mission, protecting the left flank in the general direction of Grenoble–Chambéry. The division continued its march in the direction of Lyon from its bivouac sites late in the afternoon of 20 June. By evening, the metropolis still had not been reached. Only *Hauptmann* Barth, the division intelligence officer, made it to Lyon to establish contact for the purposes of quartering and traffic regulation. (*Hauptmann* Barth received notice at the time that he had been accepted as a General Staff officer.) The division command post set up operations in Château Boullars, six kilometers west of Bourg.

The enemy no longer seemed capable of putting up organized resistance. It was only the reconnaissance and combat patrols that occasionally had it out in small skirmishes with enemy rearguards. For example, *Unteroffizier* Liebich of the 3rd Company of the motorcycle infantry was able to destroy six aircraft and a tank at an airstrip while conducting a patrol. The noncommissioned officer, who received the Iron Cross, First Class, for his efforts, had crossed the Rhone in a pneumatic craft with his squad.

Most of the division got to see a bit of Lyon on 21 June. The tankers from Berlin and Brandenburg finally got to see a large French city that had not suffered anything from the war. The columns halted before entering the Saone Valley. There were baronial villas with huge gardens, which stretched all the way up the hills. The outskirts were soon reached and the movement continued into the city center. The streets were full of people. There was movement everywhere.

The streetcars moved past, ringing their bells. French police stood at the intersections and regulated the enormous traffic. Businesses had their wares on tables in front of their stores. Many passers-by stood motionless and gaped at the field-gray columns moving by. The columns then moved across the Rhone and into the main business district. It should be noted that there were ugly, black house facades with dark rows of windows along the riverbanks. It was a picture of proletarian poverty, which the tall spires of the mighty cathedrals that dominated the skyline of the city could not hide. The movement continued without stopping past the airfields at Bron and Bourgouin. The effect of *Stuka* attacks could easily be seen there.

The division rested on the periphery of Lyon in the many small hamlets and localities. *Panzer-Regiment 6* guarded the rest area around Janneyrias. For the soldiers, it was a welcome change of pace to be able to buy fresh fruit, such as bananas and apricots, or silk goods, such as silk stockings, or smoking products while they bivouacked in the Rhone Valley. Some were happy just to see the peaks of the western Alps gleaming over from afar.

Generalmajor Stumpff summoned his commanders to a conference on 22 June at the Hotel Carlton. He briefed the officers on recently received directives concerning the situation. According to them, the *XVI. Armee-Korps (mot.)* was to be the only German corps to cross the demarcation line established between Germany and Italy. The purpose was to unhinge the French front along the Alps from the west to make it easier for the Italians to attack into the Rhone Valley.

The corps had issued orders to its divisions. On 23 June, the *3. Panzer-Division* was to form the first wave and move on Grenoble from its former assembly areas. It was to block the retreat routes leading to the city from the northeast, east and south. If possible, it was to establish contact with the Italian Army. It was directed for the *4. Panzer-Division* to guard that advance along the right flank by attacking on

both sides of the Rhone in the direction of Valence. The *13. Infanterie-Division (mot.)*, reinforced by the *II./Panzer-Regiment 6*, was to advance to a line running Montmélian–Annecy to block the egress routes for the enemy out of the Isere and Arc Valleys. There were still eight enemy divisions in the fortified area between the Mediterranean and Montblanc: the Moroccan 2nd and 3rd Infantry Divisions, the 30th Mountain Division, and the 40th, 54th, 67th, 69th, and 72nd Infantry Divisions. There were also three fortress brigades employed there. Since most of those forces had not yet done any fighting, it was anticipated that there would be an energetic resistance. That aspect was to be taken under consideration in the formation of battle groups.

The division moved its forces forward on 22 June so that *Kampfgruppe Kühn* was in the Bourgoin area, *Kampfgruppe Kleemann* in the Crémieu area, and *Kampfruppe von Manteuffel* around Bron. There was only nominal fighting that day in the division sector, with the 3rd Company of motorcycle infantry encountering slight resistance from Negroes at Crémieu. When *Obergefreiter* Krautwurst and *Gefreiter* Lewerenz captured two French officers while on patrol, they were not satisfied with their "catch." They continued scouting, but when they reached some trees, shots rang out. Undeterred, the two junior noncommissioned officers attacked courageously and brought back an additional 2 officers and 200 Negroes.

The twenty-third of June started with dreary and rainy weather. The reconnaissance battalion, reinforced by a battery from the 1st Battalion of artillery, moved out punctually. The troops moved through Ruy and Champiere in the direction of Les Abrets. The division followed with its two large battle groups. On that day, *Oberst* Kühn commanded *Panzer-Regiment 5*, the *II./Schützen-Regiment 3*, *MG-Bataillon 7*, the *I./Artillerie-Regiment 75*, the *II./Artillerie-Regiment 49*, *Panzerjäger-Abteilung 39*, the *3. Pionier-Bataillon 39*, the engineer section and bridging section from the divisional engineers, the *II./Flak-Lehr-Regiment*, and a company from

Panzerjäger-Abteilung 605. Oberst Kleemann's force, marching to the left, consisted of the *I./Panzer-Regiment 6*, the *I./Schützen-Regiment 3*, *Kradschützen-Bataillon 3*, the *I./Artillerie-Regiment 75*, *Panzerjäger-Abteilung 605*, the *2./Pionier-Bataillon 39*, and the *10./Flak-Lehr-Regiment.*

The advance guard of *Kampfgruppe Kühn* ran into a large tree abatis at the entrance of the valley leading to Grenoble, not far from Moirans. It was guarded by enemy antitank guns. The tanks took up the fight with the enemy shortly after 0900 hours and were able to breach the obstacle in the end. But the fighting vehicles were unable to advance any further that day. The terrain was too difficult, the mountain roads too steep and rocky and the meadows to the sides too marshy. Moreover, the French had posted machine guns and antitank guns at almost every bend in the road. Artillery and mortars fired from high atop the mountains on the march routes and inflicted the first casualties on the battle group. *Oberst* Kühn reported to the division that it would only be possible to advance if friendly artillery were brought forward.

The advance guard of *Kampfgruppe Kleemann* encountered stubborn resistance around 1100 hours at Pont de Beauvoisin. The road bridge had been blown up by the enemy, and the rail bridge to the south was but a mountain of rubble. Without artillery support, it proved impossible to cross with pneumatic craft, since the enemy occupied the far bank. Correspondingly, only the western portion of the locality could be taken. Fighting vehicles from the 2nd Company of *Panzer-Regiment 6*, which had been sent forward, had more success. They were able to capture an intact bridge six kilometers farther south at St. Albin.

Major Meese's 1st Battalion of the rifle regiment started crossing the demolished railway bridge near Beauvoisin by squads around 1400 hours. They approached the locality from that side. Nonetheless, the attacking riflemen received

heavy rifle fire from the houses, from behind vegetation and from trees. A hard struggle lasting several hours developed for the locality. The batteries of the 2nd Battalion of artillery, platoons from the antitank battalion and engineers had to be brought forward. There was a crashing and booming, the likes of which had not been heard since the fighting for the Dyle Position. The village was ablaze, but the enemy did not admit defeat. *Oberstleutnant* Tröger's motorcycle infantry approached. By then, it was the afternoon. The men dismounted from their bikes and pressed into the badly battered village, whose populace, almost without exception, had fled. Pockets of resistance could only be taken out in close combat. The casualties mounted. In the 3rd Company of the motorcycle infantry, *Fahnenjunker* Mertz[11] was killed, the fourteenth soldier of the company killed in the campaign.

The enemy finally started pulling back around 1800 hours. The motorcycle infantry battalion then turned north and scouted in the direction of St. Albin. The 1st Battalion of the rifle regiment pivoted to the south in the direction of St. Beron. Sections left behind in Beauvoisin needed the entire night to eliminate the last remaining machine-gun positions there.

Oberst Kühn's forces to the south had been able to work their way forward to the Voreppe after difficult fighting and movement. When the lead tanks of *Panzer-Regiment 5* worked their way through the broken terrain of the valley, which was full of dense vegetation, ditches, and stands of trees, and approached the Isère Canal, they suddenly received artillery fire of all calibers. It was nearly possible to get out of the way, since large obstacles in the road prevented any forward movement. The two lead fighting vehicles flew into the air as a result of direct hits.

Oberst Kühn ordered the 7th and 8th Companies of the rifle regiment forward to clear the obstacles. *Oberleutnant* Müller-Röhrbach's 7th Company attacked along the road, while *Oberleutnant* Engisch's 8th Company moved along

---

11. A *Fahnenjunker* was an officer candidate.

the railway line. The terrain, which formed the entrance to a narrow valley flanked on both sides by 800-meter mountains, was completely open and could be observed from the high ground. While the companies deployed, strong artillery and machine-gun fire impacted among their ranks. The French batteries were terrifically camouflaged and could barely be identified. The riflemen fought their way forward, meter by meter, along the steep slopes, through defiles and across creeks. They advanced into La Crue de Moirans, which was occupied by the enemy. A direct hit impacted at the location of the company headquarters section of the 8th Company, killing two senior noncommissioned officers and badly wounding *Oberleutnant* Engisch and many noncommissioned officers and enlisted personnel. The enemy fires continued unabated and stopped any further efforts at attacking. *Oberleutnant* Engisch, who remained up front, pulled his riflemen back to the outskirts of Moirans. Eleven dead remained on the valley floor; thirty-nine wounded dragged themselves back.

The division ordered the attack to be called off at 1900 hours. At midnight, *Oberstleutnant* von Manteuffel received orders from the division, whose headquarters was located in Château Rives that day, to cross the river at St. Quentin-sur-le-Isère and attack Veury from the west. The 3rd Battalion of the rifle regiment was directed to attempt to eliminate the artillery from there, thus allowing the two bogged-down battle groups outside of Voreppe and Beauvoisin to advance again.

Major Kratzenberg's 3rd Battalion was already leaving its former screening area around Etieene at 0100 hours and moving via Rives and Rebage to Fure. *Oberstleutnant* von Manteuffel personally briefed the Battalion Commander on the special situation. To assist the battalion, *Hauptmann* von Viereck's *3./Panzerjäger-Abteilung 39* and *Hauptmann* Stern's *1./Pionier-Bataillon 39* were attached in support. The two forward observers from the 4th and 6th Batteries had no radio contact with their batteries, so the entire operation had to be conducted without artillery preparation.

The battalion dismounted from its vehicles and advanced through the darkness of the night. The 13th Company reached Vert and was directed to take a crossing point over the Isère by means of a *coup de main*. The engineers reconnoitered and determined that a crossing was not possible because of the rapid current—three meters a second. The river was 250 meters wide, and the pneumatic craft would most likely by taken 1,000 meters downstream. Further reconnaissance was conducted at the bridge east of Tullins. The patrol received fire from several machine guns from the direction of St. Quentin. It was also determined that the bridge had been blown up. The third span was in the water and could not be repaired quickly by the engineers. After that report reached the division, *Generalmajor* Stumpff ordered the operation called off.

The attack by *Oberst* Kühn's forces on 24 June did not make any progress, despite several attempts on the part of the riflemen to penetrate into the valley west of Voreppe. Enemy fires from the outer sectors of the fortress of Grenoble were preventing the division from penetrating into the western French Alps.

Kampfgruppe Kleemann was given the mission on the morning of 24 June to establish contact with *Generalmajor* von Rothkirch und Panthen's *13. Infanterie-Division (mot.)* on the left. That was achieved late in the afternoon in the area one kilometer north of Beauvoisin. Kleemann's forces then advanced with the right wing of the motorized infantry division in the direction of the Col-de-la-Crusière. The second objective of the battle group was to attack Grenoble from the north.

The motorcycle infantry battalion was employed against La Bridoire to protect the left flank. The battalion attacked in two groups under *Hauptmann* Pape and *Oberleutnant* Beck to the north. After overcoming large obstacles and machine-gun nests, it succeeded in getting to Gunin outside of la Bridoire. Two tank platoons under the overall command of *Leutnant* Neumann-Holste supported the motorcycle infantry. That evening, the fighting vehicles took the village of Lépin on beautiful Aiguebelette Lake.

Hauptmann Hansen's *MG-Bataillon 7* eliminated the French heavy infantry weapons on the high ground north of Voreppe, thus bringing some relief to the 2nd Battalion of the rifle regiment, which was in position around La Crue de Moirans. By that afternoon, the machine-gun battalion from Saxony had taken Le Grand Bois, taking 150 prisoners in the process. Its advance then bogged down in the face of fires from enemy guns.

The main body of *Kampfgruppe Kleemann* then advanced on Les Echelles. The small village spread out at the foot of the Grand Som in a narrow valley pocket. The slopes all around the village were filled with vineyards, meadowlands and isolated farmsteads. The terrain presented a peaceful appearance. *Major* Meese's 1st Battalion of the rifle regiment, Major Wöhlermann's 2nd Battalion of artillery and *Leutnant* Fechner's *1./Panzer-Regiment 6* were earmarked for the attack on the village. The fighting vehicles advanced along the road, which was full of curves and tunnels, while the riflemen advanced to both sides. The enemy resistance appeared to grow weaker with each meter advanced. At that point, the riflemen were right outside the village.

One platoon from the tank company was sent against the village. After passing the first obstacle in the road, the fighting vehicles of *Leutnant* Müller knocked out an antiaircraft gun. The French placed well-aimed antitank fires along the road and forced the tanks to pull back.

In contrast, *Hauptmann* von Plato's 1st Company of the rifle regiment, supported by *Oberfeldwebel* Meyrhofer's platoon, had more success that day. The tankers and riflemen advanced across boulder-strewn fields, through vegetation, across narrow creek beds and along serpentines against St. Franc, located at 1,200 meters. The Germans were almost able to enter the village unnoticed. They took 100 Negroes from Senegal prisoner; the men were so surprised they had no time to offer a defense. The riflemen did not rest. Instead, they advanced through Attignat to La Bauche, which they reached before the sun set on the beautiful countryside.

Heavy rainfall made the individual engagements that flared up around les Echelles in the afternoon more difficult. The riflemen up front had been reinforced by heavy antitank guns and four howitzers from the 6th Battery of artillery, when the attack was repeated. The cannoneers brought their pieces right up to the edge of the village. The guns fired over open sights against the French pockets of resistance. Every gun had an officer in command: *Leutnant* Schaale on Gun No. 1, *Leutnant* Krause on 2, *Leutnant* Schröder on 3, and *Oberleutnant* Kersten on 4.

As a result of the concentric fires, the enemy's resistance weakened. The 2nd Company of the rifle regiment entered the first few houses of Les Echelles, which the enemy had abandoned. The enemy was simply trying to avoid the German artillery fire, however, and had reestablished himself further in the village. Based on the weapons and equipment previously captured—including five cases of dum-dum rounds—it was apparent that the 1st Battalion of the rifle regiment was facing a fairly substantial foe.

After the onset of darkness, the firing abated on both sides. The division had passed on to the battalion that it was to call off any attacks for the time being, since it was expected that a ceasefire would go into effect shortly and there was no need for unnecessary casualties. The watches of the men in the combat outposts showed 1900 hours, when a white flag started to be waved.

The mayor of Les Echelles appeared. He wore a black frock coat, over which he had placed a blue, white and red sash. He soon appeared in front of *Major* Meese and requested that his village be spared. The commander replied that he could only accept an unconditional surrender. His riflemen would otherwise be compelled to fight to the ceasefire, which was expected shortly. The mayor left with a heavy heart and disappeared through the first French lines.

An officer patrol was sent in the direction of Les Echelles. All of a sudden, the French showed no more interest in fighting. Not a shot was fired anywhere. The Germans moved down the streets without being stopped, followed by hundreds of pairs of eyes from armed Negroes. Then there was a trumpet call. Two French officers and the mayor approached the Germans. The battalion adjutant, *Oberleutnant* Mölln, greeted them and took them to the command post. During another meeting at the battalion command post, the German commander again demanded unconditional surrender. The French *Capitaine* declined, stating proudly, "A Frenchman never surrenders!" Both sides came to terms with a mutual ceasefire until 2215 hours, however.

The corps informed the division at 2130 hours that the official ceasefire would go into effect at 0135 hours.

Hardly anyone slept that night. Keyed up, everyone kept looking at their watches. The hands moved slowly across the faces, but the time finally came. The outposts up front fired signal flares into the dark skies; there was a hissing and banging like some joyous fireworks. From a distance, out of the villages of Isère Valley, came the sound of church bells. Then a faint sound mixed in that started to rise. It was a trumpet signal: *"Das Ganze halt!"*[12]

German state radio played the hymn "We Gather Together."[13] Wistfulness, joy, contemplation, and a feeling of triumph had not just a few rough-hewn warriors folding their hands.

The division remained in contact with the enemy with its outposts on that memorable day, as well as securing all important areas in its sector. As always, emphasis was placed on passive air defense measures, since there was still the sound of individual explosions in the mountains. Most of the formations rested. After positioning the necessary outposts, the rifle regiment placed its 1st Battalion in Les Echelles, its 2nd Battal-ion in Moirans and its 3rd Battalion in Tullins. The 2nd Battalion of *Panzer-Regiment 6*, which had been attached to the *13. Infanterie-Division (mot.)*, returned to the division fold.

The division headquarters issued passes to French physicians and employees of public utilities allowing those men to cross the lines and maintain everyday life for the civilians. The forces quartered in the cities and villages also took that under their wing. Not a few soldiers and officers passed up on food from the field kitchen in order to eat with *Madame*, whose food tasted a whole lot better. The businessmen did not have to worry about a loss of sales for their goods, since there were things in their shops that the tankers had learned to go without for a long time.

An officer from the division went to see the commander of the opposing forces. The French commander allowed the division to recover and evacuate the dead and wounded from the heavy fighting of the previous three days in cases where they had not been accessible. The last dead from the division were placed to eternal rest on the palace grounds at Moirans.

The commander in chief of the army, *Generaloberst* von Brauchitsch, arrived at the division command post on 29 June, and *Generalmajor* Stumpff reported to him. The commander in chief then went to Moirans, where he visited the forces positioned there. At a formation of the 6th Company of the rifle regiment, he mentioned for the first time that the division would be headed for the homeland soon.

Those words soon circulated through all of the dugouts, quarters and outposts. All of the needs and the worries of the previous six weeks were quickly forgotten. A few thought about the comrades with whom they had shared the 4,950 kilometers the division had covered in the campaign and who had paid the ultimate price. The division had been at the front from the very

---

12. It roughly means "Everyone stop!" or, in more modern terms, "Stand down!"
13. This is known in German as the *niederländisches Dankgebiet*—literally, "Dutch Prayer of Thanks"—and in the original Dutch as *Willt heden nu treden*. It was written to celebrate the Dutch victory over Spanish forces at the Battle of Turnhout in 1597.

beginning and had participated in all of the decisive battles. It had also paid a high cost. The numbers of dead suffered during the campaign in the West should be considered illustrative of all of the dead the division suffered and serve as a memorial to them: in *Panzer-Regiment 6*, 5 officers and 65 noncommissioned officers and enlisted personnel; in *Schützen-Regiment 3*, 20 officers and 134 noncommissioned officers and enlisted personnel.

The successes of the division in the campaign were not due solely to the leadership skills and tactical proficiency of the officers or to the courage and commitment of the tankers, riflemen and cannoneers who were in the frontlines, but also to those that an Armed Forces Daily Report never mentioned. Those were the innumerable radio operators, telephone operators, convoy drivers, medics, cooks, first sergeants, maintenance personnel and mechanics, bakers and butchers. Their achievements can never be measured.

In the period from May through June, the division's field post office, manned by fifteen soldiers and under the supervision of *Feldpostinspektor* Mollweide, processed the following amounts of mail: 2,851 sacks of received mail, 637 sacks of outgoing mail, 6,792 outgoing postal money transfers (389,341 *Reichsmark*), and 1,425 incoming postal money transfers (38,314 *Reichsmark*).

On 29 June, the corps passed the following order telephonically: "Effective 1 July, the *3. Panzer-Division* moves in the direction of Germany." That officially ended the employment of the division in the campaign in the West.

Command post at Asseviilers: The company commanders wait for the attack orders. From left to right: *Oberleutnant* von Baumbach, *Hauptmann* von Plato, *Oberleutnant* Stein, and other unidentified officers.

Oberst Forster, the commander of *Artillerie-Regiment 75*.

Major Zimmermann, the commander of the *II./Schützen-Regiment 3*. He was later awarded the Knight's Cross for his role in the fighting for St. Florentin.

Unteroffizier Moder led the lead squad that took the bridges.

Just before a firing mission: A 10.5-cm field gun of the *6./Artillerie-Regiment 75* at Péronne.

The bridges at St. Florentin.

The main clearing station of the
3. Panzer-Division.

Taking a breather after an engagement.
From left to right: *Leutnant* Hellinger,
Oberleutnant Stein, *Hauptmann* Haspel,
and *Leutnant* von Pfuhlstein.

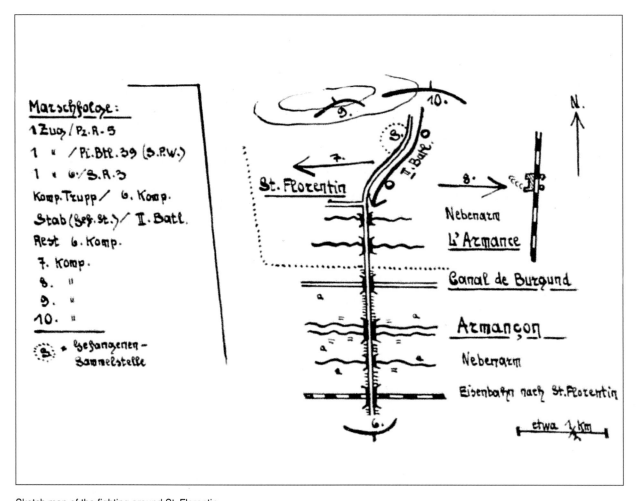

Sketch map of the fighting around St. Florentin.

A soldier's gravesite along the road in front of Arnay le Duc. Third from the left is *Leutnant Freiherr* von Werthern.

The *II./Schützen-Regiment 3* advances on Moirans.

The bridge over the St. Albin at La Bridoire.

Oberleutnant Möll, the adjutant of the *I./Schützen-Regiment 3*, receives a French emissary at Les Echelles. The war in France was over.

Panzer-Regiment 6 returns to its home garrison of Neuruppin. *Panzer II's* of the regiment pass in review in front of the regimental commander.

A parade involving the *3. Panzer-Division* in Mainz. On the tribunal are *General der Infanterie* Steppuhn, the commander of Military District XII; *Generalmajor* Stumpff; and *Generalmajor* Meyer, the local commander for Mainz and the first commander of *Panzer-Regiment 6*.

Schützen-Regiment 3 enters its home garrison of Eberswalde.

Pionier-Bataillon 39 returns home to Rathenow. In the *Panzer II* is *Leutnant* Ziegenbalg. Of interest is the fact that the order of battle for the battalion in 1940 does not indicate the issuance of any tanks.

The *III./Schützen-Regiment 3* enters the von Estorff Barracks in Hamburg-Wandsbek.

Oberst Kleemann (seen here as a *Generalmajor*), the commander of the *3. Schützen-Brigade*.

Oberst Linnarz (seen here as a *Generalleutnant*), the commander of the *5. Panzer-Brigade*.

Oberleutnant Buchterkirch was not only the first recipient of the Knight's Cross in the division (29 June 1940, as a platoon leader in the *2./Panzer-Regiment 6*), but he was also the division's first Oak Leaves recipient (31 December 1941, as the commander of the *2./Panzer-Regiment 6*).

Major Kratzenberg, the commander of the *III./Schützen-Regiment 3*. He is given credit for the taking of the Dyle Position.

CHAPTER 6

The Return Home

The first of July saw the start of the departure of the division for Germany. It was directed to take the tracked vehicles to the vicinity of Langres, where they would be rail-loaded home. All wheeled vehicles were to road march directly to their garrisons. The division started moving out of its quartering areas at 0700 hours.

It was a bright and clear morning. The mountains jutted out of the fog with their peaks and presented their final greetings to the departing soldiers. The forces rolled along familiar routes to the Rhône. The tanks rattled in the direction of the railhead at Les Abrets. The division formed three march serials and moved via Lyon to the area around Bourg and to the north. The division located its command post in Branges. *Hauptmann i.G.* Barth remained with the intelligence section in Paladru as the rear party.

The road march the next day proceeded via Châlons-sur-Sâone, Beaune, Dijon, Langres, and Chaumont. The transport trains with the tanks and tracked vehicles caught up with the march serials on 3 July, which had a day of rest. *Oberleutnant* von Brauchitsch, who had been sent to the *12. Armee* as a liaison officer, returned on 3 July with the information that a reconstitution had been ordered for the division in its peacetime garrisons. The *XVI. Armee-Korps (mot.)* remained the division's immediate superior command until the borders of the Reich, at which point the division reported to the Replacement Army.

The division assembled all of its elements on 4 July and continued its march. There was a good bit of traffic in Nancy. All of the businesses were jammed with soldiers of the occupation forces and the first brown-uniformed party functionaries. Once beyond the city, there were traces of the war: Bomb craters, graves, destroyed houses, tossed-aside weapons and vast quantities of materiel. The route then led through kilometers of peaceful, unspoiled countryside. It was not until the vicinity of the Maginot Line was reached that destroyed localities, blown-up bridges and shot-up bunkers and guns were seen again. The division moved through Saargemünd. Around 1700 hours, lead elements of the division entered Reich territory. The movement continued past bunkers, improved field fortifications, wire obstacles and tank traps and into undamaged, but depopulated Saarbrücken.

The first command post of the division on German soil was in Landstuhl. The rifle regiment took up quarters in Münchweiler, while the armored brigade did not cross the border until the next day. The next forty-eight hours were spent with sleep, leisure and maintenance. The seventh of July was a brilliant Sunday. The division marched from Saarbrücken via Kaiserslautern and arrived in Mainz that morning. The city was decorated with flowers and flags. The residents stood along the streets, looked out of their windows and waved from their balconies. Accompanied by the sounds of parade music, the regiments and battalions marched past the commanding general of the homefront command of the *XII. Armee-Korps*,[1] *General der Infanterie* Steppuhn, who was also the local military commander for Mainz, as well as *Generalmajor* Meyer, the first peacetime commander of *Panzer-Regiment 6* and *Generalmajor* Stumpff.

Advance parties from the divisional elements had already headed back to their garrisons. The tracked vehicles were loaded on trains again on 7 July and sent in the direction of Berlin. The *III./Schützen-Regiment 3* left the main body of the division the same day and moved via the Autobahn and Giessen, Göttingen, and Lüneburg to Hamburg. There, the battalion paraded in front of the cheers of thousands of people and past *Generalleutnant* Schwandtner, the commanding general of the homefront command of the *XII. Armee-Korps*. The main body of the division march through Thuringia over the next two days toward Berlin and its other home garrisons. The local populations greeted the forces everywhere with loud cheers, flowers, cakes and cigarettes. Once in their home garrisons, the various formations passed in review before their commanders.

Detachments for Africa

The fall of 1940 was a decisive time in the history of the division. After *Unternehmen "Seelöwe"* (Operation Sea Lion), the invasion of England, was called off, the German leadership attempted to force England to its knees by other means. For the immediate future, it had to help its Italian allies in North Africa.

The Army High Command ordered the division to be the first major formation trained and equipped for the new theater of war. Specialist committees started visiting the troop units at the end of September and beginning of October to determine whether soldiers were fit for duty in tropical climates. Starting in the middle of October, those soldiers, who could not be employed there due to health issues, were swapped with soldiers from other elements or from the replacement detachments. At the beginning of November, the division started exchanging equipment and vehicles and receiving special ammunition.

---

1. Germany was divided into districts, each of which was the home base to a corps. Upon mobilization, homefront commands for the districts were also activated to take care of military administrative and training matters within the respective districts. These were referred to as the "representative" (*stellvertretend*) commands, which have translated as "homefront" commands here.

Mussolini protested against the sending of a German armored division, however. Hitler acceded to his desires and the transfer of the entire *3. Panzer-Division* to Africa was halted.

The refitting of the division for tropical duty continued, however, since the German leadership entertained thoughts of using it for *Unternehmen Felix,* the proposed invasion of Morocco. Consequently, all regimental officers were sent to the military medical academy in Berlin to attend courses on tropical matters relating to the military. The division's training in garrison and local training areas continued unabated, even after orders were received on 12 November to prepare the entire division once again for tropical duty. That idea was abandoned, however.

At that point, the British started their major offensive on Cyrenaica. General Wavell's 8th Army moved out on 8 December against Marshal Graziani's 10th Army. Just one week later, Wavell's forces had pushed the Italians back across the Egyptian border. At that point, Mussolini turned to the German government and asked for expedited military support.

That caused the Army High Command to form a motorized blocking force that could accomplish just such a mission. *Oberst Freiherr* von Funck, the commander of *Panzer-Regiment 5,* was promoted to *Generalmajor* and given the task of forming the unit. *Freiherr* von Funck arrived as the first officer of the future *Deutsches Afrika-Korps* in Tripoli on 15 January 1941. He remained there four weeks before returning to Germany and assuming command of the *7. Panzer-Division* from *Generalleutnant* Erwin Rommel, who was then sent to Africa. The division was ordered to provide combat-capable elements and establish the main parts of the blocking force. Events in North Africa also took their own course. That forced the Army High Command to raise a light division,[2] instead of the originally envisioned brigade equivalent.

Consequently, the *3. Panzer-Division* lost not only combat-experienced regiments and brigades. Within the overall scheme of things, it also lost officers, noncommissioned officers and enlisted personnel, who had been in the division for years, training and growing professionally there. The loss of *Panzer-Regiment 5* was the biggest blow to the division. The regiment was not only the oldest armor regiment of the *Panzertruppe,* it had also gone through thick and thin with the division and had participated with distinction in the fighting in Poland and France. Although *Panzer-Regiment 6* had initially been earmarked for tropical duty, it had transferred all of its tropical equipment and vehicles to its sister regiment after the fall of 1940. The regiment received considerable new equipment, including seventy *Panzer III's* with the 5-centimeter main gun. The first two battalions of the regiment prepared for the transport to Africa. The 3rd Battalion of *Panzer-Regiment 28,* which had been intended for the newly activated *18. Panzer-Division,* was reassigned to *Panzer-Regiment 6* as its 3rd Battalion in March.

The divisional artillery had to give up its 1st Battalion.[3] *Panzerjäger-Abteilung 39* and *Aufklärungs-Abteilung 3* were also reassigned to the new light division.[4] Those five good formations formed the nucleus of the first German division to be employed in Africa. In addition, the division gave up the *3./Nachrichten-Abteilung 39*

2. This became the *5. leichte Division,* which was later reorganized and redesignated as the *21. Panzer-Division.*

3. This was replaced by *schwere Artillerie-Abteilung 714,* which had been a separate artillery battalion with three batteries of 10-centimeter cannon. In March 1941, it was reorganized and reissued with light howitzers and attached to the *3. Panzer-Division* as its 1st Battalion of artillery, although it maintained the numerical designation of 714 until relatively late (at least 1943, perhaps never given up). For simplicity's sake, it will be referred to as the regiment's 1st Battalion. See discussion in *Lexikon.*

4. *Panzerjäger-Abteilung 543,* a separate antitank battalion, was assigned to the division to replace the transferred *Panzerjäger-Abteilung 39.* The division received *Aufklärungs-Abteilung 1* to replace *Aufklärungs-Abteilung 3* on 29 January 1941, but that battalion was forced to give up its 2nd Troop on 29 January to help form *Aufklärungs-Abteilung (mot.) 18 (18. Panzer-Division).* The battalion was redesignated as *Panzer-Aufklärungs-Abteilung 1* in April 1941. See discussion in *Lexikon.*

and the *2./Pionier-Bataillon 39*, with the later unit becoming the 5th Company of *MG-Bataillon 2*. The signals platoon of the armored brigade had to turn in its signals equipment. *Panzer-jäger-Abteilung 605*, which had supported the division throughout the campaign in the West, was also transferred to the *5. leichte Division*.

Oberstleutnant i.G. von dem Borne, who had proven himself for years as the division operations officer and who had contributed greatly to its successes, gave up his duties to prove his abilities as the chief of staff of the newly forming *Deutsches Afrika-Korps*. The *3. Panzer-Brigade* was dissolved to provide the headquarters cadre for the *5. leichte Division*.

Generalleutnant Rommel reported to his immediate supervisor, General Gariboldi, the commander in chief of the Italian forces, in Libya at the beginning of February. The sea movement of the German forces to Tripoli started on 11 February 1941. *Oberstleutnant Freiherr* von Wechmar's *Aufklärungs-Abteilung 3* became the first German ground force to land on African soil. The armored cars and motorcycle infantry immediately headed to the front and took the British fort at El Agheila on 24 March. That started the operations of the *Deutsches Afrika-Korps*, whose first major attack took place on the last day of March between Marsa-el-Brega and the salt marshes of Marada. The fighting vehicles of *Panzer-Regiment 5*, under the command of *Oberst* Olbrich, initiated one of the most glamorous chapters of the war with their thrust into the Libyan Desert.

After a series of great victories and heroic defensive efforts, those former troop elements of the *3. Panzer-Division* found their lamentable but glorious end in 1943 as part of *Heeresgruppe Tunis* in the rocky and sandy wastes of Tunisia.

CHAPTER 7

From the Spree to the Bug, Part 2: The Eve of Operation Barbarossa

The Face of the Division Changes

All of the formations of the division were back at their home garrisons by 10 July 1940. The barracks were frequently occupied by replacement elements, however, with the result that rooms and offices had to be shared. In addition, some of the active companies were quartered privately nearby—with none of the riflemen, radio operators, cannoneers and tankers complaining one bit. For instance, the divisional signals battalion left its garrison in Stahnsdorf after a few weeks to take up residence in the Michendorf–Caputh area in farmer's and civilian's houses.

It goes without saying that many officers, noncommissioned officers, and enlisted personnel the fourteen days of leave that was due had been earned. In the process, additional training and normal duties were still carried out. Vehicles, equipment and weapons had to be cleaned, repaired and maintained. One could ask anyone assigned to the maintenance companies what all that entailed.

Once the first period of block leave was over, the quiet times were again a thing of the past. The war was still going on and new assignments were also given to the divisions that were back in their peacetime garrisons. The German command had planned first *Unternehmen Seelöwe* and then *Unternehmen Felix*. The *3. Panzer-Division* was under active consideration for both operations. For instance, a detachment of *Panzer-Regiment 5* under the command of *Major Ritter Edler* von Peter was sent to the North Sea and the Baltic to receive training on submergible tanks.[1] Most of the elements of the division were affected by reorganizations, issuances of new equipment, special duties, or courses of instruction.

The armor regiments were not the only major formations affected by reorganizations within the division. For instance, the *1./Schützen-Regiment 3*, which had previously been a motor-cycle infantry company, received armored personnel carriers. The rifle squads were organized into two machine-gun sections.

Even with the changes, the focus of daily duty continued to remain on maintaining weapons, equipment and vehicles. In the month of August, officers and enlisted personnel, who had been wounded during the Campaign in the West, returned to their units. The division returned to full strength in personnel assignments.

Major Meese, the commander of the *I./ Schützen-Regiment 3*, was transferred to the unassigned officer manpower pool of Military District III on 25 July. He was later assigned to the Ceasefire Commission. *Major* von Bosse, who had been wounded at Orp-le-Petit, returned to reassume his former command. The commander of the regiment's 1st Company, *Hauptmann* von Plato, was sent to the war academy for general-staff-officer training.

The training for the newer soldiers and the professional development of the troops intensified over time. On 16 August, the division released its training plan. Among many other things, emphasis was placed on the cultivation of discipline, march exercises, poison gas defensive training, professional development of junior leaders, weekly company exercises, and biweekly battalion exercises. The young and new officers were constantly involved in map exercises. For instance, a map exercise was conducted on 30 August that focused on the breaching of a fortified position by a battalion reinforced with tanks.

In the fall of 1940, the German Army was in the midst of both reorganization and organizational changes. Those changes especially effected the armor divisions. The direct effects on the *3. Panzer-Division* were as follows:[2]

The Headquarters, *3. Panzer-Brigade*, was used to form the headquarters of the *5. leichte Division*. In its place, the division received the Headquarters, *5. Panzer-Brigade*. The latter command-and-control entity was formed out of assets of Military District III. Since *Panzer-Regiment 5* was to be shipped in its entirety to North Africa, the division only had *Panzer-Regiment 6* remaining. Eventually, the previously reassigned personnel used to form the submergible tank battalion (*Panzer-Abteilung C*), returned to the division in a rather circuitous fashion as the *III./Panzer-Regiment 6*.[3] With the addition of a third battalion, *Panzer-Regiment 6* was one of the first armored regiments so organized.

The division also received a second rifle regiment. It was designated as *Schützen-Regiment 394*. The headquarters came from the former *Infanterie-Regiment 394* of the *209. Infanterie-Division*. The *III./Schützen-Regiment 3* was used to form the regiment's 1st Battalion. The regiment's 2nd Battalion was formed from the *II./Infanterie-Regiment 243*, which had originally been formed from *Landespolizei-Regiment*

---

1. According to *Lexikon*, both of the armored regiments provided personnel for a battalion formed under von Peter's command, with *Panzer-Regiment 6* providing its entire 2nd Company. The battalion was formed on 24 July and designated as *Panzer-Abteilung C*. In December, it was consolidated with the newly formed *Panzer-Regiment 28* (intended for the *18. Panzer-Division*) and designated as that regiment's 1st Battalion. Just three months later, in March 1941, *Panzer-Regiment 28* was disbanded and the 1st Battalion was reassigned to *Panzer-Regiment 6* as its 3rd Battalion.
2. See also the previous chapter, where some of this material overlaps.
3. See footnote 1 above.

1 in Danzig.[4] In addition, the *13./Infanterie-Regiment 325 (228. Infanterie-Division)* was used to form the regiments 13th Company. The regiment's activation took place in the Eberswalde area.

The divisional artillery did not remain unaffected. Its 1st battalion was sent to Africa. *Schwere Artillerie-Abteilung 714*, a horse-drawn artillery battalion from Swabia, was received in its place. The battalion was motorized and received the *leichte Feldhaubitze 18* and considered the regiment's 1st Battalion.[5] The divisional artillery was reorganized to have a 3rd Battalion. This was formed from the *II./Artillerie-Regiment 49*.[6] Flash-ranging support for the artillery was provided by the addition of *Beobachtungs-Batterie 325*.[7]

Since the original antitank and reconnaissance battalions of the division—*Panzerjäger-Abteilung 39* and *Aufklärungs-Abteilung 3*—were also sent to Africa, the division also received replacements for them. *Aufklärungs-Abteilung (mot.) 1*,[8] from East Prussia, became the divisional reconnaissance battalion; *Panzerjäger-Abteilung 543*, from the Rhineland, its antitank asset. The antitank battalion was moved to Teupitz, near Berlin. The reorganization for those men was difficult, inasmuch as it had been a battalion composed of reservists and older vehicles and equipment. They had to get used to the demands and pace of an active-duty armor division, which was outfitted with modern equipment. The battalion consisted of a headquarters element with signal platoon and three line antitank companies having two platoons each of 3.7-centimeter antitank guns and one platoon of 5-centimeter antitank guns. In addition, the battalion also had antiaircraft assets, consisting of one company with two platoons of 2-centimeter single-barreled *Flak* and one platoon with 2-centimeter four-barreled Flak.

Since the engineer and signals battalions each had to give up a company for the *5. leichte Division*, the battalions were reorganized to accommodate that. For instance, the 4th Company of engineers became the 2nd Company. Both of the signals companies were modernized and reorganized, so that both had the same weaponry and vehicular equipment.

The new additions and assignments to the division from previously non-organic elements, as well as the permanent and temporary reassignments of personnel, also changed the face of the division from a personnel perspective. The officers and enlisted personnel had come from all areas of the Reich and only the number reminded one that it was a Berlin and Brandenburg division. The division had been "remodeled," as the soldiers started to say.

That expression was derived from the name of the new division commander, *Generalleutnant* Model. On 13 November, a man with

---

4. That regiment was part of the *60. Infanterie-Division*, which was later motorized and end the war as *Panzergrenadier-Division "Feldhernhalle."* The regiment was inactivated as a part of the division's reorganization (motorization). This reduced its original three infantry regiments to two. Cadre from *Infanterie-Regiment 243* was also used in forming the Headquarters of *Schützen-Regiment 114* (*6. Panzer-Division*) and the *II./Schützen-Regiment 304* (*2. Panzer-Division*).

5. See the previous chapter for additional information on the numerical designation of this formation.

6. *Artillerie-Regiment 49* had been a separate artillery regiment, but its headquarters and two line battalions had been used to support differing commands after mobilization.

7. The author may be in error with regard to the additional artillery asset, inasmuch as neither *Lexikon* nor Schmitz mention this battery in this context. *Lexikon* indicates that *Beobachtungs-Abteilung 10* (*10. Infanterie-Division*) was inactivated in December 1940 and its personnel used to form three flash-ranging batteries (324, 325, and 326) which were assigned to three armored divisions (4, 7, and 15), with *Beobachtungs-Batterie* going to the *7. Panzer-Division*. See also Peter Schmitz, et al., *Die deutschen Divisionen 1939–1945*, Band 1, *Die Divisionen 1–5* (Osnabrück: Biblio-Verlag, 1993), 215 ff.

8. Not to be confused with *Aufklärungs-Abteilung 1* of the *1. Infanterie-Division*, which was also garrisoned in Königsberg (Kaliningrad). *Aufklärungs-Abteilung (mot.) 1* was formed from cavalry assets of the *3. Kavallerie-Division* and used as a separate reconnaissance battalion.

boundless zeal took the helm of the division, a man who bent it to his will, his toughness and his vision.

Generalmajor Stumpff, who had been with the division since it had been formed, was transferred to the newly formed *20. Panzer-Division* to take command there.

The operations officer for the new division commander was *Major i.G.* Pomtow. The two other General Staff positions were filled by *Hauptmann i.G.* Barth, the new division logistics officer, and *Oberleutnant* von Schubert, who took Barth's position as division intelligence officer.

Command of the armored brigade was assumed by *Generalmajor* Breith, who came from the *4. Panzer-Division*. He gave up that command in May to *Oberst* Linnarz.[9] The rifle brigade continued to be commanded by *Oberst* Kleemann. The two commanders of *Panzer-Regiment 6* and *Schützen-Regiment 3* remained in command as well, while the new commander of *Schützen-Regiment 394* was *Oberst* Erhard, who was replaced on 26 August 1940 by *Oberstleutnant* Audörsch. *Major* von Corvin-Wiersbitzki assumed command of the motorcycle infantry battalion, while *Major* Wellmann took the helm of the 1st Battalion of *Schützen-Regiment 3*. *Major Freiherr* von Türckheim zu Altdorf assumed command of *Panzerjäger-Abteilung 543*, and *Hauptmann* Ziervogel became the commander of *Aufklärungs-Abteilung 1*. In January 1941, *Oberst* Ries became the divisional artillery commander.

The year of 1941 was also marked once again by tough training. Battle drills were the focal point of the military exercises.

Starting in January, the division was uniformly equipped with vehicles of the same type, and the previously issued trucks and staff cars turned in. In February, all enlisted personnel who were born in 1909 or earlier were transferred to the replacement detachments, with the gaps in the formations being immediately filled with trained personnel. In March, the tank crews received steel helmets for the first time in their history; their marching boots were replaced by high-top, lace-up half-boots.[10]

A large-scale exercise was held on 17 May 1941 in front of *Generaloberst* Guderian at Marienwerder (near Eberswalde). A crossing over the Finow River and the Hohenzollern Canal was exercised using all available means, including the employment of close air support. *Hauptmann* Schneider-Kostalski's 3rd Battalion of the armor regiment crossed the Hohenzollern Canal using submergible tanks, while *Major* Wellmann's *I./Schützen-Regiment 3* crossed using pneumatic craft.

In the meantime, the higher command levels had already received movement directives in preparation for the campaign against the Soviet Union. The headquarters conducted the necessary map exercises within a restricted circle of commanders and staff officers. For instance, the commander in chief of the *4. Armee*, *Generalfeldmarschall* von Kluge, conducted a map exercise with his corps and division commanders in Posen, which focused on the approach march and employment of the field army. *Generalleutnant* Model, accompanied by his aide, *Leutnant* Liebrich, attended the exercise.

The division was filled to its authorized levels of personnel, weapons, equipment, and

---

9. Other sources indicate 3 June for the change of command, when Breith went to the staff of the Mobile Forces at the Army High Command. He worked there until October of that year, when he would return to the *3. Panzer-Division* as its commander. See *Die Ritterkreuzträger der Deutschen Wehrmacht und Waffen-SS* (www.ritterkreuztraeger-1939-45.de).

10. Although the helmets were issued, they were rarely worn, except for parades or field award formations. Despite the danger on the battlefield, the tankers continued to prefer cloth headgear. The iconic beret and crash helmet combination seen being worn through the campaign in the West was also turned in, since it was also generally held in disdain by the tankers.

ammunition. In the month of May, all of the companies had to provide work details that were involved in producing bundled fascines for attaching to the sides of the vehicles to aid in the negotiation of soft ground or small obstacles.

The division also received a new tactical insignia. It consisted off an upside-down "Y" with two vertical short bars to the right side of the top portion of the "Y."[11]

At the end of May, the division was ordered to be prepared to move, with its elements remaining in their garrisons and temporary quarters. The exception was the *I./Schützen-Regiment 394*, 280 kilometers from the division's areas, which was moved by rail from Hamburg to Angermünde. Rail-loading exercises were conducted, and officers and enlisted personnel on leave were summoned back.

Generalleutnant Model called his commanders together for a meeting on 25 May at the division headquarters in Buckow. The officers received the directive to look for quartering areas for their forces for the upcoming operation. To that end, the brigade and regimental commanders moved via Warsaw to Niedzyrzec to the headquarters of the *1. Kavallerie-Division*, where they were briefed on the general situation by the forces positioned along the Bug.

The division published its movement order for the East on 31 May (Order No. 0044/41, SECRET COMMAND MATTER). According to it, the wheeled elements of the division were to start moving out on 6 June, reaching Radzyn in four day and two night marches. The *3. Panzer-Division* was granted right of way along all march routes, with the exception of Posen forward, which was shared with the *4. Panzer-Division*. The rail movements, which departed at a rate of forty-eight trains a day, had absolute priority, however. There were additional directives for the tracked vehicles from the transport commands. The advance parties of the regiments and battalions left their quarters on 1 June under the command of officers. Two days later, specific movement orders were issued to each of the troop elements.

When the division started moving out on 6 June, it was greeted by radiant sunshine over Berlin and the surrounding areas. People were standing on the streets everywhere, waving in a friendly manner to the departing soldiers. The regimental bands played continuous marches in front of the garrisons, as the division left its home base in three march serials for the third time since the war started. The clocks showed 0900 hours, as the lead elements entered the Autobahn at Finowfurt. The *I./Schützen-Regiment 394* had arrived from Angermünde, as did the wheeled elements of the armored regiment. The elements of the rifle brigade were in the lead, followed by the armor brigade. Bringing up the rear was the divisional headquarters and troop units.

The movement continued without stopping. The march was used to conduct small-scale exercises and training. For instance, the vehicles were to take up concealed positions under trees when they halted, and meals were taken from the field kitchens, which also moved with the troop elements. As it started to turn dark, the division had reached its day's march objective of 225 kilometers. The wheeled vehicles of the armor regiment bivouacked in Reppen, while *Schützen-Regiment 3* set up in Drossen, to name but two locations.

The second day of movement did not proceed as smoothly, once the right-of-way for the railroads became felt. There were hour-long delays at railway crossings. The division moved via Schwiebus into the area around Tierschtiegel along the former Polish border. The movement forward from there was reminiscent of the cam-

---

11. The insignia was painted in yellow and generally appeared on the hull front, rear, and sides.

paign in Poland, as the vehicles struggled along the dusty roads under a hot sun. The move through the city of Posen was done at a fast clip. The German-Russian border of 1914 was reached and the soldiers spent the night in the villages and rural estates. Riding in his Opel (license plate: WH-512-244) along with *Leutnant* Pauckstadt, *Obergefreiter* Kohlwey, and *Gefreiter* Pape, *Generalleutnant* Model mingled with his soldiers. He frequently scolded the march discipline, since convoy movements had been practiced far too little in the previous months.

The ninth of June was another warm and cloudless day. The movement did not start until the afternoon; it moved via Kutno to Lowice. There were some delays, since march groups from the *4. Panzer-Division* had to be allowed to pass. As a result, the troop elements did not reach their march objectives until between 0200 and 0500 hours. Since the weather was warm and dry, the battalions bivouacked in the open. The division remained resting during the day; it started its movements up again that night. Around 2200 hours, the division was outside of Warsaw. The forces moved straight through the city, which was lit up as brightly as day and featured civilian and military personnel of both sexes promenading, and headed for the wooded area around Minsk–Mazowiecki. The forces bivouacked there, while the vehicles were concealed from aerial view.

Due to the night marches, all sorts of rumors surfaced. Many thought the division was simply going to be employed in border-protection duty. In the end, however, everyone noticed that there were a lot of forces on the move to both sides of their march route. Eventually, most thought they were going to move through Russia to get to Persia. Any and all available newspapers were scoured for any clues to that effect.

The divisional formations continued their night march in a pouring rain. Sometimes, the move was at a walking pace, only to be followed by a crazy tempo, so that contact with the vehicle in front would not be lost. Siedlce was crossed and, around midnight, the wooded area at Radzyn was reached. The division finally halted.

Schützen-Regiment 394 remained in the Radzyn area. The battalions were spread out along the edges of the city, with some elements staying in barns or under canvas. *Oberstleutnant* Audörsch set up his headquarters in the new school. The city consisted of peasant huts; only the district government resided in the palace. The sister rifle regiment bivouacked in and around Pluty. It was terrible in the woods, however. The innumerable masses of mosquitoes were the enemy. The soldiers cleared the thick underbrush and set it alight. Despite the warm nights, everyone ran around with thick padding. Everyone tried to find mosquito netting. The armor regiment set up a bivouac site in the area around Zabickow. Its fighting vehicles arrived by train and were unloaded at Lukow on 12 June. All of the division was in the woods west of the Bug, not far from the battlefields of the campaign in Poland, where it had fought two years previously.

The commanding general of the *XXIV. Armee-Korps (mot.)*, to which the *3. Panzer-Division* reported, was *Generalleutnant Freiherr* Geyr von Schweppenburg. The commanding general visited the division in its quartering areas on 14 June. He was satisfied with the bivouac sites and the preparations for operations. The division had issued orders that day for reconnoitering its staging areas; on 15 June, it issued a second order detailing the movement into those positions. The division's chaplains were constantly on the go, to conduct field services. The Catholic priest, Father Laub, provided general absolution in Biala Podlaska.

On 16 June, the division moved into its staging areas along the Bug. The advance parties of the battalions took off early in the day. They had the task of finding quarters for the companies that would follow and, if necessary, assume the border security mission from the regiments of the *34. Infanterie-Division*, which was stationed there. Toward evening, the lead elements of the division were along the Bug.

Major Wellmann's *I./Schützen-Regiment 3* occupied an area around Koden. Its 2nd and 3rd Companies set up outposts along the river that were run by junior noncommissioned officers. They were charged with observing all movements on the far bank and to pay especially close attention to unusual noises or light signals. The sector with the friendly forces on the right, the *4. Panzer-Division*, ran from Olszanki to Point 151.8, four kilometers east of Stradecz.

Major Dr. Müller's *II./Schützen-Regiment 394* was inserted into the line to the left of Well-mann's battalion. His observation posts were also located along the wire fence that ran the length of the river. The friendly forces on the left was the *45. Infanterie-Division*. On the far side of the river, the darkness of night was spreading, the darkness of a foreign world.

The division had occupied its designated sector. The two rifle battalions occupied a narrow frontage up front along the river. The main body of the division to the rear began to prepare for its upcoming missions by means of continuous reconnaissance, small-scale exercises, maintenance of vehicles, and issuance of ammunition. On 16 June, *Generalleutnant* Model signed the operations plan for the attack of his division across the Bug on D-Day. Only the officers of the immediate battle staff knew that that day would be next Sunday.

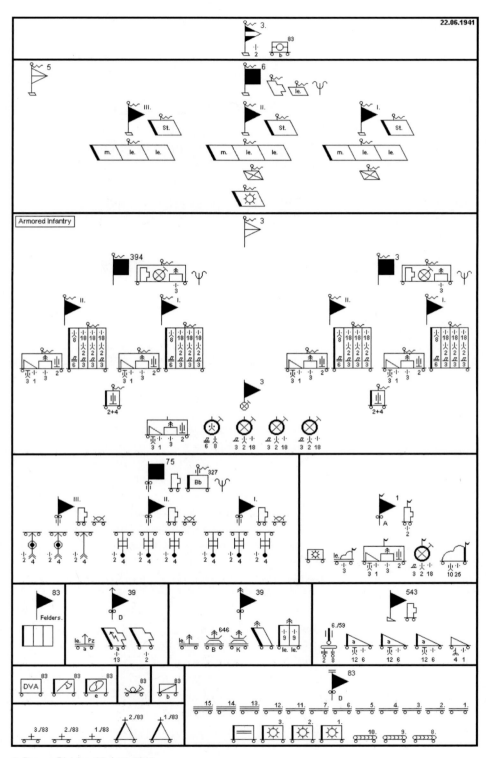

3. Panzer-Division, 22 June 1941.

CHAPTER 8

From the Bug to the Dnjepr: Fighting along the Routes of Advance, 1941

The *3. Berlin-Brandenburgische Panzer-Division* was attached to *Panzergruppe 2* (*Generaloberst* Guderian) for employment in Russia. The *Panzergruppe* was part of the *4. Armee* of *Heeresgruppe Mitte*. For the initial part of the operation, the *Panzergruppe* had received the mission of crossing the Bug on both sides of Brest-Litowsk and reaching the area bounded by Roslawl–Jelnja–Smolensk. From there, it was to turn in the direction of either Moscow or Leningrad, in conjunction with *Panzergruppe 3*.

The *XXIV. Armee-Korps (mot.)* marched over the course of the next few days with the *255. Infanterie-Division* in the area around Wlodawa, with the intent of marching on Maloryta from there. The *1. Kavallerie-Division* adjoined it and was to turn in the direction of Pinsk from Slawatycze later on. The *3. Panzer-Division* and *4. Panzer-Division* had the mission of breaking out of the area around Koden and reaching the Brest–Kobryn road. The *10. Infanterie-Division (mot.)* remained behind the armored divisions as the reserve.

The division organized itself into the following battle groups for Operation Barbarossa:

- Headquarters, *3. Panzer-Division* (*Generalleutnant* Model, with *Major i.G.* Pomtow as the division operations officer), with *Nachrichten-Abteilung 39*, *Straßenbau-Bataillon 97*,[1] and the *9.(H)/Lehr-Geschwader 2*[2] at Katy.
- *Gruppe Audörsch*, consisting of his *Schützen-Regiment 394*, *SS-Pionier-Bataillon "Das Reich"* (only for the crossing),[3] the *2./Pionier-Bataillon 39*, the *1./Panzerjäger-Abteilung 543*, the engineer platoon of *Kradschützen-Bataillon 3*, and the *1. Radfahr-Bau-Bataillon 503*.[4]

---

1. 97th Engineer Battalion (Road Construction).
2. This was the same *Luftwaffe* asset that had supported the division in France.
3. At the time, the official designation of the battalion was *Pionier-Bataillon SS-Division Reich*.
4. 1st Company of the 503rd Engineer Battalion (Bicycle), another corps asset. This formation used bicycles as its means of transport.

These formations and elements were located in the northern portion of the division sector, between Kopytow and the Bug.

- *Gruppe Kleemann* assembled in the south in the area around Koden. Belonging to *Oberst* Kleemann's forces were *Schützen-Regiment 3, Pionier-Bataillon 10,*[5] the *1./Pionier-Bataillon 39*, the *2.* and *3./Panzerjäger-Abteilung 543*, the headquarters and *2./Radfahr-Bau-Bataillon 503*, a reinforced company from the *III./Panzer-Regiment 6, Brücko 606* with the *2./403,*[6] and an assault detachment from the *3./Pionier-Bataillon 39*.
- *Gruppe Linnarz* was located around Zcuprov with *Panzer-Regiment 6, Panzerjäger-Abteilung 521,*[7] *leichte Flak-Abteilung 91,*[8] one heavy battery of the *I./Flak-Regiment 11,*[9] and the *3./Pionier-Bataillon 39*. It followed the division.
- *Gruppe von Corvin-Wierbitzki*, with *Krad-schützen-Bataillon 3, Aufklärungs-Abteilung 1*, and the *6./Flak-Bataillon 59.*[10] This *Kampfgruppe* was located in the Katy and Zcuprov area.

All of the artillery was placed under the direction of the corps artillery officer, *Oberst* Forster, and his *Arko 143.*[11] He divided his assets into three large groups. *Gruppe Nord*, under *Oberst* Ries, consisted of the *I.* and *III./Artillerie-Regiment 75*, the *III./Artillerie-Regiment 10,*[12] and the *I./Artillerie-Regiment 53.*[13] *Gruppe Süd* was commanded by the division artillery officer of the *10. Infanterie-Division (mot.)* and consisted of the *11./Artillerie-Regiment 75*, the *II./Artillerie-Regiment 10*, the *II./Artillerie-Regiment 42,*[14] and *Mörser-Abteilung 604.*[15] The artillery group in the middle was employed against long-range targets and consisted of the *I./Artillerie-Regiment 10*, the *II./Artillerie-Regiment 69,*[16] and the *7./Artillerie-Regiment 75*. Command and control of the middle group was provided by the Headquarters, *Artillerie-Regiment 623.*[17] Supporting *Oberst* Forster at the corps level was *Panzer-Beobachtungs-Batterie 327.*[18]

The logistics support elements of the division—ten supply (truck) sections, three maintenance companies, one supply company, one bakery company, one butcher company, the division rations point, the military police section, the field post office, and vehicle sections—were positioned far to the rear, while the medical company and the three ambulance platoons were attached to the three groups.

---

5. The 10th Engineer Battalion was the combat engineer battalion of the *10. Infanterie-Division (mot.)*, which was being held back as the corps ready reserve. For a forced river-crossing operation, the engineer battalions of the forces not immediately committed to the forced crossing were usually attached in direct support of the lead forces.

6. These are corps bridging assets.

7. A separate antitank battalion equipped with three companies of nine 4.7-centimeter self-propelled Czech-built antitank guns.

8. This was a *Luftwaffe* formation. It was originally an antiaircraft battalion in the Austrian military before its assimilation into the *Wehrmacht* after the *Anschluß* in 1938.

9. *Flak-Regiment 11* was also the *Luftwaffe* antiaircraft formation in direct support of the division.

10. A separate antiaircraft battalion.

11. *Artillerie-Kommando* = Artillery Command.

12. From the divisional artillery of the *10. Infanterie-Division (mot.)*.

13. Part of a separate regiment whose battalions effectively acted as separate battalions. Apparently, the battalion had three horse-drawn heavy howitzer batteries at the start of the campaign.

14. Part of a separate regiment, whose battalions effectively acted as separate battalions. Apparently, the battalion had three heavy howitzer batteries at the start of the campaign

15. The official designation of the battalion was *schwere Artillerie-Abteilung 604*. It consisted of three batteries of 21-centimeter cannon.

16. Part of a separate regiment whose battalions effectively acted as separate battalions. Apparently, the battalion had three motorized 10-centimeter cannon batteries at the start of the campaign.

17. This was strictly a command-and-control entity and had no organic line battalions assigned to it.

18. In April 1942, this flash- and sound-ranging battery was consolidated with the divisional artillery of the *3. Panzer-Division* and redesignated as *Beobachtungs-Batterie (Panzer) 75*. The *Panzer* in the designation indicates that the battery was issued *SPW's* to help accomplish its mission when observers went up front.

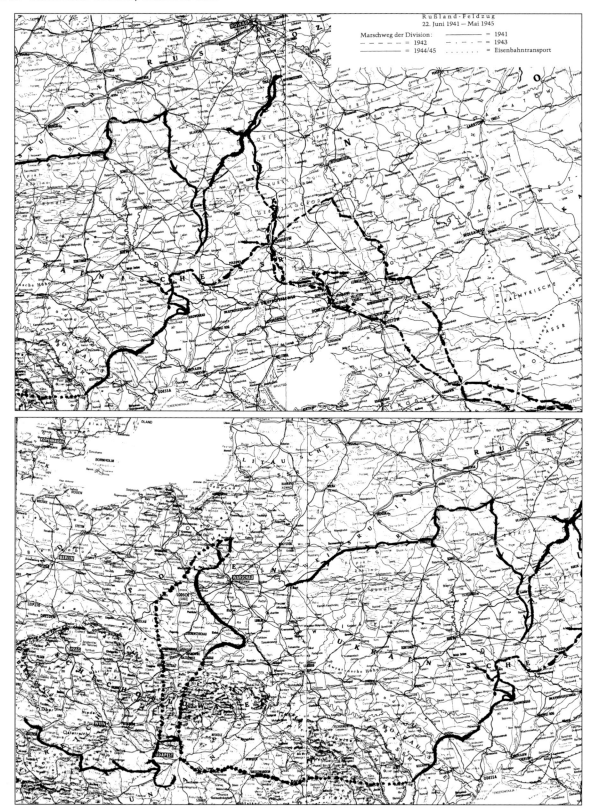

Campaign in the East, 22 June 1941 to May 1945: March Routes of the Division.

It was intended for the division to form the *Schwerpunkt* (spearhead) of the corps in the upcoming attack. The orders given to the *XXIV. Armee-Korps (mot.)* stated that the two armored divisions were to advance to the northeast once north of Miedna, after having broken through the enemy border positions on both sides of the lake area. They were to take the road between Kobryn and the crossing over the Muchawiec at Bulkowo and then advance in the direction of Sluzk. The *4. Panzer-Division* was directed to advance along "Tank Route 1," while the *3. Panzer-Division* attacked to its north. The fortress at Brest-Litowsk was to be bypassed to the right and taken down by infantry divisions.

The main effort within the attacks would lie with the armored regiments. In the case of the *3. Panzer-Division*, that would be *Panzer-Regiment 6*. The regiment had a full complement of 209 fighting vehicles: 58 *Panzer II's*, 108 *Panzer III's*, 32 *Panzer IV's*, 8 medium command-and-control tanks, and 3 light command-and-control tanks.[19] The 3rd Battalion of the regiment had tanks outfitted for deep-water wading. As with all of the other vehicles of the division, the tanks also bore the tactical sign of *Generaloberst* Guderian's *Panzergruppe*, a white "G" (about thirty centimeters high).

Starting on 19 June, all of the divisional elements started moving forward into their staging areas along the Bug. The engineers and bridging sections were divided among the individual battalions. There was no longer any doubt that the attack would take place soon. The combat outposts along the river noted increasing movements on the far side over the previous few days. That meant that the Red Army was preparing for a German attack.

The defense of the border along the Bug was the responsibility of the Western Military District of the Soviet Union. Commander in Chief Pavlov had the following forces at his disposal: the 3rd Army (Lieutenant General Kusnezow) with two motorized corps, one cavalry corps, and three rifle divisions; the 4th Army (Major General Korobkow) with one motorized corps and four rifle divisions; and the 10th Army (Major General Golubev) with one motorized corps.

The twenty-first of June confirmed everything. Division orders for movements that night arrived. A few minutes later, an appeal by the commanding general reached the forces in the field, which ended in Geyr von Schweppenburg's famous saying: "Through and forward!" The artillery liaison officers placed target reference points on their maps. The division's armor regiment, still about 100 kilometers to the rear, headed out on the more or less bad roads to the front. In the woods to the left and right of the road were the prepared and, in many cases, occupied airstrips of the *Luftwaffe*. Just before midnight, the division was in its designated staging areas.

It was 0300 hours.[20] There was still a wall of ground fog on the small island in the Bug, on which a section of engineers and riflemen were positioned. Not too far away, on the righthand side, was the bridge. *Leutnant* Möllhoff and *Unteroffizier* Hahnfeld of the 3rd Company of the divisional engineers had positioned themselves there ever since 0100 hours. An assault detachment with an assault craft had disappeared into the underbrush twenty meters downstream. Two floats were hidden on the island. The rest of the engineer platoon was 100 meters to the rear along the outskirts of Koden.

The men waited and waited and counted the minutes. Then, all of a sudden, there was the sound of engines in the air. German bombers were approaching the border. Damn it! They were five minutes too early. The enemy could be

---

19. The medium vehicle was based on the *Panzer III* chassis. Its turret was fixed in place and main gun removed to accommodate more radio equipment. A dummy gun was placed on the mantlet to simulate a normal *Panzer III*. The only close-in defensive weapons a *Panzerbefehlswagen III* had were the on-board machine guns. The light vehicle was based on the *Panzer I* chassis with the turret removed and fixed superstructure added. The latter vehicle was only used for front-line duties during the initial stages of the campaign.

20. Times given in the narrative are official German military time (corresponding to the time in Berlin) and thus two hours earlier than local Soviet time.

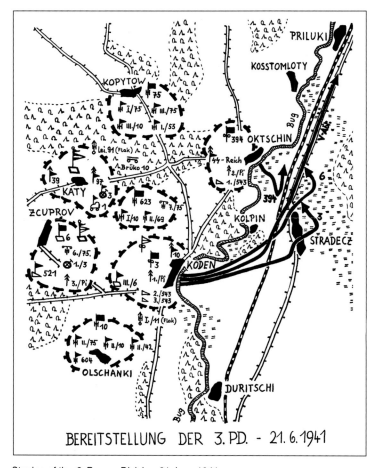

Staging of the *3. Panzer-Division*, 21 June 1941.

alerted too soon. Making a snap decision, *Leutnant* Möllhoff drew up his submachine gun and fired a burst. They were the first shots on the ground of the campaign in the East. It was the attack signal for the divisional assault forces.

Möllhoff and Hahnfeld raced across the bridge. At the same time, the engineers placed their assault craft and floats in the water and crossed over. From the direction of Koden, motorcycle infantry started racing forward. The "Spanish Riders"[21] were quickly pushed aside, and the first four Soviet soldiers overwhelmed. The engineers continued their assault. They hastened another fifty meters along the road. There was a tank ditch dug across the road. Beams were brought up quickly and tossed over it. *Feldwebel* Hasler searched the bridge for demolition charges.

The *coup de main* that had initiated the campaign had succeeded, even before the campaign had officially started.

It was 0315 hours.

At that moment, thousands of guns opened fire on the Soviet border positions from the Baltic to the Black Sea. Operation Barbarossa had started. The divisional artillery fired along with all of the batteries attached to it on the east banks of the Bug. The fires were especially concentrated around the small village of Stradecz, whose church tower was already jutting out of

---

21. Temporary barricades usually constructed from wood and strung with barbed wire.

the morning fog. The village was familiar to some of the men of the division from the campaign in Poland. It was going up in fire and flames at that point.

The lead elements of the two rifle battalions up front crossed the river at 0345 hours in pneumatic craft, while the vehicles of the motorcycle infantry and reconnaissance battalions rolled across the undamaged bridge. The sounds of individual enemy machine guns could be heard; they also caused the first losses. *Oberleutnant* Jopp, the company commander of *Panzerjäger-Abteilung 543*, was wounded while sitting in a pneumatic craft. The far banks of the river were taken rapidly. In the lead, *Oberleutnant* von Becker's 8th Company of *Schützen-Regiment 3* raced across the bridge and reached the meadowlands behind the Bug. The soldiers worked their way towards Stradecz by squad. Schützen-Regiment 394 went after the northern part of the village and encountered its first, albeit slight, resistance. The enemy bunkers were rapidly eliminated, and the attack continued into the vegetated terrain north of the village.

By contrast, *Schützen-Regiment 3*, attacking the southern part, had a more difficult time of it. The railway station for the village was protected by bunkers and the crews manning them put up a defense. Enemy artillery started firing at the forces at the same time from the village's industrial area. *Oberleutnant* Siegelmann's 2nd Company enveloped the southern part of the locality and took the Russians under crossfire. That caused the Soviet resistance to collapse. The rifle brigade's first objective was in German hands three hours after the start of the offensive. The 2nd Company lost two dead and sixteen wounded. The village itself was practically destroyed. The first twenty Soviets were taken prisoner by the riflemen. The Russians were completely flustered.

Generalleutnant Model followed his attacking soldiers with his battle staff. By 0430 hours, he had his command post established on a wooded hill north of the bridge at Koden. Five hours later, it moved to Stradecz.

The rifle regiments fought against the fleeing Russians, who offered slight resistance, in the sandy and marshy areas. The motorcycles got stuck more than once. Since no heavy vehicles had crossed over by that point, the antitank and infantry gun crews helped themselves by hooking horses up to their guns. *Oberleutnant Freiherr* von Werthern's 3rd Company of *Schützen-Regiment 3* was the first unit to reach the high ground north of Stradecz. But the riflemen's attack then bogged down in front of the moor and its damned-up creeks. The vehicles bottomed out, and not a few soldiers had to pull their boots out of the marshes.

The motorized elements of the division followed one another across the undamaged bridge. The movement forward proceeded slowly; there were a lot of traffic jams. In addition, the movement caused enormous quantities of airborne dust. The vehicle sections of all of the battalions—*Panzer-Regiment 6* started crossing the Bug at 1220 hours with its fighting vehicles—were moving along the edges of the marshland. The armored cars, motorcycles, and *SPW's* were blazing a trail with some difficulty. The division's advance guard, to which the 2nd Company of the armor regiment belonged, was attempting to find a passage point. Five kilometers had been covered; it was supposed to have been 80 by that point.

The division commander moved forward to *Oberstleutnant* Audörsch and his *Schützen-Regiment 394* in order to see for himself that all of the vehicles were getting stuck in the marshland. (The division commander's vehicle also got stuck.) An advance along the designated route was impossible. After conferring with the commanding general, Model ordered the different elements out of the marshland at 1530 hours, pivoting them to the north.

The division formed a new advance guard out of the 3rd Battalion of the armor regiment, a company of motorcycle infantry and elements of the divisional engineers. The advance guard moved out of Stradecz at 1642 hours and encountered heavy resistance a few minutes later at Przyluki, which was being defended by the enemy.

The 12th Company of the armored regiment eliminated those forces, while the motorcycle infantry held down the elements that were located in the woods and marshland between the avenue of advance and the river. The continued advance of the tanks was not held up. Around 1845 hours, the extreme southern portion of Brest-Litowsk was reached. The fighting vehicles started receiving enemy fire again. That was also eliminated, and the companies turned to the northeast, reaching the main road to Kobryn, "Tank Route 1." All of a sudden, Russian tanks appeared from the west. They were trying to get out of Brest-Litowsk, which was being attacked by the 45. *Infanterie-Division*. A short tank engagement developed, in which the stronger German tanks emerged the victor. The first Soviet tanks had been knocked out by the 3. *Panzer-Division*.

Hauptmann Schneider-Kostalski's *III./Panzer-Regiment 6* did not stop. Around 2100 hours, it was in front of the high wooden bridge on a tributary of the Muchawiec. While the German fighting vehicles rattled across the span, motorized columns of the enemy, including light tanks, attempted to get past the German vehicles and escape to the east. They were shot to pieces. Burning Soviet trucks and fighting vehicles lined the advance route of Schneider-Kostalski's battalion.

By then, all of the armored regiment had closed up. The darkness hindered the advance, and the regiment had to order a halt when the Muchawiec was reached. The bridge had been burned down by the enemy. The tanks pulled off of the road and set up an all-round defense. They were eighteen kilometers east of Brest. The rifle brigade was far to the rear. Because of the marshland, the advance was only possible along that one road that ran parallel to the Bug. Since the pontoon bridge that had been erected by the engineer battalion at Okczyn had been taken down, the trains could only cross over the bridge at Koden. As a result, the columns got jammed up everywhere.

Generalleutnant Model and his battle staff followed the forward elements of *Panzer-Regiment 6*. He ordered that the rest of the division close up as soon as possible. The trail columns, moving forward at night, were fired at by Russian forces positioned along the southern outskirts of Brest. The divisional engineers had gone all the way forward and started erecting a bridge at Bulkowo, south of the large road bridge at Chaby, just before midnight.

Hauptmann Kalkbrenner's 1st Company of engineers erected the bridge in two sixteen-ton sections, using floating supports. The engineers received no rest that night. When the morning fog of the new day lifted out of the lowlands, the bridge was finished. Divisional vehicles—armored cars, personnel carriers, and motorcycles—started rolling across it at 0500 hours. *Leutnant* Burgheim's engineers guarded the structure.

Panzer-Regiment 6 was awakened at 0430 hours, since the trains had arrived with the valuable fuel. Immediately after refueling, the tanks rumbled off. The 3rd Battalion took the lead. The advance proceeded terribly slowly. The road was very sandy, and the combat vehicles could only churn through slowly. Despite that, the lighter vehicles of the advance guard moved forward and were soon outside of Kobryn, which the Russians were defending.

Shortly after 1100 hours, the 3rd Battalion arrived. Jabbing hard, the enemy pockets of resistance on the western side of the locality were eliminated. When entering the city, Russian light tanks appeared, all of which were shot to pieces. Likewise, high-explosive rounds crashed into the houses from which Russian machine-gun fire had flared up. After a quarter of an hour, the battalion had quashed all resistance.

The motorcycle infantry had advanced into the city center and were able to take the bridge over the Bug-Dnjepr Canal through rapid action. Unfortunately, the battalion suffered its first total losses in vehicles. Killed on this day were four noncommissioned officers and one *Obergefreiter* of the 12th Company and the Headquarters Company of the 3rd Battalion.

The regiment moved through the city quickly and reached the roads leading east with all of its elements. Up front were the lead elements of *Hauptmann* Ziervogel's reconnaissance battalion and *Major* von Corvin-Wiersbitzki's motorcycle infantry battalion. That was the start of a journey that would be characteristic of this 23 June 1941.

Those vehicles of the *3. Panzer-Division* ceaselessly advanced along the broad road. There was no way to detour, since untrafficable moorland stretched to the right and left of the road. The Russians had been driven from the road. It was only the vehicles, guns, tossed away weapons and abandoned equipment that reminded one that the enemy had pulled back in flight. The tanks occasionally had difficulty in maneuvering past the enemy vehicles, which were often perpendicular to the road. The Soviet riflemen had fled into the tall cornfields and fired from there on the German columns that followed in their open cross-country vehicles. The forces had to dismount and expel the Russians with cold steel.

The *I./Panzer-Regiment 6* made a surprise contact with Russian tanks at 1540 hours at Buchowiecze. The enemy combat vehicles had broken out of nearby woods and taken the German columns under fire. *Major* Schmid-Ott[22] immediately employed his companies in an enveloping maneuver and knocked out thirty-six T-26's in the counterthrust. In the process, *Oberleutnant* Buchterkirch's 2nd Company was able to finish off twelve tanks all by itself within the space of a few minutes. Polish peasants alerted the German tank crews passing by of hidden Russian defensive positions. The light platoon of *Panzer-Regiment 6* (*Leutnant* Jacobs) was directed toward the small village of Podberje off of the avenue of advance. The combat vehicles encountered six heavy guns and tractors there. The Russian cannoneers were so surprised by the appearance of German tanks that they surrendered. The 7th Company, which had been reinforced with medium tanks, was ordered forward to the 3rd Battalion to support it in its various skirmishes with fleeing Soviet columns.

The advance guard reached the regional capital of Bereza-Kartuska on the railway line to Minsk. It was able to break the initial resistance with its own forces, before *Panzer-Regiment 6* closed up. German prisoners—they came from the *4. Panzer-Division*—were freed from the hands of the Russians. The advance guard and the tank regiment were far to the front. The rifle brigade could only follow slowly, since the solitary road was jammed. As lead regiment, *Schützen-Regiment 394* encountered no resistance. The intensity of the fighting by the divisional elements to the front could be gauged by the wrecks of enemy vehicles along the edge of the road, however.

The division command post was moved through Zabinka to Kobryn that day. The battle staff established itself in a church east of the bridge. The local populace was overwhelmingly friendly to the Germans and fed the rearward trains and supplies elements. Valuable material concerning the Soviet 4th Army fell into the hands of the division intelligence officer; the headquarters of the field army had been in Kobryn. That field army, under the command of Major General Korobkow, opposed *Panzergruppe 2* with its four rifle divisions; the 6th, the 42nd, the 49th, and the 75th. The XIV Corps (Mechanized) of Major General Oborin formed the second line of defense in the Pruzana–Kobryn area; its lines had been broken through by the *3. Panzer-Division* on 23 June.

Despite the success, *Generalleutnant* Model didn't allow his soldiers any rest. He personally went to Bereza-Kartuska and ordered the ceaseless pursuit of the fleeing enemy. *Major* Beigel, the commander of *Pionier-Bataillon 39*, quickly

---

22. Gustav Albrecht Schmidt-Ott was one of the first recipients of the newly created German Cross in Gold on 18 October 1941. He went on to receive the Knight's Cross of the Iron Cross on 3 October 1942 as an *Oberstleutnant* and acting commander of the regiment. Although this narrative spells his name as Schmid, most accounts give it as Schmidt.

reorganized the advance guard and immediately continued the advance. The combat vehicles and motorcycles advanced without regard to the withdrawing enemy elements along the road. Villages and woods were negotiated, bridges over the many small waterways were crossed and the resistance that flared up along the flanks was swiftly engaged. The Russian defenses along the railway crossing southwest of Byrten were stronger. The light armored cars fired with everything they had. The wooden freight terminal soon went up in flames. The first tanks arrived soon thereafter.

All of a sudden, well-aimed artillery fire was placed on the road. There was no getting around it, however. The tanks, followed by the motorcycles, rattled on. The forces moved three kilometers further into the night—through woods and Soviet artillery fire. The lead platoon of the *7./Panzer-Regiment 6* (*Leutnant* Rühl) was in front of the bridge at the first crossing over the Szczara at 2200 hours. The tanks rolled across the wooden bridge without incident. They then advanced a few more kilometers. The motorcycle infantry and the engineers secured the small bridgehead. The tanks then returned in the darkness and rested.

On that second day of the war, the division had broken through the enemy front and advanced 150 kilometers. One hundred seven Russian combat vehicles were destroyed and several hundred artillery pieces of all calibers were captured or destroyed. The leader of the advance guard, *Major* Beigel, became the first officer of the division to receive the Knight's Cross in the East for these actions. The official recommendation read, in part: "By means of lightning-fast action, [he] took the important bridge over the Szczara, which created the prerequisite for the rapid advance of an armored corps."

The lead elements of the division were already deep in enemy territory by the second night of the campaign. At the same time, the rear-area services of the division were still on the opposite of the border, not starting to cross it until the morning of 24 June. The formations, which were still at Koden on the east bank of the Bug were brought forward on the major supply route.[23]

Oberstleutnant Minzel's *II./Panzer-Regiment 6*, reinforced by a company of motorcycle infantry, a company of engineers, a battery of artillery and a battery of *Flak*, formed the new advance guard. The fighting vehicles moved out at a rapid pace. There were shot-up tanks and trucks along the edges of the roadway, which the forces out front had passed and destroyed. All of a sudden, the lead tank elements encountered strong enemy resistance not too far from Milowidy. The enemy's artillery also joined the fray. It was easy for the Russian batteries to hit targets, since they only had to fire on the road. The terrain on both sides was complete marshland and not trafficable for tanks. For the time being, Munzel's advance guard bogged down. Reconnaissance aircraft reported that Soviet rearguards had set up defensive positions to protect the retrograde movements of the main body of forces. Toward noon, the first few companies of *Schützen-Regiment 394* arrived to support the tanks, whose ammunition was slowly running out. *Oberstleutnant* von Lewinski ordered the 1st Battalion forward, which was able to close up quickly. By then, the armor battalion had taken the high ground at Marynowo. In the process, *Oberleutnant* Jarosch von Schweder's 5th Company, with attached elements of the 8th Company, had destroyed nine Russian tanks, two batteries, and fifteen antitank guns. *Leutnant* Dehnke of the 4th Company was killed during that operation and *Oberleutnant* Markowski of the 8th Company was wounded. The divisional engineers had two officers wounded that day: *Hauptmann* Arnold and *Leutnant* Ziegenbalg.

All of a sudden, the Red Air Force made an appearance. No one anticipated its employment,

23. This is also "Tank Route 1." The original German uses *Rollbahn*, which can often have a variety of meanings, even in the same context, such as road, route of advance, and main supply route.

since nothing had been seen of Russian aircraft the first two days. The enemy fighters and bombers attacked the road in waves starting at 1345 hours and caused the advance to falter. Even the battle staff of the division, which had followed the armored brigade as far as Niedzwiedziewa, was attacked several times.

The *II./Panzer-Regiment 6* continued the attack shortly after 1500 hours as the advance guard. Again, the tanks did not get very far. The second crossing point of the Szczara was in front of them. Although the river was only 15 meters wide, its flood plain extended for more than 800 meters and, with its ascending edges, it formed a natural basin, which was difficult to cross. The bridge, whose freshly cut pilings practically shone to the tank drivers, had been blown up in the middle. There were no routes around at that location, since everything was marshland with the exception of the road. The remaining elements of the division slowly pushed their way forward. Russian artillery fire and renewed attacks from the air brought continual delays to that approach march and caused casualties. Two *Flak* were completely destroyed.

Generalleutnant Model was unable to stand by in the rear. He had the 2nd Company of the signals battalion give him an eight-wheeled radio armored car and rode it to the front. When the general was unable to make further progress due to the congestion on the road, he dismounted to create room. At that moment, a direct hit from an artillery round tore apart the radio vehicle. The four-man crew was killed instantly; *Generalleutnant Model* was unscathed.

The hours passed, slowly. Companies from the motorcycle infantry battalion and the 1st Company of *Schützen-Regiment 394* attempted to press forward in the flood plain. The riflemen had to remain close to the road, however, since every step in the blooming meadowlands was a step into mud. The Bolsheviks defended stubbornly in the former Polish bunkers, which had been built years ago as protection against the Soviet Union.

The tanks took the individual bunkers under fire again in order to make it easier for the motorcycle infantry to work its way forward. Finally, a small section was able to make it to the bridge. It was plastered by enemy artillery and cut off. Twelve men were at the bridge and could not get back. The men were not freed from their predicament until friendly fighting vehicles pressed forward, ignoring the enemy's defensive fires.

Fighting had also broken out to the rear of the lead tank elements. Strong elements of the scattered Red detachments had fled into the woods to the right and left of the road and disrupted the columns that were closing up with ambushes. As a result, the *I./Schützen-Regiment 3* had to clear the woods at Postolowo in the afternoon. Its 3rd Company (*Hauptmann* Peschke) brought back thirty-eight prisoners and one antiaircraft gun.

Toward 2000 hours, *Generalleutnant* Model ordered the 1st Battalion of the armor regiment to move forward and form a bridgehead. *Oberleutnant* Buchterkirch's 2nd Company was reinforced by the regimental light platoon and a platoon from the 4th Company. The tanks, followed by motorcycle infantry, worked their way forward to the burning bridge by means of aggressive operations.

Oberleutnant Buchterkirch had his men halt there. He jumped down from his fighting vehicle and ran towards the bridge with a few riflemen, while the remaining tanks attempted to break the enemy resistance on the far bank through continuous fire. A few riflemen succeeded in clambering over the burning planks and establishing a foothold on the far side. An assault detachment of motorcycle infantry—using pneumatic boats from the engineer platoon of the *II./Panzer-Regiment 6*—likewise crossed the river. The bridgehead was formed.

Oberleutnant Buchterkirch's actions were praised as follows in the Armed Forces Daily Report of 6 July 1941: "distinguished himself through exemplary bravery! As a result of the fires of the 2./Panzer-Regiment 6, the Russians lost 2 light armored cars, 6 tanks, 9 antitank guns, and 25 artillery pieces at the second Szczara crossing!"

The bridging column of the engineer battalion was ordered forward that night. Its vehicles encountered an enemy ambush at Milowidy, and one man was wounded. The column reached the Szczara at Minicze intact, however. That placed the engineers one kilometer south of the burning bridge and the bridgehead formed by the motorcycle infantry. Two bridge-laying tanks were brought up to the river at the original location. The placement of the bridge took ten minutes. In the process, a portion of the original bridge was used as support. The second tank drove onto the bridge and placed the second part down to the other bank.

In the meantime, morning had dawned. Batteries from the divisional artillery had moved forward—some of them in open fields near Nibiszcze—and were firing with everything they had. Russian artillery rounds landed among the elements of the division that were waiting along the road. More effective than the artillery were the continuous attacks by Soviet bombers. The armored command vehicle of the division commander was set alight. The fire could be put out quickly, but Model's driver, *Obergefreiter* Kohlwey, died a few hours later as the result of a head wound.

Toward 1100 hours, the division ordered the continuation of the attack across the bridge that had been built by the engineers. March Group 1 consisted of a reinforced advance guard under the command of *Oberstleutnant* von Lewinski. The advance had to be postponed and did not start until after a two-hour delay. Some of the heavy tanks had to make stops on the bridge, since it was very narrow.

Oberleutnant Buchterkirch rode point again with his company. Behind him were the *3./Aufklärungs-Abteilung 1*, the *5./Artillerie-Regiment 75*, the *1./Schützen-Regiment 394*, the *I./Panzer-Regiment 6*, the *1./Panzerjäger-Abteilung 543*, the headquarters of *Panzer-Regiment 6* and *Panzer-Brigade 5*, the *1./Pionier-Bataillon 39*, the *II./Artillerie-Regiment 75*, a platoon from

Mörser-Abteilung 604, the *1./Flak-Regiment 91*, and the *6./Flak-Regiment 59*. The two remaining march groups of the division were led by *Oberstleutnant* Munzel and *Oberstleutnant* Audörsch.

The vehicles rolled through the meadowlands and reached the main road in the vicinity of the bridge. The ruins of the positions, which had been shot up by the Buchterkirch's company the previous evening, could be seen everywhere. There was no stopping his tanks. The armored vehicles churned their way through the dirt of the road with their heavy tracks. Contact had long been lost with the main body that was following. The company commander left behind a tank at each of the bridges to provide security, as he continued east with his fighting vehicles. Buchterkirch's men were able to reach Filipowicze. The houses of the locality went up in smoke and flames.

The march group following behind had been held up by enemy resistance at Siniawka. Although the fighting vehicles were able to enter the woods, the unarmored vehicles of the riflemen and cannoneers were unable to proceed. The Russians launched an immediate counterattack and hit the 1st Company of *Schützen-Regiment 394*. The 1st Company of *Panzerjäger-Abteilung 543*, under the command of *Oberleutnant* Michels, moved forward immediately and was able to turn back the Soviet assault with its self-propelled antitank guns. It was able to eliminate two fighting vehicles and seven armored vehicles of the enemy.

Oberstleutnant von Lewinski, who no longer had any radio contact to his lead company, decided to reestablish contact. He moved forward with the regimental light platoon and a few motorcycle messengers into the woods and reached his lead company around 0100 hours outside of Filipowicze. The remaining elements of the march group fought their way slowly forward. The 7th Company and the light platoon of the *II./Panzer-Regiment 6* were the first ones to enter the wooded area. They positioned themselves along the side of the road and protected the columns passing them by. The fighting vehicles fired into the woods with their main guns and machine guns and held the Russians down. As a result, the fuel and ammunition columns reached the lead tank elements at first light and the regiment could completely refuel.

Around 0525 hours on 26 June, orders came from the brigade to continue the march. The objective was Sluzk. The advance guard moved out in the same order as the previous day. The *2./Panzer-Regiment 6* moved along the road without stopping. To the north of the village of Gulicze, a Russian antitank gun position caused a temporary halt. But the resistance was quickly broken and the march continued. *Oberleutnant* Buchterkirch rattled east with his fighting vehicles. The turrets of the city of Sluzk appeared on the horizon. The tanks were two kilometers from the locality at that point.

All of a sudden, there was a howling from all sides. The Soviets intended to defend Sluzk. On orders from the Headquarters of the Western Front, they had brought artillery and antitank guns into position in order to force a stop to the German advance at all costs. Buchterkirch's company was unable to make any further advance. *Oberleutnant* Buchterkirch dismounted and rallied the riflemen forward across an embankment. Fortunately, the 1st Battalion, which was following, soon closed up. Since the terrain on both sides of the road was passable to armor, *Major* Schmidt-Ott had his battalion approach across a broad front. The fighting vehicles took the identified Russian positions under fire and held down the defenders until *Oberleutnant* Grigo's 5th Battery of artillery arrived and took out the enemy batteries. A short while later, the *1./Schützen-Regiment 394* arrived with its armored personnel carriers. Toward 1100 hours, orders were issued for an attack.

The *1./Panzer-Regiment 6* (*Oberleutnant* Vopel) advanced into the city without delay. Although the Russians offered resistance at several spots, they were surprised by the energetic attack of the lead armor elements. The wooden houses burned and collapsed like blazing torches. On more than one occasion, the fighting

vehicles had to find a way around or over the rubble. They moved rapidly through the small market place, where the Lenin memorial rose up in the middle of the sea of fire. Soviet vehicles were on the opposite side of the plaza, the crews and horses shredded by rounds. But the tank drivers didn't have any time to take that in; they continued the assault on and past the new military facilities on the outskirts of the city. Suddenly, the fighting vehicles had to halt. The wooden bridge over the small Sslutsch at Wiesiekja had been blown up. The vehicles with the engineers immediately rolled forward. Enemy antitank guns opened fire on and near the bridge and did not allow the engineers to approach. The fighting vehicles moved upstream and downstream in an effort to find a ford. In the process, *Leutnant* von Kiekebusch (*1./Panzer-Regiment 6*) was felled by a Russian sniper on the far bank.

The *I./Schützen-Regiment 394* (*Major* Kratzenberg) had moved up to Sluzk and cleared the burning city of the remaining Soviet forces with all of his companies. Sluzk was a gigantic mass of flames. They were fed by the wind which, in turn, had resulted from the large fires. The last Russian soldiers were fetched from their hiding places by noon. The few civilians hastened through their burning city, shy and agitated, and attempted to plunder the few businesses. The soldiers of *Schützen-Regiment 394* were able to capture the equipment stores in the military facilities and distributed food items, bread, flour and butter to the residents, who had been without food for two days. The battalion then moved east of the city and secured.

Up to that point, the division had only assaulted along one road. As a result, there was an immense length to the entire column. The lead elements bore themselves like an arrow into the enemy front. But the Soviets were sitting in the woods and marshland to the left and the right and did not even consider the prospect of surrendering. They attacked the supply convoys that followed again and again and inflicted considerable casualties. Correspondingly, *Schützen-*

Regiment 3 (*Oberst* von Manteuffel) was given the mission of screening the route of advance. His 1st Battalion screened in the area of Kantonowicz–Janowicze on 26 June. To the left, in the area around Siniawka, was the division field replacement battalion. The reconnaissance battalion was around Kleck. The outposts remained where they were until late in the afternoon. At that point, the lead elements of the *4. Panzer-Division* had arrived. The regiment took off after the division, which had hurried far ahead.

The lead elements were already some 300 kilometers from the borders of the Reich and had covered a fifth of the entire distance to Moscow. That stretch had left its mark on men and materiel. The vehicles rattled from top to bottom, the weapons were covered in dust and the soldiers overly tired.

Generalleutnant Model arrived in Sluzk shortly after noon and called his commanders together at the former airstrip. He scolded the march discipline of the forces. That not only caused delays in the advance, but it also offered enemy aircraft good targets.

"We have to move on! The Beresina is our next objective . . . and then Moscow is in front of us!"

There was no more advance that day. The Russians continued to block the riverbanks. It was not until the friendly artillery could be brought forward to provide covering fire that a new bridge could be built. At least the forces were able to use the transition to screening to clean some of the dirt and sand from their weapons and attend to the damage on the vehicles. The division surgeon established a main clearing station in the orphanage in Slulz with *Sanitäts-Kompanie 522*.

The division ordered the continuation of the advance at 0730 hours on 27 June. The advance guard formed two march serials to that end: one under *Oberstleutnant* von Lewinski and the other under *Oberstleutnant* Munzel. The tank regiment assembled at the outskirts of the city. The reconnaissance aircraft had noted hardly any enemy movement along the road to Brobruisk. It was assumed that rapid progress would be made that day. At least that's what the men of the division thought that morning.

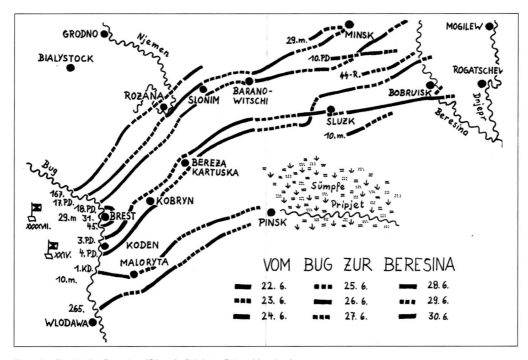

From the Bug to the Beresina (Sümpfe Pripjet = Pripet Marshes).

While taking its midday rest, the *1./Panzer-jäger-Abteilung 543* was attacked by scattered Soviet forces. The 1st Platoon immediately took up firing positions, while *Oberleutnant* Michels and ten volunteers advanced against the approaching tanks. In a short engagement, the antitank men were able to eliminate five enemy fighting vehicles. Afterwards, it was determined that the tanks in question were command tanks with valuable materiel on board, including papers, documents, 5,000 meters of film, women's silk clothing (!), and other items.

The *5./Panzer-Regiment 6* (*Oberleutnant* Jarosch von Schweder) took the lead, after the Sslutsch had been crossed. The tanks made good progress on the road, but they received fire after a few kilometers from some high ground that ran perpendicular to the road. The Russians had dug in artillery and antitank guns there. The tank company deployed north of the road into attack formation and broke the enemy resistance after a short period. Two cannons fell into German hands. The armored regiment moved out again to continue the march at 1200 hours. The march jammed up again after a short while, however. The lead elements had run into a Russian position in the woods around Stary-Hutok. That resistance was also broken rapidly, and the tanks continued to roll on through the woods and isolation.

After the fighting vehicles had passed the dangerous spot, it suddenly turned lively in the woods around Kalista, when the riflemen, engineers, *Flak* gunners, and cannoneers followed. As if on command, heavy, rapid fire from machine guns and automatic weapons broke out of the impenetrable thickets from all sides. The riflemen quickly threw themselves on the ground from their vehicles, seeking cover. Minutes passed that seemed eternally long. Friendly tanks rolled forward from the rear. It was the lead elements of the armor regiment's 1st Battalion. The fighting vehicles moved their way carefully along the wooded road. They were also showered with a hail of fire, but those rounds ricocheted off. *Generalleutnant* Model was in the middle of that group. He stood upright in his open staff car and attempted to organize a defense from there. He summoned the commander of the *I./Schützen-Regiment 394*. When *Major* Kratzenberg approached the general, he sank to the ground, badly wounded. *Hauptmann* Orts then assumed command. But he also collapsed, hit twice in the legs. He died soon afterwards at the main clearing station. *Oberleutnant Freiherr* von Werthern then assumed command of the battalion. Nothing could be seen of the enemy, but heavy fire was coming from the woods. *Oberleutnant* von Werthern issued orders: "Fix bayonets! Get up . . . go . . . go!"

The fight with the well-camouflaged opponent was conducted with determination on both sides. Every individual mound of earth that marked a Russian dug-out had to be stormed. The enemy defended strongly and could only be eliminated in close combat or by means of hand grenades. Finally, the woods around Kalista were in the hands of the von Werthern's battalion. It was a major success. Unfortunately, it had been bought with heavy casualties. *Leutnant* Berg, *Leutnant* Nebel, and *Leutnant* Bley fell leading their platoons. Leutnant Rougemont received a severe stomach wound; he died a few hours later. *Stabsarzt* Dr. Marr had his hands full. The young *Unterarzt*, Kalten, was with the riflemen, who were slowly clearing out one pocket of resistance after the other. The medic, *Unteroffizier* Sprössing, was wounded. *Unterarzt* Kalten went to help dress him and was mortally wounded.

Generalleutnant Model had witnessed the fighting of his soldiers while standing on the road and had personally issued directives and orders. When the fighting came to a conclusion, the general was able to thank the badly wounded *Major* Kratzenberg one more time for the accomplishments of his brave battalion. *Hauptmann* Pape of the motorcycle infantry battalion assumed command of the 1st Battalion. For his brave actions, *Oberleutnant* von Werthern was later awarded the Knight's Cross.[24]

---

24. Von Werthern received the Knight's Cross on 8 September 1941. He ended the war as an *Oberstleutnant* and went on to serve in the *Bundeswehr*, where he retired as an *Oberstleutnant*. He passed away on 10 January 2001 in Großhansdorf (Hamburg).

The division commander then had a convoy formed from the fighting vehicles of the *I./Panzer-Regiment 6*. They escorted the unarmored vehicles through the woods. The light platoon of the tank regiment took the lead in order to establish contact with the *II./Panzer-Regiment 6*, which had ranged far ahead. The remaining tanks were positioned at 100-meter-intervals to the left and right of the road to allow the vehicles through. This unique type of advance started around 1600 hours.

In the woods around Kalista, however, the work of the doctors, medics and chaplains continued. Fresh graves were dug. Forty-three officers, noncommissioned officers and enlisted personnel were given over to eternal rest under the trees and brush. In the evening, a large wooden cross was erected. The two divisional chaplains, Laub and Dr. Heiland, held the funeral remarks, along with the regimental commander, *Oberstleutnant* Audörsch.

In the meantime, the *II./Panzer-Regiment 6* (*Oberstleutnant* Munzel) had continued its advance, despite the fighting that had brewed up behind it. Right in front of the bridge over the Oressa, the enemy had set up an obstacle with destroyed armored vehicles. When friendly fighting vehicles showed up, they received a hail of well-aimed artillery fire. The 5th Company, moving in front, stopped briefly. *Feldwebel* Noelte moved up to the obstacle with his tank and collapsed it with the weight of his steel colossus.

Oberst Linnarz personally took the lead in the command vehicle of his brigade headquarters. They were closely followed by the 7th and 5th Companies of *Panzer-Regiment 6*. Kilometer after kilometer, the tanks churned their way forward through the roads, which had been softened by cloudbursts early in the afternoon. Then they were in front of the Ptitsch, a small tributary of the Pripjet. There was a long wooden bridge over the water at Gluscha.

Oberst Linnarz did not hesitate long. He ordered an immediate crossing. The beams on the bridge started to burn. The fighting vehicles moved through the tongues of flame to the far bank. The planks on the bridge soon went up; only the beams remained. The three command vehicles and the five tanks were already across. Right behind them, the four armored personnel carriers with the riflemen attempted to get across. They succeeded. Then, with a mighty crack, the bridge collapsed.

By then, the tanks of the 7th Company were at the river. *Leutnant* Rühl saw movement on the bridge and thought he had Russians in front of him. The vehicle of the brigade commander was inadvertently knocked out, in the process of which *Oberst* Linnarz lost his right arm. *Oberstleutnant* von Lewinski assumed acting command of the armored brigade.

The following elements of the tank regiment closed up. But there was no getting over the river in the dark night. *Generalleutnant* Model, who had ordered the attack on Brobruisk at 2100 hours, immediately ordered *Aufklärungs-Abteilung 1* to reconnoiter south for a detour. The armored cars finally located a badly worn-out road. The columns then churned their way forward through the knee-deep sand. The route was marshy in spots; as a result, some of the wheeled vehicles became stuck. They could only be pulled out of the muck by means of prime movers and tanks. A small bridge broke under the weight of the trucks, but it was able to be repaired for the time being.

Banks of fog continued to lay over the countryside, when the engines of the tanks sprang to life the next morning. They slowly pushed forward into the first outlying settlements of Brobruisk. Nothing stirred; only individual flames shot out of some of the huts. Friendly artillery had sent out its fiery greetings the previous evening. The light platoon of *Panzer-Regiment 6*, the light platoon of the *I./Panzer-Regiment 6* and the armored personnel company of *Schützen-Regiment 394* took the lead. The fighting vehicles rattled at speed over the roads. The squalid wooden houses and edifices of the party remained behind. There was hardly any resistance. It was only at the old citadel that the enemy put up a defense. The resistance was broken when all of the weapons in the lead element were brought to bear. At 0450 hours, the men of the light platoon of the *I./Panzer-Regiment 6* raised the Reich war flag on the turret of the citadel. Brobruisk had been taken.

Generalleutnant Model found himself at the edge of Brobruisk; the commander of *Schützen-Regiment 394* (*Oberstleutnant* Audörsch) arrived at the division commander's location, while the battalions of the regiment approached Brobruisk by means of detours (all of the bridges along the main road had been blown up). Reports concerning counterattacks of the Russians against the citadel arrived at the commander's location. Model issued the following order to Audörsch at that critical moment: "Assume command of all forces in the citadel. All elements of the division that arrive are attached to you. Hold the citadel and then clear Brobruisk." That order could be executed in its entirety; all of the counterattacks against the citadel were turned back, meaning that the city could then start to be cleared. The forces of *Schützen-Regiment 394*, which had arrived in the meantime, were committed by company in the various city blocks to clear them. Small skirmishes ensued. But resistance was soon broken and Brobruisk was completely clear of the enemy. The lead elements of the rifle regiment were along the banks of the Beresina. Unfortunately, the big bridge was blown up. Since the Russians held the riverbanks under continuous fire, a hasty crossing was not possible. *Oberstleutnant* Audörsch and his command post were in the bastion right along the Beresina. The artillery had also sent its observers forward to the river. They dug in behind the walls of the citadel, which were fifteen meters high right on water's edge. The divisional engineers were moved into the citadel to occupy it. The armored regiment arrived at the western portion of Brobruisk, and the tanks were refueled and rearmed.

The Soviets wanted to hold up the Germans at the Beresina at all costs. They brought up several batteries to the east bank and continuously shelled the city. The Soviet fire kept up the entire day, focusing on the citadel. The first officer from *Artillerie-Regiment 75* to be killed in this campaign—*Oberleutnant* Weihe, the battery commander of the 9th Battery—lost his life early in the afternoon.

All of a sudden, the skies darkened. A storm with flashing lightning, rolling thunder and cloudbursts let loose on the river flood plain. Despite that, the Russian fire continued across the Beresina. Enemy forces used the haze of the storm to climb across the planks of the blown-up bridge. The Soviets even succeeded in reaching the German side. They were then caught by the machine guns of the *II./Schützen-Regiment 394* and had to pull back rapidly.

The division, which also moved its command post to Brobruisk in the afternoon, ordered the *II./Schützen-Regiment 394* to form a bridgehead on the east bank of the Beresina that evening. Friendly batteries initiated the operations with a preparatory fire. The riflemen made it across the river in inflatable craft; a few took the route over the destroyed bridge. The Russians put up a bitter defense. Despite that, the battalion succeeded in establishing a small bridgehead by morning. *Major* Dr. Müller was able to enter the small village of Titowka with his companies. The 2nd Company of the divisional engineers, in support of the riflemen and led by *Oberleutnant* Roever, was the first to enter the village. Hard fighting developed, during which the engineer company lost four dead and fifteen wounded.

The 1st Company of engineers then immediately started to work on a pontoon bridge and labored the entire night. Although Russian fires disrupted the work, it continued to make progress. For the construction of this bridge and others, *Pionier-Bataillon 79*[25] was attached to the division. But the river was too wide to rapidly cross large portions of the division. The division extended its positions on the west bank of the river. In the course of those movements,

---

25. *Panzer-Pionier-Bataillon 79* was the engineer battalion of the *4. Panzer-Division*.

the airstrip south of Brobruisk was also occupied, whereby a few machines fell undamaged into German hands.

The *II./Schützen-Regiment 394* was all by itself on the far side of the Beresina and could only be supported by artillery, which sent its fiery greetings across the river. The brave riflemen urgently needed that help, since they were exposed to ongoing Russian immediate counterattacks, which concentrated on Titowka. Despite everything, *Major* Dr. Müller was able to beat back all of the Russian attacks through his own personal and brave example.

The division was held up for two days on the Beresina. It was impossible to get across the river with larger forces. Although the engineers were working constantly on the construction of both the field-expedient and the pontoon bridges, Russian aircraft attacked continuously, causing casualties and adding new damage to the work in progress. The highest command levels of the Red Army had identified the danger associated with the German offensive in the central sector of the front and attempted to prevent another breakthrough with all means available. The commander in chief of the Western Front was relieved and General Jeremenko replaced him. Jeremenko would prove to be the main antagonist to *Generaloberst* Guderian.

The friendly *Flak* elements gave it their best, but they were too weak to turn back all of the enemy air attacks. On 29 June, the batteries shot down more than twenty Soviet aircraft; on the next day, it was thirty-five. The employment of *Oberstleutnant* Mölders's wing[26] brought the riflemen considerable relief. The wing shot down so many Russian machines that soon barely any Soviet aircraft dared to show themselves on the horizon.

Schützen-Regiment 3, which had been behind the division in the second wave up to this point, moved into Brobruisk on 29 June. At the orders conference, the division commander ordered the *I./Schützen-Regiment 3* to send a patrol to the

east bank of the Beresina that very night. *Leutnant* Vormann of the 3rd Company conducted the mission and was able to determine that the Russians had apparently voluntarily evacuated their positions.

Working feverishly, *Major* Beigel's engineers were able to complete the pontoon bridge over the river during the night of 29–30 June. The division thereupon ordered that the advance was to continue the following morning. The bivouacking forces were alerted at 0600 hours and were informed to be ready to move out fifteen minutes later. But the Russians along the river did not give up and continued to place well-aimed fire on the bridge construction sites. The *Major* Dr. Müller's 2nd Battalion was still all by itself on the east bank of the Beresina, and its riflemen had been constantly defending day and night the last two days. During the morning of 30 June, the battalion finally succeeded in clearing the locality of Titowka of the enemy, thus establishing a point of departure for the continued advance.

The *1./Schützen-Regiment 394*, which was the only company of the regiment equipped with armored personnel carriers at the time, was the first unit to cross the finished bridge to the east bank of the river. The remaining companies of the 1st Battalion followed. The battalion immediately inserted itself into the marshlands next to its sister battalion, the *II./Schützen-Regiment 394*, and expanded the bridgehead in all directions, one hour at a time.

Oberst von Manteuffel's *Schützen-Regiment 3* was brought forward to the west bank of the river from Kemenka at 1000 hours. Its 2nd Battalion crossed the Beresina from the northern portion of Brobruisk. The 1st Battalion crossed the water obstacle on the pontoon bridge. Crossing the river south of the city in inflatable craft was the 3rd Company of the regiment. That company encountered heavy defensive fire in front of the railway embankment and suffered three dead and several wounded. Both of the

---

26. This was *Jagdgeschwader (JG) 51*.

middle regiments were on the east back and drove wedges into the enemy front. Finally, the Russian resistance weakened and their forces pulled back through the marshy flood plain to the east. The only thing that continued to be active was the Red Air Force, which attacked the crossing point in waves.

The continuing bomber attacks were also the reason why the armored regiment did not cross the river that day. Toward noon, the two battalions moved back to their bivouac areas west of Brobruisk, although their orders to be prepared to move continued to be in effect. An exception was a platoon of the 2nd Company under *Leutnant* von Wedel, which was attached to the reconnaissance battalion to form an advance guard. Around 1600 hours in the afternoon, the brigade provided the following situation report: "Movement east stopped. For the rest of the day, rest and maintenance." A few hours later, the armored brigade headquarters was dissolved. That meant that the armor brigade of the *3. Panzer-Division* had ceased to exist. The command vehicles of the headquarters were issued to *Oberstleutnant* von Lewinski's armored regiment, and he was placed under the direct command and control of the division.

During the day, the two rifle regiments expanded their bridgeheads. Toward 1900 hours, *Schützen-Regiment 3* reached Babin, seven kilometers east of the Beresina. At that point, the *II./Schützen-Regiment 3* and the *II./Schützen-Regiment 394* were north of the main avenue of advance, while the two other battalions were to the south of it. Forward of Babin, the *I./Schützen-Regiment 3* screened to the southeast. The Soviets continued to try to turn back the regiments by means of air attacks, but their efforts were fruitless.

The division moved across the military bridges to the east bank of the Beresina with its remaining elements. Starting at 0600 hours, the armored regiment formed up to move through Brobruisk. It started crossing the river three quarters of an hour later with its lead elements. Since the flood bridges had been blown up on the far side, long stretches of detour had to be driven through deep sand. The wheeled vehicles could only make it hooked up to tanks in front of them. After moving through badly damaged Totowka, the armored regiment bivouacked in the woods near Babin.

The division had ordered its attack in the direction of Rogatschew. A strong advance guard under *Oberst* Kleemann was established for that purpose. *Panzer-Regiment 6* detached its 3rd Battalion (*Hauptmann* Schneider-Kostalski), while *Schützen-Regiment 3* detached a mixed company under the command of *Oberleutnant* von Baumbach. The first mission for the advance guard: locate the enemy and determine his strength; determine which bridges are destroyed; take intact bridges.

The advance guard moved out at 1030 hours. The tanks, armored personnel carriers, and motorcycles made good progress until they reached Ola Creek, and a destroyed bridge there prevented their further movement. *Leutnant* Bodig's tank platoon was given the mission of reconnoitering for a detour as part of *Oberleutnant* Baumbach's mixed company. In the process, the fighting vehicles discovered an enemy airfield. Both sides were equally surprised. German tanks and Russian antiaircraft weapons opened fire at the same time. Three friendly tanks and one armored personnel carrier were knocked out and set alight. In the end, however, the enemy resistance was broken. Three "Rata" fighters and ten bombers were destroyed on the ground. *Leutnant* Haug was sent back by the commander of the advance guard to render a report. He linked up with the rifle brigade 5.5 kilometers east of Babin, where a blown-up bridge was holding up its advance. A short while later, *Oberleutnant* von Baumbach returned with his company after successfully completing his mission.

Generalleutnant Model personally moved forward to breath some life into the advance, which had bogged down. In the meantime, *Hauptmann* Ziervogel's reconnaissance battalion had discovered an intact bridge at Pawlowitschi.

At that point, *Generalleutnant* Model issued new orders. According to them, *Oberstleutnant* von Lewinski was to swing out with his 2nd Battalion to the left once across the bridge and reach the road again to the rear of the enemy. The rifle brigade was to advance on both sides of the road in two assault groups and go around the Russian position at the destroyed bridge.

A cloudburst commenced at the same time that the tanks and the riflemen started out. For the most part, the wheeled vehicles got stuck in the mud. *Oberstleutnant* Munzel thereupon had the riflemen of the *II./Schützen-Regiment 3* mount his tanks, while the 1st Battalion had to fight its way with difficulty through the marsh and molder. The *5./Panzer-Regiment 6* advanced directly east, while the remaining elements of the regiment pressed south from the far bank of the Ola. The *I./Schützen-Regiment 3* (*Major* Wellmann), supported by elements from the divisional engineers, crossed in rafts, and drove the Russians in front of it away. The riflemen linked up with the tankers of *Panzer-Regiment 6* at Bortniki. Toward 2300 hours, *Schützen-Regiment 3* transitioned to screening around Bortniki. Its 2nd Battalion (*Major* Zimmermann) was to the left of the road, the 1st Battalion to the right.

The morning of 2 July promised another warm day of weather. The armored regiment was awakened shortly after 0500 hours. *Oberstleutnant* von Lewinski only had the *II./Panzer-Regiment 6* at his disposal at the time, since the combat trains of the 1st Battalion had not made it forward yet and the battalion needed to be refueled and rearmed. The 2nd Battalion moved out at 0805 hours. The point was formed this time by its 8th Company. The company made rapid progress, but it was unable to cross the Dubysna, since the bridge had been blown up by the enemy at Liskowskaja. The fighting vehicles were able to discover a bridge capable of taking tanks to the north at Filipkowitschi. *Oberstleutnant* Munzel moved his entire battalion there, crossing the small river.

The remaining elements of the battalion followed slowly. Russian aircraft repeatedly attacked the columns in the morning. A short while later, fifteen close-support aircraft came in, followed by eight fighters. The aircraft flew at low level over the battalions and strafed, causing casualties and damage to the vehicles.

Most of the division was still bogged down in front of the Dubysna. The bridging columns of the divisional engineers were employed and built a sixteen-ton bridge. The construction did not proceed as quickly as expected, since enemy aircraft continuously forced the engineers to seek cover. It was not until around 1900 hours that the work was completed; at that point, the vehicles started rolling again. In the meantime, the division had issued orders for the next day. The advance guard of *Oberstleutnant* Munzel had advanced as far as the rail line in front of Rogatschew with its lead elements towards 1100 hours. One half hour later, it reported by radio: "Bridge over the Drut in front of Rogatschew blown up. Correspondingly impossible to advance at this time. Enemy artillery fire." At that point, *Generalleutnant* Model issued orders for a halt. The armored regiment pulled off of the road and set up security in the area around Trotzky. Smaller elements remained screening along the Drut.

The division had reached the largest natural obstacle so far in its advance. The fifty-meter-wide Drut separated the regiments from the enemy. That was followed by the marshy flood plains of the Dnjepr. The city of Rogatschew was located in the sharp corner of the confluence of the two rivers and dominated the entire region. The city was already burning. *Major* Zimmermann's *II./Schützen-Regiment 3*, reinforced by engineers and a platoon of antitank guns, attacked Rogatschew in a *coup de main*. The riflemen, some of them mounted on the antitank vehicles, assaulted along the narrow road. The resistance offered by individual machine-gun nests was rapidly broken. They reached the high ground west of the city, where they saw the enemy blow up the bridges. That meant that the objective could no longer be obtained. *Major* Zimmermann issued orders to

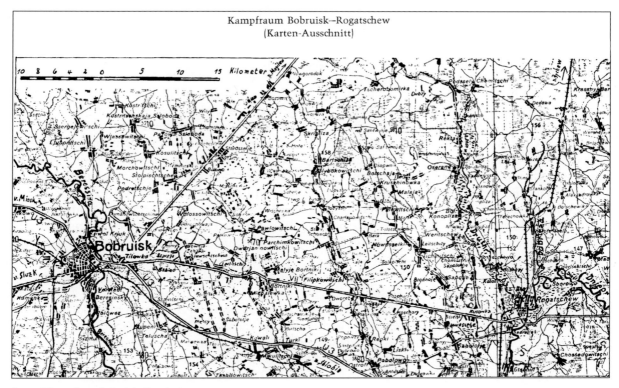

Kampfraum Bobruisk–Rogatschew
(Karten-Ausschnitt)

Area of Operations: Bobruisk–Rogatschew.

set up a hedgehog defense on the high ground. Fortunately, the milk processing plant—a fairly modern installation—remained in the hands of the riflemen, who were able to indulge in milk and cheese, before nightfall descended.

The division closed up to the river in the evening and during the night. Enemy artillery fire repeatedly disrupted friendly movements. Three large bomb craters temporarily rendered the main road useless. Patrols and route reconnaissance elements that were sent out determined that the Liskowskaja–Bartschiza–Tschgirink road, which was needed for an advance on Star-Bychow, was completely impassable to wheeled vehicles. That meant that an attack to the northeast was out of the question for the time being.

The division command therefore decided to attack Rogatschew frontally, in order to eliminate this "fire-spewing" Russian city and strongpoint and create a bridgehead to the east bank of the Dnjepr. The *II./Schützen-Regiment 3* (*Major*

Zimmermann), the *I./Schützen-Regiment 394* (*Hauptmann* Pape), and the *III./Panzer-Regiment 6* (*Hauptmann* Schneider-Kostalski) were employed to that end. In addition, there were elements from *Panzerjäger-Abteilung 543* (*Major Freiherr* von Türckheim), *Pionier-Bataillon 39* (*Major* Beigel), and the *II./Schützen-Regiment 394* (*Major* Dr. Müller). *Oberst* Ries's *Artillerie-Regiment 75*, which had closed up, started preparatory fires on burning Rogatschew and Russian positions on both sides of the river at 1800 hours on that Thursday, 3 July. The Russian artillery did not remain silent, either. It placed harassing fires all across the sector, especially along the bridge on the railway embankment.

The *III./Panzer-Regiment 6*, together with the *I./Schützen-Regiment 394*, approached the Drut through its greening vegetated flood plains, winding its way through the marshy meadows. Numerous wooden rafts were in the water, which was not deep. *Hauptmann* Streger's *Panzer-Regiment 6* initially approached the river. The tanks buttoned up. The fighting vehicles rattled into the shallow and marshy waters. The remaining companies waited a few minutes to see what happened to the fording company. When the first tank climbed out of the Drut on the far bank, *Hauptmann* Schneider-Kostalski issued orders: *"Panzer marsch!"* The entire battalion was able to get through the river without incident. The riflemen followed closely behind and, in some instances, used the wooden rafts to cross. Despite stubborn defensive fires, the tanks and the riflemen were in front of the burning wooden huts on the northern edge of Rogatschew a short while later.

At the same time, the *II./Schützen-Regiment 3*, the *II./Schützen-Regiment 394*, and the *3./Pionier-Bataillon 39* moved out to attack the city. The two battalions moved into Rogatschew fairly rapidly. The riflemen and engineers fought their way in, meter by meter. Murderous fire was received from all of the houses. The Russians defended desperately. The antitank gun crews pushed and pulled their guns by hand and individually took the pockets of resistance under fire.

The houses and the roads were burning everywhere. The battalions slowly chewed their way into the city. The platoon of *Leutnant* Möllhoff (*3./Pionier-Bataillon 39*) reached the church in the center of the city. Then the riflemen were at the Dnjepr. Extremely heavy machine gun and artillery fire was received from the far bank, forcing the riflemen to take cover. *Oberstleutnant* Audörsch (commander of *Schützen-Regiment 394*) and *Major* Zimmermann (commander of the *II./Schützen-Regiment 3*) were both in the city and discussed how to conduct the fight there as well as a possible crossing of the Dnjepr. During the night, during which the enemy artillery fire had not slowed down at all, one of the division chaplains, Dr. Heiland, made a surprise visit to the command post of *Schützen-Regiment 394*. As he had done so frequently before, he had come forward to the forward lines to care for the

wounded. For his constant presence among the lead elements and his unflappability, he was awarded the Iron Cross, First Class, that day.

It was only outside of Rogatschew that a few battle groups—the 7th and 8th Companies of *Schützen-Regiment 3*—were able to get across the river. From the regiment's 6th Company, only *Leutnant* Saathoff made it across the water. The engineers made another crossing attempt, until they were torn apart in the maelstrom of the hard fighting along the banks.

The fighting to establish a bridgehead at Rogatschew started. Since the Soviets were still defending in the city proper, our soldiers quickly got into a difficult situation. The losses mounted from hour to hour. *Oberleutnant* Spillmann, the company commander of the *6./Schützen-Regiment 394*, fell along with many of his soldiers. *Major* Zimmermann, the commander of the *II./Schützen-Regiment 3*, was wounded for the third time. *Hauptmann* Engelien assumed acting command of the battalion. The *8./Schützen-Regiment 3*, which had been employed as a flank guard in the direction of Salutje, took the heaviest casualties. The company commander, *Oberleutnant* Becker, was badly wounded; *Leutnant* Fritze was killed. *Leutnant* Gleitz, the leader of an engineer assault detachment, was mortally wounded, along with three other enlisted engineer personnel. At that point, the acting commander of the *3./Pionier-Bataillon 39*, *Leutnant* Schultze, assumed command of all surviving forces in the bridgehead and ordered a withdrawal across the river.

While the fighting vehicles of the *III./Panzer-Regiment 6* pulled back to the city's edge during the night, the riflemen remained in contact with the enemy. He was putting up particularly stiff resistance in the southern part of the city. For the time being, there was no making progress. The rifle brigade issued orders that the *I./Schützen-Regiment 3*, which had not yet been committed, reinforce the outposts in that area with some of its elements. The 1st Company of *Oberleutnant* von Zitzewitz was reinforced with platoons from the 2nd, 4th and 5th Companies, as well as a platoon from *Panzerjäger-Abteilung 543*, and given that mission. The reinforced company received its designated sector shortly after 2100 hours and dug in among the vegetated terrain southwest of the railway bridge.

The morning of 4 July saw no change to the situation. The fighting was primarily marked on both sides by the artillery fight. The Soviets had thirty-six heavy batteries on the east bank of the Dnjepr southeast of Rogatschew, which they used to shower the German movements in and around the city with heavy fire (15 centimeter). Despite the fact that forward observers had been brought as far forward as the river, the artillery was unable to successfully engage those enemy batteries.

The numbers of wounded climbed day by day, hour by hour. The wounded who could not be cared for at the forward clearing station had to be transported by ambulance to the field hospital at Brobruisk, forty-two kilometers away. *Leutnant* Schickerling, the platoon leader of the 1st Ambulance Platoon, saved a wounded man by swimming across the Dnjepr. For his actions, he was later awarded the Iron Cross, First Class.

Toward noon, the rifle brigade ordered an attack on Lutschkin by the *I./Schützen-Regiment 3*, reinforced by a platoon of tanks and two antitank companies. Major Wellmann moved out ahead with the tanks and the *2./Schützen-Regiment 3*, which had climbed aboard, and occupied it. Once there, the riflemen linked up with *Leutnant* Stegmann and his demolition party from the *5./Schützen-Regiment 3*, which had blown up the railway facilities south of the village.

The division started to form its first bridgehead on the Dnjepr at 1800 hours. A *Stuka* attack on enemy positions had already taken place at 1500 hours, but it did not succeed in silencing the enemy artillery. The *II./Schützen-Regiment 3* attacked directly from Rogatschew, in order to establish a bridgehead. It was directed for the *II./Schützen-Regiment 394*, supported by elements of the *III./Panzer-Regiment 6*, to form a bridgehead to the north, so as to then hit the

enemy in the rear, while the reinforced *3./Schützen-Regiment 3* tied down Soviets from the front at the Jedolin collective farm. Unfortunately, the operation stood under an unlucky star. The attack of the *II./Schützen-Regiment 3* bogged down at the city's edges. On his own initiative, *Hauptmann* Engelien called off the attack of his battalion. In the last few days, the battalion had lost all of its 8th Company and an additional 146 men of the other four companies! Likewise, the attack of the *3./Schützen-Regiment 3* (*Hauptmann* Peschke) was delayed. The company was unable to attack until 2000 hours, because the inflatable rafts were brought forward too late. The company's efforts then bogged down in the face of the Russian artillery. The company thereupon dug in along the Dnjepr and had to defend against the enemy's immediate counterattacks, which were directed at Lutschkin.

The *II./Schützen-Regiment 394* (*Major* Dr. Müller) had more success. The battalion, reinforced by antitank elements, was actually able to cross the 100-meter-wide river. The three submergible tanks of the *12./Panzer-Regiment 6* (under *Oberfeldwebel* Blaich) provided powerful support to the riflemen. The tanks crossed the river under the water surface and got to the far shore. Although one of the fighting vehicles was knocked out by Russian antitank guns, the remaining two tanks held down the Russian defenses long enough for the riflemen to cross. The *6./Schützen-Regiment 394* (*Leutnant* Gappel) attacked and reached the ridgeline 100 meters east of Sborowo.

At that point, *Major* Dr. Müller was at Sborowo on the east bank of the broad river with his battalion and the *1.* and *3./Panzerjäger-Abteilung 543* (*Oberleutnant* Michels and *Oberleutnant* Held). That signaled the heroic struggle of those forces, which were soon cut off from the remaining elements of the division. The Soviets placed such heavy artillery fire on the riverbanks and the destroyed bridges that not a single additional man was able to cross the Dnjepr. At the same time, Russian infantry charged the positions of the small bridgehead. Casualties mounted by the hour on the German side, and rations and ammunition were slowly running out. But the few companies held firm against all attacks. The riflemen and antitank gunners knew neither sleep nor rest nor relief over the next few days. *Major* Dr. Müller compelled his men to hold out through his personal bravery. Later on, he and *Oberfeldwebel* Blaich received the Knight's Cross for their bold actions.

The *XXIV. Armee-Korps (mot.)* radioed orders during the morning that the division was not to move any more forces into the bridgehead for the time being. In the meantime, the Drut flood plains had been made trafficable by the construction of a 1.8-kilometer-long corduroy road by the 1st and 2nd Companies of the divisional engineers under the direction of *Hauptmann* Winkler. The elements of the rifle regiments that had been employed were to remain in place, while *Panzer-Regiment 6* was to be prepared to support the *4. Panzer-Division.* But even those orders were changed. The movements of the armor regiment, which had already been initiated, were stopped. Its 1st Battalion was attached to the *10. Infanterie-Division (mot.)* in Bortniki toward noon. *Major* Schmidt-Ott immediately headed in that direction and set up in Kaschary. The *II./Panzer-Regiment 6* remained on alert, since strong enemy movements were detected along the southern flank of the division, where the motorcycle infantry battalion was screening. A platoon from the *8./Panzer-Regiment 6* was sent towards Schlobin to reconnoiter and reported motorized Russian forces. *Leutnant* Jacobs and his light platoon from the regimental headquarters reconnoitered the area between the Drut and the Dnjepr.

The overall situation that day remained unchanged. The morning was strangely quiet; it was not until the afternoon that the enemy's artillery fires increased. The division feared large-scale enemy attacks and pulled back some of the rifle companies that had been employed to screen as reserves. Only the *II./Schützen-Regi-ment 394* remained in place, involved in heavy fighting in its bridgehead position. The riflemen there had been fighting for two days without letup. It was not until 6 July that the *I./Schützen-Regiment 394* was able to cross the Dnjepr— after its companies had crossed the Drut on floating beams—and support its hard-pressed sister battalion. The casualties continued to increase, however. *Stabsarzt* Dr. Marr died after being hit in the chest, as he helped transport wounded to the rear along with *Feldwebel* Feldebert. The forward observer of the 7th Battery of artillery, *Leutnant* Schwedendieck, was mortally wounded at his observation post. The acting commander of the *6./Schützen-Regiment 394*, *Leutnant* Gappel, had to turn over his company to *Hauptfeldwebel* Holst, after being wounded by shrapnel. Holst himself was badly wounded a short while later. *Leutnant* Rosemeyer and *Leutnant* Steinmüller were likewise badly wounded. Despite all the casualties, *Schützen-Regiment 394* continued to hold. The artillery, which was being directed by the wounded *Leutnant Graf* Studnitz, provided valuable support.

After the intoxicating successes of the first few days of war, no one had thought that the Russians would be able to pull themselves together to offer such hard resistance, even though the Dnjepr was on the so-called Stalin Line. It was certain, however, that the division could not force a crossing over the Dnjepr. The corps considered sending the *4. Panzer-Division* and the *10. Infanterie-Division (mot.)* north to attack, in order to land to the rear of the enemy, who was being held down along the front by the *3. Panzer-Division.*

At that point, the Russians seized the initiative. Unnoticed, they headed out during the dark and raw night of 5–6 July from Schlobin to a point halfway to the main road. The Soviet 117th Infantry Division had the mission to cut off the 3. Panzer-Division from its logistics lines of communication at the Dubysna Bridge, over which some 250 vehicles rolled daily. The thrust landed right in the middle of the formations of the *10. Infanterie-Division (mot.)*,[27] which were staging for their own attack the next morning. The Soviets were able to penetrate into Pobolowo by surprise and wipe out the elements of the division that were there.

At 0545 hours, the division alerted the *II./Panzer-Regiment 6* for immediate employment in support of the neighboring division. Since the downpours of 5 July had made the unimproved roads almost impassable, the battalion had to first move back five kilometers to get to Pobolowo on secondary roads. All of the wheeled vehicles got stuck in the mud. The regimental headquarters likewise bogged down. *Oberstleutnant* von Lewinski had his command vehicle towed by a fighting vehicle, so as to be able to at least follow the attack, even if he had no way to lead the entire regiment by that means. A simultaneous advance by complete tank battalions in that terrain was barely conceivable. The terrain between the Dnjepr and the Dubysna formed an acute triangle leading to Schlobin A creek divided this area one more time into two parts. Embankments further restricted the terrain, which offered no extended visibility due to the high corn in the fields.

Without checking with the *3. Panzer-Division*, the command of the *10. Infanterie-Division (mot.)* immediately employed the *I./Panzer-Regiment 6* before the 2nd Battalion had arrived. *Major* Schmidt-Ott advanced with his companies and immediately encountered strong enemy forces. The 1st Company supported the advance of the *II./Infanterie-Regiment (mot.) 41* on the extreme right wing. *Oberleutnant* Buchterkirch's 2nd Company encountered enemy artillery and antitank-gun positions on the high ground southeast of Luki. *Feldwebel* Reinicke, who had lost an arm during the campaign in the West, attacked the batteries, despite their superiority. All by himself, he was able to shoot an entire battery and two additional guns to pieces. The *Panzer III* of *Feldwebel* Machens (driver: *Gefreiter* Kullrich) was hit in the drive sprocket and immobilized. The crew had to hold out in the tank during the day and was unable to bail out until it turned dark. The tank was recovered during the night.

Oberleutnant von Brodowski's 4th Company moved at high speed along a road that was not on the map directly towards Schlobin. All of the company broke through a blocking position with antitank guns, since it was impossible to leave the road. As a result, one tank followed the other towards Schlobin and the increasingly heavy enemy defensive fires. The Russian guns could barely be identified. In addition, they had camouflaged fighting vehicles in the high corn so well that they were not noticed until their fire broke into the company at pointblank range. The first German tank bogged down and the second one ran over a mine. The next three were shot to pieces by Russian fighting vehicles. The infantry had lagged behind and was prevented from closing with the tanks due to the long-range artillery fire of the Russians. The Soviets concentrated their fires on the fighting vehicles of the 4th Company. When it had moved out that morning, it had thirteen tanks. One after the other was going up in smoke and flame. *Leutnant* von Wedel was killed; a short while later, *Leutnant* Busse fell as well. *Oberleutnant* von Brodowski died a few days later from the burns he received. Along with him, twenty-two noncommissioned officers and enlisted personnel were killed. Some of the thirty-six remaining were badly wounded. Only three tanks returned from the death march of the 4th Company.

Major Schmidt-Ott ordered his 1st Company forward, which also suffered several losses. The 1st Company provided covering fire so that the remnants of the 4th Company could disengage

---

27. The division had just completed its transition to a motorized formation prior to the start of Barbarossa. As was typical with the early-war motorized infantry divisions, it did not have an organic tank formation. At the time of the actions described here, the division had two motorized rifle regiments (20th and 41st), a motorcycle battalion (40th), a motorized reconnaissance battalion (10th), a motorized artillery regiment (10th), an antitank battalion (10th), a motorized engineer battalion (10th), and the normal divisional troops.

from the enemy. Individual tanks of the 2nd Company were also there and took their wounded comrades on board, despite the enemy fire. Once again, it was *Feldwebel* Reinicke who distinguished himself. He was the last to leave the battlefield. For his aggressive actions and his already demonstrated performance, the *Feldwebel* received the Knight's Cross.[28]

By noon on that "black" day, the *I./Panzer-Regiment 6* had lost twenty-two fighting vehicles, half of its inventory. The loss could not be balanced by the destruction of nineteen Russian fighting vehicles, twenty-one guns, two antiaircraft guns, and thirteen antitank guns. For the self-sacrificing actions of his battalion, *Major* Schmidt-Ott would later receive mention in the Army Honor Roll.

The 2nd Battalion of the armored regiment heard the cries for help from the 1st Battalion on the radio. *Oberstleutnant* Munzel decided to attack east of the embankment, since he could not provide direct support. The 5th Company (*Oberleutnant* Jarosch von Schweder) took the lead, followed closely by the 7th and 8th Companies. Between Tertesch and the railway line, the lead company was able to knock out four enemy batteries, one tank and three antitank guns. The 5th and 7th Companies then covered the advance of the 8th Company (*Leutnant* Dr. Köhler) by leapfrogging. The 8th Company entered the city from the flank and advanced by surprise all the way to the bridge over the Dnjepr. Nonetheless, the enemy was able to blow it up in the nick of time. That meant that a lot of Russians were also still in the city. With his six *Panzer IV's*, *Leutnant* Dr. Köhler was able to destroy a total of twenty-two Russian tanks, two antitank guns, and one armored train. That meant that the danger of an advance by strong forces from Schlobin was thwarted for the time being.

At 0300 hours during the night, the armored regiment sent its recovery platoon out onto the battlefield, covered by the regimental light platoon, to evacuate its shot-up fighting vehicles. The work lasted through the entire next day. The men of the maintenance facility and the maintenance sections did not get any rest. *Leutnant* Jacobs, who covered the recovery operations with his light platoon, shot up an additional four enemy antitank guns.

On 7 July, the division transitioned to a screening mission along the river. The division command post was moved from Strenki back to the school in Bronnoje. Since it was anticipated the enemy would continue his efforts to break through and the events of the last few days had proven the danger posed by the enemy—the lead elements of the Soviet forces had approached very close to the quarters of the division's quartermaster section (*Hauptmann i.G.* Barth)—security around the command post was boasted by two security groups under the command of *Unteroffizier* Luft and *Unteroffizier* Junick. That was in addition to the rifle platoon and antitank platoon already there.

The armored regiment was designated the division's reserve; it located its command post in the village of Osseniki. *Hauptmann* Schneider-Kostalski's 3rd Battalion was positioned forward in the area between the Drut and Dnjepr, however, and kept in a state of readiness. *Schützen-Regiment 3* assumed responsibility for guarding along the river. The next night, during that mission, the 3rd Company was able to eliminate an officer patrol of ten men that had infiltrated. The 2nd Company of the motorcycle infantry battalion reconnoitered south in the direction of Schlobin. The northern portion of that locality was clear of the enemy, but the southern half was held by the Russians.

Oberstleutnant Audörsch's *Schützen-Regiment 394* remained in the bridgehead at Sborowo, along with its attached antitank elements, engineers and forward observers. As it started to turn dark, the first squads started crossing back over

---

28. Gerhard Reinicke was submitted for the award on 3 July and received it on 9 July. By the end of the war, he was a *Leutnant*. He passed away in Viersen on 4 July 1997.

the river in pneumatic craft. The regiment gradually disengaged form the enemy, starting with its 1st Battalion. The heroic days of fighting in Sborowo, which had seen the regiment take many casualties, was acknowledged by the inclusion of *Major* Dr. Müller in the Army Honor Roll on 9 September 1941, followed by *Feldwebel* Reiss (3rd Company) on 29 September 1941. The regiment continued its retrograde movements out of the bridgehead. The 1st Battalion was employed screening north of Rogatschew along the river. The Russian artillery took the movements under fire, with the companies taking some losses. On 9 July alone, there were eight dead.

The daily events of the other divisional elements did not change much. The outpost lines were reinforced, wherever that appeared necessary, and either pushed forward or pulled back, as deemed appropriate. The *II./Schützen-Regiment 3* was positioned northwest of Schlobin. Since the Russians were feeling their way forward against the battalion's lines with fairly strong elements, the battalion was reinforced in the afternoon by a reinforced platoon (heavy machine guns and mortars) from the 1st Battalion's 2nd Company. The platoon leader was *Leutnant* Schuppius. Those reinforcements were followed a short while later by a platoon from the 2nd Company of *Panzerjäger-Abteilung 543*. On that day, the 2nd Battalion suffered two dead and five wounded, including *Oberleutnant* von Bismarck, the commander of the 10th Company.

The *I./Schützen-Regiment 3* had been in its screening positions for days. They were constantly being covered by enemy artillery fire. *Unteroffizier* Elven's squad from the 2nd Company, which was posted far to the front, was stuck in a path of thick woods for forty-eight hours without relief.

During the morning hours of 9 July, a warning order was received that the division would be pulled out of that sector of the front, with its positions being assumed by the *1. Kavallerie-Division*. It was extremely hot that day.

As it turned night, the non-essential vehicles and equipment of the regiments was sent back to the rear area. One after the other, the companies pulled back from their positions when the advance parties of the *1. Kavallerie-Division* arrived. Strong security forces from *Schützen-Regiment 394*, the divisional artillery and the 3rd Battalion of the armored regiment remained in and around Rogatschew. The relief-in-place continued the next day. The *I./Schützen-Regiment 3* and the *II./Panzer-Regiment 6* were designated as the corps reserve. They turned hard to the northeast east of Brobruisk and marched in the direction of Sbyschin.

On the previous day, *Generalmajor Freiherr von Langermann und Erlenkamp's 4. Panzer-Division* had attacked the Russian fortifications northeast of Brobruisk. The enemy's resistance there was in the process of falling apart. The corps identified a weak spot in the enemy's frontage and earmarked the *3. Panzer-Division* to break through. That was the reason for the relief by the *1. Kavallerie-Division* around Rogatschew. The *3. Panzer-Division* assembled its forces in the fields east of Brobruisk, and the divisional engineers took down their bridge over the Dubysna. That same day, *Major* Haas, a new transfer into the division, was given command of the *I./Schützen-Regiment 394*. He replaced the acting commander, *Hauptmann* Pape, who had earned the trust and confidence of the battalion's men during the short time he had been in command.

For the *3. Panzer-Division*, this signaled the end of the first phase of its employment in the East. In an incomparable advance, the division had conquered both the enemy and the terrain. The Soviet soldier had proven himself to be an extraordinarily tough, cleaver and crafty opponent. The bloody losses sustained were painful; the materiel losses considerable. For instance, *Panzer-Regiment 6*, which had started the campaign with 210 operational tanks, had only 153 operational on 9 July.

A march halt along a Polish country road. The vehicles are maintaining a thirty-meter interval and parked under trees as concealment against aerial observation.

Camp life within *Schützen-Regiment 394* at Radzyn. From left to right: *Oberleutnant Freiherr* von Werthern, *Oberstleutnant* Audörsch, *Major* Kratzenberg, *Leutnant* Hildebrand, and *Hauptmann* Schmidt.

The first vehicles of the division arrive at Koden, along the Bug. The border has been reached.

The first captured Soviets move back over the bridge over the Bug at Koden, which was captured intact by the engineers in a *coup de main*.

On the very first day of the campaign, motorcycles were getting stuck along the sandy march routes of the division east of the Bug.

Marsh, marsh, and more marsh—by 22 June, already the most dangerous "opponent" of the *3. Panzer-Division.*

The advance was initiated on 23 June: on the road to Kobryn.

The knocked-out Sd.Kfz. 263 armored radio car of the division commander in front of the bridge at Szczara. *Generalleutnant* Model was not injured.

Observation post on the high banks of the Szczara. At the scissors scope is *Major* Kratzenberg; to his right is *Major* Dr. Weißenbruch, the commander of the *III./Artillerie-Regiment 75*.

A provisional span has been put in place over the Szczara by *Pionier-Bataillon 39*.

The commander in chief of the armored group, *Generaloberst* Guderian, visits the division and is briefed by *Generalleutnant* Model.

Generalleutnant Model talks to the commander of the lead tank company, *Oberleutnant* Buchterkirch. Next to Model are *Major* Beigel and *Leutnant* von dem Knesebeck.

A short halt among the lead elements during the advance on Sluzk.

Major Schmidt-Ott, the commander of the *I./Panzer-Regiment 6*, with *Oberleutnant* Buchterkirch.

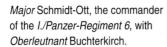

The *I./Schützen-Regiment 394* attacks Sluzk.

The main clearing station of the 1st Medical Company in Sluzk.

In the woods near Kalita. *Generalleutnant* Model discusses the situation with *Major* Schmidt-Ott.

The Beresina is reached. Here is the blown-up bridge at Brobruisk.

The *1./Schützen-Regiment 394* crosses the pontoon bridge over the Beresina.

Major Beigel, the commander of *Pionier-Bataillon 39* (seen here as an *Oberst*). For his part in the capture of the bridges over the Szczara, he was awarded the Knight's Cross.

Feldwebel Gerhard Reinicke, a platoon leader in the *2./Panzer-Regiment 6*, receives the Knight's Cross from *Generalleutnant* Model and his company commander, *Oberleutnant* Buchterkirch (9 July 1941).

Oberfeldwebel Blaich of the *12./Panzer-Regiment 6* was awarded the Knight's Cross for his actions along the Drut at Rogatschew. From left to right: *Feldwebel* Groß, *Leutnant* Heuer, *Oberfeldwebel* Blaich, *Oberleutnant* Hirschmann, and *Oberfeldwebel* Hass.

CHAPTER 9

From the Dnjepr to the Dessna: Breaking through the Stalin Line

The *3. Panzer-Division* had disengaged from its Dnjepr positions at Rogatschew with its last elements by 11 July 1941. It was located in a staging area south of Mogilew. There wasn't much time to rest, however. The free time was used to catch "forty winks," as long as the swarms of mosquitos were not buzzing too wildly or Russians that had been flushed out came running by.

At 1645 hours, the division formed a battle group from elements of both brigades under the command of *Oberst* von Manteuffel, who received orders to attack Mogilew. The designated battalions and detachments moved farther north and behind *Kradschützen-Bataillon 40* (*10. Infanterie-Division [mot.]*), which was in position there. The Russians were very active and were in the process of conducting an immediate counterattack against Nowaja Leschnewka. The *1./Schützen-Regiment 3* (*Oberleutnant* von Zitzewitz) was immediately employed against it. The riflemen advanced several kilometers to the north in their armored ersonnel carriers and were able to take Ssolanowka at 1930 hours.

At 1800 hours, *Generalleutnant* Model discussed the attack on Mogilew (population: 99,000) with his commanders.

Kampfgruppe von Manteuffel moved into its designated staging areas. The *Oberst* placed his command post on the road 400 meters southwest of Mashissjadki. The commanders of the *II./Panzer-Regiment 6* (*Oberstleutnant* Munzel) and *Panzerjäger-Abteilung 521* (*Major* Frank) reported in there, as well as the commanders of the 7th and 8th Companies of *Panzer-Regiment 6* and the commander of the headquarters company of *Schützen-Regiment 3*, whose company formed the reserve of the *Kampfgruppe*. The *6./Flak-Regiment 59* assumed area defense on both sides of Mashissjadki. The *1./Nachrichten-Abteilung 39* established radio communications with the forward elements of the division. During the day, *Pionier-Bataillon 39* employed all of its companies clearing the heavily mined terrain and completed its construction of a bridge over the Lechwa. The main clearing station was set up by both of the medical companies in Gluchaja-Seliba.

The *XXIV. Armee-Korps (mot.)* had the mission of forcing a crossing of the Dnjepr by using all of its forces. The attached divisions were given the same mission in the sectors assigned to them. As part of that, the *3. Panzer-Division* was the left-wing division and it received a dual mission: Protect the flank of the corps and take a good and armor-capable crossing point over the Dnjepr at Mogilew by rapidly taking it and its bridges.

During the night, *Artillerie-Regiment 75* brought its batteries into position, which initiated a short but intense preparation on the Soviet positions right at 0300 hours on the morning of 12 July. Shortly afterward, the men of *Kampfgruppe von Manteuffel* moved out. The initial enemy resistance was broken, but then the difficulty of the terrain and the defensive preparedness of the strong enemy forces made itself felt.

The righthand group under *Major* Wellmann advanced northeast of Mashissjadki between the road and the railway line with the 2nd and 3rd Companies of *Schützen-Regiment 3*. Against expectations, both companies were able to quickly take the railway stopping point at Krassnitza and then move out on Sselez. The 3rd Company took the meadowlands between the locality and the railway line, while the 2nd Company stormed the village. Up to that point, the *7./Panzer-Regiment 6* and the *3./Pionier-Bataillon 39* had followed the riflemen. The tanks then took the lead, swung east and reached a road running parallel to the river. They then bounded five kilometers north to Bunitschi in a single move. The Russians stubbornly defended the village and had employed their antitank guns in an especially skillful manner. Despite that, the fighting vehicles rolled through, destroying eight antitank guns and five tanks that crossed their paths. At that point, the attack bogged down. Fortunately, riflemen from the *2./Schützen-Regiment 3* showed up. They fought their way into and through the village meter by meter. In contrast, the 3rd Company of the rifle regiment hung far back, since it was unable to eliminate enemy pockets of resistance that had been established on the railway northeast of Sselez. In fact, the Soviets launched an immediate counterattack there, which was turned back with the assistance of the *1./Schützen-Regiment 3*, which was sent forward.

After noon, *Kampfgruppe Wellmann* made no progress anywhere. The enemy at Bunitschi turned active again and put a lot of pressure on his 2nd Company, since Russian forces coming from the Dnjepr attacked the company in the flank. *Oberleutnant* von Baumbach was badly wounded and died a few hours later at the main clearing station. The 3rd Company lost *Leutnant* Jobst and *Leutnant* Haug through wounds. The battalion radioed the regiment that it was unable to advance any more with its own forces and requested tanks and artillery immediately.

The lefthand *Kampfgruppe* under *Hauptmann* von Cochenhausen, consisting of his *Krad-schützen-Bataillon 3*, the *1./Schützen-Regiment 394*, the *5./Panzer-Regiment 6*, the *1./Panzer-jäger-Abteilung 521*, and the *11./Schützen-Regiment 3*, was also initially successfully that morning. The tanks, riflemen, and antitank elements quickly gained ground west of the railway line, even though they had hardly any improved roads at their disposal. Tscheinowka was taken. The tank company advanced on its own in the open terrain west of the railway embankment. The first tank then flew into the air; a second one was also quickly immobilized. A third tank lost a track, with a fourth one sharing the same fate: mines. No matter where the fighting vehicles turned and moved, they ran over mines again and again and became immobilized. The crews were forced to bail out, since the enemy was placing well-aimed antitank-gun fire on the fighting vehicles. The Russian machine-gun and antitank-gun fire caused the company considerable casualties. *Oberleutnant* Jarosch von Schweder and *Gefreiter* Schnell were killed; many were wounded. In all, eleven fighting vehicles were lost. Although the remaining tanks provided covering fire, they had to disengage from the enemy. The crew of a knocked-out tank brought back *Leutnant* Hinzpeter, the new acting company commander. Thanks to its timely appearance, the *8./Panzer-Regiment 6*, which had been called forward, was able to give powerful support to the disengagement. It also lost a few vehicles in the minefield, including the commander's tank. By noon, the 2nd Battalion had lost eighteen tanks, without making any further progress. As had been the case with the 1st Battalion at Schlobin, this was this battalion's "black day." Only the light platoon of the 2nd Battalion was able to make progress, advancing as far as Golynez, five kilometers west of Mogilew.

At that point, the division called off the unpromising attack on Mogilew. The 1st Battalion of the armor regiment was pushed forward into the area around Tumanowka, where it set up a screening position by evening. That allowed the regiment's 2nd Battalion to be pulled out of the line. The battalion's light platoon moved forward one more time to pick up survivors from the 5th Company and to recover tanks. The remaining elements of *Kampfgruppe von Manteuffel* also pulled back. The *I./Schützen-Regiment 3* reached a line running from t he railway embankment to the southern edge of Sselez to the northern edge of Ssoltanowka by 1800 hours. The motorcycle infantry battalion joined the tankers at Tumanowka in screening.

The harshness of the fighting can be demonstrated in the experience of *Assistenzarzt* Dr.

Türk (*Schützen-Regiment 394*). That evening, he wanted to recover four wounded from the 1st Company, who were lying in front of the positions. Together with ten volunteers, he moved forward in an *SPW* as it turned dark. The Russians got wind of the movement, but they were unable to deter the Good Samaritans. The medics found their comrades dead. They were lying on the ground, disfigured, stripped and plundered. They had been finished off with a round to the back of the head.

The twelfth of July ended with a setback for the division. It was only after several days of fighting that an entire corps was finally able to take Mogilew. By contrast, however, the neighboring division had more success. The *4. Panzer-Division* succeeded in taking an intact wooden bridge over the river at Star-Bychow and forming a bridgehead over the Dnjepr. The engineers then constructed a 120-meter-long bridge so that the attacking forces could remain on the heels of the enemy.

The division was directed to hold a screening line along the Lechwa until relieved, while sending some of its forces into the sector of the *4. Panzer-Division* that same night. The 3rd Battalion of the armor regiment arrived east of Star-Bychow and was designated as the corps reserve. The battle staff of the *3. Panzer-Division* marched south and bivouacked at Poplawschtschina around 0330 hours. At the same time, *Oberstleutnant* Lewinski received orders to have his armor regiment, supported by elements of artillery and *Flak*, to be prepared to move out for operations. Those orders were delayed until 0415 hours. Lewinski's forces then waited for two hours on the road to Brobruisk, before the approach march southeast to Star-Bychow commenced along the deep, sandy roads.

The rifle brigade remained in contact with the enemy that night, but there was no fighting. At noon, the Russians felt their way forward at Ssoltanowka with a large assault detachment, but it did not allow itself to be decisively engaged. Elements from the *1. Kavallerie-Division* started arriving after 1500 hours and relieved the last remaining elements of the 3. *Panzer-Division* by 1945 hours, which moved out immediately to catch up with the division.

It was Sunday, 13 July 1941. The day was hot and sunny. The division moved through the completely burned-down Star-Bychow—only the chimneys were left, in most instances—and across the Dnjepr with most of its vehicles. The east bank of the river, sandy in places and marshy in others, had extensive wire obstacles, tree abatis, wooden bunkers and machine-gun positions extending several kilometers inland. The division was in the middle of the so-called Stalin Line, which had been forced by the 4. *Panzer-Division*.

That presented the option of taking Mogilew, which had been turned into a fortress, from the east. It was directed that the division, together with the *10. Infanterie-Division (mot.)*, attempt that, while *Infanterie-Regiment (mot.) "Groß-deutschland"* and *SS-Division "Das Reich"* attempted to envelop the city from the north. But those orders were rescinded. Leaving behind screening elements oriented on Mogilew, the advance continued east.

On that 13 July, the division directed *Schützen-Regiment 394* to attack north along the Gomel–Mogilew road, while the armor regiment crossed that road to the east. It bivouacked for the night in the Kusskowitschi area, minus its 2nd Battalion, which was sent forward to support the *10. Infanterie-Division (mot.)*. The rifle regiment initiated its attack north right after crossing the river without a lot of preparation.

Its 1st Battalion moved out on foot in scorching heat. Its first mission was to relieve *Infanterie-Regiment (mot.) 41* of the motorized infantry division and then immediately advance on Studenka. The riflemen churned their way along the sandy pathways—completely exhausted. The enemy did not give up without a fight. His artillery fired on the advancing companies. It wasn't until it started to turn dark that that Soviet fires abated, only to be replaced by hundreds of swarms of mosquitoes that plagued the men.

The regiment's 2nd Battalion was inserted into the line next to its sister battalion. Later on, it provided flank guard along the left at Lykowo. The riflemen occupied makeshift foxholes and dugouts and defended against the increasing number of attacks by Russian forces over the next few days. Superior numbers of enemy forces attacked Lykowo the next morning and were able to drive the battalion out of the village in hard close combat. The battalion suffered bloody losses.

The 1st Battalion of the armor regiment, which was the last formation of the division to be relieved in the area around Mogilew, returned to the regiment. It brought a report of success with it. A company from the battalion had taken a Soviet armor garrison at Klin, ten kilometers southwest of Mogilew. In the process, it was able to secure ninety-eight light fighting vehicles.

The division was directed to remain on the enemy's heels, despite the flank threat from Mogilew. Since not all of the division's forces were across the Dnjepr to the east, the division attacked with the battalions it had at its disposal. Continuing in the lead was *Oberstleutnant* Audörsch's *Schützen-Regiment 394*. Early on 14 July, there was an orders conference in the woods east of Ssidorowitschi. *Hauptmann* Schneider-Kostalski's *III./Panzer-Regiment 6* was attached to *Major* Haas's *I./Schützen-Regiment 394*. Also in support were elements of *Major* Frank's *Panzerjäger-Abteilung 521*. The order: Attack!

The riflemen mounted the fighting vehicles and moved out. *Oberst* Kleemann was in charge of the battle group, which was churning its way through the practically primeval and forested terrain. Kostinka was taken. In the process, the tanks companies succeeded in shooting a Soviet artillery position to bits. When the column then turned toward the Mogilew–Tschaussy road, the enemy resistance suddenly grew stronger. The Soviets were positioned in deep dugouts. They let the tanks and motorized elements pass, before they ruthlessly ambushed individual vehicles. During one of those attacks, the commander of the 3rd Company of the antitank battalion, *Oberleutnant* Held, was killed.

The casualties increased by the hour. *Major* Dr. Müller's *II./Schützen-Regiment 394* had an especially tough time of it, while enduring the hard fighting in the Lykowo area as a flank guard. The 7th Company lost all of its officers. Despite being wounded, *Unteroffizier* Becker assumed command of the company and rallied the men forward in an immediate counterattack. By doing so, it was possible to seal off the enemy penetration and drive the Soviets out. The regiment sent up the 3rd Company as reinforcements. During the employment of *Oberleutnant Freiherr* von Werthern's company, he was wounded again, this time in the shoulder. *Leutnant* Schulz, who had been with the battalion one day, was killed. Von Werthern's men saved the situation. Later on, Becker[1] was awarded the Knight's Cross to the Iron Cross. The recommendation read, in part: "On his own initiative and after being wounded in the head, he took charge of the mechanized infantry, who had been rendered leaderless by the loss of all of the officers, in an engagement in the woods south of Mogilew. By means of an immediate counterattack, he prevented the penetration of the enemy and the encirclement of his own company as well as the attached units."

The attack east rolled on. *Generalleutnant* Model went forward with his battle staff at 1100 hours and had his command post established in Amchowaja, a "street" village.[2] The armor regiment followed the attack spearhead. The advance did not proceed smoothly, since enemy-occupied Mogilew forced the use of secondary roads far to the east of the city. By then, however, all of the divisional elements had closed up.

The division still needed to protect its flank in the direction of Mogilew. The Soviets attempted several attacks from that direction during the day. Individual vehicles and bogged down vehicles were the targets of enemy assault detachments. In the afternoon, the Russians attacked from the direction of Lipez. The armor regiment provided two *Panzer IV's* and one *Panzer II* to protect the moving columns. At the cemetery to the south of the village, the fighting vehicles were able to turn back two Soviet rifle companies, as well as destroy two guns and a few mortars. The armor regiment itself was ambushed at 1730 hours. The tanks had to pivot on narrow paths. That led to stoppages along the route, since other columns were rolling forward. Several Russian fighter-bombers joined in the fray, bombing and strafing, but they only caused minor casualties.

Schützen-Regiment 3 was brought forward as soon as possible. It screened north and west in the area around Kostinka. The regiment's 1st Battalion, in conjunction with the *II./Schützen-Regiment 394*, was finally able to retake Lykowo in an immediate counterattack. That eliminated the threat to the flanks for the time being. Then all of the formations of the division turned east. They had to cross a long stretch of marshland. Sections of corduroy road had to be built, which delayed rapid movement. Correspondingly, the riflemen did not arrive in Amchowaja until midnight, where the division set up an all-round defense to protect itself against any enemy attack.

In the morning, at 0500 hours, a conference was held to discuss the continued advance. The division formed a battle group under *Oberstleutnant* von Lewinski. It consisted of the *I.* and *9./Panzer-Regiment 6* and the 2nd Battalion of each of the rifle regiments. *Major* Haas's *I./Schützen-Regiment 394* moved out at 0800 hours to attack Kutjna, which was taken surprisingly rapidly. The casualties were slight, but the men were exhausted after reaching the objective.

---

1. As of 2012, Becker was still alive. He ended the war as a *Leutnant der Reserve*. He changed his last name after the war to Becker-Neetz.
2. These were villages that extended along a single road and had no depth to them.

The battalion's 3rd Company was employed to screen to the rear, in the direction of Mogilew.

Kampfgruppe Lewinski started its attack at 0940 after a short artillery preparation by the batteries. The 2nd and 4th Companies of the armored regiment moved directly along the road, while the 1st and 9th Companies moved to the right. The riflemen were mounted up on the fighting vehicles located to the rear. The Russians knew what was at stake and defended with all the means at their disposal, especially along the flank exposed to Mogilew. Despite the enemy's defensive efforts, the German forces reached the Dubrowka–Kutjna road two hours later. Up to that point, the *I./Panzer-Regiment 6* had destroyed four T-26's,[3] two guns, and ten antitank guns. Oberstleutnant von Lewinski decided to continue the advance to Wolkowitshi to ensure that the success was not temporary. After an hour of moving and fighting, that village was taken and contact was established with the *4. Panzer-Division*, which was attacking from the south. At the same time, the *9./Panzer-Regiment 6* was able to advance as far as the positions of the *10. Infanterie-Division (mot.)*, where it screened from the high ground. During a reconnaissance-in-force, the armor regiment's light platoon eliminated two enemy 15-centimeter guns in the thick woods.

The rifle brigade had moved out directly to the east from the area around Mogilew to attack in the direction of Tschaussy. The armored cars and motorcycles of the reconnaissance battalion took the lead, followed closely by the *SPW's* of the *1./Schützen-Regiment 3*. The rest of the rifle regiment followed, along with the attached engineers, antitank elements and artillery. The 2nd Company of the divisional engineers improved roads and trails in the area around Garbowitschi. To support it in its efforts, the 1st Bridging Section was pushed forward to Amchowaja and employed by *Oberleutnant* Weyler. Seljonaja-

Roschtscha was taken as well, but then the rapid attack bogged down. Enemy resistance had grown stronger and was exerting pressure, especially on the flanks, where the motorcycle infantry battalion and the *II./Schützen-Regiment 394* were screening. Both battalions registered considerable casualties.

Oberst Ries's divisional artillery fired an artillery preparation on Tschaussy and identified enemy positions at 0430 hours that made up for its shortness by its intensity. The enemy seemed to be completely surprised by the onset of sudden artillery fire during that early morning area and replied with only a few rounds. The *I./Schützen-Regiment 3* attacked the village while still being covered by the artillery and was able to report its capture to the division by 0500 hours.

The riflemen advanced through the streets and on towards the bridge over the Bassja, but it was blown up just before it could be reached. The companies bogged down, since the enemy's defensive fires from the far bank increased in intensity as it grew lighter. A few tanks from the 3rd Battalion were pushed forward and reconnoitered a ford through the watercourse. The riflemen immediately mounted up, and two tanks rolled into the water. The first one ran over a mine, and the second one was so impeded by heavy machine-gun fire that any further advance was prevented. A crossing there had to be abandoned.

The division wanted to get across that river, however. To that end, the armor regiment formed a battle group under *Oberstleutnant* Schmidt-Ott around 1100 hours. It consisted of the 2nd Company, half of the 4th and the engineer and light platoons of the 1st Battalion. It was directed to take the railway bridge six kilometers south of Tschaussy and establish a bridgehead there. The Russians put up an unexpectedly strong defense against the approaching tanks, which was especially tough around the

---

3. A Soviet light tank based on the British six-ton Vickers tank chassis. More than fifty variants were studied and more than twenty entered series production. In all, more than 11,000 were manufactured by the Soviet Union, although it was basically considered obsolescent by the time of the German invasion.

Tschaussy rail station. The fighting vehicles had to fight their way forward, meter-by-meter. When the tanks finally occupied the rail station, they had knocked out a total of fourteen guns, seven antitank guns, and three T-26's.

While the lead elements of the division that were pointed east were constantly getting involved in engagements, the elements that were screening to the north, west and south were not being spared enemy attacks and breakout attempts either. All of *Schützen-Regiment 394* was employed along the road in a screening mission, as was the 2nd Battalion of the armor regiment, which was screening west at Petrowitschi. The division's columns rolled slowly in the direction of Tschaussy under the protection of those two formations. The division command post was moved into the park in Tschaussy that afternoon.

The fighting had entered a new phase by then. Reconnaissance reported at 1400 hours that the enemy was starting to evacuate the far side of the river. The division immediately ordered *Schützen-Regiment 3* to pursue. Two engineer *SPW's* arrived with ditching beams; the regiment's 2nd Company immediately started crossing over them, while the other companies of the 1st Battalion mounted up on their vehicles and forded the Bassja. They then reached a second bridge and established a small bridgehead. The division exploited its chance and immediately ordered an expansion of the position that had been won. *Hauptmann* Schneider-Kostalski's *III./Panzer-Regiment 6* and elements of the motorcycle infantry battalion under *Hauptmann* Pape crossed over and moved out immediately. The two battalions got as far as Putjki, which was reached around 1900 hours.

In the meantime, *Kampfgruppe Schmidt-Ott* had also made progress to the south. It was able to occupy the railway bridge around 1800 hours. The engineer and light platoons, as well as an additional light platoon from one of the companies, formed a bridgehead there. The enemy, who was slow to launch immediate counterattacks, was turned back everywhere he appeared.

At 2130 hours, orders arrived to evacuate the position, since the division no longer needed the bridge for its continued advance.

On the other hand, *Major* Beigel's divisional engineers erected a bridge at Tschaussy. The bridge was started at 1300 hours, but it was not completed until around midnight. Two spans were put down, one 19.2 meters long, the other 14.4 meters. The construction was delayed by the need to construct a provisional middle support out of beams.

The division ordered a continuation of the advance while it was still night. *Kradschützen-Bataillon 3*, *Aufklärungs-Abteilung 1*, and the *III./Panzer-Regiment 6* formed the advance guard. They moved out from Putjki at 0730 hours. The hot summer weather of the previous day had turned to a light rainfall. Despite that, the advance moved rapidly, with only enemy artillery fire causing occasional delays. The enemy's resistance did not stiffen until just outside of Moljatitschi.

The motorcycle infantry and reconnaissance battalions prepared to attack from the north. The rifle brigade pushed the *I./Schützen-Regiment 3* forward, which was directed to assault the village from the south. In the face of those superior numbers, the Soviets soon vacated the area. The motorcycle infantry and reconnaissance forces pursued and occupied the village. Five antiaircraft and one antitank gun were captured in firing order. The riflemen mounted up again and advanced to the south. At the railway facilities at Kritschew, the enemy had established field fortifications. His well-aimed artillery fire forced the rifle battalion to turn off to the north. As it started to turn dark, both of the battalions of the regiment were able to make it to the area around Kalninsky.

The advance guard of the division—still comprised of the motorcycle infantry and reconnaissance battalions and the 3rd Battalion of the armored regiment—did not allow itself to be held up by considerable terrain difficulties, rain showers and enemy resistance. It reached Starosselje in complete darkness around 2030 hours. The Ssosh formed a natural barrier there and, since there were no bridges, the advance for the day came to a halt.

On 17 July, the division disengaged its last elements from the encirclement of Mogilew. The division gradually reassembled its formations, which had made it as far as Putjki in the Polna Valley. Since the bridge would only support wheeled vehicles, the tracked vehicles forded the river. The march was halted for hours on end, since the route led through marshes and dense woods. Most of the motorized elements moved into the broad meadow lowlands without being disrupted by enemy air activity. The men used the halt to bathe in the river, a pleasure that they had not enjoyed for some time. The east bank of the river proved to be a tank obstacle; it rose sharply vertically out of the water. At 2100 hours, the division command post moved forward to Moljatitschi. The *I./Schützen-Regiment 394* rested east of Tschaussy for the night, after its screening positions had been assumed by the 2nd Battalion. The *II./Panzer-Regiment 6* went to Sabolotje, to the northwest of Tschaussy, leaving its 5th Company in Petrowitschi to cover the rear. During the night, the armor regiment was sent forward to support the advance guard.

The eighteenth of July brought dreary weather with it. Everyone enjoyed the coolness, however, compared to the extended heat of the last few days. Unfortunately, the rain turned the roadways into seas of mud and muck. The German soldiers remarked that not only were the Russian people against them but the land itself.

At 0230 hours, the *III./Panzer-Regiment 6* was suddenly attacked by strong Soviet forces that had been able to approach undetected to within 150 meters of the battalion in its assembly area at Starosselje. A night fight lasting one and one-half hours developed, before the enemy was driven off. In addition to twenty infantry guns and machine guns being captured, 350 prisoners were taken.

During the course of the day, the division moved its forces up to the Ssosh. In the area around Lobkowitschi, it screened along the river.

That meant that the vehicles received a short break. They had all been in operation without a break for four weeks and had driven routes and crossed terrain that had never been intended for them. Only the rear-area services, which were in Kritschew, a town with proper brick houses and factories, used their trucks to any extent that day.

The rifle brigade screened to the north and east, with a few rifle companies remaining in contact with the tanks along the fertile banks of the river, which formed the front for the time being. There were many apple trees in the gardens, along with blooming hollyhocks and fire lilies. In the meadows, cattle, pigs and sheep could be seen.

The armored regiment was distributed throughout the division sector. The 1st Battalion rested in the Moljatitschi area. The 2nd Battalion had companies between Krotki and Petrowitschi, some eighty kilometers apart. The 9th Company forded the Ssosh and established a bridgehead at Dubrowka. The divisional engineers erected a bridge during the day. Two spans with supports and pontoons were set up for a combined total of 60.8 meters and a capacity of sixteen tons.

The enemy was unexpectedly active on 19 July and attacked the positions of the *4. Panzer-Division* at Propoisk, fifty kilometers south of Kritschew, with fighter-bombers and motorized formations. The Soviets succeeded in encircling some elements. That division had to use all of its forces to eject the enemy. The *3. Panzer-Division* received orders to assume responsibility for the bridgehead at Kritschew from the *4. Panzer-Division*. In the process, advance guards from the reconnaissance and motorcycle infantry battalions were able to establish another bridgehead east of the river at Starosselje. Late in the afternoon, the *II./Panzer-Regiment 6* was sent over the Ssosh to reinforce.

Most of the formations of the division remained where they were. The *I./Schützen-Regiment 3* was directed to occupy the bridgehead position, but it was instead turned off in the direction of Sui, to the north of Kritschew, to screen. The *I./Schützen-Regiment 394*, as well as its 11th Company, and the *II./Artillerie-Regiment 75* were attached to the *4. Panzer-Division*. Together with those formations, the *4. Panzer-Division* formed a strong battle group under *Oberst* Eberbach, which also had *Panzer-Regiment 35*, the *II./Schützen-Regiment 12*, and the *I./Artillerie-Regiment 103* at its disposal. Eberbach was given the mission of eliminating the enemy forces that had broken through and to clear the woods to the north. For all those involved, it was an uneasy night. The enemy exploited the darkness and the rain to suddenly appear at places where he was not expected. During one of those nighttime engagements, the division liaison officer to the *XXIV. Armee-Korps (mot.)*, *Hauptmann* Bernewitz (from *Panzer-Regiment 6*), was killed southwest of Tscherikoff.

That same night, a chapter in the history of the *I./Schützen-Regiment 394* started that has to be characterized as "sacrificial." Just moving somewhere during that pitch-black night was anything other than pleasant. The route taken to link up with the *4. Panzer-Division* led across extremely narrow paths, through marshes, over hills and fields and into extremely dense woods. Once at Kritschew, the main supply route was reached, heading west. The Russians had identified those movements and placed artillery fire on the bridge at Tscherikoff. A vehicle from the 5th Company received a direct hit. The battalion then found itself at the bridge over the Lobtschanka. It was there that liaison officers from the *4. Panzer-Division* brought the first specific reports: the division had taken Propoisk and was advancing. The *10. Infanterie-Division (mot.)*, which was following behind the *4. Panzer-Division*, was ejected from the city, however. In the process, the Soviets also succeeded in cutting off elements of the *4. Panzer-Division* from the main advance route. *Kampfgruppe Audörsch's* mission was to relieve those forces. Once Audörsch arrived at the command post of the *4. Panzer-Division*, he was personally briefed by the division commander, *Generalleutnant Freiherr* von Langermann, and received orders to clear the advance route and the woods to its north.

The movement to the high forest took place without significant enemy interference. It that point, the resistance increased. Audörsch issued orders to attack. The enemy defended stubbornly. The 2nd Company reported its first losses. When the battalion medical vehicle headed there, it was attacked by the Russians. The driver, *Obergefreiter* Petersen, was killed; *Unterarzt* Söntkerath was badly wounded. *Assistenzarzt* Dr. Türk, who was in the vicinity, immediately attacked the Soviets, along with his driver, *Obergefreiter* Cordes. They were able to push the Soviets back.

The battalion combed through the woods with its thick underbrush. Enemy fire was received from all directions. The snipers in the trees made the advance especially difficult. Despite that, the woods were cleared. At that point, the battle group was positioned in front of a broad meadowland that offered no cover or concealment. It had to be crossed, however, since the advance route had to be reached before it turned dark. The *SPW's* were employed up front. Enemy machine-gun and antitank-gun fire lashed out at the advancing columns from all sides. An *Unteroffizier* was struck down. Even though he himself was wounded, Dr. Türk sprang forward with two volunteers and amputated a leg in the middle of enemy fire. *Leutnant* Peters covered the Good Samaritan work with fire from his machine gun.

Oberleutnant Bachmann's 11th Company especially distinguished itself. As a result of well-aimed machine-gun fire, it was able to eliminate an enemy battery and cause the Soviet positions to waver. The *SPW's* and the riflemen picked up the tempo of the attack and took the Russian position, which meant that the last enemy resistance before the advance route had been shattered. Just before it turned dark, the road was reached. A company from *Panzer-Regiment 35* was screening there. The situation was anything but clear. Everyone was asking: "Who's encircling whom?"

A night followed that any living veteran once assigned to the *I./Schützen-Regiment 394* remembers with dread. Just before first light, there was a Russian attack from the north, that is, from the area that the *Kampfgruppe* had cleared the previous afternoon. It seemed focused on the battalion headquarters location. The Russians were attempting to break though to the south to escape their own encirclement. Despite a stiff defense on the part of the battalion, the Russians succeeded in breaking through. In addition, the battalion suffered a large number of dead and wounded.

While the fighting continued during the day both north and south of the advance route—half of the attached artillery was employed to the north, the other half south—it turned quiet toward the evening. In coordination with *Oberst* Eberbach, the advance route was evacuated over the next few nights and only screened during the day. When a large Russian column attempted to break through from the north to the south during the day, it was shot to pieces by the artillery and the infantry guns. Numerous prisoners were taken in the process.

During the time the battle group was attached to the *4. Panzer-Division*, it lost a total of 109 officers and enlisted personnel in dead and wounded. *Leutnant* Jäger, *Leutnant* Thonneger, *Feldwebel* Lange, and 37 additional noncommissioned officers and men found their last resting place at the regimental cemetery along the Lobtschanka. *Oberleutnant Freiherr* von Werthern, *Leutnant* Steinmüller, and *Leutnant* Heinz were among the badly wounded. *Assistenzarzt* Dr. Türk, who was only slightly wounded, was able to return soon to his battalion, where *Sanitätsunteroffizier* Dr. Rakowski had stepped in for him. Dr. Türk, *Stabsfeldwebel* Voss, and *Oberfeldwebel* Evers became the first men of the battalion to be awarded the Iron Cross, First Class, in the East. The high casualties suffered could not be offset by the large number of prisoners reported during that operation (6,000).

Even though the main body of the *3. Panzer-Division* had remained in the positions and bridgeheads it had won, it had not rested. It had to defend against several enemy attacks. For instance, *Hauptmann* Schneider-Kostalski's *III./Panzer-Regiment 6* beat back a strong Soviet advance at Sokoljanka in the morning. The attacks for the division, which had moved its command post back to Gorbatka, to temporarily go over to the defense. The *II./Panzer-Regiment 6* moved forward from Krotki to Bereschisstaja, bringing along the 8th Company, which had been left in Tschaussy. That evening, the *I./Panzer-Regiment 6* had to be employed in an immediate counterattack southwest of Kritschew. The Russians had reached the rear of the *4. Panzer-Division* there and were attacking that division's command post. The 1st Battalion was able to restore the situation by midnight.

The division then issued orders to *Hauptmann* Engelien's *II./Schützen-Regiment 3* to advance on Alexandrowka via Rogalnja on the morning of 21 July. The battalion advanced with its 6th and 8th Companies to the left of the advance route. It advanced past Rogalnja with practically no enemy resistance. *Oberleutnant* Mente's 7th Company formed a strongpoint. The riflemen smoked out several Russians from holes and dugouts, but they also found thirteen German dead and three burned-out tanks. After the two lead companies moved out again, strong enemy forces, reinforced by three fighting vehicles, attacked the 7th Company. The company slowly pulled back to the road. Fortunately, they encountered the lead platoons of *Leutnant* Tank's 6th Company, which had been called back by radio. They were able to take the Russians, who had approached to within 150 meters, under devastating fire. The Soviets repeated their attacks against the crossroads several times. When they did that, however, they wound up in flanking fires from the battalion. At that point, the enemy gave up his efforts. They left the following behind on the battlefield: 108 *panje* carts, 139 horses, 13 machine guns, 11 antitank guns, and 250 prisoners. The friendly losses were ten dead and ten wounded, including *Oberfeldwebel* Herbst and *Feldwebel* Edler.

The general situation did not clear up the next day, either. The Russians appeared to be everywhere at once. While our motorized columns could only move along roads and trails, the enemy understood how to establish himself in the woods and disrupt German movements from there. For that reason, the division employed a massive effort to clear the woods west of Sswadkowitschi in the morning. Under the command of *Oberstleutnant* von Lewinski, *Oberstleutnant* Munzel's *II./Panzer-Regiment 6*, *Major* Wellmann's *I./Schützen-Regiment 3*, and a company from *Panzerjäger-Abteilung 521* were committed to the undertaking. The tanks set up on the east side of the woods, while the antitank elements positioned themselves on the west side. The rifle companies entered the woods from the north and gradually cleared several enemy outposts and positions. It was a tiresome operation, since the woods were fairly dense and a short rain shower made forward progress difficult. By 1800 hours, the operation was successfully concluded. The spoils of war included five guns and one armored car; 250 prisoners were taken.

For Munzel's battalion and the 3rd Company of the rifle regiment, there was no time to rest on laurels. They were employed in a line running Kusstjokowitschi–Bowankowk, screening to the north. Prisoner statements had indicated that the enemy intended to conduct an attack south from the area west of Kritschew. None of the riflemen or tankers employed that night had time to reflect that they had prepared to cross the border along the Bug exactly four weeks previously.

Perhaps that was what the enemy was thinking of. All of a sudden, around 0200 hours, heavy artillery fire was placed on the bridgehead at Kritschew and in the city proper. At first light, the Russian riflemen stormed ahead with a loud battle cry—*Urraah!* They were units from a Russian airborne brigade, and they fought doggedly. The formations of the *4. Panzer-Division*, which were holding a bridgehead four kilometers deep and one kilometer wide, were only able to turn back the dangerous attack with difficulty. The *3. Panzer-Division* received a request for tank support. Since its tank companies were distributed across the entire front, it was not until 1900 hours that the 7th Company of the armor regiment could be sent into the eastern portion of the bridgehead.

The advance stalemated. The divisions of the *XXIV. Armee-Korps (mot.)*, which had ranged far ahead, were now facing an enemy who did not allow himself to be intimidated by tanks any more. As a result, the forward forces had to wait for the infantry divisions to close up, so that the rear areas could be cleared of the enemy, which would then allow the motorized divisions complete freedom to maneuver again. The division reinforced its outposts along the Ssosh, while the armored battalions conducted necessary maintenance.

The bridgehead at Kritschew continued to be under enemy artillery fire and subject to infantry attacks. The *7./Panzer-Regiment 6* conducted an immediate counterattack on 24 July, which brought with it valuable enemy information. The *1./Schützen-Regiment 3* was moved into the bridgehead in the evening to reinforce. *General Freiherr* Geyr von Schweppenburg, who had not had any direct contact with the division over the last few days, visited *Generalleutnant* Model for the first time in the new positions.

Generaloberst Guderian arrived at the division command post on 26 July. By then, it had been moved to Lobkowitschi. The commander in chief expressed his gratitude to Model for the performance of the division and congratulated him and *Feldwebel* Reinicke on receipt of the Knight's Cross.[4] The division intelligence officer, *Oberleutnant* von Schubert, was transferred to the reconnaissance battalion during this period to become a troop commander. His position was assumed by the assistant intelligence officer of many years, *Oberleutnant* von dem Knesebeck, whose assistant then became *Leutnant Graf* zu Dohna.

---

4. Model was officially awarded the Knight's Cross on 9 July.

The darkness was still over the woods when the Russians suddenly launched an attack in battalion strength against the Kritschew bridgehead at 0200 hours on 29 July. The enemy succeeded in completely surprising the German outposts at Sui, crossing the Ssosh and appearing at the outskirts of Kritschew by 0330 hours. The division issued a general alert. The Soviets focused their advance on the area around the rail station and the rail line to its north. Unfortunately, the prisoner collection point for both the *3.* and *4. Panzer-Divisionen* was located there. At the time, there were some 10,000 prisoners on hand. The first batches of prisoners started trying to force their way through to their own attacking forces, which were only 400 meters away on the riverbanks.

The *II./Schützen-Regiment 394* had to pull back from its positions, but the *I./Panzer-Regiment 6* soon arrived in support and was able to stabilize the front around Bel-Perwaje. The 2nd Battalion of the armor regiment established outposts east of Gorbatka. The fighting vehicles advanced on line so as to better take the terrain to the front under fire. By then, fighting had also broken out along the east side of Kritschew. A colorful mix of different divisional elements took up positions: antitank elements, *Flak* gunners, men of the maintenance and bakery companies, as well as personnel from the field post office and printing section. They fired with everything they had against the attacking Soviets.

When the enemy started to cross the railway embankment to the west, the light platoon of the *I./Panzer-Regiment 6* was employed against his flank. The armored battalion, minus its 1st Company, then launched an immediate counterattack towards the railway station at 0420 hours. The 2nd Company attacked Sui and the 4th Company to its north. The 1st Company attacked the enemy from the north. The Soviets were unable to withstand the powerful blow. They had been told before their attack that the division did not have any ammunition or fuel. They fled back to and across the Ssosh. Two hundred of them were captured. The situation settled down, and the

II./Schützen-Regiment 394 reoccupied the positions it had lost. The *1./Panzer-Regiment 6* remained in support. The division had the rear area searched for scattered enemy elements and ordered intensive reconnaissance efforts. The 1st Battalions of both rifle regiments combed through the areas in front of their outposts. *Unteroffizier* Elven and his seven-man patrol from the *2./Schützen-Regiment 3* were able to take ninety prisoners in the village of Kurolitschki on 30 July. In addition, they captured four mortars and three machine guns.

The final days of July passed by "without major incident" in the oppressive heat of the summer of 1941. Rumors started to circulate slowly that the pause would soon be over. Since 22 June, the division had taken the following numbers of casualties: 148 officers and 2,409 noncommissioned officers and enlisted personnel. During the afternoon of 30 July, the division command post was moved to Dubrowka. By then, the divisional engineers and bridging sections had erected a permanent bridge at Starosselje. Gradually, all of the divisional elements crossed over it, with the exception of the *I./Schützen-Regiment 3*, which remained behind on the west bank after it had taken over the combat-outpost line of the motorcycle infantry battalion.

During the evening of 31 July, the Morse code switches hammered away, the telephones rang, and the motorcycle messengers of the division delivered attack orders for the next day. According to the division order, all of *Panzergruppe 2* was to continue its advance on 1 August. The objective for the corps was Rosslawl. Both armored divisions were being employed against it. The *10. Infanterie-Division (mot.)* and the *7. Infanterie-Division* were employed as flank guards. The division's mission required a crossing over the Oster and an advance along the Kritschew–Rosslawl road. The righthand attack group was to be led by *Oberstleutnant* von Manteuffel, and it consisted of *Schützen-Regiment 3* and the *III./Panzer-Regiment 6*. The lefthand group was formed from the *I./Schützen-Regiment 394* and the *I./Panzer-Regiment 6* and was led by *Oberstleutnant* Audörsch. Since the broad river valley of the Ssoshenka separated the division from the neighboring division to the north, the *II./Panzer-Regiment 6*, the *II./Schützen-Regiment 394*, *Panzerjäger-Abteilung 521*, and *Aufklärungs-Abteilung 1* positioned behind von Manteuffel's forces to guard the northern flank.

The first of August 1941 promised to be another sunny and warm day. Punctually, starting at 0345 hours, the divisional artillery fired with all of its tubes on the enemy positions. The German attack was underway. Tanks and personnel carriers rattled through meadows, blooming canola fields, and the burning, squalid villages. The entire division was advancing after the *I./Schützen-Regiment 3*, which was screening from its old positions until the morning, was relieved by *Schützen-Regiment 33* (*4. Panzer-Division*). Once again, *Generalleutnant* Model found himself in the midst of his advancing soldiers. He ordered his command post in Goljejewka, which was still under enemy artillery fire, to prepare to move at 0645 hours.

The morning sun streamed over the wide land. The enemy put up a tough fight. His defense focused around the small village of Bednja, which was on dominant high ground. After a short artillery preparation, *Oberstleutnant* Schmidt-Ott's *I./Panzer-Regiment 6* attacked the village from the west and the south at the same time, capturing it. The division commander arrived with the first riflemen and had the men immediately mount up on the fighting vehicles. He ordered a continuation of the attack.

The mood improved by the hour. The men were advancing again. *Panzer-Regiment 6* started the new offensive with 103 fighting vehicles: 37 *Panzer II's*, 42 *Panzer III's*, 16 *Panzer IV's*, and 8 command tanks. That was exactly half the amount of tanks that had crossed the frontier on 22 June. The leading attack columns of the two battle groups linked up shortly after 0800 hours at the bridge over the Ssoshenka in Wabitschewka. By doing so, the first attack

objective had been reached. *Oberstleutnant* Audörsch then took over the lead elements and pressed on to the northeast against Studenez with *Schützen-Regiment 394* and the *I./Panzer-Regiment 6*. The enemy defended there; he knew that the strongpoint prevented the crossing of the German formations over the Oster. *Major* von Corvin-Witzbitzki's motorcycle infantry determined that the village was occupied, but that did not deter them from advancing. He pivoted his companies to the southeast. *Major* Wellmann's *I./Schützen-Regiment 3* was employed against the village. By 1200 hours, his 2nd Company had taken the village, establishing outposts oriented to the east.

By then, the main body of the division had advanced along the roads leading southeast from Studenez and pressed into the wooded terrain in front of the river. *Generalleutnant* Model directed the attack from Studenez; *Major i.G.* Pomtow and the battle staff had followed him there.

The next objective for the division was Mikulitschi. Both of the battle groups formed advance guards, which were then set in march in the direction of the river along the two roads. The first units to reach the city were *Oberleutnant* Vopel's *1./Panzer-Regiment 6* and *Leutnant* Schultze's *3./Pionier-Bataillon 39*. The fighting vehicles disregarded the enemy outposts and advanced right into Mikulitschi. They soon positioned themselves in front of the first bridge, which they took. The Russians had brought two long-barreled cannon into position at the second bridge, but they were so surprised by the lightning-fast appearance of the tanks that they were unable to get off a round. Machine-gun fire and high-explosive rounds kept the crews low. While the fighting vehicles continued to roll, *Oberstleutnant* Audörsch appeared with the *1./Schützen-Regiment 394* and elements of the engineer battalion. The riflemen and engineers jumped to the ground and drove off the bridge guards, who had wanted to pour fuel on the structure. They captured the bridge. A short while later, another defended bridge was taken by *Oberleutnant* Vopel's tank company and the riflemen of *Schützen-Regiment 394*. *Leutnant* Möllhoff, a company officer of the *2./Pionier-Bataillon 39*, contributed magnificently to the operation and later received a by-name mention in the Army Honor Roll. The first bridgehead over the Oster was formed in the shortest time imaginable by the assaults of all of the forces employed in that area.

Generaloberst Guderian and *Generalleutnant* Model arrived up front at the same time at Mikulitschi. They moved forward into the bridgehead and praised the participating tankers and riflemen. As a result of the rapid taking of the bridgehead, a new situation had developed, causing the entire *3. Panzer-Division* to be brought forward into the bridgehead, even though enemy forces still existed in the woods north of the river. According to prisoner statements, for example, there were strong forces in the woods between Chawrotowka and Mikulitschi, including a corps headquarters. Based on that, the *I./Schützen-Regiment 3*, *Panzerjäger-Abteilung 543*, and the *9./Panzer-Regiment 6* surrounded the woods in order to clear out the Soviets in the morning.

At the same time, the *1./Panzer-Regiment 6* received orders to pursue an enemy column that was pulling back in the direction of Schumjatschi. The company reached the column, which had been reported by aerial reconnaissance and consisted of several batteries, around 1945 hours and shot it to pieces. The fighting vehicles continued to advance and reached the Kritschew–Rosslawl road, where they established contact with the lead company of the *4. Panzer-Division*, which had moved out farther to the south. The tank company returned to the division around midnight.

As it turned dusk, *Oberstleutnant* von Lewinski ordered *Oberstleutnant* Munzel's *II./Panzer-Regiment 6* and elements of *Major* Frank's *Panzerjäger-Abteilung 521* to move from Wabitschewka directly south with the objective of taking the Kritschew–Rosslawl road, thus protecting the right flank of the *XXIV. Armee-Korps (mot.)*. By then, the *4. Panzer-Division*

had been directed east to attack Rosslawl, which it took later that night in conjunction with the *23. Infanterie-Division*.

The first day of attack had brought with it the anticipated results. The *3. Panzer-Division* was east of the Oster. The *7. Infanterie-Division* had inserted itself into the line to the right, while the *4. Panzer-Division* had advanced farther east south of the river. The Russian front started to waver, with the enemy pulling back to the south. The German command was aware of the enemy situation, with the result that orders were issued that same night that had the *3. Panzer-Division* stop its eastward movement and turn directly south. To that end, the division engineers were directed to establish additional provisional bridges across the river.

On 2 August, the division again formed two battle groups. It continued its attack at first light from the positions it had taken the previous day. *Kampfgruppe von Manteuffel* was comprised of *Schützen-Regiment 3*, elements of the *II./Panzer-Regiment 6*, the *II./Artillerie-Regiment 75*, and *Panzerjäger-Abteilung 543*. *Oberstleutnant* Audörsch had command over the *I./Schützen-Regiment 394*, the *I./Panzer-Regiment 6*, and *Panzerjäger-Abteilung 543*. *Oberstleutnant* von Lewinski led a third group, which was composed of elements of the *II./Panzer-Regiment 6*, the *II./Schützen-Regiment 394*, and *Aufklärungs-Abteilung 1*. The remaining division elements were divided among the battle groups.

The morning was very cool, and the riflemen had to put on their overcoats for the first time. *Kampfgruppe Audörsch* moved out first, with *Kampfgruppe von Manteuffel* following as soon as the elements that had been left behind to clear the woods at Mikulitschi had rejoined his forces. The objective for both battle groups was the Kritschew–Rosslawl road. The third group broke camp at 0700 hours and crossed the Oster around 1100 hours.

Toward noon, the two battle groups reached the road with their lead elements and occupied semicircle screening positions forward of the road. Reconnaissance efforts directed to the south and southwest encountered strong resistance in places and were called off. In the course of one of those patrols, the light platoon of the armor regiment eliminated one enemy artillery piece. Despite an energetic defense, the *III./Panzer-Regiment 6* assaulted Kowaljowka, shortly after the *1./Schützen-Regiment 3* had taken the Soviet mortar position along the railway embankment. The remaining companies of the rifle regiment screened in support of those operations, orienting on the dense woods. An attack on those woods in the afternoon had to be called off, when the fighting vehicles got stuck in the marsh. Nonetheless, both battalions of *Schützen-Regiment 3* were later able to comb the woods and advance as far as a line running Potapowka–Jakimowitschi, in conjunction with the motorcycle infantry battalion. The 2nd Battalion of the rifle regiment encountered the 105th Cossack Regiment at Podgassan and was able to take 100 Soviets prisoner.

Kampfgruppe Audörsch attacked Miloslawitschi, which had been set on fire by the withdrawing Russians. Elements of Audörsch's armored and rifle formations took the village and set up to defend. Any further advance that afternoon would have been senseless, since continuous rain fell starting at 1600 hours, which immediately transformed the roads and byways into muck, choking any movement.

Although the next day brought with it sunny but windy weather, the advance was not continued. The division used the time to reinforce its outposts and reorganize its forces. Contact was established with the neighboring forces. In the process, *Infanterie-Regiment 19* (*7. Infanterie-Division*) relieved elements of the armor regiment. The 2nd Battalion of the armored regiment was designated as the sector reserve, with only its 7th Company remaining in contact with the enemy at Sklimin. Early in the morning, there were engagements with Russian riflemen in front of the sector of the *7. Infanterie-Division* (halfway to Kritschew). The armored regiment's light platoon was sent to the area around Chotowisch, Ganowka and Jegorowskaja in support.

The *10. Infanterie-Division (mot.)* was inserted into the line to the left of the *3. Panzer-Division*, with the result that the corps was able to establish a front to the south of the Oster by the evening of 3 August. The most dangerous spot was on the right wing, since the German forces were jutting far into the enemy positions, which were still to the west along the Ssosh. The *XII.* and *XIII. Armee-Korps* were gradually closing up there with their infantry divisions. The command post of the *3. Panzer-Division* was in Swentschatka.

With the approach of the infantry corps, the right flank of the armored group started to stabilize. The division's rifle brigade was pulled out of the line on 4 August. By evening, both regiments had crossed back over the Oster, with the exception of their rearguards. They set up camp on both sides of the Miloslawitschi–Mikulitschi road. The rest of the division pulled back across on 5 August.

Of course, the withdrawals did not all take place without a hitch. *Oberleutnant* Klöber's *7./Panzer-Regiment 6* attacked Titowka on the morning of 4 August and took in eighty prisoners. During that action, *Oberleutnant Freiherr* von Bernewitz was killed. He had been assigned to the regiment from the operations section of the Army High Command just two weeks previously for some front-line experience. During the withdrawals, *Panzer-Regiment 6*, along with *Panzerjäger-Abteilung 521* and the divisional reconnaissance battalion, screened for the withdrawing riflemen. The next day, 5 August, the *III./Panzer-Regiment 6* was attached to the *7. Infanterie-Division*, since it was feared the enemy was going to attack in that sector. On 6 August, the armor regiment left its screening positions and pulled back across the Oster by noon. Only *Oberstleutnant* Munzel's 2nd Battalion was turned around shortly before crossing; it was kept on the far side of the river as a corset stay for the infantry still there. By then, the riflemen were resting in the assigned billeting areas. During that period, some 700 men showed up for the division as replacements.

Their trains had departed Groß-Born ten days previously.

During the evening of 6 August, the Russians launched a fairly strong attack against the road at Janowskaja-Buda. The division alerted its forces immediately. The resting forces did not need to respond, however. The *8./Panzer-Regiment 6*, along with a reserve company from the *7. Infanterie-Division*, had interdicted the enemy advance on the south bank of the river and restored the situation.

Exactly twenty-four hours later, the enemy repeated the same attack. This time, he was able to break through the infantry lines. He encountered the *II./Panzer-Regiment 6* at Schesterowka. After hours of fighting, the enemy gave up, leaving behind 110 prisoners. *Oberleutnant* Klöber's tank company pursued the withdrawing enemy in the early morning hours, occupying Hill 203.8, where *Infanterie-Regiment 61* then dug in again for the second time in as many days. The *3. Panzer-Division*, the *4. Panzer-Division*, the *10. Infanterie-Division (mot.)*, and the *7. Infanterie-Division* were all positioned south of the river and had driven a wedge into his front. The corps decided to capitalize on its advantage by launching a uniform attack to the west. It was intended to tear open the Soviet front and cause it to collapse. On 7 August, the *3. Panzer-Division* committed a raiding party under *Major* Frank, which thrust through woods and marshland almost 100 kilometers into the enemy's rear area, where it blew up the rail line at Kletnja. The elements employed—*Aufklärungs-Abteilung 1*, a company of *Panzerjäger-Abteilung 521*, a section of artillery, and a platoon from the *3./Pionier-Bataillon 39*—all returned to the divisional area five days later.

Generalleutnant Model summoned his commanders together on 8 August and briefed them on the corps order: "On 9 August 1941, the *XXIV. Armee-Korps (mot.)* attacks by surprise with the *3. Panzer-Division* on the right and the *4. Panzer-Division* on the left from the area around Miloslawitschi to the southwest against the enemy in front of the *7. Infanterie-Division*.

It then moves from the Oster through Klimowitschi to encircle the enemy forces positioned across from Kritschew as far as the Ssosh."

That meant the days of rest for the division were over. The rifle brigade started moving out of its quarters that afternoon and moved across the Oster, starting at 1600 hours. The armor regiment followed at night in rainy and stormy weather. The storms and the right-of-way exerted by the crossing columns from the *4. Panzer-Division* caused stoppages along the road that lasted for hours. The forces were still moving when it started to turn light at 0300 hours. The attack, which had been planned for 0600 hours, had to be postponed. On the right was *Oberst* von Manteuffel's battle group, consisting of *Schützen-Regiment 3* and the *III./Panzer-Regiment 6*. *Oberstleutnant* Audörsch was on the left with *Schützen-Regiment 394* and the *I./Panzer-Regiment 6*. The *II./Panzer-Regiment 6* and *Kradschützen-Bataillon 3* were held back along the road as reserves.

The division arrived in the Miloslawitschi area over the next three hours. The movements did not proceed without a hitch, since the enemy had identified the concentrations and fired into them with artillery. The first casualties were taken before the attack had even started. Finally, it was time to move out. The clocks showed 0900 hours, when the artillery batteries of the divisional artillery opened fire on the Russian positions. A short while later, both battle groups moved out. Since the attack sector was somewhat narrow and was impeded by wooded and marshy terrain, the division could not be committed all at once. *Oberstleutnant* Audörsch's forces entered the enemy positions first, followed later by the battalions of *Schützen-Regiment 3* in von Manteuffel's battle group.

The Soviets did not voluntarily give up one meter of ground and fought stubbornly. The enemy artillery fired without a break, and the casualties increased shortly after moving out. The commander of the *I./Schützen-Regiment 394*, *Major* Haas, and his adjutant, *Leutnant* Meister, were wounded. When Russian bombers and fighter-bombers also joined the fray, the casualties increased by the hour. Friendly fighters appeared only infrequently.

The attack moved through the woods to the southwest in a slow but consistent manner. The hardest enemy resistance was being offered in front of *Kampfgruppe Audörsch*. Heavy tanks, weighting fifty-two tons, were employed; the tanks of the 1st Battalion could only knock them out at close range. The riflemen then reached the point, where a German assault party had been butchered in a bestial manner by superior Soviet forces the previous day.

The terrain was so difficult that the motorized riflemen were forced to move on foot in spots. Moving through Starij Stom, the attacked continued on Titowka. The attack columns were hit several times by Russian bombers. Seven men from the *5./Schützen-Regiment 394* were killed, including *Oberfeldwebel* Ullmann. The 2nd Company of the regiment lost *Feldwebel* Nepp.

After Titowka had been taken, *Hauptmann* Schneider-Kostalski's *III./Panzer-Regiment 6* was turned in the direction of Nesnany so as to hit the enemy in front of the *7. Infanterie-Division* in the rear and eliminate his heavy artillery. *Oberstleutnant* Munzel's *II./Panzer-Regiment 6* was pushed forward to support the attack of *Schützen-Regiment 394*, which was advancing through and beyond Ostroff and Pawlowitschi. By the onset of darkness, *Oberstleutnant* Audörsch and his men were able to block the road leading from Klimowitschi to the southeast in the vicinity of Gaigowka. *Major* Wellmann's *I./Schützen-Regiment 3* screened to the north, while *Hauptmann* Engelien's 2nd Battalion oriented directly west. *Major* von Corvin-Wiersbitzki's motorcycle infantry battalion passed through the lines of riflemen starting at 2000 hours to get closer to Klimowitschi.

That night, the division ordered the city to be attacked. *Oberst* Kleemann directed the advance to move through Simniza. But by the early morning hours, the reconnaissance battalion had determined that the enemy had abandoned Klimowitschi. *Oberstleutnant* von Lewinski

thereupon decided to attack the locality with his battle group. After von Lewinski's plan had been approved, the rest of the division moved out as well. It turned into a classic attack by an armored division. At 0500 hours, two large battle groups assaulted at the same time from the east and south. The sun was beaming from a partly cloudy summer sky, as the difficult terrain was crossed and the forces entered the undefended city two hours later. It was Sunday, 10 August 1941.

The tank companies moved on ahead to screen the movement forward of the rifle regiments. *Oberleutnant* Klöber's 7th Company pressed through the fleeing Russian columns and established contact with the German forces defending the Kritschew bridgehead. The *III./Panzer-Regiment 6* protected the advance of the division against enemy forces to its north that were holding out. It drove those forces back into the woods. The 9th Company turned back a breakout attempt from Titowka, eliminating three fighting vehicles and several antitank guns in the process. An enemy battery pressing ahead ran into the defensive fires of the 1st Company of engineers. The combat engineers captured three 10.5-centimeter guns and three mortars. During the night, the division secured all around from the Kritschew area. *Schützen-Regiment 394* was responsible for guarding the city proper.

At first light the next day, patrol and assault detachments were sent in all directions in order to get a better picture of the enemy situation. There was no doubt, however, that strong Russian forces were encircled north of the city. What wasn't known was what they intended to do. The patrols returned with more or less good results. Riflemen from the *I./Schützen-Regiment 394* brought back eight guns, a few machine guns, and twenty prisoners for their efforts; the *I./Schützen-Regiment 3* took thirty-five prisoners. The battery of the divisional artillery, which had closed up around Klimowitschi, fired irregular harassment fire on the enemy forces in the pocket. In the past few days, the regiment had suffered the deaths of *Oberleutnant* Dorsch, *Leutnant* Dr. Engel, and *Leutnant* Milisch.

By then, the armored regiment had returned to an assembly area, where it performed maintenance and it refueled and rearmed. The regiment's 3rd Battalion was temporarily attached to the *10. Infanterie-Division (mot.)*. In Klimowitschi, a typical small Russian town consisting of wooden huts and dirt roads, *Schützen-Regiment 394* and *Panzerjäger-Abteilung 543* set up all-round defenses.

As the sun began to set that evening, the men of the *3./Schützen-Regiment 394* noticed all at once that several horse-mounted riders were moving from the woods towards Klimowitschi. Before the alert could be sounded, the few riders turned into an entire troop riding against the positions at a gallop and with drawn sabers. The men could only grab their carbines and machine guns in haste. Before they new it, the wild "hunting party" had descended into and between their lines. Fortunately, the guns of the antitank battalion were ready to fire, and their 3.7-centimeter rounds tore the first holes into the Soviet ranks. By then, the forward observers had also issued fire missions to their batteries. The rounds started howling in. In the hail of German fire, the Russian mounted attack vanished into thin air as quickly as it had arrived. Nonetheless, a few Soviet cavalrymen found their way into the town under the cover of darkness and made it as far as the command post of the *I./Schützen-Regiment 394*. The met their end there.

That episode was quickly forgotten, but the night would turn out to be a long one. Fireworks suddenly started in the neighboring *Infanterie-Regiment 68* of the *23. Infanterie-Division*. The Soviets were attempting to break through there as well, after the infantry regiment had pulled back its outposts when it turned dark. *Schützen-Regiment 394* was alerted. It wasn't necessary for the rifle regiment to intervene; instead, it was only called upon to assist in chasing down Russians, who had broken through and were wandering around. After an hour, it was quiet again in the Klimowitschi area.

The morning sun of 12 August had just climbed over the horizon in the east when the outposts of the *2./Schützen-Regiment 394* at Sswirelji identified enemy cavalry again. This time, it was between 150 and 200 riders, who were galloping east about 500 meters away down the slope at Sswitschewo. The riflemen and the antitank gun of the *3./Panzerjäger-Abteilung 543*, which was positioned there, immediately opened fire. The roar that arose set off the alarm in all the remaining positions. The men of the rifle regiment did not have to search long for the enemy. All of them could see a first wave of riders followed by a second and then, soon thereafter, a third. Among those columns were trains vehicles. Bringing up the rear were strong infantry forces. Rounds from the divisional artillery soon started howling in. Soon thereafter, a four-barreled *Flak* at the edge of the village started hammering away. The first approaching troop was scattered. The horses bolted, and the riders flew off and attempted to get away on foot. In the process, they intermingled with the hordes of oncoming troops, which moved out of Selzonyj–Klin in dispersed order and headed for the Klimowitschi–Sswirelj road.

The main body of *Leutnant* Dr. Lotze's *2./Schützen-Regiment 394* was holding there. It opened up with its machine guns into the massed rider elements. The leaden crack of *Oberleutnant* Michels's guns of the *3./Panzerjäger-Abteilung 543* bellowed. The wave of approximately 600 cavalrymen turned away and headed in the direction of the 3rd Company of the rifle regiment. That company was ready. Round after round whipped into the galloping cavalry. They troops swung away and turned north. The 1st Company of the rifle regiment had moved up. Behind it were the light tanks of the reconnaissance platoon of *Panzer-Regiment 6*. The machine-gun fires from the rifle company and the light tanks completely shattered the enemy attack. The riders who survived scattered in all directions. A few succeeded in getting to the artillery positions, where they also found their end.

A group of about 100 cavalrymen under the command of a lieutenant colonel made it as far as Klimowitschi by moving through a depression that was thick with vegetation. That put them to the rear of the 2nd Company of the rifle regiment. The riflemen quickly reversed positions, and *Leutnant* Peters's men launched an immediate counterattack. None of the Russians escaped. The fighting for Klimowitschi died down.

The 1st and 4th Companies of *Panzer-Regiment 6*, which had been alerted at 0435 hours, didn't need to join the immediate fighting. It had been decided by the riflemen, antitank elements, and cannoneers. The two tank companies were sent off in pursuit of the enemy, however. They caught up with the fleeing trains and a battery, which they were able to shoot to pieces. The rifle regiment sent out platoons and squads to collect the wounded laying on the battlefield and bring in prisoners. In doing so, the regiment suffered an additional sixteen casualties, including *Hauptfeldwebel* Stachowiak of the 5th Company, who was badly wounded. The casualties stemmed from the fact that the wounded Russians allowed the riflemen to approach close—they played dead—only to then fire treacherously on the Germans from the rear.

Based on that bad experience, the division had the *II./Panzer-Regiment 6* assist in the clearing of the woods northwest of Klimowitschi early in the afternoon. The 3rd Battalion of the armored regiment was ordered to comb the wooded terrain to both sides of the Titowka–Nesnanj road. It was supported in that by the *I./Infanterie-Regiment 41 (mot.)* of the *10. Infanterie-Division (mot.)*. That operations was called off around 1600 hours, since an alert was received from the *4. Panzer-Division* that the Soviet 50th Tank Division was attacking from the southwest.

Oberst Kleemann was given the mission of forming a screening front in that direction. He used *Schützen-Regiment 3*, which had been earmarked for another operation, and the *III./Panzer-Regiment 6*. The riflemen reached the woods at Putimelj by 0300 hours, while the tanks did not reach their designated assembly area around Iwanowa–Sloboda until the morning. Orders arrived that the division did not need to intervene, since the Soviets had not continued their attack. Nonetheless, route reconnaissance and contact was established with neighboring units in the course of the day.

The division had assembled most of its combat-capable forces around Miloslawitschi; only *Schützen-Regiment 394* and the antitank and artillery elements attached in support remained around Klimowitschi. On 13 August, the enemy attempted to break through a few times at the latter village, but the efforts were no longer in the same strength as the previous day and, correspondingly, could be turned back more easily. Toward evening, the rifle regiment also received orders to pull back from Klimowitschi. While most of the division was able to enjoy a day of rest, *Schützen-Regiment 394* had to undergo a few skirmishes with the enemy while it was moving back.

The armored regiment sent out a tank patrol in the morning to establish contact with *Generalleutnant* Gallenkamp's *78. Infanterie-Division*, which was twenty kilometers away. The patrol encountered the outposts of the *III./Infanterie-Regiment 283* to the east of Bessedka around 1400 hours, completing its mission.

At noon on 15 August, the division issued a warning order for the resumption of the advance. The commanders were summoned for conferences, the maps were issued and the new march routes marked on the maps. Everyone was amazed—this time, they were headed south. The warning order was short and to the point: "The *XXIV. Armee-Korps (mot.)* moves out to the south on 16 August with the *4. Panzer-Division* on the right, the *3. Panzer-Division* on the left, and the *10. Infanterie-Division (mot.)* following, in order to cut off the retreat route of the withdrawing enemy in front of the attack of the *2. Armee* to the east."

The elements of the *3. Panzer-Division* were to be ready to move starting at 1600 hours. At 1700 hours, the actual order was issued.

The nighttime approach march in the new direction could only be executed with a great deal of effort and delay. The many narrow routes were so full from the many columns that the vehicles could only advance at a walking pace. The lead elements of the division barely made it past Gabitschi; it was only *Major* von Corvin-Wiersbitzki's motorcycle infantry battalion that was able to reach Chotimsk by first light. But the bridges had to be reinforced there, so that the heavy vehicles could continue. *Kradschützen-Bataillon 3* was able to cross around 0800 hours, reaching Warwarowka, five kilometers away, in a rapid move. The motorcycle infantry and reconnaissance soldiers did not spend time there; they moved on. By then, the men of the two engineer companies that were moving toward the front cleared mines so as to enable the continuation of the move past Chotimsk. Because of the mines, the *II./Panzer-Regiment 6* was also halted in Warwarowka, so as to avoid unnecessary losses.

The lead group under *Oberst* von Manteuffel made it to Degtjarewka on the Iputj. Enemy resistance was broken, and the first bridgehead was formed after crossing in inflatable craft. *Hauptmann* Ziervogel and Major von Corvin-Wiersbitzki immediately pressed on with their companies. The engineers under *Hauptmann* Winkler and *Oberleutnant* Brandt started to erect a bridge. The bridging section was ordered to move us as quickly as possible. By 1700 hours, it had completed a 100-meter-long engineer bridge by constructing a 9.6-meter end section.

After a crossing point was created for the heavy vehicles—the terrain otherwise consisted of sandy forest soil—*Oberstleutnant* Munzel's *II./Panzer-Regiment 6* continued its march from Warwarowka starting at 1315 hours. Two hours later, the entire regiment received orders to move out and reach Degtjarewka as soon as possible. Once again, the *3. Panzer-Division* had spread out over the distance of many kilometers. The lead group was already advancing through Zynka along the good, improved road from Roslawl to Mglin, while the 1st and 3rd Battalions of the armored regiment were churning

through deep sand and marshy spots. All the while, the sun was burning hot, with the thermometer registering more than 30 degrees Celsius (86 Fahrenheit). The 2nd and 3rd Companies of *Schützen-Regiment 3* were employed screening a fifteen-kilomter stretch of road between Chotimsk and Degtjarewka.

Kampfgruppe von Manteuffel was on the road leading to Mglin. A competition to see who could move the fastest started among the tankers, the motorcycle infantry, the reconnaissance soldiers, the cannoneers, and the engineers. Enemy resistance on the road was quickly broken. The Russians frequently didn't have time to defend and had to race head over heels into the closest patch of woods. Enemy forces grew in size outside of Mglin. The battle group halted briefly and prepared to attack, while the batteries of *Oberstleutnant* Wellmann sent their fiery greetings into Mglin. The *II./Panzer-Regiment 6, Kradschützen-Bataillon 3, Aufklärungs-Abteilung 1*, and the more slowly following *II./Schützen-Regiment 3* moved out, entered the city quickly, and immediately transitioned to an all-round defense.

The main body of the division was more than twenty kilometers farther to the rear and secured the bridgehead over the Iputj from the high ground at Degtjarewka. The wheeled vehicle columns of *Kampfgruppe Kleemann* closed up there during the night. *Kampfgruppe Audörsch* found itself an additional twenty kilometers further back. The great distances of course could not be completely screened. As a result, Soviet partisans succeeded in attacking the village of Chotimsk during the night and burning it completely to the ground.

After the cool night started to yield to the first faint rays on the horizon, which indicated another hot day, *Kampfgruppe von Manteuffel* immediately moved out. The *7./Panzer-Regiment 6* arrived in Mglin at 0500 hours. By then, the remaining two battalions of the tank regiment left their bivouac areas along the Iputj, after almost all the engineer companies had improved the roads through ceaseless effort.

Since the bridges over the river were still incapable of supporting tanks, the fighting vehicles forded the river and advanced without stopping to Mglin, which they reached at 1000 hours.

At the same time, *Oberstleutnant* Munzel was advancing south with his companies and the motorcycle infantry and reconnaissance elements attached to him. The advance guard was able to get as far as the southern edge of the large forested tract outside of Unetscha without enemy contact. At that point, a Russian antiaircraft battery prevented a further advance through well-aimed fire. The fighting vehicles of the battalion formed up to conduct a concentric attack against the battery. At that point, Russian aircraft attacked the columns at low level; they were unable to defend themselves. *Leutnant* Bertram, *Gefreiter* Grund, and *Gefreiter* Sobeck were killed in the fighting.

Oberleutnant von Zitzewitz's *1./Schützen-Regiment 3* was moved forward, and the last resistance was finally broken with its assistance. The tanks immediately entered the city of Unetscha and moved to the far end without regard for any other pockets of resistance that were still holding out. Unfortunately, they were a few minutes too late. A long, fully load freight train left the railway station in front of their eyes and snorted away.

In the next two hours, the enemy remaining in Unetscha was eliminated. In the process, a portion of the city burned down. Toward 1630 hours, *Oberstleutnant* von Lewinski arrived with the other two battalions and, a short while later, *Major* Wellmann and his riflemen also arrived. The Russians did not want to give up Unetscha so easily. Soviet fighter-bombers attacked the already burning city and the entering German columns repeatedly until it turned dark. At 1930 hours, *Hauptmann* Schneider-Kostalski's *III./Panzer-Regiment 6* moved out with the *II./Schützen-Regiment 3* as the advance guard in the direction of Starodub. The quick onset of night forced the advance to be halted in the vicinity of Rjuchoff around 2300 hours. The

advance guard set up for defense and waited for morning.

The advance of the *XXIV. Armee-Korps (mot.)* turned fluid again on 17 August. In the process, the *3. Panzer-Division* had gained a surprising amount of ground to the south and was just to the east of Gomel. The *4. Panzer-Division* was able to take Gelynkowitschi and followed the *3. Panzer-Division*. The *10. Infanterie-Division (mot.)* was inserted into the line to the right of the *3. Panzer-Division* in order to establish contact with the infantry divisions, which were hanging back far to the northwest.

Generalleutnant Model issued orders at 0115 hours for the further pursuit south. The supplemental order issued by *Panzer-Regiment 6* started with the sober statement: "*Gruppe von Lewinski* reaches the area around Starodub on 18 August, starting out at 0530 hours."

At that precise moment, *Oberstleutnant* von Lewinski moved out with his strong force from the area south of Unetscha. In the lead were the companies from the *I./Panzer-Regiment 6*, followed by the vehicles of the *1./Flak-Regiment 94* and the two antitank battalions. The companies of the *I./Schützen-Regiment 3* followed that group, with the batteries of the *I./Artillerie-Regiment 75*, the *2./Pionier-Bataillon 39*, and the *1./Kradschützen-Bataillon 3* bringing up the rear of the column. *Major Freiherr* von Türckheim, the commander of *Panzerjäger-Abteilung 543*, took up the security of the avenue of advance with his guns and the attached *3./Schützen-Regiment 3*. In the process of executing that mission, his gunners knocked out seven light Russian fighting vehicles.

The advance guard of *Hauptmann* Schneider-Kostalski moved out south from Rjuchoff at 0630 hours. His 9th Company took the lead. The lead fighting vehicles arrived outside of Starodub, the large transportation hub halfway between Gomel and Brjansk, around 0900 hours. The Russians had quickly set up defenses at the outskirts and were prepared to defend the city. The German tanks did not allow the enemy any time and headed immediately in the direction of Starodub. The Soviet resistance was very tough in some places, especially where a formation of *Komsomol*, a youth group of the Communist Party, defended. The enemy could be ejected everywhere, however. At 0915 hours, the city was in German hands. The Russians were so surprised by the sudden appearance of the German tanks that they thought they were dealing with airborne forces.

Kampfgruppe von Lewinski reached the city three hours later. While the tank companies screened and established bivouac sites in the southern and western portions of Starodub, the riflemen set up for the defense to the east and north. The forward groups of the division set up hedgehog defenses. They were all by themselves, since the advance route of the division stretched all the way from Starodub to Mglin. The *4. Panzer-Division* was unable to advance as quickly that day. For that reason, elements of *Schützen-Regiment 394* had to remain behind and only slowly made their way forward.

Kampfgruppe Audörsch reached Mglin and received orders there to continue on to Unetscha, a large railway transportation hub on the Moscow line. Upon reaching Unetscha, the division commander issued orders to *Oberstleutnant* Audörsch to hold the town, although the *II./Schützen-Regiment 394* was to continue marching in the direction of Starodub to support the elements of the division employed there.

At the same time, Soviet bombs were falling on Starodub, where *Kampfgruppe von Manteuffel*, *Kampfgruppe von Lewinski*, and *Kampfgruppe Kleemann* had either arrived or were arriving. The enemy aerial attacks lasted the entire night and did not abate until first light on 19 August.

Oberleutnant Heysing, an officer assigned to a propaganda company, wrote a very interesting article about the fighting for Starodub later on. It appeared in the *Völkischer Beobachter* (issue 199), dated 18 July 1942. The first portion of the article is reprinted here:

The Celebrated Soviet Marshal and the Black Bears: How Timoschenko Escaped across the Don to the East

Oberleutnant Günther Heysing, propaganda company, July 1942. There's a "connection" between a certain German armored division, which has the symbol of its hometown, a black bear, as part of its tactical symbol, and the Bolshevik Marshal Timoschenko.

Back then, the bear division, which was the battering ram of the field army, was moving as the spearhead. It happened that this relatively unusual event took place as it reached the rural Ukrainian town of Starodub. Today, the story can be told: Telephone conversations with Timoschenko.

The advance guard of the bear division had taken Starodub in its possession. The Bolsheviks did not even have time to set everything alight prior to their retreat, as was their custom.

The armored forces in Starodub soon felt at ease in Starodub after the local populace had overcome its timidity regarding the Germans. For a few days, the town became a small garrison for the lead elements, until most of the columns had churned their way through the sand deserts of Rosslawl and the advance could continue.

When the lead elements of the German forces had entered Starodub, the signalers immediately started looking for any telephone lines that were still intact in order to destroy any contact that still existed with the enemy. A *Gefreiter*, who was cutting lines high up on a pole, happened to overhear telephone traffic being conducted by the Bolsheviks over one of the lines. A translator was quickly summoned. He also had to climb up on the pole. While eavesdropping, he determined that the conversations were without a doubt of a military nature. At the local post office, the corresponding line and switch was soon found. The leadership of the German forces was able to inform itself in the best way possible of what its counterparts were planning.

Since the post office in Starodub proper was also being called from all sorts of stations, the translator finally picked up. He initially got an earful from an unknown high-ranking Soviet officer, who wanted to know why he had been silent for so long. But the translator did not hesitate with an answer. He explained to the top-level Bolshevik that he was Sub-lieutenant Mirow and he had just finished clearing the Germans out of Starodub. His forces consisted of 250 men and a battery. The opposite number believed him, as was demonstrated that evening when listening to the Bolshevik armed forces report: Starodub had been wrested from the Germans by brave friendly forces. That also gave us some insight into the reliability of the Soviet Army reports.

The direct line to the Soviets was exploited of course by the German brigade staff located in Starodub. Despite all efforts at maintaining secrecy and using code names, it was possible to determine where the higher-level Bolshevik headquarters were located, especially a high-level Bolshevik senior command and the artillery headquarters of the Timoschenko Front. Since the telephone connection functioned magnificently on the German side, it was possible to experience the visit of German dive-bombers in the respective Soviet Bolshevik commands the following day. In addition, it was possible to eavesdrop on numerous Timoschenko orders and kept the enemy pilots away from our necks in Starodub for days on end, since our counterparts still assumed that their own forces were still there.

Whenever the translator was asked something he could not immediately answer,

he noticed "interference" on the lines, using the time to ask his commander what he should answer. He then called back, and it did not bother him that he was suddenly referred to as a "fascist pig" and a "Nazi spy." By eavesdropping on the rest of the Bolshevik landline communications, he knew that such suspicions and accusations appeared to be quite common. He would protest his own innocence and then make similar accusations, whereupon Timoschenko's general staff would be only too happy to provide information. It wasn't until two days later that the light apparently finally went on there. They cut the line and the front headquarters of the Soviet marshal could no longer be reached. Timoschenko had been able to save himself in time from the affectionate hugs of the black bears.

The Soviet command knew all too well that the breakthrough of German armor forces to the south constituted a great danger to their own front, which was still oriented to the west. For that reason, everything was then geared to defeating or at least holding up the *XXIV. Armee-Korps (mot.)*.

After *Generalleutnant* Model had taken off in the direction of Starodub, reports filtered in to *Oberstleutnant* Audörsch from the reconnaissance efforts that had been dispatched that the woods in the vicinity of Unetscha and the roadway to the rear had been occupied by Russians. At that moment, the commanding general, *Generalleutnant* Geyr von Schweppenburg, arrived at Audörsch's command post and Audörsch filled him in on the latest reports. Von Schweppenburg ordered that the *II./Schützen-Regiment 394*, which was marching through Unetscha at the time, was to remain there. The commanding general decided to remain at Audörsch's command post, since all of the roads to the corps command post were occupied by the enemy. Since it was expected that the Russians would attack Unetscha the next morning, all necessary measures for the defense of the town were taken. At first light on 19 August, the positions of *Schützen-Regiment 394* were placed under heavy Russian artillery fire; an attack by fifteen Russian fighting vehicles attempted to break through the positions. The attack hit *Leutnant* Dr. Lotze's *2./Schützen-Regiment 394* especially hard, but it did not allow itself to be shaken and bravely conducted its defense. *Oberstleutnant* Audörsch employed the three tanks that had remained in Unetscha, some of which were immobilized. *Leutnant* Büschen conducted a successful defensive engagement with his two *Panzer III's* and single *Panzer IV*. After three T-34's[5] had been knocked out, the Soviets turned away. Some of them bogged down in the marshland, where they remained stuck.

A Russian infantry attack then started against the command post of the *Kampfgruppe*. The commanding general was also there. It was supported by heavy artillery fire. All available forces, including clerks and liaison officers, were used in the defense. The commanding general personally got involved in the fighting, armed with a submachine gun. The general's liaison officer, standing next to the commanding general and *Oberstleutnant* Audörsch, was badly wounded. The enemy attack was able to be turned back.

The fighting then continued with unrelenting harshness. The responsible battle group leader, *Oberstleutnant* Audörsch, received constant reports of renewed enemy attacks or small penetrations into the positions.

It was almost miraculous that the corps landline leading forward to the *3. Panzer-Division* had not been discovered by the Russians. The commanding general was thus able to speak with *Generalleutnant* Model and ordered the immediate sending of two tank battalions to Unetscha, since that important railway hub could not be lost under any circumstances. After that conversation, Model spoke with Audörsch and asked him the following question: "Are you going to hold Unetscha or not?" After Audörsch answered the question in the affirmative, Model decided not to send the second tank battalion to Unetscha. Only *Oberstleutnant* Munzel and the *II./Panzer-Regiment 6* were sent.

The difficult defensive fighting of *Schützen-Regiment 394* continued. The disquieting information reached the command post that a fifty-two-ton fighting vehicle had just succeeded in crossing a bridge into Unetscha, after it had eliminated the German guard force on the bridge with its main gun. Audörsch gave *Leutnant* Störck of the regimental engineer platoon the mission of destroying the tank. The heavy tank was lumbering around the streets of the city, firing wildly. Previous efforts to take care of the tank with satchel charges had failed. *Leutnant* Störck jumped onto the rear deck of the tank with a satchel charge. *Gefreiter* Baldes likewise jumped up onto the rolling tank and blocked the vision ports of the turret with his hands. Störck threw open an engine compartment access grate and tossed the satchel charge inside. Both of the engineers jumped off and went into cover behind the corner of a house. The charge detonated and destroyed the tank; the Russian crew was able to dismount without any serious wounds. Störck laconically reported to the commanding general: "Tank destroyed; I brought the Russian crew." The general removed his own Iron Cross, First Class, and pinned it to the chest of *Leutnant* Störck for his brave deed.

The attacks of the Russians did not let up, but they were turned back everywhere by the brave riflemen. The difficult fighting cost a lot of casualties. *Hauptmann* Schmidt, the commander of

---

5. Nearly 1,000 early-model T-34's had been delivered to the front by the start of Barbarossa. They were employed poorly by the inexperienced crews and field commanders, besides having some mechanical problems in the early models, with the result that many of the were lost in the initial wave of German advances. Nonetheless, the tank was a formidable opponent and vastly superior in both armor and armament to anything the Germans were fielding at the time. It was fast and maneuverable, and featured a high-velocity 7.62-centimeter main gun (later upgunned to 8.5-centimeter). It became the standard Soviet main battle tank and nearly 100,000 were produced by war's end.

the *4./Schützen-Regiment 394*, and the battalion physician of the *II./Schützen-Regiment 394*, *Assistenzarzt* Bosien, were killed. *Sanitäts-Feldwebel*[6] Holler took his place. *Assistenzarzt* Dr. Türk was practically helpless in the face of all the wounded, but he was able to master the situation, as he so frequently did, with the assistance of his medical personnel. Towards noon, the heavy fighting abated somewhat, with only smaller attacks being conducted by the Russians, which were effortlessly turned back by the riflemen. *Oberstleutnant* Munzel's *II./Panzer-Regiment 6*, which arrived around noon, turned back the last Russian attacks. The riflemen, who had been in extremely difficult but ultimately successful defensive fighting since the early morning, were happy that the tanks had arrived to provide some relief for the situation.

At 0945 hours, *Oberstleutnant* von Lewinski pulled his battle group a few kilometers back from Starodub in order to set up a screening position further to the north at Janjkowa, so that contact was not lost between the two cities. Unfortunately, the enemy was so strong and the supply situation with fuel and ammunition so weak, that the Soviets could no longer be driven from the road. After the armored battle group had pulled out of its screening position between Unetscha and Starodub, the division moved another battle group into the area to prevent the enemy forces battered at Unetscha from also attempting to separate those two cities. *Oberstleutnant* Dr. Weissenbruch, the commander of the *I./Artillerie-Regiment 75*, was given the mission of forming the screening battle group. The *1.* and *2./Schützen-Regiment 3*, as well as elements of *Panzerjäger-Abteilung 521* and Weissenbruch's own battalion, moved out of Starodub at noon and occupied positions at Asskoli, ten kilometers north of the city. *Generalleutnant* Model was also at that location. The men of *Pionier-Bataillon 39* mined the railway line and the 2nd Company of the engineer battalion built a sixteen-ton bridge in Rjuchoff. The

III./Panzer-Regiment 6 and elements of the motorcycle infantry battalion and the reconnaissance battalion remained in Starodub, where they conducted patrols in all directions in the course of the day in an effort to keep the southern wing of the division from being surprised. *Kampfgruppe Frank*—consisting of *Kradschützen-Bataillon 3*, the *1./Panzerjäger-Abteilung 521*, a battery from *Artillerie-Regiment 75*, and the 4th Platoon of the *3./Pionier-Bataillon 39*—captured three artillery pieces and took fifty prisoners, among other spoils of war.

The enemy movements continued through the night and hit the widely extended division, which was fighting in all directions, with full force early on the morning of 20 August. Strong Soviet forces rolled across the crossroads north of Shetscha at 0400 hours, heading from the northwest to the southeast. Additional columns followed those initial forces in the area around Rjuchoff. Coming from *Kampfgruppe Weissenbruch*, elements of differing battalions under *Major* Wellmann immediately went into position south of Rjuchoff and engaged the enemy. The *1./Schützen-Regiment 3* encountered an enemy antiaircraft battery in the process of attempting to break through. *Obergefreiter* Schrader's rifle squad took up the fight. The soldiers approached the enemy with aggressiveness, eliminated the battery and took 192 men prisoner.

The engineers in position at Rjuchoff had a worse time of it. They had been surprised by a lightning-like attack by the Russians and lost four dead, five missing and one wounded. At the last moment, *Unteroffizier* Münchow was able to escape encirclement with four vehicles and reestablish contact with Bridging Section 1. *Major* Beigel immediately employed a motorized patrol under *Leutnant* Seefeld (*3./Pionier-Bataillon 39*) to see what had happened. Unfortunately, the engineers were unable to make it through to their encircled comrades and had to return without any tangible results.

---

6. Enlisted medical personnel generally had their specialty (medical = *Sanitäts-*) placed in front of their rank.

Generalleutnant Model directed friendly tanks to intervene as soon as possible. The *I./Panzer-Regiment 6* rolled in the direction of Shetscha. From there, the 1st Company was employed in an enveloping maneuver to the left two hours later, while the remaining companies attacked Rjuchoff from the north and felt their way forward along the road heading south that bypassed the city to the west. Two Russian fighting vehicles—T-26's—as well as an artillery piece were destroyed during the reconnaissance-in-force. The lead vehicles then linked up with the first couple of tanks from the *III./Panzer-Regiment 6*, which had moved out from Starodub to the north. As a result, contact within the divided division was reestablished at 1315 hours.

Around 1400 hours, the situation around Rjuchoff cleared up somewhat. The Soviets had disappeared from the road. They had pulled back into the thick woods between Rjuchoff and Shetscha. From there, they continued to present a danger to the columns advancing along the road. At that point, the *I./Panzer-Regiment 6* only had seven *Panzer II's*, three *Panzer III's*, and a single *Panzer IV* at its disposal. It was impossible for it to attack the enemy. The forces had to transition to the defense everywhere.

Kampfgruppe Audörsch left Unetscha around 1400 hours on 20 August with the *II./Panzer-Regiment 6* in the lead after elements of the *4. Panzer-Division* had assumed the screening mission there. The lead company encountered its first Russian formations four kilometers south of the city; they had advanced as far as the road again. The enemy had even brought artillery into position and took every vehicle under fire. The tanks succeeded in breaking through.

Schützen-Regiment 394 followed the tank battalion and, protected by it, continued its march south. All of a sudden, aircraft with the Red Star appeared above the column. The first bombs fell soon afterward and, a short while later, enemy artillery again fired into the ranks of the regiment. Exploiting the situation, the enemy came out of the woods with tanks and riflemen, scat-

tered the *I./Schützen-Regiment 394*, and pressed on farther to the east.

The next halt was at Shetscha. A camouflaged fifty-two-ton tank was positioned under trees near the roadway. It took every vehicle that rolled past under fire from pointblank range with its main gun. The first vehicle was set alight; the second one ran into it; the third one tipped over. Everything came to a standstill, and there was total confusion. The friendly infantry weapons were powerless against the steel monster.

Oberstleutnant Schlutius, the commander of the *III./Artillerie-Regiment 75*, immediately ordered a 15-centimeter battery forward. Unfortunately, the guns could not be brought into position to destroy the tank with direct fire. *Major* Haas employed the battery on both sides of the road. The riflemen were unable to advance, since the Soviets were constantly bringing up reinforcements and appeared to have appreciable amounts of ammunition.

The Soviets attacked the German outposts at 1900 hours in an effort to force a breakthrough to the east. The *III./Artillerie-Regiment 75*, the *4./Artillerie-Regiment 75*, and the *6./Flak-Regiment 59* fired with everything they had. In addition, there was the bark of infantry guns and mortars. It was a hellish concert in those gloomy woods, over which Northern Lights played that night in the bloody-red heavens. The enemy only pressed forward with riflemen. That effort could be turned back, with some of the enemy running into mines that had been laid by the *5./Schützen-Regiment 394*. The Russians did not employ any tanks that time. Toward evening, the fighting slowed down somewhat. The Soviets had suffered heavy casualties, but the friendly losses also weighed heavily. The *I./Schützen-Regiment 394* lost eight dead, including *Leutnant* Schellong, who had only been given acting command of the 3rd Company a few days earlier.

That evening, *Oberstleutnant* Audörsch received orders to immediately clear the woods of the enemy between Rjuchoff and Stietscha. Audörsch reported to the division that the orders could not be carried out in the darkness and that the attack would take place in the morning. The division placed extreme importance on driving the enemy from the road and firming up the friendly front enough so that no more Russians got through.

Audörsch, who had two tank battalions (the *I.* and *II./Panzer-Regiment 6*), as well as artillery, attached to him for the operation, scheduled the attack for 0500 hours. The planned attack had to be postponed indefinitely, however, since heavy fog took away all visibility in the bottomlands and in the woods. The batteries of *Artillerie-Regiment 75* did fire heavily into the huge woods, however, and it started to burn brilliantly in places.

Panzer-Regiment 6 had set up its screening positions as follows: the *I./Panzer-Regiment 6* along the Unetscha–Starodub railway line, blocking the woods from the west; the *II./Panzer-Regiment 6* screened along the eastern side of the woods. *Oberleutnant* Klöber, the brave commander of the 7th Company, was killed within a few minutes by a shot to the throat from short range by a sniper. The *III./Panzer-Regiment 6* continued to remain in Starodub that day to protect the division to the south and to the east (from Merinowka).

During that lull in the fighting, Model appeared at Audörsch's command post and was initially highly annoyed that the attack had not yet started. After Audörsch had rendered his report on the situation, however, Model left it up to him to determine the time of the attack. Model waited for the attack to begin. It started at 1100 hours in brutal heat after the fog had cleared. Schützen-Regiment 394 advanced on a broad front from the east along all forest trails and roadways into the large expanse of vegetation and trees. The tanks of the *II./Panzer-Regiment* rattled closely behind. The Russians had camouflaged themselves and dug in magnificently. Heavy fighting developed in some sections of woods. The enemy slowly turned weak and wanted to flee to the west. It was there that he ran into the deployed *I./Panzer-Regiment 6*,

whose concentrated fires caused even more casualties among the Russians attempting to break out. Eleven guns, including eight of 15-centimeter caliber, were destroyed by German rounds. After four hours of bitter fighting, the lead elements of *Schützen-Regiment 394* were at the western edge of the woods. The last enemy resistance collapsed at 1800 hours. Forty Russian artillery pieces and tanks—most of which had gotten stuck in the marshes—were captured. More than 900 prisoners started their way to the rear.

Under sunny and warm skies, the next day promised to be somewhat more "peaceful." The division informed all of its elements telephonically at 0900 hours that a fairly long break was in the works. The enemy, however, continued to attempt to find a "hole" somewhere along the front of the division. Early in the morning, a Russian column attempted to break through in the sector of the *3./Schützen-Regiment 3*. The attack collapsed in the defensive fires of the riflemen. One artillery piece, four trucks, one quad antiaircraft gun, and one unit flag remained in German hands.

Along the road to Rjuchoff, *Schützen-Regiment 394* combed through the woods one more time. In the process, there were additional skirmishes.

Over the next few days, the Soviets gave up their attempts to break through out of the area around Gomel and intended to escape German encirclement by going across the Dessna farther south.

The *2. Armee* had crossed the Ssosh on a broad front to the south with its infantry divisions, whereby the *1. Kavallerie-Division* on the right wing was already not too far from Gomel. The *10. Infanterie-Division (mot.)* continued to maintain contact with the forward elements of the *XXIV. Armee-Korps (mot.)*. The *3. Panzer-Division* screened from the areas it had reached and pulled its own forces closer to Starodub, since the *4. Panzer-Division* had assumed the protection of Unetscha. Behind it was the *17. Panzer-Division*, which was marching down from the northern sector of the armor group, reaching Mglin. In the course of the individual screening engagements, patrolling activities and combat raids, the *I./Schützen-Regiment 3*, together with *Kradschützen-Bataillon 3*, was able to bring in 200 more prisoners. The *9./Panzer-Regiment 6* occupied Mischkowa and Dochnowitschi to the southeast of Starodub, capturing ten Russian howitzers in the process.

Heeresgruppe Mitte issued orders on 22 August that its field armies were to move out to the south from the line running Gomel–Starodub, whereby *Panzergruppe 2* was to envelop east to prevent the enemy from escaping. The division issued its attack order at 0500 hours on 28 August: "Advance south of the *XXIV. Armee-Korps (mot.)* with the *10. Infanterie-Division (mot.)* right and the *3. Panzer-Division* left crossing the line running Cholmy–Nowgorod–Sewersk to cut off the enemy still holding out to

the southwest of Gomel. The *4. Panzer-Division* follows the *3. Panzer-Division*. Friendly east flank open; to be guarded through offensive actions and the enemy pushed back."

A Russian leaflet was scattered over the German lines during the period, which exhorted soldiers to desert. Among other things, the soldiers could read: "Just in the last three weeks alone, our forces have wiped out: The *3. Panzer-Division . . .* as a result of that fighting, there is nothing left of many of those divisions except their number." The soldiers were reading that just as they were about to start out on their boldest raid.

The division established three battle groups for the continuation of its advance. The main effort was under *Oberstleutnant* von Lewinski and consisted of the *II./Panzer-Regiment 6*, the *II./Schützen-Regiment 3*, the *III./Artillerie-Regiment 75*, *Panzerjäger-Abteilung 521*, *Aufklärungs-Abteilung 1*, and *Pionier-Bataillon 39*.

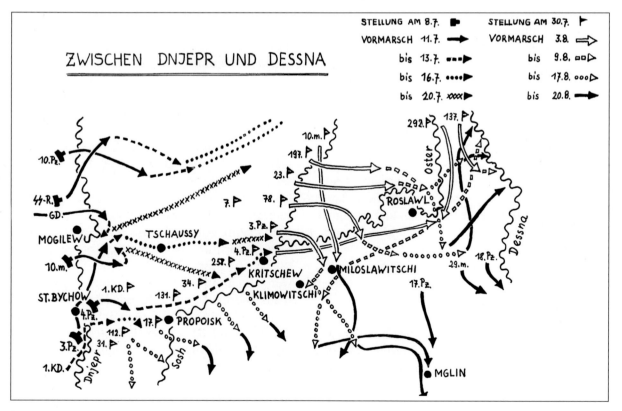

Between the Dnjepr and the Dessna.

That battle group received the mission of breaking through to Nowgorod–Sewersk. *Oberst* Kleemann's battle group followed behind. He had the *I./Panzer-Regiment 6*, *Schützen-Regiment 394*, the *II./Artillerie-Regiment 75*, elements of *Panzerjäger-Abteilung 543*, and divisional troops at his disposal. *Oberst* von Manteuffel had the third battle group. It formed the rearguard for the advance and consisted of the *III./Panzer-Regiment 6*, the *I./Schützen-Regiment 3*, and divisional troops. It also had the mission of guarding the east flank of the attacking division.

The *7./Panzer-Regiment 6* left its assembly area at 0500 hours and advanced across its line of departure at "Windmill Hill" south of Starodub as the lead element of the battle group. At the same time, the *III./Panzer-Regiment 6* moved off in the direction of Dedoff to screen those movements. The advance moved rapidly under sunny and warm weather. The slight enemy resistance was quickly broken. By around 1100 hours, the tank companies had covered forty kilometers. The reconnaissance elements in the lead reported that the direct route was very bad from that point forward. *Oberstleutnant* Munzel therefore ordered his forces to turn off to the right at Kostobobr. The fighting vehicles, *SPW's*, and artillery prime movers then churned their way along deeply sandy roads through dense woods.

There was a small, dirty sign there with Cyrillic lettering indicating the Soviet Union. The Ukraine had been reached. Strangely enough, the terrain started to look completely different. The villages appeared to be cleaner and the people friendlier. The woman stood along the side of the road and offered milk and eggs, while the men lifted their caps.

While the first battle group worked its way through the sand and the dust of the Ukraine, the second battle group left the area around Starodub–Rjuchoff around 1020 hours and followed von Lewinski's men. The forces that were employed in the flank guard mission turned back repeated attacks pressing in from the east. For instance, the *2./Schützen-Regiment 394* was suddenly hit in the flank by 200 assaulting Russian yelling *Urräh!* The company was able to turn back the attack, however. The screening forces followed the advancing columns and reached Kostobobr in the afternoon. The lead companies of the *4. Panzer-Division* arrived in Starodub in the course of the day and relieved the division rearguards.

The *3. Panzer-Division* became the first formation of *Panzergruppe 2* to enter Ukrainian territory, and its armored spearhead was approaching the Dessna. *Kampfgruppe von Lewinski* held up around 1300 hours towards the north of Petschenjugi. The supply vehicles were brought forward and the vehicles refueled. Russian fighter-bombers attacked the German tanks, dropping bombs and strafing, but they were only able to cause insignificant damage. The battle group moved out again two hours later.

The *7./Panzer-Regiment 6* was the lead company again. Outside Forostowitschi, it ran into the long stretch of ascending, barren high ground before the Dessna. The enemy had established defensive positions there. Initially, the tank company and the riflemen got bogged down. Then the rest of the 2nd Battalion closed up. *Oberstleutnant* von Lewinski summoned his commanders for a conference; the division commander was already there. A Russian gun had identified the gathering and fired. *Leutnant* Sellschopp was killed; *Oberleutnant* Darsow and Groth badly wounded; *Oberstleutnant* Munzel and *Leutnant* Kipp were slightly wounded.

Far behind the tanks, the vehicles of the riflemen and artillery of the battle group continued rolling forward. Unfortunately, the columns were not able to move fast enough along the bad roads and the attack, scheduled for 1900 hours, had to be postponed. By then, it had turned dark and it would have been senseless to advance against an enemy, whose situation was uncertain, and across terrain, which was unfamiliar. The riflemen set up security for the battle group in the positions it had reached. An all-round defense was established. The tanks pulled back to Forostowitschi, which was located in a deep defile. The Soviets had continuously observed the approaching German forces by means of observation aircraft; the formations were bombed several times during the night.

The high command of the Soviet 21st Army, which was responsible for this sector, realized the danger posed to the entire front if the Germans succeeded in crossing the Dessna and advancing deep into the Ukraine. The division was positioned only a few kilometers from that river that night, thus closing out another chapter of its operations in the east, a chapter that belonged to one of its most successful for the entire war. Since the start of the campaign, the division had covered and fought through 2,000 kilometers of Russia and had broken through strong enemy defensive positions.

Four days after crossing the Dessna on 30 August, *Feldwebel* Schröder's *SPW* from the *1./Schützen-Regiment 394* was responsible for knocking out nine tanks, one gun, and two trucks. He and his gunner, *Gefreiter* Emden (seen here), were both awarded the Iron Cross, First Class.

Schützen-Regiment 394 crossed the Seim on 7 September 1941 and established a bridgehead. The guns of the heavy infantry gun platoon of the 11th Company provided artillery support.

The interior of a platoon leader's vehicle.

The observation post of the *6./Artillerie-Regiment 75* in the water tower at Rogatschew. *Hauptmann* Kersten observes through the scissor scope.

Tanks and antitank elements push forward toward Rogatschew on 7 July.

The *2./Panzerjäger-Abteilung 543* in an assembly area outside of Rogatschew.

The church in Stary Bychow.

Kradschützen-Bataillon 3 crosses the Dnjepr at Stary Bychow.

Portrait of *Oberfeldwebel* Albert Blaich, Knight's Cross recipient in the *12./Panzer-Regiment 6.*

Unteroffizier Becker-Neetz was a squad leader in the *7./Schützen-Regiment 394*. He distinguished himself during the fighting for Lykowo and was awarded the Knight's Cross on 25 August 1941.

Major Dr. Herbert Müller, the commander of the *II./Schützen-Regiment 394*. He received the Knight's Cross on 8 September 1941, while serving in that capacity.

Oberleutnant Freiherr von Werthern was the company commander of the *3./Schützen-Regiment 394* when he received his Knight's Cross on 8 September 1941. He eventually went on to battalion and brigade command and served for some time in *Panzer-Grenadier-Division "Großdeutschland"* in the former capacity. He survived the war, reentered the German military in 1956, and retired as an *Oberstleutnant*, passing away on 10 January 2004.

CHAPTER 10

From the Dessna to the Ssula: The Battle for Kiev

On 24 August, the field army group ordered the attack of *Panzergruppe 2* to the south and into the rear of the Soviet 5th Army, which was holding out in front of Kiev. The *XXIV. Armee-Korps (mot.)* was to be the steely point of the field army once the Dessna was crossed. The corps directed the *10. Infanterie-Division (mot.)* to advance on Cholmy–Awdejwka and the *3. Panzer-Division* to force a crossing over the Dessna, while the *4. Panzer-Division* was to initially clear the west bank of the river and follow the *3. Panzer-Division*.

The *3. Panzer-Division* was about 600 to 1,000 meters in front of the broad valley of the Dessna. The city of Nowgorod-Sewersk separated the division from the river. The division closed up to the river during the night. *Oberst* Kleemann arrived with his headquarters, as did the *I./Panzer-Regiment 6*, *Kradschützen-Bataillon 3*, and *Aufklärungs-Abteilung 1*. It took longer for the batteries to make their way through the sandy roads and the deep woods in the defiles in front of the city. The commanders discussed the attack in the hours that followed. It was scheduled for 0500 hours the following morning. Since the bridge over the Dessna was marked on the bad maps available as being at the northern entrance of Nowgorod, it was directed that a reinforced tank company under *Oberleutnant* Vopel (commander of the *1./Panzer-Regiment 6*) take the bridge in a *coup de main*. The remaining companies of the *I./Panzer-Regiment 6* were to give covering fire from the high ground in front of the city while that was being done. *Kampfgruppe Kleemann* would advance against the southern entrance to Nowgorod-Sewersk, while *Kampfgruppe von Lewinski* would come in from the west.

The advance guard of *Oberleutnant* Vopel—reinforced by the *1./Schützen-Regiment 394*, the *3./Panzerjäger-Abteilung 543*, and the engineer platoon of *Schützen-Regiment 394*—left its staging area at 0345 hours. The tanks and personnel carriers were hit by artillery and mortar fire as they approached. They did not allow themselves to be deterred. The Rome Bridge was crossed and, about one kilometer to the southeast, the first Soviet roadblock broken through. The advance guard then moved two kilometers through a defile, which was dominated by enemy infantry-gun fire. The fighting vehicles approached the enemy guns at full speed and overran them.

The enemy's resistance stiffened a bit later at the fork in the road 3.5 kilometers northwest of the city. The fighting vehicles had to halt there, and the riflemen had to dismount to force the Russians to pull back in a hand-grenade duel. *Leutnant* Aye, a platoon leader in the *1./Schützen-Regiment 394*, was killed, while he was negotiating with Soviet emissaries. A short while later, the lead fighting vehicles were at the northern outskirts of Nowgorod-Sewersk. Although there were a few machine-gun nests, they were overrun in short order. But where was the bridge?

By then, *Oberstleutnant* Schmidt-Ott had worked his way forward to the high ground with his other companies. The men were offered a magnificent picture from there. To the left was the broad bed of the Dessna, with its two arms. On the right side was the pretty city, extended along the steep high ground. Behind that—about four kilometers away—was the high bridge, over which an unending stream of trucks and *panje* carts was crossing. The artillery liaison officer said he was not capable of engaging the bridge, since the batteries were so far back. At that point, Schmidt-Ott had *Kampfgruppe Vopel* informed by radio of the exact location of the bridge and issued orders that it was to be taken immediately.

The tanks, personnel carriers, and motorcycles moved out again. This time, they were hit by Russian fighter-bombers, but little damage was done. *Kompanie Vopel*, followed by the antitank elements and the riflemen, rattled in the direction of the bridge. Wherever resistance was offered, it was answered in the steely language of the main guns and machine guns. A Russian truck was destroyed right in front of the bridge. The tanks were in front of the high bridge, some 700 meters long. The clocks showed 1000 hours.

While the forwardmost elements of *Kampfgruppe Kleemann* arrived quickly at their objective, *Kampfgruppe von Lewinski* had approached the southern outskirts city from the west. The *II./Panzer-Regiment 6*, along with its attached elements, had departed Forostowitschi around 0700 hours. Artillery fire descended on the roads and defiles. The battle group reached the stubble fields, which were full of machine guns and guard outposts. While the tanks continued their way east uninterrupted, the men of the *II./Schützen-Regiment 3* swarmed out across the fields and smoked out the individual enemy groups, one after the other. The battalion was once again being led by *Major* Zimmermann, who had been released from the hospital. His predecessor, *Hauptmann* Engelien, was sent to Eberswalde, to complete General Staff officer training. (He ended the war as a regimental commander in Kurland.)

Oberstleutnant von Lewinski conducted a commanders' conference with the commanders of his battle group around 0900 hours in one of the many defiles. Coordination with the batteries was emphasized, since they could only move forward in the local terrain with difficulty. Soviet fire fell on the group of officers. The commander of *Artillerie-Regiment 75*, *Oberst* Ries, was killed. With him died another member of the divisional artillery, *Leutnant* Wöhlermann of the regiment's 1st Battery. *Unteroffizier* Lipschitz, who later became the senator for internal affairs in postwar West Berlin, was badly wounded and lost an arm.

Within *Kampfgruppe von Lewinski*, the *7./Panzer-Regiment 6* took up point again. It crossed a railway embankment just before the first houses of the city. As the tanks crossed the tracks, they ran into the positions of a Russian 15-centimeter battery. The Soviets were in the process of limbering the guns to the tall, ungainly tractors with the wide tracks that served as prime movers. The main-gun rounds crashed into the guns and the vehicles and left behind only steel skeletons and a cloud of burning oil and fuel.

A short time later—1030 hours—*Kampfgruppe von Lewinski* advanced into Nowgorod-Sewersk. *Generalleutnant* Model had moved to the head of the column in his open staff car and ordered contact be established between the two battle groups. The *II./Panzer-Regiment 6* was able to clear the area around the railway station. The division then sent the tank battalion farther to the south, in the direction of Juchnowa, to take the bridge there.

Oberleutnant Vopel's reinforced advance-guard company of the northern battle group was at the river. The terrain sloped steeply downward and rose equally steeply on the other side. The bridge stood there as the connection between the two points, jutting high into the sky on four large pilings. All of a sudden, there were bursts of machine-gun fire from the bridge guards. The two tanks in front took up the fight and shredded the machine-gun positions. Twenty to thirty Russians fled to the base of the bridge.

Leutnant Störck of the engineer platoon of *Schützen-Regiment 394* turned out to be quicker, however. He maneuvered his way through the front line of fighting vehicles and raced towards the bridge. Soviet artillery, mortars, and machine guns fired from the opposite banks. *Oberleutnant* Vopel had his tanks spread out to lend support, and the tinny reports of the main guns and machine guns could be heard firing against identified enemy positions. The engineer vehicle halted sixty meters in front of the approach ramp to the gigantic bridge, whose far side could barely be seen. Störck jumped down from his vehicle. Following behind him were *Feldwebel* Heyeres, *Unteroffizier* Strucken, *Obergefreiter* Fuhn, and *Gefreiter* Beyle. The men hurried

toward the bridge, racing bent over along the wooden planks, while the rounds of the tanks kept the enemy down. Störck and Beyle paid no attention to them. Their eyes were looking for demolitions and, indeed, they found them. The *Leutnant* discovered the first charge on one of the vertical pilings on the box-like superstructure of the bridge. The engineers dove on it, tearing the lines out and throwing the box into the water. Störck hastened on, found the second charge . . . then the third . . . then the fourth.

The rounds of individual Russian machine guns headed towards them and forced the engineers to take cover. A few Russian soldiers attempted to flee from the bridge and reach the safety of the far shore. The tank gunners took up aim and fired. Störck was then able to continue. Another charge was flung into the water, followed by another. Valuable time ticked by; no one knew how many charges were still on the bridge. Then they did it. *Oberleutnant* Vopel decided to exploit the confusion among the enemy and not wait until the engineers had completed their dangerous work. The bridge could have gone up at any minute . . . the *Oberleutnant* recognized the opportunity that was being offered. He ordered: *"Panzer—Marsch!"*

The vehicles rolled out. They rattled towards the bridge, moved past *Leutnant* Störck, who was still in the process of removing charges, and reached the far side. *Unteroffizier* Borowczek of the *4./Panzer-Regiment 6* led the first tank. With him was *Leutnant* Hiltmann, the liaison officer from the rifle brigade. Vopel followed close behind with all tanks capable of moving. Close behind were the men of *Pionier-Bataillon 39* under *Leutnant* Harzer.

It was 1100 hours, when the German tanks reached the south bank of the Dessna. The Soviets were so surprised, they fled their positions. *Oberleutnant* Vopel intended to advance farther. He advanced through the fleeing columns with his reinforced company so as to take the high ground, some 800 meters away. While the Russian infantry fled, enemy artillery and 7.62-centimeter antitank guns started firing into the approaching tanks. One fighting vehicle was lost to a direct hit from an antitank gun; the vehicle of the *Oberleutnant* was also hit. *Generalleutnant* Model arrived at the bridge at that moment and had *Oberstleutnant* Audörsch brief him. He could hardly believe that the large bridge had fallen into the division's hands intact. He ordered that Störck be recommended for a Knight's Cross immediately; he later received it from the hands of Model outside Orel.

The Soviets then noticed the great danger the loss of the bridge placed them in. They placed one artillery fire mission after the other on the bridge and the approach road. It was already too late. *Oberstleutnant* Schmidt-Ott was already there with his remaining companies. The battalion commander was the first one to race over the 700-meter-long stretch. Behind him was *Oberleutnant* von Kriegsheim with the other tanks. A fighting vehicle was hit by an antitank gun, but it was able to continue moving under its own power. One of the charges went off that the engineers had overlooked. Fortunately, it only caused light damage to the wooden beams.

The *1./Panzer-Regiment 6* underwent heavy artillery fire on the high ground 800 meters on the other side of the bridge. The rest of the battalion arrived in a timely manner, bring palpable relief. The *4./Panzer-Regiment 6* took the woods on both sides of the road under fire. The Russians quickly pulled back. At that point, the first riflemen arrived. The *1./Schützen-Regiment 394* relieved the hard-fighting tank company. Over the next few hours, *Oberstleutnant* Audörsch brought his entire regiment across to the east bank. The riflemen expanded and fortified the rapidly won bridgehead. In the process, they engaged an enemy artillery position, capturing a few guns and antiaircraft guns and taking many prisoners.

Oberstleutnant Audörsch then received orders to immediately thrust south with his battle group, which consisted of the *I./Schützen-Regiment 394*, the *I./Panzer-Regiment 6*, antitank elements, and elements of the reconnaissance battalion, and interdict the important Kiev–Moscow railway line. That meant he would be moving out into the night. The advance continued through woods and marshland. The exhaustion on the part of his forces was a consequence of the strenuous fighting of the last few days. Whenever there was a short halt, which was caused by the poor routes or fire being received from the woods, the drivers fell asleep. The commanders and company leaders went from vehicle to vehicle to keep the crews alert and ready to attack. After the small bridge at Iwot was crossed at first light, there was suddenly heavy fire received against the rearward portion of the march column. The column was immediately turned around, and the quick actions of the tanks under the command of *Oberstleutnant* Schmidt-Ott drove off the enemy attack. The battle group continued its advance. The lead element of the rifle battalion, supported by four fighting vehicles and antitank elements, reached Schostka from the north at 0800 hours. But there was little to be seen of the city. Thick, yellowish orange smoke from the burning gunpowder factory spread out for kilometers over the area. The city was taken against little resistance.

At that point, the battle group was approaching the Kiev–Moscow rail line. Just as the lead tanks and *SPW's* cleared the high ground in front of the rail line, a transport train rushed in. The fighting vehicles immediately opened fire with their main guns, and the machine guns on the *SPW's* also whipped their rounds towards the approaching steel. The train came to a stop, and the locomotive and a fuel car started to burn. Soldiers from a Russian replacement battalion jumped out of the freight cars with raised hands. They had been given the mission of taking out the German airborne forces at Nowgorod–Sewersk. The rail line was blocked by the burning train; the mission was accomplished.

Oberstleutnant Schmidt-Ott and *Oberstleutnant* Audörsch could not be held in check. All of the routes had been softened and beams frequently had to be used before the tanks could continue their advance. Soon the soldiers of the battle group were in front of Woronesch. The lead vehicles of *Hauptmann* Ziervogel's reconnaissance battalion were the first to enter the industrial city. Unfortunately, the rifle companies were not behind them. They frequently had to defend against enemy forces that were still hiding in the woods. Consequently, only the outskirts of the city were occupied by the few fighting vehicles and *SPW's*. When an enemy immediate counterattack was launched in the afternoon, it could be turned back. *Generalleutnant* Model appeared at that moment. Although he recognized the achievements of his fighting forces, he ordered Woronesch to be evacuated in light of the fact that most of the division was far to the rear. The battle group left the city at 1700 hours and screened three kilometers to the northwest.

That morning, *Kampfgruppe von Lewinski* was stalled at Juchnowa. The engineers had to improve the bridge. It proved faster for them to set up a ferry, over which the first four self-propelled guns of *Panzerjäger-Abteilung 521* were crossed at 1100 hours. Later on, the fighting vehicles were also able to be crossed, after the riflemen of the *II./Schützen-Regiment 3* had expanded the bridgehead as far as the village of Pirogowka.

The Red Air Force was very active that day and intended to destroy the large bridge over the Dessna, no matter the cost. The fighter-bombers descended on the bridge almost continuously, and the bombs howled down constantly. The biggest attack consisted of twenty-one Soviet bombers at the same time.

The division's 2nd Medical Company set up a field clearing station on Nowgorod on 26 August. The badly wounded were taken to the field hospital in Starodub, where the 1st Medical Company and the division's ambulance platoon assumed responsibility for their care.

The bad weather on 28 August considerably impeded movement. As soon as improved roads were left, vehicles and even tanks sank in the muck. The *II./Panzer-Regiment 6* was moved from Pirogowka, since the bridgehead was insufficient for starting large-scale operations from

there. The battalion was sent through Nowgorod-Sewersk and across the large bridge to the location of the armor regiment's 1st Battalion. By then, the 3rd Battalion was already in Schostka.

The *III./Panzer-Regiment 6* left its quarters around noon, after the rain had let up some, and hit the enemy in the flank at Pirogowka. Despite the nearly impassable roads, *Hauptmann* Schneider-Kostalski's crews advanced through the Russian positions, reaching the forward lines of the *II./Schützen-Regiment 3* with the lead tanks at 1700 hours. That cleared out the bridgehead. *Leutnant* Engelhardt and two junior enlisted men from the armored regiment were killed that day. The tanks and the eight self-propelled guns of *Panzerjäger-Abteilung 521* had arrived just in time. The riflemen had been attacked by strong Russian forces and torn apart. *Oberleutnant* Biegon's 9th Company did not rejoin the battalion until 0200 hours. When *Oberleutnant* Ewert was killed, the divisional artillery lost another battery commander.

On orders from the division, *Kampfgruppe Audörsch* had left its screening area in the rear in the morning and entered Woronesch around 1145 hours, with the reconnaissance battalion in the lead. The enemy attempted to take back the city with the support of tanks, but he was turned back. The battle group initiated reconnaissance to the south in the evening. It was directed that the *2./Schützen-Regiment 394* occupy the bottleneck between the lakes at Saruskawo, supported by three fighting vehicles. Contrary to expectations, the operations succeeded rapidly. The riflemen even advanced five kilometers beyond the ordered objective. The railway line there was blown up by means of mines.

The enemy then took the initiative. The Soviet high command probably recognized that the German thrust to the south was not intended to cause an envelopment along the Dessna. Instead, it was probably intended to lead into the Ukraine. Marshal Timoschenko, whose headquarters had been in Schostka only a few days previously, personally directed the operations that were intended to win back the Dessna River line.

There were constant Russian attacks on 29 August, which were supported heavily by the Red Air Force and artillery. The division's vehicles were unable to move due to a shortage of fuel. The division was left up to its own devices, since the *4. Panzer-Division* was still rolling toward Nowgorod. The armored regiment had only twenty-two *Panzer II's*, nine *Panzer III's*, and six *Panzer IV's* that day—the complement of a company.[1]

The Soviets initiated their thrust against Schostka at 0630 hours. They were able to penetrate as far as the first few houses. The German formations were in a tight squeeze, since the enemy had succeeded in crossing the main advance route, separating the battle groups. All troop elements in and around Schostka were called to arms. It was not until 0930 hours that the primary danger was eliminated, and the enemy pulled back into the woods east of the town.

When Woronesch was attacked again in the course of the sunny and warm day, the city was evacuated for the second time. The divisional formations pulled back to Schostka. The Soviets vigorously pursued. From the ranks of the *I./Schützen-Regiment 394*, *Leutnant* Hecht, *Oberfeldwebel* Müller and four enlisted personnel were killed; another three officers were wounded (*Oberleutnant* Roos, *Leutnant* Wurm, and *Leutnant* Meise). Only the reconnaissance battalion remained in the area around Woronesch to screen. The situation around the Pirogowka bridgehead eased up some. It was possible for the *II./Schützen-Regiment 3* to improve its positions there. *Major* Beigel, the commander of the divisional engineers, screened the division's frontage with a battle group composed of *Panzerjäger-Abteilung 543*, his 1st and 3rd Companies, and *Flak-Abteilung 94*.

The *XXIV. Armee-Korps (mot.)* was forced to call off the advance of the *3. Panzer-Division*

and the *10. Infanterie-Division (mot.)*. The *4. Panzer-Division* moved through Nowgorod-Sewersk to clear the Dessna river line. It then pulled behind the *3. Panzer-Division*, which, despite all of the setbacks, had taken 800 prisoners.

On 30 August, the corps ordered that the terrain to the sides of the roads be cleared, so that the armor division, which had raced ahead, would no longer face the danger of being encircled and cut off from their rearward lines of communications. Under the command of *Oberst* Kleemann, the large wooded tract east of Schostka was combed that through day. The mission was an essential one for the *3. Panzer-Division*, since its rear-area services, trains and maintenance companies were still sixteen kilometers away in Nowgorod-Sewersk or were just arriving there. Under all circumstance, the constant threat had to be eliminated.

Oberstleutnant Audörsch's *Schützen-Regiment 394* had to defend against intense enemy attacks early in the morning, which were executed from the dense woods in the direction of Lokotki and Schostka. During those operations, the enemy also employed fifty-two-ton tanks.[2] The antitank elements were powerless against them. For that reason, individual artillery pieces were brought forward to the rifle positions. (*Oberstleutnant* Dr. Weissenbruch was the divisional artillery commander at that point.) Working hard, the cannoneers attempted to render the steel giants powerless by firing over open sights.

Since the intensity of the attacks did not let up, the armored regiment was called forward. The 1st Battalion moved to Lokotki to reinforce the rifle battalions there. The 2nd Battalion was employed to clear the terrain to the east. In the process of executing that mission, the brave acting commander of the 8th Company, *Leutnant* Dr. Köhler, was killed. While the German and Russian fighting vehicles had it out, fighting also

1. The author misunderstands the combined totals, which are more like the equivalent of two companies, unless one discounts the *Panzer II's*, which were of limited value at this stage of the campaign.
2. Probably the KV-1, which weighed forty-seven tons, more than twice the weight of the heaviest German tank at that time, the *Panzer IV*. The standard German antitank gun, the 3.7-cm *PaK 36*, was totally ineffective against both this vehicle and the T-34.

erupted in the sector of *Schützen-Regiment 3*, which was still positioned in the Pirogowka area. It was directed to push the friendly positions forward in an effort to eliminate a Russian threat to the flanks. *Oberleutnant* von Zitzewitz's 1st Company was sent out to reconnoiter the enemy positions around Ssobytsch around 0900 hours. The company approached the village in a widely dispersed order and entered it from the side. The vehicles received Russian antitank-gun fire, causing the company to pull back to the hills outside the village. By then, *Unteroffizier* Simon had moved on by himself and discovered a way through the marshland from the north, which led directly into the village. *Oberleutnant* von Zitzewitz immediately sent his entire company in that direction. Those *SPW's* also entered the village undetected. The Soviets were completely surprised. *Unteroffizier* Buggert and his squad cleared the left flank, while the 2nd Platoon under *Leutnant* Braun advanced as far as the southwest corner of the village. Two vehicles were lost to mines. *Leutnant* Schuster, a platoon leader from the 7th Company, also joined the fray with his men, ending the engagement. The enemy forces manning the defenses in the village—some 200 men—surrendered.

Thanks to the determined actions of the 1st Company, it was possible to quickly occupy the actual reconnaissance objective. The higher levels of command had no idea that had been done and, as a result, *Stukas* were heading in to bomb Ssobatsch. At the same time, *Oberleutnant* Zitzewitz had his radio operator, *Obergefreiter* Prange, report to the division that the village had been taken. Finally, at the last minute, the division was able to hold back the attack by the *Luftwaffe* and have the *Stukas* directed elsewhere.

Schützen-Regiment 394 and the armored regiment started clearing the terrain around Sso-batsch after noon. The *I./Panzer-Regiment 6* swung to the south and southeast, while the 2nd Battalion covered the move. In the area just between Makoff and Woronesch alone, more than twenty-five fighting vehicles were identified. Since the friendly forces were too weak to engage, a defensive front was established that oriented to the south. The enemy tanks did not get past the railway embankment, after the first few ran over mines. The *I./Panzer-Regiment 6* and the *I./Schützen-Regiment 394* attacked Dewitschi across a practically barren plain. The enemy put up a stubborn fight. Despite all of the resistance, the German attack soon gained ground and the village could be taken. Most of the enemy escaped being encircled. The actions of *Feldwebel* Schröder and the men of his *SPW* (1st Company of the rifle regiment) were especially praiseworthy during the operation. Despite being attacked by enemy tanks, the *SPW* with the mounted 3.7-centimeter antitank gun stood its ground.[3] *Gefreiter* Eisen, the gunner, was able to knock out eight enemy tanks in the space of fifteen minutes with the small-caliber gun. *Leutnant* Peter and his crew knocked out an additional three.

The division started screening in the area it had taken that afternoon. The night was generally quiet, not counting small skirmishes by patrols on both sides. The division attempted to push its supply elements farther forward. The 2nd Platoon of the Armor Maintenance Company was able to establish shop in Nowgorod-Sewersk, although most of the company was still in Unetscha. The armored regiment received replacements that day from *Panzer-Ersatz-Abteilung 25*[4] in Erlangen. The men received could not be used right away, since they had only received training on the *Panzer I* and the *Panzer 38(t)*[5] in the homeland. Neither of the two vehicles was on hand in the division.

---

3. The *Sd.Kfz. 251/10* variant, the 3.7-cm *PaK 36*, was intended primarily as in infantry-support weapon rather than an antitank gun.

4. 25th Tank Replacement Battalion.

5. The *Panzer 38(t)* was the Czech Skoda-built tank impressed into German service at the start of the war to make up for shortfalls in German production. Some armored battalions were outfitted almost exclusively with them.

The division was unable to advance on 31 August, either, since the Soviets suddenly started assaulting Nowgorod-Sewersk from the northeast. Elements of all of the formations had to be shifted north. At the same time, the Russians attacked Woronesch. The 3./Schützen-Regiment 394 and *Aufklärungs-Abteilung 1* evacuated the city in the face of the superior numbers. The Soviets occupied the city with thirty tanks. *Schützen-Regiment 394* cleared the woods around Makoff, while *Schützen-Regiment 3* occupied the high ground southwest of Schostka. A *Stuka* attack was conducted against Woronesch early in the afternoon, laying a portion of the industrial city to waste. The Soviets took considerable losses. When the men of the reconnaissance battalion felt their way toward the city, they no longer encountered any enemy. The reconnaissance battalion then occupied the city for the third time in the space of three days.

The division was directed to move to the south, forming its point of main effort on the right. The *4. Panzer-Division* was to be to the division's right. This time, the rifle brigade was placed up front. The armored regiment was behind it, with the 2nd Battalion on the right, the 1st Battalion on the left and *Panzerjäger-Abteilung 521* in the middle. The *I./Schützen-Regiment 394* was pulled out of the line and designated as the corps reserve. The attack started at 0700 hours on 1 September after a short artillery preparation. The enemy resistance in front of the brigade was slight. The riflemen were able to advance as far as the southern part of Woronesch without any serious fighting, since the enemy had evacuated the city after the previous day's *Stuka* attack. On the far side of the city, the enemy had dug in again, however, and put up energetic resistance to *Kampfgruppe von Manteuffel.*

To the south of Woronesch, in the middle of a large wooded area, the enemy was holding rail and road bridges that led across Essanj Creek. *Major* Zimmermann's *II./Schützen-Regiment 3* was given the mission of taking both bridges. The 7th Company of the battalion, advancing on the right, reached the railway bridge around 1000 hours. It bogged down in the face of enemy fire. The 6th Company, attacking on the right, reached the road bridge with its lead platoon. Just as the first two vehicles were crossing the bridge, they were hit with well-aimed enemy machine-gun fire. The platoon leader, *Feldwebel* Moder, a Knight's Cross recipient, was wounded. One rifleman was killed. The Soviets, who were able to observe along the sandy and wide road through the woods, were able to stop every movement. Despite that, several men from the 10th Company attempted to clear enemy mines, but they were also forced to give up that effort in the face of the heavy fire. For the time being, the battalion made no progress.

By then, the division had established a strong screening ring around Woronesch. The *II./Panzer-Regiment 6* covered the southern and western edges of the city. The *1./Schützen-Regiment 3* and the *1./Pionier-Bataillon 39* were combined to form a special blocking group, to be employed wherever things were "hot." The *I./Schützen-Regiment 3* covered the flanks to the west and had to overcome energetic resistance, even after the *4. Panzer-Division*, which was moving from Ssobytsch in the direction of Klimschki, had passed by the enemy forces holding there. Supported by fighting vehicles from *Panzer-Regiment 35*, which just happened to run into the enemy in the rear, the resistance was finally broken and 350 prisoners taken in the process. To the east, the *III./Panzer-Regiment 6* screened the left flank of the division, which was growing ever longer.

Kampfgruppe von Manteuffel and *Kampfgruppe von Lewinski* moved out around 1300 hours from the rail station at Saruzkawo in an effort to finally break open the bottleneck between the lakes and take the bridge. The division had to get through that bottleneck, since the marshland on both sides of the lakes made it impossible to move with motorized vehicles. The Soviet command intended to hold that bottleneck, so that the avenue of advance to Krolewez was not lost. It was elements of the Soviet 23rd Police Division (GPU) that were positioned there. They did not allow themselves to be intimidated by either tanks or artillery.

Using all of their forces, *Oberstleutnant* Schmidt-Ott's *I./Panzer-Regiment 6* and *Major* Frank's *Panzerjäger-Abteilung 521* were able to force their way up to the second bridge. Since it was already destroyed and the enemy had good observation of the approach routes, the formations bogged down again. In contrast, the attack that afternoon by the *II./Schützen-Regiment 3* at Pissarewitschi picked up steam again, after Oberleutnant Tank's 6th Company established contact with *Oberleutnant* Mente's 7th Company. Patrols discovered another bridge right outside the village; it was also guarded by the enemy. A short way from there, however, was a wooden footbridge over the creek. Since the woods went all the way to the water, *Major* Zimmermann decided to have his battalion cross there. The lead platoon of *Leutnant* Scheffler (7th Company) encountered strong resistance almost immediately. The young officer and *Unteroffizier* Traue were mortally wounded. In the end, efforts to advance though the thick underbrush were likewise abandoned. In the middle of all that, the battalion commander received a report that a parallel track of the railway line had been discovered in the middle of the woods. It was not marked on any map. *Major* Zimmermann immediately sent the 7th Company and *Oberleutnant* von Becker's 8th Company in that direction.

Both companies reached the main track. By doing so, they found themselves approximately one kilometer behind the Russians, who were oriented to the east. The riflemen approached the railway bridge undetected. The battalion commander went forward, followed closely by his liaison officer, *Leutnant Freiherr* von Eckardstein, *Leutnant* Pauckstadt (8th Company), and *Feldwebel* Schneider (Signals Platoon). The Soviets were so surprised, they needed several minutes before they even reacted. By then, the 8th Company had tossed hand grenades at the enemy. At the same time, the battalion adjutant, *Leutnant* Brandt, had brought the 6th Company

forward, which started attacking from the flank. The railway bridge was taken. It was no longer possible to get to the road bridge, since darkness had descended.

The attack in the middle of the front had also not made any progress. The division requested *Stukas*. At 1815 hours, nine aircraft hurtled down with a howl on the enemy positions along the bottleneck and dropped their deadly cargoes. The enemy did not waver. When the riflemen and tanks felt their way forward, the received the same strong fire they had received previously. The attack could not be repeated during the night. The Red Air Force attacked Woronesch several times during the day, but it did not cause any noticeable damage. When it turned dark, the bombing raids were halted, only to be picked up against in the morning around 0500 hours.

Around 2300 hours, the corps order for the attack the next day arrived at the division command post, which was located north of Woronesch in the middle of a clover field. It required a continuation of the attack to the south. Move-out for the division was scheduled for first light on 2 September. The *I./Panzer-Regiment 6* pushed its way forward in the dense woods to the location of the *I./Schützen-Regiment 3*. In the process, the lead tanks of the 2nd Company ran over mines. The company was led by *Oberleutnant* Meyrhofer, who had distinguished himself during the campaign in the West. His predecessor, *Oberleutnant* Buchterkirch, had just left the division to assume a command in Germany.

The division reinforced the forces bogged down at the bottleneck in the course of the day. The *I./Schützen-Regiment 3* was pushed forward as far as the Essmanj. The engineers then went forward with flamethrowers and smoke pots and attached to *Oberst* von Manteuffel. The attack of the reinforced *Schützen-Regiment 3* finally started around 1400 hours, after almost all of the divisional artillery had placed an intense preparation on the enemy positions.

The riflemen attacked against a tough and wily opponent and against a marsh that was almost worse. The enemy's pockets of resistance had to be smoked out by the engineers. The 2nd Battalion of the rifle regiment succeeded in advancing through a gap in the front to the east and hitting the enemy from the rear. Fortunately, an armor patrol from the *III./Panzer-Regiment 6* had headed out at the same time in the same direction. The enemy pulled back.

Around 1845 hours, the bottleneck had been opened and a bridgehead established across the Essmanj. *Major* Wellmann's 1st Battalion immediately headed south with his 2nd Company on the right and his 3rd Company on the left. They combed through the woods on both sides of the road and shook hands with the tankers of the 3rd Battalion at the whistle stop at Andronikoff. The riflemen set up security.

The armored cars and the motorcycles of the reconnaissance battalion continued to move, reaching the area five kilometers north of Krolewez by evening. The platoons and companies had to set up an all-round defense for the night, since the woods were full of enemy. During the day, the division brought the 3rd Company of engineers and the bridging section forward to create a crossing point over the Essmanj.

During the night, the division reinforced *Kampfgruppe von Manteuffel*, which had been directed to move out against Krolewez on 3 September. The battle group consisted of *Schützen-Regiment 3*, the *I./Panzer-Regiment 6*, the *1./Panzerjäger-Abteilung 521*, the *II./Flak-Regiment 94*, and the *6./Flak-Regiment 11*. *Oberleutnant* von Zitzewitz's advance guard—consisting of a platoon of tanks, a platoon of antitank elements, a minesweeper section, the *1./Schützen-Regiment 3*, and two 10.5- and one 8.8-centimeter guns—moved out right at 0700 hours in the area around Andronikoff. The main body of the battle group followed closely behind, with Manteuffel's forces receiving additional reinforcement by the addition of *Oberstleutnant* Wöhlermann's 2nd Battalion of artillery.

Without encountering appreciable enemy resistance, the lead vehicles almost moved in a single bound as far as Podoloff, just outside Krolewez. Once again, there was a creek snaking its way across the avenue of advance— the Retj. *Major* Wellmann committed his 2nd Company against the intact railway bridge. The riflemen succeeded in taking the bridge, which had been prepared for demolition, and forming a bridgehead at Podoloff. The advance then stopped temporarily, because, unexpectedly, Russian tanks suddenly appeared on the southern outskirts of the village.

Wellmann shifted his battalion's forces to focus on that threat. Two of his companies succeeded in expanding the bridgehead to the south. At the same time, the main body of von Manteuffel's battle group had swung to the east and turned from there in the direction of Krolewez. The *I./Panzer-Regiment 6* was turned around noon and sent via Gruskoje toward Retik. It was intended for the tank companies to powerfully support the attack of the battle group from there. The bridges there were too weak to handle anything but *Panzer II's*, however. They crossed and supported the riflemen. The main body of the tank battalion remained in Retik.

Both battalions of *Schützen-Regiment 3* worked their way slowly to Krolewez from two sides, pushing the enemy back into the city. Despite the onset of darkness, the riflemen remained in contact with the enemy, even though the advance slowed down correspondingly. Both of the battalions linked up around 2330 hours in the locality.

To the rear of the battle group, the 3rd Company of engineers had arrived with the bridging section to restore the damaged bridge over the Retj in two spots. Since the open left flank of the division kept growing longer, *Kampfgruppe Audörsch* detached the 9th Company of the armor regiment, which was pushed forward to Andranikoff.

The division was blessed with good luck that day. In its sector, General Engineer Tschistoff, a recipient of the Order of Lenin, was captured. That high officer had been directed to establish defensive positions along the Dessna. He had been given wide-ranging powers and had a million workers at his disposal. He had just arrived from Moscow by train and had no idea that Nowgorod-Sewersk had been in German hands for a week. Another important prisoner that day was a captain from the operations section of the Russian XXXXV Corps, which was facing the division.

The constant rainfall transformed all of the routes into a sea of muck and demonstrated one more time how the power of nature could be dangerous for motorized formations. The armored regiment recommended to the division that its three battalions be consolidated into two, since its high losses in tanks had reduced its strength by half.

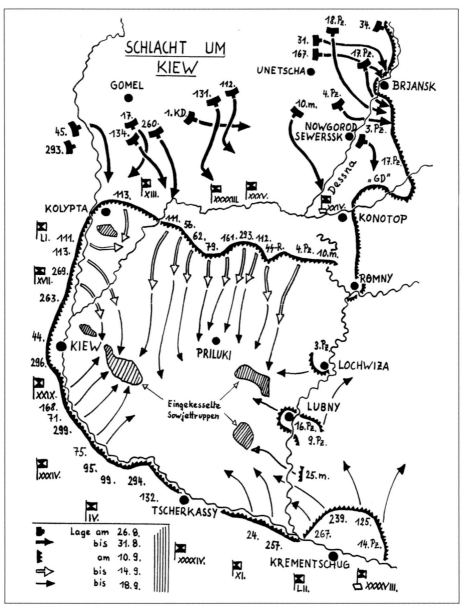

Battle for Kiev.

During the night, the *II./Schützen-Regiment 3* cleared Krolewez of stragglers and units that were still holding out. *Oberstleutnant* Schmidt-Ott's *I./Panzer-Regiment 6* left the city at 1200 hours. It had received the mission to reconnoiter as far as Sspaskoje and take the bridges over the Seim in a *coup de main*. The battalion was reinforced to that end by the attachment of the *1./Schützen-Regiment 3*, a platoon of engineers, and two artillery pieces, since its own forces—two *Panzer II's*, one *Panzer III*, and two *Panzer IV's*—were too weak to accomplish the mission on its own.

Schmidt-Ott's forces made good progress. They moved through Tscherepoff and then encountered a patch of woods right outside of Sspaskoje, which was thick with the enemy. Schmidt-Ott had his forces reorganize. While the tanks and the *SPW's* prepared, enemy artillery rounds slammed into their assembly area. A direct hit slammed into the company commander's tank of the 2nd Company. *Oberleutnant* Meyrhofer was killed instantly. A *SPW* also burned out.

The small battle group then approached the locality from the west, but it also encountered a strong defense there. A few captured Russian civilians reported that there were twenty fighting vehicles in Sspaskoje. When a patrol sent forward to the Seim determined that there was no bridge there, Schmidt-Ott called off the operation. His forces returned to Krolewez at 1900 hours.

The division had pulled its forces together, so that it could attack in concentrated form the next day. That afternoon, the *II./Panzer-Regiment 6* was pushed forward to the reconnaissance battalion at Matkowschtina, which had already been reinforced by three light fighting vehicles from the regimental headquarters. *Oberstleutnant* Munzel left the wheeled vehicles behind and pressed forward to the high ground 2.5 kilometers north of Mutino with his tanks. Unfortunately, darkness fell rapidly on the extremely cloudy day, so that the attack plan had to be abandoned.

Generalleutnant Model had his command post moved to the schoolhouse in Krolewez that afternoon. A short while later, the Red Air Force attacked the locality. A *Flak* was able to bring down one machine right over the schoolhouse. The pilot, who had bailed out, landed by parachute not too far from the command post. *Leutnant* von dem Knesebeck, the division intelligence officer, jumped on a motorcycle and raced out to the landing spot. The Russian attempted to escape, but he was shot at by the soldiers, who had responded, and killed. When his pockets were searched, important documents concerning the air defense facilities for Brjansk were discovered, as well as for the aerial defenses of Moscow. In addition, there was a situation map for the Soviet forces right in front of the division. That good catch was immediately reported to the corps and on to *Panzergruppe 2*. While examining the map, it was determined that the lead elements of the *3. Panzer-Division* were right on the boundary between the Soviet 13th and 21st Armies. *Generalleutnant* Model held a conference with his commanders that evening. He ordered the taking of Mutino the next day and the bridge over the Seim there.

Oberstleutnant Munzel's *II./Panzer-Regiment 6* and *Hauptmann* Ziervogel's *Aufklärungs-Abteilung 1*, supported by attached riflemen, antitank elements and artillery, moved out from their assembly areas up front right at 0600 hours. They took the high ground north of Mutino and pushed the enemy there down into the valley floor. The battle group then entered Mutino proper around 1300 hours. The *II./ Schützen-Regiment 3*, which had been augmented with the two *SPW* companies from the two rifle regiments, attacked the Russian positions with a loud *Hurra!* The riflemen took 244 prisoners. The battalion lost 12 men killed and 50 wounded. *Wachtmeister* Kirchgeorg, who led the attached guns from the 2nd Battery of artillery during the advance, was killed just outside of the locality. But as the tanks and the riflemen approached the river, they had to watch as the bridge flew into the air. The formations deployed along the river had to screen for the time being.

The *I./Schützen-Regiment 3* had employed *Hauptmann* Peschke's 3rd Company during the operation as a flank guard. It moved towards Sspaskoje, also with the intent of reaching the Seim. Just outside of the village, the riflemen received heavy fire from artillery and tanks, including some thirty-two-ton fighting vehicles.[6] It was unable to proceed. Since the Russians there even launched an immediate counterattack that afternoon, the motorcycle infantry battalion was quickly called forward. *Major* Pape then assumed command of the screening mission with his companies.

Since the river could not be crossed up to that point, the division ordered *Hauptmann* Schneider-Kostalski's *III./Panzer-Regiment 6* to attack Kamenj around 1200 hours. After a quick preparation along the edge of a defile, Kamenj was reached around 1530 hours. The 10th Company was even pushed forward as far as Morosowka. From Kamenj, the battalion's tanks took the enemy positions along the south bank of the Seim under fire. That afternoon, the enemy replied with heavy artillery and mortar fire.

The morning of 6 September saw rain once again. At 0900 hours, orders for the continued attack were issued. After no crossing points over the Seim could be won on the left wing and in the middle, the main effort shifted right. The bridges at Melnja were to be taken, while the *4. Panzer-Division* closed up and attacked Baturin.

Despite the softened routes, the division reorganized its forces that morning. Staging at the Tscherepoff whistle stop were the *II./Panzer-Regiment 6*, the *I./Schützen-Regiment 3*, and *Kradschützen-Bataillon 3*. They were earmarked to take Sspaskoje. The *I./Panzer-Regiment 6* and the *II./Schützen-Regiment 394* were to advance via Altinowka in the direction of Melnja. That battle group was followed in the second wave by the *III./Panzer-Regiment 6* and the *I./Schützen-Regiment 394*. The lefthand group reported to *Oberst* Kleemann, who also had the 2nd and 3rd Battalions of the divisional artillery in direct support. At exactly 1200 hours, the riflemen, tankers and motorcycle infantry moved out of the Tscherepoff area, after the two artillery battalions had placed strong preparatory fires in and around Sspaskoje.

Major Wellmann's 1st Battalion of rifles attacked the locality through a depression from the northeast. After a short, sharp fight, it was able to occupy the cemetery and take the first houses. *Oberstleutnant* Munzel's fighting vehicles were then brought forward. They pressed into the locality at the same time as the riflemen. Most of the enemy did not put up a defense. Instead, he pulled back to the south. The fighting vehicles pursued immediately.

In a short period, the tanks were able to knock out seven Russian fighting vehicles and an armored car. The 8th Company succeeded in taking out an enemy antiaircraft battery at Ljubitoff. *Major* Pape's motorcycle infantry had guarded the flank of the attacking battalions. In this he was aided by *Kampfgruppe Peschke*, which consisted of one platoon from the 3rd Company, two platoons from the 4th Company, and one platoon from the 2nd Company (all of *Schützen-Regiment 3*), as well as two antitank guns from *Panzerjäger-Abteilung 521*, one 8.8-centimeter *Flak*, and one rocket launcher. The latter forces were then rapidly committed in the direction of Ossaritschi to take the bridge over the Seim there. Just as the lead elements of the motorcycle infantry battalion reached the river, the bridge flew into the air. In addition, the last three operational tanks of the 8th Company were hit. The *7./Panzer-Regiment 6* was able to get farther, reaching the Melnja whistle stop, where it then set up an all-round defense, having expending its ammunition. The operations on the left wing of the division were successfully concluded by 1845 hours.

All of the designated objectives were also taken in the righthand attack sector. *Kampf-*

---

6. Probably T-34's.

gruppe von Lewinski had taken up its assembly areas by 1300 hours in the area between the road and the railway line not far from the Tscherepoff whistle stop. Shortly after 1300 hours, *Oberstleutnant* Schmidt-Ott's *I./Panzer-Regiment 6* and *Major* Dr. Müller's *II./Schützen-Regiment 394* commenced their attack.

The lead tanks and the 6th Company of the rifle regiment reached the village at 1500 hours and advanced all the way through to the southern edge. There were a lot of Russians hidden in the houses and the huts; they had to be driven out by the companies that followed. After an hour, Altinowka was clear of the enemy. When most of the formations had reassembled, the attack was continued.

The fighting vehicles in the lead encountered the first Soviet tanks shortly after leaving the village. They were crossing the line of advance from the east to the southwest. The enemy was driven back, after one vehicle went up in flames. The battle group pursued the withdrawing enemy. After covering two kilometers, more Soviet tanks were encountered. Those tanks had occupied good positions for defending. As the German companies moved out to attack, several enemy rifle companies attacked to the right of the road, not too far from the Ruda whistle stop.

Just as the fighting turned critical, the *12./Panzer-Regiment 6* arrived south of Ruda, since the armored regiment's 3rd Battalion was following the 1st battalion by then. It took the Russian tanks under fire at great distance. The enemy started to pull back. The Russian riflemen also started to flee. The German advance continued. But the enemy had set up defensive positions at the northern edge of Chrolynsky and offered a fight. While the *I./Panzer-Regiment 6* prepared to fight in the town, *Hauptmann* Schneider-Kostalski and his tank companies pulled a surprise and rolled past. The Russians pulled back west rapidly at that point.

When it turned dark, *Generalleutnant* Model appeared and issued orders to *Oberstleutnant* Audörsch to advance in the direction of Melnja with his battle group, which consisted of the

II./Schützen-Regiment 394, the engineer platoon of *Schützen-Regiment 394*, the *III./Panzer-Regiment 6*, a company from *Pionier-Bataillon 39*, antitank elements, and divisional artillery. He was to take the bridge over the Seim there. The advance was immediately resumed in complete darkness with the hope of reaching the river while it was still dark, since the dominant high ground on the far bank would make a daylight approach impossible. The forces only made slow progress, however, since every village was occupied by the enemy and had to be taken. Despite that, the river was reached around 2300 hours. When *Oberfeldwebel* Blaich of the *12./Panzer-Regiment 6* entered the village of Melnja in the lead tank, he received two direct hits from an antitank gun. The vehicle was no longer operational, and the senior noncommissioned officer was wounded. Nonetheless, the route was clear to the river.

Unfortunately, the riflemen of *Schützen-Regiment 394* were unable to take the bridge over the Seim in an undamaged condition. The bridge flew into the air in front of the eyes of the riflemen arriving from the lead company of the 2nd Battalion. *Oberstleutnant* Audörsch immediately made the decision to cross over the river to the far bank under the cover of darkness with the entire 2nd Battalion, using the inflatable craft from the regiment's engineer platoon (*Leutnant* Störck). Despite the heavy enemy fire, the action succeeded. To expand the bridgehead, the positions of the artillery, tanks and heavy weapons were determined during the course of the night. By then, at first light, the regiment's 1st Battalion had arrived from Woronesch. To expand the bridgehead, it also crossed over the river in inflatable craft, since the engineer company designated for the crossing had not yet arrived. It was given heavy fire support from the artillery, tanks, and *Flak*. As a result of the arrival of the 1st Battalion, the bridgehead could be expanded somewhat. A significant expansion was not possible, however, since the rifle regiment's positions were constantly under machine-gun fire and the Red Air Force was continuously in the

47

air, bombing the German forces. In order to expand his toehold and take the high ground, which the Russians still possessed, *Oberstleutnant* Audörsch requested air support through the division during the morning of 7 September. The sorties were promised at 1300 hours. As the German aircraft were closing in, *Generalleutnant* Model and *Oberst* Kleemann arrived at Audörsch's command post. With astounding precision, the bombers hit the Russian positions. The Russians wavered, and the riflemen stormed the key high ground. At that point, *Oberst* Kleemann assumed command of the forces in the bridgehead. Audörsch and his command post went forward into the bridgehead.

The division pushed *Major* Beigel's engineer battalion up to the crossing point quickly. The companies and the bridging section, which had moved forward through Altinowka, immediately started erecting a bridge. They built three sections, each with a sixteen-ton capacity. *Hauptmann* Kalkbrenner's men of the bridging section were constantly on the go and worked hard into the night.

The division reorganized over the next few hours for the continuation of the attack on 8 September. *Kampfgruppe Kleemann* consisted of *Schützen-Regiment 394*, the *1./Schützen-Regiment 3*, *Panzerjäger-Abteilung 521*, *Panzerjäger-Abteilung 543*, the *III./Panzer-Regiment 6*, *Kradschützen-Bataillon 3*, and the *6./Flak-Regiment 59*. The divisional artillery placed most of its batteries in the Melnja area and occupied firing positions under cover of darkness. *Kampfgruppe von Manteuffel* was directed to remain in its sector until a reinforced regiment from the *10. Infanterie-Division (mot.)* could relieve it. The *3./Artillerie-Regiment 75* and the *1./Panzerjäger-Abteilung 543*, which had been designated as a corps reserve, were returned to the division. *Generalleutnant* Model had his command post moved to the northeastern edge of Ksensowka. Model personally went forward with his liaison officers to Melnja, where he had a signals center set up.

Since only *Schützen-Regiment 394* was across the river at that point, the division designated the following order of priority for the crossing of the rest of its elements across the pontoon bridges: the *III./Panzer-Regiment 6*, with one company from *Panzerjäger-Abteilung 521*; the *II./Panzer-Regiment 6* and the remainder of *Panzerjäger-Abteilung 521*; the *1./Schützen-Regiment 3*; *Panzer-Regiment 35* (*4. Panzer-Division*); the *II./Artillerie-Regiment 75*; the *II./Artillerie-Regiment 42*;[7] the *III./Artillerie-Regiment 103* (*4. Panzer-Division*); the *III./Artillerie-Regiment 75*; and the combat vehicles of the formations involved. The engineers were able to bring off the completion of the bridges by 0400 hours, at least to the extent that they were for the most part usable.

Two hours later, the first tanks and *SPW's* crossed the bridge to reinforce *Kampfgruppe Audörsch*. The day slowly dawned. The riflemen and the vehicles had to bunch up in the bridgehead. The terrain was very flat and consisted primarily of meadowlands with practically no cover. From the southern end of the blown-up railway bridge, the enemy had good fields of observation into the sector, with the result that he took the pontoon bridges under constant artillery and mortar fire. At the southern edge of the meadowlands, the terrain rose to a 500-meter-long plateau that stretched to the large woods on the horizon. The sandy ridges on the northern end of the plateau offered the only concealed area for the assembly of the German forces. That spot was also under enemy fire, causing some casualties among the artillery. Ever since first light, the observation aircraft of the attached *9.(H)/ Lehrgeschwader 2* were in the air, radioing their reports to the *Luftwaffe* liaison officers below.

Then there was a sudden rushing sound in the air—it was exactly 1030 hours—*Stukas* were on their way in. They dove on the enemy positions and on the edge of the village right in front of the outposts. While the first group pulled back

---

7. A separate artillery battalion and regiment.

up, the men of the *I./Schützen-Regiment 394* emerged out of their holes and assaulted south of the railway bridge toward the enemy. They were closely followed by the fighting vehicles of the *III./Panzer-Regiment 6*. The armored regiment's 2nd Battalion and elements of *Panzerjäger-Abteilung 521* took the village in front of the positions and cleared it by 1100 hours of any enemy elements.

Oberstleutnant von Lewinski went back to the cliffs with his 2nd Battalion, the attached antitank elements and the mounted riflemen, where they then moved directly south in the direction of Werenki. They were closely followed by *Panzer-Regiment 35* of the *4. Panzer-Division*, which had also crossed by then. The continued crossing of the divisional elements was completed seamlessly in large measure to the exemplary traffic regulation provided by traffic control sections of the *I./Panzer-Regiment 6*.

Kampfgruppe von Lewinski was unable to proceed along the designated routes as a consequence of destroyed bridges; it was redirected to the east. The tanks and their mounted riflemen rattled along a deeply sandy route to the south along the rail line. Enemy forces were identified outside of Werenki. Provided strong covering fires, the tanks entered the village, scattered a truck convoy and ran into a battery that was changing positions. The battle group turned in the middle of the village to the southeast so as to take the high ground across from it. Unfortunately, the lead tank broke through a bridge when six heavy Russian tanks appeared on the high ground, moving perpendicular to the route of the German tanks. Before the enemy identified the approaching columns, the 7th Company had gone into position and opened fire, knocking out two tanks. At the same time, a light howitzer from *Oberleutnant* Weymann's 6th Battery unlimbered and a self-propelled gun of *Panzerjäger-Abteilung 521* also went into position. They each knocked out a tank. At that point, the Soviets pulled back. The battle group was unable to immediately proceed, however, since enemy forces also appeared to the southwest.

The regimental light platoon was immediately employed against those forces, stopping that attack. Two hundred prisoners were taken.

The flank guard for the attacking battle groups was provided by an *ad hoc* detachment that was formed for the purpose. Its mission was to reconnoiter in the direction of the rail line leading to Konotop. Artillery provided the necessary support, while the antitank elements, motorcycle infantry and engineers felt their way forward. Thanks to heavy machine-gun and antitank-gun fire, the enemy forced the detachment to take cover in a large cornfield. *Leutnant* Bürkner of *Panzerjäger-Abteilung 543* was killed. It was not until *Stukas* attacked that there was some relief. *Oberleutnant* Michels, the commander of the *3./Panzerjäger-Abteilung 543*, used the opportunity to have his antitank guns go into position. *Leutnant* Fischer's platoon successfully engaged the Russian trenches. The flank-guard detachment was able to complete its mission by the afternoon.

Around 1400 hours, *Kampfgruppe Audörsch* crossed the railway line. An hour later, it encountered strong enemy forces in a village that was not marked on the map. A hard struggle ensued with the Russian 777th Rifle Regiment, which was well equipped with antitank guns, thus preventing the German tanks from making a frontal assault.

Finally, the *II./Schützen-Regiment 394* was able to break the last resistance with the help of attached heavy weapons. The battalion captured one light and six heavy antiaircraft guns, four antitank guns, and ten heavy infantry guns; in addition, 200 prisoners were brought in. Among them were six uniformed girls ranging in age from fifteen to eighteen. As it started to turn dusk, the battle group set up an all-round defense in the woods two kilometers south of the rail line.

The *10./Panzer-Regiment 6* had to return to the Seim to support the crossing of the motorcycle infantry battalion over the destroyed railway bridge, starting at 1700 hours. The two battalions of *Schützen-Regiment 3* and the remaining battle groups of the division crossed the pontoon bridges in the course of the afternoon, with the result that the entire division, with the exception of the rear-area services, was across the Seim to the south.

After a cold night, where it was barely possible to still sleep in the open, a dreary day dawned. The division used the time to concentrate its forces better. *Schützen-Regiment 394* cleared Propowka. The remaining formations gradually assembled in the area around Werenki. That meant that most of the division's combat forces had shot past Konotop to the west. The large town was to be left to the *10. Infanterie-Division (mot.)*, which was still following. *Oberleutnant* Roever's 2nd Company of engineers took the airfield at Konotop, however, in a *coup de main*. Roever was wounded, and *Leutnant* Weigel assumed acting command. The company captured two aircraft and took seventeen prisoners.

The enemy attempted to attack the division from the east several times. *Kampfgruppe von Manteuffel*—the *I./Schützen-Regiment 3* and divisional troops—moved forward around 1200 hours. It was able to establish a bridgehead at Schepowalowka at 1400 hours. In the process, the 3rd Company of the rifle regiment blocked the bridges at Szarazorka and Gurewka.

The division formed a battle group under the command of *Major* Frank. Its mission was to advance as far as possible. In addition to Frank's *Panzerjäger-Abteilung 521*, the battle group heaviest combat forces consisted of the *8./Panzer-Regiment 6* and the light platoon of the same battalion. Frank and his men were able to advance as far as Korabutowo rapidly and cross the bridges there by evening. The enemy was completely surprised and needed some time to mount energetic countermeasures. The riflemen, tanks and antitank elements were able to hold off the attacks, however, and hold their bridgeheads until *Oberst* von Manteuffel's battle group with the *II./Schützen-Regiment 3* and the 2nd Battalion of divisional artillery arrived towards midnight, considerably reinforcing Frank's forces.

During the night, the division ordered the continued attack in the direction of Romny on 10 September. It was to cross the Ssula there. At that point, everyone knew what was so important about the advance—linking up with *Panzergruppe 1* coming from the south.

Around 0600 hours, the division moved out with all of its forces for the decisive thrust. Unfortunately, the skies were leaden and rain bordering on a downpour transformed all the roads and trails into muck. Many vehicles got stuck and had to be recovered by prime movers. A motorcycle was attached to each truck. It wasn't easy for the heavy trucks, either. They frequently sank to their axles in the mud. As a result, the march serials and columns were extended several times their normal length and soon the only thing that remained was a conglomerate of companies, platoons, troops, and batteries all intermingled. Despite that, the advance continued slowly forward.

The officers and men of Frank's advance guard, as well as *Aufklärungs-Abteilung 1*, *Panzerjäger-Abteilung 521*, the *II./Panzer-Regiment 6*, the *II./Schützen-Regiment 3*, the *1./Schützen-Regiment 394*, elements of *Pionier-Bataillon 39*, the *II./Artillerie-Regiment 75*, and a few *Flak* all churned their way through the mud. Toward noon, the houses of Romny appeared on the northeast edge of a ridgeline that jutted out of the valley like an island.

Major Frank raced toward the first bridge with the *3./Panzerjäger-Abteilung 521*, the *3./Pionier-Bataillon 39*, a company of riflemen, and a battery. The Soviets, who had secured the deep cut of the Romen River by tank ditches and wire obstacles, were so surprised by the sudden appearance of the Germans that they initially did not offer a defense. The lead vehicles of the division used the opportunity and did not get held up by the whistling rounds. They assaulted and took the bridge over the Bolschj-Romen and then immediately entered Romney from the northwest. They did not stop there. They continued through the city as far as the bridge over the Ssula at the far end. *Oberleutnant* Lingk, the commander of the *3./Panzerjäger-Abteilung 521*, was the first to reach the banks. Without regard for the consequences, he drove straight through the completely surprised Russians and did not stop until he knew he was on the other side of the bridge. *Leutnant* Schultze and *Leutnant* Seefeld, both from the engineer battalion, followed closely behind. The bridge fell intact into the hands of the battle group.

It was at that point that the enemy finally awakened from his surprise. There were skirmishes and tough resistance throughout the city, which had white houses and clean cobblestone streets.

Oberstleutnant Munzel's *II./Panzer-Regiment 6*, with the attached *1./Schützen-Regiment 394*, entered the city from the west and took over guarding the bridge. A freight train full of foodstuffs and clothing was captured at the rail facilities. The fighting in the city continued at an unrelenting pace. The only palpable signs of relief occurred when *Oberst* Kleemann's battle group arrived in Romny around 1700 hours. The progress of the clearing could be measured by the houses going up in flames. *Oberst* Kleemann commanded the forces in the northern part of the city; *Oberst* von Manteuffel in the south. In addition, the Red Air Force constantly attacked the lead elements of the division form the air. Despite the bad weather, the fighter-bombers constantly raced in, dropping bombs or strafing the German forces. The *Flak* were barely able to fire, since the Soviets used the cover offered by the city on the hill by flying in low and only pulling up at the last moment to then dive on the forces that had closed up to the gardens of the northern outskirts. By evening, no less than twenty-five aerial attacks had been counted. When it turned night, Romny was burning like a single torch. The 3rd Company of the divisional engineers blew up the railway tracks west of the city. The fighting was over. But the forces, overexerted and drenched to the bone, were unable to enjoy the victory. They were simply too tired.

It rained the entire night without stopping. The movement of the vehicles, which had been headed toward Romny since midday, could barely be continued. Everything was sinking in the mud. The drivers of the supply elements were the ones to be admired. With the greatest of efforts, they managed to bring supplies forward to the fighting forces. The ammunition situation was bearable. The fuel situation, on the other hand, precarious. That was also understandable when one considered the conditions of the roads and the distance to the closest rail transfer point (400 kilometers). The corps needed 1,000 tons of supplies a day. Up to this point in the campaign, every truck in the fuel sections had covered an average of 170 kilometers a day.

On 11 September, the division did not advance any further. Instead, it screened in the area it had won around Romny. With the limited number of forces available, the screening could only take place at key areas and along the roads leading into the city. Although the rain had let up, the roads were so softened that the forces in Romny were practically cut off from their rearward lines of communications. The bare minimum of fuel was brought forward on prime movers.

The outposts were extended to the south and southwest. On the high ground south of the Ssula, there were enemy field positions with bunkers and tank ditches. As a result of the rapid advance of *Major* Frank's forces, the enemy had not had time to occupy the positions. When the southern part of the city was cleared in the morning, numerous Soviet stockpiles were discovered. Four cubic meters of fuel were tracked down, as was a store of vodka and beer.

On that day as well as the next, there was no serious contact with the enemy in front of the outpost lines. There was only patrol activity on both sides in the sectors to the front. Around the city, the forty-seven oilrigs that rose up were a sign of the recently tapped oil reserves in this area. While retreating, the Soviets set thirty-six of them on fire.

The commander in chief of the field army group, *Generalfeldmarschall* von Bock, congratulated the division by radio on the capture of Romny.

The weather did not improve much. The skies were overcast, and the clouds only occasionally cleared away to allow the sun to shine. Since the rain had abated, sufficient vehicles with fuel, ammunition and rations made it forward, with the result that the combat power of the forces there increased by the hour. By the evening of 12 September, *Major* Frank was placed in charge of the advance guard to keep on the heels of the fleeing Soviets. The advance guard consisted of Frank's headquarters and 3rd Company, the *1./Schützen-Regiment 3* (which was commanded by *Leutnant* Lohse at this point), the *1./Aufklärungs-Abteilung 1*, the *6./Artillerie-Regiment 6*, two *Panzer II's* from the *II./Panzer-Regiment 6*, two light *Flak*, and a platoon from the *3./Pionier-Bataillon 39*.

The advance guard moved out from Romny prior to last light. It overran the weak Russian positions in its first attempt and bounded 45 kilometers to the south. At 2115 hours, the advance guard had reached the intact bridge over the Ssula at Mliny, across from Lochwiza. Its capture meant the retreat route for the Soviets across the Ssula had been blocked. For his deed, *Oberleutnant* Lingk, the commander of the *3./Panzerjäger-Abteilung 521*, was later inducted into the army's Honor Roll. *Leutnant* Möllhoff advanced as far as the "Stalin" rail station with his engineers, where his men shot up ten trucks. After the enemy realized the situation he was in, he did everything in his power to drive the weak German forces from the bridgehead. During the night, he remained relatively quiet, but his efforts increased in magnitude at daybreak. *Major* Frank felt compelled to radio requests for immediate support from the division.

The division put together a battle group during the morning, which was directed to relieve Frank's forces and also advance into Lochwiza. *Oberstleutnant* von Lewinski was placed in charge of the battle group, which consisted of the *III./Panzer-Regiment 6* (augmented by three *Panzer II's* from the 2nd Battalion), the *1./Panzerjäger-Abteilung 521*, the *1./Schützen-Regiment 394*, the *2. and 3./Schützen-Regiment 3*, the

4./Artillerie-Regiment 75, the *3./Pionier-Bataillon 39*, and a quad *Flak* from the *6./Flak-Regiment 59*. Around 1300 hours, a reconnaissance aircraft reported that a large armored force was approaching the advance guard. The battle group picked up its pace. The roads had dried out, so it was possible to advance rapidly. As the von Lewinski's lead vehicles approached Mliny, *Stukas* were diving on the approaching enemy armored formations. Around 1600 hours, the tanks and the *SPW's* rolled into Mliny, establishing contact with the advance guard.

Oberstleutnant von Lewinski and *Major* Frank met at the church in the village. After a short conversation, the men came to the conclusion not to wait for the more slowly moving riflemen and cannoneers. Instead, they wanted to advance into Lochwiza as soon as possible with the forces on hand. The company commanders were informed and, a short while later, the tank companies, the antitank elements and the two *SPW* companies were ready to roll. Without regard for the Russian fires that suddenly started increasing, the tankers, antitank men, and riflemen raced along the embankment that was several hundred meters long and reached all three of the bridges over the Ssula south of Mliny before the enemy recognized the threat. The men captured the bridges intact.

At that point, the Russians took the bridgeheads under heavy fire from Lochwiza, some 1,600 meters away. The fire from the heavy anti-aircraft guns was especially dangerous. By increasing intervals and varying speeds, casualties were avoided. The enemy guns took every individual vehicle under fire, but they were unable to prevent the men from crossing the bridges over to the jagged south bank of the river.

The terrain on the far side offered concealment for all of the vehicles. Because of the pace, however, the companies were all intermingled. The officers soon restored some order and the advance continued. The closer the force got to Lochwiza, the more defensive fire it received. The German tanks halted, fired, and then moved on. They received good covering fires from the self-propelled guns of the two antitank companies. The companies worked their way to the city meter by meter. The eastern portion of Lochwiza was reached around 1700 hours. The enemy did not waver; instead, he put up hard resistance against the advancing vehicles. Machine guns hammered away from all sides and the dull thud of mortars firing could be heard. But the German guns replied in kind. After half an hour, that portion of the city had been cleared.

Just as the enemy started to pull back, the *I./Schützen-Regiment 3* arrived. The riflemen received the mission to clear the houses of enemy groups. The Russians were holding out in the rest of the city and had also brought antitank, antiaircraft, and infantry guns forward. The German forces were unable to get across the intersection in the middle of the city. The enemy was firing from pointblank range against the approaching tanks and *SPW's*. Since it had turned dark by then, no one knew where the front or rear was or what was happening to the right or left.

Around 1900 hours, *Oberstleutnant* von Lewinski pulled his fighting vehicles out of Lochwiza and had them occupy screening positions in the defiles along the city's edge. Only *Major* Wellmann's riflemen remained in contact with the enemy. Over the next few hours, they had to defend against strong attacks, but they were able to hold the portions of the city they had already taken.

Far to the rear of those battle groups, the division concentrated its forces in the Romny area. The *II./Panzer-Regiment 6* was given the mission of screening the division's staging area. In carrying out that mission, *Leutnant* Rühl reconnoitered in the direction of Gawrilonka early in the morning with three *Panzer III's* and three *SPW's*. Reconnaissance aircraft had identified enemy tanks there. There was no enemy contact, so that the engineers who had come along were able to emplace a hasty minefield without any interruption, thus helping to pre-

vent any unwanted surprises around Romny from that direction.

The new day, 14 September, brought a clear morning and sunny weather. The banks of fog from the Ssula were still over Lochwiza, when the fighting started anew. *Major* Wellmann was unable to grant his riflemen a whole lot of time to sleep; he had been directed to clear the entire city on that day. Both of his companies and the fighting vehicles attached to him from the *III./Panzer-Regiment 6* moved out at first light around 0500 hours to attack the identified Russian pockets of resistance. What they had been unable to accomplish the previous day was accomplished that day. The *3./Schützen-Regiment 3* of *Hauptmann* Peschke assaulted surprisingly fast through the city and took the large northern bridge in a *coup de main*. To the amazement of the German soldiers, there were six heavy antiaircraft guns in front of the bridge, wheel-to-wheel across the entire width of the street. They were unmanned. The riflemen charged the guns with a *Hurra!* and pulled the crews that were still sleeping out from under their blankets. As quickly as that action was completed, Lochwiza was also cleared that morning, which had turned into a beautifully sunny day. The fighting vehicles of the 3rd Battalion were able to enter the city without incident around 1030 hours.

The *I./Schützen-Regiment 3* advanced across the bridge and occupied the high ground outside of Jaschniki, to the north of Lochwiza, with its 3rd Company. The 2nd Company set up on the high ground at Charjkowzi west of the city. The remaining elements of the advance guard spread out to all sides to hold open Lochwiza for *Kampfgruppe Kleemann*, which was closing on the city. It entered the locality around 1020 hours with the *II./Panzer-Regiment 6* and the *II./Schützen-Regiment 3*.

At the same time, the division ordered *Panzer-Regiment 6* to form a strong combat patrol, which was to immediately advance to the south to establish contact with the *16. Panzer-Division*, which had taken Lubny the previous day. *Oberleutnant* Warthmann, the commander of the *9./Panzer-Regiment 6*, was given the mission. Only a single fighting vehicle, a *Panzer III*, was available. Functioning as the communications center was the regimental commander's tank and a few personnel carriers. The necessary fuel had to be taken from wheeled vehicles, since the supply columns had not yet closed on the city. The patrol consisted of a total of forty-five men, including the two *Oberleutnants*, Warthmann and Müller-Hauff (commander of the *3./Panzer-Regiment 6*), and the war correspondent, Heysing, who experienced everything from the commander's tank. At that point, a short episode started in the history of the division which exemplified the boldness of the German armored arm in that summer of 1941. The action that was initiated led to the closing of one of the greatest pocket battles in history.

The small battle group started its march at the designated time. *Oberleutnant* Müller-Hauff took the lead. The weather was sunny and clear; the roads were firm and showed only a few spots of clinging mud. On top of that, it was Sunday— perfect "riding weather" or, in this case, "tank weather." The tanks and personnel carriers soon left behind the forwardmost outposts of Frank's advance guard at Iskowzy-Ssentschanskije and had the slightly rolling Ukrainian countryside in front of them. The enemy was somewhere, but no one knew his strength or his weaponry. Contact with the division could only be maintained by radio.

The first village appeared after moving for three hours. It was bypassed on the right. A Russian transport column was on the road. When the German vehicles approached, the drivers abandoned their *panje* carts and fled into the nearby sunflower fields. When some high ground was crossed, enemy trucks were crossing the road. Once again, the machine guns did the talking. And so *Lützows wilde, verwegene Jagd*[8] continued. Once again, Soviets appeared. This time it was a gigantic column consisting of bat-

teries, trains elements, construction battalions, limbers, *panje* carts, tractors, two fighting vehicles, and some Cossacks on horseback. The machine guns whistled again and shot a route through the Russian column. The tanks and other vehicles raced through the stream of vehicles at high speed.

Oberleutnant Warthmann and his men knew only one thing: Get through! And so the vehicles rolled through defiles, marshy flood plains, woods and fields and across several fragile bridges. The column crossed the Ssula in the vicinity of Titschi—that was half the way. All of a sudden, radio contact was lost with the division. The friendly vehicles were in a defile. Once they worked their way out again, the radio contact could be reestablished. In the rear, at Romny, *Generalleutnant* Model and *Major i.G.* Pomtow breathed an audible sigh of relief when they heard: "As far as Luka at 1602 hours."

The sun had already gone down, a reddish gold. Finally, however, the battle group was able to halt on a plateau and conceal its vehicles under piles of grain. The men gazed over to the silhouette of a city though binoculars, which was still offset from the evening sky. Haze and clouds of smoke crossed over the houses; in between was the whistling of machine guns and the crash of impacting artillery. There was no longer any doubt: The patrol was right behind the Russian front and a few kilometers further on were the lead elements of *Heeresgruppe Süd*!

Oberleutnant Warthmann issued orders: "*Panzer—Marsch!*" The battle group rolled out, crossed a defile, and fired at the Russians suddenly appearing out of the darkness, who scattered in shock. A creek blocked further progress. The vehicles looked for a crossing point. A bridge was seen. The *Panzer III* of the *Oberleutnant* approached. It was blown up. Gray figures sprang up. They were encrusted in dirt and had stubble beards. They waved and waved. It was

---

8. "Lützow's wild, daring hunt," a popular military song. Lützow was the stuff of German military legend in his various exploits against Napoleon.

men of the *2./Pionier-Bataillon 16* of the *16. Panzer-Division*. It was exactly 1820 hours.

The soldiers directed the battle group to a fordable location. *Oberleutnant* Warthmann crossed in his vehicle and turned toward Lubny. A short while later, he reported to *Generalmajor* Hube.[9] The fighting vehicles of the *3. Panzer-Division* with the large "G" (Guderian) on their steel walls were next to a tank with the letter "K" (von Kleist). The lead elements of the two field army groups had established contact. The Kiev Pocket was closed.

The *3. Panzer-Division* brought more of its forces closer to Lochwiza during the course of the day, since it appeared certain that the Soviets would attempt to break out of the encirclement to the east. The city was surrounded by strong enemy forces to all sides. In order to create some breathing space to the north, the divisional engineers launched an attack on Luka to blow up the bridge over the Ssula there. The effort had to be called off early in the face of the considerable enemy forces present. In contrast, the *II./Panzer-Regiment 6* had more success that afternoon when it conducted a reconnaissance-in-force in the direction of Stepali. The fighting vehicles encountered superior numbers of Russian tanks, but they were able to knock out three, as well as an armored car, while losing only one of their own. The *3./Schützen-Regiment 3*, which had been following behind, then screened the tank battalion from the high ground to the front.

The division continued to close up in the area around Lochwiza on 15 September. *Generalleutnant* Model had his command post set up in a large private house in Lochwiza. That day, additional propaganda company personnel from *Heeresgruppe Mitte* arrived to capture the historical event—the linking up of the lead elements of two field armies—in words and pictures. Included among them were Bastanier, a cameraman, who filmed for the weekly newsreel; Habedank, a photographer from the period-ical *Die Wehrmacht*; and Fritz Lucke, a reporter for the *Berliner Lokalanzeiger*. *Major Baron* von Behr, the commander of *Nachrichten-Abteilung 39*, was designated at the local area military administrative commander for Lochwiza; *Fürst*[10] Mirski was his translator. In addition to all of his military and administrative duties, Major von Behr set up a restaurant, where the soldiers could eat for free. According to an extant menu, the following was already being served on 15 September: white cabbage soup with goulash and sliced tomatoes, stewed fruit, and cake.

Major Frank screened the city to the southeast with his antitank elements and additional forces of his battle group. He had established his command post in Iskowzy-Ssentschanskija. The antitank personnel and the riflemen had to be on their toes, since Russian forces continuously tried to break in from the north and west. When one of those groups was caught, it contained the assistant senior medical officer of the Soviet 21st Army. Just before noon, dust clouds appeared to the east, which were being churned up by tanks. The antitank elements were already taking aim when the white signal flares hissed skyward. The riflemen of the *1./Schützen-Regiment 394* that were in position got up and ran toward the approaching tanks. They were the lead vehicles of *Panzer-Regiment 33* of the Austrian *9. Panzer-Division* (*Generalleutnant Ritter* von Hubicki). That division had taken the bridges over the Ssula at Ssentscha that morning at 0745 hours. When the young tank *Oberleutnant* reported to *Major* Frank, it meant that the pocket around Kiev was closed once and for all.

Oberst von Manteuffel's *Schützen-Regiment 3* had extended its outposts to the north and east by then. The regiment's 2nd Company took the bridge at Jaschiki. The friendly positions were then extended further northwest. *Schützen-Regiment 394* closed up to Lochwiza, inserting itself between divisional elements and the *4. Panzer-Division*, which was advancing on Priluki.

---

9. The commander of the *16. Panzer-Division*.
10. Count.

Hauptmann Ziervogel's reconnaissance battalion pushed the enemy back to the eastern edge of Tschernuchi. The Russians then pulled back and attempted to break out in the direction of Shdany. The division sent the available companies of *Major* Pape's motorcycle infantry battalion there. They were able to interdict the enemy forces. When *Hauptmann* Schneider-Kostalski's *III./Panzer-Regiment 6* joined the fray around 1300 hours, the enemy pulled back to Melechi.

Small reconnaissance and combat patrols from all of the employed divisional assets were sent out to all points of the compass that day to follow the enemy movements and protect the division from unwelcome surprises. In the process, *Oberfeldwebel* Kretschmar, the company headquarters section leader in the *1./Schützen-Regiment 3*, together with *Unteroffizier* Baudein's squad, linked up with *Aufklärungs-Abteilung 16* of the *16. Panzer-Division*, thus established the third firm lash-up of German forces on the eastern edge of the giant Kiev Pocket.

The night remained relatively quiet, even though more fires could be seen to the west. Around 0500 hours on 16 September, the Soviet 169th Rifle Regiment attacked in the area around Romny and pushed back the outposts guarding there. *Hauptmann* Schneider-Kostalski gathered his tanks and moved out against the Russians. The Russians fell back and the tankers pursued. That morning, they were able to occupy Melechi, with the motorcycle infantry battalion assuming the screening mission there. The *10./Panzer-Regiment 6* then had to be sent north to help the reconnaissance battalion, which was being attacked by superior enemy forces.

The rifle brigade conducted a reconnaissance-in-force to the west with both of its regiments. In doing so, *Schützen-Regiment 3* established contact with the *4. Panzer-Division*, which neighbored on the right. *Schützen-Regiment 394* remained in the area east of Pirjatin. The number of prisoners grew by the hour. Many Russians voluntarily surrendered, others only after a hard fight. The *I./Panzer-Regiment 6* established a prisoner collection point in Lochwiza. In the morning, it had 400 prisoners; by evening, the number had grown to 2,000.

The countryside was beautiful. High plateaus with woods and corn and sunflower fields were crossed. The objective on 17 September was the Udaj River. The 2nd Battalion of the armor regiment supported the advance of *Schützen-Regiment 3* against Belozerkowka and Antonowka. Both of the villages were reached in the afternoon, and outposts were established along the river. That night, the division called off any further attacks on Pirjatin. Aerial reconnaissance reported that strong enemy forces were concentrating on the west banks of the Udaj. Approximately 1,500 vehicles could be counted in the city proper. Friendly forces were insufficient to eject the enemy. Correspondingly, the outposts along the river reported the constant movements of the Soviets. They only way to significantly disrupt them was through the batteries of the divisional artillery, which had been brought forward.

Since the division's forces were still too weak to attack the Soviets at Pirjatin, the armor regiment was sent to *Infanterie-Regiment (mot.) 119*[11] to attack with it from the south. Both regiments moved out early in the afternoon with elements facing to three sides. By the onset of darkness, they succeeded in clearing the woods on both sides of Tschapatowka. In the process, numerous enemy truck columns were destroyed, including many headquarters vehicles.

During the night of 19–20 September, strong enemy elements broke through the *25. Infanterie-Division (mot.)* and attempted to escape through Melechi to the northeast. The threat to the southern flank of the *3. Panzer-Division* that resulted from that breakthrough needed to be eliminated. Major Frank and his antitank battalion, augmented by elements of the motorcycle infantry battalion, were committed. Those forces

---

11. One of the motorized infantry regiments of the *25. Infanterie-Division (mot.)*.

encountered the enemy at Welitschkowschts-china; the enemy forces were attacking to the northeast. *Oberstleutnant* Munzel's *II./Panzer-Regiment 6* was called in. His tanks advanced through the enemy and established contact with elements from the *9. Panzer-Division* one kilometer to the northeast of Melechi. The Soviets were able to escape encirclement, however, and pulled back in the direction of Shdany. The *III./Panzer-Regiment 6*, along with the rest of the motorcycle infantry battalion, advanced along both sides of the Juskowzy–Melechi road toward Hill 160. They drove the Soviets out and forced them in the direction of Drjukow-schtschina and into the woods and defiles. The *I./Panzer-Regiment 33* of the *9. Panzer-Division* joined the divisional elements in the effort.

Hauptmann von Cochenhausen's *1./Krad-schützen-Bataillon 3* and *Oberleutnant* Lingk's *3./Panzerjäger-Abteilung 521* attacked Drjukow-schtschina from the front. Despite considerable resistance, it was possible to enter the village, eject the Russians, capture two guns and six armored cars and take a number of prisoners. After the motorcycle infantry took a closer look at the Red Army men, they found out that they had captured the artillery commander of the 5th Army, Major General Ssetinski, along with his headquarters.

Most of the enemy forces were hiding in the two patches of woods and could not be driven out that evening. *Oberstleutnant* Wöhlermann's *II./Artillerie-Regiment 75* placed fires on the woods. At first light, *Hauptmann* Schneider-Kostalski's *III./Panzer-Regiment 6* and *Major* Pape's *Kradschützen-Bataillon 3* attacked the woods, while *Panzerjäger-Abteilung 521* and the *II./Panzer-Regiment 6* sealed off the area.

After five hours of struggling against stubborn resistance, the Russian defenses collapsed. The Soviets took considerable casualties. Fortunately, the German losses were negligible, although *Hauptmann* Schneider-Kostalski was wounded in the fighting. The motorcycle infantry of *Hauptmann* von Cochenhausen made a spectacular catch. When the soldiers searched

the final portions of the woods for soldiers, who were hiding, a youngish, immaculately dressed officer came out of a hole in the ground. There were gold stars and two small gold-colored tin tanks on his collar tabs. It was the commander in chief of the Soviet 5th Army, Colonel General Potapow.

By noon on 27 September, the special mission for *Oberstleutnant* Lewinski and his forces was over. The *25. Infanterie-Division (mot.)* was no longer being threatened, and the enemy had been eliminated. The captured senior officers were immediately transported to Giljzy, where the division command post had been located since 18 September. The daily logs of the intelligence section recorded the interrogations of the Russian officers in the following sequence: artillery commander of the 5th Army; quartermaster general; signals lieutenant with his wife; two Slovakian spies; commander in chief of the 5th Army; adjutant; commander of the 10th Tank Division; Red Air Force major general with daughter; commander of a rifle regiment; artillery commander of the 193rd Rifle Division; the commissars of the 9th Tank Brigade and the II Tank Corps; and others.

The fighting along the western half of the Kiev front came to an end, after German forces had thrust deep into the pocket from all sides. It was a unique and difficult fight that the forces had undergone. The Russians had attempted with all means at their disposal to escape encirclement. In some instances, the forces of the division had to fight their way out of a "hedgehog" position to withstand the pressure the Russians were exerting on all sides.

The regimental surgeon for *Schützen-Regiment 394*, *Assistenzarzt* Dr. Türk, recorded the following in his diaries: "It was a scene of horror. Human and horse remains between vehicles and equipment of all types. There was a maintenance vehicle with electric lathes, drills etc. I had never seen anything like it before. Medical vehicles with instruments . . . heavy antiaircraft guns, cannon, howitzers, tanks, trucks, staff cars. Some stuck in marshland;

some driven up in front of houses and trees, crashed down embankments, crashed into one another or burned up."

The Russian Southwest Front had ceased to exist. Among the dead were its commander in chief, Colonel General Kirponos; a member of the council of war, Burmistrenko; and the chief of staff of the 5th Army, Major General Pisarewski. The number of prisoners was immeasurable. From 18 to 22 September, *Schützen-Regiment 394* counted around 9,000 men. *Oberleutnant* Dr. Lotze's 2nd Company alone counted 2,100. During the same period, the *I./Schützen-Regiment 3* registered 1,345 prisoners. In all, the *3. Panzer-Division* counted 18,000, while the *XXIV. Armee-Korps (mot.)* had 31,000. The division had to clear its prisoner collection point in Lochwiza to make room for new arrivals. On 21 September, the *2./Schützen-Regiment 3* was detailed to escort 8,000 prisoners to Romny.

Panzergruppe 2 ordered the armored regiments to be pulled out of the line on 20 September so as not to wear them down in woodland fighting and to allow them to rest and refit. On 22 September, the division's armored regiment, along with the attached *Panzerjäger-Abteilung 521* and the *3./Pionier-Bataillon 39*, left Lochwiza. That same day, it reached Talalaler, 50 kilometers distant. A detail under the command of *Oberleutnant* Scheffler was sent to Gomel to pick up 35 new fighting vehicles. On 22 and 23 September, *Schützen-Regiment 3*, the divisional artillery and most of the remaining divisional troops disengaged from the enemy. Only *Schützen-Regiment 394* remained in the area around Lochwiza (until 24 September). The division turned around and headed back north, generally along the same routes it had taken on its advance south. Most of the division arrived in its new assembly area around Gluchow–Krolewez on 24 September.

The Pocket Battle of Kiev was over. It would go down in the history books as the largest battle of its type in the Second World War. The final report issued by the Armed Forces High Command on 27 September listed 665,000 prisoners, 884 captured or destroyed tanks, and 3,718 destroyed artillery pieces.

As a result of its bold raid through Nowgorod-Sewersk and on to Lochwiza, the *3. Panzer-Division* contributed greatly to the formation of the pocket and a proud success. The campaign had started three months previously. In that period, the division had lost 264 officers and 4,111 noncommissioned officers and enlisted personnel. That was 27 percent of its assigned strength on 22 June 1941. On 22 September, the division submitted a report on the results of its three months of uninterrupted combat: "Prisoners: 43,381. Captured or destroyed materiel: 408 tanks; 56 armored cars; 738 guns; 140 antiaircraft guns; 515 antitank guns; 265 mortars; 1,137 machine guns; 2,825 trucks; 102 staff cars; 20 motorcycles; 158 tractors; 89 destroyed, 96 shot-down and 64 captured aircraft; 1 armored trolley; 7 passenger, 25 fuel and 438 freight cars; 18 locomotives; 4 trains, etc."

The advance continues without rest. Every short halt was used to catch "forty winks."

Leutnant Reinders leads his platoon from *Schützen-Regiment 394* in preparation for an immediate counterattack at Ssidorowitschi, east of the Dnjepr.

Riflemen mount up on tanks in preparation for the attack along the Oster on 1 August 1941.

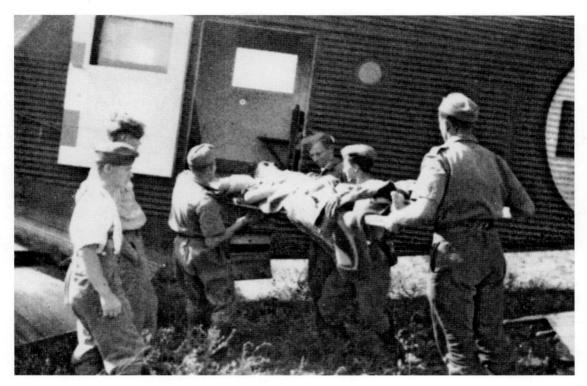

Badly wounded personnel were air transported to the homeland.

The observation post of the *6./Artillerie-Regiment 75* along the Oster. The artillery fire is helping to support the advance.

The division staff in the summer of 1941. From left to right: *Hauptmann i.G.* Barth, division logistics officer; *Generalleutnant* Model; *Major i.G.* Pomtow, division operations officer; *Major* von Oppen, division adjutant (officer personnel); and *Oberleutnant* von dem Knesebeck, division intelligence officer.

The division's bakery company at work.

Oberstleutnant Audörsch, the commander of *Schützen-Regiment 394* (seen here as a *Generalmajor*).

Oberst Ries, the commander of *Artillerie-Regiment 75*. He was killed in action on 26 August 1941.

The "Berlin Bear," the mascot of the division, in front of the division command post in Orel.

The weapons and equipment section at rest.

A cow is butchered for rations.

CHAPTER 11

From the Ssula to the Upa: The Advance on Moscow

On 26 September 1941, *Heeresgruppe Mitte* issued an operations plan for the continuation of the offensive. Its contents, inasmuch as they regarded the forces of *Panzergruppe 2*, contained the following:

> *Panzergruppe 2* advances—most likely two days before the [other] field armies move out—across a line running Orel–Brjansk. The right wing is to move along the Swop and Oka River lines. Its left wing rolls up the Dessna from the south and holds the enemy in the southeast Dessna bend, in conjunction with the *2. Armee*. The city and industrial areas of Brjansk are to be cut off initially by a mobile force and then taken later by the *XXXV. Armee-Korps* in conjunction with the *Luftwaffe*.

The plan established the date for the start of operations for the field army group as 2 October. Guderian requested his forces start two days earlier so as to receive the bulk of the initial support from the *Luftwaffe*.

The *XXIV. Armee-Korps (mot.)*, to which the division continued to be attached, was put in the main effort outside of Gluchow. The formations of the division, which had pulled out of the line in the Lochwiza–Pirjatin area, occupied bivouac and battlefield reconstitution areas around Krowelez. Although there were only a few days available, they were used to rebuild as much as possible. The division headquarters was located in Krowelez.

Since its quartering area was constantly being subjected to Soviet air attack, the battle staff moved to Pogrebki on 26 September. The terrain in the area was beautiful; less exciting, however, was the fact that there were already signs of lively partisan activity. During the day, however, the area was spared the appearance of that attendant phenomenon. The regimental and divisional bands played in the village marketplaces and the chaplains held services. Replacements came from the homeland and had to get quickly integrated into the framework of the forces.

It was intended to reorganize the armored regiment after its receipt of new tanks. Once received, the regiment would again have three full line battalions. The regiment's organization on 27 September: Each battalion had a headquarters and headquarters company; a light company consisting of approximately seventeen *Panzer III's* and two *Panzer II's*; a medium company consisting of approximately five to seven *Panzer IV's* and two to three *Panzer II's*; and a company attached from *Panzerjäger-Abteilung 521*. The battalion headquarters of the antitank battalion remained intact to process personnel and administrative matters, while the commander, *Major* Frank, assumed acting command of the *I./Panzer-Regiment 6* for *Oberstleutnant* Schmidt-Ott, who was on leave. To be able to engage heavy tanks, the armored regiment had the *5./Artillerie-Regiment 75* and a battery of 8.8-centimeter *Flak* from the *II./Flak-Regiment 11* attached to it, with each tank battalion receiving one light field howitzer and one 8.8-centimeter *Flak*. The attachment of the individual guns later proved to be ineffective. Given the poor weather conditions of the fall and the fact that they were unarmored, the guns proved to be more of a hindrance than a help. Finally, the armored regiment formed a company under *Hauptmann* Staesche, which was charged with monitoring movements and regulating traffic.

The division issued orders to occupy staging areas. *Generalleutnant* Model held a commander's conference at 1030 hours on 28 September to discuss the upcoming attack. The division issued supplemental orders as well. In one of the orders, the units were directed to take 3.5 basic loads of fuel with them. The division logistics officer was responsible for bringing that amount of fuel forward. On that day, the division had 15,050 men assigned to it.

Panzergruppe 2, on the right wing of *Heeresgruppe Mitte*, had the initial mission during the offensive of preventing any type of Russian impact on the wings of the *4. Armee* and *Panzergruppe 4*, which were attacking in the direction of Moscow from Rosslawl. Allocated to *Panzergruppe 2* on 29 September:

- *XXIV. Armee-Korps (mot.)*, with the *3. Panzer-Division, 4. Panzer-Division* and the *10. Infanterie-Division (mot.)*
- *XXXXVII. Armee-Korps (mot.)*, with the *17. Panzer-Division, 18. Panzer-Division*, and the *29. Infanterie-Division (mot.)*
- *XXXXVIII. Armee-Korps (mot.)*, with the *9. Panzer-Division, 16. Infanterie-Division (mot.)*, and *25. Infanterie-Division (mot.)*
- *XXXIV. Armee-Korps*, with the *95. Infanterie-Division* and *134. Infanterie-Division*
- *XXXV Armee-Korps*, with the *262. Infanterie-Division, 293. Infanterie-Division*, and *296. Infanterie-Division*

Two motorized corps (the XXIV and the XXXXVII) staged to break through the positions of the Soviet 13th Army, while the other corps were still closing in. It was intended for the two infantry corps to be echeloned right and left, following the motorized corps. The main effort of *Panzergruppe 2* was at Gluchow. The *XXIV. Armee-Korps (mot.)* placed both of its armored divisions in the front lines, while the *10. Infanterie-Division (mot.)* initially remained in the second wave. The first attack objective of the corps was the Orel–Brjansk road.

The weather on 29 September was anything but promising. It had rained the entire night and the routes and roads were a single mass of mud. Starting on 27 September, *Pionier-Bataillon 39* was under its new commander, *Major* Petsch, who replaced *Major* Beigel, who had been transferred to the Engineer School at Dessau-Roßlau.

Together with a battalion of *RAD*[1] personnel (*5./313*), the engineers were given the mission of constructing corduroy roads. The division took up its positions south and southwest of Gluchow, six kilometers east of Jareslawez. The main body of the division was placed under the command of *Oberst* Kleemann. The *II./Panzer-Regiment 6*, *Kradschützen-Bataillon 3*, and the *3./Pionier-Bataillon 39* were attached to the *4. Panzer-Division*, which had been directed to attack to the left of the division. Detached to the corps, as its reserve, were the *II./Schützen-Regiment 3*, one battery from *Artillerie-Regiment 42*, and one company from *Panzerjäger-Abteilung 521*. To screen the staging area, *Kampfgruppe von Manteuffel*, with the *I./Schützen-Regiment 3* and the *II./Artillerie-Regiment 42*, was employed along the Klewenj from Wjasenka to Ljachow, eight kilometers east of Gluchow.

The night passed quietly. Visibility was extremely limited, since the heavens were completely blanketed by clouds. Right at the designated minute—0530 hours—all of the batteries of the divisional artillery opened the new offensive with a barrage on the forward Russian positions. The men of the two rifle regiments then jumped out of their trenches and worked their way in bounds towards the enemy lines, which were still being covered by friendly artillery fire.

Kampfgruppe von Manteuffel was employed along the right wing to protect the flank of the division through offensive operations and maintain contact with the *XXVIII. Armee-Korps* on the right. In executing that mission, the battle group attacked Sawarkow. In the lead were the remaining armored personnel carriers of the 1st Company (*Leutnant* Lohse), on which the riflemen of the 3rd Company (*Hauptmann* Peschke) were riding. The attack took place across an open field. There were Russian positions in front of the village outskirts, which were quickly overrun. The riflemen were then among the wooden cottages, which were stubbornly defended by individual Russians. The lead elements of the *SPW* company made it to the center of the village, where they stopped at a church with a dilapidated cemetery.

All of a sudden, a few dogs sprang out of the second line of the enemy's defenses, about forty meters away. The animals ran quickly toward the *SPW's* and were not distracted by the machine-gun firing. *Obergefreiter* Müller cried out: "It's got something on its back!" His comrades identified a wooden lever, about twenty-five centimeters long. It rose vertically from a rack on the dog's body. A few of the Russians had jumped up from their positions in the trenches, encouraging the dogs. Instinctively, the machine gunner on the first vehicle, *Obergefreiter* Ostarek, took the animals under aimed fire. The lead dog continued racing. *Oberfeldwebel* Kretschmar brought his submachine gun into firing position and fired until the animal collapsed. At the same time, *Hauptmann* Peschke had finished off a dog with a carbine, and the third animal was shot by *Feldwebel* Hoffmann's machine gun. Another four dogs followed with attached two-kilogram charges, but they were also killed. *Leutnant* Lohse radioed out the new danger: "Mine dogs!"

When the Russians saw that their dogs were unable to deliver their deadly charges anywhere, they evacuated their positions behind the church and pulled completely out of Sawarkow. But as soon as our riflemen reached the edges of the village, Soviet artillery fire slammed into the wooden houses. In between were rounds of an unknown type, which rained down all at once by the dozens and had a tremendous shrapnel effect. Those were the first Stalin organs the soldiers of the division encountered.

Friendly losses mounted considerably. *Leutnant* Vetter from the *3./Schützen-Regiment 3* was badly wounded. All of a sudden, the fires

---

1. *Reichsarbeitsdienst*, or Reich Labor Service—a prewar paramilitary organization that was designed to reduce unemployment and provide inexpensive labor for government projects. Later, it worked primarily in support of the armed forces, with some units even seeing combat.

stopped around noon. An immediately launched patrol under the command of *Unteroffizier* Buggert brought in an additional forty-eight prisoners. While the 3rd Company remained in Sawarkow, the 1st Company was ordered back, with the squads of *Unteroffizier* Dreger and *Unteroffizier* Hesse then moved to screen in the direction of Cholopkowo.

Schützen-Regiment 394, which was employed as the division's main effort, quickly broke through the enemy resistance and advanced fairly rapidly. It was just that the roads and trails were a problem that could barely be solved. One was amazed that the armored personnel carriers and other vehicles were able to hold up to the demands placed on them. Since the terrain was not suited for tanks, the tank battalions remained behind for the time being. *Oberstleutnant* Audörsch believed he would be able to accomplish his mission without the support of the fighting vehicles.

By 0830 hours, the *I./Schützen-Regiment 394* had reached the high ground east of Frigoltowo, hardly encountering the enemy. The advance was then halted due to an extensive and barely identifiable mine obstacle. The engineers had to go forward to clear a lane. The situation was made even more difficult by the fact that the Russians had occupied Studenok to the east and were causing further delays through artillery fire.

By then, the *II./Schützen-Regiment 394* had reached the area two kilometers west of Klewenj. It was there that the first fighting vehicles of the *III./Panzer-Regiment 6* arrived. Both formations joined together and continued the march from Klewenj. The first obstacle appeared after four kilometers: destroyed bridges. Shortly thereafter came the second obstacle: The minefield at Studenok. The clearing of the mines took a long time, since they were almost all wood-encased, which could not be detected by electric mine detectors. The *II./Schützen-Regiment 394* lost a lot of time and was only able to continue its attack at the onset of darkness. It eventually established all-round defensive positions in the Naumowka area.

The *I./Schützen-Regiment 394* got through Studenok in the afternoon and occupied the high ground to the east at Chinel. That meant that the day's objective had been reached. A patrol advanced as far as Kutscherowka, which was reported as being clear of the enemy. In any event, the railway line to the southwest was not to be crossed.

Shortly after first light on 1 October, all of the divisional elements continued their forward advance. *Kampfgruppe Kleemann* assembled around Studenok by noon and reached Kutscherowka with *Schützen-Regiment 394* and the *II./Panzer-Regiment 6*. The completely softened ground did not allow for any rapid advance. The supply routes coming in from Gluchow were already completely ruined. Every vehicle got stuck in the mud and could only be guided out with assistance from a prime mover.

Patrols were sent out from Kutscherowka and determined that the road from Esmanj appeared more-or-less trafficable. By then, the *I./Panzer-Regiment 6* had advanced to the northeast and reached the village of Ulanow, moving through Suchodol. The tank regiment could advance no further that day, since the thirty-five new fighting vehicles had arrived and had to be distributed among the battalions, with the 3rd Battalion receiving ten *Panzer III's* and *Panzer IV's*.

Kampfgruppe Kleemann was reinforced during the day by *Kampfgruppe von Manteuffel*. The latter battle group had remained in its old positions in the morning and had turned back several Russian counterattacks, in the course of which *Leutnant* Thomas was killed and *Leutnant* Doll was badly wounded (both from the *I./Schützen-Regiment 3*). The *2./Schützen-Regiment 3* also suffered casualties, since the Soviets succeeded in breaking up Bachert's platoon. Two of the squads encircled by the enemy were able to fight their way through and make it back to the battalion. *Aufklärungs-Abteilung 1* cleared the area around Tschernewa. By noon, the *3./Schützen-Regiment 3* had to be detached to return to Studenok to take over the security there. The remaining companies followed a few hours later, after *Maschinen-Gewehr-Bataillon 5*[2] had relieved the battle group in the positions it had taken the previous day. In Studenok, *Pionier-Bataillon 39* was in the process of erecting a sixteen-ton bridge over the Klewenj. The 1st Bridging Section provided three trucks with spans and two with surface elements.

By the evening of 1 October, the lead elements of the division reached the area twenty kilometers northeast of Kutscherowka. The enemy was pulling back. *Generalleutnant* Model reported to his superior headquarters that a rapid advance could not be continued due to the bad condition of the road network. At that point, the corps decided to pull the division out of its previous sector and have it march on the better roads to Ssewsk.

The regrouping took place at night. The division turned to the north behind the *4. Panzer-Division*. On the morning of 2 October, which finally brought with it nice weather again, the division disengaged the bulk of its forces and marched through Suchodol and Polkownitschja in the direction of Ssewsk. On that day, the division command post was moved from Suchodol to Prilepy, off the side of the road. The march was frequently interrupted, since the road was completely jammed with vehicles of all types. For the first time, Russian aircraft dropped phosphorous bombs on the columns.

During the day, *Schützen-Regiment 3*, elements of *Panzerjäger-Abteilung 521*, and the *1./Pionier-Bataillon 39* provided security for those movements. In the process, the riflemen were unable to cross the railway line. During the night, the enemy had emplaced additional minefields. As a result, only reconnaissance and combat raids could be conducted. The enemy remained on the defensive and only disturbed friendly movements by means of artillery fire. Some casualties were taken. For instance, *Leutnant* Dr. Sieverling of the *4./Artillerie-Regiment 75* was killed.

As the sunny second day of October came to an end, the *XXIV. Armee-Korps (mot.)* had achieved important initial success. After the *4. Panzer-Division* had taken Ssewsk on 1 October, it not only penetrated the enemy front 130 kilometers deep, it also ripped the Soviet 13th Army apart. The Soviet 21st and 55th Cavalry Divisions, the 121st and 150th Tank Brigades and the 183rd Rifle Division were separated from the rest of their field army and were pulling back to the north.

The *3. Panzer-Division* did not conduct any major combat activity with the bulk of its forces, since it was moving behind the *4. Panzer-Division*. On the same day, the new major effort on the part of the German Army got underway. At first light on 2 October, Operation Typhoon had started. Its end objective was the capture of Moscow.

The morning of 3 October started with a haze rising out of the woods. While the forces of the division started moving out at 0800 hours, one battle group was attached to the *4. Panzer-Division*, which had been directed to attack Orel. *Panzerjäger-Abteilung 543* was ordered to join the battle group. For the first time since the start of the campaign, *Major* von Türkheim had command of his entire battalion. All three companies—the 1st under *Oberleutnant* Jopp, who had just returned a few days previously from a hospital in the homeland, the 2nd under *Oberleutnant* Michels, and the 3rd under *Oberleutnant* Möcking—participated in the attack of the neighboring division to the east. Orel, with its factory facilities and airfields, fell into German hands that day.

The division formed a strong battle group under *Oberstleutnant* von Lewinski: the *III./Panzer-Regiment 6*, the *II./Schützen-Regiment 394*, the *II./Artillerie-Regiment 75*, and the *2./Pionier-Bataillon 39*. Those forces advanced at 1100 hours from Ssewsk. A few fighting vehicles provided flank guard, but they found no appreciable resistance for fifteen kilometers. The advance proceeded slowly, since the *18. Panzer-Division* was using the same route and had

---

2. This was a general headquarters element that was not assigned to any division or corps.

"right of way" on certain parts. The battle group crossed the Ljachoff–Brjansk rail line and reached Kamarischa-Lobatowo around 1600 hours. There was no further advance for the day, and von Lewinski's forces set up an all-round defense. A large patrol from the tank battalion was sent to the northwest along the rail line. East of Schadino, it encountered an enemy cavalry patrol, which was pushed back. The motorcycle infantry battalion was ordered back to Kamarischa. The motorcycle infantry brought back prisoners from northwest of the village, who mentioned the detraining of Russian elements. The engineers then blew up the railway facilities. *Oberst* Kleemann's battle group, which was reinforced with the *II./Panzer-Regiment 6*, reached the area around Dmitrowsk, where it screened. The night passed relatively quietly.

The division pushed its forces forward in the direction of Dmitrowsk during the day. By doing so, it was adjacent to the *4. Panzer-Division* on the left. The latter division had been able to take the bridges over the Oka, but its regiments then bogged down. Elements of the *10. Infanterie-Division (mot.)* closed up to the division, relieving *Kampfgruppe von Manteuffel*, which had been screening.

At 1145 hours on 4 October, the division advanced from Dmitrowsk to the north with an advance guard that had been reinforced with the *II./Panzer-Regiment 6*. After five hours, it reached Robja in dank and chilly weather, continuously held up by bad roads and missing bridges. The lead elements of the division were then 30 kilometers north of Dmitrowsk. The three battle groups of Kleemann, von Lewinski, and von Manteuffel followed slowly. Very poor, sandy routes and stretches of sand on both sides of the bridge at Nerussa caused difficulties for the wheeled vehicles. For example, the fuel columns of *Panzer-Regiment 6* needed six hours to cover a stretch of seven kilometers that day.

The division used the day to pull its own forces closer to Dmitrowsk, replenish supplies of fuel and ammunition, erect bridges and improve roads. The division command post initially moved to Robja and then on to the schoolhouse in Molodewoje.

Soviet aircraft were very active that day and disrupted friendly movements. Some casualties were taken. The escorting *Flak* batteries could not complain about a lack of work. Just over Dmitrowsk alone, they were able to shoot down nine bombers. By evening, the elements of *Schützen-Regiment 1* and *Aufklärungs-Abteilung 1*, which had transitioned to security duties in that area, were relieved by formations of the *10. Infanterie-Division (mot.)*. They then moved on to catch up with the division. The rifle regiments cleared the villages of Schablikino and Molodewoje along the road.

On 5 October, the corps again placed its main effort in the sector of the *4. Panzer-Division*. The *II./Panzer-Regiment 6*, the *5./Artillerie-Regiment 75*, and the *2./Panzerjäger-Abteilung 521* were attached to that division. They left Robja at 1000 hours and advanced through Schablikino as far as Bunina along the Orel–Karatschew road.

The sixth of October 1941 was an event-filled day in the history of the German Army in the East. Rain showers pelted down all morning long from the low cloud cover, driven along by the strong northwest wind. In between were the first snowfalls. Those were the signs of the onset of the mud period, which would make further advance appreciably more difficult and cause delays. On that 6 October, Hitler also issued instructions that the tank groups were to be redesignated tank armies from that point forward. Likewise, the motorized corps were to be redesignated as tank corps.[3]

3. The author is in error with regard to the timeframe of the redesignations. While the tank groups started to be redesignated as field army commands and eventually as tank armies at the end of 1941 and beginning of 1942, the motorized army corps were not redesignated as tank corps until the summer of 1942. Therefore, the original designations will be used until the "official" timeframe of the redesignations.

The *3. Panzer-Division* was so held up by the rain and mushy snow on its march routes that none of its daily objectives was reached. *Panzer-Regiment 6* was stuck in the mud for three and a half hours. *Schützen-Regiment 394* was turned off in the direction of Orel to provide security for the flank of the *XXIV. Armee-Korps (mot.)* to the east.

On that day, the *17. Panzer-Division* took Brjansk, while the *18. Panzer-Division* reached Karatschew and the *10. Infanterie-Division (mot.)* fought it out with scattered enemy elements in the area west of Ssewsk. It was directed that the *XXIV. Armee-Korps (mot.)* screen the encirclement around Brjansk from the east. *Panzergruppe 2* crossed its first attack objective, the Orel–Brjansk road, and was headed for the crossings over the Ssusha at Mzensk, so as to later be able to advance from there in the direc-

tion of Tula or along the Oka. On that day, the *4. Panzer-Division*, with the attached *II./Panzer-Regiment 6*, advanced northeast of Orel in the direction of Mzensk. It was there that the fighting vehicles encountered T-34's for the first time. The *4. Panzer-Division* succeeded in bypassing those enemy formations, reaching Mzensk on 7 October and taking it. It was not possible to establish a bridgehead over the Ssusha, however, since the Soviets held the high ground on the far side. The *III./Panzer-Regiment 6*, along with *Kradschützen-Bataillon 3*, were able to advance as far as the area around Bogdanowka as the lead elements of the *3. Panzer-Division*. The attached platoon from the *1./Pionier-Bataillon 39* was able to blow up a section of the Orel–Brjansk rail line in the vicinity of Bogdanowka during the night. The engineers then found themselves surrounded by the

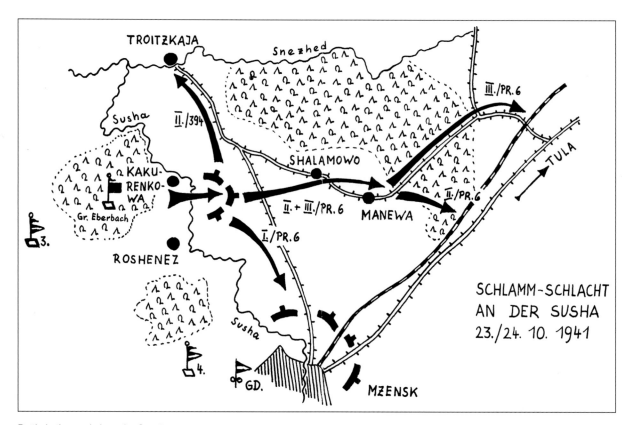

Battle in the mud along the Ssusha.

Russians a short while later, but they were able to fight their way through to the motorcycle infantry battalion.

Right at midnight during the night of 6–7 October, a violet snowstorm commenced, which quickly transformed the entire area into a winter landscape. Unfortunately, the snow did not remain on the ground, and the expected frost did not arrive. By first light, the snow had mixed with rain, and it transformed all of the roads within a short time into a morass. Driving was an unbelievable effort on men and materiel. Every truck had to be towed at the destroyed Zon Bridge by a tank. A member of *Schützen-Regiment 394* described the situation that day in the following words: "We could advance no farther. There was no more fuel. Nothing came forward. The route was long and the roads even worse than the last few days. The snow had melted again and, as a result, the mess even bigger. Rations didn't come forward, either. We sat in the muck the entire day."

The *3. Panzer-Division* reached the area around Orel and set up security. Most of the vehicles—more than 2,000—were stuck in the mud between Dmitrowsk and Kromy. Almost without exception, all of the fuel and rations vehicles were among them, as well as the entire maintenance company of *Panzer-Regiment 6*. It could not be determined with certainty when the entire column could get moving again.

After it appeared that the operations around Wjasma and Brjansk would turn out well, *Panzergruppe 2* received orders on 7 October to advance on Tula and take the crossings over the Oka there for further advance in either the direction of Kolomna or Kashira. Since the other corps were still hanging considerably back, only the *XXIV. Armee-Korps (mot.)* was available for that thrust.

For the time being, most of the division was only being employed for security missions around Orel. Only the reconnaissance and motorcycle infantry battalions were in contact with the enemy, sending patrols out in all directions. Schützen-Regiment 394 assumed the mis-

sion of guarding the Karatschew–Orel rail line. On 11 October, it moved into the area west of Orel bounded by Naryschkino and Swetiski. In Orel, a city of 120,000, there were enormous Red Army depots. Their contents indicated the Soviets were gearing up for a winter war. From external appearance, the city left a good impression. For the first time in a while, the soldiers saw multi-story homes, open shops and even a streetcar line. The *II./Schützen-Regiment 3* took up quarters in the barracks of the Soviet armor school demonstration regiment. In one of the buildings, a former Tsarist cadet academy, the riflemen discovered a two-meter-tall stuffed bear, which was a good likeness of our Berlin mascot. It was set up in front of the command post of the division and carried the general's pennant from that point forward.

Starting on 8 October, the reconnaissance battalion, augmented by the 3rd Company of the engineer battalion, was employed in the direction of Bolchow, where it encountered strong enemy forces, supported by artillery, approximately twenty-five kilometers north of Orel. The motorcycle infantry battalion and the 10th Company of the armor regiment was sent in that direction. The next day, the forces occupied the locality, thus creating a good start point for further operations.

The division ordered that the battle groups employed up front be supplied with a fuel section that had been assembled by the armor regiment. The trucks took off from Orel on the morning of 10 October. They were given a small guard force and were initially able to get 2,700 liters of fuel to Bolchow. On the way back, the trucks brought along 800 prisoners. The main body of the *4. Panzer-Division* had bogged down outside of Mzensk. *Ju 52* transporters brought in the necessary supplies during the day and air dropped the canisters, since there was no place for them to land.

There was a light snowfall on 12 October. It did not effect the course of the fighting. *Oberstleutnant* Munzel's tank battalion, still attached to the *4. Panzer-Division*, was bogged down in the western part of Mzensk and under enemy fire. Since the Soviets had turned active in the Bolchow area again, the reconnaissance battalion was reinforced that day with a mixed group comprised of the *III./Panzer-Regiment 6*, the *7./ Schützen-Regiment 394*, and the *5./Artillerie-Regiment 75*. Later on, the *I./Schützen-Regiment 3* was also brought forward. It relieved the motorcycle infantry battalion with its companies, freeing it for employment in the Mzensk area.

The division received a warning order from the corps on 13 October, that a strike force might have to be sent forward as far as the area around Schablikino, since elements of the Soviet 3rd Army had broken through in the sector of the *29. Infanterie-Division (mot.)*. The division was informed to have its forces ready to move by 0600 the following morning.

The battle group, under the command of *Oberstleutnant* Schmidt-Ott, moved out at that time. One tank, one antitank, one rifle and one battery headed off in the direction of Schablikino in the darkness. It turned out that they were not needed. On the other hand, the division had to reinforce the *4. Panzer-Division* at Mzensk, pushing all of *Panzerjäger-Abteilung 521* into the locality. The *III./Panzer-Regiment 6* continued to screen around Bolchow with the reconnaissance battalion, while *Schützen-Regiment 394* remained in the Orel area. Later on, it extended its positions in the direction of Bolchow. The division's medical forces set up a forward clearing station forty kilometers north of Orel under the direction of *Unterarzt* Rakowski of the 1st Medical Company.

On 14 October, the Army High Command issued directives for the encirclement of Moscow. Forming the main effort of the army in the East was the *4. Armee* and *Panzergruppe 4*, which were to attack the Russian capital from the north and the west, while *Panzergruppe 2* swung out far and blocked off Moscow from the south, southeast and east.

The *XXIV. Armee-Korps (mot.)* prepared for that final push along the banks of the Ssusha. Its main effort was formed by its two armored divi-

sions. The *3. Panzer-Division* was augmented by the attachment of *Infanterie-Regiment (mot.) "Großdeutschland,"* which was commanded by *Oberst* Hoernlein. The approach movements proceeded vey slowly as a result of the mud, however. Armored patrols were sent out in all directions to screen. One, for instance, was sent out on 15 October from the *I./Panzer-Regiment 6*. It moved in the direction of Snamenskoje, forty-five kilometers northwest of Orel.

Over the next few days, terrain was observed, conferences held and other types of reconnaissance conducted. It was intended to cause the heavily fortified Soviet positions around Mzensk, which were being reinforced daily, to collapse by an envelopment from the north. The *4. Panzer-Division* had reached a stalemate and could no longer advance frontally. The rifle regiments conducted combat patrols in front of the division sector. On the morning of 17 October, the *3./Schützen-Regiment 3* launched one such patrol, but it was hit hard by the enemy. The 7th Company of the same regiment had to relieve it. A platoon from the 6th Company under the command of *Leutnant* Dziallas had more luck the following day. The riflemen were able to cross the river in pneumatic craft and brought back twenty-nine prisoners from the far bank.

The Ssusha was up to forty meters across and two meters deep. The river emptied into the Oka fifty kilometers north of Mzensk. The soil between the two watercourses was very fertile, but it turned to muck after even the slightest trace of rain. The terrain was generally open. There were few woods, but they tended to be expansive. There were long and steep defiles everywhere—the so-called *balkas*—they provided an obstacle to tanks.

On 18 October, *Generalleutnant* Model held his last conference concerning the attack with his commanders. The *XXIV. Panzer-Korps* was to cross the Ssusha and generally advance on Tula. The *4. Panzer-Division* was to be on the left, the *3. Panzer-Division* on the right forming the main effort. To that end, the division formed two battle groups. The southern group consisted of the rifle brigade and would attack from the area east of Glaunowa. The northern group would be under the control of the *5. Panzer-Brigade*[4] and consisted of *Panzer-Regiment 6* and *Panzer-Regiment 18*.[5] That group had the mission of advancing in the direction of Shaljamowa and turning there onto the main road, where it was assumed that the enemy was massing his heavy artillery. It was also given the mission of guarding the flank of the rifle brigade. Since the first objective was twenty-five air kilometers from the line of departure, it was assumed that the tanks would be empty at that point and need to be refueled. Refueling by truck was not an option because of the mud. Correspondingly, each battalion was allocated a prime mover with 1,500 liters of fuel in canisters. In addition, each regiment had an additional prime mover with trailer that had 6,000 liters of fuel.

Before the division started this new chapter in its history, it also made a number of personnel changes. *Major Baron* von Behr, the Division Signals Officer, was transferred to take command of *Korps-Nachrichten-Abteilung 424*.[6] *Hauptmann* Böttge took his place. *Major* Haas, the commander of the *I./Schützen-Regiment 394*, had to give up command due to a hand wound. Acting command was assumed by *Oberleutnant* Bachmann, the commander of the 11th Company of that regiment, before he relinquished command a few days later to *Hauptmann Freiherr* von der Heyden-Rynsch. Due to health reasons, *Oberst* von Manteuffel had to return to the homeland. *Major* Zimmermann assumed command of *Schützen-Regiment 3*. *Hauptmann* Peschke took over Zimmermann's 2nd Battalion. *Oberst-leutnant* von Lewinski relinquished command of *Panzer-Regiment 6* to *Oberstleutnant* Munzel, whose 2nd Battalion was taken by *Major* Frank. *Oberstleutnant* Schmidt-Ott assumed command of the 1st Battalion.

Generalleutnant Model transferred command of the division, after he had worked out all the plans for the attack on Tula, to *Generalmajor* Breith. Breith was not an unknown factor for the division. He had been a part of the *Panzertruppe* from the very beginning. During the campaign in France, he had been the commander of the *5. Panzer-Brigade*. At the start of the campaign in the East, he was assigned to the Directorate for Fast Forces at the Army High Command.[7] Model, of course, went on to corps, field army and field-army group command by the end of the war.[8]

By the evening of 22 October, the division had reached its designated holding areas despite considerable difficulties with the roads. During the afternoon, *Panzer-Regiment 6*, departing from Tolitsche, reached the area around Roshenez. The *I./Panzer-Regiment 18* made it there from Bolchow. The division command post and the main clearing station were located in Tolitsche. The *II./Schützen-Regiment 394* arrived at Roshenez as well. These northern forces reported to *Oberst* Eberbach of the *4. Panzer-Division*. At the time, the three battalions of *Panzer-Regiment 6* each had three *Panzer II's*, sixteen *Panzer III's*, five *Panzer IV's*, and three or four self-propelled 5-centimeter antitank guns (from *Panzerjäger-Abteilung 521*). The *I./Panzer-Regiment 18* had approximately thirty tanks. Also assigned to *Kampfgruppe Eberbach* were

---

4. The brigade had been a part of the *4. Panzer-Division*. Effective 26 July 1941, the *XXIV. Armee-Korps (mot.)* ordered it attached to the *3. Panzer-Division*.

5. The armored regiment of the *18. Panzer-Division*.

6. This was the signals battalion for the *XXIV. Panzer-Korps*. Effective 15 October, it was redesignated as *Panzerkorps-Nachrichten-Abteilung 424*. It should be noted that von Behr ended the war as a *Generalmajor* commanding the *90. Panzergrenadier-Division*. He also received the Oak Leaves to the Knight's Cross of the Iron Cross as the commander of *Panzergrenadier-Regiment 200 (90. leichte Division)*. He was equally successful in the postwar German military, also achieving the rank of *Generalmajor* and commanding the *5. Panzer-Division* in the late 1950s. He passed away in Bonn in 1983.

7. In German, *General der schnellen Truppen*.

8. His immediate reassignment was as commanding general of the *XXXXI. Panzer-Korps*, which was also involved in the assault on Moscow, albeit from the northwest.

the *II./Artillerie-Regiment 75*, the *II./Artillerie-Regiment 42*, *Pionier-Bataillon 39*, the *I./Schützen-Regiment 3*, the *1./Schützen-Regiment 394*, the *5./Flak-Regiment 91*, and the *6./Flak-Regiment 11*.

The southern attack group established a bridgehead before the start of the offensive. The *6.* and *8./Schützen-Regiment 3* crossed the river at midnight on floats and moved approximately 200 meters inland, where they then dug in. The engineers from the 1st Company of the divisional engineers assisted and, by 0530 hours, had also crossed the headquarters of the 2nd Battalion. Two battalions of artillery, one battery of rocket launchers and the 10th Company of the regiment (infantry guns) set up in position behind the battalion.

All at once, the German artillery opened fire on the Russian trenches and localities with a preparation bombardment. In the north, the *I./Schützen-Regiment 3* also started to cross the Ssusha, as did the rest of the 2nd Battalion in the south. The 1st Battalion was soon able to break through the enemy positions northwest of Bobenkowo with its 2nd and 3rd Companies. After forty-five minutes, they had crossed the main road south of Nikolskaja. A halt was ordered, since the riflemen had to wait for the tanks to close up. The *II./Schützen-Regiment 3* approached Nikolskaja. Heavy defensive fires from weapons of all calibers forced the riflemen to take cover. The soldiers waited for the fighting vehicles to approach from the north, but they could not be seen. In addition, the artillery frequently fired too short, causing casualties, which were not inconsiderable. It wasn't until *Stukas* attacked around 1000 hours that there was the first palpable relief.

The hours passed slowly. The riflemen were unable to advance in the face of the heavy Russian fire. Both battalions were practically fixed in position. Only a few individuals and squads succeeded in entering the enemy positions. For instance, an unknown *Gefreiter* from the 8th Company was able to clear an entire trench line with his machine gun and take a few prisoners.

Unfortunately, the same soldier was killed a few minutes later when he went back up front. The 2nd Company made some progress, working its way slowly forward and reaching the area three kilometers southeast of Nikolskaja. But the riflemen had to dig in there as well. The weather was cold, the ground frozen in some places and the rain fell without stopping.

Kampfgruppe Nord encountered similar difficulties in its crossing of the Ssusha. The *8./Schützen-Regiment 394* crossed the river late the previous evening and established a small bridgehead on the east bank at Roshenez with the help of engineers; the 6th Company of the battalion did the same at Karukenkowo. *Leutnant* Peter and four soldiers were killed in those efforts, and the Soviets took great pains to reduce those positions. By 0700 hours, however, the riflemen succeeded in linking up the two crossing points. Because fo artillery fire, it was only possible to erect a bridge at Karukenkowo. It proved impossible to eliminate the enemy artillery fires.

The 2nd Company of engineers had been working during the night to build a bridge. It was a Sisyphus effort. Whenever they thought they had put in the final section, Russian artillery destroyed their efforts. The engineers drug materiel forward ceaselessly. They hammered, constructed and drilled. The nineteen-meter bridge, which was supposed to have been completed by 0530 hours, was four hours late. Two sixteen-ton stretches had to be put down along with a floating support.

At that point, the tanks of the *III./Panzer-Regiment 6* and the *SPW's* of the *1./Schützen-Regiment 3* approached and crossed the small river. The conditions were less than ideal in all respects. The steep far bank had been transformed into a "grease ramp" as a result of the rain. The bridge proper was partially under water and barely up to the job. It was asking almost the impossible of the vehicle drivers and their driving skills. In the case of the artillery and *Flak*, it was not just a case of getting the vehicle across, but the limbered gun as well. In one case, a *Flak* slipped off the bridge and blocked the crossing point for considerable time.

The *I./Schützen-Regiment 394* then crossed the river. It was able to expand the bridgehead as far as Triozkoje. The enemy artillery fires abated somewhat, but the crossing of the *III./Panzer-Regiment 6* lasted until noon.

Generalmajor Breith ordered the *I./Panzer-Regiment 6*, which was waiting for the bridge to be erected at Roshenez, to move north and cross behind the 3rd Battalion of the regiment. By around 1400 hours, the battalion was on the east bank. *Oberstleutnant* Schmidt-Ott turned in the direction of Nikolskaja with his companies in order to assist the riflemen. When Schmidt-Ott's tanks reached the first rise, they were already being taken under heavy fire by artillery and antitank guns. They had to turn back and go around the hill to the north. Around 1600 hours, they established contact with *Hauptmann* Peschke's *II./Schützen-Regiment 3*. The riflemen and tanks then advanced together to the southeast. The attack bogged down in front of a ridgeline that was heavily defended. The 2nd Company of the rifle regiment lost three dead and thirteen wounded; the 3rd Company, two dead and five wounded. Just on that day alone, *Schützen-Regiment 3* had three physicians wounded: *Stabsarzt* Dr. Schröder and *Stabsarzt* Dr. Schreck and *Assistenzarzt* Hoffmann. Although the tank battalion attempted to envelop the high ground from the south, it was forced to give up its efforts when it turned dark and a *balka* was encountered.

Kampfgruppe Nord immediately advanced to the northwest with *Hauptmann* Schneider-Kostalski's *III./Panzer-Regiment 6*. It crossed the first ridgeline and then reached the Mzensk–Belew road. All of a sudden, seven T-34's rolled out of Schaljamowa. A short firefight ensued, during which two T-34's were knocked out but the battalion also lost two *Panzer III's*. When the Soviets pulled back, the battalion offered an immediate pursuit and reached Schaljamowa as it turned dark. Seventy prisoners were collected; they came from the 540th Rifle Regiment. The

battle group set up an all-round defense. Around 1900 hours, *Leutnant* Rühl's 7th Company from the *II./Panzer-Regiment 6*, which had been sent forward, arrived from the west to reinforce the 3rd Battalion.

Despite the enemy fire, the engineers of the 3rd Company attempted to build a bridge at Roshenez in the afternoon. *Major* Frank's *II./Panzer-Regiment 6* was able to cross during the night, completing its move after 0600 hours. Frank's battalion moved west past its sister 1st Battalion and reached Schaljamowa around 0900 hours at the same time as the regimental and brigade headquarters. Ever since first light, the enemy had been placing heavy fire in the area around the locality. That fire, coupled with mines, which damaged two tanks, initially prevented a further advance.

The portions of the rifle brigade located to the south had suffered from the cool night. In addition, all of the landline traffic was lost, so that contact could only be maintained by means of messengers. The *I./Panzer-Regiment 6* closed up tight to the *II./Schützen-Regiment 3*, and they both moved out to assault. Five tanks were initially allocated to each rifle company.

The battle group succeeded in taking Malyje-Bersinki against practically no enemy resistance. The *I./Schützen-Regiment 3* also started its attack at 1000 hours. The battalion had no tanks in support; only the *SPW's* of the 1st Company, which had arrived from the north. *Major* Wellmann had his heavy weapons concentrate on a few positions and had his battalion attack them. Deeply echeloned, the battalion thus overran the first Russian field positions and, by noon, the positions at Krestzowo and Malyje-Bersenski.

Kampfgruppe Eberbach was still at Schaljamowa. At the moment, it did not appear that any success was possible there. The resistance was too great. *Stukas* were requested. They did not appear, however, and the attack was launched regardless. The *II./Panzer-Regiment 6* was in the first wave, with its sister 3rd Battalion right behind it. The fighting vehicles pushed forward on both sides of the Schaljamowa–Malyje-

Bersenki road to the high ground and reached the latter village around noon. The regiment set up all-round defenses there. It was out of fuel and ammunition. The *II./Panzer-Regiment 6* had to wait for *Panzer-Regiment 18*, which had not crossed the Ssusha until that morning and was carrying fuel cans for the 2nd Battalion with it. The *6.* and *9./Panzer-Regiment 18* arrived around 1500 hours.

Just after 1200 hours, the long awaited *Stukas* showed up and dove on the enemy positions. High clouds of smoke showed the tankers and riflemen the Russian trenches. As soon as the last machine turned away, the riflemen rose out of their holes and the fighting vehicles moved out. The *II./Schützen-Regiment 3*, successfully supported by *Leutnant* Vopel's *1./Panzer-Regiment 6*, advanced into the dense woods. By evening, they occupied Katuschistscha and the dominant high ground of Hill 118.7. The Soviet 401st Rifle Regiment had evacuated the field in the face of the aggressively mounted attack. The *I./Schützen-Regiment 3*, to which *Oberleutnant* von Kriegsheim's *4./Panzer-Regiment 6* had been attached, advanced to the south on Szomowo. The 2nd Company of the rifle regiment cleared the enemy's field positions. *Leutnant* Eckert, *Feldwebel* Schelinger, and *Feldwebel* Pfeiffer charged at the head of their men. The company lost five killed and twenty-six wounded during the action. The 3rd Company of the rifle regiment, under the acting command of *Leutnant* Heurich, was sent towards Saroschtscha to establish a bridgehead at Butyrki and establish contact with *Infanterie-Regiment (mot.) "Großdeutschland."* Moving form Mzensk, the latter regiment had attacked the strongly fortified Russian positions between the road and the railway and had already reached the high ground northwest of the city with its 3rd Battalion.

Oberstleutnant Munzel's *Panzer-Regiment 6* was able to take Meznewa in the afternoon. Enemy fighting vehicles fired without letup from the wooded terrain north of Gubarjowa. The *Stuka* sortie there hit the target with hair-split-

ting precision; later on, sixteen abandoned Russian tanks were found there. *Oberst* Eberbach decided to continue the attack to the northeast that night. He wanted to swing out and then block the Mzensk–Tula road, thus cutting off the withdrawal route for the Russians.

The *III./Panzer-Regiment 6* was the first battalion to refuel; it moved out at the onset of darkness, reinforced by the *1./Schützen-Regiment 3. Oberst* Eberbach and *Oberstleutnant* Munzel moved with the battalion. Moving slowly, the German vehicles approached the objective—a fork in the road with a farmstead northwest of Mzensk—despite the darkness and the unfamiliar route. The 2nd Battalion was left behind to screen the Orel–Tula railway line at Kudinowa.

The fighting vehicles approached the road through the night-darkened woods and found themselves in the middle of a Russian supply point. A wild melee ensued, which was illuminated eerily by the magical light of innumerable signal flares. Tanks moved against other tanks; stockpiles of ammunition exploded; it was a wild free-for-all. *Unteroffizier* Splettstößer of the *SPW* company went after a T-34. The mine he used didn't explode, however, and the tank withdrew in the darkness. By contrast, *Obergefreiter* Tietz of the same company had more luck. He grabbed some bundled stick grenades and leapt up on a tank. He tossed the charge in an open hatch and jumped down, right onto the back of a Red Army soldier. The turret of the KV-I flew into the air. The next "T-34" was set alight after the third round from a *Panzer IV. Oberleutnant* Möllhoff of the 3rd Company of engineers went after a fifty-two-ton KV-II and blew it up. In the end, five Soviet fighting vehicles, several armored cars and some trains vehicles were on fire, their lurid flames illuminating the nighttime scene.

Around midnight, it finally turned quiet. The Soviets had disappeared. *Kampfgruppe Eberbach* set up an all-round defense around the supply point for the night. During the early-morning hours, *Unteroffizier* Worpke unexpectedly brought forward a fuel section with the desperately needed fuel. The men had searched the ground for tank tracks and had followed their battalion there that way. *Hauptmann* Schneider-Kostalski promoted the young noncommissioned officer on the spot to *Feldwebel*.

The attack objective for the armored brigade had been reached and the Russian front broken through in that sector! The route to Tula was clear for *Panzergruppe 2*. *Oberst* Eberbach later received the Oak Leaves to the Knight's Cross for this operation.[9]

During the same night, the rifle brigade employed to the south linked up with the elements of *Infanterie-Regiment (mot.) "Großdeutschland,"* which had moved out from Mzensk. The brigade continued its attack the following morning, 25 October. The enemy had evacuated his positions, presumably as a result of the night-time tank raid. As a result, the battalions made good progress. While the *I./Schützen-Regiment 3* advanced on Chutor, the 2nd Battalion of the regiment made it through Bolschaja-Kamenka. The enemy was ejected from there and a crossing over the Ssusha forced. In the course of that fighting, the regiment lost seventeen dead and eighty wounded. The success of the operation could be measured by the taking of 1,335 prisoners, as well as innumerable quantities of captured small arms and light guns.

The division formed an advance guard under *Hauptmann* Schneider-Kostalski on the morning of 25 October. It consisted of his *III./Panzer-Regiment 6*, the *1./Schützen-Regiment 3*, elements of *Panzerjäger-Abteilung 521*, and divisional artillery. By 1600 hours, the advance guard reached the Tschern railway station and set up security. A large fuel depot was discovered. It was not possible to refuel all of the vehicles, however, since the octane quotient differed from German fuel. As a result, the advance guard was stranded there, since no fuel could be brought forward that day.

By then, *Panzer-Regiment 6* had pushed its 2nd Battalion up to the intersection. The 1st Battalion established contact with *Infanterie-Regiment (mot.) "Großdeutschland"* and rearmed in Mzensk. The regimental adjutant, *Oberleutnant* von Twardowski, brought orders for the battalion to march to the north. As it had been discovered in the course of the day that the Soviets had covered the major road to Tschern with huge minefields of up to 1,800 mines and buried aerial bombs, it turned out that a movement along that road was not possible. The battalion therefore veered off the road to the left and arrived that evening in Bolschaja-Kamenka, after having moved across completely softened ground.

The motorized companies of the division did not move the next day, with the exception of *Oberstleutnant* Schmidt-Ott's *I./Panzer-Regiment 6*, which left its quartering area at 0600 hours and reached Tschern three hours later in the midst of a downpour. The lead elements of *Infanterie-Regiment (mot.) "Großdeutschland"* had also arrived there by then. The infantry mounted up on the tanks and, after a short briefing by *Oberst* Eberbach, moved out immediately again. The movement took the elements past Gorbatschewo, where relatively light enemy resistance could be broken fairly quickly. The battle group reached the city of Plawsk before the onset of darkness; it was quickly taken.

By those movements, the breakthrough of the *XXIV. Armee-Korps (mot.)* through the enemy positions along the Ssusha was guaranteed. The enemy forces that had been employed there— the 6th Guards Infantry Division, the 41st Cavalry Division, and the 4th Tank Brigade—had pulled back to the northeast and east. The Soviets left behind 2,480 prisoners and 19 fighting vehicles.

The mud then proved to be worse than the enemy. It brought movements to a standstill. It inevitably caused all of the wheeled vehicles to

---

9. Eberbach was one of the key panzer generals of the war and eventually rose to field army command. He was the forty-second member of the German Armed Forces to be honored with the Oak Leaves, which was officially awarded to him on 31 December 1941.

get stuck; only the prime movers and the tanks were able to churn their way through the thick porridge. *Panzer-Regiment 39* of the *17. Panzer-Division* was used on 26 October, for instance, to help pull the supply columns of the battalions of *Panzer-Regiment 6* up to the front from Mzensk. After about ten kilometers, the trucks got stuck again. When it started to rain again towards midnight, any effort to continue the march proved illusory. Only *Oberst* Cuno and his *Panzer-Regiment 39* were able to make it to Tschern that night.

The division, whose command post was in Toltschje, issued orders on the evening of 26 October for the continuation of the advance on Tula. They read, in part:

1) Enemy ejected from his heavily fortified field positions north of the Ssusha by an enveloping attack of the *3. Panzer-Division* after several days of fighting under extremely difficult circumstances. Tschern occupied by *Gruppe Eberbach* on the afternoon of 25 October. *4. Panzer-Division* established contact with *Gruppe Eberbach* by means of a frontal attack from the Mzensk bridgehead.

2) *XXIV. Armee-Korps (mot.)* advances along the road on Tula with the *3. Panzer-Division* in the lead.

3) *3. Panzer-Division*, with the reinforced *Panzer-Regiment 39* in the lead, moves out from Mzensk on 26 October, advances through Tschern in the direction of Tula and takes Tula.

For the next phase of the attack, the division reorganized during the night and the next day and formed the following battle groups: *Kampfgruppe Cuno* (*Panzer-Regiment 39*); *Kampfgruppe Hoernlein* (*Infanterie-Regiment (mot.)* "*Großdeutschland*"); *Kampfgruppe Eberbach*

(*Panzer-Regimenter 6* and *35*); *Kampfgruppe Kleemann* (*Schützen-Regiment 3*, the *II./Schützen-Regiment 394*, the main body of *Artillerie-Regiment 75*, and *Pionier-Bataillon 39*); and *Sicherungsgruppe*[10] *von Türckheim* (*Aufklä-rungs-Abteilung 1* and *Panzerjäger-Abteilung 543*). For the time being, von Türckheim's forces remained in Orel and exerted command and control over all of the divisional trains elements arriving there.

The advance could not be continued on 27 October, since all of the columns remained bogged down in the muck. *Luftwaffe* transport squadrons had to be requested to get the necessary fuel forward. The heavily laden *Ju-52's* had to land at the provisional airfield at Tschern to unload their canisters and drums of fuel. Then there was the next problem. The access routes to the airfield were so muddy that only prime movers could make it through. Since there were only a limited number of them up front, the refueling of the tank battalions was considerably delayed. By then, the rifle regiments had secured their assembly areas; they were involved with the improvement of the roads and trails. Only *Oberst* Cuno's forces were able to move out that morning; *Panzer-Regiment 39* occupied Pissarjewka. After the lead elements of the regiment had crossed the bridge, it flew into the air. That armor regiment had to call off the pursuit of the enemy and set up security along the railway embankment at Pissarjewka.

Despite all that, the division intended to continue the attack. During the night, the individual battle groups were concentrated together and sent further to the front. The following account by an officer of *Schützen-Regiment 394* provides insight:

The rubbery muck clung to everything. You rocked from one side to the other. Terribly difficult. It rained; the mud grew higher and stickier. It stuck to your boots by the pound. We were sweating, despite

10. Roughly, "screening group."

the cold . . . ten minutes of a break and you started to freeze immediately. Keep going. You thought your legs couldn't do any more. The ground sucked at your boots. It got worse. . . . We frequently sank up to our knees in the mud. . . . Everyone tottered and staggered. Then you were in the muck, since your boot could no longer be pulled out. . . . Then there was a snowstorm. . . . A village after twenty kilometers. . . . But they houses had been burned down. . . . Another ten kilometers. . . . We got to a built-up area. It consisted of tiny *panje* huts. Just get in at that point. Nine hours of uninterrupted marching.

Generaloberst Guderian arrived at Pissarjewka on 28 October. He had summoned his commanders there to discuss continued operations. *General Freiherr* Geyr von Schweppenburg, *Generalmajor* Breith, *Oberst* Eberbach, *Oberst* Cuno, *Oberst* Hoernlein, and *Oberstleutnant* Munzel attended the meeting, which focused on the continuation of the advance on Tula. By then, the division was already pushing additional supply elements forward, with the result that all of the battalions could be partially rearmed and refueled that day. The armored elements of the *3. Panzer-Division* had advanced far forward and were quartering around Lapotkowo. The *I./Infanterie-Regiment (mot.) "Großdeutschland"* was attached to *Panzer-Regiment 6* there. On that clear evening of 29 October, the tanks conducting reconnaissance for *Panzer-Regiment 39* were only twenty-six kilometers south of Tula. It was intended to launch the attack on the city on 29 October in order to seal off Moscow from the south. Depending on the overall situation, the advance might be continued to Gorki (Nischi Nowgorod).

The night of 28–29 October saw frost, with the result that all of the roads and trails were trafficable. The armor brigade reorganized in the first few hours of the new day for the upcoming attack. An advance guard was formed from *Major* Frank's *II./Panzer-Regiment 6* and the

2nd Company of *"Großdeutschland."* Following closely behind was *Hauptmann* Schneider-Kostalski's *III./Panzer-Regiment 6* with the reinforced 1st Company of *"Großdeutschland."* *Oberstleutnant* Munzel and Oberst Eberbach followed with their headquarters. *Oberstleutnant* Schmidt-Ott's *I./Panzer-Regiment 6* led the second march serial, to which two batteries of the *II./Artillerie-Regiment 75*, the 3rd Company of *"Großdeutschland"*, and *Panzer-Regiment 35* also belonged.

The advance guard left the bivouac area at 0530 hours, bypassed the blown-up road bridge and advanced across the railway embankment east of Pissarjewka, only to turn towards the Jastrebzowa–Trossna road via Rebinka later on. Right near the railway station, the lead tank rolled over a mine. The engineers, who were mounted on board, also saw an obstacle. Correspondingly, the advance guard went around the village, since the advancing fighting vehicles were also receiving flanking fire by then. Russian aircraft observed the movements. German fighters were nowhere to be seen that day.

It wasn't until the regiment reached Kunaki that several flights of *Stukas* appeared. They dove on the previously identified enemy field positions there. After they had dropped their bombs, the aircraft started strafing in front of the lead tank elements. By doing so, they practically cleared the battlefield by themselves, since the tanks discovered only empty enemy positions when they entered Kunaki. The Soviets had withdrawn to the huts on both sides of the road during the aerial attacks and were very surprised by the appearance of the German ground elements. After a short firefight, the Russians came out of the huts and surrendered. Only two thirty-two-ton tanks continued to hold out at the entrance to the village. The lead company was able to eliminate them, however.

Major Frank was able to move out immediately, since the next group had arrived by then. Soviet artillery fire, coming from the left and the direction of Jassnaja-Poljana, started to impact the road. The fighting vehicles veered off the road, whereupon they started to receive antitank-gun fire from the front. Before the tanks could get into position, some of the infantry riding on the rear decks were shot.

Oberstleutnant Munzel moved up front and entered the large woods with the advance guard. It stretched across the front like a blocking position about ten kilometers outside of Tula. The companies succeeded in penetrating about 800 meters on both sides of the road into the thick underbrush without encountering enemy resistance. Then the sounds of heavy antiaircraft rounds could be heard on the road. The tanks were powerless against them as well. The exposed fighting vehicles pulled off the road to the sides and sought cover. The Russian guns could not be identified. The infantry from the 2nd Company of *"Großdeutschland"* jumped off the fighting vehicles and worked their way through the woods to the suspected enemy location. Two heavy antiaircraft guns were finally identified at extremely close range. The soldiers enveloped from the sides and eliminated the crews in close combat.

Hauptmann Schneider-Kostalski closed up with his battalion. The regimental commander issued new instructions. He directed the *III./Panzer-Regiment 6* to move to the right via Skuratowka and reach Staraja-Bassowo. Those fighting vehicles were able to make it through to the Jassnaja-Poljana rail station in a single bound without encountering the enemy. When the tanks attempted to cross the tracks, however, remotely detonated mines were set off. They did not cause any damage, but showed that the Soviets had identified the advancing columns. A few Soviet trucks were captured at the railway facilities. When the tankers had approached the vehicles, they saw that the engines were still running and the keys were still in the ignition. Apparently, the drivers had fled "head over heels" at the approach of the tanks.

After dispatching the two heavy antiaircraft guns, the *II./Panzer-Regiment 6* moved out again and advanced as far as Kossaja-Gora. After the tanks let their main guns do the talking, the Rus-

sians fled the battlefield, pulling back to the northwest. The fighting vehicles gave immediate pursuit, crossed through the village and reached the bridge at its northern outskirts. The engineers were summoned to search the bridge. They found mines and immediately started removing them. Another group was employed to the north at a railway underpass. Mines were discovered there as well. Together with eight men from the 3rd Company of engineers, *Leutnant* Seefeld cleared mines from four bridges. The fighting vehicles then moved out again.

While this was happening, the initial vehicles that were screening the following formations arrived. *Oberstleutnant* Munzel set up shop temporarily in a large smelting plant north of Kossaja-Gora. All of a sudden, there was a tremendous explosion. Dust, debris and fire. Bits of the walls, iron supports and wooden beams flew through the air. Large portions of the smelting plant had been blown up!

The regiment moved out again in the same march order. When the lead elements reached the terrain 800 meters south of Nowoje-Bassowo, they encountered antiaircraft-gun fire. In contrast to the previous encounter, the guns could be readily identified. With a few rounds from its 7.5-centimeter main gun, the lead tank was able to take out the enemy guns, with the result that the fighting vehicles that followed barely had to halt. The battalion moved into the narrow, extended village. Once again, antiaircraft-gun fire was received along the road. The fighting vehicles were unable to evade; they had to pull behind the houses. A few were able to make it to the railway station, where they then sought cover.

By then, it had turned dark. By order of the division, the attack was halted for the day. The armored regiment established security. The road signs indicated that Tula was only five kilometers away. The 3rd Battalion of the armored regiment remained in the northern part of Staraja-Bassowo, the 2nd Battalion screened from there to the middle of the village and the 1st Battalion to the southwest. Around 2130 hours, the report arrived that the attack was to be renewed the following morning at 0530 hours in order to take Tula in a *coup de main*. This was contrary to the division's previous intent.

The supply sections had performed admirably. Although the roads were rock hard with frost in the morning, they started transforming back to muck within a few hours after it started raining. The road bridge at Pissarjewka could not be negotiated until the engineers placed railway tracks on it. In some cases, the trucks did not reach the fighting elements until the morning with fuel and ammunition. That made it impossible to keep the timetable for the attack.

Gruppe Eberbach moved out at 0700 hours on 30 October. In the face of heavy fire, the battle group had to call off its attack within a few minutes and move back to the protection of the houses. *Oberstleutnant* Munzel arranged for the operation to wait until a battalion from "*Großdeutschland*" arrived. In contrast, *Hauptmann* Schneider-Kostalski and the *III./Panzer-Regiment 6* made better progress advancing from Staraja-Bassowo, but they did not make it too far, either. Russian artillery, antiaircraft guns and antitank guns placed devastating fires on all of the open terrain. The companies held up and looked for positions that offered good cover and concealment. The lack of a strong air force was felt; the few motorized forces were unable to break though the defenses established by the enemy over the course of the last two weeks.

The terrain around Tula was created by nature for the defense. The expansive industrial and mining areas, which provided the many factories and blast furnaces with raw materials, were overlaid with pockets of resistance of all types. The high ground, which was sparsely vegetated, allowed observation for kilometers on end into the defiles and valleys of the rolling terrain. Deeply echeloned field positions, covered on the far bank by artillery, antitank guns, mortars and, most of all, antiaircraft guns, had been established in a wide area all around Tula, a city of about 300,000.

The *III./Panzer-Regiment 6*, reinforced by the *1./Schützen-Regiment 3*, did not remain idle. It sent out patrols to all sides in an effort to discover a gap in the enemy's front lines. The tank commanders were able to easily observe from the hatches of their cupolas the vibrant rail and truck traffic along the approach routes to Tula. Due to the great distance, they were unable to engage.

That battalion, which was also joined by the 1st Company of "*Großdeutschland*," was able to cross a tank ditch west of the large brickworks. The Soviets attempted to stop the advance by means of antiaircraft and small arms fire. While the fighting vehicles raked the Russian positions with their main guns, the infantry worked their way forward and checkmated the enemy from the flank. The tanks rolled on and found themselves in a residential area on the southern outskirts of Tula that was not marked on the map.

There was no advancing there, since the Russians were placing heavy fire of all calibers on the terrain from the city, primarily the cemetery and the military facilities. The tank battalion had to set up an all-round defense. The commander of the 10th Company, *Oberleutnant Graf* Saurma-Jeltsch, left his fighting vehicle to reconnoiter the terrain. He did not get far. An antiaircraft round impacted next to him and shattered both of his legs. He collapsed, dead. *Unteroffizier* Ludwig and *Gefreiter* Wenz from his company were also killed. The *I./Panzer-Regiment 6* closed up and also took up positions in the workers' residential area. It likewise received heavy artillery fire. *Oberleutnant* von Kriegsheim, the acting commander of the 4th Company, and *Gefreiter* Blaschke were killed.

By 1130 hours, *Major* Frank's *II./Panzer-Regiment 6* had been reinforced by elements of "*Großdeutschland*." It was directed to continue the attack west of the road. The infantry were not in the position, however, of eliminating the two antiaircraft guns whose positions had been identified. That made it questionable whether the battalion would be able to move out, since heavy Russian fire continued to fall on the staging area.

The tricky situation was finally mastered by a young officer candidate from the *6./Flak-Regiment 11*. Despite the constantly impacting rounds, he pulled his 8.8-centimeter gun through the residential area, unlimbered and silenced the enemy antiaircraft guns after a few rounds.

Finally, at 1200 hours, the fighting vehicles of the 2nd Battalion rolled out again. Russian infantry and militia stubbornly defended the approach routes and had to be literally overrun. The companies moved through the woods east of Wyschnaja-Wolochowo and reached a defile in which a tank ditch prevented any further movement. Infantry and engineers immediately moved forward to try to bridge the ditch with tree trunks and any types of available beams.

Despite all of the obstacles and casualties, the soldiers of *"Großdeutschland"* did not give up. They remained at the throats of the Russians. Smoking out position after position, they slowly gained ground. In the lead was the 2nd Company of the elite regiment. Its commander, *Oberleutnant* Brockmann, was killed. *Leutnant* von Oppen, nineteen years old, assumed acting command of the remaining sixty men. The young officer advanced with his men, reached the first houses of the city and from his way forward, from house to house. But no one followed them. The infantry were exhausted, bleeding and freezing; in the end, they had to pull back.

By around 1700 hours, the *II./Panzer-Regiment 6* had breached the tank ditch and cleared the high ground behind it of the enemy. It then turned night. The companies had to set up all-round defenses, since fuel and ammunition had become scarce. But there was no rest during the night. The Soviet artillery, including Stalin organs, raked the entire foreground to Tula.

The last day of October dawned dreary and rainy. There was no advancing in front of Tula. *"Großdeutschland,"* with two of its battalions was right outside the southern edge of the city. Behind them were the fighting vehicles of the armor regiment. But they were condemned to inactivity. No supply columns made it forward during the night. A few *Ju-52* transporters flew in and dropped fuel canisters, some only five meters off the ground. In some cases, the canisters burst when hitting the rock-hard frozen ground.

Not only did the Soviets fire ceaselessly on the Germans positions with artillery, they also attacked from out of Tula around 1000 hours with six heavy tanks. The steel giants tore apart the thinly held infantry lines. The antitank guns of *"Großdeutschland"* knocked out four of the Russian tanks, with an 8.8-centimeter *Flak* eliminating the fifth one. At that point, the sixth tank fled the battlefield. A similar effort to penetrate the German front was made by two fifty-two-ton tanks, but they were eliminated by concentrated fires from the *II./Panzer-Regiment 6*.

The remaining hours of 31 October were spent with improving the friendly positions, which continued to suffer under the enemy's artillery fires. At the onset of darkness, the first field messes, fuel trucks and ammunition haulers made it to the regiment after three days. The men of the supply elements had made the impossible possible: they had conquered the muck.

The detachments and battalions that only had wheeled vehicles at their disposal were stuck in the mud and could neither move forward or backward. The logistics chain only worked as far as Mzensk. The engineers and the railway forces had restored the tracks that far, so that the first few trains could bring in freight. In Orel, it was almost like peacetime: Electric lights were burning in the houses and on the streets. A movie theater had been set up for the soldiers. But from Mzensk forward, nothing was working.

The division logistics officer, *Hauptmann i.G.* Barth, had all available *panje* carts commandeered, since only true horsepower could overcome the muck in some instances. The motorcycle infantry battalion had been directed to move behind the armor regiment three days previously; it was still in the city. The departure of *Schützen-Regiment 3* was also postponed daily. In the meantime, the riflemen were busy with improving roads and constructing corduroy roads. Trees were felled and half-destroyed Russian huts and bunker facilities were torn apart to create base material for driving along the roads.

Schützen-Regiment 394 was employed to screen the flanks, and its 1st Battalion reached Plawsk during that period. The *SPW's* and other vehicles remained behind in the marshland to the rear. Even the detour routes were barely passable, since the Soviets had destroyed all bridges and footpaths during their withdrawal. Despite all of the difficulties, *Schützen-Regiment 394* slowly closed up to *Panzer-Regiment 6* and reached the area ten kilometers outside of Tula, after the riflemen had simply moved and marched the last few kilometers right along the railway tracks. *Schützen-Regiment 3*, which had also been directed to move forward on 31 October, was still in its screening area. Finally, on 1 November, its two battalions moved out. It also had to leave behind its vehicles. Baggage, weapons and ammunition were loaded on the *panje* carts. The most secure route was along the railway tracks of the Mzensk–Tschern line.

Generalmajor Breith was initially up front with the armor regiment. He recognized the senselessness of a continued attack on Tula and, feeling the responsibility he had towards his men, called it off. He and his battle staff set up their command post in the former "Tolstoy" Middle School in Jassnaja-Poljana. That locality seemed to have a unique sense of peacefulness in the middle of the woods. The estate of Count Tolstoy consisted of two homes and a few administrative buildings. German soldiers took the facilities under their wing and prevented their destruction. Tolstoy's burial plot was not too far away, and it was guarded by men of the division. The first soldiers killed in the Tula area were given over to eternal rest not too far from the famous Russian poet. The medical battalion established a clearing station there with its 1st Company. There was a large influx of wounded. *Oberleutnant* von Rochow's 2nd Ambulance Platoon was constantly on the go, especially since so many vehicles had been lost, in taking

the wounded to Tschern. *Stabsarzt* Dr. Koch's 2nd Medical Company was set up there to handle the wounded soldiers. The badly wounded were flown from there to Orel.

As a result of its many vehicular losses, the division reorganized the armored regiment on 5 November. The three battalion headquarters were retained as command and cadre formations. The regiment was reorganized tactically with: a regimental headquarters; a tank section with the headquarters of the *III./Panzer-Regiment 6* (*Hauptmann* Schneider-Kostalski) and three line companies, consisting of the 1st Company (*Oberleutnant* Vopel), the 2nd Company (*Oberleutnant* Markowski), and the 3rd Company (*Oberleutnant* Müller-Hauff); and a tank supply section with the headquarters of the *I./Panzer-Regiment 6* (*Oberstleutnant* Schmidt-Ott), also with three line companies. *Panzer-jäger-Abteilung 521* was once again placed under the command of *Major* Frank with its two remaining companies and remained attached to the armor regiment.

Since the Soviets were not content with simply disrupting the assembly areas with artillery fire but also started to launch infantry attacks, the armor regiment was employed to guard the northern flank of the division on 5 November. Up to that point, only one platoon from the 5th Company of *"Großdeutschland"* had been screening a sector of three kilometers.

Under extremely difficult circumstances, *Hauptmann* von dem Heyden-Rynsch's *I./Schützen-Regiment 394* had forced its way forward through muck and woods—constantly engaging Soviet riflemen, tanks, and partisans—as far as Tula, where it went into position next to the 1st Battalion of *"Großdeutschland."* Both of those elements screened in the direction of Tula. The regimental headquarters of *Oberst* Hoernlein and *Oberstleutnant* Audörsch were located near one another. The riflemen of the *I./Schützen-Regiment 394* were exhausted, tired and dirty. In the fighting, especially in the area around Kitajewka, they had to make many sacrifices. The village was retaken by the Russians during the night of 5–6 November. The 3rd Company launched an immediate counterattack and was able to drive out the enemy in fighting that lasted for hours. In the process, 100 Russians were captured. The company was only able to hold out in the locality during the day, since the Soviets launched attacks from three sides with numerically superior forces during the night. The company evacuated the village, leaving behind all of its heavy weapons. Two men were reported missing. The riflemen were able to make it back across the railway embankment and establish contact with the 4th Company.

On 6 November, *Schützen-Regiment 3* started its move forward to relieve *"Großdeutschland."* Foot marching and vehicular movement were easier, since it had turned colder and all of the routes had frozen firmly. The 1st Battalion reached Jassnaja-Poljana that same day and relieved the first elements of *"Großdeutschland"* during the night. The battalion was guided forward by a traffic control elements that had been established by the division and which was commanded by *Hauptmann* Kersten, the commander of the 3rd Battalion of the divisional artillery. The battalions of the divisional artillery had also made it forward to Jassnaja-Poljana with great difficulty. One battalion each was dedicated to supporting the *I./Schützen-Regiment 3* and the *I./Schützen-Regiment 394*. The two *Flak* battalions up front assumed responsibility for protecting the north (*Flak-Abteilung 91*) and the south (the *II./Flak-Regiment 11*).

The reinforcement of the riflemen had come at the right time. During the night, the Soviets had launched a surprise attack on the Tolstoy estate and attempted to assault the clearing station that had just been established there. *Oberleutnant* Müller-Hauff's 3rd Tank Company, reinforced by a battery of artillery and a platoon from *Pionier-Bataillon 27*,[11] moved out against the bridge over the Upa at 0815 hours to eject the enemy and blow up the railway bridge 500

meters downstream. The Russians fled when the German fighting vehicles approached. Artillery fire then prevented further advance, however, with the result that the bridge could not be blown up. The company remained engaged with the enemy and was unable to return to the regiment until it had turned dark. At the same time that *"Großdeutschland"* was relieved, the armored regiment was also pulled out of its sector, with *Oberleutnant* Vopel's 1st Tank Company relieving the 2. and *5./Panzer-Regiment 35*. His company established outposts oriented in the direction of Tula.

Ever since the beginning of November, the Soviet command had been intent on preventing the advance of the *XXIV. Armee-Korps (mot.)*. Two cavalry corps, five rifle divisions and a tank brigade were attacking the flanks of Eberbach's brigade, in an effort to also get to the rear of the corps at the same time. The *LIII. Armee-Korps*, launching a counterattack with its main effort directed towards Teploje, pushed the enemy back slowly. Individual elements of both *Panzer-Regiment 6* and *Panzer-Regiment 35* were attached to that corps for short operations. The *II./Schützen-Regiment 394* was also cross-attached to the corps and saw heavy fighting at Krutja and Dworiki. The supreme command of the Red Army was concentrating more and more of its forces around Moscow. The Brjansk Front was dissolved and its divisions allocated to the Western and Southwestern Fronts. Facing the sector of the *XXIV. Armee-Korps (mot.)* was the Soviet 50th Army.

On 7 November, the anniversary of the October Revolution, there was enemy artillery fire all along the corps frontage. The heavy fire was concentrated on the positions of the 3rd Battalion of *"Großdeutschland"* during the morning. Around 1000 hours, several waves of enemy riflemen stormed the thinly held German lines. When the enemy tanks started to approach, the battered soldiers were no longer able to hold out,

---

11. By that time, the battalion had been redesignated as *Panzer-Pionier-Bataillon 27*. It was the engineer battalion of the *17. Panzer-Division*.

and they pulled back. The Soviets came through the gap in the line and occupied Hills 216.6 and 232.8. The enemy attack then expanded to include the sector of *Schützen-Regiment 394*. The outposts were driven out of Kitajewka and were only able to reestablish themselves along the railway embankment. Three T-34's were knocked out by antitank guns from *"Groß-deutschland."* The quickly alerted 3rd Tank Company entered the fray around 1200 hours and cleared Malejewka. The enemy artillery and antiaircraft fire continued throughout the day. Fortunately, all of the attacks could be driven off, with the front outside of Tula continuing to hold.

The enemy forces continued to be reinforced and attacked the positions of both rifle regiments during the night with his well-camouflaged riflemen. The enemy was able to take Malejewka once again. The 1st Battalion of *Schützen-Regiment 394* was especially threatened. A reconnaissance-in-force conducted by the 1st Company determined that the Russians were already in the battalion's rear. All of the drivers and trains personnel were soon engaged with the enemy. Fortunately, the 2nd Battalion of the regiment arrived in time and temporarily cleared up the situation around Kossaja-Gora. The situation was not simple, since the enemy forces were numerically superior everywhere. In addition, the enemy used searchlights in Tula to illuminate the terrain to show the attacking infantry the German positions. Since there were no heavy weapons on hand, it proved impossible to eliminate the antiaircraft searchlights. The general situation of that time is reflected in the following lines *Generaloberst* Guderian wrote in a letter: "It is misery for the troops and a great shame for our operations, since the enemy is winning time. . . . God only knows how it will all turn out."

Fortune smiled a bit more on *Schützen-Regiment 3* that day. With the exception of a few skirmishes in front of the sector of the 1st Battalion, it was quiet there. The 2nd Battalion, which had conducted successful immediate counterat-

tacks the previous day, stormed Krukowo and conducted reconnaissance-in-force in all directions. On 8 November, that battalion suffered one dead and nine wounded in the 10th Company. The battalion knocked out four tanks, captured five machine guns, and took seventy-three prisoners.

Elements of the armor regiment were also involved in the fighting in front of the positions of *Schützen-Regiment 394*. The 2nd Tank Company moved out at 0700 hours. It cleared Malejewka for the second time and advanced on Bolschaja-Jelaraja. The company encountered strong enemy forces in a defile and had to fight its way slowly back to the lines of the 1st Battalion of *"Großdeutschland."* Hauptmann Schneider-Kostalski then brought his 3rd Tank Company forward. He had the two companies attack and was able to set Bolschaja-Jelaraja alight. The enemy forces holding out there—the 2nd Siberian Regiment of the 413th Rifle Division—pulled back to the east.

While the enemy could generally be held in check along the front to east and south against the constantly attacking Russian forces, some enemy elements succeeded in infiltrating through the German positions and surfacing in the rear area. For instance, *Panzerjäger-Abteilung 521* encountered an enemy force of about 250 men quite by surprise in the area southwest of Progress. The enemy detachment had had the mission of taking Kossaja-Gora from the rear. That day, the division was threatened with being cut off. The corps and the field army were already considering whether to pull the division back, since *Infanterie-Regiment (mot.) "Großdeutschland,"* which was still attached, could hardly be considered combat capable at that stage.

The ninth of November was no different than the previous day. The Soviets were dictating the terms of the fighting outside of Tula with their artillery and aerial attacks. The enemy launched smaller-scale but energetically conducted immediate counterattacks against the positions of the 3rd Battalion of *"Großdeutschland"* and the

I./Schützen-Regiment 394. The 3rd and 4th Companies of the latter battalion were able to turn back all enemy attacks. The division then ordered the hills that had been lost to be recaptured. The Soviets beat the Germans to the punch, however, by placing strong artillery fires on the thinly held German strong-points and then attacking. The Soviets succeeded in advancing as far as Kischkino, ten kilometers east of Jassnaja-Poljana, where they ran into forces of the *II./Schützen-Regiment 3* and the *II./Schützen-Regiment 394*. In Kischkino proper that morning was only the 2nd Company of the divisional engineers. Fortunately, the enemy's rapid advance was identified and temporarily halted by fires from the heavy infantry guns of the *11./Schützen-Regiment 3*. An immediate counterattack launched by the *6./Schützen-Regiment 3* was unsuccessful. *Panzerjäger-Abteilung 521* then provided six guns to the 2nd Battalion. Early in the afternoon, the 2nd Tank Company also arrived from Kossaja-Gora. Around 1400 hours, the attack on the defile between Kischkino and Lobynskoje was started.

The thrust did not advance well in places, since the terrain, which was covered with dense woods and vegetation, gave the Soviets good covered and concealed positions. The enemy—it was the 827th Rifle Regiment—allowed the German soldiers to pass by, only to fire on them from the rear. There were considerable casualties, especially in the 6th Company. Nonetheless, the riflemen were able to occupy the defile by the onset of darkness and get to "TP" Hill. The companies of the 2nd Battalion suffered nine dead and sixteen wounded. They dug in for the night, while the tanks pulled back to Lutowinowa and the 1st and 2nd Companies of the engineer battalion moved back into Kischkino. The next morning, the 2nd Battalion moved out shortly after 0600 hours and took Lobynskoje after an hour of fighting. Two hours later, the 8th Company took Brykowa, supported by the fires of the 1st Battery of the divisional artillery. The enemy left his positions there, pulling back into the fruit orchards, which were covered in snow and allowed little visibility. It was impossible for the riflemen to penetrate into the thicket. The 1st Company of engineers then tossed smoke grenades, and the fighting vehicles of the 3rd Tank Company fired with everything they had. The 1st Battery of artillery also moved forward. The combination slowly wore down the enemy. Shortly after 1200 hours, *Hauptmann* Peschke issued orders to attack again. The 8th Company assaulted. Its commander, *Oberleutnant* von Becker, was killed, along with four other men of the company. *Leutnant* Pauckstadt then led the riflemen, who succeeded in ejecting the enemy half an hour later. In the course of the two days of fighting against the 2nd Battalion, the Soviets lost 43 machine guns, 11 infantry guns, and 600 rifles; 377 prisoners were taken.

That was the last successful operation of the division outside of Tula. The domes of the churches of the city, which had been visible up to that point, would soon disappear from the field of view of the German soldiers. At 1700 hours on 9 November, the division issued orders for a transition to the defense: "*3. Panzer-Division* transitions to the defense south of Tula. It shortens its front by withdrawing from Tula to avoid an envelopment and establish strong reserves."

That night, the first formations started to disengage from the enemy, principally "*Groß-deutschland*." They pulled back to the northern outskirts of Nowoje-Bassowo and Pirowo. The occupation of the new position was continued on 10 November and, by that evening, the new lines were occupied by the division, which had formed three battle groups.

Oberst Kleemann commanded the righthand group, which was positioned in Lobynskoje, Skuratowka, and Warwarowka. It consisted of the *II./Schützen-Regiment 3*, the *II./Schützen-Regiment 394*, *Pionier-Bataillon 39*, the *1./Schützen-Regiment 3*, the *1./Panzerjäger-Abteilung 543*, and the *6./Flak-Regiment 59*. The 1st, 2nd, 7th, and 8th Batteries of the divisional artillery were in support. The center group was commanded by *Oberstleutnant* Audörsch. It was comprised of the *I./Schützen-Regiment 3*, the *I./Schützen-Regiment 394*, *Kradschützen-Bataillon 3*, the *3./Pionier-Bataillon 39*, *Panzer-jäger-Abteilung 521*, *Artillerie-Abteilung 400* (the regimental artillery of *Infanterie-Regiment (mot.) "Großdeutschland"*), and the remaining batteries of the 2nd Battalion of artillery. Audörsch's forces were arrayed from Warwarowka to the eastern edge of the wood line east of Rwy. *Hauptmann* Ziervogel's reconnaissance battalion screened on the left of the division. *Infanterie-Regiment (mot.) "Großdeutschland"* was designated the division's ready reserve. It was pulled out of the front, leaving behind its heavy weapons to support *Schützen-Regiment 394*. The armored regiment assembled in the vicinity of the division command post. *Panzer-Regiment 35* moved to Trossna, where it was placed at the direct disposal of the corps.

The disengagement from the enemy succeeded without being noticed or disturbed. The western flank of the division turned out to be clear of the enemy, with the exception of strong elements of the Soviet 290th Rifle Division, which were in the villages northwest of the Mysa. The reconnaissance battalion established contact with the *XXXXIII. Armee-Korps*, which had reached the Tula–Aleksin road with its *31. Infanterie-Division* and *131. Infanterie-Division*. The division established its defenses in the designated sector. It formed a strong ready reserve, which could be committed whenever the situation demanded it. *Oberstleutnant* Munzel commanded the reserve forces, which consisted of the 2nd and 3rd Tank Companies, the *I./Schützen-Regiment 3*, the *1./Schützen-Regiment 394*, and a battery from the 2nd Battalion of artillery. All nonessential vehicles of the forces were concentrated that day to be sent to the Orel area later on.

By then, a deep frost had arrived. The temperature dipped to 16 degrees below zero (3.2 degrees Fahrenheit). There were new and unwelcome surprises for the forces in the field. The gas lines on the wheeled vehicles froze; it wasn't too different with the fighting vehicles. The engines had to be warmed up before they could be turned over. Even the grease in the turret traversing mechanisms froze up. The tracks on the tanks slid on the ice on the roads and in the fields. The crews placed spare track underneath to gain traction, but that also caused the spare track to be bent. A tank sometimes needed a whole hour to cover a kilometer. The logistics personnel only brought forward what the *Luftwaffe* could fly into Tschern. But it was even worse for the personnel. There were no winter uniforms; correspondingly, the first cases of frostbite appeared. On 13 November, the temperature registered 24 below (-11.2 Fahrenheit).

"General Winter" had arrived on the battlefield.

Rations are distributed within the
I./Schützen-Regiment 394.

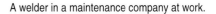

A welder in a maintenance company at work.

Winter 1941. A mail train has arrived
outside of Orel and is quickly
unloaded so that the highly desired
mail quickly reaches the units
through supply channels.

The uniform section followed the forces in the field, wherever they went. It was also "completely motorized," as the electric sewing machine attests.

Lunch is prepared for the headquarters company of the *I./Schützen-Regiment 394.*

The *3./Schützen-Regiment 394* in the attack.

Feldwebel Levermann, the rations trains leader of the 1st Battalion, supervises the distribution of personal-demand items for the *4./Schützen-Regiment 394*. *Obergefreiter* Stöver and *Obergefreiter* Seefeld are seen passing out items to *Feldwebel* Kaiser (list in hand).

Generalleutnant Model visits the auxiliary hospital in Unetscha. *Assistenzarzt* Dr. Türk is seen reporting to him.

A Soviet T-34 knocked out by *Leutnant* Störck (engineer platoon of *Schützen-Regiment 394*) in front of the corps command post in Unetscha.

Major Schneider-Kostalski, the bold commander of the *III./Panzer-Regiment 6.*

The advance of the *Panzergruppe* in 1941. Standing in the staff car on the viewer's left is *Oberstleutnant* Audörsch, the commander of *Schützen-Regiment 394.*

The main clearing station of the *3. Panzer-Division* in Meljna.

CHAPTER 12

From the Upa to the Schat: The Battle for Tula

Generaloberst Guderian's *2. Panzer-Armee* was directed to continue the offensive by going around Tula from the south and then advancing far to the east to then pivot to the northeast in the direction of Gorki. Since Tula could not be taken frontally, it was intended to take the important city, which blocked the route to Moscow, by enveloping from the east while simultaneously attacking from the west. As of the middle of November, the field army had the following forces at its disposal (from right to left): the *XXXXVII. Armee-Korps (mot.)*, commanded by *General der Artillerie* Lemelsen and consisting of the *18. Panzer-Division* and the *10., 25.*, and *29. Infanterie-Divisionen (mot.)*; the *LIII. Armee-Korps*, commanded by *General der Artillerie* Weisenberger (*Generalleutnant* Fischer von Weikertsthal, effective 1 December) and consisting of the *167.* and *112. Infanterie-Divisionen*; the *XXIV. Armee-Korps (mot.)*, commanded by *General der Panzertruppen* Geyr von Schweppenburg and consisting of the *3., 4.*, and *17. Panzer-Divisionen* and *Infanterie-Regiment (mot.) "Großdeutschland"*; and the *XXXXIII. Armee-Korps*, commanded by *General der Infanterie* Heinrici and consisting of the *31.* and *131. Infanterie-Divisionen*.

The *3. Panzer-Division* was by itself in the Tula area. On 11 November, the *4. Panzer-Division* moved to the east wing of the corps, while the *17. Panzer-Division* remained where it was, between Orel and Tschern, due to a lack of fuel. It wasn't until the onset of the deep frost that the supply columns could use the roads again and resupply began to function. Many tanks and trucks that had been stuck for weeks in the mud hole around Kromy finally began to return to their units again. The drivers had not had it easy over the past few weeks. They were bogged solidly down in the muck and could only be resupplied from the air. In the process, they were exposed to continuous attacks from the air. Some personnel were unable to pass that test of nerves. When the commander of the 1st Maintenance Company, *Hauptmann* Eikmann, drove back along the route on 19 November, he found another seventy-one stuck and abandoned vehicles.

On 13 November, the division ordered a battle group under the command of *Oberstleutnant* Munzel to clear the bend in the Upa and block the western access roads to Tula. Munzel's battle group, consisting of the reconnaissance battalion, the three *ad hoc* tank companies, the *SPW* company of *Schützen-Regiment 3*, and the 5th Battery of the divisional artillery, combed the woods at Gorjuschino in extremely difficult circumstances. The temperature registered -25 degrees Celsius (-13 Fahrenheit). It then crossed the high ground at Ugrjum and cleared the area of the enemy. The mission was already accomplished by noon, so that the battle group could be brought back to the combat outpost line, with the exception of the reconnaissance battalion, which continued to advance to the north and take the airstrip at Masslowo without encountering the enemy. The next day, a similar operation was conducted in the direction of Michalkowo. Four *Panzer IV's* under *Leutnant* von Arnim and twelve motorcycles under *Feldwebel* Gradel (the *3./Kradschützen-Bataillon 3*) started to enter the village. It was at that point that the small battle group encountered superior numbers of the enemy. Two fighting vehicles were lost to mines. *Oberfeldwebel* Ostwald, the forward observer from the 5th Battery, requested immediate fire support so that the battle group could pull back. At that point, the armored regiment was pulled

out of the front and assigned to screen Jassnaja-Poljana again.

The *XXIV. Panzer-Korps* reorganized over the next two days for an attack to the east. *Infanterie-Regiment (mot.) "Großdeutschland"* was employed to screen the road south of Tula, where it relieved the elements of the *3. Panzer-Division* that were positioned there. The corps employed the *4. Panzer-Division* on the right and the *3. Panzer-Division* on the left. The main effort was directed to be along the inner flanks, with the object of breaking through the enemy between Dedilowo and Tula and then, later on, advancing to the northeast across the Schat with the objective of Wenew. The corps had the following tank forces at its disposal: *Panzer-Regiment 6* with fifty-two vehicles (three *Panzer II's*, thirty-seven *Panzer III's*, nine *Panzer IV's*, and three command tanks), *Panzer-Regiment 35* with thirty-five vehicles, and *Panzer-Regiment 39* with fifteen vehicles. The fighting vehicles were camouflaged with a coat of whitewash. The attack was scheduled for 0500 hours on 18 November.

The division formed two battle groups. The righthand group, forming the main effort, was *Kampfgruppe Kleemann*, consisting of *Schützen-Regiment 3*, *Panzer-Regiment 6*, the *1./Panzer-jäger-Abteilung 521*, the *1./Schützen-Regiment 394*, the *2.* and *3./Pionier-Bataillon 39*, the *6./Flak-Regiment 59*, and the *I./Artillerie-Regiment 75*. The lefthand battle group, *Oberstleutnant* Audörsch's, consisted of *Schützen-Regiment 394*, *Kradschützen-Bataillon 3*, the *2.* and *3./Panzerjäger-Abteilung 521*, the *1./Pionier-Bataillon 39*, and the *III./Artillerie-Regiment 75*.

The Upa was a small river that snaked in twists and turns east of the road to Tula. It was the first objective of the *3. Panzer-Division*. It was still dark, when the batteries of *Artillerie-Regiment 75*, as well as *Artillerie-Regiment 69* and *Mörser-Abteilung 818*,[1] sent their fiery greetings over to the positions of the new

---

1. Both of these were separate artillery formation allocated to field armies and equipped with heavy howitzers of at least 15-centimeter caliber or, more likely, 21-centimeter caliber.

Siberian regiments opposite them. Our riflemen raised themselves out of their trenches and foxholes, assaulted in the direction of the river and hastened across the 10-centimeter-thick ice to the opposite bank. The engineers placed boards and beams on the ice so that the motorcycles and *SPW's* did not break through.

With the exception of the large railway bridge, all of the other bridges along the Upa had been blown up. It was the division's intent to take that bridge intact, if possible, since it was of great importance for the execution of the attack as well as future supplies. The commander of *Schützen-Regiment 394*, *Oberstleutnant* Audörsch, used his engineers, commanded by the Knight's Cross recipient *Leutnant* Störck, for that mission. The brave officer made use of a ruse. Störck took off with four men—*Unteroffizier* Strucken, *Obergefreiter* Beyle, and two Ukrainians of ethnic German descent in Russian uniforms. The rest of the engineer platoon, fourteen men under the command of the assistant platoon leader, *Feldwebel* Heyeres, followed within earshot.

The engineer platoon snuck through the thinly held Russian lines in pitch darkness, and the men reached the bridge without incident. Right in front of it, along the embankment, the men discovered foxholes on both sides, each with two men in them! The guards were sleeping! "Calmed down with a pistol butt," they continued to sleep. The two machine guns emplaced there were taken along. While Störck walked upright with his four men across the approximately eighty-meter-long bridge, the engineer platoon moved up and took the "sedated" guards under control.

The men had crossed two-thirds of the bridge, when a Russian guard approached them. They had to then use the ruse that had been discussed earlier, so that things did not go wrong. The Ukrainians then acted as though they had prisoners with them and spoke Russian to one another along the lines of: "Well, it looks like we're in a neighboring sector, but we need to get rid of these prisoners shortly." The guard was deceived by the measure and was taken prisoner himself without a sound being uttered. Despite the darkness, things did not seem quite right to another guard, who was standing at the end of the bridge. He ran before Störck could reach him. He sounded the alarm and sought cover along the embankment.

By then, however, the rest of the platoon was across the bridge, and the machine guns were quickly emplaced where ordered. In the blink of an eye, there were wild fireworks with machine guns and hand grenades. Most of the sleep-drunk Russians of the bridge guard force, who had been rendered panic stricken by the fires, surrendered. The bridge was taken. Signal flares arced skyward, the signal to the regimental commander, who had collocated his command post with the point of departure for the engineer platoon, that the operation had succeeded and that support needed to be sent to the engineer platoon. As it turned light, an immediate counterattack by the enemy lasting some thirty minutes was beaten back, since the regimental attack had also commenced by then.

In all, the Russians took losses of eighty-seven men in captured, killed and wounded. The engineer platoon was able to capture five machine guns, two antitank guns and three mortars. In the course of that risky mission, it lost one man dead and one wounded.

A similar ruse was employed by the *II./Schützen-Regiment 3*. As a result of the fluent Russian of *Unteroffizier* Roemer (6th Company), the guards were overrun and his company was able to cross the Upa without a fight.

Schützen-Regiment 3 rapidly crossed its 1st Battalion across the river and took Demidowka. *Leutnant* Heurich, the acting commander of the 3rd Company, was killed. *Leutnant* Schuppius took his place, combed through the locality with his riflemen and drove the enemy from his closest trenches. The battalion was unable to advance further, however, since the Soviets held their main field positions. The 2nd Company of the battalion screened the right flank in the direction of Malaja Sujewa, since there was a constant stream of fire coming from there. When a patrol from the company felt its way forward toward the village around noon, it entered the village without any contact, only to be suddenly engaged from all sides. The friendly riflemen had to pull back quickly; four dead and two wounded remained in the hands of the Soviets.

By early morning, the *II./Schützen-Regiment 3* had taken Dubowka. In the process, it spent its strength. The 7th Company advanced as far as Kamenka, but it was unable to move any further, despite support from the 10th and 11th Companies. It was not until *Schützen-Regiment 394* had crossed at Truschkino and Oserki that the overall advance started making progress again.

Although a *Stuka* attack late in the morning had demolished considerable portions of the enemy field fortifications, it had not broken the enemy's will to resist. The riflemen were subjected to the full fury of the Russian fire the entire time. *Panzer-Regiment 6* did not join the fray until noon, since there was still no crossing point for tanks at Truschkino. *Oberstleutnant* Munzel decided to pull his 1st and 3rd Companies back and send them over the railway bridge that had been taken by the engineer platoon of *Schützen-Regiment 394*. While the two companies rolled north, the *I./Schützen-Regiment 394* succeeded in taking Truschkino after heavy fighting. Fortunately, the Upa in the vicinity of Kamenka was not too deep, with the result that the 2nd Company of *Panzer-Regiment 6* was able to immediately start fording the ice-cold water.

The friendly advance then turned fluid again. The fighting vehicles of *Oberleutnant* Markowski and the men of *Hauptmann* Peschke attacked east. Contrary to expectations, heavily fortified Hill 292.2 could be taken. The tanks started advancing along the road between Wjewka-Staraja and Wjewka-Nowaje. The *7./Schützen-Regiment 3* had to conduct a fierce fight for the houses in Wjewka-Staraja, however, since numerically superior enemy forces had barricaded themselves there. Since it had turned dark by then, the company was stuck outside the village.

Hauptmann Schneider-Kostalski arrived on the battlefield with his two companies. His 1st Company was immediately inserted into the line on the right wing of *Schützen-Regiment 3*, while the 3rd Company prepared for operations outside of Wjewka-Staraja. Since it had turned completely dark, the advance was halted for the day. Success was great. *Schützen-Regiment 3* took in 280 prisoners, but it also lost 16 dead and 51 wounded.

As soon as morning dawned, the attack was continued. The terrain was fairly flat; there was only high ground at the edges. Chimneys and mine works were seen everywhere, a reminder of the industrial area south of Tula. The men suffered terribly under the cold, since they still did not have any winter uniforms. Moreover, they offered good targets to the enemy in their field-gray coats in the snowy landscape.

Shortly after 0700 hours on 19 November, both battle groups moved out. On the right wing, the *I./Schützen-Regiment 3* (*Major* Wellmann), along with the attached *1./Panzer-Regiment 6* (*Oberleutnant* Vopel), succeeded in occupying Malaja-Sujewa. By doing so, it eliminated the threat to the flank there. *Oberleutnant* Vopel and the *2./Schützen-Regiment 3* advanced farther to the east and established contact with the *3./Schützen-Regiment 3* (*Leutnant* Oesten) at Ssalassowka. An attack by the 3rd Company to the south was unable to develop, since the enemy opened heavy fire from the flank.

The *II./Schützen-Regiment 3*, neighboring its sister 1st Battalion on the left, had also moved out to the southeast and advanced just to the east of the main road. When contact was established with the 1st Battalion, the Russians pulled back. By noon, both battalions had reached Kalmyky-Mal. While *Major* Wellmann's riflemen screened to the south and west, *Hauptmann* Peschke's men continued advancing. His companies were able to occupy Kalmyky-Bolsch. That battalion then pushed its screening forces east as far as Markaschowa.

The main effort of the attack was with *Schützen-Regiment 394* and the two tank companies of

Hauptmann Schneider-Kostalski. The objective was Bolochowka, which was entered on the Russian general staff map with a total of four houses. Imagine how surprised the German soldiers were when they fought their way forward, kilometer after kilometer, and found out that they were dealing with an extensive industrial town. Bolochowka was no village—it was a defended industrial city.

As a result, *Schützen-Regiment 394* was unable to take the locality in a frontal attack. Instead, his men pulled back slowly to the south in an effort to penetrate from there. Although the riflemen succeeded in getting over the high ground and literally work their way into the town meter by meter, the regiment suffered considerable losses on the first day. The 1st Battalion alone lost twelve dead and fifty-eight wounded. The losses were that large because the Siberians, who were facing our units there for the first time, did not open fire until practically pointblank range. The Soviets defended stubbornly from well-concealed positions, firing at the riflemen that appeared right in front of them. An example should suffice. The *II./Schützen-Regiment 394* was bounding its way forward

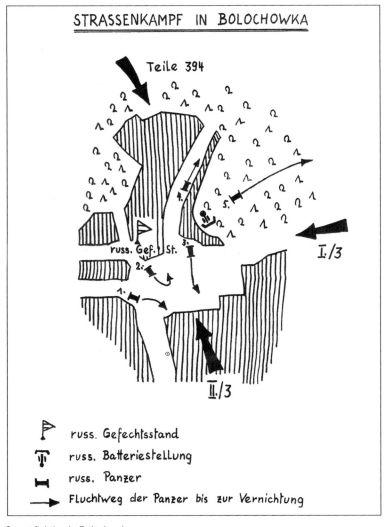

Street fighting in Bolochowka.

into the town. Its lead company encountered a wooden fence. The fence suddenly collapsed upon itself. Behind it were Siberians. They opened fire on the 7th Company at fifty meters, cutting it down. The commander, *Oberleutnant* Multhaupt, was killed, along with two other officers and many enlisted personnel. By then it was 1600 hours and night. The division transitioned to a security posture at Bolochowka and just to its south.

After Stalin was certain that Japan would not march against Russia, he withdrew the Siberian forces from the Far East and committed them to the fighting in front of Moscow.

Kampfgruppe Kleemann—consisting of *Schützen-Regiment 3*, *Panzer-Regiment 6*, the *I./Schützen-Regiment 394*, the *I./Artillerie-Regiment 75*, the *9./Artillerie-Regiment 75*, the *6./Artillerie-Regiment 69*, *Pionier-Bataillon 39*, elements of *Panzerjäger-Abteilung 521*, and elements of *Panzerjäger-Abteilung 543*—was given the mission of taking Bolochowka. The divisional engineers, who had already started erecting a bridge over the Upa on 18 November using the bridging sections of *Hauptmann* Winkler, started reconnoitering in order to establish a bridge over the Schat at Nowoje. *Oberleutnant* Möllhoff of the 3rd Company of engineers conducted the reconnaissance along the Schat. In addition, the 1st Bridging Section, under the leadership of *Leutnant* Mertens, had starting bridging the Upa at Truschkino by then. The sixteen-ton bridge later had a length of thirty-two meters and a width of 3.5 meters.

The brigade staged around Ulanowka and started its attack at 1000 hours on 20 November. The artillery preparation proved ineffective in places, since it landed too short and, as a consequence of the morning fog and the smoldering mining facilities, observation was barely possible.

The *I./Schützen-Regiment 3* moved out with its 2nd Company on the right and its 3rd on the left. The 1st Company of *Leutnant* Lohse was used to reconnoiter and also screen the flank, oriented to the east. The *SPW* company advanced from Pagassowa, which was clear of the enemy, to the north. In doing so, it encountered two Russian tanks at a large mine. The Soviets from the 413th Rifle Division pulled back in the direction of Bolochowka. The *SPW* company then swung west to reinforce the attack of the battalion. *Leutnant* Braun, moving in the lead vehicle, was able to effectively support the 2nd Company, which was struggling for some mine facilities on the east edge of Bolochowka, with his 3.7-centimeter cannon. The Soviets had set up defensively there and in the wood line to the north. They were firing with mortars and heavy antitank guns. For the time being, the battalion had to call off its attack and set up all-round security. Contact with the 2nd Battalion of the regiment was maintained by a patrol led by *Unteroffizier* Ronneberg of the 3rd Company.

The *II./Schützen-Regiment 3* of *Hauptmann* Peschke, along with the *3./Panzer-Regiment 6* of *Oberleutnant* Müller-Hauff, advanced on Bolochowka from the south. The 8th Company was able to assault the collective farm quickly and take the residential areas arrayed in front of the town from there. The 6th Company moved up alongside the 8th. The movements of both companies then bogged down, since they were receiving heavy fire from the nearby woods and the industrial facilities. The rifle battalion brought up its infantry guns and the antitank platoon that had been attached to it. For the time being, however, they were still unable to advance, since Russian tanks had rolled up in the meantime.

Major Haas's reinforced *I./Schützen-Regiment 394* had crossed the 800 meters of open ground in the southwest in the meantime and was positioned at the edge of Bolochowka. Numerous houses and factories were burning in the town proper. The Siberians put up a brave defense and could only be driven out in tough house-to-house fighting. Since heavy Soviet tanks appeared, the rifle companies were unable to advance.

The regiment ordered a 8.8-centimeter *Flak* forward. The gun was able to take out the first fighting vehicle within a few minutes, but a second one approached. After four rounds, it was also eliminated. Then a T-34 appeared in front of the *I./Schützen-Regiment 3*. It drove into a construction excavation pit and got stuck there.

The fighting for Bolochowka continued. House after house was taken in close combat. The fiercest resistance was being offered to the attacking riflemen from a two-story brick house. The headquarters of the Siberian 2nd Rifle Regiment, along with about seventy Red Army men, had barricaded itself inside. The infantry guns and a howitzer that had been brought forward fired sixty rounds into the building. A platoon from the *6./Schützen-Regiment 3* then moved out to assault. Russian rifle rounds started whistling around the ears of the German soldiers. *Hauptmann* Peschke thereupon ordered the attack called off.

The *I./Schützen-Regiment 394* had cleared the remaining houses of Bolochowka, although a few Russian tanks continued to cause unrest within the town. When the *8./Schützen-Regiment 3* combed through a nearby park, *Oberleutnant* Brandt and *Leutnant* Pauckstadt noticed an apparently abandoned KV-I. Just as the officers approached it, the heavy fighting vehicle rolled away with a howling engine and switched-on headlights. Fortunately, the 8.8-centimeter *Flak* was nearby. The cannoneers immediately took up a sight picture and, after the third round, they knocked out the tank. A fifth Russian fighting vehicle was set alight later on by antitank elements.

Darkness had descended. The Soviets continued to defend from the high brick house. *Leutnant* Weigel's engineers from the 2nd Company of engineers were brought forward. They penetrated into the house with 350 kilograms of demolitions and blew it up. Seventeen dead Russian officers remained behind; only a single first lieutenant escaped with his life. The fighting for Bolochowka was over.

The *II./Schützen-Regiment 3* lost 9 dead and 37 wounded, including *Leutnant* Zimmermann and *Leutnant* Stegemann. Victory also cost the *I./Schützen-Regiment 394* dearly. In the last two days, it had suffered 125 wounded; since the start of the attack, 63 had been killed. *Leutnant*

Dr. Lotze assumed command of the wiped-out *7./Schützen-Regiment 394*, with *Leutnant* Dürrholz taking over the regiment's 2nd Company.

The *I./Schützen-Regiment 3*, supported by the *3./Panzer-Regiment 6*, had continued to remain on the right flank. That afternoon, *Oberst* Kleemann had directed it to reconnoiter the wooded terrain to the northeast of Bolochowka. The 3rd Company took Hill 243.3, initially screening to the west and then to the north. The 2nd Company and the tank company turned towards the woods after a short artillery preparation. Despite the onset of darkness, the fighting vehicles and the riflemen entered the woods and combed through them. Around 1700 hours, the northern and eastern sides were reached. The riflemen spent the night there, after contact was established with the 3rd Company. The battalion took ninety prisoners; it lost two dead and fifteen wounded.

The night passed without any serious incident. Early in the morning, *Leutnant* Braun of the 1st Company of *Schützen-Regiment 3* was sent out on a mounted patrol in the direction of Hill 232.1 and Kurakino. Both were determined to be clear of the enemy. A second patrol advanced on Nowoje a bit later. That locality was also clear of the enemy, but enemy digging in on the high ground north of the frozen Schat was observed. At that point, a reinforced platoon from the 3rd Company occupied the village.

General der Panzertruppen Geyr von Schweppenburg met with *Generalmajor* Breith and *Oberst* Kleemann in Bolochowka on 21 November. *Hauptmann* Peschke reported on the success of his battalion the previous day. The dead were buried in a simple ceremony in the afternoon, with Father Heidland holding the eulogy. The *II./Schützen-Regiment 3* remained screening in Bolochowka that day and in the woods to the north. The *I./Schützen-Regiment 394* arrived in Bolochowka and then moved to the west and north to the southern banks of the Schat.

The *4. Panzer-Division*, attacking to the right of the division, was struggling against numerically superior enemy forces at Uslowaja. For that reason, the *II./Schützen-Regiment 394*, the *1.* and *2./Panzer-Regiment 6*, and the *2./Panzer-jäger-Abteilung 543* were attached to the *4. Panzer-Division*. The *17. Panzer-Division*, which had moved forward, had already crossed the Schat and was advancing in the direction of Wenew. In its sector, however, the strong enemy forces, which belonged to the Soviet 10th Army, were making ground gains difficult.

On 23 November, the division reached the Schat, which ran from twenty to thirty meters in width. It started screening along the river line. *Oberstleutnant* Dr. Müller's *II./Schützen-Regiment 394* returned to the division from the *4. Panzer-Division*. *Kradschützen-Bataillon 3*, which had been attached to *Infanterie-Regiment (mot.) "Großdeutschland,"* was also released from its attachment to that formation, but it was immediately designated as a corps reserve in the Dedilowo area. On the day of its return, Müller's battalion relieved *Schützen-Regiment 40* of the *17. Panzer-Division*, which was positioned in Ljachowo and Petrowka. The latter armored division moved out to advance to the north; that same day, it reached the area just south of Wenew.

It was planned to continue the attack on 24 November. To that end, the division received the following mission: "Moving out on 24 November, the *3. Panzer-Division* ejects the enemy along the west flank of the corps at least as far as a line running Panowa–Kutschina by attacking to the west and enveloping along the road from Karniki. By doing so, it is to deprive the enemy of influence along that road."

The battle group formed under *Oberst* Kleemann started the attack on a cold and misty 24 November. The main effort was along the right wing, where the tank company and elements of the antitank forces were committed. By around 0800 hours, Nowonikalkaja had been crossed. At that point, a 52-ton tank prevented further progress. The *2./Schützen-Regiment 394* remained at that location until early afternoon. A 10-centimeter cannon that was brought forward was finally able to drive away the steel monster. The *3./Schützen-Regiment 3* did not get any farther, either, and

spent the night in Krjukowa. The *II./Schützen-Regiment 3* got as far as the 3rd Company's location. Because of the early onset of darkness, Makejewka could not be taken that day.

The *LIII. Armee-Korps* had closed up to the *XXIV. Armee-Korps (mot.)* on the right and cleared the area around Stalinorgorsk. A group of enemy forces that had pulled back was encircled east of the city by elements of the *29. Infanterie-Division (mot.)* of the *XXXXVII. Armee-Korps (mot.)*, which was advancing from the south. Elements of the *4. Panzer-Division* sealed off the encirclement from the north. The *17. Panzer-Division*, which had crossed the Schat next to the *3. Panzer-Division*, advanced far to the north that day, taking Wenew. On the next day, its reconnaissance battalion advanced another twenty kilometers in a bold raid, taking it to the area three kilometers south of Kaschira. That turned out to be the northernmost point reached by elements of the *2. Panzer-Armee*. The signs to Moscow indicated it was only another eighty kilometers.

Kampfgruppe Kleemann continued its attack at 0700 hours on 25 November. *Leutnant* Lohse's *1./Schützen-Regiment 3*, which had been sent ahead to reconnoiter, determined that Makejewka was clear of the enemy. *Major* Wellmann had the rest of his battalion attack immediately, even though there was no contact with the 2nd Battalion, which had moved out to the west to envelop. Around 1030 hours, Wellmann's battalion had cleared Makejewka, followed shortly thereafter by Apeschkowo. The whitewashed tanks and *SPW's* pressed through to the west and linked up with the *II./Schützen-Regiment 3*. As they continued to move north, they encountered fleeing Russians outside Gryslowo and Maratuja, immediately opening fire.

During that period, the *XXIV. Armee-Korps (mot.)* was positioned in a salient in the front that extended east of Tula and reached as far as Kaschira. That meant that the areas the divisions had to cover were not getting any shorter. Enemy forces that were ever increasing in size were pressing against those thinly held lines. The *3. Panzer-Division* was screening the entire western flank of the corps from Wenew to the Schat. Facing the division were elements of the 154th, 413th, and 299th Rifle Divisions, the 31st Cavalry Division and militia.

The Soviets had reentered Stalinogorsk. Since it was their intention to break through from there to Tula, the corps had to take all steps necessary to eliminate that threat. The *4. Panzer-Division* was reinforced considerably. The combat elements of *Panzer-Regiment 6* were employed in that sector. The commander of those elements, *Hauptmann* Schneider-Kostalski, was wounded for the fourth time on 26 November. The brave commander of the 1st Company, *Oberleutnant* Vopel, was killed on the battlefield. He became the seventeenth officer of the regiment to be killed since the start of the campaign. During the fighting on 26 November, the 1st Company lost five *Panzer III's* and three *Panzer IV's*. *Oberstleutnant* Schmidt-Ott assumed command of the three provisional tank companies.

Oberleutnant Markowski's 2nd Tank Company was attached to the *17. Panzer-Division* that day. As there was no contact with the company, nothing is known of its activities that day. *Oberleutnant* Müller-Hauff's 3rd Tank Company was the only tank assets left in the division, with the exception of the regimental headquarters. The company, with its eight *Panzer III's* and four *Panzer IV's*, formed the division's reserve. The regimental headquarters also had three *Panzer III's*, one *Panzer IV*, and one command tank at its disposal.

The command element of the armor regiment left its quarters in Schwarzewsky on 27 November along with the men no longer capable of combat, reaching Orel by the onset of darkness. It was intended to send *Panzer-Regiment 6*, along with several other armor regiments, to

Germany for reconstitution. The headquarters occupied quarters at the same places that portions of the regiment had stayed at prior to the attack across the Ssusha and were being maintained by rear-area personnel. A small section of eleven trucks and one field mess was formed out of vehicles the regiment did not need. It was attached to the division support command.

On 1 December, *Generaloberst* Guderian appeared in Orel to bid farewell to *Panzer-Regiment 6* and *Panzer-Regiment 35* in ceremonial form. The headquarters of both regiments, along with three battalions from both regiments, assembled in an open rectangle in front of the former Russian armor garrison. The farewell ceremony commenced right at 1200 hours in biting cold. *Oberstleutnant* Munzel was the commander of troops and reported the elements. Guderian then trooped the line, accompanied by the strains of a presentation march. The commander in chief commemorated the dead—from 22 June to that day, *Panzer-Regiment 6* had lost 172 officers and enlisted personnel—praised the living and extended his best wishes for a safe reunion early in the next year.

The regiment was used over the course of the next few days to guard Orel. It reported to the local military commander, *Oberst* Usinger, who was also the commander of *Artillerie-Regiment 622*.[2] *Oberstleutnant* Munzel's forces were responsible for a multitude of tasks, including protection of bridges, waterworks, electrical plants, the leather factory, ammunition depots, the military administrative offices, the airfield etc. At his disposal were the personnel of *Panzer-Regiment 6, Feld-Ersatz-Bataillon 83*,[3] *Panzerjäger-Abteilung 543*, a company from *Panzerjäger-Abteilung 521*, and the Orel Security Group.[4] During that time, the division also

---

2. This was actually *Artillerie-Regimentsstab 622*, a regimental artillery headquarters without any line battalions. In 1942, it was used to form the basis for the divisional artillery of *Infanterie-Division (mot.) "Großdeutschland"* when that regiment was reorganized as a division.

3. This was the division field replacement battalion. It processed incoming replacements. It usually conducted some sort of additional training based on lessons learned at the front before sending replacements on to the new units.

4. It is not known whether this was a divisional *ad hoc* formation or an element attached to *Oberstleutnant* Munzel for the duration of his duties in Orel.

conducted courses for tank drivers and junior noncommissioned officer candidates in Orel. It also processed personnel replacements for onward transport to the formations at the front.

The rifle brigade of the division remained at the front in the sector between Wenew and the Schat. It had established defensive positions along that long sector. The Soviets were pressing with strong forces against the deep salient of the corps. The *17. Panzer-Division* was pulled back as far as sixteen kilometers south of Kaschira, since it was threatened with being cut off. On 27 November, the division ordered all available mobile forces pulled out of the line. These elements, such as the *I./Schützen-Regiment 3* and the 3rd Tank Company, were refueled and rearmed. They were to be prepared for employment in threatened sectors of the corps. The field army attempted to insert the *296. Infanterie-Division* in the ever-widening gap between the *XXIV. Armee-Korps (mot.)* and the *XXXXIII. Armee-Korps.* Unfortunately, only one battalion from the division was able to make it to the Upa because of the extreme difficulty of that move. Even though there were no major enemy attacks along the front of the division over the next few days, the situation was anything but quiet. Not only did the soldiers have to bear the cold, which turned worse by the day, but they were also subjected to constant air attacks. The 3rd Company of engineers suffered a particularly grievous loss on 29 November, when direct hits from Russian bombs struck an occupied building foundation. The company lost twenty dead and several wounded. In the rear areas, the partisans were also conducting more frequent operations. They temporarily occupied sections of the main supply route along the Orel–Tula road in the area around Tschern.

The German leadership thereupon decided to concentrate all of its forces one more time to bring about a change in the fighting. The *2. Panzer-Armee* was directed to cut off Tula from the east and the west and, by doing so, clearing the direct route between Moscow and Tula. The strongly fortified "strongpoint" of Tula would then be cut off from its rearward lines of communications and the *2. Panzer-Armee* freed up to attack, since the city could be encircled by infantry forces. In actual fact, the *2. Panzer-Armee* had ceased to be an armor field army for some time. It had the following numbers of tanks operational on 30 November: *Panzer-Regiment 6*, twenty-eight; *Panzer-Regiment 35*, thirty-four; and *Panzer-Regiment 39*, ten.

The thirtieth of November was the first Advent Sunday of that eventful year. The forces prepared for the reorganization and had no time for a quietly contemplative celebration. During that time, the *3. Panzer-Division* announced its achievements from 22 June to 22 November 1941: 52,289 prisoners taken; 485 tanks, 71 armored cars, 905 artillery pieces, 203 antiaircraft guns, 567 antitank guns, 366 mortars, 1,540 machine guns, 3,130 trucks, 100 staff cars, 19 motorcycles, and 157 tractors captured or destroyed; 89 destroyed, 119 shot-down, and 63 captured aircraft. The fighting forces were 1,300 kilometers from the western borders of Russia and had covered 4,500 kilometers. The ammunition columns had covered 17,000 kilometers; the fuel columns, 20,000.

The *3. Panzer-Division* occupied its assembly areas for the attack. *Oberst* Kleemann commanded the righthand battle group, which consisted of *Schützen-Regiment 3*, the *3./Panzer-jäger-Abteilung 543*, the *2./Pionier-Bataillon 39*, the *6./Flak-Regiment 59*, and the *2./Artillerie-Regiment 75*. To secure the assembly area, the *I./Schützen-Regiment 3* pushed forward on 1 December and took the localities of Djukowa and Grezewo. The lefthand battle group of *Oberstleutnant* Zimmermann consisted of the *I./Schützen-Regiment 394*, the *1./Pionier-Bataillon 39*, a battery from *Artillerie-Regiment 75*, the *1./Panzerjäger-Abteilung 543*, and a tank platoon under *Leutnant* von Arnim. *Krad-schützen-Bataillon 3* (*Major* Pape) relieved the screening group of the *II./Schützen-Regiment 394*. The motorcycle infantry were reinforced by a platoon of antitank elements. The third battle group was led by *Major* Frank. Attached to him were *Panzerjäger-Abteilung 521*, the *3./Panzer-Regiment 6*, and the *3./Pionier-Bataillon 39*. That battle group staged in the Nowosselsjskije–Wasselki–Kornitschi–Arssenjewo area on 1 December and prepared to advance west, reconnoitering routes in the direction of Makejewa–Dubki.

Kampfgruppe Audörsch was relieved by *Pionier-Bataillon 45*,[5] with only the *5./Artillerie-Regiment 75* remaining in its old positions. The *I./Infanterie-Regiment "Großdeutschland"* (*Hauptmann* Hagen) was attached to the division and prepared for operations outside of Karniki. *Oberstleutnant* Dr. Weißenbruch was directed to bring the remaining battalions of the divisional artillery—1st Battalion under *Hauptmann* Haas, 2nd Battalion under *Hauptmann* Nebel, and 3rd Battalion under *Hauptmann* Kersten—into position in such a manner that they could place harassing fires on Leshla and Iwrowka. The elements of *Major* Petsch's *Pionier-Bataillon 39* that were not attached to battle groups screened the crossings over the Schat at Petrowka and positioned all of their bridging vehicles there for immediate employment. Bridging Section 1 provided a platoon each of sixteen-ton assets to the 1st and 2nd Companies of the battalion, with the 3rd Platoon remaining the battalion's reserve. *Aufklärungs-Abteilung 1* was located in Karniki.

The night of 1–2 December was clear and illuminated by the moon. The wind had died down. As a result, it had turned colder and the temperatures registered -20 (-4 Fahrenheit) and even colder. It was still dark over the snow-covered terrain, when the batteries of the *3. Panzer-Division* and *4. Panzer-Division* opened fire on the Russian positions. *Artillerie-Regiment 75* concentrated its fires along the flanks of the attacking battle groups, in an effort to eliminate threats from that direction.

Shortly after 0400 hours, the riflemen of the two divisions moved out to attack west. *Schützen-Regiment 3* initially advanced with its 1st Battalion (*Major* Wellmann) to the southwest in the direction of Dubki. The 1st Company moved ahead in its *SPW's* and reported the locality as occupied by the enemy. The 2nd Company closed rapidly, while the 3rd Company worked its way towards the village through a depression from the north. The Russians occupying the strongpoint were surprised. Although they defended stubbornly, the fight was short. Dubki was taken and cleared. Major Wellmann immediately reorganized his companies for the continued advance. *Hauptmann* Peschke's 2nd Battalion followed closely behind the 1st Battalion with engineers and antitank elements. They moved on a route farther south. The battalion took Posslowa and pressed past Dubki to the west.

Schützen-Regiment 394 likewise broke into the first Russian position. Its 1st Battalion worked its way towards Romanowa. The Soviets were prepared for that attack and placed considerable artillery and mortar fire on the battalion. In addition, the reservoir in front of the village had been blown up. The ice had sunk, so there was only one crossing point over the defile. The battalion then had to toil across it. The *1./Pionier-Bataillon 39* constructed a ford across the Sosha for the riflemen. The company commandeer, *Hauptmann* Kalkbrenner, was wounded in the process, along with 15 enlisted personnel. *Leutnant* Harzer assumed acting command of the engineer company. The 2nd Battalion of *Oberstleutnant* Dr. Müller—whom the soldiers referred to as "Attack Müller" (*Angriffsmüller*)—attacking to the left, put down tough resistance outside Bronikowo, before it was able to penetrate into the locality. The battalion's casualties were high. In the first few hours alone, fourteen vehicles were lost, unfortunately also including the fully loaded battalion ambulance. The regiment lost forty-seven men dead and wounded in the attack; the regiment's 2nd Battalion alone accounted for thirty-five, with the 8th Company suffering nineteen.

---

5. A separate engineer battalion that frequently supported the *XXIV. Armee-Korps (mot.)* during this period.

Schützen-Regiment 3 had reached the large forest that stretched from the southwest to the northeast. The 1st Company, moving as the point element, was able to cross the woods through a well-maintained cut. It reached the village of Kolodesnaja, which was in a clearing. The riflemen were offered a spectacle there. The Russian soldiers appeared to have no idea the Germans were attacking; they were busily engaged with target practice. The company's machine guns soon scattered the Soviets, who escaped into the nearby woods, abandoning all weapons and equipment. The company took sixty prisoners.

The battalion pivoted to the northwest, combed the closest woods and took the village of Dorofejewka after eliminating an enemy battery. The electricity was still functioning. But there was little time to celebrate. The battalion continued its advance and reached Torchowo after 1300 hours. That meant the day's objective had been crossed. The Tula–Wenew road had been blocked. The 1st Battalion had achieved that success without taking any casualties.

The 2nd Battalion moved out behind the 1st Battalion again, but moved directly west from Dorofejewka, occupying Barybinka and Krjukowa. The enemy fled at those locations in undisciplined flight into the woods to the north and the west. The *I./Artillerie-Regiment 75* had to change positions in order to be able to have the range to fire. As a result of the rapid overcoming of the first Russian resistance, it was easy for the armored group of *Major* Frank to follow the riflemen.

The groups from *Schützen-Regiment 394* and *Infanterie-Regiment "Großdeutschland"* that were employed on the left encountered strong enemy forces and were still involved in heavy fighting by the onset of darkness to the southwest

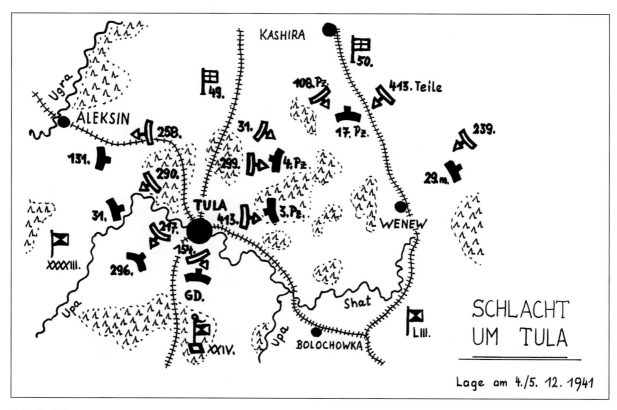

Battle for Tula.

of Dubki and Tretschtschewa. The last locality was finally taken by the *"Großdeutschland"* grenadiers, while the riflemen of *Schützen-Regiment 394* attempted to clear the large expanse of woods at Teminewa-Gamowo.

By evening, the Soviets appeared to have rapidly recovered from the shock of the initial successes of the *3. Panzer-Division*. While the battle groups set up their security for the night, the Soviets placed heavy fires—especially from Stalin organs—on the localities that had been occupied by the Germans, inflicting considerable casualties. The artillery fire disrupted all of the wire lines and, since the radios were not working either, the division headquarters had no contact with the lead elements in the evening. *General-major* Breith therefore ordered his command post moved forward the following morning.

Shortly after 0600 hours on 3 December, *Schützen-Regiment 3* conducted a reconnaissance-in-force around the occupied villages with its *SPW* company, since it had been determined that the enemy was still to the rear of the regiment. The 1st Company encountered the enemy at Olenina, to the south of its parent battalion. The enemy had even occupied the village of Kolodesnaja in the clearing in the woods the previous night. Among other things, it took the regiment's vehicle that stored the personal-demand items. The 1st Battalion committed its 3rd Company and *Leutnant* Braun's platoon (*SPW's* from the 1st Company) against the village. The riflemen were able to make good progress back through the woods, but they received considerable fire once outside the village. The acting company commander, *Leutnant* Oesten, was felled by Russian bullets. It was impossible to run through the fire and enter the locality again. The company was pulled back to Dorofejewka, where it screened.

Hauptmann Peschke's *II./Schützen-Regiment 3* started turning back strong Russian armored attacks on Krjukowa at first light. The battalion did not enjoy a single quiet hour; it also suffered terribly under the enemy fire and the cold. The division ordered the battalion to pull back to Torchowo, where the companies screened the road between that village and Wolynzewo. It was there that the lead company of the motorcycle battalion, the 2nd Company, arrived and provided welcome support. The motorcycle battalion proper occupied Iwrowka and the high ground to the west. The *I./Infanterie-Regiment (mot.) "Großdeutschland"* closed the gap between the two regiments northwest of Dubki and was able to enter the village.

Schützen-Regiment 394 advanced to the west that day in the face of heavy enemy fire. The combat vehicles were not sent forward and left east of the river. The Russians defended the village of Gamowo especially hard, using artillery and heavy mortars. Since a frontal attack promised little success, *Major* Frank attempted to bypass the village with his tank battalion. It was not possible for the tanks and the riflemen of *Schützen-Regiment 394* to take Teminewa until 1900 hours. After 2200 hours, *Leutnant* Lange led an engineer assault detachment to the west, where it entered the woods outside of Nowossjolki.

The advance of the *3. Panzer-Division* on 4 December never stood under a lucky star. From the very beginning, it was questionable whether the forces available were sufficient to accomplish the mission. The enemy grew in strength by the hour; the winter mobility and the simple needs of his Siberian forces also came to his aid. Enemy formations that had been bypassed or pushed back held out in the deeply snowed-in woods in the rear of the division.

"Großdeutschland" took the hotly contested Kolodenaja for the second time that day and relieved elements of *Schützen-Regiment 3* from their previous limit of advance. The Russians, who had transitioned to the attack, were able to take back Krjukowo in the afternoon and even felt their way forward with patrols, even though all of them were turned back. The southern battle group of *Schützen-Regiment 394* met with more success. In the morning, the regiment pressed to the northwest and took Demidowka and Nowossjolki. The success was all the more

significant, inasmuch as the Tula–Wenew road was finally blocked, once and for all. Tanks and mounted riflemen continued reconnoitering further to the south and southwest so as to block the path of any enemy forces possibly attempting to break out of Tula.

Generalmajor Breith, who temporarily established his command post at Krjukowa, ordered *Schützen-Regiment 3* and the attached *2./Artillerie-Regiment 75*, which had been pulled out of the line, to be prepared to launch an attack towards the high ground west of Meschtscherskoje, fifteen kilometers southeast of Tula. The ongoing movements could only be partially executed, since the vehicles were not cooperating. The oil and the fuel were freezing at temperatures of -27 degrees Celsius (-16.6 Fahrenheit), which went down to -31 (-23.8 Fahrenheit) at night. Even the battle staff of the *3. Panzer-Division* no longer had any operational motorized vehicles.

It turned even colder during the night of 4–5 December. The temperature registered -37 (-34.6 Fahrenheit). Technology capitulated. The engines would no longer start; the machine guns would not fire; the tank turrets would not traverse. German forces were immobilized on that morning and exposed to the onset of Russian attacks. The *4. Panzer-Division*, which was already blocking the Tula–Moscow road, had to pull back to the east, leaving behind all of its vehicles, since new Siberian regiments had inserted themselves between it and the *17. Panzer-Division*.

The *3. Panzer-Division*, which was positioned in the villages west of the Tula–Wenew road, had to defend against constant Soviet attacks, which took place all along its front. The enemy tried especially hard at Nowossjolki and Krjukowo to shatter the lines of the division. In the process, the Siberians advanced through the thick woods south of the road and reached Kolodesnaja late in the afternoon. They attacked the village and the men there by surprise, entering the locality and butchering everything that

got in their way. The commander of the *IV./Infanterie-Regiment "Großdeutschland"* was shot down with his headquarters and elements of the 17th Company. Only a few infantry were able to escape the slaughter, clothed only in their shirts and trousers. The German casualties were high. In addition to the dead officers and men of *"Großdeutschland,"* forty motorcycles, several trucks, one fuel vehicle, one assault gun, one heavy infantry gun, and numerous small arms were lost. The Soviets set up for the third time in Kolodesnaja. The division no longer had the strength to eliminate that "boil" in its front. The field army ordered the *XXIV. Armee-Korps (mot.)* to attack one more time via Krjukowo so as to establish contact with the *296. Infanterie-Division*, which had reached the Upa. *General* Geyr von Schweppenburg, who had intended to allow the *3. Panzer-Division* to rest that day, acquiesced to the order and had a battle group formed to execute the mission under the command of *Oberst* Kleemann. To that end, the *I./Schützen-Regiment 3*, an artillery battalion, a motorcycle infantry company, and the rest of *Panzer-Regiment 6* were pulled out of the front lines.

That afternoon, however, the commanding general radioed the field army headquarters in Jassnaja-Poljana. His impression of the development of the situation had changed: "Situation fundamentally changed, since the enemy has also broken into the gap between the *17.* and *4. Panzer-Divisionen*; strong enemy forces along the Sserpuchowo–Tula rail line and road. No relief is expected from the *XXXXIII. Armee-Korps* anymore. Own tanks not operational."

The fifth of December 1941 saw a change in the fortunes of the war in the East. The daily logs of the headquarters of the *2. Panzer-Armee* recorded that day: ". . . combat power of the brave forces is at an end after incredible exertions. It is imperative to preserve the force. The field army will move back to the Don–Schat–Upa position incrementally."

At the schoolyard in Lochwiza: *Generaloberst* Guderian at the command post of the *3. Panzer-Division* with *Generalleutnant* Model. It was there that the directive was issued for establishing contact with the *16. Panzer-Division*, thus effectively closing the Kiev Pocket.

Romny.

Hauptmann von Cochenhausen, the commander of the *1./Kradschützen-Bataillon 3* (seen here as a *Major*). His soldiers took the commander in chief of the Soviet 5th Army prisoner.

The *2./Schützen-Regiment 394* during a break in operations during the advance on Lochwiza. From left to right: *Oberfeldwebel* Everth, *Leutnant* Peter, *Oberleutnant* Lotze (company commander), and *Oberfeldwebel* Müller.

On 30 September, the *3. Panzer-Division* moved out to the northeast from Gluchow. Soldiers from the *2./Schützen-Regiment 394* are seen here mounted on a *Panzer II* from *Panzer-Regiment 6*.

The attack soon bogged down in the muck.

Mzensk has been taken. A knocked-out T-34 and Stalin organ are seen here on one of the streets.

The destroyed bridge at Plawsk.

Bolchow, north of Orel, has been reached.

Generaloberst Guderian and *Oberstleutnant* Munzel, the commander of *Panzer-Regiment 6*.

The Knight's Cross is presented to *Leutnant* Störck. From left to right: *Generalleutnant* Model, *Major* von Oppen, *Oberstleutnant* Audörsch, and *Leutnant* Störck.

The first trenches are dug outside Tula.

CHAPTER 13

From the Schat to the Tim: The Winter Fighting for Kursk

The fifth of December 1941 marked the culminating point for the German offensive on Moscow. The divisions had literally fought their way towards the Russian capital meter-for-meter, and their lead elements could see the high-rises of the city of millions through their binoculars. At night, the infantry could see the muzzle flashes of the antiaircraft guns firing around the pinnacles of the Kremlin.

At the time, the *XXIV. Armee-Korps (mot.)* was positioned with its divisions—the *3. Panzer-Division*, *4. Panzer-Division*, and *17. Panzer-Division* and the *25. Infanterie-Division (mot.)*—in a loose front between Tula and north of Wenew. Despite all of the previous casualties and hardships, the corps still presented the enemy with a serious threat. *Generalfeldmarschall* von Bock, the commander in chief of *Heeresgruppe Mitte*, informed the commanding general that the "*XXIV. Panzer-Korps* had been a ray of hope during these turbulent days."[1] Two decades later, Geyr von Schweppenburg wrote: "In addition to the other terrific divisions that reported to me at the time, that was especially true of the old, steely *3. Panzer-Division*."

---

1. The original passage in German is written in the subjunctive, so it is uncertain whether this is literally what von Bock or they are being paraphrased from another source. He may have actually written *Panzer-Korps* at the time, since it was common to refer to the motorized army corps as armored corps, even though the official designation was the former one.

The Russian offensive broke loose along much of the front around Moscow on 6 December. The northern field-army group started first, in an effort to defeat the *3. Panzer-Armee* and *4. Panzer-Armee*. Shortly afterward, the field armies on both sides of Moscow moved south and advanced against the infantry divisions of *Generalfeldmarschall* von Kluge. The sector around Tula was still spared from the offensive on 6 December.

In its order for the withdrawal, the *2. Panzer-Armee* had directed the following divisions disengage from the enemy and pull back across the Schat (in order of sequencing): *4. Panzer-Division, Infanterie-Regiment (mot.) "Großdeutschland,"* and *17. Panzer-Division.* The *25. Infanterie-Division (mot.)* had only a few elements on the north bank of the river at the time. For the time being, the *3. Panzer-Division* was to remain in place. It was only to pivot back to protect the flanks of the withdrawal movements later on.

That special "distinction" for the division did not fill the officers and enlisted personnel with satisfaction. They knew that the formations only had about half the combat power they once did and that they could barely be considered an armored force any more. The organization, weaponry and equipment of the division is mirrored in these numbers:

- *Schützen-Regiment 3*, with six companies of sixty men each; three antitank guns; six *SPW's*
- *Schützen-Regiment 394*, with six companies of fifty men each; no antitank guns
- *Panzer-Regiment 6*, with eighteen *Panzer III's* and four *Panzer IV's*
- *Artillerie-Regiment 75*, with nineteen light field howitzers, two heavy field howitzers, and three 10-centimeter cannon
- *Kradschützen-Bataillon 3*, with one motorized company and the remaining partially motorized companies
- *Panzerjäger-Abteilung 521*, with eleven self-propelled guns
- *Panzerjäger-Abteilung 543*, with two heavy and one light antitank gun

The division had to match the withdrawal movements of the *4. Panzer-Division* with its right wing. The sister division was pulling back in the direction of Tjoplaja. *Schützen-Regiment 3* received orders to take Kolodesnaja again in order to keep the withdrawal route through the woods to Dubki open. The withdrawal movements of that regiment were not simple, since the Soviets had already worked their way forward along the few roads and woodland paths. The 6th Company of the rifle regiment was able to enter Schurwljowka rapidly, drive out the enemy and extend outposts far enough forward that the 2nd Battery of artillery could go into position. By then, the 1st and 2nd Companies were ready to attack Kolodesnaja. They were able to assault the village and clear the lane in the woods. By accomplishing that, the regiment had established the outpost line needed for the day.

The night that followed saw not only temperatures of -38 degrees Celsius (-36.4 Fahrenheit), but also the start of the Russian offensive against the *2. Panzer-Armee*. The Soviet 10th and 50th Armies, as well as the I Guards Cavalry Corps, smashed into the thinly held German outpost lines early in the morning of 7 December. They ripped them open and forced the German formations to retreat. The field army had arranged for the crossing of Schat that day, so the movement was already planned to a certain extent. The enemy offensive struck with full force against the eastern flank of the field army. The *10. Infanterie-Division (mot.)* had to yield to the superior enemy pressure and evacuate Michailow.

Who among the soldiers and officers even stopped to think that that day was the Second Sunday of Advent? Although a large amount of personal-demand items had reached the division for the frontline troops in large quantities, there was hardly any time available to properly distribute the extensive "Christmas bonus." No one had the leisure time available to enjoy hearing the news on the radio that reported the entry of Japan into the war and its successful attack on Pearl Harbor.

On that 7 December, the division telephonically notified its elements to move back. Not all of the telephone lines were intact, however, with the result that some formations did not get the orders until late in the day. That was the case with the *I./Schützen-Regiment 3*, which only heard about the retrograde movements from its neighbors, the *4. Panzer-Division* and *Infanterie-Regiment (mot.) "Großdeutschland."*

Both of the battle group commanders, *Oberst* Kleemann and *Oberstleutnant* Audörsch, issued orders to disengage from the enemy. The companies of *Pionier-Bataillon 39* and *Pionier-Bataillon 45* started to emplace mines in the localities and prepare the non-operational vehicles to be blown up. Right at midnight on 8 December, the first rifle units disengaged from the enemy and pulled back to localities further to the rear, which had been occupied the previous afternoon by companies to protect the retrograde movements. Bridging Section 1 set up two sixteen-ton spans at Kurakino in the morning; both were also rigged to be blown up.

The retrograde movements needed to be completed by first light. The marches were an unbelievable hardship for the officers and men. The columns tramped their way through the dense woods and high snowdrifts on foot. The wounded were loaded on sleds, since only a few vehicles were still capable of moving. As soon as an element left its dwelling place, it was mined by the rearguard. Despite all of the unpleasantness that night, the movements were completed by late morning and the designated lines reached. At that point, the division was in an outpost line approximately nine kilometers southwest of Wenew that ran from there about even with Gryslowo and then as far as Prissady. An ice and snowstorm swept over the area that day and presumably prevented the enemy from following rapidly.

The forces remained in the positions they had reached on 9 December and conducted combat reconnaissance. That day, the division had to cover the retrograde movements of the other divisions. The Soviets had identified the German movements and had started attacking the *2. Panzer-Armee* again. Again, they concentrated against the eastern flank of the field army, hitting the almost twenty-kilometer-wide gap that existed southwest of Tula between the *XXIV. Armee-Korps (mot.)* and the *XXXXIII. Armee-Korps*. The attacks were directed with full fury against the already exhausted *296. Infanterie-Division*, which was reinforced that day with the first battalion of "Großdeutschland" that became available. In the afternoon, the elements of the *4. Panzer-Division* that were south of the Schat were ejected from that area. When the *17. Panzer-Division* was then withdrawn from the Schat river line, to be moved to the right wing of the *XXXXVII. Armee-Korps (mot.)*, the *3. Panzer-Division* found itself all alone in the sector and facing a hard-pressing enemy. The batteries of the divisional artillery attempted to hold back the Russians by means of continuous fire.

On 9 December, *Generaloberst* Guderian released a general order to his hard-pressed field army. The order closed with these words: "My comrades! The harder the enemy and the winter try to defy us, the more firmly you need to close ranks. Maintain iron discipline, just as you always have. Everyone is to remain with his unit. . . . Only by unified willpower and action can success be guaranteed. I know that I can rely on you. The fate of Germany is at stake."

In general, both the day and the evening passed without heavy fighting, after *Kampfgruppe Audörsch* succeeded in turning back the enemy flank attacks that were directed against the *296. Infanterie-Division* and, by their nature, brushed against the division's own front. In the process, the *7./Schützen-Regiment 394* lost three dead and four wounded. During the night, orders arrived stating that any remaining civilian populace in the villages north of the Schat were to be evacuated to the north and the northwest effective 0800 hours on 10 December.

During the night, the Soviets approached the combat outposts of the division at different places. For instance, *Leutnant* Eckardt's *2./ Schützen-Regiment 3* had to turn back strong attacks directed against Gryslowo. The Soviets succeeded in infiltrating into the depression at Iwanenkowa. They were not driven away until *Leutnant* Lohse's *1./Schützen-Regiment 3* launched an immediate counterattack.

The rear-area services of the division had already started flowing back across the Schat the previous day. Despite the many difficulties, the traffic control detachment led by Hauptmann Kersten (the *III./Artillerie-Regiment 75*) provided for a relatively fluid and disciplined rearward movement over the bridge at Kurakino. *Major* Petsch was there with his *Pionier-Bataillon 39* so that his forces would be immediately available should the situation change.

Once again, this time during the afternoon of 10 December, Kleemann's and Audörsch's battle groups disengaged from the enemy. The two *SPW* companies of the two rifle regiments formed the rearguard. They moved back and forth across the sectors, firing their 3.7-centimeter antitank guns and machine guns in an effort to portray strong forces. The pursuing Russians were deceived and did not interfere much with the retrograde movements. The companies of *Pionier-Bataillon 45* emplaced mines along the roadways and destroyed bridges. That battalion's 2nd Company (*Oberleutnant* von Drewitz) became entangled with enemy forces in the process, but it was able to successfully disengage itself.

The medical personal had an especially difficult mission. All medical vehicles were constantly on the go. The vehicles of the ambulance platoons were completely full with wounded and sick personnel. The number of wounded and cases of frostbite increased steadily. On top of that, the first cases of typhus appeared in the division on 7 December. The situation was made worse by the fact that the airstrip at Tschern had been evacuated by then and the distances the drivers had to cover grew by hundreds of kilometers. The withdrawing riflemen often found that the badly wounded were slaughtered by the Russians, who had broken through, in a bestial manner. Many of the wounded were stripped by the merciless enemy and left naked in the icy cold.

By then, the division had moved its command post back to Kalmyky-Bolsch. At 0030 hours on 11 December, it issued orders to move the division to the south bank of the Schat: "Starting at 0300 hours on 11 December, the *3. Panzer-Division* disengages from the enemy in its current positions, moves across the Schat and organizes there for the defense."

The three tanks companies under the command of *Oberstleutnant* Schmidt-Ott were the first units to pull back from their quartering areas, as soon as the moonlight allowed a rapid movement. Shortly after 0300 hours, the remaining elements followed. The roadways were covered in snow and barely recognizable due to the snowdrifts. The storm had knocked over the directional signs as well, with the result that the columns, which stretched for kilometers on end, occasionally faltered. The last combat vehicles crossed the bridge over the Schat around 0500 hours. The forces on foot that followed were guided across on a bridge made out of ice. Just as it started to turn light, the rearguards reached the southern bank, and the engineers started to tear down the bridge, completing their work at 0930 hours.

The *2. Panzer-Armee* moved back to a line running from Jefremow to the area southeast of Tula that day. The Soviets then started pressing hard all along the front, not allowing the German forces to get any rest. The division, which had been exhausted by weeks of fighting defended with the courage of desperation against the well-equipped enemy formations. Among other things, the Moscow Information Office announced on 11 December: "The forces of General Boldin have shattered the 3rd and 4th Tank Divisions of the enemy, as well as the 'Grossdeutschland' regiment. They are continuing the offensive and are enveloping the enemy's 296th Infantry Division."

The rear-area detachments of the division in the Orel area, including the headquarters of the armored regiment, also felt the effects of the

Russian winter offensive. If the officers and soldiers of the armored regiment had had hopes of being transported back to the homeland just a few days previously, those "dreams" started to rapidly evaporate. On orders of the local area commander, *Oberstleutnant* Munzel had to establish a combat outpost line and a main line of resistance along the Optucha east of the city with the regiment. There was great difficulty in doing that, since the ground was frozen up to sixty centimeters and explosives were initially not available to eliminate the layer of frost. On 12 December, Munzel discovered from *Oberstleutnant i.G. Freiherr* von Liebenstein, the chief of staff of the field army, that transport back to the homeland could not longer be anticipated due to the tense situation.

The armored regiment placed two motorcycle platoons at the disposal of the local area commander, since the appearance of enemy airborne forces were anticipated at any moment. When the *I./Panzer-Regiment 18*[2] assumed the responsibility for the guard and work details in Orel, all elements of the armor regiment were then employed in improving the defensive positions east of the city. In four days, the men of the regiment set up 23 bunkers, 16 machine-gun positions, and 50 foxholes. By 20 December, an additional 18 bunkers, 14 machine-gun positions, and 105 foxholes were added.

There was a sudden and unexpected thaw on 12 December. The snow was transformed into a white, sticky mush that sapped energy worse than the regular snow. The fighting continued with undiminished harshness. The enemy advanced into the gap between the *31. Infanterie-Division* and *296. Infanterie-Division*. The *4. Panzer-Division* was directed to interdict the enemy forces, but it was unable to do so since all of its vehicles were immobilized south of the Schat. The left wing of the *3. Panzer-Division* was also exposed to attacks, especially from cavalry, but *Schützen-Regiment 394* was able to turn back that advance by employing all of its

forces. *Schützen-Regiment 3* established contact with the *167. Infanterie-Division*, which was inserted into the line on the right.

The division, whose command post had been moved back to Gorjatschkino, directed further measures that evening to pull back the front. Its right wing was to be pulled back during the night to prepare itself for a movement to positions behind the Schirowona the following night, where it was to defend. An officer of *Schützen-Regiment 394* noted the following in his diary: "Nights very precarious. Days without rations, teeth chattering . . . we fight our way through. Horrific night. Kept the men together with extreme energy. A sad march in silence. The battalion a small band. No one can allow himself to become sick."

The battalions and detachments disengaged from the enemy at 0100 hours and moved back to the designated areas. In the course of that operation, *Kampfgruppe Zimmermann—Schützen-Regiment 3, Pionier-Bataillon 39*, the *I./Artillerie-Regiment 75*, the *1./Flak-Regiment 11*, and the *6./Flak-Regiment 59*—reached a line running southeast of Dedilowo–Chruschtschowka–northern edge of Borodino. There was contact on the right with the *167. Infanterie-Division* and *Kradschützen-Bataillon 3* on the left.

The Russians remained hard on the heels of Zimmermann's forces. By 0300 hours, they broke through the front of *Schützen-Regiment 3*, quickly reaching the rear of Oberleutnant Mente's 7th Company. *Leutnant* Lohse's 1st Company was alerted immediately, and the brave unit succeeded in reaching the 7th Company, which had pulled back to the high ground at Prokowskaja. It attacked the village proper from two sides and scattered the Soviets that had broken through. That morning, the enemy suffered 400 dead. The *SPW* Company then had to relieve *Hauptmann* von Zamory's 3rd Company, which had been surrounded by the Russians. With the assistance of three tanks, the enemy could finally be defeated there as well. By the

---

2. *18. Panzer-Division.*

afternoon, the rifle regiment's front line had stabilized. The right wing of the division formed a bridgehead at Dedilowo. The main effort of the defense centered around the *I./Schützen-Regiment 3* and *Aufklärungs-Abteilung 1*. The soft hail of the day was replaced in the evening by snow and ice. During the night, the temperature fell to as low as -20 degrees Celsius (-4 Fahrenheit).

The bridge over the Schirowon had a load capacity of twelve tons. Two spans consisting of two end and three middle elements had been placed on the fifty-centimeter-thick ice. During the night and early in the morning of 14 December, the division crossed over that bridge. Starting at 0700 hours, the engineers started destroying Dedilowo. That locality had already suffered considerably the previous day as the result of artillery fire and half of it had already burned down. *Schützen-Regiment 394* destroyed an enemy column at Ssitinka with antitank and infantry guns. Its machine guns would no longer fire due to the cold. The enemy attacked again a short while later, but he was again turned back with bloody losses. The regiment lost three battle-tested officers: *Oberleutnant* Völkel, *Leutnant* Kahl, and *Leutnant* Sajitz. The 7th Company was down to one officer and thirty-one men.

The Soviets pursued the withdrawing forces and attacked in battalion strength about 0800 hours from the north. *Leutnant* Eckardt's *2./Schützen-Regiment 3* was able to keep the enemy at bay through aimed fire, until the 1st Company and the available fighting vehicles arrived to assist. Led by *Leutnant* Lohse, the motorized elements advanced into the enemy, scattered his forces and inflicted many casualties (300 dead). One *Panzer IV* was lost to antitank-gun fire, but it could be evacuated by a fighting vehicle, albeit with great difficulty. The 1st Company also lost a vehicle, whereby one man went missing and the vehicle commander, *Feldwebel* Hoffmann, was wounded.

Starting at 0900 hours, *Schützen-Regiment 3* moved across the bridge. The 2nd Company and elements of one of the tank companies remained on the far side to fend off pursuing enemy forces.

The enemy had brought up additional forces and showed up at the bridge site around 1300 hours with two tanks coming from Bykowa. The enemy tanks took the road under fire.

By then, Soviet riflemen had occupied the high ground in front of the village and fired at the bridge site with heavy machine guns. The men of *Schützen-Regiment 3* had to try to get across the bridge as rapidly as possible. The last few *SPW's* rattled up to the bridge. One of them skidded off the slick road and was able to be blown up in time. That meant the rifle battalion was across. Later on, tanks arrived to drive off the Russians so that the rest of the division could get across the Schiworon to the near bank in a disciplined manner, albeit with a few bumps and bruises.

Schützen-Regiment 3 then screened around Panino, while the engineers scouted routes for the next bridging efforts across the Upa north and south of Kostamarowo. The fact that the roads were completely iced over made matters extraordinarily difficult. That same evening, the engineers received orders to scout another bridge site at Ikonki. The medical personnel evacuated the last of the clearing stations forward of the Upa, frequently under enemy fire. In performing that Good Samaritan duty, *Obergefreiter* Langner paid with his life. The 2nd Medical Company assumed responsibility for the hospital in Bolchow and set up its operations there.

On 15 December, the division pulled back again. It crossed the Upa with all of its forces at Krjukowa on the bridge there, with the result that another bridge was not necessary. The division was able to disengage in an orderly manner from the enemy with most of its formations. It was only along the southern wing that a crisis emerged. Towards noon, Russian tanks with mounted infantry attacked the *I./Schützen-Regiment 3*. Since the battalion no longer had any armor-defeating weapons, it had to pull back to Oslanowka. When the German resistance stiffened there, the Soviets suddenly turned off in the direction of Panino, where the 2nd Battalion of the rifle regiment was in position. The 3rd

Company was scattered as a result of the surprise attack by the enemy and lost contact with the battalion.

Additional enemy armored forces appeared outside of Smirnowka early in the afternoon. Six T-34's rolled over the German screening forces and suddenly appeared in front of the firing positions of the 1st Battery of the divisional artillery. The battery commander, *Oberleutnant* von Studtnitz, did not lose his composure. He allowed the enemy tanks to approach ever closer. When it reached the point that no shell could miss, the officer blew a whistle to commence firing. Four rounds left the German guns and four T-34's were shot aflame and stopped! The remaining two got out of there as soon as possible, receiving machine-gun fire from the *1./Schützen-Regiment 3*, which was rolling in support. By then, the 3rd Company had linked back up with the battalion, which quartered in Schandrowka for the night.

The fighting continued through the night with individual groups of enemy forces that continued to pursue. There were some losses, including *Leutnant* Kuhlow of the 7th Battery of artillery. Most of the division reached the near banks of the Upa. At 0500 hours on 16 December, the rearguards crossed the river. The division then occupied a line running Schandrowka–Ljubogoschtsch–Subarjowka–Golowina–Lipki. The division command post was located in Ogarewski that day.

On 16 December, *Generaloberst* Guderian intended to pull his field army back thirty kilometers to a line running to the west of Jefremow–Plawa River (as far as Krapiwna). The *XXIV. Armee-Korps (mot.)* was given the freedom to decide if it needed to pull back to the Solovia a day later based on enemy pressure. Guderian's intent was to pull the entire corps out of the line, if the field army was in a position to occupy a line running along the Ssusha and Oka Rivers with other elements.

Once again, the division disengaged from the enemy on the night of 16–17 December. The temperatures registered less than -17 degrees Celsius (1.4 Fahrenheit). Not a star could be seen. Occasionally, the long fingers of antiaircraft searchlights penetrated into the nighttime darkness, whenever engine noise could be heard. Muzzle flashes could be seen again and again on the enemy side; villages, individual huts and blown-up vehicles were burning.

Lining up the columns in that darkness was a difficult thing in itself. The march routes were barely marked, and the guides from the military police or the traffic control parties were not always where they needed to be. The individual battalions, companies and batteries and platoons were often separated from their march serials, sometimes with contact being completely lost. For instance, that happened to the logistics section of *Schützen-Regiment 394*. It did not rejoin the regiment until days later. The roads and trails were completely full of vehicles headed westward. To the right and left of the roads were destroyed, burned-out, blown-up, or abandoned trucks, staff cars, *SPW's*, and medical vehicles. The German Army was experiencing the horrors of a retreat. *Generaloberst* Guderian crossed the path of the retreating division that day. As always, he greeted the soldiers.

The division reached the Tula–Orel road, the first improved road along its retreat route. There were stragglers everywhere from assorted formations that were fighting in the area; they wanted to be taken along to the rear. By order of the field army, the large supply dump at Plawsk was blown up. In order to "salvage whatever was salvageable," the division sent a convoy of sixteen trucks there under the command of *Leutnant* Becker. The men loaded up whatever they could grab. Among other things were sacks of Christmas mail. All of the other troop element had also sent "retrieval details," which loaded their vehicles with precious items as the first enemy artillery rounds started impacting around the depot. *Oberleutnant* Mangelsdorff was barely able to "rescue" a crate with thirty bottles of champagne. By the time he delivered his "treasure chest" to the command post in Skuratowo, twelve of the bottles had frozen and burst because of the cold.

On 17 December, most of the formations of the division reached the area around Tschern. Guderian ordered the division pulled out of the front and move to an area thirty kilometers northeast of Orel. The division was directed to reorganize there in order to be prepared to be employed by the field army at sectors of the front that were being threatened.

The initial reorganizations started taking place during the movement there and during the few remaining afternoon hours when the forces occupied their designated quarters. It was intended to improve the leadership and movement options for the individual formations. To that end, *Oberstleutnant* Zimmermann's *Schützen-Regiment 3* formed a completely motorized battalion and a "foot" battalion starting on 18 December and extending over the course of the next two days. The motorized battalion consisted of three line companies, a heavy company, and a *SPW* company. The newly formed motorized companies generally consisted of a company headquarters, three rifle platoons, a heavy machine-gun platoon and a mortar section.

During the night of 18–19 December, the division received movement orders for new areas. The entire *XXIV. Armee-Korps (mot.)* was to be moved into the area south of Mzensk as the ready reserve of the field army. The movement there, starting after 0600 hours, did not proceed without incident. Russian fighter-bombers attacked the columns, which were barely able to defend themselves without *Flak* in support. During one of the attacks, *Leutnant* Eckert (the 3./Schützen-Regiment 3) was badly wounded, along with fourteen other men. The enemy aircraft did not have to search long to find targets. On the road to Orel, there were two motorized columns marching parallel to one another. Soldiers were marching in the two roadside ditches on foot. Gigantic trains of prisoners were headed westward along the snowed-over fields.

Most of the motorized elements of the division reached the area twenty kilometers south of Mzensk on 20 December. The foot battalions assembled south of Tschern. The neighboring *4. Panzer-Division* occupied the area around Kromy at the same time. *Generalmajor* Breith moved with his command post to Protassowa. While the troop elements took up their frequently miserable quarters, they heard on the radio sets that were still working that Hitler had relieved the commander in chief of the German Army, *Generalfeldmarschall* von Brauchitsch, and had assumed that position himself.

The division continued to reorganize its formations in the Mzensk area on 20 and 21 December. *Schützen-Regiment 394* was staged in the Gorbatschewo area and formed two battalions like its sister regiment. *Oberstleutnant* Dr. Müller assumed command of the motorized elements, which were sent to Oleschnja, east of Orel. *Major* Haas led the foot companies, while *Hauptmann Freiherr* von der Heyden-Rynsch was in charge of the collection point for damaged vehicles in Orel. Within *Schützen-Regiment 3*, *Major* Wellmann was given command of the motorized battalion: *Hauptmann* Peschke commanded the 1st Company; *Oberleutnant* Biegon, the 2nd; *Oberleutnant* Brandt, the 4th; and *Leutnant* Comberg, the heavy company. As the leader of the trains elements, *Leutnant* Hinrichs moved his sections to Rosslawlj. The armored regiment established three infantry companies. With the exception of machine guns, they had no heavy weapons. Machine-gun training for the tankers was conducted by *Hauptmann* Lanig, the regimental engineer. Two 3.7-centimeter antitank guns were mounted on sleds, forming a sort of "poor man's artillery."

Combat power decreased daily. Some troop elements registered 45 percent losses due to frostbite during the period. It had become even colder, and the howling east wind caused dense clouds of snow to blow across the countryside. The weather conditions naturally affected the progress of the preparations of field fortifications along the new main line of resistance outside of Orel. Details from the armored regiment, which had previously been in the city, were still busy with digging the trenches. By the end of the year, the men of the regiment established a trench system six kilometers in width. The regiment formed a detail of 1 officer and 100 men (in two platoons) to secure and guard the ammunition, weapons and equipment stockpiled there.

Later on, the regiment was ordered to establish additional defensive positions on both sides of the Orel–Mzensk road and in the direction of Bolchow. The armor regiment had only six operational fighting vehicles in Orel. The fighting elements under *Oberstleutnant* Schmidt-Ott continued to be attached to *Oberst* Eberbach of the *4. Panzer-Division*. The *3. Panzer-Division* was released from its attachment to the *XXIV. Armee-Korps (mot.)* and placed directly at the disposal of the Army High Command. *General der Panzertruppen Freiherr* Geyr von Schweppenburg said farewell to his old division, only himself to leave for Germany shortly thereafter to convalesce from an illness.

Generaloberst Guderian, the commander in chief of the *2. Panzer-Armee* and the creator of the German armored forces, was relieved of his post. The Supreme Commander of the Armed Forces could not get over the fact that Guderian had issued orders on his own initiative for a retreat. Nonetheless, Hitler did not punish the *Generaloberst*, since the name Guderian had a special place in the German Army. Every man in the field army was deeply affected by the relief. Guderian turned down a request by the armor regiment to give him an honor guard. The new commander in chief of the field army was *General der Panzertruppen* Rudolf Schmidt.[3]

The division celebrated Christmas in its quarters. A snowstorm had transformed the landscape with a thick layer of snow, and it continued to snow from the heavens without a letup. The supply system could not operate at full speed, but the sections were able to ensure that at least the Christmas mail made it forward. The division distributed personal-demand items for Christmas, including *Lebkuchen*,[4] cigarettes, and alcohol. It should be noted, however, that not all of the units were able to enjoy those things. For example, Haas's foot battalion was in Bludowo, which could not be reached by a field kitchen, let alone for distribution of personal-demand items. If possible, the battalions celebrated Christmas Eve at company level. Both of the chaplains started visiting all of the quarters on 23 December to hold field services. The first Christmas celebrated in the East was marked by a surprisingly clear sky, which allowed the moon to illuminate the broad, snowy terrain almost as bright as day.

The Red Army ensured that it was not quiet that night, either. Its divisions assaulted the positions of the *2. Armee* seventy kilometers southeast of Orel with undiminished ferocity. They achieved a breakthrough, resulting in that field army requesting the *2. Panzer-Armee* for help. With its own limited forces, the *2. Panzer-Armee* was unable to assist. It then requested the *3. Panzer-Division* be released; it could only be employed upon orders from the High Command.

It did not take long for permission to be granted. The *2. Panzer-Armee* passed on the following by radio and telephone late in the morning of 25 December: "By order of the *Führer*, the *3. Panzer-Division* is temporarily allocated to the *2. Armee* for the purpose of preventing a breakthrough of the enemy west of Trudki by means of a counterattack across the Nerutsch. Effective 0600 hours on 26 December, the *3.*

3. Schmidt is less well known among the German armored generals, even though his contributions to the branch were enormous. Like Guderian, he was relieved of command of the field army (1943), but not because of leadership issues. His brother was caught up in antigovernment intrigue, and Schmidt's correspondence to him, which came to light when the brother was imprisoned, also cast the leadership of the regime in a very negative light. He was court-martialed and released from military service, never to hold a command position again. To add insult to injury, he was arrested by the Soviets after the war in the Soviet Zone and then condemned to twenty-five years' imprisonment. Like most of the German senior officers incarcerated by the Soviets, he did not return to Germany until 20 September 1955. A broken man, he died in Krefeld in 1957 after an illness.
4. A traditional Christmas treat, similar to gingerbread.

Panzer-Division is prepared to move from its quartering area twenty-five kilometers south of Mzensk."

At 2030 hours, another order reached the division command post that directed a motorized battalion immediately be sent to the Nerutsch to establish a blocking position.

A battle group under the command of *Oberstleutnant* Audörsch assembled that night and marched off in the darkness. The pathways and roads were so covered with snow that a rapid movement was impossible. The columns faltered and there were hold-ups. It was until it brightened up with morning that the battle group was able to pick up the pace. During the afternoon of 26 December, the motorized battalion of *Schützen-Regiment 394* (*Oberstleutnant* Dr. Müller) reached Malo-Archangelsk with its attached antitank companies. That same morning, *Major* Ziervogel's reconnaissance battalion received orders and moved out. The troops reached the Nerutsch at Sergejewskoje in the evening after encountering untold difficulties along the route. They immediately started screening in the sector there.

While the first battle groups of the division were moving to the Nerutsch, the remaining elements of the rifle brigade had to give up their quarters on 26 December to the *293. Infanterie-Division* and draw new quarters. A short while later, the division received movement orders for the rest of its formations, with the exception of the elements of the armor regiment employed around Orel in a screening mission.

Attached to *Oberst* Kleemann for the formation of his battle group were the *I./Schützen-Regiment 3*, *Kradschützen-Bataillon 3*, the *I./Artillerie-Regiment 75*, *Pionier-Bataillon 39*, and the *6./Flak-Regiment 59*. That group departed its quarters at 0700 hours, worked its way through the huge snowdrifts to the road to Orel, reached the city around 1000 hours, refueled and rearmed and then started its road march again at 1300 hours. A half hour later, a radio message arrived from the field army stating that the *3. Panzer-Division* was attached to the *LV.*

Armee-Korps. In addition, the new mission stated that additional ground was to be taken on 27 December, as feasible, moving from Malo-Archangelsk in the direction of Droskowo. The enemy that had penetrated was to be ejected by means of a counterattack.

One of the two march serials of the division moved along the deeply snowed over road from Orel to Chotetowo, while the other serial headed south through Alexandrowka. The route past Chotetowo was impossible to negotiate because of the snowdrifts, and the columns were unable to advance. Consequently, they quartered in Chotetowo and Guropkino. The division intended to request snowplows and determine new routes via reconnaissance. But neither option worked. Instead, the individual vehicles had to be towed one after the other through the same tracks left by the lead vehicles. As a result, the march on 27 December was considerably delayed and placed a tremendous strain on both men and materiel.

The division headquarters arrived in Bogorodiskoje around 2100 hours after a march of fourteen hours that only covered a distance of sixty kilometers. At 2210 hours, a radio message was received from the *2. Armee* that stated, among other things: "It is of decisive importance that the division get to Droskowo as soon as possible!" The division directed all formations to move out again at daybreak. None of the battle group could make the departure time, since even the forward elements of *Kampfgruppe Audörsch* had only entered Malo-Archangelsk the previous evening and had suffered so many mechanical problems with its vehicles that a continuation of the march could only start around 1100 hours on 28 December. The motorized battalion of *Schützen-Regiment 3* was stranded due to a lack of fuel. Only *Oberleutnant* Biegon's company was in a position to move out at 1200 hours. Finally, shortly after noon, a sled column arrived with fuel. That enabled the tank battalion of *Oberstleutnant* Schmidt-Ott to reach Judinka, east of Malo-Archangelsk.

On the morning of 29 December, *Oberstleutnant* Audörsch assembled all of the forces that had arrived in the area and continued the march in the direction of Droskowo with elements of *Schützen-Regiment 394*, the *2./Pionier-Bataillon 39*, the *6./Flak-Regiment 59*, a company of tanks, and a battery of artillery. Despite extremely difficult road conditions (huge snowdrifts), the reinforced *Schützen-Regiment 394* reached Droskowo in the afternoon. *Oberst* Burgdorf, whose forces were desperately defending in Droskowo, breathed a sigh of relief and requested *Oberstleutnant* Audörsch to employ some tanks at the edge of the village. That never happened. The battle group commander received orders to turn around immediately, move in the direction of Senowjewka and take it. By doing so, he was to prevent the advance of the Russian forces towards the west and Malo-Archangelsk. To do that, all of the elements that had reached Droskowo or were headed there had to be intercepted and turned around. *Kampfgruppe Audörsch* was outside of Senowjewka around 1900 hours. In contrast to what was marked on the maps, it was an extended "street" village and manned by strong enemy forces. Audörsch ordered a short preparation with his heavy weapons and then an attack on the center of the village, which succeeded. The reinforced rifle regiment then set up an all-round defense in the center of the village. Following reconnaissance efforts, the right-hand portion of the village was taken in an aggressive attack, followed by the lefthand portion. By doing that, the advance of the Russian forces to the west was halted. The importance of the capture of Senowjewka for the "big picture" could be seen in the fact that a Russian division headquarters had already set up its command post in the village.

The battle group was unable to rest either that night or the next day. The Soviets, who were initially surprised and consisted of elements of three cavalry divisions, attacked the village several times from all sides. The riflemen, engineers, cannoneers, and tankers were in uninterrupted combat. They were able to turn back all of the enemy's immediate counterattacks, however.

The German forces suffered terribly from the rigors of the weather. The division had spread itself out over the area between Malo-Archangelsk and Orel. There were vehicles stuck in the snow everywhere. Only the horse-drawn sled columns were able to negotiate the snow with any speed. On top of all that, the enemy was located on both sides of the roads, and no one had any idea how strong he was. The formations of the *221. Infanterie-Division*, which had already been fighting there for days, were unable to move as a result of the cold and the snow.

Kampfgruppe Audörsch was well ahead of most of the division. On 30 December, it slowly started moving in the direction of Malo-Archangelsk. *Major* Wellmann's battalion cleared the area around Nishnjaja-Ssossna. In the process, *Oberleutnant* Biegon and his company relieved an encircled German force that was being led by a paymaster and a veterinarian. The capable commander of the 5th Battery of artillery, *Oberleutnant* Grigo, was killed during the operations of his battery around Droskowo. Once again, the medical companies had a lot to do. The 1st Ambulance Platoon was up front; *Unteroffizier* Reimann from the platoon was mortally wounded during one of the operations.

Despite all of the exertions, hardships and disappointments of the time, there were occasional happy moments. For instance, *Unteroffizier* Göschl arrived one day at the location of the *1./Schützen-Regiment 3*, which had only been able to get three *SPW's* as far as Malo-Archangelsk at that point. His vehicle had run over a mine at the beginning of December outside of Tula, and he had been reported as missing ever since. But he was back with the company after having driven nearly 400 kilometers by himself through enemy-occupied territory. And he brought his *SPW* with him. In place of one of the front wheels that had been blown off by the mine, he had mounted a sled. It was an achievement without equal.

The last day of the year arrived. There was deep snow everywhere, which severely affected all movement. Correspondingly, it took some time to assemble all of the battalions and troop elements. The enemy's strength was increasing daily. *General der Infanterie* Vierow's *LV. Armee-Korps* ordered the divisions attached to it to retake a line in a counterattack that the corps could hold for the winter. The *3. Panzer-Division* regrouped on that day, and *Pionier-Bataillon 39* relieved *Kampfgruppe Audörsch* at Senowjewka. Since the beginning of the campaign, the engineer battalion had suffered nineteen officers killed and wounded; on that day, it had sixteen officers on its rolls (its table of organization and equipment authorized twenty-six). *Schützen-Regiment 394* was pushed forward to Droskowo and staged for operations. The first elements of *Major* Pape's motorcycle infantry battalion had also arrived there by then. The battalion had marched by foot to Chotetowo, caught rail transport as far as the whistle stop at Ponyri from there and then moved on to Droskowo using all available vehicular lift capacity. The *I./Schützen-Regiment 3* cleared Werchsaja-Ssosna with Peschke's, Biegon's and Lohse's companies. *Hauptmann* Peschke assumed command of the battalion, since *Major* Wellmann was no longer able to perform duty due to frostbitten toes. On 31 December, *Bataillon Haas* attacked Nischnij Kunatsch with companies commanded by *Leutnant* Dr. Lotze (*Schützen-Regiment 394*), *Leutnant* von Sternberg (*Artillerie-Regiment 75*), *Leutnant* Schuppius (*Schützen-Regiment 3*), and *Leutnant* Stahlberg (*Schützen-Regiment 394*). The battalion, which eventually lost 90 percent of its personnel to frostbite, consisted on one company in the end. It was commanded by *Oberleutnant* Alex of the divisional artillery.

For its first attack in the New Year, the division formed a new, reinforced battle group under the command of *Oberst* Kleemann. It consisted of *Schützen-Regiment 394*, the *I./Schützen-Regiment 3*, *Kradschützen-Bataillon 3*, *Panzer-jäger-Abteilung 543*, the combat elements of *Panzer-Regiment 6*, and an artillery battalion. Its orders read that it was to advance as far as Trudy, with the main effort being the motorized battalion of *Oberstleutnant* Dr. Müller. At the same time, the motorcycle infantry battalion, to which *Major Prinz* von Waldeck's group had been attached, was to take Growsewo and screen along the creek to the east. *Major* Petsch's engineer battalion, with an attached company from *Panzerjäger-Abteilung 543* and a battery of artillery, assumed the mission of guarding the area between Sinowjewka and Wjasowoje and clearing it of scattered enemy elements and stragglers.

New Year's Eve had arrived. It was a "temperate" night. The men of the division were screening and knew that they would have to move out to attack the next day. The morning was dreary and gray. Snow was falling and the temperature had dropped to -30 degrees Celsius (-22 Fahrenheit). Ever since 0200 hours, the division's elements had been on alert. The remaining battalions moved forward.

At the stroke of 1000 hours, the cannon and howitzers of the divisional artillery roared into life again and flung their rounds against the enemy positions. *Major* Pape's motorcycle infantry attacked along the right wing from Beresowez to the northeast. To the left, *Oberstleutnant* Dr. Müller's motorized battalion from *Schützen-Regiment 394* moved forward as well. *Hauptmann* Peschke and the 3rd Tank Company of *Oberleutnant* Müller-Hauff advanced on the patch of woods north of Beretschka. *Infanterie-Regiment 133* of the *221. Infanterie-Division* and *Major* Haas's battalion were on the northern wing. They advanced along the bottom land of the Kunatsch and approached Ust-Kunatsch. The foot battalion of *Schützen-Regiment 394* numbered only 150 men at that point. As a result of the extremely difficult roadway conditions and the physical exertions attendant to that, the men were at the end of their rope and on the verge of collapsing.

The enemy was very active and showed no signs of defeat. There was such heavy defensive fire coming from the woods between Beretschka and Popowy-Dwory against *Hauptmann* Peschke's battalion that the attack by its companies bogged down. It wasn't until the four attached fighting vehicles and the *SPW* company enveloped the woods from the east that the enemy gave way. At that point, the rifle companies could advance again. They took Popowy-Dwory, Filatowka, Woltschi-Dwery, and Rasplaki one after the other. Müller-Hauff's tank company knocked out five T-34's. The Russians started pulling back to the north everywhere, leaving behind a lot of dead. *Oberstleutnant* Dr. Müller's battalion attacking on the right was west of Ust-Leski by noon and established contact with *Hauptmann* Peschke's battalion. The motorcycle infantry battalion also gained ground and took Growsewo, which was completely destroyed, by noon.

Oberleutnant Schmidt's 7th Battery of artillery with its 10-centimeter cannon rolled up front along with the motorcycle infantry and assault guns of *Major Prinz* von Waldeck, since they were they only armor-defeating weapons on the right wing of the division. *Major* Pape then approached Ust-Leski with his companies, and the motorcycle infantry finally succeeded in getting to the outskirts of the village.

By afternoon, the impetus of the attack started to wane, with the exception of the motorized battalion of *Schützen-Regiment 3*, which entered Nachalowka around 1500 hours. The village was clear of the enemy. That allowed the neighboring battalion of *Oberstleutnant* Dr. Müller to move forward as well. An assault detachment advanced in the direction of Trudy-Merjeawa at 1900 hours. There was a strong enemy force there, however. It was able to stop the attack of both battalions outside of the village outskirts for the time being. The rifle companies continued to close up, and they assaulted the western portion of Trudy around 2100 hours. Screening elements had to be established in all directions, since there was no contact with neighboring battalions. The Soviets defended stubbornly in the eastern portion of the locality and even

advanced against the German battalions with tanks in the darkness.

The enemy forces west of the *I./Schützen-Regiment 3* grew stronger by the hour. The Russians were attempting to escape to the east between Ust-Kunatsch and Trudy. In the process, they ran into the rear of the German forces that were in the village. At first light, the soldiers of the two battalion realized that they had been encircled in Trudy. The first enemy attack of regimental size took place early that morning from the north. The battalions succeeded in stopping the enemy attack on the open plain by using concentrated fires from the few infantry guns. *Leutnant* Lohse's *SPW*'s conducted reconnaissance in all directions and determined that the Soviets were growing in strength by the hour.

The division ordered Infanterie-Regiment 133 and Haas' battalion to attack Trudy to relieve the encircled battalions, which were sustaining heavy casualties. The I./Infanterie-Regiment 133 started screening at Ust-Kunatsch and along the Trudy, while *Major* Haas and his exhausted soldiers approached Trudy proper. When Haas' battalion reached Trudy at 1725 hours, his forces numbered ninety men and three machine guns. His men were immediately directed to screen to the south. Both of the battle groups already in Trudy had lost some 150 men by noon,. *Hauptmann* Peschke was badly wounded, resulting in *Leutnant* Heise assuming acting command of the *I./Schützen-Regiment 3*.

Despite all of its losses, the division had achieved all of its attack objectives for the day. In the morning, the motorcycle infantry battalion had taken Ust-Leski after one and one-half hours of fighting. The situation had been stabilized and the line for the winter fighting positions taken. *Pionier-Bataillon 39*, which was screening to the west at Sinojewka, was to be pushed forward during the night and attached to *Oberst* Kleemann's force. The engineers started work on establishing field fortifications along a general line running Hill 236.7 in Ust-Leski to Ust-Kunatsch. Trudy, which was located in a deep defile, was not included in the effort, since it could not be held in the long run. Correspondingly, the *I./Schützen-Regiment 394* left the village during the night of 2–3 January. At noon on 3 January, the *II./Schützen-Regiment 3* received orders to evacuate Trudy around 1700 hours, along with its attached tanks. The temperature registered -42 degrees Celsius (-43.6 Fahrenheit). It was the coldest night of the winter so far.

The divisional engineers were attached to *Oberst* Kleemann for building field fortifications. *Panzerjäger-Abteilung 521* was moved to Orel, since it was no longer capable of conducting operations. The corps informed the division at 1300 hours that measures were to be taken to move the motorized elements into the area around Fatesh as soon as possible. Pulling the *II./Schützen-Regiment 3* out of the line was delayed, because the evacuation of the wounded was difficult. The medical vehicles had not come forward. The German artillery, which had not been especially noticeable up to that point, fired with visible success into the eastern portion of Trudy. The battalion was finally able to pull out of the village, and the Russians did not notice. They were still firing into the village long after the division's soldiers had left. The temperatures again fell to -42, and there were many cases of frostbite.

The *221. Infanterie-Division* assumed responsibility for the northern portion of the division sector. *Infanterie-Regiment 133*, which had been given that mission, did not arrive until 0500 hours the next day; the relief was completed by 1000 hours. *Major* Pape's motorcycle infantry and *Major* Haas's foot battalion remained in the southern sector and were attached to *Kampfgruppe Moser* of the infantry division. The remaining formations of the *3. Panzer-Division* pulled back to the area around Maloarchangelsk to reorganize there. The movement to the rear was full of difficulties. Many vehicles were stranded due to the thick snow or a lack of fuel. Enemy bombers circled above the road continuously and strafed the columns with machine-gun fire. It was not until evening that Peschke's and Müller's battalions arrived in Grinew. The dis-

mounted elements were still in Droskowo, awaiting trucks or sleds. The division logistics officer, *Major i.G.* Barth, had commandeered all available vehicles for the movements. Even the bridging sections had to unload their bridge trucks to make them available for the hauling of personnel, weapons and equipment. Shuttle service was initiated from and to Maloarchangelsk and maintained, albeit with difficulty.

The division commander, who had moved to his command post in Maloarchangelsk, prepared an order on 5 January for the "Reorganization of the Motorized Elements of the Division." The first sentence of the order: "In order to make it possible for combat-capable elements to participate in operations, the motorized elements of the division are to be reorganized immediately." The restructuring and reorganization within the division started on that cold winter's day.

The *I./Panzer-Regiment 6* formed two line companies under *Oberstleutnant* Schmidt-Ott. The "new" battalion had one command tank, eleven *Panzer III's*, two *Panzer IV's*, and one *Panzer II*. The two motorized rifle battalions were consolidated under the command of *Oberstleutnant* Dr. Müller and the headquarters of the *II./Schützen-Regiment 394*. Müller received one company each from the two rifle regiments, as well as the heavy company. In addition, he received the two *SPW* companies, the *6./Flak-Regiment 59*, and *Panzerjäger-Regiment 543*. The company formed from *Schützen-Regiment 3* was led by *Oberleutnant* Dittmer. His platoon leaders were the *Leutnant* Reintjes, *Leutnant* Müller, *Leutnant* Pauli, and *Leutnant* von Ohlshausen. The company also had 35 noncommissioned officers and 220 enlisted personnel. *Oberstleutnant* Zimmermann took command of the foot battalions, using the headquarters of *Schützen-Regiment 3*. The headquarters of *Schützen-Regiment 394* and the elements of both rifle regiments that were no longer mobile because they had no vehicles were moved to Orel under the command of *Oberstleutnant* Audörsch. The noncommissioned officers and enlisted personnel sent there were reassigned to

Feld-Ersatz-Bataillon 83. The reconnaissance battalion formed a mixed company out of all of its remaining vehicles. The divisional engineer battalion kept two companies, after one bridging section was attached to the motorcycle infantry battalion and the other bridging section to the division support command. The division signals battalion remained unchanged, with one radio company and one field telephone company. The medical battalion consolidated its ambulance platoons, forming one platoon under the command of *Oberleutnant* Queck. The headquarters of *Panzerjäger-Abteilung 521* reported directly to the division, as did the headquarters of the rifle brigade in Orel.

Decisive measures were taken within the divisional artillery. The only command element left was the headquarters of the 3rd Battalion. The two battalion headquarters that were freed up were sent to Orel and then into the area around Roslawl to establish new battalions. *Panzer-Beobachtungs-Batterie 327* also moved to Orel. The remaining battalion was under the command of Hauptmann Kersten. His adjutant was *Oberleutnant* Kochan. The battalion consisted of batteries from all three battalions. They were *Oberleutnant* Speidel's 2nd Battery and *Oberleutnant* Lange's 5th Battery, both with 10.5-centimeter light field howitzers. In addition, there was *Hauptmann* Schultheiß's 7th Battery, with its cannon, and *Oberleutnant* Jahnke's 9th Battery, with its heavy 15-centimeter howitzers.

The elements of the division that had remained behind in the Orel area under *Oberstleutnant* Munzel continued to be employed digging fortifications and screening. On 4 January, a telephone message was received from the *2. Panzer-Armee* stating that a march battalion was to be formed. Munzel was given command of that battalion on express orders from *General* Schmidt. Additional instructions stated that experienced personnel, such as tank drivers, mechanics, gunners etc. were to remain in Orel

and continue with the work on the fortifications. Since the new *Kampfgruppe Munzel* was to be as mobile as possible, sleds had to be requisitioned or built. Munzel reported his battle group as operational two days later.

The remaining portions of the battalion that were immobile were loaded on columns of the *XXXXVII. Armee-Korps (mot.)* and *MG-Bataillon 5*[5] and transported to Bolchow, northeast of Orel. The sled companies and the motorized trains followed separately. Since the battalion had no heavy weapons, permission was granted by the headquarters of the field army for it to bring along two *Panzer II's*, three *Panzer III's*, and a command tank. The *ad hoc* battalion had *Oberstleutnant* Munzel in command, with *Leutnant* Ademek as his adjutant and *Leutnant* Jacob and *Leutnant* von Schell as his liaison officers. There was a signals platoon, three rifle companies, one platoon of tanks and one heavy machine-gun platoon. In all, the battalion numbered some 678 men. In addition to the tanks, there were seven staff cars, fifty-five *panje* sleds, and forty-seven horses. The forces remaining behind in Orel were under the command of *Hauptmann (Ing.)* Lanig and his adjutant, *Oberleutnant* von Twardowski.

Those rear-area elements then had to supply the widely scattered regiment. To that end, a transfer point was established in Bolchow under *Leutnant* Dr. Heuer. The very first night the last two field kitchens and two additional trucks had to be sent from Orel to make up for the vehicles *Bataillon Munzel* had already lost. The maintenance platoons continued to work on repairing vehicles—it was up to -18 degrees Celsius (-.4 Fahrenheit) in the "heated" motor bays—since *Kampfgruppe Schmidt-Ott* with the division main body continued to need vehicles. The vehicles were in such bad shape that hardly a single one could cover the stretch from Orel to Bolchow without breaking down. The second calamity was the lack of all types of fuel, which

---

5. A separate machine-gun battalion, which was later assigned to the *78. Sturm-Division* (February 1943), where it was reorganized and redesignated as *Granatwerfer-Bataillon 5*.

meant that the last drops had to be siphoned out of the vehicles that no longer could move due to mechanical problems. All of the remaining soldiers were still involved with the construction of fortifications. The regiment was especially concerned with taking care of its soldiers. Under the supervision of *Oberleutnant Graf* von Kageneck, a theater troop was assembled, which called itself the *Panzersprenggranate*.[6] In the course of more than 100 performances over the next few weeks and months, thousands of German soldiers, and not just from the division, were able to enjoy a hearty laugh once more. Despite the inexpensive cost of admission, more than 70,000 *Reichsmark* were collected in the end, which were intended to be used to erect a memorial to *Panzer-Regiment 6*.

Overcoming biting cold and a snowstorm, *Bataillon Munzel* covered ninety kilometers and reached the operational area of the *296. Infanterie-Division* on 7 January. The battalion received the mission to occupy two villages along the main line of resistance that were considered to be clear of the enemy. On approaching, the lead company of *Leutnant* Rukfuß received heavy infantry fire. The first losses were taken, including the young company commander. The village of Iwanowka could not be taken initially. It was only after *Leutnant* Becker's company came to support that it was taken.

The battalion was positioned in that sector of the front—all by itself and far removed from the *3. Panzer-Division*—halfway between Belew and Brjansk, where the Soviet 61st Army had

---

6. Armored high-explosive round.

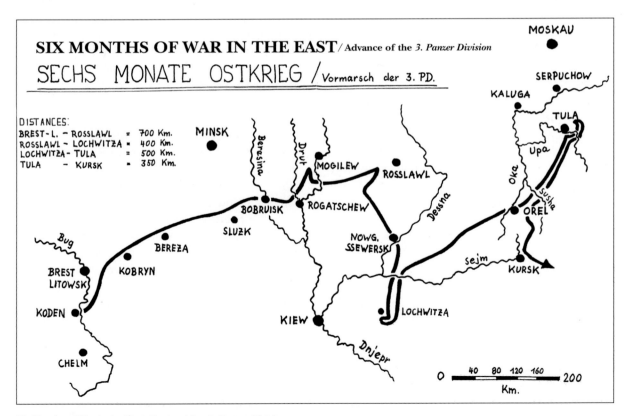

Six Months of War in the East: Route of the *3. Panzer-Division*.

driven a deep wedge into the German lines from the north. To the right and left of Munzel's forces were the battle groups of *Oberst* Kiessling and *Oberst* Rathcliffe, with Munzel initially reporting to Rathcliffe. Contact with the regiment in Orel could only be maintained through the radio in the command tank. Munzel's men were to hold Iwanowka for two months against a constantly attacking enemy.

The Soviets succeeded in entering the village twice by advancing through the "Ivan" defile; they were ejected twice. The situation was anything but enviable, since the village was frequently under mortar fire. The village sauna, which was put back into operation, could only be used at night. It was only at the Kireikowo strongpoint, where the sled section of *Leutnant* Kofel with its nearly 120 *panje* sleds defended, that the men of the battle group could get a temporary respite. The self-sacrificing actions of the battalion during that severe winter, coupled with its constant defensive skirmishes, earned special praise from the infantry division to which it was attached and from the field army. Unfortunately, many brave tankers rest in eternal peace at Iwanowka. *Leutnant* Jacob and *Leutnant* Hacker, as well as *Panzerschütz* Hoppe and *Panzerschütz* Tanke, are among them. In February, the commander of the neighboring regiment, *Oberst* Kiessling, was killed. Oberst Munzel assumed acting command of that regiment, while *Hauptmann* von Prittwitz was given command of the battalion. It was not until the March sun had conjured away the snow and replaced the iced-over landscape with mud and morass that the infantry employment of Munzel's tankers was ended.

During the severe winter of 1941–42, the division's armor regiment no longer existed as a cohesive formation. It had been split up into several battle groups and sections, which were employed at different places along the Eastern Front and up to 600 kilometers away from each other. For instance, another company was formed on 10 January in Orel from elements remaining there. It was directed to assume a security mission for the Brjansk–Orel rail line. *Leutnant* Hinpeter and 120 men, along with ten light machine guns, and two trucks, were loaded on trains and sent to be employed in Karatschew. The remaining elements of the regiment continued to establish defensive positions in the Orel area. When another thirty men had to be sent to reinforce *Kampfgruppe Schmidt-Ott*, the task of the remaining elements grew even more difficult.

The main effort of the rear-area services was in supplying the assorted battle groups of the regiment and in maintaining the vehicles. Sled of all types were constructed: five for medical purposes, one for a field mess, and twenty horse- and forty-five man-drawn sleds. In addition, recovery operations were conducted for stranded vehicles of all types, as well as courses for tank mechanics and radio operators. More and more men and materiel was detached for support elsewhere. On 17 January, for example, one *Panzer II*, two *Panzer III's*, and two command vehicles were dispatched to the two battle groups; ten days later, five fighting vehicles were sent to the *17. Panzer-Division*. By the end of January, another twenty men were sent to *Kampfgruppe Munzel*. At the same time, a security company was established under *Leutnant* Jacobs (later *Oberleutnant* Büschen), followed shortly later by a defense company, which was supposed to be employed if the city of Orel was threatened. That company was led by *Oberleutnant* Oehlrich and had 3 officers, 18 noncommissioned officers, and 160 enlisted personnel.

For a report due with an effective date of 2 February, the armored regiment had assembled the following statistics concerning its status. The number of dead suffered: 20 officers and 187 noncommissioned officers and enlisted personnel. The number of wounded totaled 40 officers and 551 noncommissioned officers and enlisted personnel. Enemy equipment and weapons captured or destroyed totaled: 317 tanks; 30 armored cars; 406 artillery pieces; 80 antiaircraft guns; 274 antitank guns; 83 mortars; 440 machine guns; 369 trucks; 5 staff cars; 40 tractors; 34 aircraft; 1 armored train; 2 transport trains; and 9 bunkers.

The headquarters of the division and its available motorized elements were sent marching towards Kursk on 6 January. The lead elements of the division arrived there after a 125-kilometer movement in the evening. *Generalmajor* Breith went ahead of his forces and received a briefing that afternoon from the commanding general of the *XXXXVIII. Armee-Korps (mot.)*, *General der Panzertruppen* Kempf, to which the division was attached. The Soviets had broken through along a broad front southeast of Kursk, and their lead elements had already reached the Kursk–Obojan road. The outskirts of Obojan had been occupied by the enemy. Up to that point, only the *I./Infanterie-Regiment 245*[7] of *Major* Schmidt, which had just arrived from France, had been employed. It was given a screening mission at Polewaja along the Kursk–Ssolnzewa road. Around Ssolnzewa proper, *Infanterie-Regiment 528* and *Aufklärungs-Abteilung 299* of the *299. Infanterie-Division* were holding. That evening, the *2./Artillerie-Regiment 75* was sent to Polewaja as the first unit of the *3. Panzer-Division* to support the infantry involved in hard fighting there.

At the same time, the enemy attacked the southern wing of *Generalmajor* Henrici's *16. Infanterie-Division (mot.)* with strong forces. He was trying to bring additional regiments through the Seim Valley, in an effort to take Kursk. The division received the mission to eliminate the threat to the *16. Infanterie-Division (mot.)* from the south and turn back additional enemy forces along the road to Wypolsowa. The next day, the division sent the first available tank companies of *Oberstleutnant* Schmidt-Ott toward Afanassjewka and the motorized infantry division, some sixy kilometers away. The companies advanced across snow-covered plains, pushed back enemy forces at Kamenskij and to the south and worked their way towards the road, constantly encountering heavy Russian resistance. Once at the road, the fighting vehicles took up defensive positions and disrupted all Russian traffic coming from the east. Although the Russians attempted to push back the German fighting vehicles by means of artillery and tanks, they did not succeed. By 8 January, the tank companies of the armor regiment were able to gain ground to the south and east and prevented any further breakthrough on the part of the enemy at that section of the front.

Generalmajor Breith was given command responsibility for the sector sough and west of the Seim on 8 January. The headquarters set up shop in Kursk. At the time, the only elements available to the commander and his operations officer, *Major i.G.* Pomtow, were the *I./Infanterie-Regiment 245*, *Infanterie-Regiment 528*, *Aufklärungs-Abteilung 299*,[8] and, from the *3. Panzer-Division*, two batteries of the divisional artillery, one troop of the reconnaissance battalion, and two companies of engineers. The general directed the *I./Infanterie-Regiment 245* to advance via Krassnikowo and reach the creek at Milidowka. The brave battalion worked its way forward through high snowdrifts, reached Krassnikowo and took the village, supported by one *Panzer IV* and two assault guns. It then moved on to the creek, achieving its attack objective.

Additional elements of the *3. Panzer-Division* arrived in Kursk during the day. They included the rifle companies of *Oberstleutnant* Dr. Müller and, a short while later, the motorcycle infantry companies of *Major* Pape, arriving by train. *Major* Ziervogel's reconnaissance battalion, whose remaining elements had arrived, worked their way forward through Polejawa to Ljubiskoje, along the completely exposed southern wing of the division, and assumed the screening mission.

The headquarters of *Oberstleutnant* Zimmermann's *Schützen-Regiment 3* (adjutant: *Hauptmann*

---

7. This was part of the *88. Infanterie-Division*, which was formed in December 1939. It was employed in France and then temporarily inactivated. It was reactivated in March 1941 and performed occupation duties in France while becoming operational again.
8. The latter two formations from the *299. Infanterie-Division*.

Haspel) was sent to Milidowka to exert command and control over the infantry forces there. The *I./Infanterie-Regiment 245* advanced through Schumakowo and towards Wypolsowa fighting both enemy resistance and terrain and weather difficulties in equal measure. The batteries of the divisional artillery supported the attack, which was crowned by the terrific battalion taking Wypolsowa. In the process, *Leutnant* Jacob of the 2nd Battery was killed. With the capture of the village, the west bank of the Seim had been reached. *Infanterie-Regiment 528*, which had been given the same objective, had not followed the attack of the other infantry forces, since it was held up by the enemy. For similar reasons, the friendly tanks had been unable to help the *I./Infanterie-Regiment 245*; they were only able to get to the west bank later on.

The Soviets had brought up reinforcements to their formations and attacked in the direction of Milidowka in the afternoon. The enemy forces encountered *Oberstleutnant* Dr. Müller's battalion, which had arrived in the meantime. In the course of the fighting, *Oberleutnant* Dittmer's company from *Schützen-Regiment 3* had to give up Ssorotschin one more time and pull back to Milidowka. That company lost one dead and four wounded during its first operation in the Kursk area.

For unknown reasons, *Infanterie-Regiment 528* evacuated Ssolnzewo during the night and moved back to the west. The division ordered the regiment to Milidowka, but the regiment did not receive the orders. As a consequence of that retrograde movement, *Kampfgruppe Zimmermann* was in danger of being cut off at Wypolsowa. The division made efforts to free up the *I./Infanterie-Regiment 245*—once from the north and once from the south—which was in acute danger. *Bataillon Müller*'s forces were unable to make it out of Milidowka, however. The enemy had been considerably reinforced during the night and turned back all attacks led by the companies of *Oberleutnant* Dittmer and *Leutnant* Schiller, which suffered casualties.

Panzergruppe Schmidt-Ott was employed in an immediate attack in the direction of Wypolsowa from the south. The 3rd Tank Company, led by *Oberleutnant* Müller-Hauff, who would be placed on the Army Honor Roll on 1 March 1942, ran into an enemy trap. The tanks were advancing on Schumakowo. All of a sudden, several T-34's appeared. The main guns of the *Panzer III's* were powerless against them. Nine German tanks were knocked out by the enemy fire. The remaining ones had to pull back to the Seim in the face of the superior enemy forces and cross the frozen river. One platoon from the 1st Company of engineers, consisting of one officer and thirty-four enlisted personnel, had followed the tank attack. Only twelve engineers returned without wounds. It was only possible to move as far forward as the knocked-out tanks in the course of an immediate counterattack launched later on. The German soldiers found out that their wounded comrades had been stabbed to death in a bestial manner and then plundered.

By then, *Infanterie-Regiment 528* had arrived completely exhausted along the Polnaja on 10 January, after having had to fight a pursuing enemy. It was able to establish contact with *Aufklärungs-Abteilung 1* there. The regiment remained attached to the division, but it was barely capable of operations. *Oberstleutnant* Zimmermann assumed temporary command of the regiment.

On 11 January, the Russians were still positioned at Ljubiskoje. They were increasing their pressure in the direction of Ssorotschin–Milidowka from the Murynowka Valley. The encircled *I./Infanterie-Regiment 245* and the tank battalion continued to fight against numerically superior forces. The Soviets at Wypolsowo attempted to break out to the east to escape the attacks of the *2. Armee* and the *6. Armee*, which were slowly starting to gather steam. The next two days were spent in patrol activates on both sides, without a change to the basic situation. Unfortunately, the commander of the 3rd Tank Company, the brave and exemplary *Oberleut-*

nant Müller-Hauff, was killed during one of those operations.

The thirteenth of January saw *Infanterie-Regiment 528* involved in hard fighting that resulted in a lot of casualties. It was only possible for the motorcycle infantry battalion to temporarily relieve the encircled *I./Infanterie-Regiment 245* at Wypolsowa. The motorcycle infantry companies attacked in the direction of Machnino to the right of *Bataillon Müller*. Despite considerable terrain difficulties, the motorcycle infantry were able to take the enemy positions, which were being held by elements of an entire cavalry division. Major Pape and the commander of the 3rd Company, *Hauptmann* von Cochenhausen, served as examples in driving their men forward to attack. The enemy suffered a considerable setback. The rifle platoon of *Oberfeldwebel* Kruse, which was employed as a flank guard, was able to gain ground in the direction of Bynino and Schumakowo. After the successful attack of the motorcycle infantry battalion was concluded, Kruse's platoon heading back to Milidowka that evening. The *I./Infanterie-Regiment 245* was still on its own, however. Only *Hauptmann* Markowski, who had taken over the 3rd Tank Company, was able to escort supplies to the infantry battalion.

A renewed attempt by *Infanterie-Regiment 528* to break open the enemy front and advance on Ssorotschin was unsuccessful and resulted in heavy casualties. At that point, the division ordered *Bataillon Müller* to attack south one more time. Fortunately, *Major* Haas's foot battalion had arrived in Milidowka that day. It was able to assume responsibility for securing the village, albeit with only 120 men. *Oberstleutnant* Dr. Müller's two rifle companies conducted an enveloping attack against Ssorotschin. *Oberleutnant* Dittmer and his platoons succeeded in entering the locality from the north, establishing contact with the lead elements of *Infanterie-Regiment 528*. That evening, *Oberstleutnant* Zimmermann took over the security responsibilities for Ssorotschin with his battle group.

The enemy did not slacken in his efforts. During the morning of 15 January, he launched a surprise attack by ten T-34's, which smashed into the positions of the battered and completely burned out *I./Infanterie-Regiment 245* at Wypolsowa. The commander, *Major* Schmidt, was killed in that fighting. The battalion, or more accurately, what was left of the battalion, pulled back under the command of an *Oberleutnant*, since it no longer had any armor-defeating weapons and the fighting vehicles that had been up front were also out of commission. The brave infantry, who had to leave behind 39 dead comrades and 126 wounded or missing ones, was passed through the lines by the companies of the motorcycle infantry battalion at Machnino.

As a consequence of retaking Wypolsowo, the enemy was once again along the road. The division ordered a temporary cessation of all movement and a transition to the defense, until an attack could be launched on 17 January in conjunction with *Generalleutnant* Neuling's *239. Infanterie-Division*.

In accordance with its orders, *Oberstleutnant* Dr. Müller's battalion moved out at 0600 hours, after the batteries of *Hauptmann* Kersten fired a short preparation on the enemy positions. Six fighting vehicles supported the attack of the riflemen, who immediately started receiving heavy enemy fire. Once again, *Oberfeldwebel* Kruse and his platoon were up front and entered Schumakowo at 0750 hours. A short while later, the remaining platoons of *Oberleutnant* Dittmer's company had closed up and occupied the locality. The riflemen established contact by 1130 hours with the motorcycle infantry battalion in Machnino, thus achieving their attack objective. The company lost two dead and fifteen wounded, including *Leutnant* von Ohlshausen. *Oberst* Schmidt, the commander of *Infanterie-Regiment 245*, assumed command of the forces in the Schumakowo area; *Bataillon Müller* was attached to him.

The Soviets did not give up, however. Starting in the afternoon, they conducted counterattacks that were preceded by waves of bombers.

The enemy pressure was especially focused on Machnino, where the motorcycle infantry battalion knocked out two T-34's and ejected the Russians, who had already entered the village. The enemy continued his efforts during the night and showered the terrain and the positions of the motorcycle infantry with heavy artillery fire. An attack on the Machnino positions on 18 January was turned back; an 8.8-centimeter *Flak* knocked out a KV-I.

The enemy was present in superior numbers everywhere. Heavy artillery fire was placed on all of the localities occupied by the German forces, which were also repeatedly attacked by fighter-bombers. It was directed for the *3. Panzer-Division* to advance against Ssolnzewo, as soon as the attack to the south by the neighboring *XXIX. Armee-Korps* of *General der Infanterie* von Obstfelder started to show an effect.

Since the promised *Stuka* support did not materialize—as was frequently the case—the operation was not started. In its place, the Soviets became active and advanced one more time against the positions of the motorcycle infantry at Machnino with tanks. Once again, the motorcycle infantry had to save their skins, forcing the enemy back and knocking out two T-34's in the process. Apparently, it was the Russians' plan to cut off the elements of the division that were echeloned forward. To counter that, *Infanterie-Regiment 528* was moved to Bynino and employed as a flank guard. That regiment relieved the badly battered motorcycle infantry the next day. The headquarters of *Schützen-Regiment 3* under *Oberstleutnant* Zimmermann, which had been involved in the defensive fighting since day one, returned to Orel.

On 20 January, the Soviets made it their point to try to take Machnino and Milidowka. They attacked at first light, but they were turned back by 0700 hours. Another attempt by the enemy to roll up the German front in the afternoon also fell apart after an hour. A mine obstacle that had been emplaced by the German engineers blew up as a result of sympathetic explosions caused by a direct hit. Friendly losses were considerable.

By then, strong Russian formations had broken through the winter positions along the Tim and at the boundary between the *LV. Armee-Korps* and the *XXXXVIII. Armee-Korps (mot.)*. They were advancing with cavalry and rifle divisions in the direction of Schtschigry. *Oberstleutnant* Dr. Müller's battalion, along with an attached battery of artillery and an engineer company, were pulled out of the line and sent by motor transport to the sector of *Generalleutnant Ritter* von Hubicki's *9. Panzer-Division*. In the course of the day, the headquarters of the *3. Panzer-Division* followed, as did all of the divisional elements that had been employed in that sector. Only *Major* Pape's motorcycle infantry battalion and *Major* Haas's foot battalion remained where they had been, in contact with the enemy. Haas had to detail one officer (*Leutnant* Schupius) and thirty men to reinforce Müller's force, however. Major Frank led the security battalion, which was then taken over by *Major* von Türckheim. The battalion remained at Ssobatschenko until 21 February as *Sperrverband Türckheim*.[9] *Generalmajor* Gollwitzer's *88. Infanterie-Division*, which was gradually arriving from France, assumed command of the sector around Milidowka from *Generalmajor* Breith.

That signaled the end of the first round of fighting around Kursk for the *3. Panzer-Division*. The unfavorable situation dictated that the division could not be employed as such. Instead, it had had to fight with formations it had never worked with before. In the time from 4 to 21 January, the division had fought against the Russian 2nd Guards Rifle Division, the 62nd and 293rd Rifle Divisions, and the 14th Tank Brigade. All of those forces belonged to the 40th Army. The enemy lost five tanks and four guns; 281 prisoners were taken. Friendly losses during the same period consisted of 13 officer and 271 enlisted personnel dead; 15 officer and 610 enlisted personnel wounded; 102 enlisted per-

9. Blocking Formation Türckheim.

sonnel missing; and 585 sick personnel. Materially, the division lost eight fighting vehicles, one command tank, two self-propelled guns, and one *Flak*.

Since the Soviets were continuing their offensive aimed at Kursk, there was no time for the division to take a break. During the night of 21–22 January, the Russians broke open the boundary between the *9. Panzer-Division* and the *95. Infanterie-Division* and advanced far to the west. As a result, orders were immediately issued to the elements of the division in the Kursk area—artillery, engineers, tanks, and the reconnaissance battalion—to screen the area to the front of Kursk. At the same time, the *2. Armee* brought a march battalion forward. It was attached to *Major* Frank and was directed to immediately start screening the railway line between Orel and Kursk. On 23 January, *Major* Ziervogel's reconnaissance battalion moved to Wedjanoje, to reconnoiter in the valleys that were running from the south to the north. *Oberstleutnant* Dr. Müller's battalion was already engaged with the enemy and was located along the south bank of the Olchowatka. By 23 January, the Soviets were attacking the newly occupied positions. *Oberleutnant* Dittmer's and *Leutnant* Schiller's companies were able to hold on to their positions around Werch–Olchowatoje.

During the morning of 24 January, the corps ordered the movement of all of the division's elements in the Kursk area to Alekssandrowka along the Tuskarij. It was intended to interdict the enemy's breakthrough there by means of an immediate counterattack. An attack launched by the *9. Panzer-Division* prior to the completion of the movements failed. That resulted in the companies of the *3. Panzer-Division* that were already in position having to be pulled back. That evening, the division received orders to launch an immediate counterattack with all available forces in the direction of Schtschigry.

Major Frank was directed to move east with his battalion through the Tuskarj Valley. He was to depart form Budanowka and attempt to cover 10 kilometers a day. He was to reach Kriw-

zowka, while simultaneously reconnoitering along the avenue of advance and in the valleys. Both *Oberleutnant* Fredenhagen's and *Oberleutnant* Hagenguth's companies from *Schützen-Regiment 394* were to temporarily remain at the bridges over the Tuskarj in a screening mission, and the companies of *Oberleutnant* Mente and *Oberleutnant* von Studnitz were to advance east south of the river, while *Oberleutnant* Dziallas was to move north of the river. The advance was made difficult by the deep snow, the icy east wind and temperatures that went as low as -40 degrees Celsius [-40 Fahrenheit]. Nevertheless, Nisch-Demkino, about twelve kilometers away, was reached by the evening. *Leutnant* Berg assumed command of the *7./Schützen-Regiment 3* there. The next day, the battalion moved as far as Kartaschowka. *Feldwebel* Bachert's platoon from the *2./Schützen-Regiment 3* screened there, while the three companies went into position around Propowetz. The enemy pulled back in the face of the battle group, which was being commanded by *Major Freiherr* von Türckheim by then. On 27 January, Romaschowka was reached. By doing so, the gap that had previously existed along the western side of the front was closed. The battalion stayed there two days.

The division was then moved to the railway station at Ochotschewka, with the reconnaissance battalion in the lead. *Generalmajor* Breith arrived at the location of the command post of the *9. Panzer-Division* during the afternoon of 25 January. With him were the lead elements of *Kampfgruppe Schmidt-Ott*, which consisted of all available tanks, three self-propelled antitank guns, one battery of the divisional artillery and one 8.8-centimeter *Flak*. The situation grew more critical by the hour. Just east of Ochotschewka, the Soviets had already pressed across the rail line and were already in the northern portion of Schtschigry, while additional forces were rolling towards the rail line.

Major Ziervogel's reconnaissance battalion moved straight from its line of march without regrouping against the enemy forces along the railway embankment. As soon as *Oberstleutnant*

Schmidt-Ott arrived with his battle group, his tanks and guns advanced on Schatalowka in order to clear the road to Schtschigry. The *9. Panzer-Division* also committed two infantry companies in that direction. The fighting for the locality was fairly hard, but the Russians were forced out. At the same time, a hastily assembled battle group, comprised of elements from the rear-area services and under the command of *Oberleutnant* Bachmann of *Schützen-Regiment 394*, drove the enemy out of Schtschigry by means of an aggressively led attack. Exploiting the success, the reconnaissance battalion advanced to the north and occupied a patch of woods two kilometers southeast of Alekssandrowka. The Russians pulled back in the face of the hammer blows of the German attack towards Poschidajewka.

The division intelligence officer summarized the reports and reconnaissance results as follows:

> The overall situation showed that the attack of the *9. Panzer-Division* to the north had failed and that it had been abandoned farther to the east along the Koserscha River between Butyrki and Stakanowo. The counterattack had not been resumed, since enemy was present in Tuskarj Valley at Kriwzowka and in the valley at Masslowka. As the result of aerial reconnaissance and statements from the local populace, strong enemy cavalry forces had been determined especially in Terebusch Valley, but also at Karschaka and at Kasinowka.

Those few words also include the brave and self-sacrificing fighting of *Bataillon Müller* (*Schützen-Regiment 394*), which was attempting to take Stakanowo as part of the *9. Panzer-Division*. On 25 January, at the onset of darkness, *Oberleutnant* Dittmer's company succeeded in taking Stakanowo. The company encountered stubborn resistance, and suffered four dead, including the company headquarters section leader, *Feldwebel* Nitz, and seven wounded. Since the company was all by itself and had no contact at all with the neighboring elements, it had to be pulled back during the night. After a few hours, the riflemen had to attack again, but the effort did not succeed. *Leutnant* Schiller's company, which had closed up in the meantime, suffered twenty-two dead and wounded that day. The enemy was stronger. The battalion transitioned to the defense around Nisch-Olchowatoje.

On 26 January, the division was able to score a nice success with its two battle groups. *Major* Ziervogel and his reconnaissance battalion advanced from Schtschigry, along with some tanks and artillery, while *Oberstleutnant* Schmidt-Ott headed in the direction of Alekssandrowka with his battle group, consisting of elements of the armor regiment and *Infanterie-Regiment 133*,[10] from Poschidajewka, which had been taken that morning. The Russians were hit on two sides and ejected from Alekssandrowka after a short firefight. The battle groups exploited the success and continued the advance in the direction of Kriwzowka, which was reached in the evening. The enemy lost the will to fight and fled back.

The next mission for the division was the clearing of the valley depressions around Kriwzowka. On 27 January, the motorcycle infantry battalion, transported by trucks, arrived in Werch-Olchowatoje from Wodjanoje. Once there, *Major* Pape assumed command of a battle group consisting of his battalion, an SS infantry battalion,[11] tanks, and antitank elements. Shortly after 1330 hours, the men of the battle group assaulted from Werch-Olchowatoje, overran the initial enemy strongpoints and positions and entered Solowjewka by surprise. Pape's men

---

10. This was part of the *45. Infanterie-Division*, which was composed primarily of Austrians.

11. Based on additional information provided below, this was undoubtedly the *III./SS-Infanterie-Brigade 1 (mot.)*, which *SS-Hauptsturmführer* Alfons Zeitler commanded during this period.

sustained few casualties—only three wounded. The regiments of the Soviet 32nd Cavalry Division that were holding there were completely surprised by the power and aggressiveness of the German attack. Despite that, they stubbornly defended in the impoverished huts and houses of the locality. *Major* Pape led from the front and rallied his men forward. The Soviet cavalrymen started to scatter in all directions. Their division commander was among those taken prisoner. The attached tanks continued rolling forward with their last few liters of fuel and were able to chase the remnants of a Soviet division out of Nikolskoje.

The thirtieth of January was marked by the crowning achievement of all of the heavy fighting and previous sacrifices. The division concentrated its forces for a concentric attack aimed at defeating the enemy forces in the Butyrki–Judinka–Stakanowo area. The main effort was with *Kampfgruppe Pape*, which was directed to advance on Stakanowo. The battle group staged for the attack with half of the *II./Infanterie-Regiment 246* and its tanks in Solowjewka and with the motorcycle infantry battalion and *SS-Bataillon Zeitler* in Rudino. *Oberst* Neubauer intended to only move his battalions out in the direction of Butyrki after *Kampfgruppe Pape* was successful.

Hauptmann Kersten's batteries, which had closed up, opened the attack with a short preparation on the enemy trenches. It was still dark across the snow-covered terrain when the men of *Kampfgruppe Pape* rose out of their trenches and advanced against the Russian positions. By 0630 hours, they had succeeded in entering Nowo-Danilowka; half an hour later, the attached tanks had reached Moskwinka. Both of the localities were in German hands after a short fight. The enemy left his positions fairly quickly. The battle group gained more ground by the hour and reached Stakanowo by 1100 hours with the tanks in the lead.

Kampfgruppe Neubauer moved out at 0800 hours and had to "chew" its way into Butyrki meter-by-meter against extremely tough resistance. The *I./Infanterie-Regiment 133* took heavy casualties, before it was able to take the village in hard house-to-house fighting. The *III./Infanterie-Regiment 156*,[12] which was employed on the right wing and supported by tanks from the *9. Panzer-Division*, moved through Orljanka and quickly closed on Judinka, although the tanks were then held up by the bottomland of the Kosorscha and the infantry could no longer follow.

At that point, the fighting vehicles of *Hauptmann* Markowski joined the fray. They advanced from Stakanowo to the southeast in the direction of Judinka, rallying *Kampfgruppe Neubauer* in the process. The enemy took extremely heavy casualties in the fighting and evacuated the battlefield. The battalions of *Oberstleutnant* Dr. Müller and *Major* Frank no longer needed to be committed; they remained to the rear to secure the area that had been taken. By the afternoon, the division had reached its attack objectives.

The weather that day was anything but nice. An icy wind from the east brought with it more snow, which was already meters deep. Fuel, ammunition and rations just did not make it forward. The men of the divisional signals battalion had to master extraordinary difficulties, just to lay wire. The radio sections were bogged down somewhere.

As a result, it was only possible to use tanks to reconnoiter as far as Chochlowka that afternoon. The results demonstrated, however, that the enemy was beaten everywhere. The same results were obtained when the reconnaissance battalion and *Kampfgruppe Frank* sent out patrols. The Soviets were pulling back along the northern flank of the division.

The Armed Forces Daily report of 31 January 1942 announced the following: "A counterattack by German infantry and tanks led by Generalmajor Breith in the area northeast of Kursk has led to a complete success after several days of

---

12. This was one of the motorized infantry regiments of the *16. Infanterie-Division (mot.)*.

fighting. A group of enemy forces consisting of several [infantry] division and armored formations that had broken into the German lines was defeated, suffering heavy losses, and thrown back."

Major Pape, whose battle group formed the main effort of those operations, received the Knight's Cross for the performance of his forces and his personal leadership.[13] The entire division was honored by a personal telegram from the Supreme Commander of the Armed Forces, which *Generalmajor* Breith received on that same day: "In grateful appreciation for your heroic leadership in the course of successful counterattacks against superior enemy forces, I am awarding you the Oak Leaves to the Knight's Cross of the Iron Cross as the sixty-ninth soldier of the German Armed Forces."

The weather did not change of 1 February. Heavy snowstorms howled across the countryside that did not abate somewhat until the afternoon. The continuation of the advance was scheduled for 3 February. The second of February had to be used for establishing supply lines of communication and bringing up tanks and other motorized sections to Isakowo and Judinka in order to have sufficient forces on hand for the new attack.

The operations started right at 0700 hours on 3 February. *Oberstleutnant* Schmidt-Ott advanced with his tanks and *SS-Bataillon Zeitler* from Isakowo to the southeast and into Dolgaja Valley. One hour later, *Kampfgruppe Neubauer* moved out from Judinka, advancing on Chochlowka. The advance gained ground rapidly after 1000 hours, when the *I./Infanterie-Regiment 133* reinforced Schmidt-Ott's forces. The Soviets only put up minor resistance and were pulling back. After receipt of the aerial observation report of the withdrawal, the division ordered Neubauer to move his forces beyond the originally designated attack objective. By 1700 hours, all of the localities in Dolgaja Valley were

retaken. In the end, a small battle group from the *9. Panzer-Division* also joined the operation.

The Russian front was losing its cohesiveness. The formations of the III Guards Cavalry Corps that were employed—the 5th and 6th Guards Cavalry Divisions, the 32nd Cavalry Division, and the 34th Rifle Brigade—were in a state of dissolution or were pulling back across the Tim. The enemy left six tanks, eleven guns, ten antitank guns (including five German ones), six heavy machine guns, fourteen trucks, and an untold quantity of horses, wagons and sleds on the battlefield. In addition, 130 prisoners were taken.

The *3. Panzer-Division* exploited the important success and assaulted Urynok on the Tim on 4 February with the infantry battalions of *Oberst* Neubauer. That meant that the winter position that had been designated by the field army had been reached. The *2. Armee* could set up its defenses there. In the area of operations around Kursk, the division suffered the following losses from 22 January to 4 February: 3 officers and 34 noncommissioned officers and enlisted personnel killed; 4 officers and 165 noncommissioned officers and enlisted personnel wounded; 2 missing enlisted personnel; and 156 sick personnel.

The successes allowed the division to be relieved in its sector over the next few days by infantry divisions and be moved to the rear. The battle groups and all of the separate elements of the division moved back into the area around Kursk by the middle of February, where the division reassembled.

Not all elements of the *3. Panzer-Division* were involved in the winter fighting around Kursk. A number of elements remained in and around Orel. Along with all of the other elements positioned around the city, they had to form a battalion on 27 January, which reported directly to *Oberst* Usinger, the local area commander. *Hauptmann* von Zamory, the company

---

13. Pape was officially presented with the award on 10 February 1942. He later went on to become the 301st recipient of the Oak Leaves to the Knight's Cross of the Iron Cross (15 September 1943). He passed away in his native town of Düsseldorf on 21 January 1986.

commander of the *3./Schützen-Regiment 3*, was entrusted with command of the battalion. He was assisted by the headquarters of the 1st Battalion of the rifle regiment; his adjutant was *Leutnant* Heise. The battalion consisted of elements from the two rifle regiments, the armor regiment, the divisional artillery and supply sections of the *2. Armee*. Employed in defensive fighting ninety kilometers farther north was the sled battalion of the armor regiment.

The battalion in Orel received orders on 30 January to establish combat outposts twenty kilometers west of the city that were oriented to the west. The enemy had dramatically reinforced his forces northwest of the city over the last few days, and the danger was manifest that he could advance towards Orel across the Orel–Karatschew rail line. The battalion moved out the next day with its three companies under *Leutnant* Schulze (*Schützen-Regiment 394*), *Leutnant* Jacobs (*Panzer-Regiment 6*), and *Oberleutnant* Krallmann (*Nachschub-Bataillon 583*). An advance party under *Feldwebel* Nawrath had already been dispatched to look for quarters.

The battalion reached the area around Naryschkino, where it established its outposts. The weather was very bad. High snowdrifts prevented any type of rapid march movements, with the result that all of the vehicles of the companies had to remain behind in Naryschkino. It was almost impossible to send out patrols or build bunkers. As a consequence of the snowstorms, elements were constantly getting lost. Resupply was conducted on the fly. It was not until February that the weather improved. The companies started to construct bunkers and field positions and conduct patrols into Orlik Valley. There was no enemy contact, so the battalion was summoned back to Orel on 5 February by *Oberst* Usinger. A few days later, Soviet forces broke through at Kirow, to the north of Orel. The commander of the rear area, *Generalleutnant* von Unruh, formed a battle group which pushed the enemy back by 21 February. The *3. Panzer-Division* participated in that operation with one company under the command of *Oberleutnant* Heuke of the division headquarters. Although it suffered heavy casualties, it took 80 prisoners.

The second half of February and the first two weeks of March were used by the division to gradually reassemble its forces in the area around Kursk in order to allow them to rest, refit and reorganize. The division headquarters was located in the city. A personnel replacement battalion of 1,000 men arrived on 12 February. In addition to the assignment and training of the new personal and issuance of materiel, "normal" duties were also conducted.

From 9 February to 12 March 1942, the division reported directly to the Army High Command. Those few weeks of essential rest also saw changes in the personnel structure and commands of the division. *Oberst* Kleemann, the longtime commander of the *3. Schützen-Brigade*, was promoted to *Generalmajor* and took command of the *90. leichte Division*, which was fighting in North Africa. *Oberst* Westhoven followed him in command. That officer was closely associated with the armor branch through his work in the Army Personnel Office and had been the commander of *Schützen-Regiment 1* of the *1. Panzer-Division*, fighting around Leningrad, Kalinin and Moscow. *Oberst* Munzel remained commander of the armored regiment and *Oberstleutnant* Zimmermann continued to command *Schützen-Regiment 3*. *Oberst* Audörsch gave up command of *Schützen-Regiment 394* to be reassigned to the Weapons Directorate of the Army High Command. He was replaced by Oberst Chales de Beaulieu. From his duties as the chief of staff of the *XVI. Armee-Korps (mot.)* in France, he was well known to the *3. Panzer-Division*. Prior to being reassigned to the division, he was the chief of staff of the *4. Panzer-Armee* of *General* Hoepner. *Major i.G.* Barth, the industrious division logistics officer, was transferred at the end of February. Starting on 5 March, *Hauptmann i.G.* Dankworth from the Army High Command assumed duties as the division logistics officer.

Oberstleutnant Audörsch with officers of his regiment outside Tula.

Even the tanks no longer made things happen. The enemy has become stronger and winter has arrived.

The main clearing station of the division was located in the Tolstoy Estate in Jassnaja-Poljana.

Supply elements of the division on the road between Brjansk and Orel. These men performed in an exemplary manner. Without them, the fighting elements would have had to have laid down their arms.

Firing position of a 10-centimeter battery in Bolochowka.

The reserves of *Schützen-Regiment 394* advance toward the front around Bolochowka under the leadership of *Leutnant* Schickerling.

The "mounted squadron" of the *3. Panzer-Division* brings weapons and ammunition to Tula. The commander of the provisional element was *Hauptmann* Höpfner.

Between Tula and Wanew.

East of Tula.

The Battle of Tula is over—hopelessly bogged down in the snow and ice. Victor: Winter.

Generalmajor Breith, who assumed command of the division during the difficult times outside Tula.

Oberstleutnant i.G. Pomtow, the division operations officer.

APPENDIX 1

Rank Table

U.S. Army	German Army	Waffen-SS	English Equivalent
Enlisted			
Private	Schütze	SS-Schütze[1]	Private
Private First Class	Oberschütze	SS-Oberschütze[2]	Private First Class
Corporal	Gefreiter	SS-Sturmmann	Acting Corporal
(Senior Corporal)	Obergefreiter	SS-Rottenführer	Corporal
(Staff Corporal)	Stabsgefreiter	SS-Stabsrottenführer[3]	
Noncommissioned Officers			
Sergeant	Unteroffizier	SS-Unterscharführer	Sergeant
(None)	Unterfeldwebel	SS-Scharführer	Staff Sergeant
Staff Sergeant	Feldwebel	SS-Oberscharführer	Technical Sergeant
Sergeant First Class	Oberfeldwebel	SS-Hauptscharführer	Master Sergeant
Master Sergeant	Hauptfeldwebel	SS-Sturmscharführer	Sergeant Major
Sergeant Major	Stabsfeldwebel		
Officers			
2nd Lieutenant	Leutnant	SS-Untersturmführer	2nd Lieutenant
1st Lieutenant	Oberleutnant	SS-Obersturmführer	1st Lieutenant
Captain	Hauptmann	SS-Hauptsturmführer	Captain
Major	Major	SS-Sturmbannführer	Major
Lieutenant Colonel	Oberstleutnant	SS-Obersturmbannführer	Lieutenant Colonel
Colonel	Oberst	SS-Standartenführer	Colonel
(None)	(None)	SS-Oberführer	(None)
Brigadier General	Generalmajor	SS-Brigadeführer	Brigadier General
Major General	Generalleutnant	SS-Gruppenführer	Major General
Lieutenant General	General der Panzertruppen, etc.	SS-Obergruppenführer	Lieutenant General
General	Generaloberst	SS-Oberstgruppenführer	General
General of the Army	Feldmarschall	Reichsführer-SS	Field Marshal

1. *SS-Mann* before 1942.
2. Not used before 1942.
3. Rank did not officially exist but has been seen in written records.

APPENDIX 2

Major Command and Duty Positions, 1935–42

The Division Headquarters

Division Commander

Fessmann	*Generalleutnant*	15 October 1935–30 September 1937
Freiherr Geyr von Schweppenburg	*Generalleutnant*	1 October 1937–14 February 1940
Stumpff	*Generalmajor*	15 February 1940–12 November 1940
Model	*Generalleutnant*	13 November 1940–30 September 1941
Breith	*Generalleutnant*	1 October 1941–30 September 1942

Division Operations Officer (Ia)

Graf von Sponeck	*Major i.G.*
Von dem Borne	*Oberstleutnant i.G.*
Pomtow	*Oberstleutnant i.G.*
Voss	*Oberstleutnant i.G.*

Division Logistics Officer (Ib)

Keppel	*Rittmeister*
Krasà	*Hauptmann i.G.*
Barth	*Hauptmann i.G.*
Dankworth	*Hauptmann*

Division Intelligence Officer (Ic)

Materne	*Major*
Barth	*Hauptmann*
Von Schubert	*Oberleutnant*
Von dem Knesebeck	*Hauptmann*

Adjutant General (Officers) (IIa)

Von Necker	*Rittmeister*
Von Wietersheim	*Major*
Von Oppen	*Major*
Düwel	*Hauptmann*
Menard	*Oberleutnant*
Graf Pilati	*Major*
Von Alvensleben	*Major*

Adjutant General (Officers) (IIa) *continued*

Von Brauchitsch	*Hauptmann*
Markowski	*Hauptmann*

Judge Advocate (III)

Dr. Schweinsberger	*Kriegsgerichtsrat*
Dr. Clemens	*Kriegsgerichtsrat*
Dr. Koch	*Kriegsgerichtsrat*
Dr. Gramm	*Kriegsgerichtsrat*
Fischer	*Inspektor*

Administrative Officer (IVa)

Dr. Zur Neiden	*Stabsintendant*
Dr. Angermann	*Oberstabsintendant*
Blümel	*Intendanturrat*
Falk	*Oberstabsintendant*

Division Surgeon (IVb)

Prof. Dr. Muntsch	*Oberstabsarzt*
Dr. Böhm	*Oberstabsarzt*
Dr. Zinsser	*Oberfeldarzt*
Dr. Stribny	*Oberfeldarzt*

Division Chaplains (IVd)

Dr. Heidland	Protestant
Sieburg	Protestant
Drews	Protestant
Laub	Catholic
Ruzek	Catholic

Division Transportation Officer (V)

Brätsch	*Regierungs-Baurat*
Rein	*Hauptmann (Ing.)*
Lanig	*Major (Ing.)*
Riessberger	*Major (Ing.)*

Panzer-Brigade 3

Kühn, Georg	*Generalleutnant*	15 October 1935–31 December 1937
Stumpff	*Oberst*	1 January 1938–14 February 1940
Crüwell	*Oberst*	Acting commander, Fall 1938
Kühn, Fritz	*Generalmajor*	15 February 1940–12 October 1940
Freiherr von Funck	*Oberst*	13 October 1940–1 May 1941 (transfer to Africa)

Panzer-Brigade 5

Linnarz	*Oberst*	1 May 1941–31 August 1941 (deactivation of the brigade)

Schützen-Brigade 3

Kühn, Fritz	*Oberst*	Summer 1935–14 October 1935
Bernard	*Oberst*	15 October 1935–end of 1936
Stumpff	*Oberst*	1 January 1937–31 December 1937
Gawantka	*Oberst*	1 January 1938–1 August 1938
Angern	*Oberst*	2 August 1938–31 December 1939

Schützen-Brigade 3 *continued*

Kleemann	Oberst	1 January 1940–31 January 1942
Westhoven	Oberst	1 February 1942–30 September 1942 (deactivation of the brigade)

Panzer-Regiment 6

Meyer	Oberst	
Crüwell	Oberst	
Rothenburg	Oberstleutnant	
Von Lewinski	Oberst	
Munzel	Oberst	
Schmidt-Ott	Oberstleutnant	
Freiherr von Liebenstein	Oberst	
Munzel	Oberst	

Panzer-Regiment 5

Zuckertort	Oberst	
Nehring	Oberst	
Conze	Oberstleutnant	Acting commander
Freiherr von Funck	Oberst	Transfer to Africa

Schützen-Regiment 3

Stumpff	Oberst	
Kleemann	Oberstleutnant	
Von Manteuffel	Oberstleutnant	
Zimmermann	Oberst	
Wellmann	Oberst	

Schützen-Regiment 394

Erhard	Oberst	
Audörsch	Oberstleutnant	
Chales de Beaulieu	Oberst	

Artillerie-Regiment 75

Weidling	Oberst	
Forster	Oberst	
Ries	Oberst	
Dr. Weissenbruch	Oberst	
Lattmann	Oberst	

Kradschützen-Bataillon 3

Von Manteuffel	Major	
Tröger	Oberstleutnant	
Von Manteuffel	Major	
Von Corvin-Wiersbitzki	Major	
Pape	Major	

Aufklärungs-Abteilung 3

Paulus	Oberst	
Schroetter	Major	
Freiherr von Wechmar	Major	Transfer to Africa

Aufklärungs-Abteilung 1

Ziervogel	*Major*	

Panzerjäger-Abteilung 521 (Sfl)

Frank	*Major*	
Streger	*Major*	Battalion deactivated

Panzerabwehr-Abteilung/ Panzerjäger-Abteilung 39

Von Tippelskirch	*Major*	
Von Bernuth	*Major*	Transfer to Africa

Panzerjäger-Abteilung 543

Freiherr von Türckheim zu Altdorf	*Oberstleutnant*	
Hoffmann	*Hauptmann*	

Pionier-Bataillon 39

Von Mertens	*Major*	
Beigel	*Major*	
Petzsch	*Major*	

Heeres-Flak-Abteilung 314

Fleischer	*Major*	

Feld-Ersatz-Bataillon 83

Peschke	*Major*	
Biegon	*Hauptmann*	

Nachrichten-Abteilung 39

Kempf	*Major*	
Negendank	*Oberstleutnant*	
Baron von Behr	*Major*	
Böttge	*Major*	

Division Support Command

Haker	*Hauptmann*	

APPENDIX 3

Winners of the Knight's Cross while Assigned to the Division

OAK LEAVES				
Buchterkirch	*Oberleutnant*	Company Commander	*2./Panzer-Regiment 6*	31 December 1941
Breith	*Generalmajor*	Division Commander	*3. Panzer-Division*	31 January 1942
KNIGHT'S CROSS				
Buchterkirch	*Oberleutnant*	Platoon Leader	*2./Panzer-Regiment 6*	29 June 1940
Kühn	*Oberst*	Brigade Commander	*3. Panzer-Brigade*	4 July 1940
Kratzenberg	*Major*	Regiment Commander	*III./Schützen-Regiment 3*	15 August 1940
Zimmermann	*Major*	Regiment Commander	*II./Schützen-Regiment 3*	4 September 1940
Moder	*Unteroffizier*	Squad Leader	*6./Schützen-Regiment 3*	28 November 1940
Model	*Generalleutnant*	Division Commander	*3. Panzer-Division*	9 July 1941
Beigel	*Major*	Battalion Commander	*Pionier-Bataillon 39*	9 July 1941
Schneider-Kostalski	*Hauptmann*	Battalion Commander	*III./Panzer-Regiment 6*	9 July 1941
Reinicke	*Feldwebel*	Platoon Leader	*2./Panzer-Regiment 6*	9 July 1941
Blaich	*Oberfeldwebel*	Platoon Leader	*12./Panzer-Regiment 6*	24 July 1941
Becker-Neetz	*Unteroffizier*	Platoon leader	*7./Schützen-Regiment 394*	25 August 1941
Dr. Müller	*Major*	Battalion Commander	*II./Schützen-Regiment 394*	8 September 1941
Freiherr von Werthern	*Oberleutnant*	Company Commander	*3./Schützen-Regiment 394*	8 September 1941
Störck	*Leutnant*	Platoon leader	Headquarters, *Schützen-Regiment 394*	22 September 1941
Kleemann	*Oberst*	Brigade Commander	*3. Schützen-Brigade*	13 October 1941
Pape	*Major*	Battalion Commander	*Kradschützen-Bataillon 3*	10 February 1942

APPENDIX 4

Winners of the Knight's Cross Assigned to the *3. Panzer-Division* at One Time

OAK LEAVES					
Crüwell	*Generalleutnant*	Commander, *11. Panzer-Division*[1]	Commander, *Panzer-Regiment 6*[2]	1 September 1941	34[3]
Model	*General der Panzertruppen*	Commander in Chief, *2. Panzer-Armee*	Commander, *3. Panzer-Division*	13 February 1942	74

KNIGHT'S CROSS				
Angern	*Oberst*	Commander, *11. Schützen-Brigade*	Commander, *Schützen-Brigade 3*	5 August 1940
Bayerlein	*Oberstleutnant i.G.*	Chief of Staff, *Deutsches Afrika-Korps*		25 December 1941
Behr	*Oberleutnant*	Company Commander, *Aufklärungs-Abteilung 3*		14 May 1941
Crüwell	*Generalmajor*	Commander, *11. Panzer-Division*	Commander, *Panzer-Regiment 6*	14 May 1941
Fenski	*Major*	Commander, *Panzer-Regiment 10*		31 December 1941
Freiherr von Funck	*Generalmajor*	Commander, *7. Panzer-Division*	Commander, *Panzer-Regiment 5*	15 July 1941
Freiherr Geyr von Schweppenburg	*General der Panzertruppen*	Commanding General, *XXIV. Armee-Korps (mot.)*	Commander, *3. Panzer-Division*	9 July 1941
Gierga	*Hauptmann*	Commander, *5./Panzer-Regiment 5*		27 June 1941
Gorn	*Major*	Commander, *I./Schützen-Regiment 10*	*5./Kradschützen-Bataillon 3*	20 April 1941
Nehring	*Generalmajor*	Commander, *18. Panzer-Division*	Commander, *Panzer-Regiment 5*	24 July 1941
Rode	*Oberleutnant*	Company Commander, *Kradschützen-Bataillon 34*	Commander, *I./Panzergrenadier-Regiment 394*	17 September 1941
Rödlich	*Oberstleutnant*	Commander, *II./Panzer-Regiment 4*	*Panzer-Regiment 6*	5 August 1940
Rothenburg	*Oberst*	Commander, *Panzer-Regiment 25*	Commander, *Panzer-Regiment 6*	15 August 1940
Senfft von Pilsach	*Oberleutnant*	Commander, *5./Panzer-Regiment 5*		27 June 1941
Stumpff	*Generalleutnant*	Commander, *20. Panzer-Division*	Commander, *3. Panzer-Division*	29 September 1941
Thomale	*Oberstleutnant*	Commander, *Panzer-Regiment 27*	*Panzer-Regiment 5*	10 February 1942
Toll	*Leutnant der Reserve*	Platoon Leader, *Pionier-Bataillon 200*	*Pionier-Bataillon 39*	10 June 1941

KNIGHT'S CROSS *continued*				
Freiherr von Wechmar	*Oberstleutnant*	Commander, *Aufklärungs-Abteilung 3*		13 April 1941
Wendenburg	*Major*	Battalion Commander, *Panzer-Abteilung 67*	*4./Panzer-Regiment 5*	15 August 1940
Wendt	*Hauptfeldwebel*	Company First Sergeant, *5./Panzer-Regiment 5*		30 June 1941
Von Wietersheim	*Oberstleutnant*	Commander, *Schützen-Regiment 113*	Division Adjutant (Officer Personnel), *3. Panzer-Division*	10 February 1942
Zugehör	*Hauptmann*	Commander, *II./Artillerie-Regiment 19*		12 September 1941

1. Translator's Note: Position at time of receipt of award.
2. Translator's Note: Position held when assigned to the *3. Panzer-Division*.
3. Translator's Note: Indicates sequencing number of the award.

APPENDIX 5

Recipients of the German Cross in Gold

Brandes	*Leutnant*	Company Officer	*Kradschützen-Bataillon 3*	10 October 1941
Schmidt-Ott	*Major*	Commander	*I./Panzer-Regiment 6*	18 October 1941
Rühl	*Leutnant*	Company Officer	*7./Panzer-Regiment 6*	27 October 1941
Wöhlermann	*Major*	Commander	*II./Artillerie-Regiment 75*	27 October 1941
Engelien	*Hauptmann*	Company Officer	*6./Schützen-Regiment 3*	5 November 1941
Kruse	*Feldwebel*	Platoon Leader	*7./Schützen-Regiment 3*	19 January 1942
Seefeldt	*Leutnant der Reserve*	Platoon leader	*3./Pionier-Bataillon 39*	23 January 1942
Schulz	*Leutnant*	Acting Company Commander	*Aufklärungs-Abteilung 1*	23 January 1942
Pape	*Major*	Commander	*Kradschützen-Bataillon 3*	23 January 1942
Fischer	*Oberleutnant*	Company Commander	*Schützen-Regiment 394*	23 January 1942
Michels	*Oberleutnant der Reserve*	Company Commander	*2./Panzerjäger-Abteilung 543*	23 January 1942
Hass	*Oberfeldwebel*	Platoon Leader	*12./Panzer-Regiment 6*	23 January 1942
Kaufmann	*Oberfeldwebel*	Platoon Leader	*7./Schützen-Regiment 3*	23 January 1942
Von Lewinski	*Oberstleutnant*	Commander	*Panzer-Regiment 6*	23 January 1942
Vopel	*Oberleutnant*	Company Commander	*I./Panzer-Regiment 6*	16 February 1942

APPENDIX 6

Induction in the Army Honor Roll

Name	Rank	Unit	Date	Location	Induction Date
Buchterkirch	*Oberleutnant*	Commander, *2./Panzer-Regiment 6*	22–24 June 1941	Niwische	30 August 1941
Reiss	*Feldwebel*	Platoon Leader, *3./Schützen-Regiment 394*	5 July 1941	Sborowo	29 September 1941
Dr. Müller	*Major*	Commander, *II./Schützen-Regiment 394*	5–7 July 1941	Sborowo	9 September 1941
Schmidt-Ott	*Major*	Commander, *I./Panzer-Regiment 6*	6 July 1941	Shlobin	19 August 1941
Möllhoff	*Leutnant*	Platoon Leader, *3./Pionier-Bataillon 39*	1 August 1941	Mikulitschi	6 November 1941
Störck	*Leutnant*	Platoon Leader, *Schützen-Regiment 394*	19 August 1941	Unetscha	28 August 1941
Balde	*Gefreiter*	*Schützen-Regiment 394*	19 August 1941	Unetscha	28 August 1941
Lingk	*Oberleutnant*	Commander, *3./Panzerjäger-Abteilung 521*	12 September 1941	Lochwiza	20 October 1941

APPENDIX 7

Accredited Skirmishes, Engagements, and Battles of the *3. Panzer-Division*, 1939–42

Entries in the Wehrpaß

1–23 September 1939	Campaign in Poland
1–5 September 1939	Battle in West Prussia
1–2 September 1939	Fighting for the Brahe
2–5 September 1939	Engagements in the Tuchel Heath
11–21 September 1939	Pursuit in Eastern Poland
14–17 September 1939	Capture of the Fortress of Brest
14–18 September 1939	Engagements at Zabinka-Kobryn
17–19 September 1939	Engagements at Wlodawa and to the south
23 September 1939–28 January 1940	Duties in the Homeland War Zone
29 January–10 May 1940	Duties in the Operational Area of the Western Front
11 May–2 July 1940	**Campaign in France**
	Breakthrough to the English Channel as Part of the *6. Armee*
11 May 1940	Breakthrough across the Albert Canal west of Maastricht
12–13 May 1940	Armored engagement at Hannut
14–16 May 1940	Breakthrough through the Dyle Position
17–18 May 1940	Pursuit from the Dyle to the Charleroi Canal
	Breakthrough to the English Channel as Part of the *4. Armee*
19–22 May 1940	Fighting around the Mormel Woods
	Fighting in Flanders and as part of the *4. Armee*
22–26 May 1940	Fighting along the La Bassée Canal at Bethune
28–29 May 1940	Fighting at Armentieres and Bailleul
	Fighting in France as part of the *6. Armee*

11 May–2 July 1940	Campaign in France
5–9 June 1940	Battle to Breakthrough along the Somme and the Oise
5–6 June 1940	Breakthrough through the Weygand Line at Péronne
7–9 June 1940	Fighting along the Avre to both sides of Roye
	Fighting in France as part of the *9. Armee*
11–14 June 1940	Fighting for the Marne and pursuit as far as the Seine
12–13 June 1940	Fighting along the Petit-Morin at Montmirail
13–14 June 1940	Pursuit across the Petit-Morin as far as the Seine
13 June 1940	Capture of the bridges over the seine in the area of Nogent sur Seine and Romilly sur Seine
15–17 June 1940	Pursuit from the Seine to the Cote d'Or
17 June 1940	Capture of Dijon and Beaune
	Fighting in France as part of the *12. Armee*
18–22 June 1940	Pursuit on both sides of the Cote d'Or
18–20 June 1940	Blocking the Burgundian Gate; crossing of the Saone and the Doubs
23–25 June 1940	Fighting along the Isére and the Western Alps
	Occupation of France as part of the *12. Armee*
26 June–2 July 1940	Screening of the demarcation line
3 July 1940–21 June 1941	Allocated to the Commander in Chief of the Replacement Army in the Homeland War Zone
22 June 1941–4 February 1942	**Campaign in the East**
22 June–9 July 1941	Battles of Bialystok and Minsk
22 June 1941	Breakthrough through the border positions (Crossing of the Bug)
23–28 June 1941	Fighting in the Pripjet area east of Brest (Pursuit to the Beresina)
29 June–9 July 1941	Advance against and across the Swistosch and the Beresina: 29 June–1 July: Crossing of the Beresina at Brobruisk 2–9 July: Fighting at Rogatschew and Shlobin
10–31 July 1941	Fighting at Smolensk
10–14 July 1941	Breakthrough through the Dnjepr Position (Dnjepr crossing at Stary Bychow and breakthrough through the Stalin Line)
15–31 July 1941	Defensive fighting along the Ssosh (Fighting at Propoisk)
1–8 August 1941	Battle of Roslawl
2–20 August 1941	Battle of Kritschew and Gomel (Fighting to eliminate the enemy at Klimowitsch–Miloslawitsch)
21 August–26 September 1941	Fighting at Kiev
21 August–5 September 1941	Pursuit as far as the Dessna (Penetration of the Dessna Position. Envelopment of the enemy forces around Gomel)
6–26 September 1941	Pursuit in the Battle of Kiev: 6–15 September: Battles at Konotop, Romny and Lochwiza; Closing the Kiev Pocket 16–29 September: Defensive fighting at Romny
27 September–3 October 1941	Battles at Wjasma and Brjansk
27 September–3 October 1941	Battle at Brjansk (Breakthrough to Orel)
4 October–5 December 1941	Advance against Moscow and Woronesh. In detail:
4–31 October 1941	Advance on Tula
1–17 November 1941	Fighting at Jefremow and Tula
18 November–5 December 1941	Battle of Tula and advance on Rjasan and Kaschira
5 December 1941–4 February 1942	Defensive fighting outside of Moscow
6–20 December 1941	Defensive fighting in the areas around Jefremow and Tula
21–25 December 1941	Defensive fighting along the Oka
26 December 1941–2 January 1942	Defensive fighting northwest of Liwny
6 January–4 February 1942	Defensive fighting for Kursk: 6–25 January: Defensive fighting in the area around Wypolsowa 26 January–4 February: Defensive fighting north of Schtschigry